T0305097

PUBLIC POLICY IN THE ENTREPRENEURIAL SOCIETY

Wherever possible, the articles in these volumes have been reproduced as originally published using facsimile reproduction, inclusive of footnotes and pagination to facilitate ease of reference.

For a list of all Edward Elgar published titles visit our website at
www.e-elgar.com

Public Policy in the Entrepreneurial Society

David B. Audretsch

Distinguished Professor and Ameritech Chair of Economic Development and Director, Institute of Development Strategies, Indiana University, USA, Honorary Professor of Industrial Economics and Entrepreneurship, WHU-Otto Beisheim School of Management, Germany and Visiting Professor at King Saud University, Saudi Arabia

Edward Elgar
Cheltenham, UK • Northampton, MA, USA

Published by
Edward Elgar Publishing Limited
The Lypiatts
15 Lansdown Road
Cheltenham
Glos GL50 2JA
UK

Edward Elgar Publishing, Inc.
William Pratt House
9 Dewey Court
Northampton
Massachusetts 01060
USA

A catalogue record for this book is available from the British Library

Library of Congress Control Number: 2013949888

ISBN 978 1 78347 223 9

Printed and bound in Great Britain by T.J. International Ltd, Padstow

Contents

Acknowledgements

The editor and publishers wish to thank the authors and the following publishers who have kindly given permission for the use of copyright material.

Blackwell Publishing Ltd for articles: David B. Audretsch and Max Keilbach (2007), 'The Theory of Knowledge Spillover Entrepreneurship', *Journal of Management Studies*, **44** (7), November, 1242–54; Rajshree Agarwal, David Audretsch and M.B. Sarkar (2007), 'The Process of Creative Construction: Knowledge Spillovers, Entrepreneurship, and Economic Growth', *Strategic Entrepreneurship Journal*, **1** (3–4), December, 263–86.

Elsevier for articles: David B. Audretsch and Erik E. Lehmann (2005), 'Do University Policies Make a Difference?', *Research Policy*, **34** (3), April, 343–47; David B. Audretsch and Jürgen Weigand (2005), 'Do Knowledge Conditions Make a Difference? Investment, Finance and Ownership in German Industries', *Research Policy*, **34** (5), June, 595–613; David B. Audretsch and Erik E. Lehmann (2005), 'Does the Knowledge Spillover Theory of Entrepreneurship Hold for Regions?', *Research Policy*, **34** (8), October, 1191–202; David B. Audretsch and Max Keilbach (2008), 'Resolving the Knowledge Paradox: Knowledge-Spillover Entrepreneurship and Economic Growth', *Research Policy*, **37** (10), December, 1697–705; Taylor Aldridge and David B. Audretsch (2010), 'Does Policy Influence the Commercialization Route? Evidence from National Institutes of Health Funded Scientists', *Research Policy*, **39** (5), June, 583–88; Julie Ann Elston and David B. Audretsch (2010), 'Risk Attitudes, Wealth and Sources of Entrepreneurial Start-Up Capital', *Journal of Economic Behavior and Organization*, **76** (1), October, 82–89; T. Taylor Aldridge and David Audretsch (2011), 'The Bayh–Dole Act and Scientist Entrepreneurship', *Research Policy*, **40** (8), October, 1058–67; David B. Audretsch, Werner Bönte and Prashanth Mahagaonkar (2012), 'Financial Signaling by Innovative Nascent Ventures: The Relevance of Patents and Prototypes', *Research Policy*, **41** (8), October, 1407–21.

Oxford University Press via the Copyright Clearance Center's Rightslink Service for article: David B. Audretsch (2007), 'Entrepreneurship Capital and Economic Growth', *Oxford Review of Economic Policy*, **23** (1), Spring, 63–78.

Springer Science and Business Media B.V. for articles: David B. Audretsch and Dirk Dohse (2007), 'Location: A Neglected Determinant of Firm Growth', *Review of World Economics*, **143** (1), April, 79–107; Christine A. Gulbranson and David B. Audretsch (2008), 'Proof of Concept Centers: Accelerating the Commercialization of University Innovation', *Journal of Technology Transfer*, **33** (3), June, 249–58; Zoltan J. Acs, Pontus Braunerhjelm, David B. Audretsch and Bo Carlsson (2009), 'The Knowledge Spillover Theory of Entrepreneurship', *Small Business Economics*, **32** (1), January, 15–30; David B. Audretsch, Erik E. Lehmann and

Lawrence A. Plummer (2009), 'Agency and Governance in Strategic Entrepreneurship', *Entrepreneurship Theory and Practice*, **33** (1), January, 149–66; David B. Audretsch (2009), 'The Entrepreneurial Society', *Journal of Technology Transfer*, **34** (3), June, 245–54; Pontus Braunerhjelm, Zoltan J. Acs, David B. Audretsch and Bo Carlsson (2010), 'The Missing Link: Knowledge Diffusion and Entrepreneurship in Endogenous Growth', *Small Business Economics*, **34** (2), February, 105–25; David Audretsch, Dirk Dohse and Annekatrin Niebuhr (2010), 'Cultural Diversity and Entrepreneurship: A Regional Analysis for Germany', *Annals of Regional Science*, **45** (1), August, 55–85; David Audretsch and Taylor Aldridge (2012), 'Transnational Social Capital and Scientist Entrepreneurship', *Journal of Management and Governance*, **16** (3), August, 369–76; Julie A. Elston and David B. Audretsch (2011), 'Financing the Entrepreneurial Decision: An Empirical Approach Using Experimental Data on Risk Attitudes', *Small Business Economics*, **36** (2), February, 209–22.

Taylor and Francis Ltd (http://www.informaworld.com) for article: David B. Audretsch and Erik E. Lehmann (2006), 'Do Locational Spillovers Pay? Empirical Evidence from German IPO Data', *Economics of Innovation and New Technology*, **15** (1), January, 71–81.

Foreword

The open society, the unrestricted access to knowledge, the unplanned and uninhibited association of men for its furtherance – these are what may make a vast, complex, ever growing, ever changing, ever more specialized and expert technological world, nevertheless a world of human community.
                                                                                                — J. Robert Oppenheimer

David Audretsch has accomplished in this collection what few of us will be likely to accomplish during our careers. He has not only shared within the pages that follow codified knowledge though an extant collection of previously published scholarship, but he has also allowed us to glean, through the subtle complementarity of the papers in the collection, tacit knowledge about the more interesting and important aspects of entrepreneurship.

The title of this volume, *Public Policy for the Entrepreneurial Society*, raises at least two interesting questions, the first of which is: What is an entrepreneurial society?

The amount of effort taken by Professor Audretsch to prepare this collection, thematically integrating the papers within it into an Introduction was not trivial, and through the Introduction one gleans tacit knowledge about entrepreneurship and thus how to define an entrepreneurial society. While many have written about who the entrepreneur is and what he/she does (in other words, entrepreneurship), there is still not a widely accepted definition within the academic community. And, I should point out that the academic community extends beyond those of us trained in economics. It encompasses learned individuals within the fields of business, education, management, political science, public administration, and sociology.

While much of my academic career has been spent searching for and writing about the entrepreneur (Hébert and Link 1988, 2009), I am constantly enlightened by Professor Audretsch's insight about the actions of the entrepreneur, that is, his insight about what influences a person's ability and desire to perceive opportunity and also have the ability to act on that perception.

One might thus conclude that an entrepreneurial society is one characterized by perception and action by at least some of its members or some of its institutions. Now, the second question raised by the title is: Can public policy affect how, or how many, individuals or institutions perceive opportunities and act on them? I do not think so, at least not directly. What public policy can do is to provide incentives for entrepreneurial interactions to occur, and through these interactions networks arise and knowledge spillovers result.

Professor Audretsch is in the early afternoon of his research career. For many of us that would mean that our production functions had long adopted a logarithmic or even declining path. But this has not been the case for Professor Audretsch, as this collection clearly indicates. The included papers that are related to his knowledge spillover theory of entrepreneurship alone have more than 1,000 citations.

But why have these papers, that is, why has this theory, been so influential on the academic community? At one level, Professor Audretsch has transcended a static view of the role of the entrepreneur and introduced a more dynamic role. At yet another and more important level, these views have influenced, and will long continue to influence, economics at both the micro as well as macro levels. At the micro level, the knowledge spillover theory introduces into economic analysis the role of networks and their influence on optimizing behavior. At the macro level, at which endogenous growth models have long recognized the connection between knowledge spillovers and growth, it was the insight of Professor Audretsch that taught us that such spillovers alone do not generate growth. Rather, such spillovers must be transmitted through entrepreneurial actions.

Albert N. Link
University of North Carolina at Greensboro

References

Hébert, Robert F. and Albert N. Link (1988), *The Entrepreneur: Mainstream Views and Radical Critiques*, New York: Praeger.
Hébert, Robert F. and Albert N. Link (2009), *A History of Entrepreneurship*, London: Routledge.

Introduction

David B. Audretsch

Economics attracted me as a young student because of its promise to address the most compelling issues confronting society at that time. Coming of age during the post-World War II economic boom left a heady impression of the great impact that scholars could contribute in eradicating society's most pressing problems. A bold new approach to macroeconomics developed by John Maynard Keynes and his disciples had revolutionized the view that business cycles and their devastating downturns were inevitable. The insights of Keynesian economics held the promise of sparing subsequent generations the misery and despair inflicted by the Great Depression. 'Never again' was the confident mantra of what the journalist David Halberstam (1972) termed as the 'Best and the Brightest' – young minds who were summoned by President John F. Kennedy to ensure not only that economic prosperity would become the norm, but with an unprecedented array of microeconomic and social problems, that poverty and social injustice would also be eradicated.

This was an era when the leading minds in economics unraveled the seemingly impossible puzzle of how best to foster economic growth, jobs, and a high standard of living. Robert Solow, in his famous growth model that ultimately won him the Nobel Prize in Economics, uncovered the secret to generating economic growth – physical capital. Investments in plants, factories, and machines would spur productivity to unprecedented levels, unleashing an unprecedented era of economic prosperity.

While the field of macroeconomics was content with recognizing the primacy of physical capital as driving economic growth, analyses at the microeconomic level revealed a dilemma inherent in a capital-driven economy – high levels of productivity could be attained only through such large-scale production as to pre-empt the possibilities for a competitive market structure. The Holy Grail underlying the Vallejo of economic performance – efficiency, productivity, and competition – was threatened to unravel due to an organization of industry where production and sales were dominated by just a handful of large companies. It became the task of scholars in the emerging field of industrial organization to explicitly identify the options confronting public policy to remedy what Oliver Williamson (1968) termed optimistically as a tradeoff between less government intervention and greater allocative inefficiency but also higher productive efficiency on the one hand, versus greater government intervention which would result in less allocative inefficiency but only at the cost of reduced productive efficiency. Through the enlightened application of the leading tools of microeconomic analysis, a generation of industrial organization scholars could guide public policy makers in choosing among such policy instruments as antitrust, regulation, and government ownership to mitigate the impact of inherently flawed market structures.

Determined to join the ranks of the 'Best and the Brightest', I charted my course through graduate school to set this policy tradeoff in industrial economics straight by writing a Ph.D. Dissertation on the impact of antitrust policy on market efficiency in the field of industrial organization. However, even before the Dissertation was completed and the doctoral degree had been procured, the promise of economics began to unravel. The 1970s saw the advent of what became popularly known as *stagflation*, or the simultaneous existence of high inflation and high levels of unemployment. The emergence of stagflation posed a contradiction to the widely accepted premise of the Phillips Curve, which took the logic inherent in the Keynesian Model to conclude that there is an inevitable tradeoff between unemployment and inflation. While such a policy trade-off between unemployment and inflation had defined the post-war macroeconomic policy paradigm, the increases in both unemployment and inflation that were pervasive in the 1970s undermined the entire policy approach along with the theoretical underpinning.

A profound shift occurred away from the demand side of the economy to the supply side. Along with this shift came the recognition that the 'missing' element or residual inherent in the Solow growth model – technological change, or what today is referred to as knowledge – is actually the key to the capacity of a modern, developed economy to supply goods and sustain competitiveness in an era of globalization. Clearly the endogenous growth models placed investments in knowledge at the heart of the capacity for an economy to grow. Not only did such knowledge investments represent a key factor that had previously been missing in the Solow growth model, but what made knowledge particularly potent in its impact was its propensity to spill over for use by third-party firms and entities. That is, knowledge created and used by one firm could also be used by other firms, enjoying the benefits without incurring the costs accrued by knowledge externalities.

Thus, together with Zoltan Acs, I began to develop my research towards innovative activity, and in particular how industrial organization affects innovation (Acs and Audretsch, 1990). Our findings that small firms were at least as innovative as larger firms enjoying market dominance were surprising. In *Capitalism, Socialism and Democracy*, Schumpeter (1942, p. 132) concluded that, due to scale economies in the production of new economic knowledge, large corporations would not only have the innovative advantage over small and new enterprise, but that ultimately the economic landscape would consist only of giant corporations, 'Innovation itself is being reduced to routine. Technological progress is increasingly becoming the business of teams of trained specialists who turn out what is required and make it work in predictable ways.'

Schumpeter (1942, p. 106) believed the large corporation to be the engine of technological change and innovative activity, 'What we have got to accept is that (the large-scale establishment or unit of control) has come to be the most powerful engine of … progress and in particular of the long-run expansion of output not only in spite of, but to a considerable extent through, this strategy which looks so restrictive.'

Similarly, Galbraith ([1967] 1979, p. 61), concluded that the entrepreneur 'is a diminishing figure in the planning system. Apart from access to capital, his principal qualifications were imagination, capacity for decision, and courage in risking money, including, not infrequently, his own. None of these qualifications is especially important for organizing intelligence or effective in competing with it.' As Galbraith ([1967] 1979, p. 61) argued, 'power' has shifted from entrepreneurs to the large organization, 'So it is with organization – organized competence – that the power now lies'.

Galbraith (1956, p. 87) viewed the large corporation as having an inherent innovative advantage, 'Because development is costly, it follows that it can be carried on only by a firm that has the resources which are associated with considerable size'. In unequivocally rejecting the Schumpeter of 1911 while endorsing the Schumpeter of 1942, Galbraith (1956, pp. 86–87) concluded that, 'There is no more pleasant fiction than that technical change is the product of the matchless ingenuity of the small man forced by competition to employ his wits to better his neighbor. Unhappily, it is a fiction. Technical development has long since become the preserve of the scientist and engineer. Most of the cheap and simple inventions have, to put in bluntly and unpersuasively, been made.'

Similarly, Galbraith, in *The New Industrial State* (1979, p. IX), concurred with Schumpeter's view in *Capitalism, Socialism and Democracy* that the large corporation was the most efficient form of organization. In describing the economy as he saw it,

> This was the world of great corporations – a world in which people increasingly served the convenience of those organizations which was meant to serve them. It was a world in which the motivation of those involved did not fit the standard textbook mold. Nor did the relationship between corporation and state. Nor did markets. So far from being the controlling power in the economy, markets were more and more accommodated to the needs and convenience of the great business organizations.

What became known as the Schumpeterian Paradox, which reflected the greater investment in knowledge made by large corporations but the high propensity for small and new firms to innovate, posed the question, 'How are new and small firms able to be so innovative given their paucity of knowledge resources?'

It was difficult to reconcile the static view that access to knowledge resources drive innovative output with the empirical evidence highlighting the vigorous innovative performance of small firms. Reconciliation of the Schumpeterian Paradox resulted from the dynamic lens provided by the knowledge theory of entrepreneurship. The model of the knowledge production function, formalized by Zvi Griliches (1979), had linked the output of innovative activity to the resources of knowledge, in the form of research and development and human capital within a static context. The knowledge investment of the firm was assumed to be exogenous, which endogenously generated innovative output. By contrast, the knowledge spillover theory of entrepreneurship starts with knowledge that has been created in some organizational context. If that knowledge is not completely commercialized, the residual knowledge creates an opportunity for entrepreneurship. Thus, seen through the dynamic lens of the knowledge spillover theory of entrepreneurship, the knowledge is exogenous and the startup of a new firm is the endogenous response by individuals to best appropriate a return on their knowledge or ideas.

Seen through the dynamic lens of the knowledge spillover theory of entrepreneurship, entrepreneurship plays a key role in generating innovative activity and ultimately economic growth by serving as a conduit for the spillover of knowledge created in the organizational context of an incumbent firm but actually commercialized in the organizational context of a new startup (Audretsch, 1995 and Audretsch, Keilbach and Lehmann, 2006). Since knowledge spillovers play a pivotal role in models of economic growth, entrepreneurship provides a missing link to economic growth by serving as a conduit for knowledge spillovers.

What is meant by *The Entrepreneurial Society* is a society where entrepreneurship serves as a driving force generating economic growth, jobs, and competitiveness in global markets (Audretsch, 2007). The papers contained in the ensuing chapters explore the appropriate role for the public, not just to enhance entrepreneurship, but rather to enhance economic performance in an economy where entrepreneurship serves as a driving force for economic performance.

References

Acs, Zoltan and David B. Audretsch (1990), *Innovation and Small Firms*, Cambridge: MIT Press.

Audretsch, David B. (1995), *Innovation and Industry Evolution*, Cambridge: MIT Press.

Audretsch, David B. (2007), *The Entrepreneurial Society*, New York: Oxford University Press.

Audretsch, David B., Max Keilbach and Erik Lehmann (2006), *Entrepreneurship and Economic Growth*, New York: Oxford University Press.

Galbraith, John Kenneth (1956), *American Capitalism*, Boston: Houghton Mifflin.

Galbraith, John Kenneth (1967), *The New Industrial State* (1979 edn), Boston: Houghton Mifflin.

Griliches, Zvi (1979), 'Issues in Assessing the Contribution of Research and Development to Productivity Growth', *Bell Journal of Economics*, **10**, 92–116.

Halberstam, David (1972), *The Best and the Brightest*, New York: Random House.

Schumpeter, Joseph A. (1911), *Theorie der wirtschaftlichen Entwicklung*, Berlin: Duncker und Humblot.

Schumpeter, Joseph A. (1942), *Capitalism, Socialism and Democracy*, New York: Harper.

Williamson, Oliver (1968), 'Economies as an Antitrust Defense: The Welfare Tradeoffs', *American Economic Review*, **58**, 18–36.

[1]

Research Policy 34 (2005) 343–347

Do University policies make a difference?

David B. Audretsch [a,*], Erik E. Lehmann [b]

[a] Department Entrepreneurship, Growth and Public Policy; Max Planck Institute Jena for Research into Economic Systems,
Indiana University and CEPR, Kahlaische Strasse 10, D-07745 Jena, Germany
[b] Max Planck Institute Jena for Research into Economic Systems, Kahlaische Strasse 10, D-07745 Jena, Germany

Received 9 September 2004; received in revised form 12 January 2005; accepted 21 January 2005

Abstract

The purpose of this paper is to examine whether the technical universities have been more successful in facilitating the spillover and commercialization of knowledge. We compare the impact of technical and general universities on the performance of knowledge-based firms. Based on a unique data set consisting of publicly held high technology firms, the empirical evidence suggests that, in fact, firm performance is not influenced by the type of university. Technical universities do not have a differential impact on firm performance from more general universities.
© 2005 Elsevier B.V. All rights reserved.

JEL classification: M13; L 20; R30

Keywords: University spillover; Firm growth

1. Introduction

Much attention has recently been focused on the so-called European Paradox. On the one hand, Europe has consistently made one of the highest amounts of investment in new knowledge, in the form of research and development, university research and human capital. On the other hand, commercialization, innovation and ultimately economic growth emanating from those knowledge investments has been relatively low, and in

* Corresponding author. Fax: +49 3641 68 6710.
  E-mail address: audretsch@mpiew-jena.mpg.de
(D.B. Audretsch).

any case disappointing. Germany has not escaped the European Paradox. Investments in German universities have ranked among the highest in Europe. Still, the ensuing commercialization has been disappointing.

The European Commission has responded to the European Paradox by calling for a European standard of a minimum of 2.5% of GDP invested in research. Such a policy response to inadequate commercialization assumes that the bottleneck lies in the magnitude of the investment. However, a different approach focuses on institutions involved in research, and in particular, in their efficacy as serving as conduits for the spillover of knowledge. A number of policy makers in Germany have suggested that the technical universities are better

0048-7333/$ – see front matter © 2005 Elsevier B.V. All rights reserved.
doi:10.1016/j.respol.2005.01.006

suited as conduits of knowledge spillovers than are general universities.

The purpose of this paper is to examine whether the institutional difference in universities makes a difference in the spillover and commercialization of knowledge. In particular, we compare the impact of two different institutional types of universities in Germany – general universities and technical universities – on the performance of firms, measured in terms of economic growth. The results suggest that, in fact, despite the claims to the contrary, the institutions of technical university have no better impact on firm performance. This might suggest that policy reform is needed to stimulate greater knowledge spillovers and the commercialization of university-based knowledge.

2. Linking university policy to firm growth

Left to themselves the scientific research community and the market are likely to achieve less in terms of economic value and new jobs. Thus, university policy matters. Recently, the Federal Ministry of Research and Education proclaimed a policy that provides the setting for innovations and for the creation of new jobs because only state-of-the-art research policy promotes sustainable growth (FMER, 2004, p. 13). The technical universities have generally been assigned the role of generating more commercial spillovers emanating from university research. Originally, and as the name implies, the technical oriented universities restricted their teaching and to technical and engineering disciplines. However, during the course of time, they have developed into more comprehensive higher education institutions. Hence, students can now also study arts and humanities degree courses. Nevertheless, the focus of their activities in both research and teaching continues to be directed towards engineering and sciences. The technical universities have therefore played a key role in German research policy in their more applied nature, and have been assumed to be institutions more adept and fostering knowledge spillovers, commercialization and ultimately economic growth. As a result of their presumed role in generating technology commercialization and economic growth, the technical universities have been funded through public policy more generously when compared to more general on the premise that they are uniquely suited to fos-

ter and promote spillovers from new technologies to firms.

However, studies evaluating university policies are rare (see Link and Scott, 2005, for public sector R&D programs, Hall et al., 2003 for universities as research partners and Link and Scott, 2003 for research parks, or Feldman and Desroche, 2003 for John Hopkins University).

To test the hypothesis that technical universities are more adept at serving as a conduit of knowledge spillovers and facilitating the commercialization of university knowledge, we compare the impact of technical and general universities on firm growth. The starting point for such a comparison is the well known relationship between size and growth provided in the literature testing the basic assumption of Gibrat's Law (Sutton, 1997, Caves, 1998). We then extend this basic relationship by including the type of universities on growth.

Gibrat's law assumes that the present size of firm i in period t may be decomposed into the product of a "proportional effect" and the initial firm size as:

$$\text{Size}_{i,t} = (1 + \varepsilon_t)\text{Size}_{i,t-1} \tag{1}$$

where $(1 + \varepsilon_t)$ denotes the proportional effect for firm i in period t. Here, the random shock ε_t is assumed to be identically and independently distributed. Taking the natural log and assuming that for small ε, $\ln(1+\varepsilon) \approx \varepsilon_t$,

$$\ln(\text{Size}_{i,t}) = \ln(\text{Size}_{i,0}) + \sum_{k=1}^{t} \varepsilon_{ik} \tag{2}$$

It can be observed that as $t \to \infty$ a distribution emerges which is approximately log normal with properties that $\ln(\text{Size}_{i,t}) \sim N(t\mu_\varepsilon, t\sigma_\varepsilon^2)$. Firm growth can then be measured as the difference between the natural log of the number of employees as:

$$\text{Growth}_{it} = \ln(S_{i,t}) - \ln(S_{i,t-1}) \tag{3}$$

where the difference in size for firm i between the current period t and the initial period $(t-1)$ equals Growth_{it}.

This equation can be empirically estimated by:

$$\text{Growth}_{i,t} = B_1 \ln(\text{Size}_{i,t-1}) + B_2 \ln(\text{Size}_{i,t-1})^2 \\ + B_3 \text{Age}_{i,t-1} + \varepsilon_i \tag{4}$$

where growth for firm i in period t is a function of initial firm size, size^2, age, and ε_i a stochastic error term.

D.B. Audretsch, E.E. Lehmann / Research Policy 34 (2005) 343–347   345

Sutton (1997) and Caves (1998) survey and report on the large number of empirical studies estimating Eq. (4). The evidence is systematic and compelling that both size and age are negatively related to firm growth.

Note that Eq. (4) only considers characteristics specific to the enterprise. We extend this approach by including a dummy variable indicating a technical oriented university.

$$\text{Growth}_{i,t} = B_1 \ln(\text{Size}_{i,t-1}) + B_2 \ln(\text{Size}_{i,t-1})^2$$
$$+ B_3 \text{Age}_{i,t-1} + \varepsilon_i B_4 \text{ Technical oriented}$$
$$\text{University}_{t-1} B_5 \text{Age}_{t,t-1} + \varepsilon_t$$

where D_{ind} is a vector of industry dummies controlling, for example, for the knowledge intensity of production in a specific sector. Knowledge$_{r,t-1}$ represents knowledge spillovers from universities.

3. Data set and descriptive statistics

To test the hypothesis that firm growth depends not only on firm size and age but also university spillovers, we use a unique dataset of 276 IPO firms in Germany (see Audretsch and Lehmann, in press; Audretsch et al., in press-a,b). The dataset are collected combining individual data from IPO prospectuses, along with publicly available information from on-line data sources including the *Deutsche Boerse AG* (www.deutsche-boerse.com). We pooled this dataset by adding university-specific variables, which are individually collected from the 73 public universities in Germany. From those 73 public universities, 6 universities are defined as Technical oriented Universities (TU).

We take the *log growth rates* of employees 1 year after the IPO as the dependent variable. The first two exogenous variables are firm age (*AGE*) and firm size (*SIZE*). Age is measured in years from foundation to IPO, and firm size by the number of employees before IPO.

In the first model (model I), we estimate the following basic regression

(I) ln Growth = const. + β_1 ln Size + β_2 ln Size^2
    + β_3 ln Age + β_4 ln Age^2 + ε
    Secondly, we test for the impact of technical oriented universities.

(II) ln Growth = const. + β_1 TU + ε
    And then we test the combination from (I) and (II):

(III) ln Growth = const. + β_1 ln Size + β_2 ln Size^2
    + β_3 ln Age + β_4 ln Age^2 + β_5 TU + ε

Finally, take the regression model (III) and run different regressions, each for one type of universities (models IV and V) (Table 1). Table 1 shows some descriptive statistics from the top 20 universities in Germany, ranked by the number of firms located closest to this university.

The descriptive statistics are depicted in Table 2. The data also demonstrate that most of the firms are strikingly young. Half of the firms in our samples are 8-year-old or less. The firms also differ extremely in their size as measured by the number of employees before IPO. The mean firm before IPO employed about 180 workers. Finally, the table shows that on average the log growth rate is about 0.53. Firms, which are located nearest to a technical oriented university, did not significantly differ in growth rates and age. However, they significantly differ in there patent activities, in that the firms located within geographic proximity to the technical universities exhibit a significantly greater propensity to patent. Thus, while the simple mean growth rates do not vary between firms located within geographic proximity to technical and general universities, the patent activity of firms located close to technical universities is considerably higher.

4. Empirical evidence

The regression results from estimating firm growth are presented in Table 3. In the first model (I), only the standard measures found in the Gibrat's Law literature, size and growth, are included in the estimation. As has been commonly found throughout the literature, the negative and statistically significant coefficient suggests that firm growth is negatively related to firm size.

When the dummy variable is included in the model, the significance of the other variables does not greatly change. The coefficient of the dummy variable is not statistically significant, which suggests that, in fact, knowledge-based firm accessing spillovers from technical universities do not have any performance

Table 1
List of the top 20 universities in Germany

University	Firms[a]	Økm[b]	Staff[c]	Grants[d]	SSCI students[e]	SCI students[f]
LMU München	51	17.9	412,633	83,681	43,633	8,119
Uni Frankfurt	26	19.5	265,845	50,976	26,324	5,715
Uni Hamburg	24	13.25	87,924	8,870	1,361	329
Uni Stuttgart	16	16.2	403,180	203,489	4,779	12,104
HU Berlin	14	7.78	352,676	55,167	20,769	4,936
Uni Köln	12	5.9	299,294	51,409	47,112	9,395
TU München	**10**	**8.8**	**462,522**	**205,463**	**1,619**	**14,976**
TU Karlsruhe	**9**	**36.7**	**322,389**	**120,261**	**4,102**	**11,818**
Uni Düsseldorf	7	18.57	145,912	19,382	14,697	4,762
Uni Erlangen-Nürnberg	6	14	290,793	103,212	12,861	7,144
Uni Freiburg	6	40.33	212,177	40,121	12,334	4,942
FU Berlin	5	5.5	435,784	73,023	30,290	6,260
TU Aachen (RWTA)	**5**	**3.4**	**473,740**	**205,389**	**7,884**	**20,570**
Uni Jena	5	15.8	198,905	34,142	7,615	2,864
U-GH Paderborn	4	17	161,200	40,386	6,993	8,676
Uni Bielefeld	4	15.5	190,698	39,114	15,831	4,400
Uni Bremen	4	25.5	224,573	82,507	11,749	4,800
UdB München	4	14.25	131,395	7,858	1,054	1,104
Uni Kiel	4	40.75	238,427	63,196	13,000	6,513
Uni Regensburg	4	40	153,090	26,069	11,192	3,696

As measured by the firms located around this university, TU means technical oriented university (in bold).
[a] Measured by the number of firms located closest to this university.
[b] Økm is the average distance of the firms located to this university.
[c] Staff are expenditures on personnel (in 1000 DM).
[d] Grants are research grants.
[e] Number of students in the social sciences.
[f] Number of students in the natural sciences.

advantage over firms accessing spillovers from general universities.

An important qualification of representing the impact of university type by using the dummy variable to indicate a technical university is that the effect is assumed to shift the intercept, but have no impact on the coefficients of the size and age variables. A different specification is provided in the last two columns, which decomposes the sample into firms within close geographic proximity of a technical university and those

Table 2
Descriptive statistics

	Mean	S.D.	Ha		
			diff<0	diff=0	diff>0
Log growth rates			0.0379	0.0379	0.0379
TU	0.528	0.344			
U	0.542	0.101			
Firm age (in years)			0.429	0.429	0.429
TU	11.288	7.166			
U	10.383	10.298			
Firm patents			1.782**	1.782*	1.782
TU	7.12	12.813			
U	3.023	10.77			

Differences between Technical Oriented Universites (TU) and traditional Universities (U), *t*-test of means over the whole sample, $N=276$; Ho: mean (TH) − mean (U) = diff = 0, *t*-values, (*, **, ***) statistically significant at the 10, 5 1, % level, respectively.

Table 3
Regressions on firm growth

	(1)	(2)	(3)	(4)	(5)
ln Size	−0.7895 (2.75)**		−0.8575 (3.01)***	−0.9762 (1.98)**	−0.7349 (1.58)
ln Size^2	−0.0152 (0.47)		−0.0056 (0.17)	0.0099 (0.19)	−0.03359 (0.62)
ln Age	0.0859 (1.29)		0.08511 (1.28)	0.1061 (1.32)	−0.3195 (2.92)***
ln Age^2	−0.0114 (0.41)		−0.0159 (0.58)	−0.0152 (0.51)	0.0243 (0.37)
Technical oriented university		−0.01285 (0.04)	0.1429 (0.564)		
Const.	4.3187 (7.03)***	0.54118 (5.32)***	4.4197 (7.22)	4.577 (4.18)***	5.1784 (5.01)***
R^2	0.4749	0.0001	0.4784	0.7413	0.4571
N	281	281	281	253	28

This table presents the result from OLS on firm growth. The endogenous variable is growth rates of employees one year after the IPO. All OLS-estimations are done using the White-heteroskedasticity robust estimator. Absolute *t*-values in parentheses, (*, **, ***) statistically significant at the 10, 5 1, % level, respective.

close to a general university. Using this specification it is possible for the impacts of age and size to be affected by the type of university. No such impact is observed for the firms within close geographic proximity to a general university. However, for those firms accessing knowledge spillovers from technical universities, the negative and statistically coefficient of firm age suggests that age plays a greater role in shaping firm performance than does firm size.

5. Conclusion

Perhaps in a response to what is now referred to as The European Paradox, or the relatively low propensity for investments in knowledge to result in innovative activity, the technical universities of Germany were targeted to generate knowledge spillovers and commercialization. This paper has examined whether the particular type of university – technical or more general – actually makes a difference in impacting the performance of knowledge-based startups. Based on a data set consisting of publicly listed high technology firms, the empirical evidence suggests that, in fact, the technical universities do not bestow any locational advantage to firm performance. This may suggest that it will take more than just technical universities within the context of German institutions to generate knowledge spillovers. In this case, university policy does not make a difference, at least not in terms of influencing the performance of knowledge-based startups.

Acknowledgement

Financial support by the German Research Foundation (DFG) through the research group #FOR454 "Heterogeneous Labor" at the University of Konstanz and the ZEW, Mannheim, is gratefully acknowledged.

References

Audretsch, D.B., Lehmann, E., 2005. Do locational spillovers pay? Empirical evidence from German IPO data. Economics of Information and New Technology, forthcoming.

Audretsch, D.B., Lehmann, E., Warning, S., 2005. University spillovers and new firm location. Research Policy, forthcoming.

Audretsch, D.B., Keilbach, M., Lehmann E., 2005. Entrepreneurship and Growth, Oxford University Press, forthcoming.

Caves, R., 1998. Industrial organization and new findings on the turnover and mobility of firms. Journal of Economic Literature 36, 1947–1982.

Federal Ministry of Education and Research, 2004. Facts and Figs. 2002 (http://www.bmbf.de).

Feldman, M., Desroche, P., 2003. Research universities and local economic development: lessons from the history of the John Hopkins University. Industry and Innovation 10, 5–24.

Hall, B., Link, A., Scott, J., 2003. Universities as research partners. Review of Economics and Statistics 85, 485–491.

Link, A., Scott, J., 2003. The growth of research triangle parks. Small Business Economics 20, 167–175.

Link, A., Scott, J., 2005. Evaluating public sector R&D Programs: the advanced technology program's investment in wavelength references for optical fiber communications. Journal of Technology Transfer 30, 241–251.

Sutton, J., 1997. Gibrat's Legacy. Journal of Economic Literature 35, 40–59.

[2]

research
policy

Research Policy 34 (2005) 595–613

Do knowledge conditions make a difference?
Investment, finance and ownership in German industries

David B. Audretsch [a,b,c], Jürgen Weigand [d,*]

[a] *Indiana University, Institute for Development Strategies, Bloomington, IN, USA*
[b] *Max-Planck Institute for Research into Economic Systems, Jena, Germany*
[c] *Centre for Economic Policy Research (CEPR), London, UK*
[d] *WHU Beisheim School of Management, Burgplatz 2, Vallendar 56179, Germany*

Received 13 September 2000; received in revised form 25 November 2004; accepted 5 December 2004
Available online 28 April 2005

Abstract

This paper examines the impact of industry knowledge conditions, the mode of corporate control and firm size on tangible investments and its financing. Based on a large panel data set of German firms we investigate whether financing constraints exist for tangible investment and whether there is systematic variation across firms engaged in activities reflecting different knowledge conditions. In particular, we compare the extent of financing constraints for firm in knowledge intensive (*hi-K*) industries with those in less knowledge-based (*lo-K*) industries. This distinction is important because knowledge-based economic activity tends to be subject to high degrees of uncertainty, asymmetric information and spillovers of newly created knowledge, making access to external sources of finance difficult. Our surprising empirical finding is that firms in *hi-K* industries are less finance constrained than are their counterparts in *lo-K* industries. However, the mode of corporate control and firm size play an important role. After controlling for firm size and manager versus owner control, we observe that the small manager-controlled firms in both *hi-K* and *lo-K* industries are most finance constrained. By contrast, no financing constraints seem to exist for the smaller owner-controlled firms in *hi-K* industries. This latter result contrasts sharply with results of Anglo-Saxon studies.
© 2005 Elsevier B.V. All rights reserved.

JEL classification: G3; L2; 03

Keywords: Determinants of investment; Financing constraints; Corporate governance

1. Introduction

* Corresponding author.
E-mail addresses: daudrets@indiana.edu (D.B. Audretsch),
jweigand@whu.edu (J. Weigand).

0048-7333/$ – see front matter © 2005 Elsevier B.V. All rights reserved.
doi:10.1016/j.respol.2004.12.004

One of the reasons why the determinants of firm investment remain clouded is that the role of finance has been ambiguous. From a neoclassical perspective, a firm's investment decisions are independent of capital structure choice (except for tax considerations) because perfect capital markets guarantee all firms equal access to external finance (Modigliani and Miller, 1958). However, a more recent literature argues that, arising from asymmetric information, capital markets imperfections render external finance an imperfect substitute for internal finance. Thus, financial factors, such as the reservoir of internally generated funds or the availability of new debt or equity, determine a firm's investment decisions. An important implication of this "new theory of the firm" (Greenwald and Stiglitz, 1990) is that firms may face financing constraints for investment.[1]

The ensuing empirical research, triggered by the seminal article by Fazzari et al. (1988), has looked into the existence of financing constraints, primarily by examining the impact of firm-specific characteristics on the relationship between cash flow and investment.[2] In essence, young and smaller firms seem to suffer

most from financing constraints.[3] Little is known, however, about how industry and systemic characteristics, such as knowledge conditions and the financial system, affect the link between firm size and financing constraints.[4] Answers to this question are important, not the least because of the recent policy discussion on how the design of financial and governance systems matters for economic growth and the competitiveness of countries. In particular, the innovative thrust of small firms is often viewed as an important growth factor. Financing investments may be more difficult for small firms in R&D or knowledge intensive (*hi-K*) industries than for their counterparts in less knowledge intensive (*lo-K*) industries since *hi-K* industries typically involve more uncertainty and asymmetric information as well as problems of appropriating the returns from investment based on newly created knowledge.[5] The financing problem may be aggravated in a bank-centered financial system due to a higher degree of risk aversion.

The purpose of this paper is to fill the gap in the empirical literature by investigating how industry knowledge conditions in conjunction with firm-specific factors affect the extent of financing constraints, as measured by the relationship between tangible investment and cash flow. Most of the available empirical evidence is based on firm data for market-oriented (Anglo-Saxon) financial systems. By looking at a large panel data set of German firms we provide an empirical analysis for a bank-centered financial system.

Our empirical analysis suggests that small firms with specific knowledge may be finance constrained in a bank-centered financial system. More precisely, we

---

[1] Stiglitz and Weiss (1981) pointed out that, unlike in most other markets, the credit market is exceptional in that the price of the good – the rate of interest – is not necessarily at a level that equilibrates the market. They attribute this to the fact that interest rates influence not only the demand for capital but also the risk inherent in different borrowers. As the rate of interest rises, so does the riskiness of borrowers, leading suppliers of capital to rationally decide to limit the quantity of loans they make at any particular interest rate. Most potential lenders have little information of the managerial capabilities or investment opportunities of firms and are unlikely to be able to screen out poor credit risks or to have control over a borrower's investments. If lenders are unable to identify the quality or risk associated with particular borrowers, credit rationing will occur (Jaffe and Russel, 1976). The existence of asymmetric information prevents the suppliers of capital from engaging in price discrimination between riskier and less risky borrowers. The implied agency costs raise the firm's cost of external finance relative to the cost of internally generated funds (Jensen and Meckting, 1976), implying a hierarchy ("pecking order") of finance (Myers and Majluf, 1984). Firms prefer to finance investments internally due to lower agency costs. If the volume of planned investment exceeds internal financing capabilities, firms will seek external finance, favoring debt over equity due to higher agency costs of new equity.

[2] Changes in cash flow do not affect firms' investment spending in perfect capital markets. If capital markets are imperfect, investment spending should be sensitive to changes in cash flow. On the basis of firm-specific factors, such as dividend payouts and firm size, Fazzari et al. (1988) split their sample of firms into the subsets of unconstrained and potentially financing constrained firms. The existence of financing constraints is then inferred from investment-cash-flow regressions by comparing the regression coefficients of cash flow across the two subsets.

[3] Fazzari et al. (1988), for instance, report a significantly greater cash flow sensitivity of investment for smaller firms. For surveys and discussions of the empirical evidence see e.g. Chirinko (1993), Schiantarelli (1996), Hubbard (1998), Hall (2002).

[4] See e.g. Allen and Gale (2001) for a discussion of systems of finance and corporate governance. We understand governance systems as "the design of institutions that induce or force management to internalize the welfare of stakeholders" (Tirole, 2001, p. 4). See Laeven (2003) and Love (2003) for cross-country evidence on how financial liberalization and development relieve financing constraints for small firms.

[5] See for a seminal discussion Arrow (1962) who pointed out that the knowledge conditions underlying an industry vary systematically across industries and may crucially affect investment. In some industries innovation depends more on basic scientific knowledge and systematic R&D than in others.

D.B. Audretsch, J. Weigand / Research Policy 34 (2005) 595–613   597

find that firms in *hi-K* industries are less constrained than are their counterparts in *lo-K* industries. Taken for itself, this outcome may not be startling. It could simply be driven by the fact that many *hi-K* industries include large established and profitable firms which usually do not have financing problems.[6] However, when we control for firm size and the mode of firm control, we get the surprising result that in the *hi-K* industries also the small, owner-controlled firms were not finance constrained. This finding contrasts sharply with empirical evidence for comparable U.S. firms (Himmelberg and Petersen, 1994). As an explanation for our counterintuitive finding, we provide a signaling theory of cash flow in which the ability of small firms with specific knowledge to generate cash flow in a *hi-K* market environment demonstrates to external investors the firm's viability and up-side potential, thus improving the availability of external finance. A caveat is warranted. Due to the lack of data we only consider tangible investment, not firm-level R&D investment which may better indicate knowledge intensity than our distinction in *hi-K* versus *lo-K* industries.[7]

The remainder of the paper is organized as follows. Section 2 discusses the potential links between financing investment, industry characteristics and the mode of corporate control in detail. Section 3 introduces the data set of 361 listed and non-listed German firms, sets up the empirical model, discusses measurement issues and formulates the hypotheses. Section 4 presents the empirical results. We summarize and conclude in Section 5.

2. Knowledge conditions, the mode of corporate control, and corporate investment

Why should knowledge conditions make a difference for corporate finance and investment? Stephan

(1996) and Dasgupta and David (1994) argue that firms engaging in knowledge intensive activities are typically associated with a greater degree of uncertainty and knowledge asymmetries about the potential economic value of their investments. The implication is that financing the investments of knowledge intensive or innovating firms may be more difficult.[8]

There are compelling theoretical reasons to suspect that in knowledge intensive market environments cash flow serves as a signal of a firm's viability and success. The theory of noisy selection introduced by Jovanovic (1982) argues that new firms do not know whether the idea upon which the firm is launched is viable in the market or not. Rather, they discover the viability of the idea through the process of learning from the firm's actual post-entry performance. As a result of the uncertainty, knowledge asymmetries, and potential non-exclusive nature of a firm's investments in a *hi-K* environment, it is more difficult to evaluate the expected value of such a firm as compared to a significantly less knowledge-based firm. The generation of cash flow in a highly uncertain environment, however, does signal firm success and viability. As Arrow (1962) and later Sah and Stiglitz (1986) argue, the cost of acquiring a signal to learn about the underlying economic performance in the presence of uncertain, asymmetric knowledge is not trivial. Thus, by serving as a signal that the firm is being positively selected in the market process, the generation of sufficient cash flow should in fact make it easier to attract external finance. This consideration leads us to predict that the impact of cash flow on investment will actually be weaker for firms in *hi-K* environments, due to the signaling effect of cash flow.[9]

The value of the signal that a firm has been positively selected, should matter more for small and new

---

[6] As correctly pointed out by one reviewer, the industries identified in this paper as *hi-K* industries "include many established high-growth ones, such as autos and chemicals. If Volkswagen applies for a bank loan, not surprisingly there is no problem, even if VW is 'hi research'. In fact, VW's access should be easier than that of a large firm in a mature industry, such as paper".

[7] As emphasized by the same reviewer: "The real way to test for this – which I believe cannot be done [with this German data set, added by the authors] – would be to differentiate 'hi/lo research' by the R&D data for the individual firms in the sample.

---

[8] Recent empirical research provides some supporting evidence. Sterken et al. (2001) find for Dutch companies that financing investment from internally generated funds is more important for firms facing high uncertainty. Baldwin et al. (2002) find that small R&D or knowledge intensive Canadian firms are significantly less debt-financed than their non-R&D or less knowledge intensive counterparts.

[9] There is recent empirical evidence providing indirect support for our argument. Planes et al. (2001) do not find significant differences in financing constraints between innovating and non-innovating French firms. Von Kalckreuth (2004) provides evidence based on survey data that innovating German firms were subjected to milder financing constraints or adjustment problems than non-innovating firms.

firms than for their larger, more established counterparts. Larger firms tend to be older, more diversified and more established in product markets than smaller firms, allowing for a more stable cash flow to avoid being subjected to financing constraints.[10] Access to external finance should be easier for larger firms because they generally can put up more collateral, have a longer track record (credit reputation), and can take advantage of established informal relations to capital providers.

The extent of informational and knowledge asymmetries may be affected by the mode of how the firm is governed. In the neoclassical theory of the firm, perfect markets and informational symmetries ensure that the allocation of risk capital across firms will be Pareto-optimal, irrespective of industry- or firm-specific knowledge conditions and of who owns or runs the firm. Utility-maximizing owner-managers can do no better than managers hired to maximize shareholder value. As shareholders have the same information as managers, the latter cannot deviate from the goal of shareholder value maximization. With asymmetric information however, managers enjoy an information advantage over shareholders and have the incentive to pursue their own interests. Appropriate governance mechanisms are then called for to align managers' and shareholders' interests.

Conflicts of interest may arise from the separation of ownership and control in dispersely held companies in particular. In such companies individual shareholders hold only small equity interests so that control over the firm is in the hands of hired managers and honorary outside supervisors. This separation of control from ownership gives managers discretion to pursue personal investment objectives (see Berle and Means, 1932). "Manager control" may foster free cash flow to be diverted for pet projects, staff expansion, empire building, etc. (Jensen, 1986). It has been argued in the governance literature that the presence of large shareholders (ownership concentration, board membership) may improve corporate governance. Large shareholders have sufficient control over the firm's assets (such as a blocking interest) to actually govern the firm by exercising their voting rights. Since they aim

at maximizing their return on investment, they have a strong interest in the selection of top-level managers, monitoring their progress, and intervening when they fail. "Owner control" thus may reduce agency conflicts and facilitate access to external finance for investment. Banks as monitoring creditors may exert as much control as a large shareholder – even more so in a bank-oriented financial system such as Germany where banks can hold equity stakes in industrial firms. The mode of corporate governance may thus affect financing constraints if tighter governance reduces the transaction or agency costs associated with knowledge asymmetries.[11]

There is sound empirical evidence that the degree of financing constraints is negatively related to firm size (see Fazzari et al., 1988). Smaller firms typically appear to be significantly more constrained. Only a few studies have examined the role of ownership structures for corporate investment.[12] Comparing majority-held and diffusely-owned U.S. companies Holdemess and Sheenan (1988) found no significant differences in tangible and intangible investment patterns. More recently, Cho (1998) provided evidence for a sample of large U.S. manufacturing firms that ownership structure does not matter for tangible and R&D investment. Rather, investment induces changes in ownership structures by changing corporate value. Firms with profitable investment decisions become more attractive to investors and the highly liquid U.S. stock markets facilitate changes in share ownership.

A couple of recent studies examine firm financing constraints across different financial systems, such as the bank-centered systems of France or Germany ver-

---

[10] Clementi and Hopenhayn (2002) show theoretically that borrowing constraints are a feature of optimal long-term lending contracts and relax with the success, age and size of the firm.

[11] There may also be costs involved with having large shareholders or strong banks. For example, if the interests of large shareholders deviate from the interests of other investors in the firm, wealth may be redistributed inefficiently. According to Shleifer and Vishny (1997, pp. 755), 'straightforward expropriation of other investors, managers, and employees; inefficient expropriation through pursuit of personal (non-profit-maximizing) objectives; and finally the incentive effects of expropriation on the other stakeholders' may result from having large shareholders. Banks could exploit an exclusive main-bank relationship and make a client firm more finance constrained (Sharpe, 1990; Rajan, 1992). Further, recent cases of firm bankruptcies and scandals (Metallgesellschaft, Philip Holzmann, Kirch Media Group) cast German banks in an unfavorable light with respect to their ability and willingness to exercise good corporate governance.

[12] Most studies have explored the impact of ownership structure on profitability or capital structure. See Short (1994) for a recent survey.

D.B. Audretsch, J. Weigand / Research Policy 34 (2005) 595–613   599

sus the market-oriented Anglo-Saxon systems. Comparing a matched sample of firms from the U.K. and Germany for the late 1980s and early 1990s, Bond et al. (1999) find that German firms were not finance constrained, while their British counterparts were. Hall et al. (1999) and Mulkay et al. (1999) find a significantly stronger investment cash flow relationship for U.S. firms than for French firms. Elston and Albach (1995), Bond et al. (2003), and Reimund (2002, 2003), comparing bank-owned and non-bank-owned German firms, find that the bank affiliated firms experienced weaker financing constraints, implying that affiliation with banks mitigated information problems through more effective corporate governance.

With respect to knowledge conditions Himmelberg and Petersen (1994) find for U.S. firms that small owner-managed firms in R&D-intensive environments suffer most from financing constraints. Having a large corporation as the main shareholder or being a member of a business group may provide substantial backup finance and collateral for the investment of a small firm. Gangopadhyay et al. (2001) find that Indian companies which were members of business groups were less finance constrained. However, the findings of Lang and Stulz (1994) as well as Shin and Stulz (1998) imply that subsidiaries of large, diversified U.S. firms may be finance constrained.

Summing up, theoretical arguments and empirical evidence suggest that both industry and firm characteristics as well as the orientation of the financial system should systematically affect corporate investment. This will be explicitly tested in the remainder of the paper.

3. Measurement

3.1. The data

To estimate if the liquidity constraints of firms in *hi-K* industries differ from firms in *lo-K* industries and how governance structures and firm size link in, we apply a data set of 361 firms of the German mining and manufacturing sector. Most of the sample firms have the legal form of stock corporation (*Aktiengesellschaft*); 182 of them were publicly traded companies. In addition to stock corporations, we include a number of private limited liability companies (GmbH companies),

as well as limited partnerships, for which accounting data were available. Accounting data for constructing empirical variables were taken from the firms' annual reports, while secondary sources had to be consulted for identifying owners, distributions of shares outstanding, composition of managing and supervisory boards.[13] Annual observations were available for each firm between 1991 and 1996, making it possible to construct a balanced panel data set. For a subset of firms also observations for 1987–1990 and 1997–1998 could be included, allowing us to check the regression results found for the shorter time-series of the balanced panel with the unbalanced panel.[14]

3.1.1. hi-K versus lo-K industries

Our classification of industries as being knowledge intensive or not is based on survey results reported by Beise and Licht (1996, pp. 4–6, Tables 2.1 and 2.2).[15] The survey reveals that chemicals (including pharmaceuticals and biotechnology), machinery, motor vehicles, electronics (including information technology), and instruments (including laser technology, cameras, watches and clocks) had the highest R&D ratios and the highest share of firms with R&D budgets and in-house R&D laboratories. Further, economic activities in these industries are specifically based on knowledge generated in the natural sciences. Therefore, we define these industries as well as the aerospace industry, which is not listed separately in Beise and Licht, as *hi-K* industries. All other industries are regarded as *lo-K*. Table 1 shows industries, classifications and the distribution of our sample firms. According to their core economic activity we classified 223 firms into *hi-K* industries and 138 into *lo-K* industries.

---

[13] The sources used are Commerzbank's, Wer gehört zu wem?, Hypobank's Wegweiser durch deutsche Aktiengesellschaften, and Hoppenstedt's Börsenführer.

[14] Adding observations for the earlier 1980s is not feasible because (1) data for many smaller firms in our sample – if they existed at all before 1987 – were not available and (2) there was a change in German corporate law in 1986 regarding the standards for financial statement data. Thus, data from before 1987 cannot fully be compared to data from later years.

[15] The survey Mannheimer Innovationspanel conducted for the first time in 1992/1993 by the Mannheim-based Zentrum für Europaische Wirtschaftsforschung (ZEW) contains data on innovation and investment collected from more than 43,000 West German manufacturing firms.

D.B. Audretsch, J. Weigand / Research Policy 34 (2005) 595–613

Table 1
Knowledge intensive vs. less knowledge intensive industries

Industry	Industry R&D intensity (%)[a]	Percentage of firms in the industry with R&D activities (%)[b]	Number of sample firms from the respective industry (average firm size)[c]
Knowledge intensive (*hi-K*) industries			223 (13216)
Chemicals and related products	8.1	57	60 (13667)
Electric and electronic equipment	6.0	63	56 (14556)
Motor vehicles and related products	5.3	40	18 (10148)
Instruments and related products	5.1	41	10 (5328)
Machinery, except electrical	3.3	44	76 (7105)
Aircraft and aerospace technologies	NA	NA	3 (2988)
Other (*lo-K*) industries			138 (7584)
Steel and light metal construction	2.9	9	4 (2520)
Leather and leather products, textile mill products, apparel	1.9	25	3 (2660)
Rubber and plastic products	1.6	45	4 (14586)
Primary metal industries	1.1	30	37 (6098)
Fabricated metal products	0.9	37	16 (1975)
Lumber, paper, printing, and related products	0.9	12	4 (3191)
Stone and clay, pottery and glass products	0.8	17	33 (4080)
Food and kindred products, tobacco manufacturers	0.6	7	4 (4751)
Other manufacturing	NA	NA	33 (17810)

[a] Total expenditures for R&D and innovation in 1993 in per cent of sales revenues, source: Beise and Licht (1996), based on the ZEW innovation survey (Mannheimer Innovationspanel, Zentrum fur Europaische Wirtschaftsforschung), including 43,300 West German firms.
[b] In per cent of all reporting firms, source: Beise and Licht (1996).
[c] Average firm size of the sample firms is measured by the number of employees averaged over the period 1991–1996.

3.1.2. Firm size

To compare small and large firms, we define small (and medium-sized) firms as having less than 500 employees during the observation period. The definition of a small and medium-sized firm as having 500 employees or less, while confirming to government definitions, is arbitrary but unavoidable here because smaller firms are underrepresented in our sample. However, due to the fact that only stock corporations and larger private limited companies are obliged by German law to publish financial statements this shortcoming cannot be overcome easily. Nevertheless future work should examine how the determinants of liquidity constraints vary systematically as firm size changes.

3.1.3. Asset ownership and mode of corporate control

A striking feature of the ownership structure of German firms is the presence of very large shareholders and a high degree of ownership concentration. As Table 2 shows, more than two-thirds of the sample firms

had just one large shareholder who, on average, commanded a dominating share of the voting capital. Only in 71 firms the largest shareholder did not have at least a majority block of the voting capital. Further, owners and ownership concentration barely change over time. In the balanced-panel period 1991–1996 we find only 26 firms that changed large blockholders. Further, a mere six per cent of the sample variation of ownership concentration results from time series (within) variation, while 94% is attributable to variation across firms.

Since ownership is so highly concentrated for an overwhelming part of our sample firms and has so little time-series variation, we capture the mode of corporate control by distinguishing between manager-controlled and owner-controlled firms. We define a firm as *owner-controlled* if individuals, families or banks have equity stakes (or accumulated proxy voting rights in the case of banks) exceeding at least 5% of the voting capital and there is no independent company identifiable that commands a *larger* share. All other firms with no iden-

D.B. Audretsch, J. Weigand / Research Policy 34 (2005) 595–613

Table 2
Ownership and size characteristics of the sample firms

Number of large shareholders (more than 5% of voting capital)	Number of firms (average number of employees)	Mean (st. dev.) of largest shareholder's share in voting capital (%)	Mean (st. dev.) share of dispersed owner-ship (%)	Number of owner-controlled firms (average number of employees)
0	6 (52422)	0.55 (1.35)	99.45 (1.39)	0
1	243 (10977)	87.34 (23.18)	10.01 (19.13)	105 (16532)
2	65 (7576)	55.65 (16.21)	16.84 (17.52)	25 (7666)
3	28 (9814)	44.43 (18.33)	24.68 (23.56)	5 (1510)
>3	19 (8155)	55.58 (28.28)	21.23 (24.73)	8 (4478)
Overall	361 (10972)	75.19 (28.78)	14.45 (22.76)	143 (15824)

Voting power of the largest shareholder	Number of firms (average number of employees)	Mean (st. dev.) of largest shareholder's share in voting capital (%)
Minority interest[a]	27 (59214)	11.72 (9.89)
Blocking interest[b]	44 (18759)	39.67 (8.80)
Majority interest[c]	77 (4289)	59.57 (7.84)
Dominating interest[d]	213 (7081)	96.22 (7.00)

[a] Minority interest less than 25.0% of voting capital.
[b] Blocking interest between 25% of voting capital plus one vote and 50.0% of voting capital.
[c] Majority interest between 50% of voting capital plus one vote and 75.0% of voting capital.
[d] Dominating interest 75% of voting capital plus one vote and more.

tifiable large shareholder or with an another industrial company as large shareholder are defined as *manager-controlled* (see Lehmann and Weigand, 2000, for more discussion).

For the manager-controlled firms we assume that hired managers exercise control rather than the ultimate owners. About 40% of the sample firms are owner-controlled. In most of these firms owners were members of either the board of directors or the board of supervisors, sometimes of both.[16]

3.2. *Some descriptive statistics*

Table 3 compares the means of selected firm variables for *hi-K* versus *lo-K*, manager-controlled versus owner-controlled, as well as large versus small firms. For each variable and pair of sub-groups we report the absolute *t*-statistics of testing for differences in means.[17]

As measured by sales and employment, *hi-K*, owner-controlled and, of course, larger firms are significantly larger than their counterparts. The annual rate of change

in employment was negative in all subgroups. However, employment downsizing was significantly less severe for the owner-controlled firms and for the small firms. The owner-controlled firms also experienced significantly higher rates of sales growth.

hi-K firms as compared to *lo-K* firms display significantly lower ratios of investment and cash flow to total assets but the sales/assets ratio is also lower, implying less opportunities for additional investments. This lower tangible investment ratio might reflect a greater emphasis of the *hi-K* firms on R&D investment. Unfortunately, we cannot investigate R&D investment directly due to the lack of firm-specific R&D data. The net working capital ratio and their share of pension liabilities is significantly higher, whereas the ratio of long-term debt is lower. This pattern indicates that the *hi-K* firms may be better able to smooth investment spending in the face of cash flow shocks by reducing net working capital and tapping the reservoir of funds built up to satisfy pension schemes. The lower long-term debt ratio may also reflect that firm investment in *hi-K* industries is preferably financed internally because of higher uncertainty.

Owner-controlled firms as compared to manager-controlled firms have significantly higher ratios of investment and cash flow but the sales/assets ratio is also higher so that investment opportunities might not have

---

[16] See e.g. Baums (1994, pp. 425) for a discussion of the German dual-boards (two-tier) system.

[17] The *t*-test assumes that variances differ across the subsets. Degrees of freedom are given in brackets behind the *t*-statistic.

Table 3
Summary statistics, balanced sample, 1991–1996

Variable (in per cent if not noted otherwise)[a]	Mean (standard error)			
	All firms	hi-K industries, lo-K industries, t-statistic (d.f.)	Manager-controlled, owner-controlled, t-statistic (d.f.)	Large, small, t-statistic (d.f.)
Investment ratio[b]	7.61 (0.15)	6.76 (0.16), 8.98 (0.29), 6.73 (1125)***	7.07 (0.15), 8.17 (0.1), 4.48 (1765)***	7.71 (0.15), 7.14 (0.47), 1.16 (400)
Cash flow ratio[c]	11.56 (0.27)	10.51 (0.32), 13.26 (0.47), 4.89 (1296)***	10.40 (0.30), 12.39 (0.33), 4.48 (1974)***	11.28 (0.28), 12.80 (0.71), 2.01 (441)***
Sales-to-assets ratio[d]	156.71 (1.76)	154.10 (2.21), 160.93 (2.91), 1.87 (1420)*	153.80 (2.41), 161.15 (2.51), 2.12 (1694)**	153.46 (1.75), 171.25 (5.54), 3.06 (397)***
Net working capital ratio[e]	31.89 (0.46)	34.35 (0.59), 27.92 (0.70), 7.03 (1533)***	31.95 (0.56), 32.21 (0.60), 0.73 (2000)	31.06 (0.47), 35.64 (0.13), 3.23 (413)***
Change in net working capital ratio	2.23 (0.35)	2.50 (0.47), 1.79 (0.50), 1.03 (1431)	1.12 (0.41), 0.61 (0.44), 0.81 (1670)	2.12 (0.90), 2.71 (0.38), 0.61 (450)
Long-term debt ratio	11.70 (0.32)	10.75 (0.40), 13.23 (0.52), 3.76 (1440)***	10.65 (0.43), 13.30 (0.46), 4.19 (1682)***	11.94 (0.36), 10.65 (0.71), 1.61 (507)
Change in long-term debt	0.50 (0.24)	0.52 (0.32), 0.49 (0.37), 0.06 (1563)	0.04 (0.33), 1.21 (0.35), 2.44 (1686)**	0.56 (0.28), 0.26 (0.47), 0.56 (585)
Pension liabilities ratio	28.30 (0.36)	29.52 (0.48), 26.31 (0.50), 4.61 (1671)***	29.93 (0.47), 25.81 (0.54), 5.78 (1599)***	29.52 (0.39), 22.84 (0.85), 7.14 (472)***
Change in pension liabilities	1.51 (0.13)	1.64 (0.17), 1.32 (0.21), 1.19 (1537)	1.54 (0.18), 1.48 (0.20), 0.22 (1614)	1.63 (0.15), 0.98 (0.28), 2.07 (540)***
Sales (in millions DM)	3316 (239)	3820 (344), 2502 (282), 2.96 (1799)***	2578 (189), 4357 (467), 3.60 (1154)***	4020 (289), 171 (21), 13.30 (1488)***
Sales growth (annual log change in real sales)	2.19 (0.53)	2.46 (0.67), 1.76 (0.88), 0.63 (1425)	0.93 (0.74), 4.23 (0.72), 3.18 (1737)***	2.07 (0.59), 2.74 (1.26), 0.48 (480)
Employment	10972 (803)	13094 (1217), 7543 (719), 3.93 (1693)***	7940 (557), 15824 (1648), 4.53 (1053)***	13369 (972), 263 (8), 13.49 (1474)***
Employment change (annual log change in total employment)	−1.96 (0.46)	−1.42 (0.55), −2.83 (0.80), −1.46 (1319)	−3.24 (0.53), −0.00 (0.82), 3.28 (1319)***	−2.39 (0.48), −0.04 (1.26), 1.78 (430)*
Firms (pooled observations)	361 (1805)	223 (1115), 138 (690)	218 (1090), 143 (715)	295 (1475), 66 (330)

[a] Beginning-of-the-year book value of total assets.
[b] Current-period expenditure for tangible investment/assets.
[c] (Operating income + depreciation + the year-to-year change in liability reserves)/assets.
[d] Current-period sales revenues.
[e] (Current assets (cash, short-term securities, receivables, inventories) − current liabilities)/assets.
* Significant at the 0.10 level.
** Significant at the 0.05 level.
*** Significant at the 0.01 level.

D.B. Audretsch, J. Weigand / Research Policy 34 (2005) 595–613

been fully exploited. They rely more on long-term debt, and this ratio has increased significantly over the observation period. By contrast, their ratio of pension liabilities is significantly lower.

Large firms as compared to small firms have significantly lower ratios of cash flow and net working capital than small firms but the sales-assets ratio is also significantly lower, indicating more exploited investment opportunities. They have a higher ratio of pension liabilities, and the ratio has increased significantly more over the observation period.

3.3. The empirical model

We estimate the following panel regression model:

$$\frac{I_{it}}{A_{i,t-1}} = \beta_1 \frac{CF_{it}}{A_{i,t-1}} + \beta_2 \frac{S_{it}}{A_{i,t-1}} + \beta_3 \frac{\Delta_t WC_i}{A_{i,t-1}}$$
$$+ \beta_4 \frac{\Delta_t LTD_i}{A_{i,t-1}} + \beta_5 \frac{\Delta_t PL_{it}}{A_{i,t-1}} + \mu_{it} \qquad (1)$$

The subscripts $i = 1,\ldots,361$ and $t-1 = 1987,\ldots,1998$ denote individual firms and time periods, respectively, Δ is the first-difference operator. Regression equation (1) regresses a firm's investment ratio on the cash flow ratio and a set of control variables. I is the current-period expenditure for tangible investment. A, the beginning-of-the year book value of total assets, serves as a scaling factor.[18] CF denotes cash flow defined as operating income plus depreciation charges plus the year-to-year change in liability reserves. S is current-period sales. ΔWC, ΔLTD and ΔPL stand for the year-to-year changes in net working capital (current assets minus current liabilities), long-term debt LTD and pension liabilities PL, respectively. The potential effect of these variables on corporate investment will be discussed in more detail below.

We take advantage of the data set's panel structure to allow for unobserved heterogeneity across firms and time periods which may be introduced by systematic variations in the user cost of capital or bias due to the non-randomness of sample selection. The regression disturbance μ_{it} decomposes into a classical white noise error $v_{it} \sim (0, \sigma_v^2)$ and effects specific to individual firms, α_i, and time, λ_t. Regression equation (1) is

estimated using standard panel regression techniques (see e.g. Baltagi, 2001). Details on estimation techniques and specification tests will be provided in the tables.

To test for the *individual* impact of either firm size, knowledge conditions or the mode of corporate control on the investment cash flow relationship we use Eq. (2).

$$\frac{I_{it}}{A_{i,t-1}} = \beta_1 \frac{CF_{it}}{A_{i,t-1}} + \delta_1 D_i \times \frac{CF_{it}}{A_{i,t-1}} + \beta_2 \frac{S_{it}}{A_{i,t-1}}$$
$$+ \delta_2 D_i \times \frac{S_{it}}{A_{i,t-1}} + \cdots + \mu_{it} \qquad (2)$$

The dummy variable D_i equals 1 if firm i operates in a *hi-K* industry (is manager-controlled or large, respectively), and 0 otherwise. The β coefficients measure the impact of the respective variables on investment of the *lo-K* (owner-controlled, small) firms, whereas the δ coefficients measure the difference between the β coefficients and the slope coefficients of the *hi-K* (manager-controlled, large) firms.[19]

To test for *joint* effects of firm size, knowledge conditions or the mode of corporate control on the investment cash flow relationship we employ the same methodology as for regression equation (2) but split the firms into the eights subsets defined as large manager-controlled firms in *hi-K* industries (LMH), large owner-controlled firms in *hi-K* industries (LOH), small manager-controlled firms in *hi-K* industries (SMH), small owner-controlled firms in *hi-K* industries (SOH), large manager-controlled firms in *lo-K* industries (LML), large owner-controlled firms in *lo-K* industries (LOL), small manager-controlled firms in *lo-K* industries (SML), and small owner-controlled firms in *lo-K* industries (SOL).

---

[18] Replacement values of assets were not available and could not be calculated either, since the investment series is too short for most sample firms.

[19] Adding δs to βs, or estimating the equation with the dummy variable defined the other way around, yields the slope coefficients for the *hi-K* (manager-controlled, large) firms. Estimating model (2) yields exactly the same regression coefficients as those that would result from estimating model (1) separately for the subgroup of *hi-K* firms and the subgroup of *lo-K* firms. However, given that the variance of the regression errors is constant over the sample period, a coefficient estimate from model (2), since being based on all available observations, is efficient, whereas the estimates obtained from two separate subgroups are not.

4. Regression analysis

4.1. Hypotheses

For firms operating under a regime of financial constraints we expect the following pattern of coefficients

$$\beta_1 > 0, \qquad \beta_2 > 0, \qquad \beta_3 > 0,$$
$$\beta_4 > 0, \qquad \beta_5 > 0 \qquad\qquad (3)$$

estimated at a statistically significant level. In the following, we substantiate the underlying hypotheses.

4.1.1. The cash flow effect and investment opportunities

The importance of cash flow for corporate investment is reflected in Eq. (1) by the coefficient β_1. With imperfect capital markets, we expect $\beta_1 > 0$ if investment opportunities are properly controlled for. This is the cash flow hypothesis.

H1. Firm investment is positively related to cash flow.

Many studies in the literature control for investment opportunities by including Tobin's Q in the estimating equation. Unfortunately, in this study Tobin's Q cannot be constructed because of the relatively large number of non-quoted firms (179) in our sample. In order to control for investment opportunities, we instead use the sales-to-total assets ratio which indicates the utilization of a firm's total assets and thus the need for additional investment (see Brealey and Myers, 2000, p. 827). We expect $\beta_2 > 0$ which reflects the second hypothesis.

H2. Firm investment is positively related to investment opportunities.

An important qualification is that these proxy measures may introduce measurement bias. Studies have identified average Tobin's Q as well as the sales/assets ratio or sales growth as being less than perfect indicators of investment opportunities.[20] To the extent that the regression coefficient is biased, a positive coefficient estimate on cash flow may then simply indicate shifts in investment demand and expected future profitability

rather than financing constraints. Different solutions to overcome these measurement problems (e.g. estimating the Euler equation, accelerator or error correction models) have been suggested in the literature. However, these approaches often call for rather long time-series data.[21] An alternative to identifying the potential liquidity role of cash flow was suggested by Fazzari and Petersen (1993). They point out that a firm confronted by financing constraints typically adjusts net working capital to smooth investment relative to cash flow shocks if adjusting tangible or R&D investment entails higher costs than adjusting the difference between current assets (cash, short-term securities, receivables, inventories) and current liabilities. They recommend including the change in net working capital to separate the profitability effect of cash flow from the liquidity effect. Therefore, for a financially constrained firm, we expect an inverse relationship between investment and the change in net working capital, $\beta_3 < 0$. However, if cash flow signals investment opportunities rather than liquidity, we should also observe a positive coefficient for the change in net working capital in the investment equation, $\beta_3 > 0$, since the change in net working capital tends to be positively correlated with profits or sales. This suggests the third hypothesis.

H3. Firm investment should be negatively related to the change in net working capital.

Of course, as we assume that investment in tangible investment is financed from current cash flow, investment in net working capital is also an endogenous variable. To account for the simultaneity of tangible investment and net working capital investment we use two-stage least square estimation techniques (2SLS-Within), instrumenting the change in net working capital by the lagged working capital ratio plus all other right-hand side variables from regression equation (1).[22]

---

[20] See e.g. Chirinko (1993), Kaplan and Zingales (1997), Hubbard (1998) for a discussion of measurement issues.

[21] Estimation techniques for dynamic panel data models (e.g. GMM) consume a substantial amount of degrees of freedom. While taking care of contemporaneous simultaneity and measurement error, the dynamic panel data estimators tend to have large standard errors due to the fact of weak instruments. See Baltagi (2001) on estimators for static and dynamic panel data models.

[22] See Fazzari and Petersen (1993) for a detailed discussion of instrumenting the change in working capital.

D.B. Audretsch, J. Weigand / Research Policy 34 (2005) 595–613   605

4.1.2. Controlling for other sources of finance

We include the changes in long-term debt and pension liabilities as indicators of firms' access to finance other than cash flow. It is often argued for the bank-centered German financial system that bank loans are more readily available than other forms of external finance. The reason could be that German banks may have been better informed and more effective monitors due to close relationships to industrial firms (e.g. through equity holdings, proxy voting rights, board representation).[23] Although not reported separately by most firms in our sample, long-term debt presumably reflects bank loans to a high degree.[24]

A peculiarity of the German accounting system is that pension assets and pension liabilities are not netted out in companies' balance sheets. Moreover, pension liabilities are not paid into a trust (pension fund) but remain within the firm and are available to the firm as a source of long-term finance. If German firms suffer from financing constraints despite the potential advantages of a bank-centered financial system we expect the changes in long-term debt and pension liabilities to be positively related to investment, $\beta_4 > 0$ and, $\beta_5 > 0$ which reflect H4 and H5.

H4.   Firm investment is positively related to changes in long-term debt.

H5.   Firm investment is positively related to pension liabilities.

Compared to small firms in the U.S. and U.K., smaller enterprises in Germany traditionally have relied heavily on banks as a source of finance. However, by the 1990s, new forms of finance, such as venture capital, started to emerge. The increased access of smaller German firms to these non-traditional sources of finance may have reduced the extent of financing constraints in the 1990s.[25] Further, deregulation and liberalization of the entire financial sector in Germany, as

well as throughout the European Union set in in the 1990s. This provided large enterprises direct access to the capital markets, thereby leaving more funds available for lending to small enterprises.[26] The implication is that financing constraints were alleviated in the course of the 1990s.

H6.   Financing constraints relax over the sample's time period due to financial deregulation and the emergence of new sources of finance.

4.1.3. Controlling for individual and joint effects of firm size, knowledge conditions and mode of corporate control

Based on our discussion in Section 2 we expect the following hypothesis to hold.

H7a.   Firm size, knowledge conditions and the mode of control affect the extent of financing constraints individually. Therefore, the coefficient pattern in (3) differs significantly among the defined subsets of firms.

Smaller firms should be significantly more finance constrained than larger ones. Also firms in *hi-K* industries and manager-controlled firms should be more constrained. However, there are obvious interactions between the respective variables. For example, separation of ownership and control, and thus manager control, is more likely in larger firms. Therefore, we expect the following hypothesis to hold.

H7b.   Firm size, knowledge conditions and the mode of control affect the extent of financing constraints jointly. Therefore, the coefficient pattern in (3) differs significantly among the defined subsets of firms.

4.2. Full-sample results

The regression results from estimating model (1) for the full sample of firms and from model (3) considering differences in firm size, knowledge conditions and mode of control are shown in Tables 4 and 5. Table 4 contains the estimates for the balanced

---

[23] See Edwards and Fischer (1994), Baums (1994), or Roe (1994) for a more comprehensive discussion.

[24] Studies using aggregate data show that bank loans have by far been the most important source of external firm finance in Germany (Edwards and Fischer, 1994; Weigand, 1998).

[25] Hall (2002), in reviewing the available empirical evidence, concludes that small and new innovative firms face high costs of capital which are only partly lowered by the availability of venture capital.

[26] Bank borrowing of large firms in Germany decreased significantly from the 1980s to the 1990s, while lending to smaller firms increased (see Weigand, 1998).

D.B. Audretsch, J. Weigand / Research Policy 34 (2005) 595–613

Table 4
Investment and financing constraints: balanced sample, 1992–96

Explanatory variable predicted coefficient for financing constraints	Dependent variable: investment ratio			
	Estimated coefficients (absolute t-ratios)			
	All firms	hi-K industries, lo-K industries, coefficient difference	Manager-controlled, owner-controlled, coefficient difference	Large, small, coefficient difference
Cash flow ratio, $\beta_1 > 0$	0.1116 (5.59)***	0.0932 (3.43), 0.1441 (4.53)***, −0.0508 (1.21)	0.0965 (3.83)***, 0.1532 (4.14)***, −0.0567 (1.27)	0.0950 (4.40)***, 0.2656 (4.52)***, −0.1706 (2.72)***
Sales-to-assets ratio, $\beta_2 > 0$	0.0376 (7.98)***	0.0369 (5.75)***, 0.0393 (5.74)***, −0.0024 (0.25)	0.0305 (5.45)***, 0.0585 (6.49)***, −0.0280 (2.63)***	0.0393 (7.14)***, 0.0319 (3.86)***, 0.0074 (0.74)
Change in net working capital ratio, $\beta_3 > 0$	−0.1237 (5.01)***	−0.0671 (1.92)*, −0.1936 (5.77)***, 0.1264 (2.61)***	−0.1087 (3.75)***, −0.1675 (3.48)***, 0.0587 (1.04)	−0.1081 (4.38)***, −0.2681 (3.65)***, 0.1600 (2.07)**
Change in long-term debt, $\beta_4 > 0$	0.1608 (7.27)***	0.0868 (2.76)**, 0.2589 (8.66)***, −0.1720 (3.96)***	0.1387 (4.64)***, 0.2046 (7.36)***, −0.0658 (1.58)	0.1322 (5.89)**, 0.4008 (6.34)***, −0.2686 (4.00)***
Change in pension liabilities, $\beta_5 > 0$	0.0433 (1.68)*	0.0320 (0.92), 0.0493 (1.26), −0.0173 (0.33)	0.0560 (1.65)*, −0.0169 (0.40), 0.0731 (1.36)	0.0223 (0.84), 0.2247 (3.07)***, −0.2023 (2.60)***
Time effect 1993	−0.0099 (2.91)***	−0.0143 (3.31)***, −0.0033 (0.60), −0.0110 (1.59)	−0.0112 (2.59)**, −0.0077 (1.43), −0.0035 (0.51)	−0.0090 (2.49)*, −0.0112 (1.45), 0.0022 (0.26)
Time effect 1994	−0.0125 (3.64)***	−0.0179 (4.14)***, −0.0032 (0.58), −0.0147 (2.10)**	−0.0165 (3.77)***, −0.0051 (0.95), −0.0114 (1.63)	−0.0133 (3.62)***, −0.0103 (1.37), −0.0030 (0.36)
Time effect 1995	−0.0128 (3.79)***	−0.0136 (3.20)***, −0.0096 (1.78)*, −0.0040 (0.57)	−0.0139 (3.20)***, −0.0106 (2.03)**, −0.0033 (0.48)	−0.0160 (4.44)***, 0.0014 (0.18), −0.0174 (2.06)**
Time effect 1996	−0.0146 (4.32)***	−0.0151 (3.56)***, −0.0136 (2.47)**, −0.0015 (0.22)	−0.0214 (4.93)***, −0.0035 (0.66), −0.0179 (2.61)***	−0.0176 (4.86)***, −0.0028 (0.37), −0.0148 (1.77)*
Firms (pooled observations)	361 (1805)	223 (1115), 138 (690)	218 (1090), 143 (715)	295 (1475), 66 (330)

Notes: Heteroskedasticity-consistent 2SLS-Within regression estimates from the balanced panel with 361 fixed firm-specific effects (coefficients not reported). The coefficient difference is the estimated coefficients for the knowledge-based (manager-controlled, large) firms minus the coefficients for the non-knowledge-based (owner-controlled, small) firms. Instruments for *Working capital ratio*: all other right-hand side variables plus the working capital ratio ($t − 1$).

* Significant at the 0.10 level.
** Significant at the 0.05 level.
*** Significant at the 0.01 level.

Table 5
Investment and financing constraints: unbalanced sample, 1988–1998

Explanatory variable predicted coefficient for financing constraints	Dependent variable: investment ratio			
	Estimated coefficients (absolute *t*-ratios)			
	All firms	hi-K industries, lo-K industries, coefficient difference	Manager-controlled, owner-controlled, coefficient difference	Large, small, coefficient difference
Cash flow ratio, $\beta_1 > 0$	0.1489 (3.11)***	0.1160 (3.12)***, 0.1721 (2.80)***, -0.0561 (2.07)**	0.1119 (3.23)***, 0.1609 (3.77)***, -0.0590 (1.53)	0.0932 (4.10)***, 0.2439 (4.65)***, -0.1407 (2.64)***
Sales-to-assets ratio, $\beta_2 > 0$	0.0534 (2.51)**	0.0492 (3.18)***, 0.0564 (4.02)***, -0.0072 (0.34)	0.0480 (5.16)***, 0.0611 (5.22)***, -0.0131 (1.34)	0.0426 (3.12)***, 0.0577 (2.92)***, -0.0152 (0.61)
Change in net working capital ratio, $\beta_3 < 0$	-0.1900 (6.62)***	-0.0766 (2.11)**, -0.2514 (5.77)***, 0.1748 (3.44)***	-0.1212 (2.35)**, -0.2691 (2.43)**, 0.1479 (2.69)***	-0.1198 (3.05)***, -0.2976 (2.58)***, 0.1778 (1.96)**
Change in long-term debt, $\beta_4 < 0$	0.2098 (4.55)***	0.1437 (2.76)***, 0.3008 (6.06)***, -0.1571 (3.51)***	0.1601 (4.09)***, 0.2900 (6.45)***, -0.1299 (1.67)*	0.1477 (4.47)***, 0.4941 (2.81)***, -0.3464 (3.22)***
Change in pension liabilities, $\beta_5 < 0$	0.0726 (2.09)***	0.0684 (1.72)*, 0.0843 (1.81)*, -0.0159 (0.28)	0.0689 (1.66)*, 0.0202 (0.39), 0.0487 (0.88)	0.0081 (0.06), 0.2386 (3.17)***, -0.2305 (2.98)***
Time effect 1989	0.0001 (0.98)	0.0033 (1.21), -0.0021 (0.60), 0.0012 (0.59)	0.0038 (1.08), -0.0052 (0.28), -0.0014 (0.77)	0.0001 (0.49), 0.0008 (0.72), -0.0007 (0.11)
Time effect 1990	0.0248 (5.01)***	0.0304 (2.17)*, 0.0199 (1.69)*, 0.0105 (1.54)	0.0255 (1.92)*, 0.0213 (1.88)*, 0.0042 (0.30)	0.0278 (3.62)***, 0.0182 (2.57)*, 0.0096 (1.45)
Time effect 1991	0.0078 (2.72)***	0.0100 (3.33)***, 0.0019 (1.72)*, 0.0081 (2.16)**	0.0082 (2.80)***, 0.0002 (0.08), 0.0080 (1.90)*	0.0100 (3.31)***, 0.0042 (1.39), 0.0058 (1.20)
Time effect 1992	-0.0046 (3.01)***	-0.0020 (2.51)**, -0.0052 (1.19), 0.0032 (0.74)	-0.0030 (2.84)***, -0.0061 (1.99)**, 0.0031 (1.50)	-0.0034 (3.13)***, -0.0066 (1.96)**, 0.0022 (0.70)
Time effect 1993	-0.0119 (2.77)***	-0.0113 (4.09)***, -0.0125 (2.32)**, 0.0012 (0.87)	-0.0110 (3.04)***, -0.0125 (1.79)*, 0.0015 (0.86)	-0.0110 (3.27)***, -0.0136 (1.52), 0.0026 (0.24)
Time effect 1994	-0.0128 (2.82)***	-0.0121 (2.49)**, -0.0139 (2.42)**, 0.0018 (0.68)	-0.0128 (3.01)***, -0.0132 (2.56)**, 0.0004 (0.02)	-0.0126 (4.08)***, -0.0141 (1.56), 0.0015 (0.47)
Time effect 1995	-0.0110 (3.09)***	-0.0110 (5.12)***, -0.0119 (3.63)***, 0.0009 (0.23)	-0.0102 (4.45)***, -0.0124 (2.34)**, 0.0022 (0.88)	-0.0106 (4.20)***, -0.0118 (1.09), 0.0012 (0.22)
Time effect 1996	-0.0125 (3.63)***	-0.0119 (2.15)**, -0.0134 (1.66)*, 0.0015 (0.51)	-0.0111 (2.41)**, -0.0131 (2.38)**, 0.0020 (0.48)	-0.0120 (4.42)***, -0.0129 (0.97), 0.0009 (0.05)
Time effect 1997	-0.0004 (0.27)	-0.0002 (0.14), -0.0012 (0.32), 0.0010 (0.51)	-0.0120 (0.38), -0.0131 (1.24), 0.0011 (0.17)	-0.0080 (0.50), -0.0106 (0.69), 0.0026 (0.62)
Time effect 1998	-0.0111 (1.72)*	-0.0094 (2.01)*, -0.0142 (1.94)*, 0.0048 (0.67)	-0.0089 (1.77)*, -0.0094 (1.92)*, 0.0005 (0.00)	-0.0075 (1.65)*, -0.0126 (1.97)*, 0.0051 (1.44)
Firms (pooled observations)	361 (3729)	223 (2296), 138 (1433)	218 (2339), 143 (1390)	295 (3108), 66 (621)

Notes: Heteroskedasticity-consistent 2SLS–Within regression estimates from the unbalanced panel with 361 fixed firm-specific effects (coefficients not reported). The coefficient difference is the estimated coefficients for the knowledge-based (manager-controlled, large) firms minus the coefficients for the non-knowledge-based (owner-controlled, small) firms. Instruments for *Working capital ratio*: all other right-hand side variables plus the working capital ratio ($t - 1$).
* Significant at the 0.10 level.
** Significant at the 0.05 level.
*** Significant at the 0.01 level.

D.B. Audretsch, J. Weigand / Research Policy 34 (2005) 595–613

panel 1992–1996, Table 5 for the unbalanced panel 1988–1998.

The full-sample estimates for both the balanced and unbalanced panel suggest that our sample firms were facing financing constraints. The coefficients $\beta_1 > 0$, $\beta_2 > 0$, $\beta_3 < 0$, $\beta_4 > 0$ and $\beta_5 > 0$ are indeed statistically significant as suggested by H1–H5 for a regime of financing constraints. Calculated at mean values (taken from Table 3), the elasticity of investment with respect to cash flow is 0.17 (0.16 at median values) in the balanced sample and 0.19 in the unbalanced sample (0.18 at median values). Thus, the inclusion of observations from the late 1980s and late 1990s does not change the cash flow effect greatly.

Table 6 reports the estimates of the cash flow effect when the balanced-sample period 1992–1996 is successively extended forward (adding 1997, 1998) and backward (adding 1991, 1990, 1989, 1988). Starting from the balanced-sample estimates, the cash flow effect increases when observations for 1997 and 1998 are added. It decreases when we add 1991 and 1990 but increases again for 1989 and 1988. This is inconsistent with H6 which claims an alleviation of financing constraints over time due to financial deregulation and venture capitalism. Rather, it seems as if the German reunification boom 1990/1991 reduced the investment cash flow correlation. This interpretation is also supported by the significantly positive time effects for 1990 and 1991. The negative time effects for 1992 and later pick up the downward trend in firm investment that set in after the reunification boom, aggravated by the 1993 recession, the most severe downturn since the oil crises of the 1970s.

4.3. Subset comparisons

The subsample regressions test H7a and H7b. Tables 4–6 show in columns (3)–(5), respectively, the results of the empirical test for the individual effects. Table 7 presents the results of the joint-effects analysis.

4.3.1. Firm size effects

In accordance with Anglo-Saxon studies we find small firms to be significantly more constrained than large firms. The small-firm cash flow elasticity calculated at mean values is 0.48 for the balanced and 0.54 for the unbalanced sample. The availability of long-term financing sources is significantly more important

for the small firms. The cash flow elasticity estimates are very close to what studies for the United States have found for financially constrained firms (cash flow elasticities of 0.50 and greater, see, e.g., Fazzari et al., 1988; Himmelberg and Petersen, 1994).

4.3.2. Do knowledge conditions matter?

Differences in knowledge conditions seem to matter. The cash flow coefficient for the *hi-K* firms tends to be significantly smaller. However, the *lo-K* firms smoothed tangible investment significantly more by adapting net working capital. The coefficient of the change in net working capital is highly significant as is the coefficient difference. Further, the availability of long-term debt is significantly more important for the *lo-K* firms.

Therefore, we may conclude that financing constraints were *less* severe in *hi-K* industries. As Jovanovic (1982) theory of noisy selection would predict, in an uncertain environment cash flow may serve to signal market success, facilitating access to external finance and making investment less depending on the availability of internal finance. After accounting for knowledge conditions, we find cash flow elasticities of 0.14 (0.16, unbalanced) for the *hi-K* firms and of 0.21 (0.22, unbalanced) for the *lo-K* firms.

4.3.3. Does the mode of corporate control matter?

Both manager- and owner-controlled firms exhibit the coefficient pattern expected in the presence of financing constraints. For the balanced panel, there is no statistically significant difference between the two subsets except for the coefficients of the sales/assets ratio, although the relevant coefficients tend to be smaller for the manager-controlled firm. In the unbalanced case, the cash flow, working capital and debt effects are significantly more pronounced for the owner-controlled firms, implying somewhat greater financing constraints.

4.3.4. Are there joint effects?

Table 7 presents the results of testing for joint effects of firm size, knowledge conditions and the mode of corporate control. We take the subset of large manager-controlled firms in *hi-K* industries (LMH) as the baseline group to which the other subsets of firms are compared.

Table 6
The cash-flow effect over time

Estimation period	Estimated cash flow coefficient (absolute t-ratio)			
	All firms	hi-K industries, lo-K industries, coefficient difference	Manager-controlled, owner-controlled, coefficient difference	Large, small, coefficient difference
From Table 4				
1992–1996	0.1116 (5.59)***	0.0932 (3.43)***, 0.1441 (4.53)***	0.0965 (3.83)***, 0.1532 (4.14)***, −0.0567 (1.27)	0.0950 (4.40)***, 0.2656 (4.52)***, −0.1706 (2.72)***
1992–1997	0.1304 (4.98)***	0.0702 (1.78)*, 0.1687 (2.64)***, −0.0985 (2.33)**	0.1042 (2.26)**, 0.1316 (2.38)**, −0.0274 (0.27)	0.0830 (3.59)***, 0.2755 (4.17)***, −0.1925 (2.77)***
1992–1996	0.1419 (5.38)***	0.1000 (3.02)***, 0.1495 (4.41)***, −0.0495 (1.69)*	0.0975 (3.18)***, 0.1364 (3.62)***, −0.0389 (0.72)	0.0779 (3.01)***, 0.2523 (3.88)***, −0.1744 (2.84)***
1991–1998	0.1077 (3.66)***	0.0884 (2.59)**, 0.1277 (3.08)***, −0.0393 (1.11)	0.0921 (2.63)***, 0.1277 (3.08)***, −0.0356 (0.81)	0.0865 (4.19)***, 0.2656 (4.52)***, −0.1706 (2.72)***
1990–1998	0.1122 (4.11)***	0.0966 (3.11)***, 0.1414 (3.20)***, −0.0448 (0.98)	0.1088 (2.77)***, 0.1668 (3.20)***, −0.0580 (1.57)	0.0943 (3.13)***, 0.1956 (4.52)***, −0.1013 (1.95)*
1989–1998	0.1605 (2.47)**	0.1117 (2.59)***, 0.1989 (3.08)***, −0.0872 (2.44)**	0.1117 (2.83)***, 0.1904 (2.86)***, −0.0787 (2.19)**	0.0811 (4.22)***, 0.2466 (4.52)***, −0.1655 (2.55)**
From Table 5				
1988–1998	0.1489 (3.11)***	0.1160 (3.12)***, 0.1721 (2.80)***, −0.0561 (2.07)**	0.1119 (3.23)***, 0.1609 (3.77)***, −0.0590 (1.53)	0.0932 (4.10)***, 0.2439 (4.65)***, −0.1407 (2.64)***

* Significant at the 0.10 level.
** Significant at the 0.05 level.
*** Significant at the 0.01 level.

Table 7
The joint impact of size, control mode and knowledge conditions on the investment – finance relationship

Explanatory variable	Dependent variable: investment ratio	Coefficient difference (absolute t-ratio)						
	Estimated coefficient (absolute t-ratio) 1992–96 1988–98							
	(1) LMH[a]	(2) LOH[b]	(3) SMH[c]	(4) SOH[d]	(5) LML[e]	(6) LOL[f]	(7) SML[g]	(8) SOL[h]
Cash flow ratio	0.0773 (2.24)**, 0.0855 (2.19)**	−0.0183 (0.31), 0.0034 (0.17)	0.1786 (1.92)*, 0.2038 (2.02)**	−0.0280 (0.16), −0.0274 (0.09)	−0.0059 (0.12), −0.0018 (0.01)	0.1660 (2.12)**, 0.1721 (2.14)**	0.2904 (1.98)**, 0.3133 (2.16)**	−0.0062 (0.05), −0.0005 (0.00)
Sales-to-assets ratio	0.0232 (2.81)***, 0.0221 (2.56)**	0.0419 (2.49)**, 0.0351 (2.18)**	0.0366 (2.00)**, 0.0289 (2.06)**	−0.0107 (0.41), −0.0009 (0.32)	0.0125 (0.96), 0.0111 (0.78)	0.0467 (2.90)***, 0.0342 (2.68)***	−0.0131 (0.79), −0.0009 (0.20)	0.0854 (2.99)***, 0.1004 (2.61)**
Change in net working capital ratio	−0.0489 (1.02), −0.0628 (0.98)	−0.0317 (0.43), −0.0414 (1.02)	−0.1491 (1.34), −0.1226 (1.57)	0.0267 (0.43), 0.0232 (0.39)	−0.0778 (1.34), −0.0828 (1.42)	−0.3530 (3.19)***, −0.3884 (3.22)***	−0.4355 (2.14)**, −0.5319 (2.77)***	−0.6043 (4.95)***, −0.6405 (3.17)***
Change in long-term debt	0.0605 (1.15), 0.0490 (1.01)	0.0134 (0.22), 0.0112 (0.28)	0.3093 (2.51)**, 0.4521 (2.34)**	0.0771 (0.53), 0.0803 (0.58)	0.0732 (1.19), 0.0686 (1.11)	0.5544 (6.42)***, 0.5212 (5.99)***	0.5559 (3.68)***, 0.5907 (2.66)***	0.5509 (5.01)***, 0.5399 (2.89)***
Change in pension liabilities	0.0367 (0.63), 0.0422 (0.98)	−0.0593 (0.75), −0.0470 (0.55)	0.1263 (0.96), 0.1504 (1.38)	0.2181 (1.51), 0.1930 (1.32)	−0.0268 (0.37), −0.0194 (0.26)	0.0544 (0.49), 0.0388 (0.29)	0.5497 (2.94)***, 0.4928 (2.36)***	0.6798 (3.41)***, 0.6300 (2.72)***
Firms (pooled observations)	111 (555), 111 (1140)	74 (370), 74 (786)	21 (105), 21 (201)	17 (85), 17 (169)	73 (365), 73 (781)	37 (185), 37 (401)	13 (65), 13 (117)	15 (75), 15 (134)

Notes: Heteroskedasticity-consistent 2SLS–Within regression estimates from the balanced panel with 361 fixed firm- and four time specific effects (coefficients not reported). Adding the coefficient difference in columns (2)–(8) to the coefficient estimate in column (1) yields the coefficient for the respective group of firms. Instruments for *Working capital ratio*: all other right-hand side variables plus the working capital ratio ($t − 1$).

[a] Large manager-controlled firms in *hi-K* industries.
[b] Large owner-controlled firms in *hi-K* industries.
[c] Small manager-controlled firms in *hi-K* industries.
[d] Small owner-controlled firms in *hi-K* Industries.
[e] Large manager-controlled firms in *lo-K* industries.
[f] Large owner-controlled firms in *lo-K* industries.
[g] Small manager-controlled firms in *lo-K* industries.
[h] Small owner-controlled firms in *lo-K* industries.
* Significant at the 0.10 level (two-tailed test).
** Significant at the 0.05 level (two-tailed test).
*** Significant at the 0.01 level (two-tailed test).

D.B. Audretsch, J. Weigand / Research Policy 34 (2005) 595–613   611

The coefficient estimates in column (1) cast considerable doubt on the presence of financing constraints for this subset of firms. The cash flow coefficient is indeed significantly positive but small. Moreover, the coefficients of the changes in net working capital, long-term debt and pension liabilities are clearly insignificant. Columns (2)–(8) contain the coefficient differences to the other subsets of firms. There are no significant differences for the large owner-controlled *hi-K* firms (LOH) as well as the large manager-controlled firms from *lo-K* industries (LML). Most surprisingly, this is also true for the small owner-controlled firms in *hi-K* industries (SOH). The cash flow coefficients of these three subsets of firms are even slightly smaller than for the baseline group. The coefficient of the change in net working capital is even insignificantly positive for the SOH firms, implying that the investment-cash flow correlation may reflect better investment opportunities rather than financing problems. As we have argued above, the generation of cash flow may signal to external financiers that a small but *hi-K* firm is positively selected in the market process. Certainly, caution in interpretation is warranted because of the small number of firms in the small firm subsets.

Obvious differences exist with respect to the small manager-controlled firms in both *hi-K* and *lo-K* industries (SMH, SML) as well as the large and small owner-controlled firms in *lo-K* industries (LOL, SOL). These subsets of firms appear to be finance constrained. The cash flow coefficients (with one exception, SOL) and the coefficients of the change in long-term debt are significantly larger than for the baseline group. Even if the cash flow coefficient for the small owner-controlled *lo-K* firms SOL is very small, the highly significant and large differences of all other coefficients suggests the presence of financing constraints.

5. Summary and conclusion

The neoclassical view of perfect capital markets has been replaced by a more recent literature providing convincing evidence that financing constraints exist and that they vary according to the characteristics of the firm. A theoretical literature has emerged arguing that the core reason for financing constraints is uncertainty and asymmetric information. However, empirical studies have not systematically examined whether the degree to which financing constraints exist varies across different institutional settings and industries characterized by different degrees of uncertainty and knowledge asymmetries.

In this paper we have explicitly focused on how financing constraints vary according to the knowledge conditions underlying industries, the mode of corporate control and firm size, and how such constraints have changed in the bank-centered financial system of Germany over the time period 1987–1998. In particular, we compared the extent of financing constraints between firms from knowledge intensive (*hi-K*) and less knowledge intensive (*lo-K*) industries. The evidence on the impact of cash flow on tangible investment suggests that the extent of financing constraints is significantly smaller for the firms in *hi-K* industries. Further, two firm-specific characteristics, the mode of corporate control and firm size, play a crucial role as determinants of investment and the extent of financing constraints. Ignoring knowledge conditions, we find small firms to be more constrained than large firms. This is consistent with the Anglo-Saxon evidence. However, the importance of the knowledge base in conjunction with the mode of corporate control affects the extent of estimated financing constraints. Surprisingly, our regressions have revealed that smaller firms in *hi-K* industries are *less* constrained than are their *lo-K* counterparts, even the larger ones. Owner control reinforces this mitigation effect. *hi-K* industries presumably provide a better environment for small, well-governed firms to demonstrate entrepreneurial skill and excellence, to grow by continuously investing in innovation, and to attract external capital (Audretsch, 1995).

Looking at the dynamics involved, we find that the estimated cash flow effects do not change greatly over the analyzed time period. The implication is that the advent of venture capitalism in the 1990s did not affect the financing behavior of our sample firms greatly. The relaxation of the investment cash flow relationship we do observe, is for the years of the German reunification boom. Taken together and compared to the empirical evidence from Anglo-Saxon firm data, our results concerning the cash flow elasticity of tangible investment imply that the larger part of our sample firms faced only very modest financing constraints. This finding may support the opinion often put forward in the literature that the bank-centered German system of corporate finance mitigates financing constraints. Alternatively, it may reflect the favorable impact of financial deregulation in the European Union which started in the 1980s, leading up to the Single Market in 1993.

An important qualification for our findings is that the inferences and interpretations are based on a "truncated" non-random sample excluding the smallest-sized firms. The inherent data restrictions, such as unavoidable survivor bias may extenuate the efficiency of firm financing in the German financial system. Nonetheless, from our viewpoint, the findings in this study indicate that the relationship between investment and finance, and thus the extent of financing constraints, is shaped by the joint influence of industry characteristics, firm size, and the mode of corporate control. The results presented in this paper suggest that knowledge intensive industries may offer more windows of opportunities for new and smaller firms than do less knowledge intensive industries. Summing up, we may argue that knowledge intensive economic activities foster entrepreneurial success, and entrepreneurial success in turn breeds finance for investment.

Acknowledgments

We would like to thank the anonymous reviewers for their very helpful comments. Further thanks for comments on earlier versions of this paper go to Rajshree Agarwal, Philippe Aghion, Jan Boone, Bob Carpenter, Julie Ann Elston, Hariolf Grupp, Bronwyn Hall, Dietmar Harhoff, Doug De Jong, Boyan Jovanovic, Dilek Karaomeriioglu, Alexander Karmann, Jan-Pieter Krahnen, Gordon Murray, Bruce Peterson, Claudia Ploetscher, Anne-Gael Vaubourg, and participants in conferences, workshops, and seminars at Indiana University (Bloomington), the University of Central Florida, the University of Hannover, University of Warwick, ZEW Mannheim, as well as participants in the annual conferences of the Econometric Society (Summer Meetings 1999, Madison), the European Economic Association (Santiago de Compostela 1999), and the European Association of Researchers in Industrial Economics (EARIE, Torino 1999). We are particularly indebted to Erik Lehmann for providing us with a subset of the data.

References

Allen, F., Gale, D., 2001. Comparing Financial Systems. MIT Press, Cambridge, MA.

Arrow, K., 1962. Economic welfare and the allocation of resources for invention. In: Nelson, R.R. (Ed.), The Rate and Direction of Inventive Activity. Princeton University Press, Princeton.

Audretsch, D.B., 1995. Innovation and Industry Evolution. MIT Press, Cambridge, MA.

Baldwin, J., Gellaty, G., Gaudreault, V., 2002. Financing Innovation in New Small Firms: New Evidence from Canada. Working Paper No. 190, Statistics Canada.

Baltagi, B.H., 2001. Econometric Analysis of Panel Data, 2nd ed. Wiley, New York.

Baums, T., 1994. The German banking system and its impact on corporate finance and governance. In: Aoki, M., Patrick, H. (Eds.), The Japanese Main Bank System. Oxford University Press, Oxford.

Beise, M., Licht, G., 1996. Innovationsverhalten derdeutschen Wirtschaft. Beitrag zur Erweiterten Berichterstattung zur technologischen Leistungsfahigkeit Deutschlands im Auftrag des Bundesministeriums fur Bildung, Wissenschaft. In: Forschung und Technologie. Zentrum fur Europaische Wirtschaftsforschung ZEW, Mannheim.

Berle, A., Means, G., 1932. The Modern Corporation and Private Property. Macmillan, New York.

Bond, S., Elston, J., Mairesse, J., Mulkay, B., 2003. Financial factors and investment in Belgium, France, Germany and the UK: a comparison using company panel data. Review of Economics and Statistics 85, 153–165.

Bond, S., Harhoff, D., Van Reenen, J., 1999. Investment, R&D and Financial Constraints in Britain and Germany. IFS Working Paper W99/5, London.

Brealey, R., Myers, S., 2000. Principles of Corporate Finance, 6th ed. McGraw-Hill, New York.

Chirinko, R., 1993. Fixed business investment spending: modeling strategies, empirical results, and policy implications. Journal of Economic Literature 31, 1875–1911.

Cho, M.-H., 1998. Ownership structure, investment, and the corporate value: an empirical analysis. Journal of Financial Economics 47, 103–121.

Clementi, G., Hopenhayn, H., 2002. A Theory of Financing Constraints and Firm Dynamics. Working Paper, Carnegie Mellon University GSIA, Pittsburgh.

Dasgupta, P., David, P.A., 1994. Toward a new economics of science. Research Policy 23, 487–521.

Edwards, J., Fischer, K., 1994. Banks Finance and Investment in Germany. Cambridge University Press, Cambridge.

Elston, J.A., Albach, H., 1995. Bank affiliations and firm capital investment in Germany. Ifo Studien 41, 3–16.

Fazzari, S.M., Hubbard, G.R., Petersen, B.C., 1988. Financing constraints and corporate investment. Brookings Papers on Economic Activity, 141–195.

Fazzari, S.M., Petersen, B.C., 1993. Working capital and fixed investment: new evidence on financing constraints. RAND Journal of Economics 24, 328–342.

D.B. Audretsch, J. Weigand / Research Policy 34 (2005) 595–613   613

Gangopadhyay, S., Lensink, R., van der Molen, R., 2001. Business groups, financing constraints, and investment. CCSO Quarterly Journal, 3.

Greenwald, B., Stiglitz, J., 1990. Asymmetric information and the new theory of the firm: financial constraints and risk behavior. In: American Economic Review 80, Papers and Proceedings, pp. 160–165.

Hall, B.H., 2002. The financing of research and development. Oxford Review of Economic Policy 18, 35–51.

Hall, B., Mairesse, J., Branstetter, L., Crepon, B., 1999. Does cash flow cause investment and R&D? An exploration using panel data for French, Japanese, and United States scientific firms. In: Audretsch, D.B., Thurik, A.R. (Eds.), Innovation, Industry Evolution, and Employment. Cambridge University Press, Cambridge, UK.

Himmelberg, C.P., Petersen, B.C., 1994. R&D and internal finance: a panel study of small firms in high-tech industries. Review of Economics and Statistics 76, 38–51.

Holdemess, C., Sheenan, D., 1988. The role of majority shareholders in publicly held corporations: an explanatory analysis. Journal of Financial Economics 20, 317–346.

Hubbard, R.G., 1998. Capital market imperfections and investment. Journal of Economic Literature 26, 193–225.

Jaffe, D., Russel, T., 1976. Imperfect information, uncertainty, and credit rationing. Quarterly Journal of Economics 90, 651–666.

Jensen, M.C., 1986. Agency costs of free cash flow, corporate finance and takeovers. American Economic Review 76, 323–329.

Jensen, M.C., Meckting, W., 1976. Theory of the firm: managerial behavior, agency costs, and capital structure. Journal of Financial Economics 3, 305–360.

Jovanovic, B., 1982. Selection and evolution of industry. Econometrica 50, 649–670.

Kaplan, S., Zingales, L., 1997. Do investment – cash flow sensitivities provide useful measures of financing constraints. Quarterly Journal of Economics 112, 169–215.

Laeven, L., 2003. Does financial liberalization reduce financing constraints? Financial Management 32, 5–34.

Lang, L.H.P., Stulz, R., 1994. Tobin's Q, corporate diversification, and firm performance. Journal of Political Economy 102, 1248–1280.

Lehmann, E., Weigand, J., 2000. Does the governed corporation perform better? Governance structures and corporate performance in Germany. European Finance Review 4, 157–195.

Love, I., 2003. Financial development and financing constraints: international evidence from the structural investment model. Review of Financial Studies 16, 765–791.

Modigliani, F., Miller, M., 1958. The cost of capital, corporation finance and the theory of investment. American Economic Review 48, 261–297.

Mulkay, B., Hall, B.H., Mairesse, J., 1999. Investment and R&D in France and in the United States. In: Deutsche Bundesbank (Ed.), Investing Today for the World of Tomorrow. Springer, Berlin.

Myers, S., Majluf, N., 1984. Corporate financing and investment decisions when firms have information that investors do not have. Journal of Financial Economics 13, 187–221.

Planes, B., Bardos, M., Sevestre, P., Avouyi-Dovi, S., 2001. Innovation, Financing and Financing Constraints, Bank of France Working Paper, BIS Working group on "IT innovations and financing patterns: implications for the financial system".

Rajan, R., 1992. Insiders and outsiders: the choice between informed and arm's length debt. Journal of Finance 47, 1367–1400.

Reimund, C., 2002. Internal Capital Markets, Bank Borrowing and Investment: Evidence from German Corporate Groups, Paper Presented at the EFMA 2002 Meetings, London.

Reimund, C., 2003. Liquiditätshaltung und Unternehmenswert (Liquidity and Corporate Value). DUV, Wiesbaden.

Roe, M., 1994. Some differences in corporate governance in Germany, Japan, and America. In: Baums, T. (Ed.), Institutional Investors and Corporate Governance. Springer, New York.

Sah, R., Stiglitz, J.E., 1986. The architecture of economic systems: hierarchies and polyarchies. American Economic Review 76, 716–727.

Schiantarelli, F., 1996. Financial constraints and investment: methodological issues and international evidence. Oxford Review of Economic Policy 12, 90–108.

Sharpe, S., 1990. Asymmetric information, bank lending, and implicit contracts: a stylized model of customer relationships. Journal of Finance 45, 1069–1087.

Shin, H.-H., Stulz, R., 1998. Are internal capital markets efficient? Quarterly Journal of Economics 113, 531–552.

Shleifer, A., Vishny, R.W., 1997. A survey of corporate governance. Journal of Finance 52, 737–783.

Short, H., 1994. Ownership, control, financial structure, and the performance of firms. Journal of Economic Surveys 8, 203–249.

Stephan, P., 1996. The economics of science. Journal of Economic Literature 34, 1199–1235.

Sterken, E., Lensink, R., Bo, H., 2001. Investment, cash flow, and uncertainty: evidence for the Netherlands. CCSO Quarterly Journal, 3.

Stiglitz, J., Weiss, A., 1981. Credit rationing in markets with imperfect information. American Economic Review 64, 851–866.

Tirole, J., 2001. Corporate governance. Econometrica 69, 1–39.

Von Kalckreuth, U., 2004. Financial Constraints for Investors and the Speed of Adaptation: Are Innovators Special? Deutsche Bundesbank Discussion Paper No. 20, Series 1, Frankfurt.

Weigand, C., 1998. Der Einfluss der Bankkreditvergabe auf den Unternehmenswettbewerb (The Impact of Bank Lending on Product Market Competition). Kovac, Hamburg.

[3]

Research Policy 34 (2005) 1191–1202

Does the Knowledge Spillover Theory of Entrepreneurship hold for regions?

David B. Audretsch [a,*], Erik E. Lehmann [b]

[a] Department Entrepreneurship, Growth, and Public Policy, Max-Planck Institute of Economics, Jena,
Kahlaische Strasse 10, 07745 Jena, Germany
[b] University of Augsburg and Max-Planck Institute of Economics, Jena, Universitätsstrasse 16, 86159 Augsburg, Germany

Received 21 November 2004; received in revised form 12 March 2005; accepted 15 March 2005
Available online 19 July 2005

Abstract

The purpose of this paper is to test whether the Knowledge Spillover Theory of Entrepreneurship holds for regions. We do this by linking investments in knowledge by universities and regions to the amount of entrepreneurial activity associated with each university. Using binomial regressions we estimate how the number of young and high-tech firms located around universities depends on regional factors and the output of universities. The results clearly show that the number of firms located close to a university is positively influenced by the knowledge capacity of this region and the knowledge output of a university. Thus, there is considerable evidence suggesting that the Knowledge Spillover Theory of Entrepreneurship holds for regions as well as for industries.
© 2005 Elsevier B.V. All rights reserved.

Keywords: University spillover; Firm location

1. Introduction

As described by Audretsch and Thurik (2001), globalization is shifting the comparative advantage in the OECD countries away from being based on traditional inputs of production toward knowledge. As the comparative advantage has become increasingly based on new

* Corresponding author. Fax: +49 3641 68 6900.
  E-mail address: audretsch@mpiew-jena.mpg.de
(D.B. Audretsch).

0048-7333/$ – see front matter © 2005 Elsevier B.V. All rights reserved.
doi:10.1016/j.respol.2005.03.012

knowledge, public policy has responded enabling the creation and commercialization of knowledge. Furthermore, new policy approaches are emerging shifting the focus from national and international focuses towards regions and regional clusters. Examples of such policies include encouraging R&D spillovers, venture capital and new firm startups. In this new entrepreneurship based policy, universities play a key role in providing spillovers by academic research and human capital in the form of well trained and educated students. The success of a number of different technology clusters is the

1192   *D.B. Audretsch, E.E. Lehmann / Research Policy 34 (2005) 1191–1202*

direct result of enabling policies, such as the provision of research support by universities.

The traditional view of knowledge and innovation is that the firm exists exogenously and then invests in research and development or the augmentation of human capital through training and education of workers to endogenously create new knowledge and ideas. This view was formalized by Griliches (1979) in what he termed as the Model of the Firm Knowledge Production Function.

While Griliches' model of the knowledge production function was statistically confirmed through a plethora of econometric studies linking knowledge inputs to innovative outputs at the levels of the country and the industry, the relationship proved to be considerably more ambiguous at the level of the firm, particularly when new and small enterprises were included in the sample. Small firms were found to contribute more to innovative output than would have been expected from their rather meager investments in R&D and other knowledge inputs.

This paradox of the high innovative output of small enterprises given their low level of knowledge inputs that seemingly contradicts the Griliches model of the firm knowledge production function was resolved by Audretsch (1995), who introduced the Knowledge Spillover Theory of Entrepreneurship, "The findings in this book challenge an assumption implicit to the knowledge production function—that firms exist exogenously and then endogenously seek out and apply knowledge inputs to generate innovative output. It is the knowledge in the possession of economic agents that is exogenous, and in an effort to appropriate the returns from that knowledge, the spillover of knowledge from its producing entity involves endogenously creating a new firm" (pp. 179–180).

What is the source of this entrepreneurial knowledge that endogenously generated the startup of new firms? The answer seemed to be through the spillover of knowledge from the source creating to commercialization via the startup of a new firm, "How are these small and frequently new firms able to generate innovative output when undertaking a generally negligible amount of investment into knowledge-generating inputs, such as R&D? One answer is apparently through exploiting knowledge created by expenditures on research in universities and on R&D in large corporations" (p. 179). While policy makers have no direct influence on

large corporations as a source of spillovers, they can, more or less, influence universities as a promoter for entrepreneurship and important source of spillovers. As an example for Germany, the Federal Ministry for Education and Research established regions where startups from universities and government research laboratories are encouraged (Federal Ministry of Education and Research, 2004). Strongly influenced by federal and state policies, universities can alter their curricula, initiate research, and participate in collaborations that serve these ventures and thus allowing the startups to be more competitive with larger and better financed competitors.

The empirical evidence supporting the Knowledge Spillover Theory of Entrepreneurship was provided from analyzing variations in startup rates across different industries reflecting different underlying knowledge contexts. In particular, those industries with a greater investment in new knowledge also exhibited higher startup rates while those industries with less investment in new knowledge exhibited lower startup rates, which was interpreted as the mechanism by which knowledge spillovers are transmitted.

Thus, compelling evidence was provided suggesting that entrepreneurship is an endogenous response to the potential for commercializing knowledge that has not been adequately commercialized by the incumbent firms. This involved an organizational dimension involving the mechanism transmitting knowledge spillovers—the startup of new firms. In addition, Jaffe (1989), Audretsch and Feldman (1996) and Audretsch and Stephan (1996) provided evidence concerning the spatial dimension of knowledge spillovers. In particular their findings suggested that knowledge spillovers are geographically bounded and localized within spatial proximity to the knowledge source. None of these studies, however, identified the actual mechanisms which actually transmit the knowledge spillover; rather, the spillovers were implicitly assumed to automatically exist (or fall like Manna from heaven), but only within a geographically bounded spatial area.

The purpose of this paper is to bring these two literatures together by asking whether the Knowledge Spillover Theory of Entrepreneurship also has a spatial component in that the startups tend to cluster within geographic proximity to knowledge sources. The second section explains why the knowledge spillover theory should also have a spatial component in that the

D.B. Audretsch, E.E. Lehmann / Research Policy 34 (2005) 1191–1202 1193

knowledge startups cluster geographically around the knowledge source. The third and fourth sections provide an empirical test within a spatial context—the region around a university. Finally, in the last section a summary and conclusion are provided. In particular, the empirical evidence suggests that those universities with a greater investment in knowledge and where the regional investment in knowledge is higher tend to generate more technology startups. This supports the view that the spillover theory of knowledge holds for regional contexts as well as for industries.

2. Localizing the Knowledge Spillover Theory of Entrepreneurship

That entrepreneurial activity varies across geographic space has long been observed. Efforts to systematically link spatial variations in entrepreneurship with locational specific characteristics showed that such spatial activity is not at all random but rather shaped by factors associated with particular regions (Reynolds et al., 1994). A series of studies, dating back at least to Carlton (1983) and Bartik (1985) and more recently Reynolds et al. (1994), have tried to identify characteristics specific to particular regions that account for inter-spatial variations in entrepreneurship. However, while a large literature exists linking new-firm startup activity to region-specific characteristics and attributes (Fritsch, 1997; Reynolds et al., 1994; Carlton, 1983; Bartik, 1985; Audretsch and Fritsch, 1994), virtually none of these studies provided a theory linking knowledge spillovers to new-firm startup activity, nor did any of these studies provide a measure of knowledge spillovers.

For example, Audretsch and Fritsch (1994), examine the impact that location plays on entrepreneurial activity in (West) Germany. Using a database derived from the social insurance statistics, which covers about 90% of employment, they identify the birth rates of new startups for each of 75 distinct economic regions. These regions are distinguished on the basis of planning regions, or *Raumordungsregionen*. They find that, for the late 1980s, the birth rates of new firms was higher in regions experiencing low unemployment, which have a dense population, a high growth rate of population, a high share of skilled workers, and a strong presence of small businesses.

The Knowledge Spillover Theory of Entrepreneurship provides a focus on the generation of entrepreneurial opportunities emanating from knowledge investments by incumbent firms and public research organizations which are not fully appropriated by those incumbent enterprises. It is a virtual consensus that entrepreneurship revolves around the recognition of opportunities and the pursuit of those opportunities (Shane and Eckhardt, 2003). Much of the more contemporary thinking about entrepreneurship has focused on the cognitive process by which individuals reach the decision to start a new firm. According to Sarasvathy et al. (2003, p. 142), "An entrepreurial opportunity consists of a set of ideas, beliefs and actions that enable the creation of future goods and services in the absence of current markets for them". Sarasvathy, Dew, Velamuri and Venkataraman provide a typology of entrepreneurial opportunities as consisting of opportunity recognition, opportunity discovery and opportunity creation.

While much has been made about the key role played by the recognition of opportunities in the cognitive process underlying the decision to become an entrepreneur, relatively little has been written about the actual source of such entrepreneurial opportunities (see Audretsch and Stephan, 1999). The Knowledge Spillover Theory of Entrepreneurship identifies one source of entrepreneurial opportunities—new knowledge and ideas. In particular, the Knowledge Spillover Theory of Entrepreneurship posits that it is new knowledge and ideas created in one context but left uncommercialized or not vigorously pursued by the source actually creating those ideas, such as a research laboratory in a large corporation or research undertaken by a university, that serves as the source of knowledge generating entrepreneurial opportunities. Thus, in this view, one mechanism for recognizing new opportunities and actually implementing them by starting a new firm involves the spillover of knowledge. The source of the knowledge and ideas, and the organization actually making (at least some of) the investments to produce that knowledge, is not the same as the organization actually attempting to commercialize and appropriate the value of that knowledge—the new firm. If the use of that knowledge by the entrepreneur does not involve full payment to the firm making the investment that originally produced that knowledge, such as a license or royalty, then the entrepreneurial act of starting a new firm serves as a mechanism for knowledge

1194   *D.B. Audretsch, E.E. Lehmann / Research Policy 34 (2005) 1191–1202*

spillovers. However, theories of localization suggest that just because universities are the sources of knowledge spillovers does not mean that knowledge transmits costlessly across geographic space. In particular, these theories argue that geographic proximity reduces the cost of accessing and absorbing knowledge spillovers. Thus, a basic tenet in the literature is that university spillovers lower the costs of firms to accessing and absorbing knowledge spillovers. If an entrepreneur decides to locate nearby a university, the benefits must outweigh the costs. Locating close to universities, mostly in the center of a city, is associated with high costs of living, housing, and others. Though, firms also have to pay higher wages to their employees since their costs of living. If the basic resources gathered from a university are not essential to bear those costs, it is more advantageous to locate outside such a metropolitan area.

There are at least two principle mechanisms facilitating the knowledge spillovers from universities to firms. The first one involves scientific research published in scholarly journals. Such published research is codified knowledge. This is because knowledge provided by articles can be transferred and transmitted with low cost, or with costs which are independent from the location. Academic papers can be downloaded from the Internet, obtained from publishers or found in libraries. However, an important qualification is that not all university knowledge is the same. In fact, the knowledge output of a university is heterogeneous. One useful distinction differentiates natural and social science knowledge. Social science knowledge is not based on a unified and established scientific methodology, but it rather is idiosyncratic to very specific disciplines, sub-disciplines and even research approaches. Compared to the natural sciences, research in the social sciences is considerably less codified. Thus, geographic proximity to high output universities may be more important for accessing social science research than for accessing natural science research.

This suggests that an important testable hypothesis is that the amount of scientific articles published by a university has no effect on firm location, since accessing (codified) knowledge is more or less invariant to locational distance from the university producing that knowledge. Strict adherence to the scientific method assures that academic research embodies a high component of codified and specific knowledge in the nat-

ural sciences (Stephan, 1996). By contrast, the more limited applicability of the scientific method implies that research in the social sciences will embody less codified knowledge (Stephan, 1996). In contrast, academic research in the natural sciences is more codified. Because of its high codification, scientific knowledge can be largely accessed by (competently) reading scientific journals. Thus, we assume that knowledge in the social sciences is more tacit and less codified.

The second type of spillover mechanism involves human capital embodied in students graduating from the university. As Saxenien (1994) points out, one of the important mechanisms facilitating knowledge spillovers involves the mobility of human capital, embodied in graduating students, as they move from the university to a firm. Spatial proximity to universities can therefore generate positive externalities that can be accessed by the firm through the spillover mechanism of human capital. As Varga (2000) shows, university graduates may be one of the most important channels for disseminating knowledge from academia to the local high technology industry. In addition, other related externalities may result from close geographic proximity. For example, local proximity lowers the search costs for both firms and students. This may lead to some competitive advantage over similar firms which are not located close to universities, especially when high skilled labor is a scarce resource and there is intense competition about high potentials.

If a universities graduate's educational background corresponds to the needs of a firm, the probability of employment is higher which lowers the costs of matching for both students and firms. This contains to educate students and prepare them for later employment in the economy and academic research activities and thus provides spillovers. The business sector receives inputs from universities in the form of highly educated human capital. Although these individuals may require further training, university education provides the foundation for subsequent specialized industrial training. Universities may also provide further training of employees. Thus, it seems that the most frequent types of interactions between firms and universities are the employment of university graduates (Schartinger et al., 2001, p. 259).

Why should entrepreneurship play an important role in the spillover of new knowledge and ideas? And why should new knowledge play an important

D.B. Audretsch, E.E. Lehmann / Research Policy 34 (2005) 1191–1202 1195

role in creating entrepreneurial opportunities? In the Romer (1986) model of endogenous growth new technological knowledge is assumed to automatically spill over. Investment in new technological knowledge is automatically accessed by third-party firms and economic agents, resulting in the automatic spill over of knowledge.[1] The assumption that knowledge automatically spills over is, of course, consistent with the important insight by Arrow (1962) that knowledge differs from the traditional factors of production – physical capital and (unskilled) labor – in that it is non-excludable and non-exhaustive. When the firm or economic agent uses the knowledge, it is neither exhausted nor can it be, in the absence of legal protection, precluded from use by third-party firms or other economic agents. Thus, in the spirit of the Romer model, drawing on the earlier insights about knowledge from Arrow, a large and vigorous literature has emerged obsessed with the links between intellectual property protection and the incentives for firms to invest in the creation of new knowledge through R&D and investments in human capital.

However, the preoccupation with the non-excludability and non-exhaustability of knowledge first identified by Arrow and later carried forward and assumed in the Romer model, neglects another key insight in the original Arrow (1962) article. Arrow also identified another dimension by which knowledge differs from the traditional factors of production. This other dimension involves the greater degree of uncertainty, higher extent of asymmetries, and greater cost of transacting new ideas. The expected value of any new idea is highly uncertain, and as Arrow pointed out, has a much greater variance than would be associated with the deployment of traditional factors of production. After all, there is relative certainty about what a standard piece of capital equipment can do, or what an (unskilled) worker can contribute to a mass-production assembly line. By contrast, Arrow emphasized that when it comes to innovation, there is uncertainty about whether the new product can be produced, how it can be produced, and whether sufficient demand for that visualized new product might actually materialize.

In addition, new ideas are typically associated with considerable asymmetries. In order to evaluate a proposed new idea concerning a new biotechnology product, the decision maker might not only need to have a Ph.D. in biotechnology, but also a specialization in the exact scientific area. Such divergences in education, background and experience can result in a divergence in the expected value of a new project or the variance in outcomes anticipated from pursuing that new idea, both of which can lead to divergences in the recognition and evaluation of opportunities across economic agents and decision-making hierarchies. Such divergences in the valuation of new ideas will become greater if the new idea is not consistent with the core competence and technological trajectory of the incumbent firm.

Thus, because of the conditions inherent in knowledge – high uncertainty, asymmetries and transactions cost – decision making hierarchies can reach the decision not to pursue and try to commercialize new ideas that individual economic agents, or groups or teams of economic agents think are potentially valuable and should be pursued. The basic conditions characterizing new knowledge, combined with a broad spectrum of institutions, rules and regulations impose what Acs et al. (2003) term *the knowledge filter*. The knowledge filter is the gap between new knowledge and what Arrow (1962) referred to as economic knowledge or commercialized knowledge. The greater is the knowledge filter, the more pronounced is this gap between new knowledge and new economic, or commercialized, knowledge.

The knowledge filter is a consequence of the basic conditions inherent in new knowledge. Similarly, it is the knowledge filter that creates the opportunity for entrepreneurship in the Knowledge Spillover Theory of Entrepreneurship. According to this theory, opportunities for entrepreneurship are the duality of the knowledge filter. The higher is the knowledge filter, the greater are the divergences in the valuation of new ideas across economic agents and the decision-making hierarchies of incumbent firms. Entrepreneurial opportunities are generated not just by investments in new knowledge and ideas, but in the propensity for only a distinct subset of those opportunities to be fully pursued by incumbent firms.

Thus, the knowledge theory of entrepreneurship shifts the fundamental decision making unit of observation in the model of the knowledge production function

---

[1] For more recent models of endogenous growth combining both new economic geography models and R&D investments see Fujita and Thisse (2002, Chapter 11) or Baldwin and Forslid (2000).

1196   *D.B. Audretsch, E.E. Lehmann / Research Policy 34 (2005) 1191–1202*

away from exogenously assumed firms to individuals, such as scientists, engineers or other knowledge workers — agents with endowments of new economic knowledge. As Audretsch (1995) pointed out, when the lens is shifted away from the firm to the individual as the relevant unit of observation, the appropriability issue remains, but the question becomes, *How can economic agents with a given endowment of new knowledge best appropriate the returns from that knowledge?* If the scientist or engineer can pursue the new idea within the organizational structure of the firm developing the knowledge and appropriate roughly the expected value of that knowledge, he has no reason to leave the firm. On the other hand, if she places a greater value on his ideas than do the decision-making bureaucracy of the incumbent firm, he may choose to start a new firm to appropriate the value of his knowledge.

In the Knowledge Spillover Theory of Entrepreneurship the knowledge production function is actually reversed. The knowledge is exogenous and embodied in a worker. The firm is created endogenously in the worker's effort to appropriate the value of his knowledge through innovative activity. Typically an employee from an established large corporation, often a scientist or engineer working in a research laboratory, will have an idea for an invention and ultimately for an innovation. Accompanying this potential innovation is an expected net return from the new product. The inventor would expect to be compensated for his/her potential innovation accordingly. If the company has a different, presumably lower, valuation of the potential innovation, it may decide either not to pursue its development, or that it merits a lower level of compensation than that expected by the employee.

In either case, the employee will weigh the alternative of starting his/her own firm. If the gap in the expected return accruing from the potential innovation between the inventor and the corporate decision maker is sufficiently large, and if the cost of starting a new firm is sufficiently low, the employee may decide to leave the large corporation and establish a new enterprise. Since the knowledge was generated in the established corporation, the new start-up is considered to be a spin-off from the existing firm. Such startups typically do not have direct access to a large R&D laboratory. Rather, the entrepreneurial opportunity emanates from the knowledge and experience accrued from the R&D laboratories with their previous employers. Thus, the

knowledge spillover view of entrepreneurship is actually a theory of endogenous entrepreneurship, where entrepreneurship is an endogenous response to opportunities created by investments in new knowledge that are not commercialized because of the knowledge filter.

As investments in new knowledge increase, entrepreneurial opportunities will also increase. Contexts where new knowledge plays an important role are associated with a greater degree of uncertainty and asymmetries across economic agents evaluating the potential value of new ideas. Thus, a context involving more new knowledge will also impose a greater divergence in the evaluation of that knowledge across economic agents, resulting in a greater variance in the outcome expected from commercializing those ideas (see Audretsch et al., 2006). It is this gap in the valuation of new ideas across economic agents, or between economic agents and decision-making hierarchies of incumbent enterprises, that creates the entrepreneurial opportunity.

As already discussed, a vigorous literature has already identified that knowledge spillovers are greater in the presence of knowledge investments. Just as Jaffe (1989) and Audretsch and Feldman (1996) show, those regions with high knowledge investments experience a high level of knowledge spillovers, and those regions with a low amount of knowledge investments experience a low level of knowledge spillovers, since there is less knowledge to be spilled over. Bode (2004) shows that in general interregional spillovers contribute significantly to regional knowledge production. Also Anselin et al. (1997) conclude that the geographical scope of knowledge spillovers is restricted to a limited number of neighboring regions or to regions within a given maximum distance from the region of interest.

The Knowledge Spillover Theory of Entrepreneurship analogously suggests that, ceteris paribus, entrepreneurial activity will tend to be greater in contexts where investments in new knowledge are relatively high, since the new firm will be started from knowledge that has spilled over from the source actually producing that new knowledge. A paucity of new ideas in an impoverished knowledge context will generate only limited entrepreneurial opportunities. By contrast, in a high knowledge context, new ideas will generate entrepreneurial opportunities by exploiting (potential) spillovers of that knowledge. Thus, the knowledge spillover view of entrepreneurship provides a clear link, or prediction that entrepreneurial

D.B. Audretsch, E.E. Lehmann / Research Policy 34 (2005) 1191–1202 1197

activity will result from investments in new knowledge and that entrepreneurial activity will be spatially localized within close geographic proximity to the knowledge source.

3. Dataset, methodology, and descriptive statistics

To test the hypothesis that knowledge-based startups are located within close proximity to knowledge sources, we examine the spatial relation between knowledge-based startups and their proximity to universities. We do this by analyzing a unique dataset consisting of 281 firms which made an initial public offering (IPO) in Germany between March 1997 and March 2002. The dataset was collected combining individual data from IPO prospectuses, along with publicly available information from on-line data sources including the *Deutsche Boerse AG* (www.deutsche-boerse.com). We pooled this dataset by adding university-specific variables, which are individually collected from the 73 public universities in Germany (see Warning, 2004). The dependent variable is the number of firms located closest to a university (Firms). We do this by measuring the distance (in kilometers) between a firm and the surrounding universities. The distance is measured in kilometers using the online database of the *German Automobile Club* (www.adac.de). All firms located within a radius of 1.5 km are classified as belonging in the distance category of 1 km. Thus, the variable "Firms" contains all firms for which the distance towards this respective university is the closest one. No firm is allocated to more then one university.

To analyze the amount of knowledge investment that has been made by the university and elsewhere in the region, we include a measure that should reflect the potential supply of knowledge spillovers. This variable (regional capacity) is an index constructed by using spending in R&D and technological innovations in a specific region (see Sternberg and Litzenberger, 2003). This variable serves also as a measure for the "knowledge filter", which is significantly influenced by the structure of the innovation system within a regional context.

As university output we measure the number of students in the natural sciences (StudentsSCI) and in the social sciences as well as the articles published in the natural sciences (SCI) and the social sciences (SSCI). Information about the number of students is provided by the Federal Statistical Office. Since those data are provided sporadically we take 1997 as the base year where we have information of all universities. Publication data are hand-collected from the research database ISI (Information Sciences Institutes). We included the number of listed papers for each university published from 1993 until 2000.[2]

These measures are shown for the top 20 universities in Germany in Table 1. Using four distinct measures of university output enables us to examine any potential heterogeneous impact of university output.

We further include several control variables which may influence the degree of technology entrepreneurship located around a university. First, we include a dummy variable indicating a technical university (TU) (see Audretsch et al., in press). Technical universities are assumed to play a special role in the technology transfer, since their focus is especially on engineering and natural sciences (Audretsch and Lehmann, 2005). Those universities get more funds compared to other universities to foster and promote spillovers from new technologies to firms. Thus, technical universities may attract more young and high-tech firms. Secondly, we include the age (Age) of a university as measured in years to control for reputation effects. Thirdly, we use the number of inhabitants as the size of the city (City) of the respective university as well as the number of universities of applied sciences (universities). Those universities differ from the included public universities since their main goal is to educate students and are not engaged in academic research. They also do not have the status of a "university" in Germany. However, they also provide human capital and are thus included for this effect. Most of the included cities have a couple of such universities of applied sciences. Finally, a dummy variable is included to control for re-unification effects (West).

We employ the negative binomial regression model as the analytical technique for estimating the impact of the technology index and university research output on the role of geographic proximity. The underlying assumption is that the number of knowledge

---

[2] The publications in social science and natural science did not vary across the universities during time.

Table 1
List of the top 20 universities in Germany

University	Firms[a]	ϕ (km)[b]	SSCI Students[c]	SCI Students[d]
LMU München	51	17.9	43,633	8,119
Uni Frankfurt	26	19.5	26,324	5,715
Uni Hamburg	24	13.25	1,361	329
Uni Stuttgart	16	16.2	4,779	12,104
HU Berlin	14	7.78	20,769	4,936
Uni Köln	12	5.9	47,112	9,395
TU München	10	8.8	1,619	14,976
TU Karlsruhe	9	36.7	4,102	11,818
Uni Düsseldorf	7	18.57	14,697	4,762
Uni Erlangen-Nbg.	6	14	12,861	7,144
Uni Freiburg	6	40.33	12,334	4,942
FU Berlin	5	5.5	30,290	6,260
TU Aachen (RWTA)	5	3.4	7,884	20,570
Uni Jena	5	15.8	7,615	2,864
U-GH Paderborn	4	17	6,993	8,676
Uni Bielefeld	4	15.5	15,831	4,400
Uni Bremen	4	25.5	11,749	4,800
UdB München	4	14.25	1,054	1,104
Uni Kiel	4	40.75	13,000	6,513
Uni Regensburg	4	40	11,192	3,696

[a] Measured by the number of firms located closest to this university.
[b] ϕ (km) is the average distance of the firms located closest to this university.
[c] Number of students in the social sciences.
[d] Number of students in the natural sciences.

spillover startups located within geographic proximity to a university could be interpreted as count data. Since ordinary least squares regression is inappropriate for the count dependent variables that have large numbers of the smallest observation and remaining observations taking the form of small positive numbers, Poisson-regression seems to be more appropriate. However, the assumption for a Poisson-regression, the equality of mean and variance of the exogenous variable, is rejected by several tests. Thus, we apply the negative binomial regression model to overcome this problem of over-dispersion (Greene, 2003, pp. 740–752). Also, this statistical technique is designed for maximum likelihood estimation of the number of occurrence of nonnegative counts like the event of location.

In the first model (Model (1)), we estimate the following basic regression with the technology indices:

Number of firms

$$= \text{const.} + \beta_1 \text{regional technology capacity}$$
$$+ \text{Controlvariables} + \varepsilon \qquad (1)$$

Secondly, we test for the impact of university spillovers on the number of firms located to a university:

Number of firms

$$= \text{const.} + \beta_1 \text{StudentsSCI} + \beta_2 \text{StudentsSSCI}$$
$$+ \beta_3 \text{SSCI} + \beta_4 \text{SCI} + \text{Controlvariables} + \varepsilon \qquad (2)$$

then we test the combination from (1) and (2):

Number of firms

$$= \text{const.} + \beta_1 \text{regional capacity} + \beta_2 \text{StudentsSCI}$$
$$+ \beta_4 \text{StudentsSSCI} + \beta_5 \text{SSCI}$$
$$+ \beta_6 \text{Controlvariables} + \varepsilon \qquad (3)$$

Finally, we estimate model (3) for selected industries. Our base hypotheses is that in models (1) and (3) $\beta_1 > 0$, that the numbers of firms clustered around a respective university depends on the regional capacity.

From the 73 public universities in Germany, only 54 universities are chosen as the closest university for the included firms. The descriptive statistics, as presented in Table 1, show the highly skewed number of

D.B. Audretsch, E.E. Lehmann / Research Policy 34 (2005) 1191–1202   1199

firms located around universities. From the included 281 firms, 51 of them are located closest to the LMU Munich. The median distance of all firms located around the closest university is 7 km and the average distance is about 16 km. It could also be shown that the universities differ highly in their number of students in the natural sciences and the social sciences (see Warning, 2004, for more details).

4. Empirical evidence

In this section, we provide the results of the negative binomial regressions with the number of firms clustered around a university as the dependent variable. The empirical results for the negative binomial regression equations estimating the number of knowledgebased-startups located within geographic proximity to each university are presented in Table 2. The dependent variable is the number of firms located within geographic proximity to a university. As explained in the previous section, the first model includes only the technology index, the second model includes only the measures of university outputs, and the third model includes both types of measures.

In the first model, as the positive and statistically significant coefficient of the measure of technology capacity of the region in which the university is located suggests, the greater the technological capacity of the

region, the greater are the number of firms locating in that region.

The negative coefficient of university age does not support the hypothesis that university reputation, at least measured by age, has a positive influence on startups. Rather, the younger a university is, the more firms tend to locate with close geographic proximity. This finding could be explained by the fact that old and traditional universities are more focused on the social sciences, resources which are not really necessary for young and high-tech firms. The same holds for technical oriented universities which are mainly focused on the traditional research in engineering and machineries. While the size of the city is insignificant, the number of firms is also explained by the number of universities.

The results of the second estimation model show that university output influences the location decision of firms. As found by others (Schartinger et al., 2001; Stephan, 2001) the amount of university educated human capital is one of the major factors influencing firm location. Proximity offers the possibility of linking students to industry more efficiently, by providing industry and students a pre-employment look at each other. Thus, universities with a high output of students tend to generate more knowledge-based startups.

New technology oriented firms are particularly dependent on technological innovations and scientific progress and are therefore more than others

Table 2
Negative binomial estimating regional technology startups

	Model I	Model II	Model III
Regional knowledge capacity	0.03753 (10.19)***		0.4279 (16.95)***
SCI students		0.0004 (3.77)***	0.0001 (1.36)
SSCI students		0.00003 (10.03)***	0.0003 (14.36)***
SSCI		−0.0009 (8.43)***	−0.0009 (11.06)***
SCI		0.1100 (3.13)***	0.1149 (3.99)***
Age	−0.0004 (2.27)**	0.0005 (2.30)**	−0.00057 (2.90)**
TU	−1.4786 (10.20)***	−1.1976 (6.65)***	−1.389 (9.53)***
City	−1.17E07 (1.10)	−0.856E07 (10.09)***	−3.06E07 (3.96)***
Universities and universities of applied sciences	0.4047 (6.24)***	1.1935 (20.90)***	0.681 (12.90)***
West	−0.2029 (0.93)	−0.6351 (3.32)***	−0.5320 (3.61)***
Const.	0.4892 (1.65)*	1.7352 (6.65)***	0.6887 (3.07)***
Pseudo R2	0.1792	0.2067	0.3412
LL-ratio	−897.76	−850.11	−705.998

The endogenous variable is the number of technology startups located within geographic proximity to a university. Z-values are in brackets. The asterisks, *, **, and *** indicate significance at the 10%, 5%, and 1% level, respectively. The dataset includes 281 firms and 54 universities.

inclined to engage in interactions with research intense universities. Thus, research intense universities especially in the natural sciences are more attractive for high-tech firms. This could be confirmed by the positive significance of the coefficient indicating the number of articles published in the natural sciences. However, research intensity in the social sciences seems to be less important for attracting high-tech firms.

The third regression model includes both the regional innovation capacity measures and the university output measures and is consistent with the previous results, indicating that the results are robust. The number of new knowledge-based firms located within close geographic proximity to a university is positively influenced by the knowledge output of the respective university and the innovative capacity of the region. In both regressions, the dummy variable controlling for the reunification effect is significant negative for West Germany. This could be explained by the entrepreneurial policy which is concentrated around universities in East Germany, especially Dresden in Saxony and Thüringen (see Acs, 2002, p. 190).

This third model is also estimated for major technology industries or groups. As the results in Table 3 suggest, the evidence suggests that not all of the knowledge measures have a homogeneous impact on entrepreneurship across the particular industries. The results show that the demand for high skilled labor, as expressed by the number of students, differs across the industries. Especially in the high-technology and knowledge intense industries, the amount of students in the natural sciences enters the regressions significantly. While research activities in the social sciences seem to have no impact on the number of firms clustered around a university, the results differ for research in the natural sciences. The number of articles published in this field is significant and positive in the Hardware and Technology sector as well as in the Biotechnology and Medicine Technique sector. This strongly supports the thesis that university research in those fields can provide knowledge spillovers in high-technology and knowledge based industries.

Thus, there is no reason to think that knowledge spillover entrepreneurship is invariant to the type of knowledge or the industry context. Still, these results confirm that there is compelling evidence suggesting that knowledge-based startups tend to cluster within geographic proximity to the knowledge source.

Table 3
Negative binomial estimating regional technolology startups

	Software	Service	Media and Entertainment	Hardware/technology	Biotec/medtec
Regional capacity	0.0437 (7.59)***	0.0402 (7.81)***	0.04377 (4.50)***	0.06128 (8.08)***	0.0706 (2.36)**
SCI students	-1.50E06 (0.09)	0.0001 (0.98)	0.0001 (2.30)***	0.0002 (2.59)***	0.0003 (3.04)***
SSCI students	0.00002 (3.17)***	0.0003 (8.84)***	0.0004 (3.35)***	0.0004 (4.49)***	0.0006 (3.69)***
SSCI	-0.001 (1.13)	-0.012 (1.39)	-0.001 (1.13)	-0.0005 (1.52)	-0.0018 (1.35)
SCI	-0.1971 (0.92)	0.2076 (0.71)	-0.0043 (0.08)	0.2356 (2.05)**	0.0103 (1.67)*
Age	0.00002 (0.05)	-0.0004 (1.16)	-0.006 (1.12)	-0.003 (2.96)***	0.0025 (0.85)
TU	-1.0577 (3.46)***	-0.9135 (3.15)***	-2.284 (3.01)***	-0.5618 (1.59)	1.468 (1.67)*
City	-0.282E07 (5.34)***	-4.74E07 (2.85)***	-3.45E07 (1.48)	-1.17E07 (0.24)	-1.18E06 (1.47)
West	-0.4105 (1.01)	-0.5606 (1.67)*	-0.4876 (1.12)	-0.7883 (0.88)	-3.130 (1.45)
Number of universities	0.8234 (5.34)***	0.9007 (7.66)***	0.7666 (3.42)***	0.4493 (1.26)	0.7164 (1.72)*
Const.	0.3309 (0.62)	0.7129 (1.41)	0.3122 (0.23)	0.2576 (0.22)	3.5109 (2.12)*
Pseudo R2	0.3722	0.3560	0.4042	0.3999	0.4143
LL-ratio test (χ^2)	-130.485	-164.059	-93.357	-110.326	-51.769
Number of firms in each industry	55	67	37	47	25

The endogenous variable is the number of technology startups located within geographic proximity to a university. Z-values are in brackets. The asterisks, *, **, and *** indicate significance at the 10%, 5%, and 1% level, respectively. $N = 54$ universities. We dropped all industries with less than 20 firms and matched Hardware and Technology as well as Biotech and Medtec to increase the number of firms in the regressions.

D.B. Audretsch, E.E. Lehmann / Research Policy 34 (2005) 1191–1202   1201

5. Conclusion

The Knowledge Spillover Theory of Entrepreneurship suggests that investment in the creation of new knowledge will generate opportunities for entrepreneurship as a mechanism for knowledge spillovers. While empirical evidence has already been provided supporting the Knowledge Spillover Theory of Entrepreneurship for the different contexts provided by industry specific knowledge investments, little was known about the spatial dimension. This paper has found that those universities in regions with a higher knowledge capacity and greater knowledge output also generate a higher number of technology startups. Thus, at least on the basis of data from Germany, there is considerable evidence that the Knowledge Spillover Theory of Entrepreneurship holds for regions as well as for industries.

As comparative advantage has become increasingly based on new knowledge, the results show that public policy can respond in two fundamental ways. First, by providing an infrastructure that enables young firms to absorb necessary resources. This is shown by the positive effect of the regional knowledge capacity on firm location. Secondly, by influencing universities to increase their research activities, especially in the natural sciences and in providing well educated students.

Acknowledgements

Financial support by the German Research Foundation (DFG) through the research group #FOR454 "Heterogeneous Labor" at the University of Konstanz and the ZEW, Mannheim, is gratefully acknowledged. We also would like to thank Adam Lederer, two anonymous referees and Michael Fritsch for helpful comments and suggestions.

References

Acs, Z., 2002. Innovation and the Growth of Cities. Edward Elgar, Cheltenham.

Acs, Z., Audretsch, D.B., Braunerjhelm, P., Carlsson, B., 2003. The Missing Link: The Knowledge Filter and Endodenous Growth. Center for Business and Policy Studies, Stockholm, Sweden.

Anselin, L., Varga, A., Acs, Z., 1997. Local geographic spillovers between university research and high technology innovations. Journal of Urban Economics 42, 422–448.

Arrow, K., 1962. Economic welfare and the allocation of resources for invention. In: Nelson, R. (Ed.), The Rate and Direction of Inventive Activity. Princeton University Press, Princeton.

Audretsch, D.B., 1995. Innovation and Industry Evolution. MIT Press, Cambridge/Mass.

Audretsch, D.B., Lehmann, E.E., 2005. Mansfields's missing link: the impact of knowledge spillovers on firm growth. Journal of Technology Transfer 30 (1/2), 207–210.

Audretsch, D.B., Keilbach, M., Lehmann, E.E., 2006. Entrepreneurship and Growth. Oxford University Press, in press.

Audretsch, D.B., Feldman, M.P., 1996. R&D spillovers and the geography of innovation and production. American Economic Review 86, 630–640.

Audretsch, D.B., Fritsch, M., 1994. The geography of firm births in Germany. Regional Studies 28 (4), 359–365.

Audretsch, D.B., Stephan, P.E., 1996. Company-scientist locational links: the case of biotechnology. American Economic Review 86 (3), 641–652.

Audretsch, D.B., Stephan, P.E., 1999. How and why does knowledge spill overs in biotechnology? In: Audretsch, D.B., Thurik, R. (Eds.), Innovation, Industry Evolution, and Employment. Cambridge University press, Cambridge, pp. 216–229.

Audretsch, D.B., Thurik, R., 2001. What is new about the new economy: sources of growth in the managed and entrepreneurial economies. Industrial and Corporate Change 19, 795–821.

Baldwin, R.E., Forslid, R., 2000. The core-periphery model and endogenous growth: stabilizing and destabilizing integration. Economics 67, 307–324.

Bartik, T., 1985. Business location decisions in the United States: estimates of the effects of unionization, taxes, and other characteristics of the states. Journal of Business and Economic Statistics 3 (January), 16–22.

Bode, E., 2004. The spatial pattern of localized R&D spillovers: an empirical investigation for Germany. Journal of Economic Geography 4, 43–64.

Carlton, D.W., 1983. The location and employment choices of new firms: an econometric model with discrete and continuous endogenous variables. Review of Economics and Statistics 65 (3), 440–449.

Federal Ministry of Education and Research, 2004. Facts and Figures 2002 (http://www.bmbf.de).

Fritsch, M., 1997. New firms and regional employment change. Small Business Economics 9 (5), 437–448.

Fujita, M., Thisse, J.-F., 2002. Economics of Agglomeration. Cities, Industrial Location, and Regional Growth. Cambridge University Press, Cambridge.

Greene, W.H., 2003. Econometric Analysis, fifth ed. Prentice Hall, New York.

Griliches, Z., 1979. Issues in assessing the contribution of research and development to productivity growth. Bell Journal of Economics 10, 92–116.

Jaffe, A.B., 1989. Real effects of academic research. American Economic Review 79, 957–970.

Reynolds, P., Storey, D.J., Westhead, P., 1994. Cross-national comparisons of the variation in new firm formation rates. Regional Studies 28 (4), 443–456, July.

Romer, P.M., 1986. Increasing returns and long-run growth. Journal of Political Economy 94, 1002–1037.

Sarasvathy, S.D., Dew, N., Ramakrishna Velamuri, S., Venkataraman, S., 2003. Three views of entrepreneurial opportunity. In: Acs, Z., Audretsch, D.B. (Eds.), Handbook of Entrepreneurship Research. Kluwer Academic Publishers, Dordrecht, pp. 141–160.

Saxenien, A., 1994. Regional Advantage: Culture and Competition in Silicon Valley and Route 128. Harvard University Press, Cambridge, MA.

Schartinger, D., Schibany, A., Gassler, H., 2001. Interactive relations between universities and firms: empirical evidence for Austria. Journal of Technology Transfer 26 (3), 255–268.

Shane, S., Eckhardt, J., 2003. The individual-opportunity nexus. In: Acs, Zoltan J., Audretsch, D.B. (Eds.), Handbook of Entrepreneurship Research. Kluwer Academic Publishers, Dordrecht, pp. 161–194.

Stephan, P., 1996. The economics of science. Journal of Economic Literature 34 (3), 1199–1235.

Stephan, P., 2001. Educational implications of university-industry technology transfer. Journal of Technology Transfer 26 (3), 199–205.

Sternberg, V.R., Litzenberger, T., 2003. Regional clusters—operationalisation and consequences for entrepreneurship. Working paper, University of Cologne.

Varga, A., 2000. Local academic knowledge transfers and the concentration of economic activity. Journal of Regional Science 40, 289–309.

Warning, S., 2004. Performance differences in the German Higher Education System: empirical analysis of strategic groups. Review of Industrial Organization 24, 393–408.

[4]

Econ. Innov. New Techn., 2006, Vol. 15(1), January, pp. 71–81

DO LOCATIONAL SPILLOVERS PAY? EMPIRICAL EVIDENCE FROM GERMAN IPO DATA

DAVID B. AUDRETSCH[a,b,*] and ERIK E. LEHMANN[a,†]

[a]*Department Entrepreneurship, Growth and Public Policy, Max-Planck Institute for Research into Economic Systems, Jena, Kahlaische Strasse 10, 07745 Jena, Germany;* [b]*Indiana University Bloomington, Indiana, USA*

(Received 11 February 2004; Revised 1 July 2004; In final form 16 November 2004)

This study examines the impact that locational spillovers have on firm performance. On the basis of a uniquely created data set consisting of high-technology start-ups publicly listed in Germany, this paper tests the proposition of locational spillovers positively affecting firm performance, as measured by abnormally high profits on the stock market. The results provide evidence that geographic proximity and university spillovers are complementary determinants of firm performance. Although neither geographic proximity nor academic research spillovers alone can explain firm performance, a combination of both factors results in significant higher stock market performance. The results also show that academic spillovers are heterogeneous in their impact, depending on the type. In particular, spillovers from social sciences have a different impact on firm performance than do spillovers from natural sciences.

Keywords: University spillover; Firm performance; University–firm collaboration

JEL Classification: M13; L 20; R30

1 INTRODUCTION

'Munich was the only city which offered us a location on the Campus of the University'[1]

It has long been thought that when people work in close geographic proximity, the likelihood that they will collaborate together increases dramatically (Finholt, 2003; Olson and Olson, 2003; Audretsch, *et al.*, 2005). Such forms of collaboration – interacting with colleagues, accessing instrumentation, exchange of students and graduates and sharing data and computational resources, among others – have to be among the most important mechanisms of transmitting the spillover of knowledge. However, depending upon the specific kind of knowledge, geographic proximity matters for accessing such spillovers. An important empirical result that has consistently emerged in the literature on the geography of knowledge spillovers is that, although geographic proximity seems to be less important for codified knowledge, it seems to be more important for tacit knowledge. For example, Audretsch and Stephan

---

* Corresponding author. E-mail: audretsch@mpiew-jena.mpg.de

† E-mail: lehmann@mpiew-jena.mpg.de

[1]Armin Pfoh, Head of the Global Research Center of General Electric, reply to the question why General Electric decided to build up the Global Research Center in Munich, cited in Focus, October 2004, No. 41, p. 118.

ISSN 1043-8599 print; ISSN 1476-8364 online © 2006 Taylor & Francis
DOI: 10.1080/1043859042000332187

(1996, 1998) found that the importance of spatial proximity between scientists and biotechnology firms depended on whether the scientist was involved in the transfer of codified or tacit knowledge.

Although a huge amount of empirical studies tried to analyze the determinants of spillover effects, this paper addresses the question of how firm performance is shaped by the spillover of knowledge from universities. In particular, we analyze whether firm performance on the stock market of newly listed and high-tech firms is shaped by both geographical proximity to universities and magnitude and quality of the university research output. Production, acquisition, absorption, reproduction and dissemination of knowledge are seen as the fundamental characteristics of contemporary competitive dynamics and help in fostering innovative activities (Anselin *et al.*, 1997; 2000; Sorensen and Audia, 2000; Varga, 2000; Santoro and Chakrabarti, 2002; Stuart and Shane, 2002; Baum and Sorensen, 2003). However, little is known about how exactly and why geographic proximity to universities influences firm performance.

Thus, the purpose of this paper is to address these questions focusing on whether knowledge spillovers and geographic proximity actually influence firm performance, and if so, what is the exact nature of the impact of knowledge spillovers and geographic proximity on firm performance. We do this by linking the stock market performance of firms in terms of abnormal profits to the proximity to a university along with the different elements of university research and educational outputs.

The paper is organized as follows. Section 2 summarizes the literature and introduces the testable hypotheses raised in this paper. Section 3 contains the description of the database, and the estimation techniques. The empirical results are presented in Section 4. In Section 5, the summary and conclusions are presented. In particular, we find compelling evidence suggesting that performance is shaped by both geographic proximity and university research. However, the impact of these two factors is complementary in that both are required to generate high levels of firm profitability.

2   UNIVERSITY SPILLOVERS, GEOGRAPHICAL PROXIMITY AND FIRM PERFORMANCE

Although the importance of spillovers on firms has entered mainstream economics only recently, the important productivity effects of spillovers has been recognized for a long time (Romer, 1986; Grossman and Helpman, 1991). There is an ongoing debate on fostering university spillovers to enhance economic growth. University spillovers could be defined as an externality accessed by firms, for which the university is the source of the spillover but not fully compensated (Harris, 2001). Because firms access external knowledge at a cost that is lower than the cost of producing this value internally, or of acquiring it externally from a larger geographic distance (Harhoff, 2000), they will exhibit higher expected profits. The cost of transferring such knowledge is a function of geographic distance and gives rise to localized externalities (Siegel, *et al.*, 2003).

However, little is known about the actual mechanisms transmitting the spillover of knowledge. Studies have identified that knowledge spillovers may arise from personal networks of academic and industrial researchers (Liebeskind *et al.*, 1996; MacPherson, 1998; Feldman and Desroche, 2003), participation in conferences and presentations or pre-employment possibilities with students are important channels for disseminating the latest knowledge from academia to high-technology industry (Varga, 2000). University research, as the source of such spillovers, is typically measured by the amount of money spent on research and development (R&D), the number of articles published in academic and scientific journals and the number of employees or patents (Henderson *et al.*, 1998; McWilliams and Siegel, 2000;

Varga, 2000; Hall *et al.*, 2003). The overwhelming part of the empirical literature confirms the positive effects of university spillovers (Acs *et al.*, 1992; 1994; Jaffe *et al.*, 1993; Audretsch and Feldman, 1996; Anselin *et al.*, 1997; Varga, 2000; Mowery and Ziedonis, 2001; Audretsch *et al.*, 2004), although there are barriers of partnering, like unclear property rights (Hall *et al.*, 2001).

Although there exists a huge amount of empirical work analyzing the existence of geographical proximity and university spillovers (Audretsch *et al.*, 2004), there is only scarce evidence on the effects of knowledge spillovers on firm performance. One way to measure performance is whether university spillovers reduce the cost of R&D for the firms (Harhoff, 2000). Another method is introduced by Griliches (1979). He suggested using hedonic price functions to analyze whether the quality of new products increases owing to spillovers relative to the old product. One branch of research analyzes the productivity effects of spillovers (see Nadiri, 1997 for a survey). However, whether geographic proximity and access to knowledge spillovers improve firm performance remains relatively unexplored. This is the main question of this paper.

Perhaps the most prevalent and established finding in the spillover literature is that innovative output and growth is higher in the presence of knowledge inputs (Feldman, 2000). However, this literature has been established for a region or city as the unit of observation. As already emphasized, little is known about the impact of geographic proximity on the performance at the firm level. As Jaffe (1989) points out, geographical location is important in capturing the benefits of spillovers when the mechanism of knowledge is informal conversation, as is the case for tacit knowledge. Then, '….geographic proximity to the spillover source may be helpful or even necessary in capturing the spillover benefits' (Jaffe, 1989, p. 957). Thus, the limited geographic reach of such channels for the exchange of information and know-how is assumed to be one of the main reasons why geographic proximity promotes firm performance as it leads to a competitive advantage over similar firms which are not located close to universities. During the innovation process, firms are confronted with a wide range of possible problems and difficulties which may be beyond the firm's own problem solving capacity. Close location then gives support to both management capacity and technological input. Otherwise, spatial distance between firms and universities is likely to act as the major barrier of interaction (Schartinger *et al.*, 2001). Thus, our first hypothesis is that locational proximity positively influences firm performance. The closer is the distance towards the nearest university, the higher is the likelihood that people will collaborate by personal interaction. Therefore, we would expect that firm performance decreases with distance from the nearest university.

However, our analysis is based on the assumption that stock markets are not perfect. A number of studies (Ritter, 1991) assume that agents are not able to evaluate every piece of information and therefore that stock market prices did not reflect full information in the prices. Like our paper, his analysis is based on initial public offering (IPO) and the pricing of firms with different quality. Thus, the underlying null-hypothesis would be that there is no impact of geographic proximity on stock market performance. If, however, geographic proximity towards universities is important for those firms, proximity would be priced in the IPO and thus would have no impact on abnormal returns.

The first hypothesis states that distance alone has an impact on firm performance, whereas the second hypothesis states that the research output of universities enhances firm performance, especially when high-skilled labor is a scarce resource and there is intense competition for human capital and other knowledge inputs (Porter and Stern, 2001). Schartinger *et al.* (2001) conclude that mobility of human capital is the main channel of knowledge transfer from universities to the business sector. This leads us to formulate our second hypothesis, which is that research-intensive universities and those with a high number of fresh graduates and students will enhance firm performance positively.

The third hypothesis is based on the distinction between codified and tacit knowledge (Kogut and Zander, 1992). Elements of know-how and operations cannot be codified easily in a blueprint, a contractual document (Mowery and Ziedonis, 2001) or a published article (Audretsch and Feldman, 1996). Tacit knowledge needs oral communication and reciprocity, which may be ineffective or infeasible over longer distances. Audretsch *et al.* (2004) and Audretsch and Stephan (1996, 1998) find that also the kind of science – codified or tacit knowledge – matters for spillover effects. Although locating spatially close towards universities is not necessary to transmit and disseminate findings where knowledge is codified, it is important where knowledge is tacit. Knowledge in the natural sciences is characterized by a greater degree of codification. Strict adherence to the scientific method assures that academic research embodies a high component of codified and specific knowledge in the natural sciences (Stephan, 1996). In contrast, the more limited applicability of the scientific method implies that research in the social sciences will embody less codified knowledge and is there more tacit in nature (Stephan, 1996). Thus, the third hypothesis states that firm performance will be positively related to geographic proximity for research in the social sciences but not necessarily in the natural sciences.

Finally, our fourth hypothesis states that neither the magnitude of research output nor the geographical proximity to the university alone enhances firm performance significantly. Only in combination will locational proximity and high research university output, positively affect firm performance.

3   DATA SET AND DESCRIPTIVE STATISTICS

3.1   Measurement and Methodology

To test the hypothesis that firm performance depends on geographical proximity to a university, we use a unique data set of high-technology German firms publicly listed on the *Neuer Markt*. The total number of German firms listed on the *Neuer Markt*, Germany's counterpart of the NASDAQ, was 295 between 1997 and 2002. From these firms, we dropped all banks (5) and holding companies (9) as they differ in their production function significantly from the other firms.[2] The data set is collected by combining individual data from IPO prospectuses, along with publicly available information from on-line data sources including the *Deutsche Boerse AG* (www.deutsche-boerse.com). We pooled this data set by adding university-specific variables, which are individually collected from the 73 universities in Germany. For each of these universities, we collected the number of articles listed in the research database from Information Sciences Institutes (ISI). Although this research database includes a small amount of all the journals in one field, it ensures that it only contains the high-quality research journals.

We take the log of abnormal profits as the dependent variable. This is a wide-spread measure of firm performance on the stock market. We calculated the abnormal annual log-rents on the stock market from IPO until 30 June 2002. This time-period captures both the prominent and the well-known effects, the so called internet bubble on the stock markets and the rapid decline in 2001 and 2002.

The abnormal annual log-profit is measured as:

$$\frac{[(\ln \text{price}30.06.02 - \ln \text{IPOprice}) - (\ln \text{NEMAX}30.06.02 - \ln \text{NEMAXIPO})]52}{\text{number of weeks}}$$

ln IPOprice is the natural logarithm of the stock price at the first day when the firm was listed on the stock market and thus reveals the demand and supply for the firm's shares. Therefore, this

---

[2] We dropped banks like Comdirect, Consors and holding companies like BB-Biotech.

price is the market determined price on the first day of trading. ln NEMAXIPO is the logarithm of the market index at IPO. ln price 30.06.02 and ln NEMAX 30.06.02 are the values taken on 30 June 2002. Capital increases and dividend payments are considered in the stock prices. The term is divided by the number of weeks from IPO to 30 June 2002. Multiplying by 52 gives the annual abnormal profit. The underlying performance measure of abnormal profits measures long time performance from IPO up to the first half of the year 2002. Although no new IPOs are observed in the years 2001 and 2002, we increased the time horizon until June 2002. This time horizon includes both dramatical ups – until March 2000 – and downs – from March 2000 until March 2002 – on the stock market.

We take the distance to the closest university as the first exogenous variable. As universities in Germany are more geographically concentrated compared with the US, we need a measure that is sensitive to small variations. The distance is measured in kilometers using the on–line database of the German Automobile Club (www.adac.de). All firms located within a radius of 1.5 km are classified as belonging to the distance category of 1 km to capture 'on campus' effects of tacit knowledge.

To capture effects of excellence in academic research, we rank German universities according to their academic papers published in highly ranked journals as included in the ISI database (Rank SCI, Rank SSCI). This ranking is published by the Center of University Evaluation (CHE, Warning, 2004).[3] In contrast to traditional rankings, the better the university, the higher the ranking. As technical universities, with their focus on engineering and machinery, differ from the traditional universities, we include a dummy variable to control for this special type of university (TU). We also control the age of a firm (AGE), which is measured in years from foundation to IPO, and the number of employees before IPO to control for size effects (SIZE).

As the dependent variable is highly skewed, we apply median regression methods to test our hypothesis. Just as one can define the sample mean as the solution to the problem of minimizing a sum of squared residuals, one can define the median as the solution to the problem of minimizing a sum of absolute residuals. This semi-parametric technique provides a general class of models in which the conditional quantiles have a linear form. In its simplest form, the least absolute deviation estimator fits medians to a linear function of covariates. The method of quantile regression is potentially attractive for the same reason that the median or other quantiles are a better measure of location than the mean. Other useful features are the robustness against outliers and the fact that the likelihood estimators are, in general, more efficient than least square estimators. Besides the technical features, quantile regressions allow for potentially different solutions at distinct quantiles to be interpreted as differences in the response of the dependent variable, namely the distance, to changes in the regressors at various points in the conditional distinction of the dependent variable. Thus, quantile regressions reveal asymmetries in the data, which could not be detected by simple OLS estimations (Koenker and Hallock, 2001; Fitzenberger, 1999 for more details of quantile regressions). Specifically, we estimate three nested models to extract the influence of geographical distance and university spillovers on firm performance.

In the first model (Model I), we estimate the following regression to test the first three hypotheses:

$$\text{Performance} = \text{const.} + \beta_1 \text{ distance} + \beta_2 \text{ RankSSCI} + \beta_3 \text{ RankSCI} + \beta_4 \text{ studentsSCI}$$
$$+ \beta_5 \text{ studentsSSCI} + \beta_6 \text{ technical university} + \beta_7 \text{ firmage} + \beta_8 \text{ firm size}$$
$$+ \beta_{9-15} \text{ industry dummies} + \beta_{16-18} \text{ IPO dummies} + \varepsilon$$

[3] We experimented with the number of articles published in both the social and the natural sciences. The results that include the relative performance or excellence of universities, as summarized by the ranking in both fields, provide better results. However, the bivariate correlation coefficients between the ranking positions and the number of articles published in the natural science (social science) is 0.921 (0.951) (Tab. II).

To test the fourth hypothesis we estimate the following reduced form (Model II):

$$Performance = const. + \beta_1 distance \times RankSSCI + \beta_2 distance \times RankSCI$$
$$+ \beta_3 distance \times studentsSCI + \beta_4 distance \times studentsSCI + \varepsilon$$

Finally, we estimate the third model (Model III):

$$Performance = const. + \beta_1 distance \times RankSSCI + \beta_2 distance \times RankSCI$$
$$+ \beta_3 distance \times studentsSCI + \beta_4 distance \times studentsSSCI + \beta_5 firm\ age$$
$$+ \beta_6 firm\ size + \beta_7 technical\ university + \beta_{8-14} industry\ dummies$$
$$+ \beta_{15-17} IPO\ dummies + \varepsilon$$

3.2   Descriptive Statistics

Some descriptive statistics are depicted in Tables I and II. The closest location between firms and universities is 1 km and the maximum distance is 177 km from the nearest university. The skewed distribution of the data is reflected by the difference between the mean and the median values. Although the arithmetic mean distance is ~17 km, the median shows that 50% of the firms are located within an area of radius 7 km. Table I indicates that research activities and the number of students and fresh graduates vary considerably across universities. A comparison between the mean and the median also exhibits the skewed number of articles in both the social sciences and the natural sciences. On an average, each university published about 250 papers in social sciences and more than 5100 articles in natural sciences. However, the number of articles published by 50% of the universities is lower. In addition, the number of graduates differs across universities (Tab. I).

Interestingly, the number of articles and graduate students varies not only across universities but also across the two fields. The mean university publishes 20 times more articles in

TABLE I   Descriptive statistics.

Variable	Mean	Std. Dev.	Min	Max	Median
Distance (km)	16.69	23.45	1	177	7
SCI-Articles	5139.43	4603.16	0	14,176	4069
SSCI-Articles	253.86	220.01	0	659	204
SCI-Students	20,321.17	15,409.63	0	47,112	15,741
SCI-Students	7304.89	3988.45	0	20,570	7725
SCI-Rank	2.042	1.119	1.3	11.38	1.93
SSCI-Rank	1.824	0.269	1.39	2.668	1.75
Firm size (No. of employees)	180.20	256.52	2	1700	94
Firm age (years)	10.27	11.11	0.1	107	8
Abnormal log-rent	−1.70565	0.9431	−6.551	0.259	−1.615

TABLE II   Correlation matrix.

Variable	Size	Age	SCI-Grads	SSCI-Grads	SCI-Rank	SSCI-Rank	SSCI-Articles	SCI-Articles
Age	0.328	1.000	–	–	–	–	–	–
SCI-Grads	0.0352	0.1016	1.000	–	–	–	–	–
SSCI-Grads	−0.0056	−0.0276	0.118	1.000	–	–	–	–
SCI-Rank	0.1267	0.0916	0.0767	−0.1924	1.000	–	–	–
SSCI-Rank	−0.0015	0.0835	−0.0756	0.1070	0.3469	1.000	–	–
SSCI-Articles	−0.008	−0.0019	0.0690	0.8771	0.4019	0.9514	1.000	–
SCI-Articles	0.024	−0.011	0.1807	0.8042	0.8771	0.1661	0.921	1.000
Distance (km)	0.078	−0.1010	−0.0236	−0.0622	0.1939	0.0142	−0.0012	0.0011

the natural sciences when compared with the social sciences; this difference increases with the number of published papers. However, articles in the natural sciences and those in the social sciences differ in their length, number of co-authors and referee time, and are thus not comparable. While 50% of the universities publish about 200 articles in social sciences, there are more than 4000 articles in natural sciences. The opposite can be found for the number of students. On an average, more than 20,300 students are studying social sciences, whereas only about one-third, 7300, are enrolled in the natural sciences.

The data presented in Table I also demonstrate that most of the firms are strikingly young. Half of the firms in our sample are 8 years old or less. The firms also differ greatly in their size as measured by the number of employees before IPO. The median firm employs about 94 people, whereas the mean firm is about twice as large with 253 employees.

Finally, the table shows that on an average the abnormal annual log-profit is negative. This, however, is due to the fact that the benchmark, the NEMAX 50 Index, covers a subsample of firms which are larger in size and are assumed to be of higher 'quality', like non-IPOs, firms from abroad, and the excluded banks or holding companies.

Table II provides the correlation between the included variables. The high correlation between the articles published in SCI and in SSCI demonstrates that universities are either research active or not, independently from the academic field. Interestingly, there is a high correlation between the articles published in social sciences and the number of graduates in these fields, but not for natural sciences. Although research in the social sciences seems to be not affected by the number of students in the natural sciences, there is a high correlation between the articles published in the natural sciences and the students in the social sciences. One explanation may be that the natural sciences restrict the number of students. The high correlation between the number of students in the social sciences and the number of articles published in this field may also be due to size effects.

4   EMPIRICAL EVIDENCE

The results of the median regressions are presented in Table III. In Model I, distance and university output enter the regression separately. From the coefficients it is seen that neither geographic proximity nor university research rankings show any significant effect on firm performance. Most of the variance in firm performance is explained either by industry effects or by time to IPO. The latter indicates the phenomenon of the 'window of opportunities': the longer the IPO period, the lower the quality of firms which are brought to the stock markets. The pseudo R^2 is 0.334, which can be interpreted in the same way as the traditional R^2 in OLS regressions, as it also shows the proportion of the explained variance about the specified quantile. Thus, ~33% of the variance of firm performance could be explained by our model.

In the second model (Model II), we only included the interaction terms. Although only ~4% of the variance could be explained by the four variables, three of them have a statistically significant coefficient. With a given level in the SSCI-Rank, firm performance increases, the closer its location is to the university. The same also holds significantly for the amount of fresh graduates and students in the natural sciences. However, the opposite holds for research activities in the natural sciences. This result is in line with findings from Audretsch and Stephan (1996, 1998) and Schartinger *et al.* (2001). The latter study showed that the employment of high-skilled, university educated personnel is the most important input for the innovation process of high-tech firms. Codified knowledge, as embodied in academic articles in the natural science, did not need short distance to enhance firm performance. In this case, firms could lower their costs and thus increase profits by choosing a location outside the inner circle of a city and thus lower costs of living and housing.

78   D. B. AUDRETSCH AND E. E. LEHMANN

TABLE III   Geographic proximity, university research and performance.

	Model 1	Model 2	Model 3
Distance (km)	$-0.0007^{\dagger}$ $(0.36)^{\ddagger}$	–	–
SSCI-Ranking	0.0514 (0.28)	–	–
SCI-Ranking	0.1001 (0.37)	–	–
SSCI-Students	−0.000001 (0.36)	–	–
SCI-Students	0.00001 (0.86)	–	–
SSCI-Ranking × Distance	–	−0.02084 (5.06)***	−0.0104 (2.79)**
SCI-Ranking × Distance	–	0.0270 (5.16)***	0.0136 (3.11)***
SSCI-Students × Distance	–	−0.000001 (1.20)	−0.0000002 (0.29)
SCI-Students × Distance	–	−0.000001 (2.43)**	−0.000001 (1.91)**
Technical university	−0.1236 (0.53)	–	0.096 (0.59)
Age	0.0066 (1.30)	–	0.0048 (1.26)
Size	0.00019 (1.03)	–	0.00019 (1.37)
Software	−0.0703 (1.71)*	–	−0.0766 (2.39)**
Service	−0.1712 (1.29)	–	−0.2171 (2.02)**
E-commerce	−0.3214 (1.51)	–	−0.4096 (2.47)**
Telecommunication	−0.21016 (1.08)	–	−0.2474 (1.58)
Biotechnology	−0.20204 (0.91)	–	−0.1481 (0.80)
MedTec	0.21509 (0.92)	–	0.1833 (0.96)
Media and entertainment	−0.3307 (1.94)*	–	−0.3256 (2.49)**
IPO 97	1.6175 (6.20)***	–	1.6709 (8.64)***
IPO 98	1.2307 (8.11)***	–	1.2243 (9.53)***
IPO 99	0.8052 (7.67)	–	0.7908 (9.53)***
Constants	−2.4214 (4.83)	−1.6231 (27.88)***	−2.0771 (20.08)***
Pseudo R^2	0.334	0.0330	0.3375
N	259	259	259
Pseudo median	−1.6032	−1.6032	−1.6032

Note: This table presents the result from median regression on firm performance. The endogenous variable is abnormal annual log-profits on the stock market. *Statistically significant at 10% level; **Statistically significant at 5% level; ***Statistically significant at 1% level.
†Estimated median regression coefficients.
‡Absolute *t*-values.

As shown in column 3, these results are also robust in the full model. In contrast, geographic proximity may be less important for accessing knowledge transmitted by recent graduates in the social sciences than in the natural sciences. This is because of the generic nature of university education in the social sciences in Germany. Social science programs are standardized throughout the country, which produces graduates with a relatively homogeneous degree of human capital. However, such standardization is not found in the natural sciences; therefore, geographic proximity is important to access knowledge embodied in recent graduates in the natural sciences. Therefore, the number of fresh graduates in social sciences would not really affect the firms' decision to locate close towards the next university and thus has no significant effect on firm performance. In the natural sciences, however, universities differ in their specific research specialization like life science, biochemistry, physics or engineering. Thus, the human capital of fresh graduates and students in the natural sciences is likely to be more 'specific' than 'general' (Audretsch *et al.*, 2004).

The first important result of our study is that geographical proximity alone has no significant impact on firm performance. Thus, we reject hypothesis 1. We also reject hypothesis 2 that research-intense universities and those with a high amount of students and graduates significantly enhance firm performance.

The second important result is that firm performance is significantly higher when both geographic proximity and strong university research output are present. This suggests an interactive relationship between geographic proximity and university output, on the one hand, and firm performance on the other.

Finally, the third important result involves the roles of tacit and codified knowledge. The negative and statistically significant coefficient of SSCI-Rank in Models II and III suggests the contribution of geographic proximity to the university will play a more important role for firm performance in the social sciences than in the natural sciences. However, the regressions suffer from an endogenous problem as firms are located close to universities to capture those spillovers and from spillover effects between those firms.

5   CONCLUSIONS

An important literature has emerged identifying the role that knowledge spillovers play in shaping the economic performance of cities and regions. A significant contribution of this literature is that, because of the localized nature of knowledge spillovers, geographically bounded regions with higher knowledge resources also tend to exhibit a stronger economic performance. However, a limitation of this literature is that the findings apply for spatial units of observation, such as cities and regions, while less is known about the impact of geographic proximity and knowledge spillovers at the firm level.

By utilizing a new and unique data set consisting of high-technology and knowledge firms in Germany, this paper has posed the question 'Does the relationship between geographic proximity to knowledge sources and performance hold at the firm level?' The answer found in this paper is that it depends. In particular, the impact of geographic proximity on firm performance depends on the type of knowledge produced at a particular university. If the spillover involves knowledge in the natural sciences, geographic proximity is less important. In contrast, if the spillover involves knowledge in the social sciences, geographic proximity is seen to be a necessary condition for generating abnormally high profits. Thus, the results of this paper suggest that the relationship between geographic proximity to universities and economic performance at the firm level is more complicated than might appear from the literature at the more aggregated spatial levels and depends on the nature of the particular type of spillover involved.

An important limitation of this paper is that only two types of knowledge, and therefore knowledge spillovers – social science and natural science – are considered. The results show a different impact between the social and the natural sciences on stock market performance. However, this difference could also be that the spillover effects of the codified scientific knowledge are easier to anticipate by market participants and priced at the IPO than the spillover effects from social science knowledge.[4] Thus, the results show that spillovers matter for firm performance. However, it depends on whether the impact of geographic proximity on firm performance is anticipated and priced in the IPOs.

Future research might be well served to further investigate the heterogeneous nature of cooperation and knowledge spillovers. Only then can progress continue to be made in disentangling the relationship among firm performance, location and collaboration.

Acknowledgements

We are grateful to two anonymous referees and comments from Frank A. Rothaermel, Don Siegel, Taylor Aldrigdge, and Paula Stephan.

---

[4] We are grateful to an anonymous referee for his point. In fact, it seems that codified knowledge could be priced easier. If we use the IPO-returns (difference between the fixed price before IPO and the first market determined price), the results differ in that the coefficients of the interaction terms show the opposite signs. Another explanation is that firms overestimate their future returns from spillovers in the sciences, which are then reflected by higher IPO prices.

References

Acs, Z.J., Audretsch, D.B. and Feldman, M.P. (1992) Real Effects of Academic Research (Comment). *American Economic Review*, **82**, 363–367.

Acs, Z.J., Audretsch, D.B. and Feldman, M.P. (1994) R&D Spillovers and Innovative Activity. *Managerial and Decision Economics*, **15**, 131–138.

Anselin, L., Varga, A. and Acs, Z. (1997) Local Geographic Spillovers between University Research and High Technology Innovations. *Journal of Urban Economics* **42**, 422–448.

Anselin, L., Varga, A. and Acs, Z. (2000) Geographical Spillovers and University Research: A Spatial Econometric Perspective. *Growth and Change*, **31**(4), 501–515.

Audretsch, D.B. and Feldman, M.P. (1996) R& D Spillovers and the Geography of Innovation and Production. *American Economic Review*, **86**, 630–640.

Audretsch, D.B. and Stephan, P.E. (1996) Company-Scientist Locational Links: The Case of Biotechnology. *American Economic Review*, **86**(3), 641–652.

Audretsch, D.B. and Stephan, P.E. (1999) Knowledge Spillovers in Biotechnology: Sources and Incentives. *Journal of Evolutionary Economics* **19**, 97–107.

Audretsch, D.B., Lehmann, E. and Susanne W. (2004) University Spillovers: Does the Kind of Knowledge Matter? *Industry and Innovation*, in press.

Audretsch, D.B., Keilbach, M. and Erik E. L. (2005) *Entrepreneurship and Growth*. Oxford University Press in press.

Baum, J.A.C. and Sorenson, O. (2003) *Advances in Strategic Management: Geography and Strategy*, Vol. 20. JAI Press: Greenwich CT. in press.

Feldman, M.P. (2000) Location and Innovation: The New Economic Geography of Innovation, In: Clark, G. Feldman, M.P. and Gertler, M. (eds.), *Handbook of Economic Geography*. Oxford: Oxford University Press.

Feldmann, M. and Desroche, P. (2003) Research Universities and Local Economic Development: Lessons from the History of the John Hopkins University. *Innovation and Industry*, **10**, 5–24.

Finholt, T.A. (2003) Collaboratories as a New Form of Science Organization. *Economics of Innovation and New Technology*, **12**(19), 5–25.

Fitzenberger, B. (1999) *Wages and Employment Across Skill Groups*. Heidelberg: Physica.

Griliches, Z. (1979) Issues in Assessing the Contribution of Research and Development to Productivity Growth. *Bell Journal of Economics*, **10**, 92–116.

Grossman, G.M. and Elhanan H. (1991) *Innovation and Growth in the Global Economy*. (Cambridge MA: MIT Press).

Hall, B.H., Link, A.N. and Scott, J.T. (2001) Barriers Inhibiting Industry from Partnering with Universities: Evidence from Advanced Technology Program. *Journal of Technology Transfer* **26**, 87–98.

Hall, B.H., Link, A.N. and Scott, J.T. (2003) Universities as Research Partners. *Review of Economics and Statistics*, **85**, 485–491.

Harhoff, D. (2000) R&D Spillovers, Technological Proximity, and Productivity Growth – Evidence from German Panel Data. *Schmalenbach Business Review*, **52**, 238–260.

Harris, R.G. (2001) The Knowledge-Based Economy: Intellectual Origins and New Economic Perspectives, *International Journal of Management Review*, **3**, 21–41.

Henderson, R., Jaffe, A. and Trajtenberg, M. (1998) Universities as a Source of Commercial Technology: A Detailed Analysis of University Patenting 1965–1988. *Review of Economics and Statistics*, **65**, 119–127.

Jaffe, A.B. (1989) Real Effects of Academic Research. *American Economic Review*, **79**, 957–970.

Jaffe, A.B., Trajtenberg, M. and Henderson, R. (1993) Geographic Localization of Knowledge Spillovers as Evidenced by Patent Citations. *Quarterly Journal of Economics*, **63**, 577–598.

Koenker, R. and Kevin F.H. (2001) Quantile Regression. *Journal of Economic Perspectives*, **15**, 143–156.

Kogut, B. and Zander, U. (1992) Knowledge of the Firm, Combinative Capabilities, and the Replication of Technology. *Organizational Science*, **3**, 383–397.

Liebeskind, J., Amalya, O.L., Zucker, L.G. and Brewer, M. (1996) Social Networks, Learning, and Flexibility: Sourcing Scientific Knowledge in New Biotechnology Firms. *Organizational Science*, **7**, 428–443.

Link, A.N. (1980) Firm Size and Efficient Entrepreneurial Activity: A Reformulation of the Schumpeterian Hyothesis. *Journal of Political Economy*, **88**, 771–782.

McWilliams, A. and Siegel, D.S. (2000) Corporate Social Responsibility and Financial Performance: Correlation or Misspecification? *Strategic Management Journal*, **21**, 603–609.

Mowery, D.C. and Ziedonis, A.A. (2001) The Geographic Reach of Market and Non-Market Channels of Technology Transfer: Comparing Citations and Licenses of University Patents, *NBER Working Paper*, No 8568.

Nadiri, M.I. (1997) Innovations and Technological Spillovers, *BNER Working Paper*, No 4423.

Olson, G.M. and Judith S.O. (2003) Mitigating the Effects of Distance on Collaborative Intellectual Work. *Economics of Innovative and New Technology*, **12**(1), 27–42.

Porter, M.E. and Stern, S. (2001) Innovation: Location Matters. *MIT Sloan Management Review*, Summer, 28–36.

Romer, P.M. (1986) Increasing Returns and Long-Run Growth. *Journal of Political Economy*, **94**, 1002–1037.

Santoro, M.D. and Chakrabarti, A.K. (2002) Firm Size and Technology Centrality in Industry-University Interactions. *Research Policy*, **31**, 1163–1180.

Siegel, D.S., Westhead, P. and Wright, M. (2003) Assessing the Impact of Science Parks on the Research Productivity of Firms: Exploratory Evidence from the United Kingdom. *International Journal of Industrial Organization*, **21**(9), 1357–1369.

Sorensen, O. and Audia, G. (2000) The Social Structure of Entrepreneurial Activity: Geographic Concentration of Footwear Production in the U.S, 1940–1989. *American Journal of Sociology*, **106**, 324–362.
Stephan, P. (1996) The Economics of Science. *Journal of Economic Literature*, **34**(3), 1199–1235.
Stephan, P.E., Sumell, A.J., Black, G.C. and Adams, J.D. (2002) Public Knowledge, Private Placements: New Ph.D.s as a Source of Knowledge Spillovers. Working Paper, Georgia State University.
Varga, A. (2000) Local Academic Knowledge Transfers and the Concentration of Economic Activity. *Journal of Regional Science*, **40**, 289–309.

Oxford Review of Economic Policy, Volume 23, Number 1, 2007, pp.63–78

Entrepreneurship capital and economic growth

David B. Audretsch*

Abstract This paper shows how and why the Solow growth accounting framework is useful for linking entrepreneurship capital to economic growth. The knowledge filter impedes the spillover of knowledge for commercialization, thereby weakening the impact of knowledge investments on economic growth. By serving as a conduit for knowledge spillovers, entrepreneurship is the missing link between investments in new knowledge and economic growth. Entrepreneurship is an important mechanism permeating the knowledge filter to facilitate the spillover of knowledge and ultimately generate economic growth. The emergence of entrepreneurship policy to promote economic growth is interpreted as an attempt to promote entrepreneurship capital, or the capacity of an economy to generate the start-up and growth of new firms.

Key words: entrepreneurship, growth, knowledge spillovers, Solow

JEL classification: O4, O3, E0, L26

I. Introduction

In his seminal article, Robert Solow (1956) provided a framework that not only explicitly linked key factors of production to economic growth but also framed the public policy discourse on how best to achieve growth. The Solow growth accounting framework included two explicit factors, physical capital and labour, as well as the implicit factor of technological change. While the specification of these factors has seen considerable evolution, such as the endogenization of knowledge investments generating technological change, public policy for growth has generally remained remarkably constant and focused on these three factors in the decades subsequent to Solow's pathbreaking article.

Thus, it may have come as a startling surprise when Romano Prodi (2002, p. 1), who at the time served as President of the European Commission, proclaimed that the promotion of entrepreneurship was a central cornerstone of European economic growth policy: 'Our lacunae in the field of entrepreneurship needs to be taken seriously because there is mounting evidence

*Max Planck Institute of Economics and Indiana University, e-mail: daudrets@indiana.edu

doi: 10.1093/icb/grm001

that the key to economic growth and productivity improvements lies in the entrepreneurial capacity of an economy.' With the 2000 Lisbon Proclamation, the European Council made a commitment to becoming not just the leader in knowledge but also the entrepreneurship leader in the world by 2020 in order to ensure prosperity and a high standard of living throughout the continent.

Europe was not alone in focusing on entrepreneurship as a key factor generating economic growth. From the other side of the Atlantic, Mowery (2005, p. 1) observes,

> During the 1990s, the era of the 'New Economy', numerous observers (including some who less than 10 years earlier had written off the US economy as doomed to economic decline in the face of competition from such economic powerhouses as Japan) hailed the resurgent economy in the United States as an illustration of the power of high-technology entrepreneurship. The new firms that a decade earlier had been criticized by such authorities as the MIT Commission on Industrial Productivity (Dertouzos *et al.*, 1989) for their failure to sustain competition against large non-US firms were seen as important sources of economic dynamism and employment growth. Indeed, the transformation in US economic performance between the 1980s and 1990s is only slightly less remarkable than the failure of most experts in academia, government, and industry, to predict it.

At first glance, the emergence of entrepreneurship as a focus of growth policy would seemingly have little to do with the Solow growth accounting framework. Just as physical capital was generally considered to be best organized for large-scale production to exhaust scale economies (Chandler, 1977, 1990), knowledge capital in general, and R&D in particular, was similarly considered to be a large corporation phenomenon. A generation of scholars had arduously and systematically documented painstaking empirical evidence that supported the conclusion of Joseph A. Schumpeter (1942, p. 106), 'What we have got to accept is that the large-scale establishment or unit of control has come to be the most powerful engine of progress and in particular of the long-run expansion of output.' John Kenneth Galbraith (1956, p. 86) provided a post-war interpretation, 'There is no more pleasant fiction than that technological change is the product of the matchless ingenuity of the small man forced by competition to employ his wits to better his neighbor.'

The purpose of this paper is to show that not only is the recent emergence of entrepreneurship as a central focus of growth policy compatible with the Solow model, but actually to use the lens provided by the Solow growth accounting framework to link entrepreneurship to economic growth. By endogenously facilitating the spillover of knowledge created in an incumbent organization and perhaps for a different application, entrepreneurship makes an important contribution to economic growth.

Confronted with what is termed the knowledge filter (Acs *et al.*, 2004; Audretsch *et al.*, 2006), or barrier impeding the spillover of knowledge from the firm or organization where it was originally generated, for commercialization by third-party firms, public policy instruments to promote investment in knowledge, such as human capital, R&D, and university research, may not adequately generate economic growth. One interpretation of the 'European Paradox', where such investments in new knowledge have certainly been substantial and sustained, while vigorous growth and the reduction of unemployment have remained elusive, is that the presence of such an imposing knowledge filter chokes off the commercialization of those new knowledge investments, resulting in diminished innovative activity and ultimately stagnant growth.

By serving as a conduit for knowledge spillovers, entrepreneurship is the missing link between investments in new knowledge and economic growth. Entrepreneurship is an important mechanism that permeates the knowledge filter, facilitating the spillover of knowledge and ultimately generating economic growth. The emergence of entrepreneurship policy to promote economic growth is interpreted as an attempt to create entrepreneurship capital, or the capacity of an economy to generate the start-up of new firms.

The starting point of this paper, presented in the second section, revolves around the link between knowledge spillovers and economic growth. Why knowledge might not automatically spill over is attributable to the knowledge filter, which is explained in the third section. The fourth section analyses the role of entrepreneurship as a conduit of knowledge spillovers to penetrate the knowledge filter.

The fifth section shows how measures of entrepreneurship capital have been included along with the traditional factors in the Solow growth accounting framework to link entrepreneurship to economic growth. The emergence of entrepreneurship policy, which is interpreted as the attempt to create entrepreneurship capital, is the focus of the sixth section. In the last section a summary and conclusions are provided. In particular, this paper concludes that the lens provided by the Solow growth accounting framework has proven remarkably robust and flexible, enabling an interpretation of the recent emergence of public policy to create entrepreneurship capital as a means for generating economic growth.

II.   Knowledge spillovers and economic growth

Robert Solow (1956, 1957) was awarded the Nobel Prize for his model of economic growth based on what became termed as the neoclassical production function. There are two key factors of production in the Solow model, physical capital and (unskilled) labour. Solow, of course, did acknowledge that economic growth was influenced by technical change. However, in terms of his formal model and the econometric estimation, it was considered to be an unexplained residual, which 'falls like manna from heaven'. As Nelson (1981, p. 1030) points out, 'Robert Solow's 1956 theoretical article was largely addressed to the pessimism about full employment growth built into the Harrod–Domar model. . . . In that model he admitted the possibility of technological advance.'

Solow's pathbreaking research inspired a subsequent generation of economists to apply his growth accounting framework based on the model of the production function to link various measures of physical capital and labour to economic growth. As Nelson (1981, p. 1032) pointed out,

> Since the mid-1950s, considerable research has proceeded closely guided by the neoclassical formulation. Some of this work has been theoretical. Various forms of the production function have been invented. Models have been developed which assume that technological advance must be embodied in new capital. . . . Much of the work has been empirical and guided by the growth accounting framework implicit in the neoclassical model.

Growth policy, if not shaped by the Solow theoretical growth model, certainly corresponded to the view that inducing investments in physical capital in particular was the key to generating economic growth and advances in worker productivity. Both the economics literature and the corresponding public policy discourse were decidedly focused on instruments designed to induce investment in physical capital and ultimately promote growth. While these debates may never have been satisfactorily resolved, their tenacity reflected the deep-seated belief about the primacy of capital investment as the fundamental source of economic growth.

It would be a mistake to think that knowledge was not considered as a factor influencing economic growth prior to the 'new endogenous growth theory'. In fact, one of the main conclusions of the Solow model was that the traditional factors of physical capital and labour did not account for much of the variation in growth performance. Rather, most of the variation in economic growth was explained by the residual, which was considered to reflect technological change. As Nelson (1981, p. 1033) concludes, the research 'provided evidence that neoclassical variables do not account for all of the differences among firms in productivity'.

The explicit introduction of knowledge into macroeconomic growth models was formalized by Romer (1986) and Lucas (1993), who argued that as a result of externalities and spillovers, knowledge was particularly important. In the Romer (1986) and Lucas (1993) models of endogenous growth, knowledge is assumed automatically to spill over from the firm or organization generating that knowledge for commercialization by third-party firms. While the more traditional concept of technology transfer identified knowledge as flowing across different organizations for a market price, knowledge spillovers could be procured for free.

Including the spillover of knowledge in growth models shifted the focus of policy to knowledge, which became particularly potent in terms of its impact on growth when compared to the traditional factors of physical capital and labour, where no such spillovers and free access by third-party firms was possible. Thus, while knowledge was characterized as falling like 'manna from heaven' in the Solow model, the analogous characterization in the endogenous growth models is that it blows over from the neighbours.

The endogenous growth models are consistent with the predominant theory of innovation at the firm level. Rather, than falling like manna from heaven, in what Griliches (1979) formalized as the model of the knowledge production function, innovative output is the result of systematic investment by firms to create knowledge and new ideas, and subsequent efforts to appropriate the returns accruing from those investments through commercialization. Such investments to create new knowledge involve R&D and the enhancement of human capital through training and education. Thus, according to the model of the knowledge production function (Griliches, 1979), innovative opportunities are endogenously created by purposeful and dedicated investments and efforts by firms. As in the macroeconomic models of endogenous growth, Griliches (1992) also recognized that knowledge would spill over from the firm making the investments in new knowledge for use by third-party firms at low or no cost.

Corresponding to the explicit recognition that investments in knowledge were a driving force of economic growth, particularly because of the propensity for knowledge to spill over, the policy debate accordingly shifted away from instruments to promote physical capital and focused increasingly on knowledge capital, such as university research, R&D, and education. Policy focusing on knowledge was increasingly viewed as the key to generating economic growth.

III. The knowledge filter

As Griliches (1992) pointed out, investments in new knowledge by firms and other organizations not only generate the inputs for innovation for the organization making those investments, but also because of the propensity for knowledge to spill over, for other third-party firms as well. Such externalities are consistent with the basic properties inherent in what Arrow (1962) referred to as information. According to Arrow (1962), information is distinct from the traditional factors of production in that it is non-exclusive and non-rivalrous. Thus, not only does such information generate externalities, but it also incites what has become known as the appropriability problem for any firm generating that new information. Responding to Arrow's distinction between information and traditional factors, scholars have generated a daunting literature exploring the role of various intellectual property regimes and strategies optimally to ensure firm appropriation of its investments.

Writing back in 1962, it would have required extraordinary prescience to realize that information would become a concept distinct from knowledge. Information refers to facts that can be codified. By contrast, knowledge involves tacit ideas that not only defy codification, but whose economic value remains highly uncertain and asymmetric. The expected value of any new idea is highly uncertain, and has a much greater variance than would be associated with the deployment of traditional factors of production. After all, there is relative certainty about what a standard piece of capital equipment can do, or what an (unskilled) worker can contribute to a mass-production assembly line. However, when it comes to potential innovation, there is uncertainty about whether the new product can be produced, how it can be produced, and whether sufficient demand for that visualized new product might actually materialize.

In addition, new ideas are typically associated with considerable asymmetries. For example, in order to evaluate a proposed new idea concerning a new biotechnology product, the decision-maker might not only need to have a Ph.D. in biotechnology, but also a specialization in the exact scientific area. Differences in education, background and experience can result in divergences in the expected value of a new project or the variance in outcomes anticipated from pursuing that new idea, both of which can lead to divergences in the recognition and evaluation of opportunities between economic agents and decision-making hierarchies. Such divergences in the valuation of new ideas will become even greater if the new idea is not consistent with the core competence and technological trajectory of the incumbent firm.

Thus, the expected economic value of a new idea, or knowledge, varies significantly across economic agents. What seems like a good idea to one economic agent may not seem so good to her boss or her boss's boss. New ideas, technical or otherwise, are likely to generate a divergence of assessments about their potential value. While information tends to converge to a singular expected value across economic agents, by contrast new knowledge can generate a divergence in expected values across diverse economic agents.

Thus, because of the conditions inherent in knowledge—high uncertainty, asymmetries, and transactions costs—decision-making hierarchies can reach the decision not to pursue and try to commercialize new ideas that individual economic agents, or groups or teams of economic agents think are potentially valuable and should be pursued. The characteristics of knowledge distinguishing it from information, a high degree of uncertainty combined with non-trivial asymmetries, combined with a broad spectrum of institutions, rules, and regulations, impose what Audretsch *et al.* (2006) and Acs *et al.* (2004) term *the knowledge filter*. The knowledge filter is the gap between knowledge that has a potential commercial value and knowledge that is actually commercialized. The greater is the knowledge filter, the more pronounced is the gap between new knowledge and commercialized knowledge.

Thus, the knowledge filter serves as a barrier impeding investments in new knowledge from spilling over for commercialization. In contrast to the assumption implicit in the Romer (1986) model that knowledge will automatically spill over from the source generating that knowledge for commercialization by third-party firms, incorporation of the knowledge filter suggests that knowledge spillovers are at least partially impeded. Investments in new knowledge do not automatically spill over, thus dampening the impact that such investments in new knowledge, such as university research, R&D, and human capital, have on generating economic growth.

IV. Knowledge spillover entrepreneurship

According to the Griliches (1979) model of the knowledge production function, the firm will invest in knowledge inputs, such as R&D and human capital, in order to generate innovative output. The knowledge filter can impede such knowledge investments from resulting in commercialized new products and/or processes. In some cases the firm will decide against developing and commercializing the new ideas emanating from its knowledge investments, even if an employee, or group of employees, think they have a positive expected value. As explained above, the inherent conditions of uncertainty, asymmetries, and high transactions costs leading to the knowledge filter can result in a divergence in the expected value of a new idea between the incumbent firm or organization creating that knowledge and a worker, or economic agent employed by the firm.

While Griliches's model of the knowledge production function focuses on the decision-making context of the firm concerning investments in new knowledge, Audretsch (1995) proposed shifting the unit of analysis from the firm to the individual knowledge worker (or group of knowledge workers). This shifted the fundamental decision-making unit of observation in the model of the knowledge production function away from exogenously assumed firms to individuals, such as scientists, engineers, or other knowledge workers—agents with endowments of new economic knowledge. Shifting the lens away from the firm to the individual as the relevant unit of observation also shifts the appropriability problem to the individual, so that the relevant question becomes how economic agents with a given endowment of new knowledge can best appropriate the returns from that knowledge. If an employee can pursue the new idea within the context of the organizational structure of the incumbent firm, she has no reason to leave the firm. On the other hand, if she places a greater value on her ideas than does the decision-making hierarchy of the incumbent firm, she may face forgoing what she has evaluated as a good idea. Such divergences in the valuation of new ideas force the worker to choose between forgoing her idea or else starting a new firm to appropriate the value of her knowledge.

By focusing on the decision-making context confronting the individual, the knowledge production function is actually reversed. Knowledge becomes exogenous and embodied in a worker. The firm is created endogenously in the worker's effort to appropriate the value of his knowledge through innovative activity. Typically an employee in an incumbent large corporation, often a scientist or engineer working in a research laboratory, will have an idea for an invention and ultimately for an innovation. Accompanying this potential innovation is an expected net return from the new product. The inventor would expect compensation for his/her potential innovation accordingly. If the company has a different, presumably lower, valuation of the potential innovation, it may decide either not to pursue its development, or that it merits a lower level of compensation than that expected by the employee.

In either case, the employee will weigh the alternative of starting her own firm. If the gap in the expected return accruing from the potential innovation between the inventor and the corporate decision-maker is sufficiently large, and if the cost of starting a new firm is sufficiently low, the employee may decide to leave the large corporation and establish a new enterprise. Since the knowledge was generated in the established corporation, the new start-up is considered to be a spin-off from the existing firm. Such start-ups typically do not have direct access to a large R&D laboratory. Rather, the entrepreneurial opportunity emanates from the knowledge and experience accrued from the R&D laboratories of their previous employers. Thus, entrepreneurship is an endogenous response to opportunities created by investments in new knowledge that are not commercialized because of the knowledge filter. By resorting to the start-up of a new firm to actualize the commercialization of ideas that otherwise might remain dormant in the incumbent firm, entrepreneurship serves as a conduit for knowledge spillovers.

Knowledge created in one organizational context that remains uncommercialized owing to the knowledge filter provides an important source generating new entrepreneurial opportunities. It is new knowledge and ideas created in one context but left uncommercialized or not vigorously pursued by the organization actually creating those ideas, such as a research laboratory in a large corporation or research undertaken by a university, that serves as the source of knowledge-generating entrepreneurial opportunities. Thus, entrepreneurship can serve as an important mechanism facilitating the spillover of knowledge. The incumbent organization creating the knowledge and opportunities is not the same firm that actually exploits the opportunities. If the exploitation of those opportunities by the entrepreneur does not involve full payment to the firm for producing those opportunities, such as a licence or royalty, then the entrepreneurial act of starting a new firm serves as a mechanism for knowledge spillovers.

Thus, new knowledge generating opportunities for entrepreneurship is the duality of the knowledge filter. The higher is the knowledge filter, the greater are the divergences in the valuation of new ideas across economic agents and the decision-making hierarchies of incumbent firms. Entrepreneurial opportunities are generated not just by investments in new knowledge and ideas, but in the propensity for only a distinct subset of those knowledge opportunities to be fully pursued and commercialized by incumbent firms. Thus, entrepreneurship is important to economic growth by serving as an important conduit of knowledge spillovers.

V. Entrepreneurship capital

The existence of perceived entrepreneurial opportunities resulting from the knowledge filter may be necessary to induce knowledge spillover entrepreneurship, but it is not sufficient. Rather, barriers to entrepreneurship can impede knowledge spillover entrepreneurship. Such barriers range from legal restrictions and impediments to the existence and availability of early stage finance, or to a social and institutional tradition discouraging entrepreneurship and a stigma associated with failed attempts at entrepreneurship. The capacity of an economy to generate entrepreneurial behaviour is shaped by the extent of its underlying entrepreneurship capital.

Entrepreneurship capital should not be confused with social capital. The concept of social capital (Coleman, 1988; Putnam, 1993) injected a social component to the traditional factors shaping economic growth and prosperity. According to Putnam (2000, p. 19),

> Whereas physical capital refers to physical objects and human capital refers to the
> properties of individuals, social capital refers to connections among individuals—social

networks and the norms of reciprocity and trustworthiness that arise from them. In that sense social capital is closely related to what some have called 'civic virtue'. The difference is that 'social capital' calls attention to the fact that civic virtue is most powerful when embedded in a sense network of reciprocal social relations. A society of many virtues but isolated individuals is not necessarily rich in social capital.

Putnam (2000, p. 19) extended the standard neoclassical growth model by arguing that social capital is also important in generating economic growth, 'By analogy with notions of physical capital and human capital—tools and training that enhance individual productivity—social capital refers to features of social organization, such as networks, norms, and trust, that facilitate coordination and cooperation for mutual benefits.'

However, while Putnam was providing a link between social capital and economic performance, this link did not directly involve entrepreneurship. The components of social capital Putnam emphasized the most included associational membership and public trust. While these may be essential for social and economic well-being, it is not obvious that they involve entrepreneurship, *per se*.

Thus, entrepreneurship capital is a concept distinct from social capital,[1] and involves a number of aspects such as social acceptance and valuation of entrepreneurial behaviour, along with attitudes towards risk and failure.[2] Hence, entrepreneurship capital reflects a broad spectrum of different legal, institutional, and social factors. Taken together, these factors and forces constitute the entrepreneurship capital of an economy, which shapes the capacity for entrepreneurial activity.

The relevant spatial unit for measuring entrepreneurship capital has generally been considered to be a city or region. This reflects a large empirical literature suggesting that knowledge spillovers tend to be localized within a geographically bounded region (Jaffee, 1989; Jaffee *et al.*, 1993; Audretsch and Feldman, 1996; Audretsch and Stephan, 1996). While Jaffe (1989) and Audretsch and Feldman (1996) made it clear that spatial proximity is a prerequisite to access such knowledge spillovers, they provided no insight about the actual mechanisms transmitting such knowledge spillovers. As for the Romer (1986) and Lucas (1993) models, the Jaffe (1989) and Audretsch and Feldman (1996) studies assumed that investment in new knowledge automatically generates knowledge spillovers that lead to commercialization. If knowledge spillovers are spatially bounded within close geographic proximity to the source generating that entrepreneurship, transmitting those spillovers should also be spatially bounded in that local access is required to access the knowledge facilitating the entrepreneurial start-up. Thus, knowledge spillover entrepreneurship will tend to be spatially located within close geographic proximity to the source of knowledge actually producing that knowledge.

An example of a region rich in entrepreneurship capital, Silicon Valley in California, is provided by Saxenian (1990, pp. 96–7), who observed:

---

[1] According to Putnam (2000, p. 19), 'Social capital refers to connections among individuals—social networks and the norms of reciprocity and trustworthiness that arise from them. In that sense social capital is closely related to what some have called "civic virtue". . . . Social capital calls attention to the fact that civic virtue is most powerful when embedded in a sense network of reciprocal social relations. . . . Social capital refers to features of social organization, such as networks, norms, and trust, that facilitate coordination and cooperation for mutual benefits.'

[2] As Gartner and Carter (2003) state, 'Entrepreneurial behavior involves the activities of individuals who are associated with creating new organizations rather than the activities of individuals who are involved with maintaining or changing the operations of on-going established organizations.'

It is not simply the concentration of skilled labor, suppliers and information that distinguish the region. A variety of regional institutions—including Stanford University, several trade associations and local business organizations, and a myriad of specialized consulting, market research, public relations and venture capital firms—provide technical, financial, and networking services which the region's enterprises often cannot afford individually. These networks defy sectoral barriers: individuals move easily from semiconductor to disk drive firms or from computer to network makers. They move from established firms to start-ups (or vice versa) and even to market research or consulting firms, and from consulting firms back into start-ups. And they continue to meet at trade shows, industry conferences, and the scores of seminars, talks, and social activities organized by local business organizations and trade associations. In these forums, relationships are easily formed and maintained, technical and market information is exchanged, business contacts are established, and new enterprises are conceived. . . . This decentralized and fluid environment also promotes the diffusion of intangible technological capabilities and understandings.

According to Saxenian (1994), even the language and vocabulary used can be particular to the entrepreneurship capital associated with that region: 'a distinct language has evolved in the region and certain technical terms used by semiconductor production engineers in Silicon Valley would not even be understood by their counterparts in Boston's Route 128' (Saxenian, 1990, pp. 97–8).

Several studies have added measures of entrepreneurship capital to the more traditional measures of physical capital, labour, and knowledge capital, included in the Solow growth accounting framework, to link entrepreneurship to economic growth. The unit of observation for these studies is at the spatial level—a city, region, state, or, in several cases, a country. These studies have tried to link various proxy measures of entrepreneurial capital to economic growth.

Measurement of entrepreneurship capital is no less complicated than is measuring the traditional factors of production. Just as measurement of physical capital, labour, and knowledge invokes numerous assumptions and simplifications, creating a metric for entrepreneurship capital has also presented a challenge. Many of the elements that constitute entrepreneurship capital defy quantification. In any case, entrepreneurship capital, like all of the other types of capital, is multifaceted and heterogeneous. However, entrepreneurship capital manifests itself in a singular way—the start-up of new enterprises. Thus, Audretsch *et al.* (2006) propose using new-firm start-up rates as a proxy indicator reflecting what is essentially an unobservable (i.e. latent) variable. Higher levels of entrepreneurship capital are reflected by higher start-up rates, *ceteris paribus*.

Audretsch *et al.* (2006) include measures of entrepreneurship capital along with measures of physical capital, knowledge capital, and labour to estimate a production function for German regions in the 1990s. Their results confirm the positive relationships between physical capital and output, and labour and output, as suggested in the original Solow model (1956). They also find a positive relationship between knowledge capital and output, as suggested by the Romer (1986) model. In addition, entrepreneurship capital is also found to have a positive impact on regional economic growth. Holding the amount of physical capital, knowledge capital, and labour in the region constant, those regions with a greater degree of entrepreneurship capital are found to exhibit a higher level of economic growth.[3] These results suggest that, at least in the German context, those regions exhibiting a greater degree of entrepreneurship tend to have a higher level of economic performance.

There is also evidence from the United States linking entrepreneurship to economic growth. For example, Holtz-Eakin and Kao (2003) examine the impact of entrepreneurship on growth. Their spatial unit of observation is the state. Their measure of growth is productivity change over time. A vector autoregression analysis shows that variations in the birth rate and the death rate for firms are related to positive changes in productivity. They conclude that entrepreneurship has a positive impact on productivity growth, at least for the United States.

Acs and Armington (2006) similarly link the extent of entrepreneurship to growth for US regions in the 1990s. Their evidence shows that, even after controlling for agglomeration effects, those regions with higher entrepreneurial activity exhibited higher growth rates.

The relationship between entrepreneurship and economic growth at the country level is examined by Acs *et al.* (2004). Using OECD country-level data for the 1990s, they find that, holding constant measures of physical capital and knowledge capital, those countries exhibiting higher rates of growth also had higher rates of entrepreneurship.

Thus, considerable empirical evidence is mounting identifying a positive relationship between entrepreneurship and economic growth. This relationship has been found to hold at the regional level for several countries, as well as in a panel of OECD countries. The empirical results are consistent with the view that, by serving as a conduit for knowledge spillovers, entrepreneurship is conducive to economic growth.

VI.   The emergence of entrepreneurship policy

Economic growth policy centred on instruments to promote investment in physical capital during the post-war era. This corresponded with the interpretation of the original Solow (1956) model that physical capital was the driving force of economic growth. For example, Charlie 'Engine' Wilson, the one-time General Motors top executive, who went on to become the secretary of defence under President Dwight D. Eisenhower, was widely quoted as declaring, 'What's good for General Motors is good for America.'[4] It seemed to be a capital-driven economy. At the macroeconomic level, public policy revolved around instruments to induce investments in physical capital. At the microeconomic, or industry level, this was the era of targeting of capital-intensive industries in Japan and industrial policies to enhance the competitiveness of capital-intensive industries in Europe.

Public policy towards small firms and entrepreneurship generally reflected the view of economists and other scholars that they were a drag on economic efficiency and growth, generated lower-quality jobs in terms of direct and indirect compensation, and were generally threatened by long-term extinction. Some countries, such as the former Soviet Union, but also Sweden and France, adopted the policy stance of allowing small firms to disappear gradually and account for a smaller share of economic activity.

---

[3] The positive relationship between entrepreneurship capital and economic growth holds even when the measure of entrepreneurship capital is also estimated endogenously as an instrumental variable.

[4] In fact, Halberstam (1993, p. 118) points out, 'That is what he probably thought, but what he actually said was: "We at General Motors have always felt that what was good for the country was good for General Motors as well.".'

The public policy stance of the United States reflected long-term political and social valuation of small firms that seemed to reach back to the Jeffersonian traditions of the country. After all, in the 1890 debate in Congress, Senator Sherman vowed:

> If we will not endure a King as a political power we should not endure a King over the production, transportation, and sale of the necessaries of life. If we would not submit to an emperor we should not submit to an autocrat of trade with power to prevent competition and to fix the price of any commodity.[5]

Thus, in the post-war era, small firms and entrepreneurship were viewed as a luxury, perhaps needed by the West to ensure a decentralization of decision-making, but in any case obtained only at a cost to efficiency. Certainly the systematic empirical evidence, gathered from both Europe and North America, documented a sharp trend towards a decreased role of small firms during the post-war period.

Public policy towards small firms and entrepreneurship in the United States was oriented towards preserving what were considered to be inefficient enterprises, which, if left unprotected, might otherwise become extinct—for example, in creating the US Small Business Administration. In the Small Business Act of 10 July 1953, Congress authorized the creation of the Small Business Administration, with an explicit mandate to 'aid, counsel, assist and protect. . . the interests of small business concerns'.[6] The Small Business Act was clearly an attempt by the Congress to halt the continued disappearance of small businesses and to preserve their role in the US economy.

Nor did small firms and entrepreneurship seem to play any important role with the addition of knowledge capital to the traditional factors of physical capital and labour in growth models. Commensurate with the new emphasis on knowledge as a factor of production, instruments fostering the creation of new knowledge, such as industry R&D, university research, intellectual property protection, education, and human capital enhancement, became central to economic growth policy (Romer, 1986; Lucas, 1993), but there did not seem to be any apparent role for small firms and entrepreneurship.

For example, writing in the *Harvard Business Review* shortly before the fall of the Berlin Wall, Ferguson (1988, p. 61), argued that entrepreneurship would actually reduce rather than increase economic growth. He condemned entrepreneurship in the Silicon Valley context for imposing a drag on economic performance,

> because the fragmentation, instability, and entrepreneurialism are not signs of well-being. In fact, they are symptoms of the larger structural problems that afflict US industry. In semiconductors, a combination of personnel mobility, ineffective intellectual property protection, risk aversion in large companies, and tax subsidies for the formation of new companies contribute to a fragmented 'chronically entrepreneurial' industry. US semiconductor companies are unable to sustain the large, long-term investments required for continued US competitiveness. Companies avoid long-term R&D, personnel training, and long-term cooperative relationships because these are presumed, often correctly, to yield no benefit to the original investors. Economies of scale are not sufficiently developed. An elaborate infrastructure of small subcontractors has sprung up in Silicon Valley. Personnel turnover in the American

---

[5] Quoted from Scherer (1970, p. 980).
[6] http://www.sba.gov/aboutsba/sbahistory.html

merchant semiconductor industry has risen to 20 per cent compared with less than 5 per cent in IBM and Japanese corporations. . . . . Fragmentation discouraged badly needed coordinated action—to develop process technology and also to demand better government support.

Despite the policy implications commensurate with the endogenous growth models, policy-makers increasingly discovered that investments in knowledge capital provided no panacea for stagnant economic growth and sustained high levels of unemployment. For example, throughout the post-war era, Sweden has consistently ranked among the highest in the world in terms of investments in new knowledge. Whether measured in terms of private R&D, levels of education, university research, or public research, Sweden has exhibited strong and sustained investments in knowledge. As recently as 2003, Sweden had the highest share of GDP invested in R&D in the world. Yet, with such massive investments in knowledge, the return in terms of employment creation and economic growth has been modest, at best, and disappointing to the Swedish public policy community. The persistence of stagnant economic growth and rising unemployment, even in the face of substantial and sustained investments in new knowledge, led policy-makers in Sweden to coin a new term—'the Swedish Paradox'. Similar examples of high investments in new knowledge combined with a persistently low performance in terms of economic growth and unemployment could be found throughout Europe, spanning Germany and France, leading the European Union to adapt the term for the European failure adequately to commercialize her massive investments in new knowledge—the European Paradox.

As described in the above section, it is the knowledge filter that impedes investments in knowledge from spilling over for commercialization that leads to the so-called Swedish Paradox and European Paradox. Examples of high investments in knowledge but a low growth performance are not restricted to Europe. An Asian example is Japan. Investments in private R&D and human capital have ranked among the highest in the world. Still, Japan has been bogged down with low and stagnant growth for over a decade. It would seem that Europe does not have a monopoly on the European Paradox.

The United States has also not been able to avoid the knowledge filter. In fact, the knowledge filter impeding the commercialization of investments in research and knowledge can be formidable. As Senator Birch Bayh warned, 'A wealth of scientific talent at American colleges and universities—talent responsible for the development of numerous innovative scientific breakthroughs each year—is going to waste as a result of bureaucratic red tape and illogical government regulations.'[7] It is the knowledge filter that stands between investment in research on the one hand, and its commercialization through innovation, leading ultimately to economic growth, on the other.

Seen through the eyes of Senator Bayh, the magnitude of the knowledge filter is daunting, 'What sense does it make to spend billions of dollars each year on government-supported research and then prevent new developments from benefiting the American people because of dumb bureaucratic red tape?'[8]

[7] Introductory statement of Birch Bayh, 13 September 1978, cited from the Association of University Technology Managers Report (AUTM, 2004, p. 5).
[8] Statement by Birch Bayh, 13 April 1980, on the approval of S. 414 (Bayh–Dole) by the US Senate on a 91–4 vote, cited from AUTM (2004, p. 16).

In an effort to penetrate such a formidable knowledge filter, the Congress enacted the Bayh–Dole Act in 1980 to spur the transfer of technology from university research to commercialization.[9] The goal of the Bayh–Dole Act was to facilitate the commercialization of university science. Assessments about the impact of the Bayh–Dole Act on penetrating the knowledge filter and facilitating the commercialization of university research have bordered on the euphoric:[10]

> Possibly the most inspired piece of legislation to be enacted in America over the past half-century was the Bayh–Dole Act of 1980. Together with amendments in 1984 and augmentation in 1986, this unlocked all the inventions and discoveries that had been made in laboratories through the United States with the help of taxpayers' money. More than anything, this single policy measure helped to reverse America's precipitous slide into industrial irrelevance. Before Bayh–Dole, the fruits of research supported by government agencies had gone strictly to the federal government. Nobody could exploit such research without tedious negotiations with a federal agency concerned. Worse, companies found it nearly impossible to acquire exclusive rights to a government-owned patent. And without that, few firms were willing to invest millions more of their own money to turn a basic research idea into a marketable product.[11]

An even more enthusiastic assessment suggested that,

> The Bayh–Dole Act turned out to be the Viagra for campus innovation. Universities that would previously have let their intellectual property lie fallow began filing for—and getting—patents at unprecedented rates. Coupled with other legal, economic and political developments that also spurred patenting and licensing, the results seems nothing less than a major boom to national economic growth.[12]

As the traditional policy instruments focusing on either physical capital or knowledge capital failed to generate sustainable economic growth, employment, and competitiveness in globally linked markets, policy-makers began to look elsewhere. The political mandate for entrepreneurship capital was to replace or at least augment physical capital, and augment knowledge capital with the missing link—a mechanism facilitating the return on investments made in knowledge that were not being accrued in terms of economic growth and employment by those regions making such knowledge investments. That missing link is entrepreneurship capital.

Schumpeter (1911) had identified entrepreneurship as triggering creative destruction, where the new start-ups displace the large incumbent corporations through innovative activity. However, in a global economy, the destruction of jobs is more typically the result of globalization-induced downsizing, outsourcing, and offshoring. By contrast, because it serves as a conduit of knowledge spillover from investments that might otherwise not have

---

[9] Public Law 98–620.

[10] Mowery (2005, pp. 40–1) argues that such a positive assessment of the impact on Bayh–Dole is exaggerated, 'Although it seems clear that the criticism of high-technology startups that was widespread during the period of pessimism over US competitiveness was overstated, the recent focus on patenting and licensing as the essential ingredient in university–industry collaboration and knowledge transfer may be no less exaggerated. The emphasis on the Bayh–Dole Act as a catalyst to these interactions also seems somewhat misplaced.'

[11] 'Innovation's Golden Goose', *The Economist*, 12 December 2002.

[12] Mowery (2005, p. 64).

become commercialized, entrepreneurship contributes to growth. Schumpeter's penetrating analysis was generally restricted to a single, closed economy. But in the globalized economy of this century, entrepreneurship may be more about creative construction in that it elevates the return from (knowledge) investments already made. Perhaps this is why entrepreneurship policy has emerged and diffused so quickly throughout the OECD countries. The public policy challenge confronting the leading developed countries in the global era has become how to generate an adequate return in terms of economic growth and employment creation from the massive investments in new knowledge. Entrepreneurship policy has emerged as an attempt to meet that challenge.

Whether or not specific policy instruments will work in their particular contexts is not the point of this paper. What is striking, however, is the emergence and diffusion of an entirely new public policy approach to generate economic growth—entrepreneurship policy.

VII. Conclusions

The seminal contribution of Robert Solow (1956) served formally to link the most salient factors of production to economic growth. His model of growth accounting provided a timeless framework not just for analysing economic growth but also for focusing and framing the ensuing public policy debates.

This paper has shown how Solow's model was sufficiently general and flexible to absorb changes in the world that would have been unimaginable in 1956—the end of communism, the emergence of personal computers and the Internet, and globalization, to name just a few. The Solow growth accounting framework has demonstrated a remarkable robustness to decipher how and why growth policy has evolved over time. The policy focus on instruments to induce investments into physical capital corresponded best to the era in which the original article was published. As globalization shifted the comparative advantage of the advanced industrial nations away from the factor of physical capital and towards knowledge capital, the focus of the growth debate accordingly shifted towards instruments to promote investments in knowledge capital, such as R&D, education, and university research.

This paper has explained the emergence of an additional factor that is important for economic growth—entrepreneurship capital. The knowledge filter impedes the spillover of knowledge investments from automatically resulting in commercialized new products and processes and therefore growth. As the European Paradox suggests, knowledge investments alone will not guarantee high growth and a reduction of unemployment.

Public policy has responded with a new focus on a factor of production not discussed in Solow's original paper—entrepreneurship capital. A growing consensus among policy-makers has emerged that investment in new economic knowledge alone will not guarantee economic growth. Rather, key institutional mechanisms are a pre-requisite for such knowledge investments to become transmitted and transformed into economic knowledge, through the process of spillovers and commercialization. Entrepreneurship has emerged as a driving force of economic growth by serving as an important conduit of knowledge spillovers and commercialization.

Thus, as knowledge has become more important as a factor of production, knowledge spillovers have also become more important as a source of economic growth. Entrepreneurship capital takes on new importance because it serves as a key mechanism by which knowledge created in an existing incumbent organization becomes commercialized in a new enterprise, thereby contributing to the economic growth, employment, and vitality of the overall economy.

References

Acs, Z., and Armington, C. (2006), *Entrepreneurship, Agglomeration and US Regional Growth*, Cambridge, Cambridge University Press.
— Audretsch, D., Braunerhjelm, P., and Carlsson, B. (2004), 'The Missing Link: The Knowledge Filter and Endogenous Growth', Discussion Paper, London, Center for Economic Policy Research (CEPR).
Arrow, K. (1962), 'Economic Welfare and the Allocation of Resources for Invention', in R. Nelson (ed.), *The Rate and Direction of Inventive Activity*, Princeton, NJ, Princeton University Press, 609–26.
Audretsch, D. (1995), *Innovation and Industry Evolution*, Cambridge, MA, MIT Press.
— Feldman, M. (1996), 'R&D Spillovers and the Geography of Innovation and Production', *American Economic Review*, **86**(3), 630–40.
— Stephan, P. (1996), 'Company-scientist Locational Links: The Case of Biotechnology', *American Economic Review*, **86**(3), 641–52.
— Keilbach, M., and Lehmann, E. (2006), *Entrepreneurship and Economic Growth*, Oxford, Oxford University Press.
AUTM (2004), *Recollections: Celebrating the History of AUTM and the Legacy of Bayh–Dole*, Washington, DC, Association of University Technology Managers.
Chandler, A. (1977), *The Visible Hand: The Managerial Revolution in American Business*, Cambridge, MA, Belknap Press.
— (1990), *Scale and Scope: The Dynamics of Industrial Capitalism*, Cambridge, MA, Harvard University Press.
Coleman, J. (1988), 'Social Capital in the Creation of Human Capital', *American Journal of Sociology*, **94**, 95–121.
Dertouzos, M., Lester, R., and Solow, R. (1989), *Made in America: Regaining the Productive Edge*, Cambridge, MA, MIT Press.
Ferguson, C. H. (1988), 'From the People Who Brought You Voodoo Economics', *Harvard Business Review*, **66**, 55–62.
Galbraith, J. (1956), *American Capitalism*, Boston, MA, Houghton Mifflin.
Gartner, W., and Carter, N. (2003), 'Entrepreneurial Behaviour and Firm Organizing Processes', in Z. Acs and D. Audretsch (eds), *International Handbook of Entrepreneurship*, New York, Springer.
Griliches, Z. (1979), 'Issues in Assessing the Contribution of Research and Development to Productivity Growth', *Bell Journal of Economics*, **10**, 92–116.
— (1992), 'The Search for R&D Spillovers', *Scandinavian Journal of Economics*, **94**, 29–47.
Halberstam, D. (1993), *The Fifties*, New York, Villard Books.
Holtz-Eakin, D., and Kao, C. (2003), 'Entrepreneurship and Economic Growth: The Proof is in the Productivity', Center for Policy Research, Syracuse University.
Jaffe, A. (1989), 'The Real Effects of Academic Research', *American Economic Review*, **79**, 957–70.
— Trajtenberg, M., and Henderson, R. (1993), 'Geographic Localization of Knowledge Spillovers as Evidenced by Patent Citations', *Quarterly Journal of Economics*, **63**, 577–98.
Lucas, R. (1993), 'Making a Miracle', *Econometrica*, **61**, 251–72.
Mowery, D. (2005), 'The Bayh–Dole Act and High-technology Entrepreneurship in US Universities: Chicken, Egg, or Something Else?', paper presented at the Eller Centre Conference on 'Entrepreneurship Education and Technology Transfer', University of Arizona, 21–22 January 2005.
Nelson, R. (1981), 'Research on Productivity Growth and Differences: Dead Ends and New Departures', *Journal of Economic Literature*, **19**, 1029–64.
Prodi, R. (2002), 'For a New European Entrepreneurship', public speech, Madrid, Instituto de Empresa.
Putnam, R. (1993), *Making Democracy Work. Civic Traditions in Modern Italy*, Princeton, NJ, Princeton University Press.
— (2000), *Bowling Alone: The Collapse and Revival of American Community*, New York, Simon & Schuster.
Romer, P. (1986), 'Increasing Returns and Long-run Growth', *Journal of Political Economy*, **94**, 1002–37.
— (1994), 'The Origins of Endogenous Growth Theory', *Journal of Economic Perspectives*, **8**(Winter), 3–22.
Saxenian, A. (1990), 'Regional Networks and the Resurgence of Silicon Valley', *California Management Review*, **33**, 89–111.

Saxenian, A. (1994), *Regional Advantage*, Cambridge, MA, Harvard University Press.
Scherer, F. (1970), *Industrial Market Structure and Economic Performance*, Chicago, IL, Rand McNally.
Schumpeter, J. (1911), *Theorie der wirtschaftlichen Entwicklung. Eine Untersuchung über Unternehmergewinn, Kapital, Kredit, Zins und den Konjunkturzyklus*, Berlin, Duncker & Humblot.
— (1942), *Capitalism, Socialism and Democracy*, New York, Harper.
Solow, R. (1956), 'A Contribution to the Theory of Economic Growth', *Quarterly Journal of Economics*, **70**(1), 65–94.
— (1957), 'Technical Change and the Aggregate Production Function', *Review of Economics and Statistics*, **39**, 312–20.

[6]

Location: A Neglected Determinant of Firm Growth

David B. Audretsch and Dirk Dohse

Indiana University, MPI Jena and CEPR; Kiel Institute for the World Economy

Abstract: This paper links the performance of new technology firms, measured in terms of employment growth, to geographic location. We introduce a model of firm growth that is specific to characteristics of the location as well as the firm and industry. The model is estimated using a unique data set identifying the growth performance of small technology-based firms in Germany. We find that firm performance, as measured by employment growth, does appear to be influenced by locational characteristics as well as characteristics specific to the firm and the industry. In particular, the empirical evidence suggests that being located in an agglomeration rich in knowledge resources is more conducive to firm growth than being located in a region that is less endowed with knowledge resources. These results suggest the economic value of location as a conduit for accessing external knowledge resources, which in turn, manifests itself in higher rates of growth. JEL no. L10, R11, O12, O30
Keywords: Agglomeration; knowledge resources; firm growth

1 Introduction

The last two decades have seen an explosion of interest in economic growth for a diversity of units of observation. While the Endogenous Growth Theory (Romer 1986, 1990; Lucas 1988) and New Economic Geography (Krugman 1991, 1998; Fujita et al. 1999) focus on growth at the macroeconomic level, a complementary literature has emerged examining the growth of cities (Glaeser et al. 1992; Henderson et al. 1995; Rosenthal and Strange 2003). One of the most important findings is that knowledge externalities, or what has become known as knowledge spillovers, provide a mechanism generating a superior economic performance, measured in terms of growth, in spatially concentrated areas rather than when economic activity is geographically dispersed. Both the endogenous growth literature as well as the studies on

Remark: Please address correspondence to Dirk Dohse, Kiel Institute for the World Economy, Düsternbrooker Weg 120, 24105 Kiel, Germany; e-mail: dirk.dohse@ifw-kiel.de

DOI: 10.1007/s10290-007-0099-7

city growth suggest that agglomerations of economic activity have a positive impact on economic growth.

However, the actual mechanisms by which this growth takes place are less clear. An important step was made in penetrating the black box of urban space by Glaeser et al. (1992) and Feldman and Audretsch (1999), who demonstrated that not only is growth influenced by the spatial concentration of economic activity, but also the manner in which that activity is organized. In particular, they found that a diversity of complementary economic activity is more conducive to growth than specialization. Still, there is very little known about the impact of location on growth at the micro or firm level (Acs and Armington 2004: 270).

Does location make a difference in terms of firm growth? Are there systematic differences in growth rates of firms engaged in the same industry across geographic space? While the recent theories and empirical evidence about the linkages between agglomerations and growth at the spatial level would certainly imply that this relationship should also hold at the micro or firm level, in fact, very little is known about the locational impact on firm performance, as measured in terms of growth. This is because both the conceptual framework and empirical analyses have been aggregated to spatial units such as cities or industries located in cities, such that insights about the impact of location in general, and agglomerations in particular on firm growth have been limited.

It is important to note that this omission cannot be attributed to a lack of theories and empirical evidence about growth at the firm level in general: In fact, a large literature has been compiled providing both a conceptual framework as well as compelling evidence as to why performance, measured in terms of growth, varies systematically across firms (Sutton 1997; Caves 1998). While the literature on Gibrat's Law and industry dynamics has produced stylized facts about the roles that characteristics specific to the firm, such as size and age, and industry, such as high tech versus low tech, play in shaping growth, locational aspects have been overlooked in these studies.

This paper is a modest attempt to reduce these gaps in the literatures on spatial growth on the one hand and firm growth on the other, by explicitly linking the performance of new technology firms, measured in terms of growth, to the geographic location. To do this, we will combine the conceptual frameworks developed in these two distinct literatures to introduce a model of growth that is specific to characteristics of the location as well as the firm and industry. The model will be estimated using a new data set identifying the growth performance of small technology-based firms.

The paper is organized as follows: The next section deals with the determinants of firm growth, discusses why location might be an important (but overlooked) driver of firm growth and presents the two fundamental hypotheses to be tested in this paper. Section 3 provides the econometric model, introduces the data set and discusses the variables used in the estimations. Section 4 presents the results of the econometric analysis. Section 5 concludes.

2 Determinants of Firm Growth—Why Should Location Matter?

In response to a literature that focused on static relationships, Mansfield (1962: 1023) made a plea some 40 years ago for a greater emphasis on understanding the dynamic performance of industries that underlies the process of economic growth: "Because there have been so few econometric studies on the birth, growth, and death of firms, we lack even crude answers to the following basic questions regarding the dynamic processes governing an industry's structure: What are the quantitative effects of various factors on the rates of entry and exit? What have been the effects on a firm's growth rate?" Scholars responded to Mansfield's plea by undertaking a wave of studies to uncover the various dimensions of industry dynamics. The resulting literature on industry evolution examined the process by which new firms enter an industry, either survive or exit, and ultimately grow. This literature has become so thorough and compelling that it required two recent articles in the *Journal of Economic Literature* (Sutton 1997 and Caves 1998) to summarize what has been learned about the entry, growth, survival, and mobility of firms.

The starting point for much of the empirical work in this area is a relationship known as "Gibrat's law". In his exhaustive survey in the *Journal of Economic Literature*, Sutton (1997: 43) interpreted Gibrat's law not as a prima facie law but rather pragmatically as an assumption by which "the probability that the next opportunity is taken up by any particular active firm is proportional to the current size of the firm." From this simple proposition follows the equally simple prediction of proportional effect, that growth rates should be independent of size, which Mansfield (1962: 1030–1031) characterized as "the probability of a given proportionate change in size during a specified period is the same for all firms in a given industry, regardless of their size at the beginning of the period."

A wave of empirical studies has tested the validity of Gibrat's law (Sutton 1997; Caves 1998). The earlier studies seemed to provide empirical evidence supporting the law in that firm growth was independent of size. However, these studies were generally based on samples of large corporations. When subsequent studies included a broader range of firm size, Gibrat's law was found not to hold. In fact, when small firms were included in the sample, firm growth was found to be negatively related to size. In addition, younger firms are found to grow at a higher rate than their more mature counterparts.

Resolution to this paradox was provided by Jovanovic (1982), who introduced a model in which new entrants, which he terms entrepreneurs, face costs that are not only random but also differ across firms. A central feature of his model is that a new firm does not know with certainty what its cost function, or relative efficiency is, but rather discovers this through a process of learning from the actual post-entry performance. The new firm will typically have a small start-up size. Those firms that learn the most will enjoy the greatest growth. Pakes and Ericson (1998) include active learning into the model and show that entrants that are able to actively learn, through R&D activities, will experience greater growth rates. Thus, the models by Jovanovic (1982) and Pakes and Ericson (1998) suggest that firm growth tends to be systematically higher in smaller firms that are able to learn.

Interest in industry dynamics also spread to regional economics. A large literature has developed examining the determinants of entry across geographic space (Carlton 1983; Bartik 1989; Acs and Armington 2004). Similarly, a series of studies have identified the impact that entry rates have on subsequent regional or city growth (Fritsch 1997). While studies in regional economics have identified the determinants and impact of new-firm entry, no analogous studies have been undertaken about the role that location plays in the subsequent post-entry performance. Several scholars have realized this and emphasize that there is urgent need for studying whether the economic and human capital characteristics of regions influence the growth and survival of young firms (Acs and Armington 2004: 270).

The reason for this omission may be both conceptual and empirical. At the conceptual level, there have not been models linking the post-entry performance of individual firms to regional growth. At the empirical level, linking entry to growth was feasible for data sets aggregated to geographic units of observation, such as cities or regions. However, analyzing the post-entry performance of firms in a spatial context requires longitudinal data at the establishment or enterprise level.

Despite the omission of locational aspects from studies focusing on firm growth, there are a number of reasons to expect that location should play an important role in shaping the growth of enterprises. Theories dating back to at least Marshall (1890) suggest that location within a geographically concentrated area, or an agglomeration, results in greater firm efficiencies. The first type of benefit accrues from labor market pooling. The second type is the provision of non-traded inputs, or the development of specialized intermediate goods. The third source emanates from knowledge externalities or knowledge spillovers. As Glaeser et al. (1992: 1127) point out, knowledge spills over within a geographically bounded space because, "After all, intellectual breakthroughs must cross hallways and streets more easily than oceans and continents." That is, location and proximity matter. While the costs of transmitting information may be invariant to distance, the cost of transmitting knowledge rises with distance.[1]

Undoubtedly among these three forces which are hypothesized by Marshall to increase firm growth in agglomerations, localized knowledge externalities have gained the most prominence in the empirical literature (see Feldman 1999 for a survey). The most influential of these studies have been based on the knowledge production function. As introduced by Griliches (1979), the knowledge production function links inputs in the innovation process to innovative outputs. Griliches pointed out that the most decisive innovative input is new economic knowledge, and the greatest source that generates new economic knowledge is generally considered to be R&D. Jaffe (1989), Jaffe et al. (1993), and Audretsch and Feldman (1996) provided empirical evidence supporting the theory that knowledge spills over spatially bounded regions.

The results of this literature identifying the propensity for knowledge inputs and spillovers to cluster geographically would suggest that firms using knowledge inputs will exhibit a superior performance if they are located in an agglomeration. A firm located within an agglomeration will

---

[1] New knowledge is often unstructured and highly complex and can thus best be transferred "face to face" (Polanyi 1958). Furthermore, new knowledge is often produced cooperatively in joint ventures or innovation networks. In these cases the advantage of spatial proximity is not so much the reduction of information costs but the fact that only close personal relationships allow for the evolution of incentive and sanction mechanisms necessary for the keeping of the implicit cooperation contracts (Bröcker 1995).

have superior access to both knowledge resources as well as knowledge spillovers. This leads us to the two *fundamental hypotheses* of this proposal:

1. *The performance of a high-technology firm should be superior if the firm is located within an agglomeration containing knowledge sources complementary to its economic activity.* This would suggest that the growth performance of technology firms should be systematically related to locational characteristics.
2. *The impact of location on firm growth should be greater in industries that are more knowledge intensive.* Industries where knowledge is not an important factor of production depend less on knowledge inputs and provide less of a potential for knowledge spillovers and for learning from others.

3 The Empirical Approach

3.1 The Econometric Model

To identify the locational impact on firm growth, we propose a model linking firm growth to characteristics specific to the *firm*, *industry*, and *location*.

Our starting point is the most prevalent model for identifying the determinants of growth at the level of the firm, which has been used to test Gibrat's law. As mentioned before, Gibrat's law is a proposition stating that the probability of a given proportionate change in firm size during a specified period is the same for all firms in a given industry—regardless of their initial size. This means that, according to Gibrat's law, firm growth is regarded as a purely stochastic phenomenon resulting from the chance operation of a large number of forces acting independently of each other. The economic motivation behind this may be expressed as follows: "The chances of growth or shrinkage of individual firms will depend on their profitability as well as on many other factors which in turn depend on the quality of the firm's management, the range of its products, availability of particular inputs, the general economic environment, etc. During any particular period of time, some of these factors would tend to increase the size of the firm, others would tend to cause a decline, but their combined effect would yield a probability distribution of the rates of growth (or decline) for firms of each given size. It is commonly asserted that this probability distribution is the same for all size-classes of firms." (Singh and Whittington 1975: 16).

Formalizing the relationship between size and growth, Gibrat's law implies that the present size of firm i in period t may be decomposed into the product of firm size in some previous period $t-1$ and a "proportional effect" as represented in equation (1):

$$SIZE_{i,t} = (1 + \varepsilon_{i,t})SIZE_{i,t-1} \,. \tag{1}$$

In (1) the term $(1 + \varepsilon_{i,t})$ denotes the proportional effect for firm i in period t and $\varepsilon_{i,t}$ is a random shock which is assumed to be identically and independently distributed with mean μ_{ε} and variance σ_{ε}^2. Following the process in (1) to its origin we may as well write:

$$SIZE_{i,t} = SIZE_{i,0}(1 + \varepsilon_{i,1})(1 + \varepsilon_{i,2})...(1 + \varepsilon_{i,t}) \,. \tag{2}$$

Taking the natural log and making use of the fact that for small ε, $\ln(1 + \varepsilon) \approx \varepsilon$ yields:

$$\ln(SIZE_{i,t}) = \ln(SIZE_{i,0}) + \sum_{k=1}^{t} \varepsilon_{ik} \,. \tag{3}$$

As we have assumed the increments $\varepsilon_{i,t}$ to be independent variates with mean μ_{ε} and variance σ_{ε}^2, we have that as $t \to \infty$, so the term $\ln(SIZE_{i,0})$ will be small compared to $\ln(SIZE_{i,t})$, that the distribution of $\ln(SIZE_{i,t})$ is approximated by a normal distribution with mean $\mu_{\varepsilon}t$ and variance $\sigma_{\varepsilon}^2 t$.[2] In other words: The limiting distribution of $SIZE_{i,t}$ is lognormal.[3]

Firm growth can then be expressed as the difference in the log of firm size (i.e., the number of employees) between the current period t and some previous period $(t-1)$:

$$GROWTH_{it} = \ln(SIZE_{i,t}) - \ln(SIZE_{i,t-1}) \,. \tag{4}$$

A simple way to examine the relationship between firm growth and size in a regression framework is to estimate an equation of the following form:

$$GROWTH_{i,t} = B_0 + B_1 \ln(SIZE_{i,t-1}) + \varepsilon_{i,t} \,, \tag{5}$$

where B_1 represents the effect of initial size on the subsequent rate of a firm's growth. If $B_1 = 0$ then firm growth is independent of initial firm size and the central tenet of Gibrat's law of proportionate effect holds.[4] If $B_1 < 0$ this

---

[2] Derived by applying the "Central Limit Theorem".
[3] Almus and Nerlinger (2000) confirm this distributional assumption via kernal density estimates for German firms 1990–1996.
[4] Tschoegel (1983) argues that robust acceptance of Gibrat's law also requires that growth does not persist from one period to the next and that the variability of growth is independent of firm size.

implies that small firms on average grow faster than their larger counter-parts, whereas when $B_1 > 0$ then large firms tend to grow faster than smaller firms.

There are, however, good reasons to assume that firm growth is more than just a purely stochastic phenomenon and that there are other factors—apart from firm size—that may have a systematic influence on the growth performance of firms. Based on the seminal papers by Hall (1987) and Evans (1987) the empirical growth equation for testing the counter-hypothesis that characteristics specific to the individual firm such as size and age impact firm growth can be specified as:

$$GROWTH_{i,t} = B_0 + B_1 \ln(SIZE_{i,t-1}) + B_2 \ln(SIZE_{i,t-1})^2$$
$$+ B_3 \ln(AGE_{i,t-1}) + \varepsilon_{i,t}, \qquad (6)$$

where growth for firm i in period t is a function of initial firm size, size^2, age, and a stochastic error term $\varepsilon_{i,t}$. Sutton (1997) and Caves (1998) survey and report on the large number of empirical studies estimating (6). The evidence is systematic and compelling that both size and age are negatively related to firm growth.

Note that (6) only considers characteristics specific to the firm. In this pa-per, we extend the classical firm-specific approach by considering industry-specific and location-specific determinants of growth as well. In particular, we will include the types of location-specific measures used by Carlton (1983), Bartik (1989), and Reynolds et al. (1994). The location-specific variables will include measures reflecting the importance of knowledge and technology at that location. Our econometric model (basic version) has the form

$$GROWTH_{i,t} = B_0 + B_1 \ln(SIZE_{i,t-1}) + B_2 \ln(SIZE_{i,t-1})^2$$
$$+ B_3 \ln(AGE_{i,t-1}) + B_4 D_{ind}$$
$$+ B_5 KNOWLEDGE_{r,t-1} + B_6 X_{r,t-1} + \varepsilon_{i,t}, \qquad (7)$$

where D_{ind} is a vector of industry dummies controlling, for example, for the knowledge intensity of production in a specific sector. $KNOWLEDGE_{r,t-1}$ is a region-specific knowledge or agglomeration variable and $X_{r,t-1}$ is a vector of other region specific variables hypothesized to have an impact on firm growth.

While the existing literature on firm growth, as represented by (6), has implicitly assumed that location plays no role in shaping growth, (7) reflects the major hypothesis of this paper whereby firm performance is enhanced in locations providing greater access to knowledge resources.[5] If the assumption that location plays no role is true, then the coefficients of the variables reflecting location-specific characteristics will be equal to zero. However, if the hypotheses posed here are correct, and firm growth is influenced by locational factors, then the coefficients will not be equal to zero. In particular, if knowledge externalities improve firm performance, then the coefficients will be greater than zero.

In a nutshell, positive coefficients on measures of knowledge factors and the degree of agglomeration would suggest that firm growth is systematically and positively shaped by being located in regions rich in knowledge.

3.2 Data and Measurement

There are many indications from the empirical literature that knowledge activities tend to benefit more from agglomeration than do non-knowledge activities, at least in manufacturing (Audretsch and Feldman 1996; Zucker et al. 1998; Maurel and Sédillot 1999). Therefore, a data set consisting of young knowledge intensive (technology) firms appears to be particularly well-suited to examine the impact of location on firm performance. By examining the records from the Initial Public Offering (IPO) of 212 knowledge-based firms that were publicly listed on the "Neuer Markt" (New Market) in Germany between 1997 and 2002, we created such a data set.[6] Only firms with their headquarters in Germany were considered. Most of the relevant data were publicly available from online data sources such as Deutsche Boerse AG (2003), Onvista AG (2003) or SdK e.V. (2003). However, for a number of (particularly smaller) firms there were no employment data available online. In these cases we performed a supplementary e-mail survey to complete the data base.

---

[5] Our hypothesis is, in other words, that knowledge-rich locations provide a particularly fertile soil for the growth of young, technology-oriented firms.

[6] The "Neuer Markt", launched in 1997 by Deutsche Boerse, the German stock exchange, has been Europe's most important growth stock market and Europe's closest equivalent to the Nasdaq. In conjunction with the fundamental restructuring of Deutsche Boerse AG the "Neuer Markt" has been closed in June 2003. The restructuring had no impact on the tradability of stocks formerly listed on the "Neuer Markt" (Deutsche Boerse AG 2002: 3). The firms still exist—and most of them continue to grow—although they are no longer bundled in a single index. They are now listed on the newly created indices TECDAX (for Blue Chips), Technology All Share Index and SDAX (a small cap index not restricted to technology firms).

Total employment with the firms included in the data set increased from 26,845 employees in 1997 to 104,917 employees in 2002, which illustrates that the mean employment growth of the firms included in our sample was very high (Table 1). Also reflected in Table 1 is the fact that firm growth rates were highly specific to the particular sector. However, the question addressed in this paper is not why the growth of these high-technology enterprises is so high,[7] but, rather, whether the growth performance of these firms is shaped by location.

Table 1: *Employment Growth Rates, Employees and Number of Firms by Sector*

	Compound annual growth rate (percent)		Number of employees	Number of firms
	1998–2002	2000–2002	September 2002	September 2002
Biotech	46.5	17.2	3,005	14
Media&Entertainment	42.2	−12.4	4,560	26
Internet	40.7	−4.0	14,364	31
IT Services	31.2	8.3	15,297	26
Financial Services	29.4	−9.5	2,231	2
Telecommunications	29.0	−1.3	10,465	12
Technology	26.2	11.8	23,354	47
Medtech&Health	24.0	21.1	1,804	9
Industrials&Industrial Services	21.3	10.4	18,801	13
Software	17.5	−2.6	11,036	32
All sectors	27.6	3.9	104,917	212

Source: Deutsche Boerse AG (2003), Onvista AG (2003), SdK e.v. (2003), own survey.

The geographical breakdown used in our analysis is planning regions. The whole of Germany consists of 97 such planning regions ("Raum-ordnungs-" or "Analyseregionen") intended to be comparable regions "that reflect in acceptable approximation the spatial and functional inter-relation between core cities and their hinterland." (BBR 2001: 2). For the purpose of our investigation planning regions are better suited than "Kreise"[8] as they are more homogeneous and as they are large enough

---

[7] Klodt (2001) and Klodt et al. (2003) provide an excellent discussion of possible reasons for such an accelerated growth.

[8] "Kreise" are smaller units than planning regions. There are 440 "Kreise" in Germany. See BBR (2001) for more information about spatial planning and the different regional units in Germany.

to assume that spillovers are primarily intraregional in nature. It is noteworthy that the geographical spread of "Neuer Markt" firms and "Neuer Markt" employment is very uneven: In 2002, while several planning regions hosted no "Neuer Markt" firms at all, the leading region (Munich) had more than 20,000 employees in "Neuer Markt" firms (see Figure A1 in the Appendix for illustration).

In order to empirically test for the impact of location on the growth performance of knowledge-intensive firms, variables reflecting knowledge characteristics specific either to the industry or the location need to be added to the basic model linking firm characteristics to growth as discussed in Section 3.1. Therefore, in addition to the usual measures of firm age[9] and firm size (employment in 1997), industry- and region-specific measures are included in the estimations (see Tables 2 and 3 for some descriptive statistics).[10]

Table 2: *Descriptive Statistics*[a]

	Mean	Std.Dev.	Minimum	Maximum
GROWTH	1.433820	0.923475	−.699456	4.90528
AGE	1.712890	1.343200	−.693147	4.67282
SIZE	4.166830	1.421420	0.000000	7.12528
SIZESQRD	19.373400	11.499000	0.000000	50.76970
KIS	0.349057	0.477800	0.000000	1.00000
EAST	0.113208	0.317596	0.000000	1.00000
VC	0.844340	0.363391	0.000000	1.00000
HC	0.674528	0.469660	0.000000	1.00000
NME	8.242160	1.444320	3.713570	9.96801
INDENS	−2.379230	0.299320	−3.248500	−1.71679
POPDENS	6.313300	0.869304	4.669030	8.24280
STUPINT	0.316070	0.130215	0.105152	0.68400

[a] All independent variables except for the dummies in logarithms. 212 cases (firms in the sample).

Source: BBR (2001), BVK e.V. (2003), Deutsche Boerse AG (2003), Onvista AG (2003), SdK e.v. (2003), ZEW (2003), own survey.

---

[9] The average firm age in 1997 was 10.5 years. 40 percent of firms in the sample were younger than 5 years and more than 60 percent were younger than 10 years. Only 13 percent were older than 20 years.

[10] Note that, as we investigate firm growth in the period 1997–2002, our year "$t − 1$" is 1997.

Table 3: *Correlation Matrix*

	1	2	3	4	5	6	7	8	9	10	11	12
GROWTH	1.00											
AGE	−0.44	1.00										
SIZE	−0.67	0.47	1.00									
SIZESQRD	−0.59	0.44	0.97	1.00								
KIS	0.06	0.13	0.10	0.12	1.00							
EAST	−0.11	−0.01	0.09	0.08	−0.07	1.00						
VC	0.01	−0.02	−0.02	−0.01	−0.15	0.07	1.00					
HC	0.16	−0.15	−0.12	−0.11	−0.17	0.25	0.37	1.00				
NME	0.10	0.02	0.00	0.03	−0.15	−0.08	0.51	0.66	1.00			
INDDENS	0.00	0.04	0.01	−0.01	0.12	−0.67	−0.33	−0.25	−0.10	1.00		
POPDENS	0.05	−0.08	−0.07	−0.05	−0.26	0.27	0.36	0.45	0.35	−0.43	1.00	
STUPINT	0.03	0.02	−0.05	−0.06	0.01	−0.27	0.00	0.02	0.32	0.38	−0.29	1.00

Source: Same as for Table 2. Own calculations.

We use an *industry-specific* dummy variable KIS (short for knowledge intensive sector), which takes a value of 1 if the firm belongs to an industry with an above average share of knowledge workers in its labor force and a value of 0 otherwise. The share of knowledge workers in an industry's labor force is proxied by the share of academics or, alternatively, by the share of scientists and technicians (see Table A1 in the Appendix for details). Sectors with an above-average share of knowledge workers according to these definitions are highlighted in Table A1.

The rationale for using this measure of knowledge intensity (apart from data availability) is threefold: First of all, a high share of knowledge workers in the labor force indicates a high dependence of the firms' production process on knowledge—be it produced internally (within the firm) or externally. Second, the higher the share of highly qualified knowledge workers the higher is ceteris paribus the firms' ability to absorb knowledge produced elsewhere. And third, a particularly high share of permanently employed knowledge workers may be interpreted as an investment in active learning, which is seen as a key determinant of firm growth and profitability in the literature (Pakes and Ericson 1998; Dosi et al. 1995; Ballot and Taymaz 1997).[11]

We use two *region-specific* measures reflecting the knowledge resources and other spillover sources of the region, including a dummy variable for

---

[11] Although this interpretation is straightforward it should be noted that it only holds ceteris paribus as other factors might have an impact on the share of knowledge workers as well.

regions with a highly qualified labor force share in the highest 20 percent (HC = human capital)[12], and the amount of employment in the region accounted for by "Neuer Markt" firms (NME = "Neuer Markt" employment). The reason we use two distinct measures of agglomeration is that human capital is a relatively broad measure for the stock of knowledge capital in a region, as it is aggregated over all sectors. "Neuer Markt" employment, by contrast, is narrower as it is restricted to what may be called the "new economy" sector of the economy. Thus, the distinction between the two is in a way similar to the distinction between the broader concept of urbanization economies and the narrower concept of localization economies, introduced by Hoover (1937).

It should be noted that it is beyond the scope of this paper to empirically discriminate between knowledge spillovers and the pooling of highly-skilled labor as determinants of firm growth. The central question of this paper is a more basic one: Does the availability of localized knowledge resources impact firm growth or not?

Following Rauch (1993) one may interpret the average level of human capital in a region as a local public good entering the resident firms' production function. This interpretation is straightforward but rather abstract as it leaves open the exact description of the mechanism by which human capital contributes to higher growth. Such a mechanism is provided by Jovanovic and Rob (1989). In their model, individual agents (e.g., entrepreneurs) augment their knowledge through pairwise meetings with a finite number of randomly chosen other agents. The higher the average level of human capital, the higher is the likelihood that these meetings prove successful and the more rapid will be the diffusion and growth of knowledge.[13] Acs and Armington, in the same vein, argue that "higher education trains individuals to rationally assess information, and to seek new ideas. Therefore more educated people are more likely to acquire useful local knowledge spillovers from others who are involved in reseach or in managing some service business." (Acs and Armington 2004: 256). One might add that more educated people are also more likely to produce knowledge—part

---

[12] Regionally disaggregated data on highly qualified employees are available from the German Federal Office for Building and Regional Planning (BBR). Highly qualified employees are—according to the definition used by the BBR—employees who hold a university degree, a degree by a technical college (Fachhochschule) or who have graduated from a higher vocational school (Höhere Fachschule).

[13] See Bröcker (2004) for a theoretical treatment of the interrelation between agglomeration and knowledge diffusion.

of which is locally bound for the reasons discussed in footnote 1—that proves to be useful to others. Therefore, we have good reason to expect that firms in agglomerations rich in human capital have access to superior knowledge which increases their profitability (and accelerates their growth) relative to competitors in regions less well endowed with human capital.

The interpretation of the variable "Neuer Markt" employment *(NME)* in the region is analogous to the interpretation of the variable human capital *(HC)*, with the slight difference that "Neuer Markt" employees represent a rather specific form of human capital and therefore provide a somewhat different local public good. One may also argue that a high number of Neuer Markt employees in a region makes knowledge spillovers between them more likely.

Apart from these variables measuring region-specific knowledge resources we employ several region-specific control variables. Included in the basic model version is a dummy variable *VC* for the presence of venture capital firms in the region, taking into account that new ideas are most likely to occur and to be put in practice "where knowledge workers ... hook up with venture capitalists—the suppliers not only of money but of management expertise of the kind most technology-based start-ups lack" (Norton 2000, ch. 3). Further included is a dummy variable *EAST* for firms with a location in one of the five new eastern states (the former East Germany). The latter variable is considered because the structure of the East German economy still differs substantially from the structure of the West German economy.

In an extended model version we control for the impact of agglomeration in general (without special reference to knowledge resources) by including variables measuring population density *(POPDENS)* and industry density *(INDDENS)*. Finally, we include the high-technology start-up rate of the region *(STUPINT)* as a measure of the region's entrepreneurial dynamics in the technologically most advanced industries .[14]

As can be seen from Table 3, the correlation between the explanatory variables is relatively low, such that multicollinearity issues should not cause major problems in the regressions.

---

[14] The exact definition of *POPDENS, INDDENS* and *STUPINT* is given in Section 4.3.

4 Results

4.1 Growth Conditional on Survival

Table 4 shows the results of estimating the impact of location on firm growth,[15] 1997–2002, for the publicly listed German firms. To estimate the

Table 4: *Regression Models Estimating Firm Growth and Survival*

Dependent Variable	Agglomeration variable: *HC*			Agglomeration variable: *NME*		
	Model (1) OLS *GROWTH*	Model (2) Heckit *GROWTH*	Model (3) Probit *SURVIVAL*	Model (4) OLS *GROWTH*	Model (5) Heckit *GROWTH*	Model (6) Probit *SURVIVAL*
Constant	4.206*** (0.339)	3.950*** (0.466)	0.557 (0.494)	3.770*** (0.410)	3.325*** (0.585)	0.557 (0.494)
AGE	−0.086** (0.037)	−0.086** (0.039)	0.016 (0.096)	−0.097*** (0.037)	−0.097** (0.042)	0.016 (0.096)
SIZE	−1.049*** (0.155)	−1.019*** (0.139)	0.143* (0.087)	−1.030*** (0.158)	−0.980*** (0.143)	0.143* (0.087)
SIZESQRD	0.083*** (0.017)	0.082*** (0.016)	–	0.080*** (0.018)	0.078*** (0.016)	–
KIS	0.230** (0.089)	0.300** (0.138)	–	0.234*** (0.089)	0.344** (0.146)	–
EAST	−0.205* (0.121)	−0.192 (0.140)	–	−0.091 (0.111)	−0.064 (0.140)	–
VC	−0.081 (0.103)	−0.064 (0.128)	–	−0.134 (0.113)	−0.121 (0.137)	–
HC	0.218*** (0.084)	0.222** (0.102)	–	–	–	–
NME	–	–	–	0.075** (0.033)	0.082** (0.036)	–
LAMBDA	–	0.485 (0.699)	–	–	0.741 (0.744)	–
OTNMF	–	–	0.446 (0.367)	–	–	0.446 (0.367)
IISMS	–	–	−0.610** (0.238)	–	–	−0.610** (0.238)
	$R^2 = 0.561$ Adj. $R^2 = 0.546$ F[7,204] = 37.25	$R^2 = 0.562^a$ Adj. $R^2 = 0.545$ F[8,203] = 32.58	McFadden: 0.072 Veall/Zim: 0.1205	$R^2 = 0.561$ Adj. $R^2 = 0.546$ F[7,204] = 37.26	$R^2 = 0.563^a$ Adj. $R^2 = 0.546$ F[8,204] = 32.76	McFadden: 0.072 Veall/Zim: 0.1205
	N = 212	N = 212	N = 243	N = 212	N = 212	N = 243

Note: Standard errors, robust to heteroskedasticity, are reported in parentheses. ***, **, * indicate significance at the 1, 5, and 10 percent level, respectively.
[a] Not using OLS. R^2 is not bound in [0,1].

Source: Same as for Table 2. Own calculations.

---

[15] Remember from equation (4) that growth is measured as $\ln(SIZE)_t - \ln(SIZE)_{t-1}$. We set $t = 2002$ and $t - 1 = 1997$.

growth equation, the natural logs of each independent variable is used, other than for the dummy variables.

In a first step we estimated firm growth using OLS estimation (see models (1) and (4) in Table 4). Concerning the impact of the firm-specific variables (*SIZE* and *AGE*) the estimation of models (1) and (4) yielded standard results: The negative coefficient for firm age is consistent with the so-called "stylized finding" that firm growth tends to decline as the firm evolves over its life cycle. While the negative and statistically significant coefficient of firm size indicates that growth tends to decline with firm size, the positive coefficient of the squared term (*SIZESQRD*) suggests that growth tends to decrease more slowly as the firms become larger.[16]

Most important in the context of our investigation is the impact of the variables representing regional knowledge resources. The positive and highly significant coefficient of human capital *(HC)* in the region suggests that firms experience higher growth rates in agglomerations characterized by a high density of highly qualified employees (model 1). The same result emerges when the alternative measure, the log of "Neuer Markt" employment (*NME*) in the region, is used (model (4)). Thus, both measures indicate that firm growth is positively influenced by being located in an agglomeration rich in knowledge resources.

As concerns the region-specific control variables, there is no evidence that the presence of venture capital firms in the region (*VC*) influences the growth rates. The East Germany dummy (*EAST*) has a negative sign and is weakly significant (at the 10 percent level) in model (1), but is insignificant in all other model specifications.

However, as the positive and statistically significant coefficients suggest, firm growth is positively influenced by the knowledge intensity of the sector (*KIS*), which we think is another remarkable result. A possible interpretation of this result—which is in line with theoretical models such as Ericson and Pakes (1995), Dosi et al. (1995) or Ballot and Taymaz (1997)—is that young firms that have *invested in active learning* by employing (on average) a particularly high proportion of knowledge workers in their labor force experience faster growth.

---

[16] The above estimates of the growth model implicitly assume that firm size is exogenous and growth is endogenous. To challenge this assumption of exogeneity, a Hausman test for the endogeneity of the size variable was undertaken. Following the method proposed by Durbin, the rank of the size variable was used as an instrument. The result of the Hausman test gave no hint on endogeneity of the size variable.

4.2 Unconditional Growth

In models (1) and (4) we have only considered the 212 "Neuer Markt" firms that survived until September 2002, i.e., we have analyzed *growth conditional on survival*. However, an important qualification is that various "Neuer Markt" firms closed or went bankrupt in the period under consideration (1997–2002). This neglect of exit might lead to a sample selection bias in our results.

We have therefore re-calculated our basic regressions using the two-stage Heckit (after Heckman 1976) procedure. This procedure consists of two steps: (i) a probit estimate of survival from the whole sample (including the 212 survivors plus 31 further firms that closed or went bankrupt before September 2002) and (ii) an estimate of growth from the selected sample of "survivors" using the estimated expected error (the inverse mills ratio *LAMBDA*) obtained from step 1 as a correction factor (see Wooldridge 2002: 564 for details).

We follow Evans (1987) by using firm age and size as arguments in the survival function. Additional identifying variables are a dummy for the availability of other "Neuer Markt" firms in the region (*OTNMF*) and a sector dummy for Internet, IT Services, Media and Software firms (*IISMS*) which are hypothesized to have a higher likelihood of failure than firms belonging to other sectors.

As can be seen from Table 4, the most important variable in explaining survival[17] (or exit, respectively) is the sector dummy for Internet, IT Services, Media and Software firms (IISMS), which has a negative sign and is significant at the 5 percent level. This partly reflects the "death of the dot.coms" phenomenon that could be observed in 2000 and 2001. Size has a positive impact on the probability of survival and is weakly significant (at the 10 percent level). All other variables have no significant impact on survival.[18]

Moreover—and most important in the context of our investigation—the results of the Heckit estimation of firm growth (models (2) and (5) in Table 4) reveal that the inverse mills ratio term (*LAMBDA*) is statistically insignificant in both cases and that the differences between the OLS and Heckit estimates are practically small. Thus, our basic results on the impact

---

[17] The variable *SURVIVAL* takes a value of 1 if firm *i* has survived until September 2002 and a value of 0 if that firm hasn't survived.

[18] Note that models (3) and (6) in Table 4 are identical since the different agglomeration variables do not enter the survival function.

of agglomeration ("knowledge clustering") on firm growth presented in Section 4.1 do not only apply to "growth conditional on survival" but still hold after we have controlled for sample selection bias.

4.3 Is It Density or Entrepreneurial Dynamics Rather Than Knowledge Resources?

One might argue that the strong results obtained for the regional knowledge variables *HC* and *NME* in Sections 4.1 and 4.2 just reflect the general advantages of a high density of economic activities, i.e., one might suspect that agglomeration in general and not the agglomeration of knowledge resources runs the story. In that case the positive and significant variables *HC* and *NME* would just reflect the impact of left out agglomeration variables without particular relation to knowledge.

Moreover, there is an emerging literature linking entrepreneurship to regional growth, i.e., it is hypothesized that a vivid entrepreneurial environment (usually measured in terms of start-up intensity) accelerates regional growth (see, for example, Audretsch and Keilbach (2004) or Fritsch and Müller (2005)). Clearly, if this holds at the regional (macro) level it should also be observable at the micro or firm level.

We have therefore extended the models used in Sections 4.1 and 4.2 to include additional explanatory variables measuring agglomeration in general as well as regional entrepreneurial dynamics. The variable *POPDENS* measures population density (inhabitants per square kilometer) in the German planning regions in 1997,[19] whereas *INDDENS* (= industry density) relates a region's manufacturing employment to the number of inhabitants in 1997.[20] Entreprenuerial dynamics is measured by the regions high-tech start-up rate (*STUPINT*).[21]

As can be seen from Table 5 neither the density variables nor the high-tech start-up rate have a significant influence on firm growth. Moreover, a comparison of Tables 4 and 5 reveals that the results derived in Sections 4.1 and 4.2 change only marginally when including additional explanatory variables.

---

[19] The data source is Statistisches Bundesamt (1999).
[20] The data are taken from Statistische Ämter des Bundes und der Länder (2005).
[21] Start-up intensity (*STUPINT*) is defined as regional high-tech start-ups per 10,000 employed persons. The data source is ZEW Mannheim (2003).

Audretsch/Dohse: Location: A Neglected Determinant of Firm Growth   97

Table 5: *The Impact of Additional Explanatory Variables*

	Agglomeration variable: *HC*		Agglomeration variable: *NME*	
Dependent Variable	Model (7) OLS *GROWTH*	Model (8) Heckit *GROWTH*	Model (9) OLS *GROWTH*	Model (10) Heckit *GROWTH*
Constant	3.934*** (0.646)	3.671*** (0.782)	3.969*** (0.507)	3.256*** (0.798)
AGE	−0.086** (0.037)	−0.086** (0.038)	−0.097*** (0.037)	−0.097** (0.041)
SIZE	−1.044*** (0.155)	−1.016*** (0.140)	−1.017*** (0.156)	−0.974*** (0.142)
SIZESQRD	0.083*** (0.017)	0.082*** (0.016)	0.078*** (0.017)	0.076*** (0.016)
KIS	0.227** (0.090)	0.295** (0.141)	0.233** (0.092)	0.333** (0.146)
EAST	−0.299* (0.166)	−0.280 (0.191)	−0.147 (0.138)	−0.127 (0.191)
VC	−0.111 (0.115)	−0.096 (0.139)	−0.167 (0.121)	−0.150 (0.145)
HC	0.231** (0.091)	0.230** (0.108)	−	−
NME	−	−	0.087** (0.037)	0.093** (0.040)
INDDENS	−0.164 (0.207)	−0.157 (0.220)	−0.953 (2.026)	−0.084 (0.221)
POPDENS	−0.017 (0.055)	−0.012 (0.063)	−0.017 (0.057)	−0.015 (0.063)
STUPINT	0.004 (0.333)	0.043 (0.370)	−0.265 (0.369)	−0.230 (0.406)
LAMBDA	−	0.455 (0.708)	−	0.679 (0.737)
	$R^2 = 0.562$ Adj. $R^2 = 0.541$ F[10,201] = 25.82	$R^2 = 0.563^a$ Adj. $R^2 = 0539$ F[11,200] = 23.44	$R^2 = 0.563$ Adj. $R^2 = 0.541$ F[10,201] = 25.88	$R^2 = 0.565^a$ Adj. $R^2 = 0.541$ F[11,200] = 23.59
	N = 212	N = 212	N = 212	N = 212

Note: Standard errors, robust to heteroskedasticity, are reported in parentheses. ***, **, * indicate significance at the 1, 5, and 10 percent level, respectively. The probit estimation of survival is the same as in Table 4.
[a] Not using OLS. R^2 is not bound in [0,1].

Source: Same as for Table 2. Own calculations.

In addition, various other sensitivity analyses were performed.[22] We have, for example, run regressions in which the knowledge-related variables

---

[22] Results are available from the authors upon request.

HC and *NME* were not complemented (as in Table 5) but replaced[23] by *POPDENS*, *INDDENS*, and *STUPINT*. Dropping the regional knowledge variables clearly worsened the fit of the model and resulted (again) in insignificant coefficients of the general (non knowledge-related) density and entrepreneurship variables.

In sum, it appears that our results on the importance of regional knowledge resources derived in Sections 4.1 and 4.2 are very robust to changes in the model specification.

4.4 High-Knowledge versus Low-Knowledge Sectors

Since the availability and the spillover of knowledge are presumably less important in sectors where knowledge does not play an important role, in Table 6 firms in the high knowledge-intensive sectors are separated from low-knowledge sectors.[24] "High-knowledge" is defined as the subsample of firms belonging to sectors with an above-average employment share of academics.

As may be seen from Table A1 in the Appendix, these high-knowledge sectors are Biotech, Software, Internet, Industrials&Industrial Services and IT Services.[25] Accordingly, sectors with a below-average employment share of academics are labelled "low-knowledge" sectors.[26]

As the positive and statistically significant coefficients of regional human capital (*HC*) indicate, the growth of knowledge intensive firms is higher in regions with a high agglomeration of knowledge assets (models (11) and (12) in Table 6). The same holds when we use "Neuer Markt" employment (*NME*) as agglomeration variable, as can be seen from Table A2 in the Appendix.

However, this does not appear to be the case in the low-knowledge sectors (see models (14) and (15) in Table 6 and Table A2 in the Appendix):

---

[23] One by one as well as in groups.

[24] For the sake of convenience we present the results for the basic model version here. The extended version (including POPDENS, INDDENS and STUPINT) yields similar results.

[25] In order to control our results we also worked with a different definition of high knowledge, including only sectors with an above-average employment share of natural scientists and technicians (Biotech, Industrials&Industrial Services, Technology, according to Table A1 in the Appendix). The results for this more narrow definition of knowledge intensive sectors resemble those given in Table 4 and are available from the authors upon request.

[26] These are the sectors Financial Services, Media&Entertainment, Technology, Telecommunications, MedTech&Health Care.

Table 6: *Regression Models Estimating Firm Growth for High- and Low-Knowledge Sectors (agglomeration variable: HC)*

	Subsample of particularly knowledge intensive sectors			Subsample of sectors with below average knowledge intensity		
Dependent Variable	Model (11) OLS *GROWTH*	Model (12) Heckit *GROWTH*	Model (13) Probit *SURVIVAL*	Model (14) OLS *GROWTH*	Model (15) Heckit *GROWTH*	Model (16) Probit *SURVIVAL*
Constant	4.599*** (0.472)	5.067*** (0.693)	0.814 (0.735)	4.373*** (0.383)	4.748*** (0.545)	0.545 (0.759)
AGE	−0.099** (0.050)	−0.089 (0.073)	−0.013 (0.130)	−0.028 (0.055)	−0.051 (0.076)	0.065 (0.145)
SIZE	−1.189*** (0.217)	−1.234*** (0.256)	0.179 (0.121)	−1.101*** (0.191)	−1.125*** (0.212)	0.082 (0.132)
SIZESQRD	0.098*** (0.024)	0.097*** (0.028)	−	0.090*** (0.023)	0.088*** (0.027)	−
EAST	−0.269* (0.157)	−0.280 (0.247)	−	−0.077 (0.179)	−0.098 (0.216)	−
VC	−0.083 (0.151)	−0.068 (0.199)	−	−0.163 (0.149)	−0.146 (0.223)	−
HC	0.341*** (0.121)	0.324** (0.163)	−	−0.015 (0.122)	−0.012 (0.171)	−
LAMBDA	−	−1.120 (0.905)	−	−	−1.007 (0.819)	−
OTNMF	−	−	0.334 (0.5013)	−	−	0.553 (0.555)
IISMS	−	−	−0.815* (0.471)	−	−	−0.690** (0.342)
	$R^2 = 0.555$ Adj. $R^2 = 0.531$ F[6,110] = 22.87	$R^2 = 0.567^a$ Adj. $R^2 = 0.539$ F[7,109] = 32.58 20.39	McFadden: 0.0650 Veall/Zim.: 0.1105	$R^2 = 0.585$ Adj. $R^2 = 0.556$ F[6,88] = 37.26 20.63	$R^2 = 0.596^a$ Adj. $R^2 = 0.563$ F[7,87] = 32.76 18.32	McFadden: 0.0971 Veall/Zim.: 0.1572
	N = 117	N = 117	N = 135	N = 95	N = 95	N = 108

Note: Standard errors, robust to heteroskedasticity, are reported in parentheses. ***, **, * indicate significance at the 1, 5, and 10 percent level, respectively.
[a] Not using OLS. R^2 is not bound in [0,1].

Source: Same as for Table 2. Own calculations.

Neither the degree of regional human capital (*HC*) nor the amount of "Neuer Markt" employment (*NME*) has a statistically significant impact on the growth of firms in low-knowledge sectors.

These results corroborate our second hypothesis that the impact of location on firm growth is greater in industries that are more knowledge intensive. We consider this a plausible result since industries where knowledge is not an important factor of production provide ceteris paribus less of a potential for knowledge spillovers and possess less absorptive capacity than knowledge-rich industries.

5 Conclusions

Two highly prominent literatures have generated something of a paradox. On the one hand, the new economic geography and endogenous growth literature suggest that spatial growth will be greater where knowledge spillovers are higher. However, the actual mechanisms by which this growth takes place at the microeconomic or firm level have remained vague and unclear. On the other hand, there is an extensive literature focusing on growth at the firm level, which has virtually ignored spatial externalities and instead focused almost exclusively on firm-specific characteristics, such as size and age, and to a lesser degree on industry specific characteristics.

The results of this paper suggest that it is useful to bring these two literatures together. In fact, firm performance, as measured by growth, does appear to be influenced by locational characteristics as well as characteristics specific to the firm and the industry. In particular, the empirical evidence suggests that being located in an agglomeration rich in knowledge resources is more conducive to firm growth than being located in a region that is less endowed with knowledge resources. In other words: *Regions abundant in knowledge resources appear to provide a particularly fertile soil for the growth of young, technology-oriented firms.* These results suggest the economic value of location as a mechanism for accessing external knowledge resources, which in turn, manifests itself in higher rates of growth.

An important qualification is that these results are most apparent for German publicly listed small and young firms in the most knowledge-intensive industries. Whether location has a similar impact on firm performance in a different sectoral (e.g., traditional industries) and institutional setting remains to be determined by subsequent research.

Appendix

Table A1: *Knowledge-Intensive Sectors According to Different Definitions*

	Definition 1 Above average percentage of academics	Definition 2 Above average percentage of natural scientists and technicians
Biotech	**51.5**	**68.5**
Financial Services	37.0	0
Internet	**48.1**	13.9
Industrials&Industrial Services	**43.9**	**54.8**
Media&Entertainment	28.4	8.8
Technology	30.7	**38.6**
IT Services	**55.2**	7.0
Telecommunications	n.a.	21.5
MedTech&Health Care	14.5	14.5
Software	**56.6**	17.2
"Neuer Markt" average	42.1	29.1

Source: Survey by RBSC (2002).

Table A2: *Regression Models Estimating Firm Growth for High- and Low-Knowledge Sectors (agglomeration variable: NME)*

Dependent Variable	Subsample of particularly knowledge intensive sectors			Subsample of sectors with below average knowledge intensity		
	OLS *GROWTH*	Heckit *GROWTH*	Probit *SURVIVAL*	OLS *GROWTH*	Heckit *GROWTH*	Probit *SURVIVAL*
ONE	4.061***	4.560***	0.814	4.160***	4.562***	0.545
	(0.545)	(0.807)	(0.735)	(0.504)	(0.704)	(0.759)
AGE	−0.113**	−0.103	−0.013	−0.028	−0.050	0.065
	(0.051)	(0.073)	(0.130)	(0.056)	(0.075)	(0.145)
SIZE	−1.196***	−1.241***	0.179	−1.093***	−1.119***	0.082
	(0.217)	(0.257)	(0.121)	(0.195)	(0.211)	(0.132)
SIZESQRD	0.096***	0.094***	–	0.090***	0.088***	–
	(0.024)	(0.029)		(0.023)	(0.026)	
EAST	−0.064	−0.085	–	−0.071	−0.093	–
	(0.140)	(0.246)		(0.166)	(0.207)	
VC	−0.171	−0.151	–	−0.226	−0.199	–
	(0.159)	(0.217)		(0.170)	(0.234)	
NME	0.113**	0.107*	–	0.028	0.024	–
	(0.045)	(0.059)		(0.047)	(0.058)	
LAMBDA	–	−1.130	–	–	−0.991	–
		(0.911)			(0.813)	
OTNMF	–	–	0.334	–	–	0.553
			(0.501)			(0.555)
IISMS	–	–	−0.815*	–	–	−0.690**
			(0.471)			(0.342)
	$R^2 = 0.552$	$R^2 = 0.564^a$	McFadden:	$R^2 = 0.586$	$R^2 = 0.597^a$	McFadden:
	Adj. $R^2 = 0.528$	Adj. $R^2 = 0.536$	0.0650	Adj. $R^2 = 0.558$	Adj. $R^2 = 0.564$	0.0971
	F[6,110] = 22.61	F[7,109] = 20.18	Veall/Zim.: 0.1105	F[6,88] = 20.75	F[7,87] = 18.40	Veall/Zim.: 0.1572
	N = 117	N = 117	N = 135	N = 95	N = 95	N = 108

Note: Standard errors, robust to heteroskedasticity, are reported in parentheses. ***, **, * indicate significance at the 1, 5, and 10 percent level, respectively.
^{a} Not using OLS. R^2 is not bound in [0,1].

Source: Same as for Table 2. Own calculations.

Figure A1: *Geographic Distribution of Employment
in "Neuer Markt" Firms, 2002*

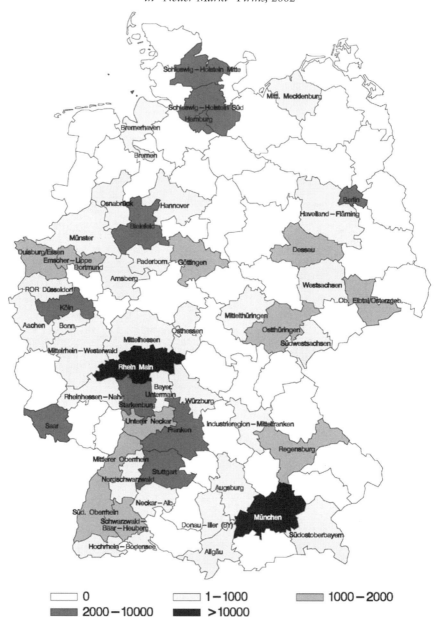

Data source: See Table 1.

References

Acs, Z., and C. Armington (2004). The Impact of Geographic Differences in Human Capital on Service Firm Formation Rates. *Journal of Urban Economics* 56 (2): 244–278.

Almus, M., and E. A. Nerlinger (2000). Testing 'Gibrat's Law' for Young Firms— Empirical Results for West Germany. *Small Business Economics* 15 (1): 1–12.

Audretsch, D. B., and M. P. Feldman (1996). R&D Spillovers and the Geography of Innovation and Production. *American Economic Review* 86 (3): 630– 640.

Audretsch, D. B., and M. Keilbach (2004). Entrepreneurship Capital and Economic Performance. *Regional Studies* 38 (8): 949–959.

Ballot, G., and E. Taymaz (1997). The Dynamics of Firms in a Micro-to-Macro Model: The Role of Training, Learning and Innovation. *Journal of Evolutionary Economics* 7 (4): 435–457.

Bartik, T. S. (1989). Small Business Start-Ups in the United States: Estimates and the Effects of Characteristics of States. *Southern Economic Journal* 55 (4): 1004– 1018.

Bröcker, J. (1995). Korreferat zum Referat Agglomerationen und regionale Spillovereffekte von D. Harhoff. In B. Gahlen, H. Hesse and H. J. Ramser (eds.), *Neue Ansätze zur Regionalökonomik.* Wirtschaftswissenschaftliches Seminar Ottobeuren Band 24. Tübingen: Mohr.

Bröcker, J. (2004). Agglomeration and Knowledge Diffusion. In R. Capello and P. Nijkamp (eds.), *Urban Dynamics and Growth: Advances in Urban Economics.* Amsterdam: Elsevier.

Carlton, D. W. (1983). The Location Employment Choices of New Firms: An Econometric Model with Discrete and Continuous Endogenous Variables. *Review of Economics and Statistics* 65 (3): 440–449.

Caves, R. (1998). Industrial Organization and New Findings on the Turnover and Mobility of Firms. *Journal of Economic Literature* 36 (4): 1947–1982.

Deutsche Boerse AG (2002). What's Changing in Deutsche Börse's Market Segments? *Stocks & Standards* 8/2002.

Dosi, G., O. Marsili, L. Orsenigo, and R. Salvatore (1995). Learning, Market Selection and the Evolution of Industrial Structures. *Small Business Economics* 7 (6): 411–436.

Ericson, R., and A. Pakes (1995). Markov-Perfect Industry Dynamics: A Framework for Empirical Work. *Review of Economic Studies* 62 (1): 53–82.

Evans, D. (1987). Tests of Alternative Theories of Firm Growth. *Journal of Political Economy* 95 (4): 658–674.

Feldman, M. P. (1999). The Economics of Innovation, Spillovers and Agglomeration: A Review of Empirical Studies. *Economics of Innovation and New Technology* 8 (1): 5–25.

Feldman, M. P., and D. B. Audretsch (1999). Innovation in Cities: Science-Based Diversity, Specialization and Localized Competition. *European Economic Review* 43 (2): 409–429.

Fritsch, M. (1997). New Firms and Regional Employment Change. *Small Business Economics* 9 (5): 437–448.

Fritsch, M., and P. Müller (2005). The Evolution of Regional Entrepreneurship and Growth Regimes. In M. Fritsch and J. Schmude (eds.), *Entrepreneurship in the Region*. New York: Springer.

Fujita, M., P. Krugman, and A. Venables (1999). *The Spatial Economy—Cities, Regions and International Trade*. Cambridge, Mass.: MIT Press.

Glaeser, E., H. Kallal, J. Scheinkman, and A. Shleifer (1992). Growth of Cities. *Journal of Political Economy* 100 (6): 1126–1152.

Griliches, Z. (1979). Issues in Assessing the Contribution of R&D to Productivity Growth. *Bell Journal of Economics* 10 (1): 92–116.

Hall, B. (1987). The Relationship between Firm Size and Firm Growth in the US Manufacturing Sector. *Journal of Industrial Economics* 35 (4): 583–604.

Heckman, J. J. (1976). The Common Structure of Statistical Models of Truncation, Sample Selection, and Limited Dependent Variables and a Simple Estimator for Such Models. *Annals of Economic and Social Measurement* 5: 475–492.

Henderson, J. V., A. Kuncoro, and M. Turner (1995). Industrial Development in Cities. *Journal of Political Economy* 103 (5): 1067–1090.

Hoover, E. M. (1937). *Location Theory and the Shoe and Leather Industries*. Cambridge, Mass.: Harvard University Press.

Jaffe, A. B. (1989). Real Effects of Academic Research. *American Economic Review* 79 (5): 957–970.

Jaffe, A. B., M. Trajtenberg, and R. Henderson (1993). Geographic Localization of Knowledge Spillovers as Evidenced by Patent Citations. *Quarterly Journal of Economics* 108 (3): 577–598.

Jovanovic, B. (1982). Selection and the Evolution of Industry. *Econometrica* 50 (3): 649–670.

Jovanovic, B., and R. Rob (1989). The Growth and Diffusion of Knowledge. *Review of Economic Studies* 56 (4): 569–582.

Klodt, H. (2001). *The Essence of the New Economy*. Kiel Discussion Papers 375. Kiel Institute for the World Economy, Kiel.

Klodt, H., C. M. Buch, B. Christensen, E. Gundlach, R. P. Heinrich, J. Kleinert, D. Piazolo, K. Sailer, and J. Stehn (2003). *Die neue Ökonomie: Erscheinungsformen, Ursachen und Auswirkungen*. Kiel Studies 321. Kiel: Springer.

Krugman, P. (1991). Increasing Returns and Economic Geography. *Journal of Political Economy* 99 (3): 483–499.

Krugman, P. (1998). What's New About the New Economic Geography? *Oxford Review of Economic Policy* 14 (2): 7–17.

Lucas, R. E. (1988). On the Mechanisms of Economic Development. *Journal of Monetary Economics* 22 (1): 3–42.

Mansfield, E. (1962). Entry, Gibrat's Law, Innovation, and the Growth of Firms. *American Economic Review* 52 (5): 1023–1051.

Marshall, A. (1890). *Principles of Economics* London: Macmillan.

Maurel, F., and B. Sédillot (1999). A Measure of the Geographic Concentration in French Manufacturing Industries. *Regional Science and Urban Economics* 29 (5): 575–604.

Norton, R. D. (2000). The Geography of the New Economy. In Scott Loveridge (ed.), *The Web Book of Regional Science.* Morgantown, WV: Regional Research Institute, West Virginia University ⟨www.rri.wvu.edu/regscweb.htm⟩.

Pakes, A., and R. Ericson (1998). Empirical Implications of Alternative Models of Firm Dynamics. *Journal of Economic Theory* 79 (1): 1–46.

Polanyi, M. (1958). *Personal Knowledge. Towards a Post-Critical Theory.* Chicago: University of Chicago Press.

Rauch, J. E. (1993). Productivity Gains from Geographic Concentration of Human Capital: Evidence from the Cities. *Journal of Urban Economics* 34 (3): 380–400.

Reynolds, P., D. Storey, and P. Westhead (1994). Cross-National Comparisons of the Variation in New Firm Formation Rates. *Regional Studies* 28 (4): 443–456.

Romer, P. (1986). Increasing Returns and Long-Run Economic Growth. *Journal of Political Economy* 94 (5): 1002–1037.

Romer, P. (1990). Endogenous Technological Change. *Journal of Political Economy* 94 (1): 71–102.

Rosenthal, S., and W. Strange (2003). Geography, Industrial Organizations and Agglomeration. *Review of Economics and Statistics* 85 (2): 377–393.

Singh, A., and G. Whittington (1975). The Size and Growth of Firms. *Review of Economic Studies* 42 (1): 15–26.

Sutton, J. (1997). Gibrat's Legacy. *Journal of Economic Literature* 35 (1): 40–59.

Tschoegel, A. E. (1983). Size, Growth, and Transnationality Among the World's Largest Banks. *Journal of Business* 56 (2): 187–201.

Wooldridge, J. M. (2002). *Econometric Analysis of Cross Section and Panel Data.* Cambridge, Mass.: MIT Press.

Zucker, L. G., M. R. Darby, and M. B. Brewer (1998). Intellectual Human Capital and the Birth of U.S. Biotech Enterprises. *American Economic Review* 88 (1): 290–306.

Data Sources

BBR (Bundesamt für Bauwesen und Raumordnung) (2001). Aktuelle Daten zur Entwicklung der Städte, Kreise und Gemeinden. Berichte. Band 8. Bonn.

BVK (Bundesverband Deutscher Kapitalbeteiligungsgesellschaften) e.V. (2003). Mitgliederdatenbank. Electronic document ⟨http://www.bvk-ev.de⟩, accessed on April 25, 2003.

Deutsche Boerse AG (2003). Neuer Markt. Electronic document ⟨http://www. neuer-markt.de⟩, accessed on March 30, 2003.

Onvista AG (2003). Einzelwerte NEMAX 50 Performance-Index. Electronic database ⟨http://index.onvista.de/stocks.html?ID_NOTATION=2580608⟩, accessed on March 30, 2003.

RBSC (Roland Berger Strategy Consultants) (2002). Der Beitrag der am Neuen Markt gelisteten Unternehmen für die Beschäftigung in Deutschland. (Studie im Auftrag des Bundesministeriums für Wirtschaft und Technologie) Berlin.

SdK (Schutzgemeinschaft der Kleinaktionäre) e.V. (2003). HV-Info: Informationen rund um die Hauptversammlungen aller börsennotierten deutschen Aktiengesellschaften, Unternehmensberichte und –meldungen. Electronic database ⟨http://www.hv-info.de⟩, accessed on April 15, 2003.

Statistisches Bundesamt (1999). Statistisches Jahrbuch 1999 für die Bundesrepublik Deutschland. Wiesbaden.

Statistische Ämter des Bundes und der Länder (var. issues). Statistik regional— Daten für die Kreise und kreisfreien Städte Deutschlands auf CD-ROM. Wiesbaden.

ZEW Mannheim (2003). ZEW-Gründungspanels Ost und West. Gründungsintensitäten 1997–2000 nach Kreisen und Raumordnungsregionen. Mannheim.

7

Journal of Management Studies 44:7 November 2007
0022-2380

The Theory of Knowledge Spillover Entrepreneurship*

David B. Audretsch and Max Keilbach

Max-Planck Institute of Economics, Jena, Germany and Indiana University; Max-Planck Institute of Economics, Jena, Germany

ABSTRACT   The prevailing theories of entrepreneurship have typically revolved around the ability of individuals to recognize opportunities and then to act on them by starting a new venture. This has generated a literature asking why entrepreneurial behaviour varies across individuals with different characteristics while implicitly holding constant the external context in which the individual finds herself. Thus, where the opportunities come from, or the source of entrepreneurial opportunities, is also implicitly taken as given. By contrast, in this paper an important source of entrepreneurial opportunities is identified – knowledge and ideas created in an incumbent organization. By commercializing knowledge that otherwise would remain uncommercialized through the start-up of a new venture, entrepreneurship serves as a conduit of knowledge spillovers. According to the theory of knowledge spillover entrepreneurship, a context with more knowledge will generate more entrepreneurial opportunities. By contrast, a context with less knowledge will generate fewer entrepreneurial opportunities. Based on a data set linking entrepreneurship to the knowledge context, empirical evidence is provided that is consistent with the proposition that entrepreneurial opportunities are not exogenous but rather systematically created by investments in knowledge by incumbent organizations.

INTRODUCTION

Both the motivation for, as well as the impact from, entrepreneurship has been a concern of management scholars.[1] In particular, why is it that some individuals choose to start a new venture, while yet others abstain from entrepreneurial activity?[2] According to Shane and Venkataraman (2000, p. 218), the field of entrepreneurship is concerned with 'the sources of opportunities; the process of discovery, evaluation, and exploitation of opportunities; and the set of individuals who discover, evaluate, and exploit them'.[3] Thus, entrepreneurship scholarship is focused on the recognition of opportunities and the cognitive process of deciding to act upon those opportunities (Venkataraman, 1997).[4]

In asking the question of why some individuals act entrepreneurially, while others do not, scholars have remained fixated, on the one hand, on taking the existence of

Address for reprints: David B. Audretsch, Max-Planck Institute of Economics, Entrepreneurship, Growth and Public Policy Group, Kahlaische Straße 10, 07745 Jena, Germany (audretsch@econ.mpg.de).

Knowledge Spillover Entrepreneurship   1243

the entrepreneurial opportunity for granted, while, on the other hand, asking what individual-specific characteristics account for differences in entrepreneurial behaviour across individuals. For example, Krueger (2003, p. 105) concludes that 'the heart of entrepreneurship is an orientation toward seeing opportunities', which frames the research questions, 'what is the nature of entrepreneurial thinking and what cognitive phenomena are associated with seeing and acting on opportunities?'.

Thus, as Plummer et al. (2007) point out, 'a notable lack of research focused on the origins of opportunity'. Rather, the traditional approach to entrepreneurship essentially holds the entrepreneurial opportunity as given and fixed and proceeds to ask how the cognitive process inherent in the entrepreneurial decision varies across different individual characteristics and attributes (McClelland, 1961; Shaver, 2003). As Shane and Eckhardt (2003, p. 187) conclude, entrepreneurship has been primarily concerned with 'the process of opportunity discovery', thereby helping to explain 'why some actors are more likely to discover a given opportunity than others'. The entrepreneurial opportunity itself is taken as given and implicitly fixed, enabling variations in the propensity to become an entrepreneur across people to be explained by individual-specific characteristics, such as the need for autonomy, the willingness to incur risk, as well as a superior access to scarce and costly resources, such as financial capital, human capital and social capital.

While holding the entrepreneurial opportunity implicitly fixed and focusing on differences across individual characteristics has generated a number of valuable insights, such as the importance social networks, education and training, and familial influence (Acs and Audretsch, 2003), Companys and McMullen (2007), warn that, 'Despite the advances and the importance of entrepreneurial opportunities to strategy and entrepreneurship, there have been surprisingly few recent studies that explore the nature of opportunities . . . Currently, scholarly understanding of the origins of entrepreneurial opportunities remains limited owning to the fact that most studies have taken opportunities for granted when exploring strategic and entrepreneurial processes.'

The purpose of this paper is to provide one theory explaining a particular source of entrepreneurial opportunities. Rather than taking the entrepreneurial opportunity as exogenous and given, and then examining how variations across individual attributes shape the cognitive process underlying the decision to become an entrepreneur, this paper instead assumes the individual characteristics to be constant and then analyses how the cognitive process inducing the entrepreneurial decision is influenced by context, and in particular the opportunities for entrepreneurship afforded by the specific context. Thus, the approach and contribution of this paper is to invert the traditional approach prevalent in the entrepreneurship literature by holding the characteristics of the individual constant but allowing the extent of entrepreneurial opportunities to vary systematically.

In particular, the entrepreneurial response to contexts that are rich in knowledge is compared to those with impoverished knowledge contexts. Alvarez (2003), Barney (1986) and Alvarez and Barney (2005, 2007) have provided a compelling theoretical basis suggesting that entrepreneurial opportunities tend to be greater in contexts characterized by a high degree of uncertainty as compared to risk. As we will explain in the second section of this paper, Arrow (1962), among other scholars, clearly identified economic activity based on knowledge as being inherently more uncertain. Thus, linking together the greater degree of uncertainty inherent in knowledge posited by Arrow (1962) with the greater extent of entrepreneurial opportunities emanating from contexts characterized by high uncertainty by Alvarez (2003) and Alvarez and Barney (2005, 2007), the theory of knowledge spillover entrepreneurship (Acs and Armington, 2006; Acs et al., 2004; Audretsch et al., 2006) posits that those contexts rich in knowledge will inherently be characterized by a greater degree of uncertainty, leading to greater entrepreneurial opportunities. Thus, building on the uncertainty theory of Alvarez (2003) and Alvarez and Barney (2005, 2007), this paper suggests that entrepreneurship is an endogenous response to opportunities generated by investments in new knowledge made by incumbent firms and organizations but which are unable to completely and exhaustively commercialize. In this paper, we show how entrepreneurship can be an endogenous response to investments in new knowledge where commercialization of that knowledge is constrained by uncertainty confronting incumbent firms (Alvarez, 2003; Alvarez and Barney, 2005, 2007), thus leading to incomplete commercialization of the new knowledge.

The next section explains how entrepreneurship combines the cognitive process of recognizing opportunities with pursuing those opportunities by starting a new venture. The third section explains the theory of knowledge spillover entrepreneurship, which links the greater entrepreneurial opportunities under uncertainty as compared to risk identified in Alvarez's (2003) theory of entrepreneurship with the greater degree of uncertainty inherent in knowledge-based economic activity, as identified by Arrow (1962). The fourth section provides an empirical test of the knowledge spillover entrepreneurship theory. Finally, a discussion of the main findings and their implications is provided in the last section. In particular, there is compelling empirical evidence consistent with the proposition that entrepreneurial opportunities are not exogenous but rather endogenously created by contexts rich in knowledge.

ENTREPRENEURSHIP AS OPPORTUNITY RECOGNITION AND NEW VENTURE CREATION

In this paper, entrepreneurship is operationalized according to the definition posited by Gartner and Carter (2003): 'Entrepreneurial behavior involves the activities of individuals who are associated with creating new organizations rather than the activities of individuals who are involved with maintaining or changing the operations of on-going established organizations.' Krueger (2003) accordingly views entrepreneurial thinking and the cognitive process associated with the identification of an opportunity in conjunction with the decision to engage in entrepreneurial action. As Companys and McMullen (2007) point out, 'An *entrepreneurial* opportunity is more accurately described as an opportunity to engage in entrepreneurial action, in which entrepreneurial denotes a sub-class of some broader category of human action.'

The focal point of entrepreneurship research has been on the cognitive process by which the individual discovers a given entrepreneurial opportunity, combined with the decision to act on that opportunity. The existence of a perceived entrepreneurial opportunity and the intent to act on that opportunity triggers entrepreneurship. According to Companys and McMullen (2007), 'Opportunities then become the Where and When of entrepreneurial action – i.e., a situation in which one can attempt to profit by creating new goods or services.'

Most of the research examining why the propensity for entrepreneurship varies across people has focused on differences across individuals, and in particular, characteristics specific to those individuals. For example, personal attitudes and attributes such as self efficacy (the individual's sense of competence), collective efficacy, prior experience and social norms have all been found to influence the ability of an individual to perceive an entrepreneurial opportunity and then subsequently to act upon that opportunity (Shane, 2000). Similarly, Shane and Eckhardt (2003) show how the cognitive process in reaching the entrepreneurial decision is influenced by a differential access to information sources across individuals. In particular, heterogeneous access to information, along with differences in cognitive abilities, psychological differences, and access to financial and social capital all serve to explain why entrepreneurial activity varies across individuals. However, the entrepreneurial opportunity itself is implicitly assumed to be exogenously given and therefore implicitly constant across individuals.

Empirical studies examining why entrepreneurship varies across individuals also implicitly assume the entrepreneurial opportunity to be exogenous and therefore constant. For example, the Panel Study of Entrepreneurial Dynamics (PSED) provides longitudinal observations on individuals that were considering becoming entrepreneurs (Reynolds, 2007). The PSED has generated a number of studies enabling scholars to link characteristics specific to the individual, such as financial resources in the form of household income and wealth, and human capital, in the form of education, prior work experience, entrepreneurial experience, and influence from family and friends, to the decision to start a new business.

Thus, the tradition in the entrepreneurship literature has been to take the entrepreneurial opportunity as exogenous, and then to link entrepreneurial activity to characteristics specific to the individual. However, virtually nothing is learned about where the entrepreneurial opportunity comes from in the first place, leading the reader with the uneasy feeling that entrepreneurial opportunities are simply ubiquitous and unbounded. Such a conclusion seemingly implies that variations in the likelihood of becoming an entrepreneur are attributable solely to differences in the propensities, proclivities, and inclinations of individuals. However, McMullen et al. (2007) warn against such a conclusion: 'For management scholars and economists alike a lack of clarity regarding entrepreneurial opportunity presents a significant theoretical dilemma. Specifically, without a clear understanding of the nature of opportunity, formulating logically consistent prescriptions for both policy and practice is problematic.' Thus, in the next section, a theory is introduced explicitly identifying where (at least some) entrepreneurial opportunities come from and why they may be systematically different for different individuals.

THE THEORY OF KNOWLEDGE SPILLOVER ENTREPRENEURSHIP

The entrepreneurship literature has generally focused on the key role played by the ability of the individual to discover exogenously given entrepreneurial opportunities and then to act upon them through undertaking entrepreneurial activity. Thus, variation in the observed propensity for entrepreneurship across people has generally been attributable to differences in measurable characteristics specific to individuals and not to any differences in the entrepreneurially opportunities available to individuals. That is,

D. B. Audretsch and M. Keilbach

virtually nothing is known about the actual *source* of such entrepreneurial opportunities, that is where entrepreneurial opportunities come from, and how and why entrepreneurial opportunities might vary systematically across individuals.

The theory of knowledge spillover entrepreneurship posits one source of entrepreneurial opportunities – new knowledge and ideas (Acs and Armington, 2006; Acs et al., 2004; Audretsch et al., 2006). According to the theory of knowledge spillover entrepreneurship, ideas and knowledge created in one organizational context such as a firm or university research laboratory, but left uncommercialized as a result of the uncertainty inherent in knowledge, serve as a source of knowledge generating entrepreneurial opportunities. In this paper we refer to this knowledge source as being characterized by *incomplete commercialization* in incumbent organizations. When such incomplete commercialized knowledge in incumbent organizations serves as the basis for the entrepreneurial opportunity, the actual entrepreneurial activity, that is the start-up of a new venture, provides the conduit for the spillover of knowledge from the source organization creating that knowledge to the new, entrepreneurial organization (venture) actually exploiting and commercializing that knowledge. Thus, just as the incomplete knowledge generated in an incumbent organization generates the entrepreneurial opportunity, the entrepreneurial activity provides, in turn, the conduit facilitating the spillover and commercialization of that knowledge.

Knowledge

In his path-breaking paper, Arrow (1962) pointed out that knowledge was distinct from the traditional factors, or resources, available for economic activity, in that it is characterized by two fundamental conditions. The first involves non-excludability, or the inability to exclude others from accessing and using that knowledge. The second involves the non-exhaustibility of knowledge. Use of ideas by one party does not preclude others from using that same knowledge. An important implication of Arrow's propositions concerning knowledge was pointed out by Griliches (1992) – that in contrast to investments in traditional resources, such as physical capital, investments in knowledge have a high propensity to spill over for commercialization by third-party firms which do not pay for the full cost of accessing and implementing those ideas. Thus, a crucial distinction between the firm resource of knowledge and the more traditional resources is the high propensity for knowledge to spill over.

The preoccupation with the non-excludability and non-exhaustibility of knowledge first identified by Arrow (1962), which Griliches (1992) and others identified as resulting in knowledge spillovers, neglects another key insight in the original Arrow (1962) article. Arrow (1962) also identified another dimension by which knowledge differs from the traditional factors of production. This other dimension involves the greater degree of *uncertainty* and larger extent of *asymmetries*, and greater *cost of transacting* new ideas. First, the outcome associated with any new idea is more highly uncertain than would be associated with the deployment of traditional resources for firms, such as physical capital. After all, there is relative certainty about what a standard piece of capital equipment can do, or what an (unskilled) worker can contribute to a mass-production assembly line. By contrast, Arrow (1962) emphasized that when it comes to innovation, there is uncertainty about whether the new product can be produced, how it can be produced, and whether sufficient demand for that visualized new product might actually materialize.

Thus, an important implication emanating from Arrow's (1962) paper is that as knowledge becomes more important as a source of competitive advantage, the degree of uncertainty involving economic activity also increases. However, as the next sub-sections suggest, the organizational form of economic activity is not neutral with respect to a greater degree of uncertainty. Rather, as Alvarez (2003) and Alvarez and Barney (2005, 2007) suggest, as the extent of uncertainty increases, the organizational form of entrepreneurship tends to gain the competitive advantage. This is because some of the opportunities generated by new knowledge manifest themselves in the form of entrepreneurial opportunities in that they are rejected and not perceived and pursued as opportunities by incumbent firms.

Uncertainty

In developing the uncertainty theory of entrepreneurship, Alvarez (2003) makes a sharp distinction between uncertainty and risk. Risk is calculable, and an expected value can be imputed for a distribution of outcomes. By contrast, under uncertainty, no such distribution of outcomes or expected value can be calculated. As Alvarez (2003) and Alvarez and Barney (2005, 2007) emphasize, a high level of uncertainty makes it difficult, if not impossible, for firms to assign an expected value to various outcomes. According to Alvarez, decision making under uncertainty is more likely to trigger entrepreneurship in the form of creating a new organization or firm. While decision making under risk enables the incumbent firm to calculate expected outcomes along with a probability distribution associated with those outcomes, decision-making under uncertainty more typically is associated with organizational inertia. Confronted with uncertainty, decision-making hierarchies tend towards maintaining the status quo rather than choosing to act upon new ideas for which no expected value and commensurate probability distribution corresponding to possible outcomes can be calculated.

The inertia inherent in decision-making under uncertainty within incumbent organizations reflects what has been termed as the knowledge filter (Acs et al., 2004; Audretsch et al., 2006). Because new ideas and knowledge are characterized by uncertainty, they may not be pursued and will remain uncommercialized by incumbent firms. The knowledge filter is a consequence of the basic conditions inherent in new knowledge.

Knowledge Spillovers as Entrepreneurial Opportunities

As Alvarez (2003) and Alvarez and Barney (2005, 2007) emphasize, it is the uncertainty inherent in new ideas and knowledge that creates opportunities for entrepreneurship. If the incumbent organization making the investments to create new ideas and knowledge chooses not to commercialize those ideas, an opportunity is created for someone to start a new firm in order to commercialize that knowledge. According to the theory of knowledge spillover entrepreneurship, opportunities for entrepreneurship are the duality of the knowledge filter. The greater is the knowledge filter, the greater are the divergences in the valuation of new ideas across economic agents and the decision-making

D. B. Audretsch and M. Keilbach

hierarchies of incumbent firms. Entrepreneurial opportunities are generated not just by investments in new knowledge and ideas, but in the propensity for only a distinct subset of those opportunities to be fully pursued and commercialized by incumbent firms. That is, not only do investments in knowledge generate new opportunities, but because of the knowledge filter, some subset of these opportunities constitute entrepreneurial opportunities. Thus, the source of the knowledge and ideas and the organization actually making (at least some of) the investments to produce that knowledge may not the same as the organization actually attempting to commercialize and appropriate the value of that knowledge (e.g. the new venture). If the use of that knowledge by the entrepreneur does not involve full payment to the firm making the investment that originally produced that knowledge, such as a license or royalty, then the entrepreneurial act of starting a new venture is a mechanism for knowledge spillovers. The act of founding a new venture to commercialize knowledge generated in an incumbent organization serves as a conduit for the spillover of knowledge.

This discrepancy between the organization *creating* opportunities and the new venture actually *exploiting* the opportunities was pointed out by Audretsch (1995), who introduced the knowledge spillover theory of entrepreneurship. In posing the question, 'How are these small and frequently new firms able to generate innovative output when undertaken a generally negligible amount of investment into knowledge-generating inputs, such as R&D? One answer is apparently through exploiting knowledge created by expenditures on research in universities and on R&D in large corporations', he concludes that these 'findings challenge an assumption implicit to the knowledge production function – that firms exist exogenously and then endogenously seek out and apply knowledge inputs to generate innovative output . . . It is the knowledge in the possession of economic agents that is exogenous, and in an effort to appropriate the returns from that knowledge, the spillover of knowledge from its producing entity involves endogenously creating a new firm' (Audretsch, 1995, pp. 179–80).

The empirical evidence supporting the theory of knowledge spillover entrepreneurship was provided by analysing how different industries reflecting different underlying knowledge contexts impacted entrepreneurial activity in that industry, as reflected by new-firm start-ups. The empirical results provided compelling evidence suggesting that entrepreneurial activity was systematically greater in those industries with a greater investment in new knowledge, but lower in industries with low investments in knowledge.

Thus, compelling evidence was provided suggesting that entrepreneurship is an endogenous response to opportunities created but not exploited by the incumbent firms, which we refer to in this paper as incomplete commercialization. This involved an organizational dimension involving the mechanism transmitting knowledge spillovers, the start-up of a new venture.

Knowledge Spillover Entrepreneurship

In the lens provided by the theory of knowledge spillover entrepreneurship, the knowledge filter will impede and pre-empt at least some of the knowledge from being completely commercialized, which in turn generates entrepreneurial opportunities. An important implication is that entrepreneurial opportunities will be systematically greater in those contexts characterized by more knowledge. By contrast, entrepreneurial opportunities will be systematically lower in those contexts characterized by less knowledge. This would suggest that for any particular context, observing a high rate of entrepreneurial activity may not necessarily reflect an underlying population of people who are inherently different in their attitudes, capabilities and proclivities towards entrepreneurship than are their counterparts in contexts exhibiting less entrepreneurial activity. Rather, the greater extent of entrepreneurial activity in the former context may reflect a higher prevalence of entrepreneurial opportunities generated by an abundance of knowledge. Thus, the main proposition to emerge from the theory of knowledge spillover entrepreneurship is:

> *Knowledge Spillover Entrepreneurship Proposition*: Contexts rich in knowledge should generate more entrepreneurship, reflecting more extensive entrepreneurial opportunities. By contrast, contexts impoverished in knowledge should generate less entrepreneurship, reflecting less extensive entrepreneurial opportunities.

EMPIRICAL EVIDENCE

The Spatial Context

In this section, empirical evidence is provided in support of the knowledge spillover entrepreneurship proposition. This test is made by linking the knowledge investments within a spatial context, that is a region, to the start-up activity associated with that region.

Combining the insight of Arrow (1962) that knowledge is characterized by a greater degree of uncertainty with that of Alvarez (2003) and Alvarez and Barney (2005, 2007), that greater uncertainty tends to bestow the competitive advantage to new ventures, leads to the central proposition emanating from the theory of knowledge spillover of entrepreneurship, that contexts richer in knowledge investment will generate more entrepreneurial activity than those contexts that are poor in knowledge. But which type or dimension of context is most relevant to testing this proposition?

One insight is provided by Jaffe (1989) and Audretsch and Feldman (1996), who found that knowledge spillovers tend to be spatially bounded within close geographical proximity to the source of that knowledge. Since we have just identified one such mechanism by which knowledge spillovers are transmitted, the start-up of a new venture, it follows that knowledge spillover entrepreneurship is also spatially bounded in that local access is required to access the knowledge facilitating the entrepreneurial start-up. Thus, one important way to test the knowledge spillover entrepreneurship proposition is by linking measures of entrepreneurial activity to knowledge investments within the context afforded by geography corresponding to the dimension found to spatially bound knowledge spillovers – regions.

Measurement and Model Specification

The dependent variable is entrepreneurial activity, which is measured by the start-up rate, and is defined and measured the number of start-ups divided by the population in each German region between 1998 and 2000.[5] To test the knowledge spillover entrepreneurship proposition, four alternative measures of entrepreneurship are used. These four different measures allow for variation in the scope of what is included in the definition and measure of entrepreneurial activity. The first measure includes new-firm start-ups in all industries and is therefore the more general. The second measure includes only new-firm start-ups in high-technology industries, which are defined as having a mean R&D-sales ratio exceeding 2.5 per cent.[6] The third measure includes only new-firm start-ups in the ICT-industries, which includes both manufacturing and service industries. Finally, the fourth measure includes new-firm start-ups in low-tech industries. It should be emphasized that the label of 'low-tech' refers to the degree of R&D intensity of the industry and not to the capabilities or extent of human capital of the founder(s).

The theory of knowledge spillover entrepreneurship does not imply that knowledge spillovers, alone, are the only factor influencing the extent of entrepreneurial activity in a region. Rather, the traditional factors that both are conducive to as well as impede regional entrepreneurship need to be controlled for. In fact, considerable insight has been made identifying factors influencing regional entrepreneurial activity.

A rich literature has accumulated linking start-up rates to regional-specific character-istics, such as growth, population density, unemployment, and the skill levels of the labour force. The empirical evidence accumulated from this literature has generally found a positive impact on entrepreneurial activity by population density, growth, skill and human capital levels of the labour force. The empirical evidence concerning the relationship between unemployment rates and start-up activity is considerably more ambiguous (Reynolds et al., 1994; Storey, 1991).

Entrepreneurial activity has been found to be greater in regions with higher growth than in those with less growth. In the model tested in this study, regional growth is measured as the percentage change in regional gross domestic product between 1992 and 2000. A positive regression coefficient would suggest that entrepreneurship is enhanced in higher growth regions. The regional rates of unemployment are also included in the estimation model. However, as Storey (1991) concludes, a vast literature has identified an ambiguous relationship between unemployment and entrepreneurship, which has been interpreted to reflect the contradictory impacts of lower opportunity costs associated with entrepreneurship by the unemployed on the one hand, but the reduced entrepreneurial opportunities on the other hand in regions with high unemployment.

Jacobs (1979) has argued that the degree of diversity in the workforce is an important source of entrepreneurship. People with different backgrounds and experiences will tend to evaluate any given set of information differently. Thus, entrepreneurial activity should be greater in regions with a more diverse population, since more entrepreneurial oppor-tunities would be expected to be identified as a result of diversity. One aspect of diversity is reflected by social diversity, which is measured by an entropy index of the voting behaviour on the occasion of the 1998 parliament election. The entropy index is nor-malized to range between zero and one, where zero indicates the absence of diversity and one indicates the maximum extent of diversity. The extent of human capital diversity is measured by constructing a Herfindahl index for the share of three different levels of vocational education – no formal vocational education, high level of vocational education (college degree or master craftsmanship), or intermediate level (neither of the other two categories).

Spatial agglomerations facilitate the flow of ideas (Audretsch and Stephan, 1996; Feldman and Audretsch, 1999). Hence, entrepreneurial activity should be greater in agglomerations, or more densely populated regions, than in less agglomerated regions. The provision of ancillary services and inputs is also greater in agglomerated regions. The extent of regional agglomeration is measured by the regional population density. A positive coefficient would reflect a positive relationship between the extent to which a region is agglomerated and entrepreneurial activity. Regions that are attractive to people may also be more conducive to entrepreneurial activity. However, while controlling for locational attractiveness may be important, measurement is anything but obvious. Locational attractiveness is measured by the number of hotel beds in the region relative to the total surface area. A positive relationship between locational attractiveness and entrepreneurship is expected.

To these different control measures, a variable reflecting the regional knowledge context is also included. The amount of investment in knowledge in the region is measured by R&D intensity, or the share of the regional labour force accounted for by scientists and engineers. According to the *Knowledge Spillover Entrepreneurship Proposition*, those geographical contexts, or regions, which are rich in knowledge, should generate more entrepreneurial opportunities, and therefore exhibit higher rates of observed entrepreneurship. By contrast, those geographical contexts, or regions, which are poor in knowledge, will generate fewer entrepreneurial opportunities, and therefore should exhibit lower rates of observed entrepreneurship.

Results

The knowledge spillover entrepreneurship proposition is tested by linking knowledge within the spatial context of the region to entrepreneurship using OLS estimation for regional entrepreneurship rates. The empirical results are presented in Table I. The results estimating general entrepreneurship are presented in the first column, high-technology entrepreneurship in the second column, ICT entrepreneurship in the third column, and low-technology entrepreneurship in the fourth column.

As the positive and statistically significant coefficients on knowledge suggest, those regions which are rich in knowledge also exhibit higher rates of both high-technology and ICT entrepreneurship. Thus, there is evidence supporting the *Knowledge Spillover Entrepreneurship Proposition*, but the evidence is limited to knowledge-based entrepreneurship. In fact, no statistically significant relationship can be inferred for the measures of general entrepreneurship and low-technology entrepreneurship. Of course, it should also be emphasized that it is exactly these results that are implied by the theory of knowledge spillover entrepreneurship. Only those types of new ventures based on knowledge and ideas generated in the organizational context of an existing incumbent firm or other organization would be expected to be endogenously induced. More general new ventures, and low-technology new ventures in particular, would not be expected to be influenced by potential knowledge spillovers, which is consistent with the findings in Table I.

Table I. Regression results for entrepreneurship (OLS)

	General	*High-technology*	*ICT*	*Low-technology*
Regional growth	2.631***	0.388***	0.170	2.073**
	(2.83)	(3.99)	(1.58)	(2.54)
Knowledge	1.828	4.359***	4.313***	−6.845
	(0.21)	(4.84)	(4.32)	(−0.90)
Unemployment	−0.003	−0.034***	−0.034***	0.065***
	(−0.13)	(−11.89)	(−10.90)	(2.71)
Agglomeration	6.874***	1.447***	1.138***	4.290**
	(2.80)	(5.64)	(4.00)	(1.99)
Location attractiveness	1.787	0.099	0.285**	1.402
	(1.61)	(0.85)	(2.22)	(1.44)
Social diversity	−0.807	−0.792***	−0.116	0.100
	(−0.66)	(−6.22)	(−0.82)	(0.09)
Skill diversity	8.931***	0.855***	0.968***	7.109***
	(6.71)	(6.15)	(6.28)	(6.08)
Constant	−3.921*	0.242	−0.308	−3.855**
	(−1.81)	(1.07)	(−1.23)	(−2.03)
R^2	0.2490	0.5256	0.5221	0.2052

Notes: t-statistic in brackets.
* Statistically significant at the two-tailed test for 90% level of confidence.
** Statistically significant at the two-tailed test for 95% level of confidence.
*** Statistically significant at the two-tailed test for 99% level of confidence.

As for the control variables, regional growth is found to have a positive and statistically significant impact, with the exception of ICT entrepreneurship. The negative and statistically significant coefficients of unemployment on High-Technology Entrepreneurship as well as on ICT Entrepreneurship suggest that regions exhibiting high rates of unemployment are not conducive to generating knowledge spillover entrepreneurship. By contrast, the positive and statistically significant coefficient on low-technology entrepreneurship suggests that unemployment has a positive impact on low-technology entrepreneurship.

Agglomeration, as measured by population density, is found to have a positive and statistically significant effect on all four of the measures of entrepreneurship. There is at least some evidence suggesting that the attractiveness of a location will generate more entrepreneurship.

There is also at least some evidence suggesting that social diversity is conducive to entrepreneurship, albeit only high-technology entrepreneurship. Finally, the diversity of human capital, as measured by labour skills, is found to have a significant impact on all four measures of entrepreneurship.

DISCUSSION

The prevailing theories of entrepreneurship have typically revolved around the ability of individuals to recognize opportunities and then to act on them by starting a new venture.

This has generated considerable insights into why entrepreneurial behaviour varies across individuals. In particular, the literature has focused on variations of individual-specific characteristics to explain why some individuals become entrepreneurs, while implicitly holding the external context in which the individual finds herself to be constant. Thus, where the opportunities come from, or the source of entrepreneurial opportunities, is also implicitly taken as given.

This paper has posited a theory suggesting a key source of entrepreneurial opportunities – knowledge created in an incumbent firm or organization but not completely or exhaustively commercialized by that organization. In particular, the theory of knowledge spillover entrepreneurship suggests that knowledge and new ideas created but not completely or exhaustively commercialized by incumbent firms and organizations provide an important source of entrepreneurial opportunities.

Based on a data set linking entrepreneurial activity to the extent of knowledge within the spatial context of geographical regions, higher knowledge contexts are found to generate more entrepreneurial opportunities, where the new venture serves as a conduit for knowledge spillovers. By contrast, lower knowledge contexts are found to generate fewer entrepreneurial opportunities. Thus, the empirical evidence is consistent with the proposition that entrepreneurial opportunities are not exogenous but rather systematically created by investments in knowledge by incumbent organizations.

NOTES

*Paper prepared for the *JMS* Special issue Conference, Columbus (OH), 28–29 October 2005. We thank the participants of the conference and the editors of the special issue for the valuable and insightful comments and suggestions.

[1] Examples of how this concern for entrepreneurship has been manifested within the various scholarly disciplines are included in Acs and Audretsch (2003).
[2] Link and Herbert (2007) identify three distinct scholarly traditions that form the intellectual basis of the modern entrepreneurship literature. The German Tradition is based on von Thuenen and Schumpeter, the Chicago Tradition is based on Knight and Schultz, and the Austrian Tradition is based on von Mises, Kirzner and Shackle.
[3] According to Shane and Venkataraman (2000), entrepreneurial opportunities involve the discovery of new means–ends relationships in which resources are combined to generate economic value that otherwise would not have existed.
[4] According to Sarasvathy et al. (2003, p. 142), 'An entrepreneurial opportunity consists of a set of ideas, beliefs and actions that enable the creation of future goods and services in the absence of current markets for them.'
[5] The data on start-ups are provided by the ZEW (Mannheim) foundation panels. This database was created from biannual observations by *Creditreform*, which is analogous to Dun and Bradstreet and ranks among the largest German credit-rating agencies. Virtually all businesses are included in the database, including start-ups, in the German Trade Register.
[6] The classification provided by the Federal Ministry of Education and Research is followed.

REFERENCES

Acs, Z. J. and Armington, C. (2006). *Entrepreneurship, Agglomeration and US Regional Growth*. Cambridge: Cambridge University Press.
Acs, Z. J. and Audretsch, D. B. (Eds) (2003). *Handbook of Entrepreneurship Research*. New York: Springer.
Acs, Z. J., Audretsch, D. B., Braunerhjelm, P. and Carlsson, B. (2004). *The Missing Link: The Knowledge Filter and Entrepreneurship in Endogenous Growth*. Centre for Economic Policy Research (CEPR) Discussion Paper. London: Centre for Economic Policy Research.

Alvarez, S. A. (2003). 'Resources and hierarchies: intersections between entrepreneurship and business strategy'. In Acs, Z. J. and Audretsch, D. B. (Eds), *Handbook of Entrepreneurship Research*. New York: Springer, 247–66.

Alvarez, S. A. and Barney, J. B. (2005). 'How do entrepreneurs organize under conditions of uncertainty?'. *Journal of Management*, **31**, 776–93.

Alvarez, S. A. and Barney, J. B. (2007). 'Guest editors' introduction: The entrepreneurial theory of the firm'. *Journal of Management Studies*, **44**, 1057–63.

Arrow, K. J. (1962). 'Economic welfare and the allocation of resources for invention'. In Nelson, R. R. (Ed.), *The Rate and Direction of Inventive Activity*. Princeton, NJ: Princeton University Press, 609–26.

Audretsch, D. B. (1995). *Innovation and Industry Evolution*. Cambridge, MA: MIT Press.

Audretsch, D. B. and Feldman, M. P. (1996). 'R&D spillovers and the geography of innovation and production'. *American Economic Review*, **86**, 630–40.

Audretsch, D. B. and Stephan, P. E. (1996). 'Company-scientist locational links: the case of biotechnology'. *American Economic Review*, **86**, 641–52.

Audretsch, D. B., Keilbach, M. and Lehmann, E. (2006). *Entrepreneurship and Economic Growth*. New York: Oxford University Press.

Barney, J. E. (1986). 'Strategic factor markets: expectations, luck and business strategy'. *Management Science*, **42**, 1231–41.

Companys, Y. R. and McMullen, J. S. (2007). 'Strategic entrepreneurs at work: the nature, discovery, and exploitation of entrepreneurial opportunities'. *Small Business Economics*, **28**, 302–22.

Feldman, M. and Audretsch, D. (1999). 'Innovation in cities: science-based diversity, specialization and localized competition'. *European Economic Review*, **43**, 409–29.

Gartner, W. B. and Carter, N. M. (2003). 'Entrepreneurial behaviour and firm organizing processes'. In Acs, Z. J. and Audretsch, D. B. (Eds), *Handbook of Entrepreneurship Research*. New York: Springer, 195–222.

Griliches, Z. (1992). 'The search for R&D spillovers'. *Scandinavian Journal of Economics*, **94**, 29–47.

Jacobs, J. (1979). *The Economy of Cities*. New York: Vintage Books.

Jaffe, A. B. (1989). 'Real effects of academic research'. *American Economic Review*, **79**, 957–70.

Krueger, N. F. Jr (2003). 'The cognitive psychology of entrepreneurship'. In Acs, Z. J. and Audretsch, D. B. (Eds), *Handbook of Entrepreneurship Research*. New York: Springer, 105–40.

Link, A. and Hebert, R. F. (2007). 'Historical perspectives on the entrepreneur'. *Foundations and Trends in Entrepreneurship*, **2**, 4, 1–86.

McClelland, D. (1961). *The Achieving Society*. New York: Free Press.

McMullen, J. S., Plummer, L. A. and Acs, Z. J. (2007). 'What is an entrepreneurial opportunity?'. *Small Business Economics*, **28**, 273–83.

Plummer, L. A., Haynie, J. M. and Godesiabois, J. (2007). 'An essay on the origins of entrepreneurial opportunity'. *Small Business Economics*, **28**, 363–9.

Reynolds, P. (2007). 'Firm creation in the United States: a PSID I overview'. *Foundations and Trends in Entrepreneurship*, **3**, 1–164.

Reynolds, P., Storey, D. J. and Westhead, P. (1994). 'Cross-national comparisons of the variation in new firm formation rates'. *Regional Studies*, **28**, 443–56.

Sarasvathy, S. D., Dew, N. S., Velamuri, R. and Venkataraman, S. (2003). 'Three views of entrepreneurial opportunity'. In Acs, Z. J. and Audretsch, D. B. (Eds), *Handbook of Entrepreneurship Research*. New York: Springer, 141–60.

Shane, S. (2000). 'Prior knowledge and the discovery of entrepreneurial opportunities'. *Organizational Science*, **11**, 448–69.

Shane, S. and Eckhardt, J. (2003). 'The individual-opportunity nexus'. In Acs, Z. J. and Audretsch, D. B. (Eds), *Handbook of Entrepreneurship Research*. New York: Springer, 161–94.

Shane, S. and Venkataraman, S. (2000). 'The promise of entrepreneurship as a field of research'. *Academy of Management Review*, **25**, 218–28.

Shaver, K. G. (2003). 'The social psychology of entrepreneurial behaviour'. In Acs, Z. J. and Audretsch, D. B. (Eds), *Handbook of Entrepreneurship Research*. New York: Springer, 331–58.

Storey, D. J. (1991). 'The birth of new firms – does unemployment make a difference? A review of the evidence'. *Small Business Economics*, **3**, 167–78.

Venkataraman, S. (1997). 'The distinctive domain of entrepreneurship research'. In Katz, J. and Brockhaus, R. (Eds), *Advance in Entrepreneurship, Firm Emergence, and Growth*. Greenwich, CT: JAI Press, 119–38.

8

Strategic Entrepreneurship Journal
Strat. Entrepreneurship J., **1**: 263–286 (2007)

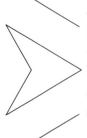

THE PROCESS OF CREATIVE CONSTRUCTION: KNOWLEDGE SPILLOVERS, ENTREPRENEURSHIP, AND ECONOMIC GROWTH

RAJSHREE AGARWAL,[1]* DAVID AUDRETSCH,[2] and M. B. SARKAR[3]
[1]*College of Business, University of Illinois at Urbana Champaign, Champaign, Illinois, U.S.A.*
[2]*Max-Planck-Institut für Ökonomik, Jena, Germany and Indiana University, Bloomington, Indiana, U.S.A.*
[3]*Department of Management, College of Business Administration, University of Central Florida, Orlando, Florida, U.S.A.*

Questioning the underlying assumptions of the process of creative destruction, we conceptualize an alternative process of creative construction that may characterize the dynamics between entrants and incumbents. We discuss the underlying mechanism of knowledge spillover strategic entrepreneurship whereby knowledge investments by existing organizations, when coupled with entrepreneurial action by individuals embedded in their context, results in new venture creation, heterogeneity in performance, and subsequent growth in industries, regions, and economies. The framework has implications for future research in entrepreneurship, strategy, and economic growth. Copyright © 2008 Strategic Management Society.

INTRODUCTION

The fundamental question in the emerging field of strategic entrepreneurship is how firms combine entrepreneurial action that creates new opportunities with strategic action that generates competitive advantage (Hitt *et al.*, 2002). We confront this question by developing the creative construction approach, which identifies knowledge spillovers as a key mechanism that underlies new venture formation and development at the micro level, and economic growth at the macro level. The development of this framework flows from the recognition that although strategy and entrepreneurship theory abounds with

Keywords: entrepreneurship; economic growth; creative destruction; knowledge spillovers
*Correspondence to: Rajshree Agarwal, University of Illinois at Urbana Champaign, 350 Wohlers Hall, College of Business, 1206 S. Sixth St., Champaign, IL 61820, U.S.A.
E-mail: agarwalr@uiuc.edu

Schumpeterian accounts of creative destruction and incumbent displacement by new entrants, our understanding of new venture emergence and associated externalities is less acute.

By specifying the process whereby ideas, technologies, and structures are rendered obsolete and displaced by new and superior ones, Schumpeter's idea of creative destruction has become the dominant framework for entrepreneurship and economic development. The concept highlights the tension between innovation and selection: innovations by new firms unleash selection pressures on existing firms. The view is particularly powerful in explaining *what* happens as economic structures change from within; however, it is remarkably silent with regard to mechanisms identifying *how* new entrants emerge, *why* the process of displacement occurs, and *whether* increasing returns to knowledge investments could benefit entrants, incumbents, and the economy alike. We identify some implicit assumptions in this approach, and juxtapose these against insights from accepted frameworks in the strategy and entrepreneurship literature to describe aspects of an emerging paradigm that we call *creative construction*, with knowledge spillovers as the underlying mechanism.

The literature that links knowledge spillovers to entrepreneurship emphasizes that incumbent organizations are an important source of new entrants, particularly when they underutilize the knowledge they create (Agarwal *et al.*, 2004; Klepper, 2007; Klepper and Sleeper, 2005; Shane and Stuart, 2002). Building on this work, we identify the endogeneity of entrepreneurial opportunities and action, and the intriguing possibility that knowledge can be leveraged back to incumbents as *spillins* from entrants. In doing so, we relate knowledge investments to a virtuous cycle of growth at multiple levels. Positing this cycle as one of creative construction, we suggest that in the face of the strategic management of knowledge spillovers across incumbents and entrants alike, displacement and value destruction are less likely as an outcome, as is growth of both entrants and incumbents in a virtuous loop of value creation. In doing so, we discuss how the process of creative destruction is but one end of the continuum; with the other end representing a process of creative construction—a process wherein entrants benefit from new knowledge created by incumbent organizations that may otherwise be left unexploited, but where such knowledge spillovers do not necessarily result in the destruction of incumbents. As entrants build on knowledge and networks developed by incumbent organizations to create new novel combinations that in a Schumpeterian sense causes the destruction of lesser entities, reverse flows from entrants to incumbents can lead to a dynamic process of growth, and thereby a win-win scenario where the positive externalities of knowledge spillovers are highlighted in the process of both value creation and appropriation.

In identifying knowledge spillover-based strategic entrepreneurship (KSSE) as the key mechanism behind the process of creative construction, we make three central arguments. First, in the context of entrepreneurship literature, we identify the symbiotic relationship between individuals (potential founders who are employees) and their knowledge environments, and contend that entrepreneurial opportunities, instead of being exogenously available, are endogenously created through knowledge investments. Second, by highlighting that the cocreators of knowledge (incumbent organizations and the

individuals who work for them) may each be able to appropriate the value, we contribute to the strategy literature by linking the genesis of firm capabilities to performance, and identifying existing boundaries to value appropriation. Further, due to the intriguing possibility that knowledge spillins can be strategically managed, we discuss how incumbents may effectively benefit from knowledge spillovers that originate from entrants, and in the process enhance their own competitiveness.

Third, we connect new venture origin, entrant, and incumbent performance, and regional and industry growth through the cycle of creative construction. Our contribution to the macroeconomic growth literature is, thus, in identifying *two* endogenous mechanisms—incumbents' knowledge investments and subsequent entrepreneurial venturing—that enable knowledge spillovers and value creation. In contrast to existing growth models that assume passivity in human action and/or exogenous technological advances, we emphasize the need for entrepreneurial action in both generation and appropriation of value and, thus, macro-level growth. Importantly, we contribute to all three literature streams by drawing attention to the intersection of different units of analyses, since the process of creative construction is enabled when entrepreneurial individuals choose to build on extant knowledge to innovate and found new firms that contribute to macro-level growth by becoming hotbeds of further entrepreneurial activity themselves.

The article proceeds in the following manner: we first provide a brief review of the process of creative destruction. We then develop the knowledge spillovers view of strategic entrepreneurship (KSSE) by linking the endogenous creation of opportunities to new firm formation due to the intersection of entrepreneurship and knowledge spillovers. The mechanism of KSSE, we argue, underlies the process of creative construction, where linkages to extant knowledge translate, through the founders, to firm level capabilities, growth, and competitive advantage. We proceed to link the process of creative construction to regional- and industry-level growth, since spillover benefits of the initial knowledge investments are reaped due to strategic entrepreneurship. We then discuss how our work integrates parallel literature streams that have typically focused on different units of analyses, and contribute to each as a result. The integrative model also sheds light on important research gaps that need to be addressed, and our final section is a call for additional

Strat. Entrepreneurship J., **1**: 263–286 (2007)
DOI: 10.1002/sej

effort to help explicate the processes, underlying mechanisms, and boundary conditions for growth through knowledge spillovers and strategic entrepreneurship.

CREATIVE CONSTRUCTION AND THE KNOWLEDGE SPILLOVER VIEW OF STRATEGIC ENTREPRENEURSHIP

A brief review of the process of creative destruction

According to Schumpeter (1934), entrepreneurship triggers *creative destruction*. The process of creative destruction and ensuing churn results from the creation of value through innovations in new products, services, and organizations that inevitably cause displacement or diminishing of the value of incumbent products, services, and organizations. The Schumpeterian view implicitly assumes that the value creation generated by the entrepreneurial agent exceeds that contributed by the status quo incumbent; otherwise, the entrepreneurial firm would not survive through the Darwinian process long enough to displace the incumbent(s). Creative destruction highlights the relationship between innovation and selection: innovations of new entrants generate selection pressures on existing firms. Thus, entrepreneurial creation and incumbent displacement (or destruction) are intertwined, leading scholars to comment that 'destruction, however painful, is the necessary price of creative progress toward a better material life' (McCraw, 2007: 501).

Focusing on the destruction aspect has led some scholars to posit that the net benefits of entrepreneurship may be less positive than Schumpeter believed (Aghion and Howitt, 1992; Ferguson, 1988). Implicit in this approach is the assumption of a competitive, zero-sum game where entrant wins are juxtaposed against incumbent losses. If the destruction effect is sufficiently high, the net value creation accruing from entrepreneurship may be very low or even negative; thus, having a dampening effect on longer term growth. This view is perhaps best exemplified by Ferguson (1988) who comments on *vulture capitalism* and focuses on the fragmentation, incumbent displacement, and instability of economy that is wrought by the *chronically entrepreneurial* semiconductor industry. In this view of mere redistribution of wealth from incumbents to entrants, not only is there no positive contribution to overall growth and employment, there could be a long-term

detrimental effect if future growth opportunities are dampened due to underinvestment in R&D, lack of scale economies, and lack of coordinated action for development of process technologies and government support. This perspective has found theoretical support in the literature related to the information paradox (Arrow, 1962), wherein the public nature of information—its nonrival and nonexcludable properties—cause firms to underinvest in knowledge-generating investments due to the negative externalities of knowledge spillovers and creative destruction (Aghion and Howitt, 1992). Moreover, at a macro level, the policy implication of the view is that cities, regions, and nations should pay more attention to preventing destruction, and less on creation ensuing from entrepreneurship, potentially leading them to erect barriers to entrepreneurship to encourage long-term investments by status quo incumbents (Hart, 2003).

A second assumption of the creative destruction view is that entrants avail themselves of exogenously available entrepreneurial opportunities, much like manna from heaven. In modeling the process of creative destruction, Aghion and Howitt (1992) assume that innovations occur randomly and entrants arrive at a constant Poisson rate. Indeed, while recognizing that economic structure changes from within, Schumpeter himself is silent on the following questions: Where do the new entrants come from? How do they create value?

In summary, scholarly work on creative destruction rests on twin assumptions of potential zero-sum games and exogenous entrepreneurial opportunities. Even though Schumpeter himself focused on the overall economic structure changing from within, subsequent work at the firm-level unit of analysis has focused on the invasion from outside industry and/or regional boundaries, which results in the destruction of incumbents. While not discounting this possibility, the relaxation of these assumptions permits other potential paths of economic progress, wherein destruction of incumbents is not an inevitable result. In order to develop a better understanding of the alternative paths, we first describe the underlying mechanism relating to the knowledge spillover view of strategic entrepreneurship.

The knowledge spillover view of strategic entrepreneurship

Viewing organizations as knowledge producing and exchanging subsystems (Schulz, 2001), the knowledge-based view of the firm argues that competitive heterogeneity is caused by the creation and application of privately held, tacit knowledge (Grant, 1996; Spender, 1996; Teece, Pisano and Schuen, 1997). Implicit, therefore, is the notion that wealth creation in a firm is a function of its ability to create new knowledge and exploit it in the market. However, as research indicates, the investment that a firm makes in knowledge-related activities has important implications beyond its boundaries. On the one hand, organizations often falter in transforming their scientific or industrial knowledge into what Arrow (1962) terms economic or commercialized knowledge, thus suffering from an *abundance of underexploited knowledge* (Agarwal *et al.*, 2004). On the other hand, organizations are imperfect repositories of knowledge, due to which private knowledge tends to leak into the environment and become the source of new ventures. These two forces, as captured in our *knowledge spillover view of strategic entrepreneurship*, together have profound implications for entrepreneurship, strategy, and growth.

Existing organizations as knowledge fountainheads

Existing organizations systematically undertake knowledge investments to generate innovative activity to fulfill their strategic mission. Griliches (1979) formalized the model of the knowledge-production function, wherein organizations engage in the pursuit of new economic knowledge as an input to innovative activity. Such efforts to create opportunities involve creating firm-specific intangible knowledge resources by undertaking investments in research and development. However, not all value created through scientific discoveries is fully appropriated within the investing organization's boundaries. Various constraints on extant organizations' abilities to deploy resources prevent them from fully exploiting the inherent value of their knowledge assets (Moran and Ghoshal, 1999). In fact, evidence shows that many large established companies find it difficult to take advantage of all the opportunities emanating from their investment in scientific knowledge (Christensen and Overdorf, 2000). For example, Xerox's Palo Alto Research Center is a poster child of a firm that succeeded in generating a large number of scientific breakthroughs—a superior personal computer, the facsimile machine, the Ethernet, and the laser printer, among others—yet failed to commercialize many of them (Smith and Alexander, 1988; Chesbrough and Rosenbloom, 2002).

As a result, existing organizations may be characterized as having an abundance of underexploited knowledge (Agarwal *et al.*, 2004). Much of the knowledge created may lay dormant within the organizational boundaries, since the constraints that result from existing organizational capabilities, orientation, or cognition may prevent them from pursuing all potential opportunities. Knowledge, however, is different from other resources given its public good characteristic of being nonrival and nonexcludable (Arrow, 1962), thus creating spillover opportunities. While spillovers refers broadly to the transfer of economic benefits between parties without compensating payment, knowledge spillovers relate specifically to the external benefits from the creation of knowledge that accrue to parties other than the creator.[1] Since organizational investments in knowledge lead to the enhancement of human capital in the form of technological, social, and cultural capital (Becker, 1964; Yli-Renko, Autio, and Sapienza, 2001), important conduits for spillovers are the people engaged in the knowledge-producing activities. Since human capital resides in the heads of individuals, this knowledge is inherently mobile—personnel are under limited organizational control and free to quit at will (Coff, 1997).

New venture creation: knowledge spillovers and entrepreneurial action

Individuals who perceive unexploited opportunities created by imcumbent organizations' knowledge investments may choose to venture out armed with the human capital they acquired during their tenure at the knowledge-generating organization. Thus,

---

[1] Knowledge spillovers have long been recognized as an important element in stimulating economic development. While knowledge spillovers are critical to models of multicountry development (Aghion and Howitt 1992), international trade (Keller 1988), agglomeration and de-agglomeration (Krugman 1991), they are central to modern growth theories (Romer 1990; Aghion and Howitt, 1992). Broadly, research has highlighted the potential of knowledge flowing from its generating source (firms or universities and public research establishments) to benefit others, resulting in an acceleration of economic growth. In fact, in a review of the empirical literature on spillovers, Griliches (1992) concludes that not only is the magnitude of R&D spillovers quite large, but that their social rates of return are significantly above private rates.

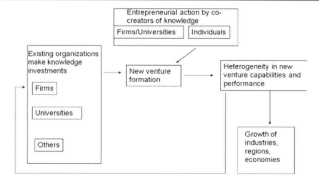

Figure 1.   The knowledge spillover view of strategic entrepreneurship

individuals working for existing firms and scientists at research institutions facilitate knowledge spillovers when they engage in the entrepreneurial act of new venture formation. In the earlier example of the dormant knowledge created by Xerox PARC, each of the breakthroughs made fortunes for many Silicon Valley start-ups (Smith and Alexander, 1988; Chesbrough and Rosenbloom, 2002). In fact, the notion that knowledge is mobile and, at the end of the day can walk out of the door with a firm's employees, is reported in research by Bhide (2000), who found that 71 percent of 100 founders of the 1989 *Inc.* 500 fastest-growing private companies in the United States had replicated or modified an idea encountered through previous employment.

New ventures are a manifestation of the intersection of knowledge spillovers and entrepreneurial action. For example, 'the potential of employee entrepreneurship results from incumbent firms being imperfect and permeable repositories of knowledge, [causing] new organizations to emerge from other organizations' (Agarwal *et al.*, 2004: 502). The rich literature streams on *university-based spinoffs* (Audretsch and Stephan, 1996; Lockett *et al.*, 2005; Louis *et al.*, 1989; O'Shea *et al.*, 2005; Zucker, Darby, and Brewer, 1997) and *firm-based spinouts* (Agarwal *et al.*, 2004; Burton, Sorensen, and Beckman, 2002; Chatterji, 2005; Klepper, 2007; Klepper and Sleeper, 2005; Shane and Stuart, 2002) illuminate the role that new firm start-ups play in the commercialization of knowledge investments by academic institutions and existing firms

respectively,[2] By starting a new venture, entrepreneurs not only create new firms, but they provide a conduit for the spillover of knowledge that otherwise might have remained dormant in the incumbent firm or organization creating that knowledge in the first place.

The KSSE framework

Knowledge spillover strategic entrepreneurship (KSSE), illustrated in Figure 1, can be defined as the creation of entrepreneurial opportunity based on knowledge generated by investments made by incumbent organizations. It stems from the symbiotic relationship between incumbent firms and other organizations and the people they employ in

---

[2] In academic entrepreneurship literature, new ventures are consistently defined as *university spinoffs*. This nomenclature also extends to other science based organizations (e.g. NASA spinoffs). However, in the employee entrepreneurship literature, there is less consistency in the usage of the terms. Different authors have used different terms—spinoffs, entrepreneurial spinoffs, spinouts, etc. We prefer the term 'spinout' to denote new ventures formed due to employee entrepreneurship for the following reasons. 'Spinoffs' is also widely used in diversification and finance literature to indicate *intended* divestments of business units by existing organizations. While the term 'entrepreneurial spinoffs' mitigates this issue to some extent, it is less illuminating in the context of entrepreneurship literature, where all new ventures are entrepreneurial. Accordingly, we use the term 'spinout,' which has been used in popular press and by some academic researchers (Agarwal *et al.*, 2004; Franco and Filson, 2007) to denote new ventures resulting from employee entrepreneurship.

Strat. Entrepreneurship J., **1**: 263–286 (2007)
DOI: 10.1002/sej

the knowledge-generation process, since knowledge investments by existing institutions enable individuals to jointly create new knowledge, some of whose benefits may be appropriated outside of current organizational structure.[3]

KSSE results not only in new venture formation, but also in heterogeneity in their capability and performance. Imprinted by their experience in extant organizations (Stinchcombe, 1965), founders of new ventures shape new venture capability and performance due to scientific, market-based, psychological, and social knowledge that they bring from their parent organizations, thus resulting in systemic heterogeneity in entrant capabilities (Carroll *et al.*, 1996; Helfat and Lieberman, 2002; Klepper and Simons, 2000). Path dependency in firm evolution (Cyert and March, 1963; March and Simon, 1958; Nelson and Winter, 1982) and endogenous processes of learning by doing (Nonaka, 1994; Zollo and Winter, 2002; Winter, 2003) can result in sustained interfirm variance in structure, strategy, routines, and culture (Sastry and Coen, 2001), suggesting that the knowledge stocks at founding leaves a long-lasting imprint on a firm's future competitiveness.

These ventures then represent the extant organizations who engage in knowledge investments. The resultant feedback loop fuels industry, regional, and economic growth. In contrast to the assumption of zero costs of location choice in spatial models (Hotelling, 1929; Lancaster, 1966; Salop, 1979), KSSE implies that the costs of choosing a location in technological or geographical space are nonzero.[4]

The knowledge linkages of new entrants to extant organizations can constrain their ability to occupy nonoverlapping segments in the industry or geographical space, due to costs related not only to learning and innovating, but also to those that stem from agglomeration economies and supply chain and infrastructure development. Importantly, since entrepreneurial entrants are embedded in their particular institutional contexts, they are more likely to locate closer to this space (geographical, technological, or preferences scale). It may also be that consumers learn as well, and that their preferences may be revealed/developed, in part, due to their interaction with the firms that offer the products. Thus, in contrast to the model by Salop (1979), where new entrants locate farthest away from existing organizations in a circular space, KSSE results in a gradual spread of firms from anchor points on the circle that represent existing institutions and organizations.

Support for such evolutionary patterns in industries and regions stems from the industry life cycle literature. Scholars have consistently documented the importance of new entrants in the takeoff and growth of industries (Agarwal and Bayus, 2002; Audretsch, 1995; Carroll *et al.*, 1996; Gort and Klepper, 1982; Klepper, 2002), since they are a key vehicle for introducing new innovations into the market (Audretsch, 1995; Gort and Klepper, 1982). In subsequent work, Agarwal *et al.* (2004) and Klepper (2002) found systematic differences in entrant success rates, with spinout firms having the highest levels of performance. Importantly, Klepper (2007) documented evidence that spinouts from existing firms tend to be spatially clustered within close geographic proximity to their parents. In particular, Klepper examined the formative stages of the automobile industry and found that not only did they generate considerable growth for the surviving new ventures, but also for the region in which those new ventures were spawned. Thus, just as the industry evolves over a life cycle, so too does a region in which such an industry is located. The simultaneous growth of a region and an industry is

---

[3] We note here that the spillover of knowledge is being defined at the organizational level, with the individual scientist or employee acting as the conduit of knowledge spillovers. The actual creation of knowledge or innovation may have been entirely the brainchild of the individual, or it may have had limited input by the individual(s) who ultimately found the new company (In academic entrepreneurship, for example, the first case relates to the academic inventor, while the other may relate to say, a graduate student exposed to the innovation who later seeks to commercialize the invention). However, since the commercial benefits, at least in part, stem from knowledge that originated at another organization, the new venture is termed as stemming from KSSE.

[4] Spatial models are useful to conceptualize not just geographical space, but also technological or consumer preference space (Carlton and Perloff, 2006), and can thus help illuminate growth dynamics in industries or regions. In particular, the Salop (1979) model examines competitive dynamics and optimal entry locations when consumers are assumed to be located around a circle representing their geographical or preference space. To maximize monopoly rents, entering firms

have the incentive to locate as far away from incumbents as possible, i.e., when two firms compete, they will locate at the end points of a diameter. In general, if the circumference of the circle is unity, the distance between n firms will be $1/n$. However, the model makes a critical assumption that entrant firms incur zero costs in their choice of location. In the context of industries and technologies, this is similar to the assumptions that innovations stem from a random process, as in Aghion and Howitt (1992).

fueled by spinouts, as is evidenced by Detroit and the automobile industry (Klepper, 2007), and Silicon Valley and the semiconductor industry (Brittain and Freeman, 1986; Moore and Davis, 2004).

Similarly, knowledge spillovers emanating from universities have also been acknowledged to generate not only new venture growth and entire new industries, but also the regions in which they are located. For example, the turnaround in San Diego from a highly depressed region due to naval base closings and downsizings to a high-growth region has been attributed to the efficacy of spinoffs from the University of California at San Diego.

KSSE can generate regional and industry growth (and hence growth at more aggregate macro levels of nations and continents) due to two endogenous processes: the first relates to the knowledge investments made by existing organizations, while the second relates to the entrepreneurial action of individuals embedded in these contexts that result in new venture formation. The implication of the dual need for human action is that there are *nonrandom* patterns of innovation. Subsequent innovations result from initial investments, and further, path dependencies in origins and growth of capabilities imply that industries and regions where these firms operate are going to be differentially advantaged than others. An unequal access to initial knowledge investments by parent organizations creates unequal rates of growth of industries and regions. Thus, differences in technological intensity, for instance, will result in differences in levels of sales achieved in the industry at its peak; just as regional differences in location will result in different levels of economic growth.

The process of creative construction

As reviewed in the earlier section, the process of creative destruction depicts entrants empowered by exogenous sources of innovation as displacing incumbents in an interaction characterized by zero-sum and win-lose dynamics. KSSE highlights that entrants often emerge endogenously from existing organizations, armed by knowledge created but underutilized within incumbents. At first glance, KSSE would thus seem very consistent with creative destruction, inasmuch as it relates to entrants appropriating the value created by incumbents. However, KSSE is also consistent with creative construction, wherein the growth of entrants is not necessarily at the expense of the incumbent. We elaborate on this alternative path, which while

acknowledged implicitly in scholarly writings, has never fully been articulated as a process wherein synergies develop through the creation of larger pies and win-win dynamics. Creative construction is similar to creative destruction in highlighting the creation of value through entrepreneurial entry; however it differs from creative destruction in two critical ways. First, it identifies the *construction* of these new entrants due to incumbent investments in knowledge. Second, it questions whether incumbents are necessarily *destroyed* in the process, given the potential for simultaneous growth of both incumbents and entrants alike, and for incumbents' strategic management of the knowledge spillovers that may result in spillins.

There are at least two reasons for a win-win rather than a win-lose outcome. The first stems from agglomeration and legitimacy effects, which can lead to an increase in demand that permits simultaneous growth of both the parent and the progeny. As discussed earlier, industry life cycle scholars have documented the growth of both industries and regions due to entrepreneurial entry (Agarwal and Bayus, 2002; Klepper, 2007). Agarwal and Bayus (2002) show that sales takeoff and growth in the industry are linked to a critical mass of entry in the industry, an empirical fact also documented by organizational ecology scholars who theorize about the legitimacy-building role of early entrants in the industry (Hannan and Freeman, 1989). Further, scholars have explicitly linked the growth of regions and industries to spinout activity (Brittain and Freeman, 1986; Klepper, 2007; Saxenian, 1994). They document the positive synergies and agglomeration economies caused due to geographical clusters enabled by knowledge spillover strategic entrepreneurship. As industries and regions grow due to KSSE, they attract not only additional human capital, but also supporting infrastructure related to the supply chain and venture financing. Not only does this serve to reinforce the supply side effects for the incumbent organization, but it can lead to enhanced demand of the products they sell. Thus, particularly in the growth stages of the industries, both parent and progeny organizations may grow, and the growth of one is not at the expense of the other.

The second stems from *spillin* or capability enhancement effects which arise when spinouts occupy complementary rather than competitive positions, and their growth in capabilities provides a potential for learning (and even subsequent acquisition of the spawned firm) by the parent organization.

Strat. Entrepreneurship J., **1**: 263–286 (2007)
DOI: 10.1002/sej

As an example, Gordon Moore stated that 'at Fairch-ild, we began to encourage and support spinoffs that could provide us with necessary components to our research and manufacturing processes. Later, Intel adopted an outright technology policy that we would use none of our own equipment. We knew we couldn't keep up with too many technologies, or dedicate the resources to be at the leading edge in all areas simultaneously' (Moore and Davis, 2004: 11). Thus, an incumbent firm may be able to lever-age off the capabilities of a spinout it has spawned, and use it as a complementary asset. While much has been documented about spinouts occupying com-peting positions in the supply chain, recent work by Somaya, Williamson and Lorinkova (2007) has systematically documented that employee mobil-ity to firms that are vertically linked, or produce complements, can have beneficial effects on the incumbents. The incumbent can access new knowl-edge, competencies, and capabilities created in the new venture by relying on social capital links to the new venture (Somaya *et al.*, 2007). Such linkages, either formally through contractual agreements, or informally through interactions of personnel from both the incumbent and new venture, can facilitate the access of valuable know-how and competencies generated by the new venture, thereby enabling the *spillin* of knowledge from the new venture generated by the spillover back to the spawning incumbent.

The alternative paths of creative construction and creative destruction are illustrated in Figure 2, which represents time on the horizontal axis and performance of a firm on the vertical axis. An incum-bent's potential performance path is depicted as ini-tially increasing over time. An entry event occurs at time t_1; if the entrant is a spinout from an exist-ing organization, this is illustrated by the dashed arrow exhibiting the linkages from the incumbent to the new venture. Creative destruction assumes that the incumbent organization follows the path A, while the entrant follows the path B, and in the case of a zero-sum, the gains in performance of the entrant exactly equal the loss in performance of the incumbent.

The interlinkages among the incumbents and entrants through individuals and knowledge spill-overs imply some alternative paths. One potential, particularly when incumbents' investments result in the creation of more knowledge than they can pos-sibly employ themselves, is that as entrants follow path B, and incumbents progress along path C. KSSE suggests that entrepreneurship may not displace incumbents as much as commercialize ideas that otherwise would have remained dormant and unused by incumbents. The assumption that there is a high, immediate opportunity cost of knowledge spillovers to the incumbent may not be valid in some, if not in most, cases of entrepreneurial ventures. In instances where the knowledge has no *a priori* economic value to the existing organization, but is deemed poten-tially highly valuable by the individual, entrepre-neurship is a constructive force because it increases the value of knowledge and ideas that otherwise might not have been developed and commercialized.

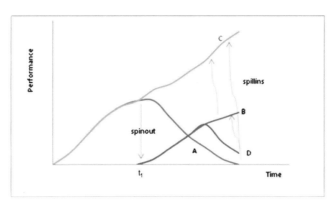

Figure 2.   Creative destruction and creative construction

Strat. Entrepreneurship J., **1**: 263–286 (2007)
DOI: 10.1002/sej

By serving as a conduit of knowledge spillovers, entrepreneurial ventures do not displace or detract from the incumbent firms and industries, but rather create new alternatives. This represents creative construction at its most beneficial manifestation, particularly if spillins from spinout entrants fuel incumbent growth through mutually advantageous synergies resulting from agglomeration economies, gains from expanded social networks, and complementarities of positions in the value chain.

Importantly, even in situations where incumbents or entrants have less rosy outcomes, knowledge spillovers between firms ensure knowledge that is created is constructively used. If entrant firms exhibit pattern D, which is characteristic of liability of newness or adolescence, their experimentation and failure provides for knowledge that continues to live on past their exit from the industry (Hoetker and Agarwal, 2007). Similarly, in the event that incumbents (for reasons discussed in a later section) fail to systematically harness and appropriate the value they created through their knowledge investments and follow path A, the gains from the investments are not lost to society due to employee mobility and entrepreneurship.

The dynamics at the firm level also have implications at the more macro levels of regions, industries, and economies. The implications for regional growth and performance arise from the idea that greater amounts of KSSE will generate greater spillovers and resultant commercialization of knowledge. As endogenous growth theory (Romer, 1990) suggests, knowledge spillovers spurs higher rates of growth, employment, and international competitiveness. Entrepreneurial new ventures are an important mechanism for knowledge spillovers, since their use of knowledge and ideas serves as the crucial resource driving the competitive advantage of the industries, regions, and economies that they are associated with. Regions and industries with a high degree of entrepreneurial activity will also facilitate more knowledge spillovers, which will ultimately increase economic growth, employment creation, and international competitiveness.

In sum, whether or not KSSE crowds out incumbents, industries, regions, and economies or reinforces their competitiveness depends on whether the positive effects of spinouts on incumbent capability and industry and regional growth are offset by the negative effects due to increased competition. Indeed, whether KSSE results in creative construction or creative destruction of firms, regions, and

economies rests upon a course dictated by *from each according to their ability (to create), and to each according to their ability (to appropriate)*.

IMPLICATIONS FOR ENTREPRENEURSHIP, STRATEGY, AND ECONOMIC GROWTH LITERATURE

The preceding section highlighted the virtuous process of *creative construction* and the underlying mechanism of knowledge spillover strategic entrepreneurship. We now turn to the implications of KSSE for core concepts in entrepreneurship, strategy, and economic growth literature.

Origin of entrepreneurial opportunities

While the concept of entrepreneurial opportunities is fundamental to both entrepreneurship and strategy literature, the literatures have widely divergent views on their origin. In the entrepreneurship literature, opportunities are generally viewed as being given, or exogenous. Nelson (1992) traces this bias back to Schumpeter, who specifically eschewed the entrepreneur's role in creating opportunities. According to Nelson (1992: 90), 'Schumpeter is curiously uninterested in where the basic ideas for innovations, be they technological or organizational, come from. Schumpeter does not view the entrepreneur as having anything to do with their generation.' Recent entrepreneurship work echoes this view with research revolving around the questions of how entrepreneurs perceive existing opportunities and how these opportunities manifest themselves as being credible versus being an illusion. For example, recent literature on individual opportunity nexus has tended to focus on the process of opportunity discovery so as to explain why some actors are more likely to discover a given opportunity than others (Shane and Eckhardt, 2003). Others have tried to uncover the covariance between individual characteristics and attributes and cognitive processes underlying the entrepreneurial decision (Shaver, 2003; McClelland, 1961), assuming that entrepreneurship is an orientation toward opportunity recognition (Stevenson and Jarillo, 1990).

In other words, there is a tendency to view opportunities as a given in models of entrepreneurship. The focus is on how heterogeneity in willingness to incur risk, preference for autonomy and self-

Strat. Entrepreneurship J., **1**: 263–286 (2007)
DOI: 10.1002/sej

direction, and differential access to scarce and expensive resources influences entrepreneurship at the individual level. After reviewing the entrepreneurship literature, Plummer, Hanie, and Godestabois (2007: 363) conclude 'a notable lack of research focused on the origins of opportunity,' while Companys and McMullen (2007: 302) suggest that 'despite the advances and the importance of entrepreneurial opportunities to strategy and entrepreneurship, there have been surprisingly few recent studies that explore the nature of opportunities . . .'

In contrast to the entrepreneurship literature view of the nascent entrepreneur as a taker of the exogenous opportunity, strategy has long viewed firms as creating or making opportunities. Growth through new entry in markets and products is considered to be a key objective and the heart of any economic enterprise (Mintzberg, 1973; Abell, 1980; Penrose, 1959). The quest for *Ricardian rents*—returns that accrue due to scarcity of the resource (Ricardo, 1817)—causes firms to invest in the production of resources such as knowledge that may provide competitive advantage due to their uniqueness, imperfect mobility and lack of imitability (Barney, 1991; Penrose, 1959; Wernerfelt, 1984). In the strategy literature, sustained heterogeneity of firms is the cause of sustained competitive advantage (Mahoney and Pandian, 1992), and much of the research has focused on both how firm heterogeneity may be created (Ghemawat, 1991; Teece, 1986; Teece, Pisano, and Schuen, 1990) and sustained (Rumelt, 1984; Lippman and Rumelt, 1992). According to Mahoney and Pandian (1992: 374), 'A major advancement in the strategy field is the development of models where firm heterogeneity is an endogenous creation of economic actors.' Mahoney and Pandian discuss the potential of both equilibrium (Lippman and Rumelt, 1992; Penrose, 1959) and disequilibrium models (Iwai, 1984; Teece, Pisano, and Schuen, 1990) to shed light on this issue.

Incorporating views of strategic action into the equation brings up the intriguing possibility that rather than being opportunity takers as espoused in the entrepreneurship literature, organizations are actually opportunity makers. The key to reconciling entrepreneurship's view on opportunities vs. the strategy view of entrepreneurship is to adopt the assertion from the strategy literature that opportunities are endogenously created by strategic investments by incumbent firms and research institutions, but then to ask who, and in which organizational context, is able to take advantage of that opportunity.

The knowledge spillover view of strategic entrepreneurship posits that knowledge investments by existing organizations create an abundance of entrepreneurial opportunities, not all of which are fully enacted upon by the parent organization itself. As we will discuss later in this article, there are many reasons why incumbent organizations—particularly firms that generate knowledge primarily to appropriate its benefits—do not capture all the returns. Thus, in addition to generating *Ricardian rents*, endogenous investments in knowledge generate *entrepreneurial rents*—returns that are achieved in an uncertain or complex environment due to risk taking and entrepreneurial insight (Cooper, Gimeno-Gascon, and Woo, 1991; Rumelt, 1987; Schumpeter, 1934). These entrepreneurial rents accrue to those individuals who may have cocreated the knowledge in the existing organizations and who additionally engage in the entrepreneurial process of harnessing the potential of opportunities that are created, but left unexploited.

Firm performance

Strategy has been defined as a theory about how to gain competitive advantage, where competitive advantage is the ability to create more economic value than rival firms (Barney and Hesterly, 2006). Since the focus of strategy is on the individual firm, value that is created, but not appropriated, does not enter into the measurement of firm performance. Indeed, this definition of competitive advantage would place the economic value attributed to the spinout as value created by *rival* firms, since it misses the link of KSSE between the parent and progeny organizations. However, just as calls for balanced scorecards of organizational performance (Kaplan and Norton, 1992) draw attention to nonfinancial measures of performance, the knowledge spillover view of strategic entrepreneurship highlights the fact that the traditional shareholder value maximization measure of firm performance may underestimate the value created by an organization by not accounting for the spillover benefits it generates.

Brittain and Freeman (1986) conducted an insightful study that examined value creation of two firms—Texas Instruments and Fairchild Semiconductor—in the semiconductor industry. They showed that the Silicon Valley phenomenon can be genealogically traced back to Fairchild (and its own parent, Shockley Transistor) due to 351 employee entrepreneurs during the 1955–81 period.

Strat. Entrepreneurship J., 1: 263–286 (2007)
DOI: 10.1002/sej

The inclusion of the inception and growth of these *Fairchildren* in Fairchild's creation of value, relative to its rival Texas Instruments that generated very few spinouts during the same period, greatly increases the value beyond the traditional performance measures of profitability or survivability. Hoetker and Agarwal (2007) similarly document the benefits of innovative firms, even after they have exited the industry, in terms of sustained post-exit knowledge diffusion.

Indeed, the knowledge spillover view of strategic entrepreneurship is similar to strategy's view of firm diversification that hails back to Penrose (1959). Mahoney and Pandian (1992) draw attention to the *nonrandomness of the direction of a firm's diversification.* Their review of the literature, which includes prior work by Lemelin (1982), MacDonald (1985), Montgomery and Hariharan (1991), and Stewart, Harris, and Carleton (1985) provides compelling evidence for Penrose's thesis that resources are a selective force determining the direction of firm diversification. Interestingly, Mahoney and Pandian (1992: 367) also comment that 'while the resource-based view has developed a viable approach for explaining and predicting growth and diversification, a 'resource-based theory of divestment' is clearly lacking.' While not a resource-based theory of divestment as such, the knowledge spillover view of strategic entrepreneurship clearly highlights the role of knowledge spillovers—in the presence of underexploited knowledge at the parent organization—plays in the *nonrandomness of the direction of entrepreneurial new venture formation,* when incumbent organizations choose to forgo opportunities that they created, thus passively divesting their resources.

Boundary conditions to value appropriation

In discussing the process of creative construction and KSSE in the preceding section, we had refrained from addressing the question of why incumbent organizations permit spinout generation and appropriation of the value of their knowledge investments by others. Indeed, systematic underutilization of opportunities created by knowledge investments will result in creative destruction, rather than creative construction, since incumbents fail to appropriate the value for improving their own performance and survival. For example, among the two types of firms studied by Brittain and Freeman (1986), Shockley Transistor and Fairchild Semiconductor ceased to exist in 1968

and 1979 respectively, while Texas Instruments still lives on.

KSSE provides a rich context within which to examine boundary conditions to value appropriation. In particular, it can complement extant theories of the firm for contributions within each stream. Three theories of the firm are particularly salient in the context of KSSE. These relate to theories of 1) managerial diseconomies of scale or the *Penrose Effect* on the limits to firm growth; 2) behavioral aspects of the firm that relate to bounded rationality or cognitive limits of managers to perceive opportunities; and 3) agency issues or incentive alignment of individual and firm objectives.

One explanation of knowledge spillover strategic entrepreneurship is limited access to managerial resources for appropriating value, which limits the growth potential of the organization (Penrose, 1959). In fact, incumbent firms may be constrained by resources, managerial in particular, in appropriating the benefits of *all* the knowledge that is created. In examining diversification and expansion efforts of firms, scholars have highlighted the dual pulls on managerial resources—the need to manage current operations and maintain size, and the need to engage in expansion efforts to create and identify new opportunities (Agarwal *et al.*, 2004; Gort, 1962; Hay and Morris, 1979; Marris, 1964; Mahoney and Pandian, 1992). Given specialized skills and the need for prior experience, managerial capabilities of the firm may grow at a smaller rate than the opportunities generated, thus causing project and top management teams to have to choose among multiple positive NPV projects. Accordingly, *even in the absence of limited cognition, strategic disagreements, or lack of incentive alignment,* existing organizations may be unable to fully appropriate value, resulting in KSSE by individuals who are in the organizational context.

A second reason relates to organizational inertia, which can be linked to the behavioral theory. Firms often fail to realize their full potential due to various constraints on their ability to deploy resources and exploit the inherent value of their knowledge assets (Moran and Ghoshal, 1999). Inertial behavior has been attributed to competency traps (Leonard-Barton, 1992; Nelson and Winter, 1982) and cognitive limits that constrain managerial decision making (Barr, Stimpert, and Huff, 1992; Tripsas and Gavetti, 2000; Henderson and Clark, 1990). Interpreting routines as an embodiment of codifying microeconomic incentives and constraints, as well as being a locus of

Strat. Entrepreneurship J., **1**: 263–286 (2007)
DOI: 10.1002/sej

conflict and governance, Kaplan and Henderson (2005) integrate disparate views on routines, cognitions, and incentives to argue that routines and capabilities reflect both 'a cognitive (how things are done) and motivational (what gets rewarded) dimension' (Kaplan and Henderson, 2005: 513). Accordingly, due to an interaction of existing capabilities, cognitions, incentives, and governance issues, incumbent firms face a certain rigidity that renders them unable to take advantage of all the opportunities emanating from their investment in scientific knowledge (Christensen and Overdorf, 2000). Due to certain inertial properties that result, they are impeded in their ability to fully realize the value of their knowledge investments (Hannan and Freeman, 1984).

From a behavioral perspective, the goals, expectations, and risk averseness of top managers may diverge significantly from those of R&D personnel in the firm. While top management typically emphasizes goals salient to external stakeholders that provide critical resources to the organization (Audia and Greve, 2006; Greve, 1998), scientific personnel are more likely to be driven by aspirations linked closely to the performance of their subunit, or the specific technology they are working on. Reflecting such thoughts, the organizational learning literature describes various pathologies ascribed to competency and learning traps (March, 1991; Levinthal and March, 1993) that serve to constrain and localize search for solutions in proximate areas (Ahuja and Lampert, 2001; Cyert and March, 1963). For example, Christensen (1993) shows how a firm's dependence on existing customers hampered efforts to reorient market strategies and frustrated engineers who did not see their technological inventions being commercialized. Such differences between resource allocating managers and R&D scientists create a tension between exploitation activities that have a far more certain return and exploratory investments that are riskier, longer term, and uncertain. Such risk averseness can inhibit experimentation and leads to situations where organizations fail to act on radical new solutions (Greve, 1998; Greve and Taylor, 2000).

Another reason stems from incentive alignment and agency issues. Organizational theorists have long acknowledged the importance of both formal and informal incentives facing a firm's employees, stressing that the political economy and the social context in which economics and incentive systems of a firm are embedded play a major role in shaping

decisions made (Ancona *et al.*, 1999; Pfeffer, 1990). The economic literature suggests that employment contracts place only limited restrictions on an employee's freedom to leave a firm. While firms can impose exit costs on their employees by imposing *golden handcuffs* or long-term incentives that defer the timing at which the employee receives payments for her knowledge (Milgrom and Roberts, 1992; Liebeskind, 1996), these mechanisms are subject to agency costs. Problems of moral hazard (Wiggins, 1995), and information asymmetries (Anton and Yao, 1995) are associated with long-term incentive plans, such as deferred stock options and promises of promotions. These contractual problems make it lucrative for the employee to develop the discovery in her own entrepreneurial venture rather than contracting with the employer to develop it.

Thus, all these theories help address why organizations are limited in their ability to appropriate all the value they create. As Agarwal *et al.* (2004: 505) state, 'an abundance of underutilized knowledge can beget spinouts, such incidents are deterred when the knowledge of a firm is put to use.' We note that the first of the these explanations—managerial diseconomies of scale—is not necessarily a cause of the firm's eventual failure. Indeed, managerial diseconomies to scale as a boundary condition to value appropriation is entirely consistent with creative construction, rather than creative destruction, since abounding opportunities generated through knowledge investments permit both the parent and progeny organizations to grow. In fact, to the extent that spillins from spinout activity can be effectively leveraged by incumbent firms, the synergies relax some of the managerial constraints and allow each firm to focus strategically on what to do, and equally importantly, what not to do. However, the latter explanations—organizational inertia due to behavioral limits and misalignment of incentives— may lead to spinout growth at the expense of the parent, and in the long run, cause the parent organization's failure (Christensen, 1997). An incumbent's inertia and resultant inability to fully exploit its know-how, combined with contractual failures to prevent employees from leaving leads to potential situations where spinouts may form with the raison d'être of exploiting the slack incumbent's scientific and technological knowledge in the market. These boundary conditions to value appropriation will result in creative destruction, not creative construction.

Strat. Entrepreneurship J., **1**: 263–286 (2007)
DOI: 10.1002/sej

Heterogeneity of firm capabilities and performance

Turning to a core issue in strategy research—namely heterogeneity in firm capabilities and performance—the knowledge spillover view of strategic entrepreneurship links the growth of capabilities and, hence, performance of firms to differences in their founding conditions, or the fountainheads of their knowledge.

Numerous sources generate competitive heterogeneity among firms and, thus, result in enduring and systematic differences among close rivals (Hoopes and Madsen, 2007). From the dominant perspective within the strategy literature, the varied competitive positions that firms enjoy are influenced by the heterogeneous distribution of capabilities across firms. While much has been written about the consequences of capabilities, there has been comparatively little scrutiny on where these heterogeneous capabilities came from in the first place. This is analogous to the paucity of studies identifying where entrepreneurial opportunities come from, which was discussed in an earlier section. This lacuna is more apparent in the case of entrepreneurial firms. While firms' histories, market positions, beliefs, and preferences can all generate and, thereby, explain competitive heterogeneity (Rumelt, 1984), such legacy-based explanations do not explain much as far as start-up firms are concerned.

Further, while the *micro* strand within entrepreneurship research focuses on individual traits that explain new venture creation, the dominant *macro* studies focus on the environmental characteristics. While studies of innovation and market evolution emphasize the role of entrants as agents of structural market transformations (Gort and Klepper, 1982; Tushman and Anderson, 1986), the origin of entrepreneurial ventures has garnered little attention (Klepper and Simons, 2000). Studies have related new firm formation to market structure (Geroski, 1995), technology (Gort and Klepper, 1982; Shane, 2000), and population dynamics (Hannan and Freeman, 1987), but there has been little research addressing their origin, or the implications of genealogy.

KSSE fills this gap in the literature, since it posits that the entrepreneurial source impacts evolutionary churn by influencing entrant capabilities. Venture origin determines heterogeneity in entrant capabilities (Carroll *et al.*, 1996; Klepper and Simons, 2000) and initial endowments not only help new ventures

withstand competitive pressures during their especially vulnerable initial years, but also imprint on their subsequent behavior and performance (Stinchcombe, 1965). Literature related to the evolutionary theory of the firm (Nelson and Winter, 1982), endogenous experiential learning by doing, and vicarious learning from other referent firms (Irwin and Klenow, 1994; Ingram and Baum, 1997) document the path dependency in the development of capabilities. By linking the origin of capabilities within existing organizations to the path dependency of capabilities, the knowledge spillover view of strategic entrepreneurship links new ventures benefits from incumbent experience in their formation to subsequent heterogeneity in their capabilities and performance due to path dependent growth.

When employees leave existing organizations to found a new organization, it is argued that the founders transfer some of the parent's routines to the progeny organization. So, the capabilities of progeny organizations are, in part, determined by those of their parent organizations. Thus, the literature suggests that when a new venture is founded, a firm's capabilities and subsequent performance are influenced by the founder's capabilities and knowledge acquired within the context of an incumbent organization. The genesis of firm capabilities, at least to some extent, has its roots in the capabilities and knowledge of a parent organization. The link between firm performance and the parent organization is KSSE.

Considerable empirical evidence exists supporting the hypothesis that KSSE responds positively to the organizational knowledge context. Holding the degree to which an organization can actually take advantage of the new opportunities it generates from knowledge investments as a given, the greater the amount of investment in knowledge resources in an organization, the greater the entrepreneurial opportunities generated. Thus, an organization context rich in scientific knowledge would be expected to generate a high degree of knowledge spillover entrepreneurship. By contrast, an organization context low in knowledge would not be expected to generate significant knowledge spillover entrepreneurship. For example, Agarwal *et al.* (2004) analyze spinouts from firms in the disk drive industry and find compelling evidence that the performance was greater in spinouts from high-performing firms than from low-performing firms. The high-performing firms provide a more fertile seedbed for entrepreneurial opportunities than do the low-performing

Strat. Entrepreneurship J., **1**: 263–286 (2007)
DOI: 10.1002/sej

firms. Klepper (2007) similarly finds for the automobile industry that the knowledge capabilities of an incumbent firm influence the subsequent performance of spinouts. A growing literature links the pre-entrepreneurial experience of founders to the actual entrepreneurial performance of the new venture (Burton *et al.*, 2002; Shane and Stuart, 2002). In particular, studies point to two distinct types of knowledge sources that entrepreneurs can draw from to launch a new venture. Burton *et al.* (2002) find compelling evidence suggesting that entrepreneurs are able to leverage prior career experience in higher performing and status firms into a strategic advantage in terms of obtaining external finance used to launch the new venture. Klepper and Simons (2000), Phillips (2000), Agarwal *et al.* (2004) and Chatterji (2005) all show that the acquisition of skills, technological capabilities, experience, and know-how in a high-performing incumbent company provide the knowledge basis for spawning a new venture from a high-performing incumbent.

Nonrandomness in patterns of economic growth

When David Birch (1981) uncovered his startling (at the time) evidence that small firms created more jobs than large firms, a number of attempts were made to use the Birch analysis to link small business dynamics to regional economic development. However, such studies suffered from a fatal flaw. Among other things, the growth accounting was assumed to take place within distinct firm-size classes, typically large (over 500 employees) and small (fewer than 500 employees). This ignored the possibility of inter-firm externalities, that one firm's actions could influence productivity and growth in a firm in a different size class. This flaw was particularly glaring in light of the rich scholarly tradition in macroeconomics, which has analyzed why some spatial units of analysis perform better than others. After all, public policy does not care which type of firm—large or small—generates growth. The main thing is that growth is generated. However, the mechanism that generates growth in the knowledge spillover view of strategic entrepreneurship is different than those in the traditional macroeconomic growth models.

Neoclassical economics models focus heavily on the *production-function approach*, where output is modeled as a function primarily of capital and labor. Within this context, early economic growth models related growth in productivity as arising primarily from growth in the underlying inputs: population growth results in an increase in the supply of labor, and savings from current consumption increases future capital stock (Harrod, 1939; Domar, 1946).

Solow (1956) departed from this tradition by calling attention to the empirical evidence that growth rates in capital and labor accounted for only half of the total output growth. Solow's model of exogenous technical change introduced a multiplier term *A* in the traditional production function approach, where *A* related to the exogenous technological advance parameter that permitted higher economic growth than could be accounted for by natural rates of growth in the underlying inputs (Solow, 1956). In other words, in Solow's model, economic growth was a result of *manna from heaven*. Thus, early economic growth models explained the growth in the wealth of nations as either caused due to natural rates of growth in the underlying inputs or determined by exogenous shocks of technological advance. A key feature missing in both models is the lack of relevance of human action, other than the passive notion of abstinence from current consumption (which leads to savings and increases in capital).

Endogenous growth models represented a marked departure from this tradition. Building on the insights provided by Arrow (1962) regarding the nonexcludable and nonrival nature of information, Romer (1990) modeled economic growth as resulting from endogenous investments in knowledge and the subsequent spillover benefits. In Romer's model of horizontal innovation—where new products and varieties are introduced to expand the existing set—the increasing returns to R&D activity stem from spillover benefits captured by organizations other than those making the initial investment in knowledge. Thus, in Romer's model, economic growth is a consequence of positive externalities of knowledge investments; rather than manna falling from heaven, it blows over from the neighbor.

Another variant of the endogenous growth model is by Aghion and Howitt (1992) who focus on vertical innovation consisting of improvements to existing products and services. They explicitly model creative destruction through the *business-stealing effect* or the negative externalities imposed by the innovators on the incumbents in the industry. Aghion and Howitt (1992), nonetheless, abstract away from the source of the innovation, assuming that innovations arrive randomly (as dictated by a Poisson process)

Strat. Entrepreneurship J., **1**: 263–286 (2007)
DOI: 10.1002/sej

due to research investments. Rather than receiving manna from heaven or it blowing over from the neighbor, their model posits economic growth as resulting from innovative activity of new entrants. But who exactly enters and how they come to enter is never explicitly specified, especially in terms of human actions.

Thus, endogenous growth models improve on the earlier models of growth by providing insights regarding the underlying mechanisms, and importantly, focus on economic growth as being caused by explicit firm action—either due to investments in knowledge by existing organizations, or due to research activity undertaken by new entrants. They advance our understanding of the underlying mechanisms by relating growth to *exogenous* spillovers of *endogenous* investments in knowledge. However, they assume that spillovers merely happen or are randomly generated. Our conceptualization highlights the active role of human or entrepreneurial action in the spillover process; thus, in addition to endogenous investments in knowledge by incumbent organizations, spillovers occur due to subsequent endogenous pursuit of innovation by individuals immersed in these institutional contexts. As a result, economic growth is not a consequence of manna that comes from heaven or blows over from your neighbor, but is due to deliberate investment and activity both by incumbent organizations and by entrepreneurial individuals within these organizations (who then carry it over to new entities through founding new ventures). Entrepreneurship is an important conduit of knowledge spillovers, absent which the knowledge would not have been commercialized and no growth would emanate from the investments in knowledge made by incumbent organizations. Importantly, such a conceptualization draws attention to the fact that economic growth occurs due to *path dependent* action that is local or *nonrandom* in nature.

As a result, growth at the spatial levels, ranging from city to region and country levels, is related to the inception and growth of specific industries and regions. Thus, growth at more macro levels can be understood only by relating it to the more micro-level activity that occurs within industries and regions that may be seeded due to institutions and organizations occupying the specific space. Entrepreneurship creates not just growth for individuals and new ventures that are launched, but also for the entire region where the KSSE occurs.

AVENUES FOR FUTURE RESEARCH

The emphasis of this article—that resources are the cornerstone for strategic entrepreneurship in shaping competitiveness and performance and, in particular, knowledge resources—is neither surprising nor novel, given the widespread acceptance of the resource-based view of the firm (Barney and Clark, 2007; Mahoney and Pandian, 1992; Penrose, 1959). Even the observation that these knowledge resources may be accessed via spillovers has been around since Arrow (1962), and the notion of absorptive capacity (Cohen and Levinthal, 1990) explicitly identifies what firms can do to access knowledge spillovers.

However, in both the resource-based view and the notion of absorptive capacity, the firm is assumed to exist exogenously, and the questions relate to strategic enhancement of its performance. By contrast, our knowledge spillover view of strategic entrepreneurship shifts the focus away from knowledge accessed by incumbent firms, both the one creating it as well as other firms making strategic investments to externally access that knowledge. Instead, employees and other individuals endogenously create a new venture to commercialize knowledge that is not highly valued by incumbent organizations. By taking knowledge and capabilities created in the context of one organization to launch a new venture, entrepreneurship serves as a valuable conduit of knowledge spillovers. KSSE not only links the knowledge generated in one organization with the knowledge accessed and used for commercialization and innovation, and ultimately a strong performance in a different organization, but also the literatures of entrepreneurship and strategy as they coalesce into the scholarly field of strategic entrepreneurship and its implications for economic growth.

In integrating these diverse literature streams, we have attempted to highlight core implications for extant thought. These also present exciting avenues for future research. In particular, we identify three key areas where efforts to develop the scholarly field of strategic entrepreneurship would be particularly beneficial.

From knowledge spillovers to new venture formation

The first set of questions for future research relate to the linkages from knowledge generation and spillovers in the form of new venture formation, and

Strat. Entrepreneurship J., **1**: 263–286 (2007)
DOI: 10.1002/sej

the strategic decisions in incumbent organizations that are confronted by the inevitability and/or the desirability of KSSE.. While recent attention on the reasons for KSSE (Agarwal *et al.*, 2004; Franco and Filson, 2007; Klepper, 2007; Lockett *et al.*, 2005; Louis *et al.*, 1989; Shane and Stuart, 2002; Shane, 2004; Zucker *et al.*, 1997) has significantly improved our understanding of why employees and scientists venture on their own, more work is needed to explore additional reasons and, importantly, to reconcile extant explanations for new venture formation. For instance, in the case of employee entrepreneurship, scholars have highlighted selection (Franco and Filson, 2007), abundance of underexploited knowledge (Agarwal *et al.*, 2004) and strategic disagreements (Klepper, 2007) as causes for new venture formation. However, rather than acting in isolation, these factors may work in tandem, and even reinforce each other. For example, in his account of the reasons for leaving Fairchild to create Intel, Gordon Moore states that 'while the catalyst for our Fairchild departure was the politics of internal control, the decision to leave Fairchild was motivated, in large part, by the fact that it had ceased to be the responsive and flexible firm we set out to build' (Moore and Davis, 2004: 8). Similarly, research on academic entrepreneurship highlights differences in scientist likelihood to create start-ups rather than license their technology, particularly when they perceive the true value of their invention is not recognized by existing firms (Lowe and Ziedonis, 2006). Research that examines the motives behind KSSE, particularly using a mixture of qualitative and quantitative analysis, would be very valuable in increasing our understanding of factors that enable or constrain KSSE.

Additionally, the effect of individual, organizational, and environmental factors on the incidence and type of KSSE is an important avenue for future research. At the individual level, there is a need to reconcile KSSE with the parallel stream of literature that examines knowledge spillovers through employee mobility (Almeida and Kogut, 1999; Rosenkopf and Almeida, 2003). While some labor economics models have attempted to address issues of individual choice among alternative options, additional research on the determinants of the choice to engage in KSSE would be fruitful. Also, since new ventures are often founded by *teams* of individuals, rather than lone inventors, further research is also needed on the selection process of the founding team members. Matching models (Becker and Murphy, 1992) may be a useful tool to gauge how individual complementarities may result in optimal selection choices. At the organizational level, while extant research has examined the effect of parent status and capabilities on the KSSE (Agarwal *et al.*, 2004; Burton *et al.*, 2002; Lockett *et al.*, 2005; Louis *et al.*, 1989; Shane and Stuart, 2002; Shane, 2004; Zucker *et al.*, 1997), additional factors, such as team composition in terms of size and heterogeneity at the parent organization, may impact the incidence of spinout formation. Similarly, environmental-level contingency conditions include the technological intensity of the industry and region, as well as whether the industry is in the growth or mature stage. Importantly, individual, organizational, and environmental factors may interact with each other—for example, KSSE may be more likely when individuals perceive an abundance of such opportunities due to a confluence of organizational (i.e., complementary rather than competitive positioning with parent firm) and environmental support (i.e., growth versus mature stage of industry life cycle). Alternatively, organizational level strategic decisions regarding intellectual property protection (Ziedonis, 2004) may interact with environmental-level policy regarding enforcement of noncompete clauses (Kim and Marschke, 2005) to impact knowledge spillover strategic entrepreneurship. Answers to such questions clearly have both strategic and policy implications, since they would not only shed light on the tension between knowledge creation and appropriation inherent in situations of cocreation of knowledge by organizations and the individuals embedded in their context, but also highlight the boundary conditions that enable creative construction versus creative destruction.

Measures of performance and growth

New firm entry is a fundamental construct in the Schumpeterian framework (1934), where an exogenous event, such as a scientific discovery, triggers entrepreneurial entry in the form of both *de novo* and *de alio* firms (Carroll *et al.*, 1996).[5] As agents of

---

[5] Although *de novo* (new start-up entrants) and *de alio* (diversifying entrants from other industries) firms have some conceptual differences, fundamentally they both represent entrepreneurial activity. They reflect differences in modes through which an entrepreneurial opportunity may be exploited (Shane and Venkataraman, 2000), but, in essence, are both Schumpeterian agents.

Strat. Entrepreneurship J., **1**: 263–286 (2007)
DOI: 10.1002/sej

change, these industry entrants increase innovative activity and stimulate growth and development not only within the industry, but also in specific regions where such entrepreneurial activities are located due to spillover effects (Geroski, 1995). However, spillovers are a function of resident knowledge in the first place, and if one assumes that today's new ventures are tomorrow's incumbents, the type of knowledge that entrants possess has important implications for the dynamics of spillover-led growth. Now, entrants differ with respect to the knowledge they possess at the time of entry, which has been shown to impact the evolution of firm capabilities over time. For example, there is preliminary evidence suggesting that spinouts, or new firms that are founded by employees of existing organizations as a direct result of knowledge spillovers from incumbents, seem to develop knowledge trajectories that are substantively different from other entrants (Agarwal *et al.*, 2004). Accordingly, one important avenue for research relates to understanding the long-term implications for innovation and regional growth as a function of the type of entrants that populate the entrepreneurial landscape. A starting point would be to explore the performance of spinouts in terms of their innovation input, quality, and productivity, as compared to other entrants. Do spinouts have higher innovation productivity compared to their counterparts? Given their heritage, are they more open to disruptive innovations? Accordingly, are the search patterns of spinouts in knowledge space different from that of other entrants? Behaviorally, having resulted partially from incumbent inertia, are spinouts more exploratory in nature? Being more cognizant of the possibility of someone else benefiting from the knowledge that one has invested in, are the internal incentive systems and resource allocation processes different from other entrants? Do they emphasize a different set of performance criteria, which are less likely to cause a focus on exploitation and drive our experimentation? A corollary would be to investigate whether the innovation performance of spinouts relative to nonspinouts is contingent on the knowledge intensity of the industry. These questions have larger implications for the regional growth aspect, which, as we argued before, is conditioned by the type of knowledge generated in a given context, and are, therefore, important beyond the immediate issue of competitive heterogeneity.

On the other hand, an emerging stream of literature that related past experiences and affiliations of the founding team on the type of innovation pursued

by new firms argues that firms whose teams have diverse prior company affiliations are more likely to pursue explorative behaviors and become technical pioneers, compared to a founding team from the same parent, which is more often involved in extending and utilizing knowledge from the parent company (Beckman, 2006). This raises the intriguing question whether the spillover of parental knowledge is a double-edged sword in that while spillovers empower the spinout, it may also have a debilitating effect through constraining the firm through the type of innovation it creates. This tension is fruitful grounds for new research.

Another important arena for future research relates to the way that exit or failure is typically viewed in both the strategy and entrepreneurship literature. When the focus is on the performance of the exiting venture, it is difficult to interpret failure in a positive light. However, emerging literature questions the prevalent bias against firm failure (Hoetker and Agarwal, 2007; Knott and Posen, 2005). Not only is the demise of less effective organizations or those that engaged in unsuccessful experimentation an integral part of a well-functioning market system (Davidsson, 2003), but creative construction or destruction can be fueled by failed ventures as much as it is by successful ones (Knott and Posen, 2005). While Audretsch and Thurik (2001) and Acs *et al.* (2004) show that the process of creative destruction creates value at a localized level, recent research has identified spillovers as a mechanism through which failure creates value. Hoetker and Agarwal's (2007) findings that the knowledge contributions of firms live on after their death support the idea articulated by Knott and Posen (2005: 618) that 'the knowledge produced by excess entrants while 'wasted,' in that it is no longer appropriable by the failed firm, may be captured by survivor firms through spillovers.' Arguing that failure attracts entrepreneurial entry through the release of resources into a local economy, Pe'er and Vertinsky (2007) make a case for a localized depiction of the process because of immobility of resources and lower search and transaction costs for local entrepreneurs. In other words, a negative entrepreneurial experience of an individual entrepreneur or investor when viewed from a spillover perspective may be a positive value-creating event when considered from the perspective of lessons learned by serial entrepreneurs or in the context of the local economy where the exit occurred. Additional research, however, is needed to unravel the mechanisms of such spillovers and

Strat. Entrepreneurship J., **1**: 263–286 (2007)
DOI: 10.1002/sej

quantify the magnitude and extent to which spillovers from failed ventures can act as triggers of growth and renewal.

Similarly, research that explores the linkages between the creation of entrepreneurial opportunities, their implementation through launching a new venture, and the subsequent impact on regional economic growth and development will help quantify the overall performance consequences and social welfare gains of knowledge spillover strategic entrepreneurship. Such research can also examine questions related to strategies pursued by communities, cities, regions, and countries to generate hothouses nurturing investments into knowledge along with KSSE that will trigger growth, employment creation, and competitiveness. The research agenda shedding light on these questions will be of importance and value not just to scholars of strategic entrepreneurship, but also the public policy community charged with creating viable and sustainable economic development. Finally, an important avenue of research is one that is in contrast to the Birch (1981) model of accounting for job generation by small versus large firms. Such research could formally quantify the *joint* effect of small and large firms on firm performance and in macro models of job generation, to identify synergies in job creation due to complementarities between small and large firms, rather than substitutability.

Knowledge spillovers and open innovation

The rise of vertically integrated innovation systems within firms where large firms internalized their R&D, product development, and commercialization processes was largely to create entry barriers through economies of scale and scope (Teece, 1986; Chandler, 1990). The business model revolved around developing a rich technology base through internal R&D and then developing a commercialization machine within the organization in order to exploit the accumulated knowledge through marketable products. One unintended consequence of this closed system of innovation was that basic research generated spillovers, which, as Nelson (1959) noted, was beyond the limited ability of funding firms to commercialize and, therefore, appropriate value. Behavioral and cognitive barriers to innovation, such as the *not invented here* syndrome (Katz and Allen, 1985) were recognized as organizational pathologies that accompanied the Chandlerian model of vertically integrated R&D and hindered the exploitation

of new technology. The consequences, when the technology was not licensed, were unexploited technologies until employees walked out and founded their own firms.

The open innovation model has been portrayed as the antithesis of the traditional vertically integrated model of R&D, product development, and marketing. By treating R&D as an open system—where valuable ideas can come from inside or outside the company and can be commercialized from within the company or by another entity—open innovation assumes that valuable knowledge is widely dispersed, and that, regardless of how capable the R&D system of an organization, it must identify, connect, and leverage external knowledge sources as a core process in innovation. In the closed innovation model, however, organizations invested in internal R&D to develop new products and services. Spillovers, a regrettable—yet necessary—cost of doing business, were an unintended by-product of the process. In the open innovation system, spillovers are integrated into the company's business model, and are treated as an opportunity to expand a firm's core activities or to spin off a technology and, thus, create a new business model (West *et al.*, 2006).

In other words, with innovation becoming more complex and recombinant in nature, and with the R&D paradigm shifting toward open systems, the notion of spillovers is under scrutiny. Instead of being considered a cost of doing business, the open innovation system suggests the intriguing possibility that spillovers need to be strategically managed. Traditionally, the imperative has been on firms to design *golden handcuffs* to prevent employees from leaving the firm with private knowledge, and to create structural and procedural barriers to the spillover of internally generated knowledge. Emerging views suggest that spillover potentials be identified, and leveraged through mechanisms such as corporate venture capital or spinoffs, or as through active IP management techniques that treat knowledge as a new class of revenue-generating assets (Rivette and Klein, 2000).

A whole set of research questions emerge around the notion of knowledge spillover and strategic entrepreneurship in the context of evolving R&D paradigms. What kind of institutional mechanisms can promote open innovation and the strategic use of knowledge spillovers? What is the changing role of the financial innovation machine in commercializing spillovers in an open innovation system? As

Strat. Entrepreneurship J., **1**: 263–286 (2007)
DOI: 10.1002/sej

more R&D gets outsourced and innovations become more complex and recombinant in nature, incumbent and potential entrepreneurs are likely to take on more of system integrator roles. With the strategic management of spillovers, is the balance likely to shift towards intrapreneurship—or being an entrepreneur within an incumbent organization—rather than spinout from an organization to start one's own venture? Will the long-term effect of open innovation be, quite counterintuitively, to stifle the *free* spillover of knowledge to the environment, and instead to keep it circulating within a tight network of incumbent corporate entities? From a recipient organization perspective, the traditional view has emphasized how internal R&D enables absorptive capacity, or the ability to identify, assimilate, and exploit externally created knowledge (Cohen and Levinthal, 1990). Fundamentally though, the firm has always been the locus, and internally generated knowledge the driver, of innovation. However, when external knowledge is afforded an equal role in innovation as internally generated knowledge, the ability of a firm's internal organization to systematically capture spillovers and develop knowledge integration capabilities assumes center stage. Although university-based research has long been recognized as a fountainhead of public knowledge characterized by open disclosure and rapid dissemination, the current trend is toward formal property protection of knowledge, associated secrecy, and slowing down technology transfer. Similar questions arise with regard to social welfare and the spillovers from academic research.

A long tradition of research has connected knowledge spillovers to macroeconomic growth. Regional clusters or the 'concentration of interconnected companies and institutions in a particular field' (Porter, 1998: 78) are important for spillovers. Recently, however, we have seen a trend toward fragmentation of clusters and de-agglomeration. Partly due to the increasing complexity of knowledge underlying innovation, and partly through forces of globalization that has seen the rise of knowledge clusters in Bangalore, India and Hsinchu, China, knowledge sources have increasingly dispersed away from traditional knowledge clusters. This has important implications for spillover-led innovation for firms. While earlier the imperative was to ensure that a firm was located in the main cluster, say Silicon Valley, so as to take advantage of knowledge spillovers that occurred through formal and informal interactions, and then *project* products and services based on such

knowledge to the rest of the world, the task is far more complicated now.

Fragmentation of innovation clusters, dispersion of knowledge to geographically diverse locations around the world, and technological convergence are combining to create imperatives on firms to capitalize on the diversity of knowledge sources from around the world and connect them into global innovation processes. The requirement now, due to increasing complexity of knowledge and fragmentation of regional knowledge clusters, is to develop what Doz, Santos, and Williamson (2001) termed *metanational* capabilities. With emerging markets serving as *learning laboratories* of innovation capabilities (Hitt, Li, and Worthington, 2005), developing a global footprint is becoming critical to searching out and mobilizing untapped pockets of technology and market intelligence that are dispersed across the globe. In parallel, along with pluralism in knowledge clusters, powerful new paradigms of innovation are emerging, such as open sourcing, crowd sourcing, peer-to-peer production, consumer-generated content, and collaborative creation.

Voluntary sharing of private knowledge and spillovers form the bedrock of these emerging business models of innovation. Innovation ecosystems, instead of trying to strategically throttle spillovers, are fundamentally based on externalities and the hope that others find value in the pursuit of knowledge created by a focal entity. In other words, the business model of revenue generation is increasingly dependent on strategically managing spillovers so as to create ecosystems around emerging technologies. All these contemporary developments bring into question not only fundamental producer-consumer relationships, conventional theories of firm boundaries, and concomitantly, but also bring into sharp focus the need to better understand the evolving role of spillovers as fountainheads of not only new firms, but also of powerful forces that are reshaping geopolitical power and global economies.

CONCLUSION

Recent research in academic and employee entrepreneurship has identified the key role of knowledge spillovers in the formation of new ventures and subsequent growth of industries and regions. In this article, we present our optimistic view of the process of creative construction due to what we term as the *knowledge spillover* view of strategic

Strat. Entrepreneurship J., **1**: 263–286 (2007)
DOI: 10.1002/sej

entrepreneurship. In reconciling literature streams across entrepreneurship, strategy, and growth (of regions, industries, and macroeconomies), we have identified areas in which knowledge spillover strategic entrepreneurship has already contributed to extant literature, and also highlight exciting ways in which the field of strategic entrepreneurship may develop. We hope that other scholars share our vision of the untapped opportunities in the area and heed our call for additional attention to questions that will inform our understanding of how strategy and entrepreneurship may interface to provide economic growth opportunities.

ACKNOWLEGEMENTS

All three authors contributed equally, and the names are arranged in alphabetical order. The research is supported by a grant from the E. Marion Kauffman Foundation. The manuscript has benefited from comments received from the editor, Jay Barney, as well as Janet Bercovitz, Joseph Mahoney, Steven Michael, Robert Strom, and participants at the *Strategic Entrepreneurship Journal* Conference in Oak Brook, Illinois, in 2007. The usual disclaimer applies.

REFERENCES

Abell DF. 1980. *Defining the Business: the Starting Point of Strategic Planning*. Prentice-Hall: Englewood Cliffs, NJ.

Acs ZJ, Audretsch DB, Braunerhjelm P, Carlsson B. 2004. The missing link: the knowledge filter and entrepreneurship in endogenous growth. Discussion paper 4783, Centre for Economic Policy Research, London.

Agarwal R, Bayus BL. 2002. The market evolution and sales takeoff of product innovations. *Management Science* 48(8): 1024–1041.

Agarwal R, Echambadi R, April F, Sarkar M. 2004. Knowledge transfer through inheritance: spin-out generation, development and performance. *Academy of Management Journal* 47: 501–522.

Aghion P, Howitt P. 1992. A model of growth through creative destruction. *Econometrica* 60(2): 323–351.

Ahuja G, Lampert C. 2001. Entrepreneurship in the large corporation. *Strategic Management Journal* 22(6–7): 521–543.

Almeida P, Kogut B. 1999. Localization of knowledge and the mobility of engineers in regional networks. *Management Science* 45(7): 905–917.

Ancona DG, Kochan TA, Scully M, Maanen JV, Westney DE. 1999. *Managing for the Future: Organizational Behavior and Processes*. South Western College Publishing: Cincinnati, OH.

Anton J, Yao D. 1995. Start-ups, spin-offs, and internal projects. *Journal of Law, Economics, and Organization* 11: 362–378.

Arrow KJ. 1962. Economic welfare and the allocation of resources for invention. In *The Rate and Direction of Inventive Activity*, Nelson RR (ed). Princeton University Press: Princeton, NJ; 609–626.

Audia PG, Greve HR. 2006. Less likely to fail: low performance, firm size, and factory expansion in the shipbuilding industry. *Management Science* 52(1): 83–94.

Audretsch DB. 1995. *Innovation and Industry Evolution*. MIT Press: Cambridge, MA.

Audretsch DB, Stephan PE. 1996. Company-scientist locational links: the case of biotechnology. *American Economic Review* 86(3): 641–652.

Audretsch DB, Thurik R. 2001. What's new about the new economy? Sources of growth in the managed and entrepreneurial economies. *Industrial and Corporate Change* 10(1): 267–315.

Barney JE, Hesterly WS. 2006. *Strategic Management and Competitive Advantage*. Pearson Prentice-Hall: Upper Saddle River, NJ.

Barney JE. 1991. Firm resources and sustained competitive advantage. *Journal of Management* 17(1): 99–120.

Barney JE, Clark DN. 2007. *Resource-Based Theory: Creating and Sustaining Competitive Advantage*. Oxford University Press: New York.

Barr PS, Stimpert JL, Huff AS. 1992. Cognitive change, strategic action, and organizational renewal. *Strategic Management Journal* 13(Special Issue): 15–36.

Becker GS. 1964. *Human Capital*. National Bureau of Economic Research: New York.

Becker GS, Murphy KM. 1992. The division of labor, coordination costs, and knowledge. *Quarterly Journal of Economics* 107: 1137–1160.

Beckman C. 2006. The influence of founding team company affiliations on firm behavior. *Academy of Management Journal* 49: 741–758.

Bhide AV. 2000. *The Origin and Evolution of New Businesses*. Oxford University Press: New York.

Birch DL. 1981. Who creates jobs? *The Public Interest* 65: 3–14.

Brittain JW, Freeman J. 1986. Entrepreneurship in the semiconductor industry. Unpublished manuscript from the 46th Annual Meetings of the Academy of Management, New Orleans, LA.

Burton MD, Sorensen J, Beckman C. 2002. Coming from good stock: career histories and new venture formation. *Research in the Sociology of Organizations* 19: 229–262.

Carlton D, Perloff JM. 2006. *Modern Industrial Organization*. Longman Publishing: Boston, MA.

Carroll GR, Bigelow LS, Seidel ML, Tsai LB. 1996. The fates of de novo and de alio producers in the American

Strat. Entrepreneurship J., **1**: 263–286 (2007)
DOI: 10.1002/sej

automobile industry 1885–1981. *Strategic Management Journal* **17**(Summer): 117–137.

Chandler A. 1990. *Scale and Scope: The Dynamics of Industrial Capitalism*. Harvard University Press: Cambridge, MA.

Chatterji AK. 2005. Spawned with a silver spoon?: Entrepreneurial performance and innovation in the medical device industry. Working paper, Duke University.

Chesbrough H, Rosenbloom RS. 2002. The role of the business model in capturing value from innovation: evidence from Xerox Corporation's technology spin-off companies. *Industrial and Corporate Change* **11**(3): 529–555.

Christensen CM, Overdorf M. 2000. Meeting the challenge of disruptive change. *Harvard Business Review* **78**(2): 66–76.

Christensen CM. 1993. The rigid disk drive industry: a history of commercial and technological turbulence. *Business History Review* **67**(Winter): 531–588.

Christensen CM. 1997. The Innovator's Dilemma. Harvard Business School Press: Cambridge, MA.

Coff RW. 1997. Human assets and management dilemmas: coping with the hazards on the road to resource-based theory. *Academy of Management Review* **22**: 374–402.

Cohen W, Levinthal DA. 1990. Absorptive capacity: a new perspective on learning and innovation. *Administrative Science Quarterly* **35**: 128–152.

Cohendet P, Llerena P. 2003. Routines and incentives: the role of communities in the firm. *Industrial and Corporate Change* **12**(2): 271–297.

Companys YE, McMullen JS. Strategic entrepreneurs at work: the nature, discovery, and exploitation of entrepreneurial opportunities. *Small Business Economics Journal* **28**(4): 301–322.

Cooper AC, Gimeno-Gascon FJ, Woo CY. 1991. A resource-based prediction of new venture survival and growth. Academy of Management Best Paper Proceedings.

Cyert RM, March JG. 1963. *A Behavioral Theory of the Firm*. Blackwell Publishers, Inc.: Malden, MA.

Davidsson P. 2003. The domain of entrepreneurship research: some suggestions. In *Advances in Entrepreneurship, Firm Emergence, and Growth* (Volume 6), Katz J, Shepherd S (eds). Elsevier/JAI Press: Oxford, U.K.; 315–372.

Domar E. 1946. Capital expansion, rate of growth, and employment. *Econometrica* **14**(2): 137–147.

Doz Y, Santos J, Williamson P. 2001. *From Global to Metanational: How Companies Win in the Knowledge Economy*. Harvard Business School Press: Cambridge, MA.

Franco A, Filson D. 2007. Spin-outs: knowledge diffusion through employee mobility. *Rand Journal of Economics*. Forthcoming.

Ferguson C. 1988. From the people who brought you voodoo economics. *Harvard Business Review* **66**(3): 55–62.

Geroski PA. 1995. What do we know about entry? *International Journal of Industrial Organization* **13**: 421–440.

Ghemawat P. 1991. *Commitment: The Dynamic of Strategy*. Free Press: New York.

Gort M. 1962. *Diversification and Integration in American Industry*. Princeton University Press: Princeton, NJ.

Gort M, Klepper S. 1982. Time paths in the diffusion of product innovations. *Economic Journal* **92**: 630–653.

Grant RM. 1996. Prospering in dynamically-competitive environments: organization capability as knowledge integration. *Organization Science* **7**(4): 375–387.

Greve HR. 1998. Performance, aspirations, and risky organizational change. *Administrative Science Quarterly* **43**(1): 58–86.

Greve HR, Taylor A. 2000. Innovations as catalysts for organizational change: shifts in organizational cognition and search. *Administrative Science Quarterly* **45**(March): 54–80.

Griliches Z. 1979. Issues in assessing the contribution of research and development to productivity growth. *Bell Journal of Economics* **10**: 92–116.

Griliches Z. 1992. The search for R&D spillovers. *Scandinavian Journal of Economics* **94**(Supplement): 29–47.

Hannan MT, Freeman J. 1984. Structural inertia and organizational change. *American Sociological Review* **49**: 149–164.

Hannan MT, Freeman J. 1987. The ecology of organizational founding: American labor unions, 1836–1985. *American Journal of Sociology* **92**: 910–943.

Hannan MT, Freeman J. 1989. Organizational Ecology. Harvard University Press: Cambridge, MA.

Harrod R. 1939. An essay in dynamic theory. *The Economic Journal* **49**(193): 14–33.

Hart D. 2003. *The Emergence of Entrepreneurship Policy: Governance, Start-Ups, and Growth in the U.S. Knowledge Economy*. Cambridge University Press: Cambridge, N.Y.

Hay DA, Morris DJ. 1979. *Industrial Economics*. Oxford University Press: Oxford, U.K.

Helfat CE, Lieberman M. 2002. The birth of capabilities: market entry and the importance of pre-history. *Industrial and Corporate Change* **11**(4): 725–760.

Henderson RM, Clark KB. 1990. Architectural innovation: the reconfiguration of existing product technologies and the failure of established firms. *Administrative Science Quarterly* **35**(1): 9–30.

Hitt MA, Li H, Worthington WJ. 2005. Emerging markets as learning laboratories: learning behaviors of local firms and foreign entrants in different institutional contests. *Management and Organization Review* **1**: 353–380.

Hitt MA, Sexton DL, Ireland RD, Camp SM. 2002. Strategic entrepreneurship: integrating entrepreneurial and strategic management perspectives. In *Strategic Entrepreneurship: Creating a New Mindset*, Hitt MA, Sexton DL, Ireland RD, Camp SM (eds). Blackwell Publishers: Oxford, U.K.; 1–16.

Strat. Entrepreneurship J., **1**: 263–286 (2007)
DOI: 10.1002/sej

Hoetker G, Agarwal R. 2007. Death hurts, but it isn't fatal: the Post-exit diffusion of knowledge created by innovative companies. *Academy of Management Journal* **50**(2): 446–467.

Hoopes D, Madsen TL. 2007. A capability-based view of competitive heterogeneity. Working paper, Santa Clara University.

Hotelling H. 1929. Stability in competition. *Economic Journal* **39**: 41–57.

Ingram P, Baum JAC. 1997. Opportunity and constraint: organizations learning from the operating and competitive experience of industries. *Strategic Management Journal* **18**(Summer Special Edition): 75–98.

Irwin DA, Klenow PJ. 1994. Learning by doing spillovers in the semiconductor industry. *Journal of Political Economy* **102**: 1200–1227.

Iwai K. 1984. Schumpeterian dynamics: an evolutionary model of innovation and imitation. *Journal of Economic Behavior and Organization* **5**: 159–190.

Kaplan RS, Norton DP. 1992. The balanced scorecard: measures that drive performance. *Harvard Business Review* **70**: 71–79.

Kaplan S, Henderson R. 2005. Inertia and incentives: bridging organizational economics and organizational theory. *Organization Science* **16**(5): 509–521.

Katz R, Allen T. 1985. Project performance and the locus of influence in the R&D matrix. *Academy of Management Journal* **28**: 67–87.

Keller W. 1998. Are international R&D spillovers trade related? Analyzing spillovers among randomly matched trade partners. *European Economic Review* **42**: 1469–1481.

Kim J, Marschke G. 2005. Labor mobility of scientists, technological diffusion, and the firms patenting decision. *Rand Journal of Economics* **36**(2): 298–317.

Klepper S. 2002. The capabilities of new firms and the evolution of the U.S. Automobile industry. *Industrial and Corporate Change* **11**: 645–666.

Klepper S. 2007. Disagreements, spinoffs, and the evolution of Detroit as the capital of the U.S. automobile industry. *Management Science* **53**(4): 616–631.

Klepper S, Simons K. 2000. Dominance by birth right: entry of prior radio producers and competitive ramifications in the U.S. television receiver industry. *Strategic Management Journal* **21**: 997–1016.

Klepper S, Sleeper S. 2005. Entry by spinoffs. *Management Science* **51**(8): 1291–1306.

Knott A, Posen H. 2005. Is failure good? *Strategic Management Journal* **26**(7): 617–641.

Krugman P. 1991. Increasing returns and economic geography. *Journal of Political Economy* **99**(3): 483–499.

Lancaster KJ. 1966. A new approach to consumer theory. *Journal of Political Economy* **74**:132–157.

Lemelin A. 1982. Relatedness in the patterns of interindustry diversification. *Review of Economics and Statistics* **64**: 646–657.

Leonard-Barton D. 1992. Core capabilities and core rigidities: a paradox in managing new product development. *Strategic Management Journal* **13**(Special Issue): 111–125.

Levinthal DA, March JG. 1993. The myopia of learning. *Strategic Management Journal* **14**(Winter): 95–112.

Liebeskind J. 1996. Knowledge, strategy and the theory of the firm. *Strategic Management Journal* **17**(Winter Special Issue): 441–452.

Lippman S, Rumelt R. 1992. Demand uncertainty and investment in industry-specific capital. *Industrial and Corporate Change* **1**(1): 235–262.

Lockett A, Siegel D, Wright M, Ensley D. 2005. The creation of spin-off firms at public research institutions: managerial and policy implications. *Research Policy* **34**(7): 981–993.

Louis KS, Blumenthal D, Gluck ME, Stoto MA. 1989. Entrepreneurs in academe: an exploration of behaviors among life scientists. *Administrative Science Quarterly* **34**: 110–131.

Lowe RA, Ziedonis AA. 2006. Overoptimism and the performance of entrepreneurial firms. *Management Science* **52**: 173–186.

Mahoney JT, Pandian JR. 1992. The resource-based view within the conversation of strategic management. *Strategic Management Journal* **13**(5): 363–380.

March JG. 1991. Exploration and exploitation in organizational learning. *Organization Science* **2**(1): 71–87.

March JG, Simon HA. 1958. *Organizations*. John Wiley and Sons: New York.

Marris R. 1964. *The Economic Theory of Managerial Capitalism.* Free Press of Glencoe: New York.

McCraw TK. 2007. *Prophet of Innovation: Joseph Schumpeter and Creative Destruction.* Belknap Press of Harvard University Press: Cambridge, MA.

McClelland D. 1961. *The Achieving Society.* Free Press: New York.

MacDonald JM. 1985. R&D and the directions of diversification. *The Review of Economics and Statistics* **67**: 583–590.

Milgrom P, Roberts J. 1992. *Economics, Organizations, and Management.* Prentice-Hall: Englewood Cliffs, NJ.

Mintzberg H. 1973. Strategy-making in three modes. *California Management Review* **16**(2): 44–53.

Montgomery CA, Hariharan S. 1991. Diversified expansion by large established firms. *Journal of Economic Behavior and Organization* **15**: 71–89.

Moore G, Davis K. 2004. Learning the Silicon Valley way. In *Building High-Tech Clusters: Silicon Valley and Beyond*, Bresnahan T, Gambardella A (eds). Cambridge University Press: Cambridge, MA.

Moran P, Ghoshal S. 1999. Markets, firms and the process of economic development. *Academy of Management Review* **24**(3): 390–412.

Nelson R. 1959. The simple economics of basic scientific research. *Journal of Political Economy* **67**: 297–306.

Strat. Entrepreneurship J., **1**: 263–286 (2007)
DOI: 10.1002/sej

Nelson R. 1992. *National Innovation Systems: A Comparative Analysis.* Oxford University Press: New York.

Nelson R, Winter SG. 1982. *An Evolutionary Theory of Economic Change.* The Belknap Press of Harvard University Press: Cambridge, MA.

Nonaka I. 1994. A dynamic theory of organizational knowledge creation. *Organization Science* **5**(1): 14–37.

O'Shea RP, Allen TJ, Chevalier A, Roche F. 2005. Entrepreneurial orientation, technology transfer and spinoff performance of U.S. universities. *Research Policy* **34**(7): 994–1009.

Pe'er AA, Vertinsky I. 2007. Firm exits as a determinant of new entry: is there evidence of local creative destruction? *Working paper,* Dartmouth College.

Penrose E. 1959. *The Theory of the Growth of the Firm.* Oxford University Press: Oxford, U.K.

Pfeffer J. 1990. Incentives in organizations: the importance of social relations. In *Organization Theory: From Chester Barnard to the Present and Beyond,* Williamson OE (ed). Oxford University Press: New York.

Philips DJ. 2002. The Parent-progeny transfer and organizational mortality: the case of Silicon Valley law firms, 1946–1996. *Administrative Science Quarterly* **47**(3): 474–506.

Plummer LA, Haynie JM, Godesiabois J. 2007. An essay on the origins of entrepreneurial opportunity. *Small Business Economics Journal* **28**(4): 363–379.

Porter ME. 1998. Clusters and the new economics of competition. *Harvard Business Review* **76**(6): 77–90.

Ricardo D. 1817. *On the Principles of Political Economy and Taxation.* Empiricus Books: London.

Rivette K, Klein D. 2000. *Rembrandts in the Attic: Unlocking the Hidden Value of Patents.* Harvard Business School Press: Cambridge, MA.

Romer PM. 1990. Endogenous technological change. *Journal of Political Economy* **98**(October, Part 2): 71–102.

Rosenkopf L, Almeida P. 2003. Overcoming local search through alliances and mobility. *Management Science* **49**(6): 751–766.

Rumelt RP. 1984. Towards a strategic theory of the firm. In *Competitive Strategic Management,* Lamb RB. Prentice-Hall: Engelwood Cliffs, NJ; 566–570.

Rumelt RP. 1987. Theory, strategy and entrepreneurship. In *The Competitive Challenge,* Teece D (ed). Ballinger: Cambridge, MA.

Salop SC. 1979. Monopolistic competition with outside goods. *Bell Journal of Economics* **10**: 141–156.

Sastry A, Coen C. 2001. Beyond the beginning: building a theory of organizational imprinting. Working paper, University of Michigan.

Saxenian A. 1994. *Regional Advantage: Culture and Competition in Silicon Valley and Route 128.* Harvard University Press: Cambridge, MA.

Schulz M. 2001. The uncertain relevance of newness: organizational learning and knowledge flow. *Academy of Management Journal* **44**(4): 661–681.

Schumpeter JA. 1934. *The Theory of Economic Development.* Harvard University Press: Cambridge, MA.

Shane S. 2000. Prior knowledge and the discovery of entrepreneurial opportunities. *Organizational Science* **11**: 448–469.

Shane S. 2004. *Academic Entrepreneurship.* Edward Elgar Publishing: Cheltenham, U.K.

Shane S, Eckhardt J. 2003. The individual-opportunity nexus. In *Handbook of Entrepreneurship Research,* Acs ZJ, Audretsch DB (eds). Springer: New York; 161–194.

Shane S, Stuart T. 2002. Organizational endowments and the performance of university start-ups. *Management Science* **48**(1): 154–170.

Shane S, Venkataraman S. 2000. The promise of entrepreneurship as a field of research. *Academy of Management Review* **25**(1): 218–228.

Shaver KG. 2003. The social psychology of entrepreneurial behaviour. In *Handbook of Entrepreneurship Research,* Acs ZJ, Audretsch DB (eds). Kluwer Law International: London; 331–357.

Smith DK, Alexander RC. 1988. *Fumbling the Future.* William Morrow: New York.

Solow RM. 1956. A contribution to the theory of economic growth. *Quarterly Journal of Economics* **70**: 65–94.

Somaya D, Williamson IO, Lorinkova N. 2008. Gone but not lost: the different performance impacts of employee mobility between cooperators versus competitors. *Academy of Management Journal* (in press).

Spender JC. 1996. Making knowledge the basis of a dynamic theory of the firm. *Strategic Management Journal* **17**(10): 45–62.

Stevenson HH, Jarillo JC. 1990. A paradigm of entrepreneurship: entrepreneurial management. *Strategic Management Journal* **11**(Summer Special Issue): 17–27.

Stewart JF, Harris RS, Carleton WT. 1984. The role of market structure in merger behavior. *Journal of Industrial Economics* **32**: 293–312.

Stinchcombe AL. 1965. Social structure and organizations. In *Handbook of Organizations,* March JG (ed). Rand McNally: Chicago, IL; 142–193.

Teece DJ, Pisano G, Schuen A. 1990. *Firm Capabilities, Resources, and the Concept of Strategy,* University of California, Berkeley: Berkeley, CA.

Teece DJ. 1986. Profiting from technological innovations. *Research Policy* **15**(6): 285–306.

Teece DJ, Pisano G, Shuen A. 1997. Dynamic capabilities and strategic management. *Strategic Management Journal* **18**(7): 509–533.

Tripsas M, Gavetti G. 2000. Capabilities, cognition, and inertia: evidence from digital imaging. *Strategic Management Journal* **21**(10–11): 1147–1161.

Tushman ML, Anderson P. 1986. Technological discontinuities and organizational environments. *Administrative Science Quarterly* **31**: 439–465.

Wernerfelt B. 1984. A resource-based view of the firm. *Strategic Management Journal* **5**(2): 171–180.

West J, Vanhaverbeke W, Chesbrough H. 2006. Open innovation: a research agenda. In *Open Innovation: Researching a New Paradigm*, Chesbrough H, Vanhaverbeke W, West J (eds). Oxford University Press: Oxford, U.K., 2006; 285–307.

Wiggins SN. 1995. Entrepreneurial enterprises, endogenous ownership, and the limits to firm size. *Economic Inquiry* **33**: 54–69.

Winter SG. 2003. Understanding dynamic capabilities. *Strategic Management Journal* **24**(10): 991–995.

Yli-Renko HK, Autio E, Sapienza H. 2001. Social capital, knowledge acquisition, and knowledge exploitation in young technology-based firms. *Strategic Management Journal* **22**(6/7): 529–613.

Ziedonis R. 2004. Don't fence me in: fragmented markets for technology and the patent acquisition strategies of firms. *Management Science* **50**: 804–820.

Zollo M, Winter SG. 2002. Deliberate learning and the evolution of dynamic capabilities. *Organization Science* **13**: 339–351.

Zucker LG, Darby MR, Brewer MB. 1997. Intellectual human capital and the birth of U.S. biotechnology enterprises. *American Economic Review* **88**: 290–306.

Strat. Entrepreneurship J., **1**: 263–286 (2007)
DOI: 10.1002/sej

9

J Technol Transfer (2008) 33:249–258
DOI 10.1007/s10961-008-9086-y

Proof of concept centers: accelerating the commercialization of university innovation

Christine A. Gulbranson · David B. Audretsch

Published online: 8 February 2008
© Springer Science+Business Media, LLC 2008

Abstract Innovation drives economic growth. Economic growth leads to longer, healthier lives by transforming yesterday's luxuries into better, cheaper, and more efficient goods and services. University research is a key component of our nation's innovative capacity. In an increasingly dynamic and global economy, the institutional infrastructure is inefficient at moving university innovations to the marketplace. University researchers often face convoluted procedures with insufficient guidance to commercialize their innovations. As angel investors and venture capitalists increasingly invest in later stage enterprises (See PricewaterhouseCoopers, and National Venture Capital Association. *MoneyTree*^{TM} *survey report.* 2007. and VentureOne, "Venture Capital Industry Report." DowJones 2006), researchers face difficulty finding early stage funding to develop and test prototypes and conduct market research. In order to fill this funding gap and accelerate the commercialization of university innovations, a new type of organization has emerged—the proof of concept center. An analysis of the Deshpande Center at MIT and the von Liebig Center at UCSD provides valuable insight into how proof of concept centers can facilitate the transfer of university innovations into commercial applications.

Keywords Innovation · Research and development · Scientists · Entrepreneurship · Venture capital

JEL Classifications 03 · L26

C. A. Gulbranson
The Kauffman Foundation, Kansas City, MO, USA
e-mail: cgulbranson@kauffman.org

D. B. Audretsch (✉)
Max Planck Institute of Economics, Jena, Germany
e-mail: audretsch@econ.mpg.de

D. B. Audretsch
Indiana University, Bloomington, IN, USA

1 Introduction

Globalization has shifted the competitiveness of leading developed economies away from standardized manufacturing activities towards knowledge-based industries and services (Friedman 2005). As Thurow (2002, pp. 38–39) observes, "The world is moving from an industrial era based on natural resources into a knowledge-based era based on skill, education, and research and development." Knowledge has emerged as a crucial source of employment and economic growth in the global economy because it is the basis for innovation.[1]

Where does the crucial resource of knowledge come from? While investments by private firms in research and development (R&D) are a crucial source of knowledge, so too are investments made in research and education at universities. However, as Senator Birch Bayh observed some three decades ago, investments in university research do not automatically spill over to generate innovative activity and economic growth. "A wealth of scientific talent at American colleges and universities—talent responsible for the development of numerous innovative scientific breakthroughs each year—is going to waste as a result of bureaucratic red tape and illogical government regulations..."[2] Audretsch et al. (2006) suggest that it is the knowledge filter that stands between investment in university research on the one hand, and its commercialization through innovation, leading ultimately to economic growth, on the other.

Seen through the eyes of Senator Bayh, the magnitude of the knowledge filter is daunting, "What sense does it make to spend billions of dollars each year on government-supported research and then prevent new developments from benefiting the American people because of dumb bureaucratic red tape?"[3]

Thus, if university research does not passively spill over for commercialization and innovation, then institutions are needed to facilitate the spillover of university research. As Litan, Mitchell and Reedy (2007, p. 57) emphasize, "A perennial challenge related to university/driven innovation has been to ensure that university structures help, not hinder, innovation and its commercialization."

The purpose of this paper is to examine two important examples of institutions devoted towards facilitating the spillover and commercialization of university research, the Deshpande Center at MIT and the von Liebig Center at the University of California San Diego (UCSD). Both of these centers are mechanisms designed to fill the "funding gap" of seed stage investing as angel investors and venture capital funds shift their focus to larger and later stage investments (Fishback et al. 2007). In order to fill this funding gap and accelerate the commercialization of university innovations, a new type of organization has emerged—the proof of concept center.

The proof of concept center accelerates the commercialization of innovations out of the university and into the marketplace. It does this by providing seed funding to novel, early-stage research that most often would not be funded by any other conventional source. Unlike some accelerators, there is no central shared laboratory space; each of the funded investigators continues to perform their research in their own respective laboratories. The proof of concept center facilitates and fosters the exchange of ideas between the university innovators and industry via various mentors associated with the center. An analysis of the

---

[1] Investments in knowledge are the driving force of economic growth in Romer (1986) and Lucas (1993).

[2] Introductory statement of Birch Bayh, September 13, 1978, cited from the Association of University Technology Managers Report (AUTM) (2004, p. 5).

[3] Statement by Birch Bayh, April 13, 1980, on the approval of S. 414 (Bayh-Dole) by the U.S. Senate on a 91–94 vote, cited from (AUTM 2004, p. 16).

Deshpande Center at MIT and the von Liebig Center at UCSD provides valuable insight into how proof of concept centers can facilitate the transfer and spillover of university research into innovative activity and commercial applications.

2 The von Liebig Center at UCSD

In 2001, the William J. von Liebig Foundation awarded UCSD's Jacobs School of Engineering a $10 million gift in order to create the William J. von Liebig Center. The von Liebig Center's stated mission is "to accelerate the commercialization of UCSD innovations into the marketplace, foster and facilitate the exchange of ideas between the University and industry, and prepare engineering students for the entrepreneurial workplace."[4] In order to accomplish these goals, the Center uses three complimentary approaches: seed funding, advisory services, and educational programs.

2.1 Seed funding

The von Liebig Center provides seed funding ranging from $15,000 to $75,000 to support the commercialization of UCSD discoveries with near-term market prospects. These funds are not used for basic research, but rather to evaluate the commercial potential of existing research. Von Liebig funding allows recipients to focus on development, testing, or prototype construction, and/or conduct specific market research. This evaluation may lead to industry collaboration, licensing, the formation of a new company, or the abandonment of the technology for commercial application.

The von Liebig Center typically funds ten to twelve projects annually, which ranged from 35–60% of the proposals submitted to the center. In order to be considered for funding, a project must include at least one Jacobs School of Engineering faculty member.[5] The first step in the funding process is to submit a Statement of Intent,[6] which outlines the project. After the Statement of Intent is submitted, the Center Commercialization Director assigns an advisor to the faculty member to help prepare the proposal and presentation to the review panel. The following month the full funding application[7] is submitted. A five to eight member review panel, with both technical and business expertise, then reviews the application. The review panel recommends candidates to the Center based on the technology's novelty and need, the potential market size, the market definition, the technology's maturity, the utility of the grant, the intellectual property position, and the Principle Investigator's credibility. The final funding decision is made with input from Advisors and Center Staff.

---

[4] From the Center's website, available at http://www.vonliebig.ucsd.edu/about/mission.shtml.

[5] The center will work with researchers in other disciplines to find a partner in the Jacobs school who may be interested in collaboration. The Center is planning to expand beyond the Engineering school to engage researchers across the campus in 2008.

[6] A Statement of Intent includes the name of the Principle Investigator (PI), the project title, and a brief outline of up to 500 words describing the project.

[7] The full funding application requests that the PI describe the project goals, the project plan, the commercialization potential of the technology, the backgrounds of the team members, any intellectual property associated with the technology, and a preliminary budget summary. The budget may include only direct project expenses, including the salaries and fees of graduate and undergraduate students, but may not include faculty salaries, patent and legal costs, UCSD overhead costs, or equipment costs over $5,000.

After a grant is awarded, a von Liebig advisor works with the principle investigator to prepare a commercialization plan that includes technical and business milestones as well as the budget needed to complete the milestones over a period of twelve months. The advisor then requests the authorization of funds corresponding to the first milestone from the commercialization director. Further payments are contingent on reaching established milestones. Upon completion of the project, PIs are requested to submit a two-page summary of the major findings of the project.

2.2 Advisory services

As of 2007 the von Liebig Center had six paid advisors[8] that work at the Center part-time These advisors support approximately ten projects each. Advisors are selected based on their backgrounds in a technical discipline, having considerable experience in start-up and early stage technology ventures, and possessing significant connections to local companies and investment sources. These connections are extremely valuable because they link the technology and researchers to important external networks. The Advisors and Center staff work in partnership with representatives from the university technology transfer office (TechTIPS) who are responsible for protecting the intellectual property, and negotiating and executing the license agreements to the startups or licensees. The Center also works in coordination with external community organizations (CONNECT, Tech Coast Angels, and others to coach, offer guidance and to identify entrepreneurs and investment capital that will help the nascent companies move down the commercialization pipeline. The von Liebig Center makes these advisory services available to all researchers at the Jacobs School even if they do not receive funding from the Center. The Center also provides incubation space and needed meeting locations for pre-companies to operate before they secure capital and execute the license agreement.

2.3 Educational programs

The Center's educational programs can be divided into three categories: courses, lectures and seminars, and conferences. The von Liebig Center currently supports four graduate level courses[9] designed by engineers to prepare students for the challenges of an entrepreneurial work environment. Instructors with both academic and industry experience teach these courses. Approximately 400 students have completed one or more of the courses and a small number of students have also had the opportunity to work for the Center as interns. Of these, at least ten have started companies, and another six have gone into non-traditional fields, such as technology investment banking and strategy consulting.

The Center hosts lectures and seminars to educate students, faculty, and researchers. The Center's most prominent series is the von Liebig Forum, which brings in high-profile innovators from industry and academia to give presentations and interviews.

---

[8] The Center's current six advisors are Hal DeLong (Life Sciences), Mike Elconin (IT), Steve Flaim (Life Sciences), Roger Moyers (IT/Materials), Jack Savidge (Structural Materials) and Mary Zoeller (IT).

[9] The Center offers four courses: ENG 201-Venture Mechanics, ENG202-Enterprise Dynamics, ENG203-Applied Innovation, and ENG207-Corporate Entrepreneurship for Global Competitiveness. Detailed information for these courses is available on the Center's website at http://www.vonliebig.ucsd.edu/education/education_courses/.

The von Liebig Center also hosts conferences for faculty, researchers, and graduate students such as the National Collegiate Inventors and Innovator Alliance's "Invention to Venture" conference in San Diego. These educational programs are all designed to further the student and faculty levels of awareness, education and familiarity with relevant and practical issues related to early stage commercialization.

3 The Deshpande Center at MIT

The Deshpande Center was founded at the MIT School of Engineering in 2002 from an initial $17.5 million donation by Jaishree and Gururaj Deshpande. The center was created with the mission to increase the impact of MIT technologies on the marketplace. The Deshpande Center achieves its mission through the Grant Program, Catalyst Program, Innovation Teams (I-Teams) and Events.[10]

3.1 Grant program

The Deshpande Center provides up to $250,000 to prepare MIT technology projects for commercialization. The Center holds two rounds of grant proposals each year and awards two types of grants. The Deshpande Center provides Ignition Grants (up to $50,000) for novel projects that may be used for exploratory experiments and proof of concept. Innovation Grants (up to $250,000) are also awarded to take an innovation into full development. Innovation Grants are only awarded once a project has established proof of concept and has identified an R&D path and an IP strategy. This allows a project to attract venture capitalists or companies interested in investing in its technology.

The Deshpande Center typically awards sixteen grants each year,[11] which is approximately 18 percent of the proposals submitted to the center.[12] Originally the Center was exclusively focused on research created in the School of Engineering, but in spring 2005 the Center began accepting proposals from all MIT faculty. A multidisciplinary committee selected from inside the Institute and from the Catalyst (mentors) program evaluates all applications. After the committee recommends grant candidates, a catalyst is assigned to each project and a full proposal is submitted.[13] Grant recipients are required to participate in the Catalyst Program, attend Center events, establish IP if appropriate, communicate the project's progress through various means, and avoid conflicts of interest.

3.2 Catalyst program

Unlike the von Liebig Center, the Deshpande Center uses volunteers to provide advisory services through its Catalyst Program. The center has approximately 50 Catalysts with

---

[10] From the Center's website, available at http://web.mit.edu/deshpandecenter/about.html.

[11] Fourteen projects have been awarded multiple grants.

[12] Since 2002, 64 projects have been funded out of over 365 reviewed proposals.

[13] The full proposal is similar to the von Liebig proposal and should be no longer than ten pages in length and includes an executive summary, the market opportunity of the innovation, the proposed approach to innovation, the commercialization process, the impact of the technology, similar or previous technologies, the progress to date of the research, the research plan and milestones, resources and budget, other funding provided, team and collaboration information, and a budget proposal.

technology innovation and entrepreneurial experience. Catalysts do not represent any company interests; they provide mentorship and assistance to MIT research teams in order to facilitate the commercialization process. Catalysts also agree to keep discussions in confidence and manage conflict of interest.

3.3 Innovation teams and events

The educational aspect of the Deshpande Center is divided into events and Innovations Teams. The Center hosts several events for grant recipients including IdeaStream, Open House, and the Catalyst Party. IdeaStream is an annual networking event that showcases MIT technologies to venture capitalists, entrepreneurs, and other researchers. Open House and the Catalyst Party are informal events that promote the exchange of ideas and the formation of new collaborations.

The Center's involvement in Innovation Teams (I-Teams) is part of a three-way partnership with the School of Engineering and the MIT Entrepreneurship Center. The I-Teams program is open to graduate students across MIT and is always filled. Six Deshpande grantees are chosen to be part of the I-Teams program each year and are given the opportunity to work with student teams to discover and define their commercialization plan. Data is not available to assess the number of I-team participants who pursue entrepreneurial careers after graduation.

4 Comparing and evaluating the centers

Table 1 provides a comparison between the Deshpande and von Liebig Centers. While both centers were initially funded from philanthropic donations, the initial funding of the Deshpande Center was 75% greater than for the von Liebig Center. However, both centers have funded about the same number of projects.

There are many obstacles in evaluating the performance of the two centers with respect to quantitative metrics of success. First, both centers have only been in existence for approximately five years; thus, there has not been enough time to evaluate the end result of many projects. Second, there are no accepted benchmarks to define success. While the formation of a business or the licensing of a technology are easy to identify as successes, it is difficult to determine failures. For example, if a researcher receives funding and ultimately discovers that there is no clear market opportunity for a particular technology, this allows the researcher to obtain quicker feedback and begin working on new technologies. Furthermore, there is no quantitative way to measure how much faster a particular technology reached the market by using a center or other intangibles such as the likelihood that a student will pursue an entrepreneurial endeavor later in life as a result of involvement with a center sponsored course, lecture, seminar, or project. Third, as is typical of entrepreneurship promotion programs, there are no clearly defined time expectations for proposals to come to fruition. Certain technologies require more time than others to develop and cross industry comparisons must account for market conditions that are unique to each industry.

Despite these difficulties in precise measurements, there are many clear indications of success at the von Liebig Center and Deshpande Center. Both centers exhibit a well-defined organizational structure that provides capital, guidance, and contacts to university innovators. This basic framework accelerates the commercialization process because it

Table 1 Comparison between the von Liebig and Deshpande Centers as of November 2007

	The von Liebig Center	The Deshpande Center
Location	UCSD—Jacobs School of Engineering	MIT—School of Engineering
Initial Funding	$10 million	$17.5 million
	Gift in 2001 from the William J. von Liebig Foundation	Donation in 2002 from Jaishree and Gururaj Deshpande
Budget	~$1.2 million per year	~$1.7 million per year
	• Administrative staff ~$475 K	• Administrative Staff ~$320 K
	• Grants ~$420 K	• Grants ~$1.3 M
	• Advisors' salary ~$240 K	• Operational expenses ~$80 K
	• Academic courses ~45 K	
Amount of grants	Seed funding—$15–$75 K	Ignition grants—≤$50 K
		Innovation grants—≤$250 K
Total amount of grants awarded	Over $2.8 million	Over $7 million
Number of proposals funded	66 projects	64 projects (78 grants, 39 ignition grants, 39 innovation grants)
	Approximately 11 grants per year	Approximately 16 grants per year
	35–60% approval rate of proposals	Approximately 18% approval rate of proposals
Time period of accepting proposals	1–2 proposal rounds per year (spring and fall)	2 proposal rounds per year (spring and fall)
Advisory services	6 Advisors work at the center approximately 1 day a week	Pool of 50 volunteers that are assigned as advisors in the catalyst program
	Advisory services available to all faculty and research staff at Jacobs School independent of funding considerations	
Networking events	The "von Liebig Forum: Profiles in Innovation"—speaker series that showcases entrepreneurs, scientists, and innovators	IdeaStream Symposium—networking event for grant recipients, venture capitalists, entrepreneurs, and other researchers
	Open house—informal gathering for UCSD and business community	Open house—informal gathering for MIT and business community
	Community workshops—i.e. IP transfer between University and Industry	Catalyst party—informal gathering of grant recipients and catalysts
	Lunches—Awardee luncheon/networking event	Other optional events including ignition forum, joint seminars with student groups, and teambuilding events
	Other events including seminars and additional speaker/presentation events	
Educational programs	4 Graduate level courses to introduce engineering students to entrepreneurism (Venture Mechanics, Enterprise Dynamics, Applied Innovation, Corporate Entrepreneurship for Global Competitiveness)	I-Teams Course—Collaboration with MIT Entrepreneurship Center that consists of teams with 3–5 science, engineering, and management graduate students evaluating the commercial feasibility of innovation research emerging from MIT research labs
	Over 400 students and graduate student interns have enrolled in at least one of these courses	

Table 1 continued

	The von Liebig Center	The Deshpande Center
Number of startups and licenses	16 startups, 4 licenses	10 startups, 1 license
Number of employees in startups	64+	150+
Capital leverage	Spinouts have acquired over $71 million in private capital	Spinouts have acquired $88.7 million in private capital
Sustainability	Percentage of University royalty income from the commercialization of any technologies that receive Center services, University support and private donations, targeting $2 million by 2008 and $10 million by 2010	Donations from companies that have spun out Future private donations

provides customizable support for researchers and fills an early-stage funding gap. Anecdotal evidence via interviews supports this claim. For example, one project interviewed was denied funding from a governmental agency yet received funding from the proof of concept center. The proof of concept center funding allowed the concept to be proved. Once this occurred many outside investors became interested in funding the project's further development. Furthermore, the success of the centers can be seen in the power they have given grantees to leverage more capital for their technologies. By legitimizing a researcher's technology, both centers have enabled and accelerated the acquisition of private capital for university technology. Together the centers have awarded nearly $10 million in grants and have already seen 26 spinout companies accumulate over $159 million in capital.

There are also areas where both centers can improve their efficiency and usefulness. Some participants felt that the Catalysts provided by the Deshpande Center were not appropriate for their technology. This might be a sign that the von Liebig Center model of paying advisors ensures that they provide better assistance. Some participants also questioned the amount and number of proposals funded by each center as being too few, but in general respondents spoke positively about both centers.

5 Conclusions

Both the von Liebig and Deshpande centers originally focused on the cultivation of innovation in the engineering schools. This concentration allowed the centers to maximize their effectiveness by limiting the areas of expertise needed by advisors. Attempting to fund proposals from multiple disciplines creates the need for a center to have advisors who are experts in multiple fields, but neglecting non-engineering disciplines does not yield the maximum impact in terms of commercialization. This also creates a challenge in determining which proposals to fund since comparing prospective technological innovations among disciplines is difficult without extensive knowledge of all the fields that could submit proposals. Perhaps the most important cost for these centers is the opportunity cost of the proposals they choose not to fund. By limiting the proposals to the school of engineering, a proof of concept center can minimize missed opportunities resulting from selection bias with review boards only funding technologies they are familiar with. However, this concerted approach comes at the cost of missing opportunities to fund technologies that originate outside the engineering schools. The von Liebig Center has combined the need for a concerted approach with a desire to fund the best technologies at the university by opening proposals to all UCSD faculty members but requiring them to partner with a Jacobs School of Engineering faculty member. The Deshpande Center has opened proposals to all MIT faculty members, which necessarily increases the difficulty of proposal evaluation.

In order to replicate and improve on the successes of the von Liebig and Deshpande Centers, it is important to understand the unique conditions that allowed each to prosper. Both centers benefit from locating at universities that excel in research and are located within a strong network of angel investors and venture capitalists. It is important to recognize that the strength of both centers comes from providing far more than capital. Both centers combine seed funding with advisory services, educational initiatives, and plug innovators into outside funding and collaboration networks. This unified approach is vital to ensure the commercialization of university technology because each component is complimentary.

With this in mind, the creation of a new proof of concept center must be located in a university that (1) produces innovative and marketable technology, (2) is not adverse to collaboration with external networks and groups, and (3) has technology transfer offices that are willing to work with a center to assist in the commercialization process. Furthermore, locating the center in the engineering school, at least initially, allows the center to focus its efforts on research that has a greater likelihood of translation into products.

The proof of concept center must also be able to find an administrative team and advisors who are "hubs" in the local venture capital, technology, and industry networks. The localized knowledge of a center's staff may actually be more useful in accelerating the commercialization of university technology than the seed funding. It is also important that a strong social network exists in the surrounding community including advisors, angel investors, venture capitalists, and interested firms for grantees to partner with. This component is necessary to allow proof of concept centers to invest in risky or unproven technologies with the realization that an outside supportive infrastructure is present for further development and commercialization. By providing the initial seed funding to reach proof of concept, these centers allow researchers the ability to then obtain follow-on funding.

With these considerations in mind, there are a number of locations that may be best suited for new proof of concept center including, but not limited to UT-Austin, Johns Hopkins, University of Illinois, Northwestern, and University of Wisconsin-Madison. Regardless of the center's location, its success will be determined by the strength of its staff and its surrounding social network infrastructure.

References

Association of University Technology Managers (AUTUM). (2004). *Recollections: Celebrating the history of AUTM and the legacy of Bayh-Dole*. Northbrook, Ill.: Association of University Technology Managers.

Audretsch, D. B., Keilbach, M., & Lehmann, E. (2006). *Entrepreneurship and economic growth*. New York: Oxford University Press.

Fishback, Bo., Christine, A., Gulbranson, R. E., Litan, L. M., & Marisa P. (2007). *Finding business "idols": A new model to accelerate start-ups*, Kauffman Foundation Report, 4.

Friedman, T. L. (2005). *The world is flat*. London: Lane.

Litan, R. E., Lesa M., & Reedy E. J. (2007). The University as innovator: Bumps in the road, *Issues in Science and Technology,* Summer, 57–66.

Lucas, R. (1993). Making a miracle. *Econometrica, 61,* 251–272.

Romer, P. (1986). Increasing returns and long-run growth. *Journal of Political Economy, 94,* 1002–1037.

Thurow, L. (2002). *Fortune favors the bold.* New York: HarperCollins.

[10]

Research Policy 37 (2008) 1697–1705

Research Policy

Resolving the knowledge paradox: Knowledge-spillover entrepreneurship and economic growth

David B. Audretsch [a,b,c,*], Max Keilbach [a]

[a] Max Planck Institute of Economics, Research Group on Entrepreneurship, Growth and Public Policy, Kahlaische Str. 10, 07745 Jena, Germany
[b] Indiana University, Bloomington, IN 47405, USA
[c] Centre for Economic Policy Research, London, UK

ARTICLE INFO

Article history:
Available online 8 October 2008

JEL classification:
M13
O32
O47

Keywords:
Entrepreneurship
Knowledge
Growth
Innovation

ABSTRACT

The knowledge paradox suggests that high levels of investment in new knowledge do not necessarily and automatically generate the anticipated levels of competitiveness of growth. In particular, knowledge investments do not automatically translate into balanced growth and competitiveness. The purpose of this paper is to explain why knowledge investments are inherently unbalanced, so that the competitiveness and growth ensuing from knowledge are not equally spread across individuals, firms, and spatial units of observation, such as regions and countries. Based on a data set linking entrepreneurial activity to growth within the context of German regions, this paper shows that entrepreneurship serves a conduit of knowledge spillovers.

© 2008 Elsevier B.V. All rights reserved.

1. Introduction

Knowledge has emerged as a crucial source of competitiveness for virtually all of the traditional units of economic analysis, spanning from the individual to the firm, region and nation. However, how these various levels of economic analysis create knowledge, access that knowledge, and ultimately benefit from that knowledge is less than clear. In endogenous growth theory it is assumed that the entire geographic context, typically a country, will automatically benefit from investments in new knowledge (Lucas, 1988; Romer, 1986, 1990). The general underlying assumption of this approach is that newly created knowledge is automatically available to all agents in the economic process. Since knowledge behaves like a public good, all agents will benefit from it ('knowledge spillovers') which will increase the rate of economic growth in a knowledge-based economy.

However, as first the 'Swedish Paradox' and subsequently the 'European Paradox' have suggested, investments in new knowledge do not automatically translate into competitiveness and growth. Both of these euphemistically describe a more general paradox associated with knowledge, that high levels of investment in new knowledge do not necessarily and automatically generate the anticipated levels of competitiveness or economic growth. That is, knowledge investments do not automatically translate into higher levels of balanced growth and competitiveness.

The purpose of this paper is to explain why knowledge investments are inherently unbalanced, so that the competitiveness and growth ensuing from knowledge are not equally spread across individuals, firms, and spatial units of observation, such as regions and countries. Following Acs et al. (2004), this paper posits that a filter exists between investments in new knowledge and its commercialization,

---
* Corresponding author at: Max Planck Institute of Economics, Research Group on Entrepreneurship, Growth and Public Policy, Kahlaische Str. 10, 07745 Jena, Germany.
  E-mail addresses: audretsch@econ.mpg.de (D.B. Audretsch), keilbach@econ.mpg.de (M. Keilbach).

0048-7333/$ – see front matter © 2008 Elsevier B.V. All rights reserved.
doi:10.1016/j.respol.2008.08.008

1698   *D.B. Audretsch, M. Keilbach / Research Policy 37 (2008) 1697–1705*

so that, in contrast to the models of endogenous growth, knowledge does not automatically spill over and result in increased competitiveness and growth. Rather, conduits are required to facilitate spillovers from the organization, or firm, creating that knowledge, to its commercialization.

By taking knowledge created within the context of one organization or incumbent firm as a basis for starting a new firm, 'knowledge-spillover entrepreneurship' serves as one such conduit of knowledge spillovers. The economic implication of that process is the transformation of knowledge within the context of an incumbent organization into a new product or service that is produced in a new organization, which is the essence of knowledge-spillover entrepreneurship. Hence entrepreneurship can be considered as an important, though in our view neglected, mechanism in the transmission of knowledge and the actual spillover process. By commercializing knowledge and ideas that otherwise would not be pursued and commercialized, entrepreneurship serves as one mechanism facilitating the spillover of knowledge.

Why and how entrepreneurship can serve as a conduit of knowledge spillovers, along with its impact on economic growth and performance, is explained in Section 2 of this paper. In Section 3, an econometric model is specified which will be empirically estimated to test the simultaneous relationship between entrepreneurship on the one hand and economic growth on the other. Measurement issues are explained in Section 4. In Section 5, measures of entrepreneurship are combined with the more traditional factors of production, labor, physical capital and knowledge capital, in the estimation context of a three-stage regression model, where first entrepreneurial activity and then economic performance are estimated. Finally, in Section 6, a summary and conclusions are provided. In particular, the empirical evidence suggests that not only is entrepreneurial activity greater in regions with higher investments in new knowledge, but that also those regions with more entrepreneurship exhibit higher growth.

2. Linking knowledge-spillover entrepreneurship to growth

It has long been observed that knowledge is inherently different from the more traditional inputs of production, such as labor and physical capital (Arrow, 1962a,b) for at least two main reasons: (1) knowledge has a public good characteristic, and (2) the economic value of knowledge is intrinsically uncertain and its potential value is asymmetric across economic agents.

The first aspect is an essential part of the theory of endogenous growth and has been extensively addressed and formalized (e.g. Romer, 1990, p. S73). There, the most important, although not the only source of knowledge spillovers is considered to be research and development (R&D). Other key factors include human capital or skilled labor force (Romer, 1986, 1996; Lucas, 1988). The dynamics of knowledge creation in these models lead to constant or increasing returns to scale in production. However, these theories do not necessarily refer to returns at the level of observation most familiar in the industrial organization literature – the plant, or at least the firm – but rather at the

level of a spatially distinguishable unit, say a nation state or smaller regional units. In fact, it is assumed that it is externalities across firms and even industries that yield convexities in economic activity on the regional level.

The second aspect of knowledge differing from traditional production factors is uncertainty combined with asymmetries across economic agents. Endogenous growth theory implicitly assumes that knowledge, once it has been generated, spills over more or less automatically to other firms.[1] This is not the case. Transforming generally available new economic knowledge into viable new products or technologies requires investment with uncertain outcomes and therefore bears risks (Arrow, 1962b). This uncertainty inherent in new knowledge increases with the extent to which the ideas are incrementally or radically different from the existing stock of knowledge. While some aspects of the new knowledge are incremental in nature, easy and therefore less risky to implement, others are more radical in nature and are difficult to understand, so that their implementation is more risky. Furthermore, asymmetries with respect to the backgrounds, experiences and intuitions of decision-makers imply that what one economic agent infers is a new idea with a positive expected value, another agent may be less positive about. Confronted with uncertainty and asymmetries about new knowledge and ideas, especially more radical ones, decision-making hierarchies in incumbent firms tend to stick to the status quo. It is well known that decision-making in a group context tends to result in selecting safe and less risky alternatives.

Marshall (1920) considered 'risk-taking' as one of the central functions of entrepreneurship and as equally important as the role of what we know as the production factors. In the 4th book of his *Principles*, he considered four 'agents of production'—land, labor, capital and organization. He understood 'organization' not just in a structural sense (i.e. in the sense that the notion 'industrial organization' reflects) but also in the sense of an activity (i.e. in the sense of 'management'). Referring to entrepreneurs as 'business men' or 'undertakers' he states that:

> "They [i.e. the entrepreneurs] 'adventure' or 'undertake' its risks [i.e. of production]; they bring together the capital and the labour required for the work; they arrange or 'engineer' its general plan, and superintend its minor details. Looking at business men from one point of view we may regard them as a highly skilled industrial grade, from another as middlemen intervening between the manual worker and the consumer." (Marshall, 1920, p. 244)

Hence for Marshall, the function of the entrepreneur is to organize and control the production process and to bear the risks involved with it.

A typical pattern of entrepreneurship is that employees with a strong vision on the usability of new knowledge that they cannot push forward within the incumbent firm leave that firm and create a new one (i.e. they become entrepreneurs) with the aim of realizing their vision.

---

[1] This view has been challenged by the literature on absorptive capacity. See, e.g. Cohen and Levinthal (1990).

D.B. Audretsch, M. Keilbach / Research Policy 37 (2008) 1697–1705   1699

By developing new knowledge into new products the entrepreneurs: (a) confront the risk that is involved in the process due to the inherent uncertainty, and (b) create new knowledge, specifically on the feasibility and marketability of the new technology.

Such a new-firm startup reflects knowledge-spillover entrepreneurship in that the knowledge used to start the new organization or firm was actually created in a different, incumbent firm or organization. Several authors (e.g. Agrawal et al., 2004; Burton et al., 2002; Chatterji, 2005; Klepper, 2001, 2006; Shane and Stuart, 2002) have provided industry case studies of knowledge-spillover entrepreneurship resulting from spin-offs from incumbent firms. However, knowledge-spillover entrepreneurship not only serves as a conduit for knowledge spillovers, it also generates competitiveness for the individual entrepreneur, the new firm, and the region.

Perhaps for this reason, Baumol (2002b) considers innovation as an integrated process based on a division of labor between small firms, who launch new products and introduce new technologies based on the riskier parts of the new knowledge, and large firms, who take on these ideas and develop them in an incremental innovation process. Hence entrepreneurial firms and large firms coexist in what Baumol (2002a) calls a 'David-Goliath Symbiosis'. In this view, the investment in the development of the riskier parts of new technological knowledge is usually made by entrepreneurs. By starting up a business, an entrepreneur literally 'bets' on the product she offers (or will be offering) and thus is willing to take the risk that this process bears. She starts a new firm on the basis of her belief that the potential returns are greater than the potential loss. An important implication of the knowledge-spillover theory of entrepreneurship (Audretsch, 1995; Audretsch et al., 2006) is that contexts rich in knowledge will generate more entrepreneurial opportunities. By contrast, those contexts that have less knowledge will generate fewer entrepreneurial opportunities. Thus, as knowledge has become more important over time in developed countries, so too has entrepreneurship (Audretsch, 2007).

However, the willingness and potential of individuals to serve as a conduit of knowledge spillovers via entrepreneurship is not homogeneous or constant across geographic space. Rather, it is a function not only of personal and idiosyncratic preferences but also of regional characteristics and factors, such as social acceptance of entrepreneurial behavior, and also individuals who are willing to deal with the risk of creating new firms[2] and the activity of bankers and venture capital agents that are willing to share risks and benefits involved. We denote a region in which these legal, institutional and social factors and forces are conducive to entrepreneurship as being endowed with a high level of 'entrepreneurship capital'.[3]

Regions characterized by a high degree of entrepreneurship capital are conducive to entrepreneurs recognizing and seizing opportunities to take knowledge that would otherwise not be commercialized and use it to launch a new firm. On the other hand, regions characterized by a paucity of entrepreneurship capital impede the ability of individuals to start new firms. Since, as explained above, new-firm startups can serve as a conduit of knowledge spillovers, those regions with a high level of entrepreneurship capital would be expected to exhibit high levels of economic growth, *ceteris paribus*.

In the literature, a number of other mechanisms are identified on how entrepreneurship is conducive to economic growth. The first involves increasing the level of competition as a result of the entry of new firms and subsequent selection processes that ultimately lead to economic growth. This argument is made, e.g. by Geroski (1989) or in the collection by Roberts and Tybout (1996). Studies of this effect are inconclusive in that they do not find coherent evidence on a positive effect of entry or turbulence (i.e. entrepreneurship) on economic growth. The second – and broader – mechanism involves the impact of the external effects of new knowledge on other economic agents, here driven through entrepreneurship. As Jacobs (1979), Glaeser et al. (1992) and Feldman and Audretsch (1996) emphasize, it is rather the large variety of new ideas that drives economic growth. With higher propensity to start up new ventures on the basis of new economic knowledge, more of this knowledge is being processed and therefore more variety is made available. Moreover, if a new venture that was based on new knowledge fails, the failure in itself creates new knowledge, specifically on the usability of this new knowledge. Through this path, entrepreneurship can generate a learning effect within the economy. Thus, entrepreneurship capital has a three-fold impact on economic growth: it facilitates knowledge spillovers, injects new competition in the input market for ideas, and enhances regional diversity, all of which are hypothesized to contribute to economic growth.[4]

While a high level of entrepreneurship capital can be expected to be conducive to economic growth, the inverse relationship can be expected to hold as well: regional economic growth is conducive to entrepreneurial opportunities. Thus, in moving towards a tractable econometric model, economic growth is not only influenced by the extent of entrepreneurial activity, but entrepreneurship in turn is influenced by economic growth.

It can be argued that opportunities for knowledge-spillover entrepreneurship are created through more complex processes, which are inherently more burdened by greater uncertainty and asymmetries across economic agents. As previously emphasized, entrepreneurship involves the transformation of the riskier parts of new knowledge into the creation of new organizations and firms, since it is these aspects of new ideas and knowl-

---

[2] As Gartner and Carter (2003) state, entrepreneurial behavior involves the activities of individuals who are associated with creating new organizations rather than the activities of individuals who are involved with maintaining or changing the operations of on-going established organizations.

[3] Saxenian (1994) argues in similar directions, referring to regional networks and specific knowledge. In that respect the notion of entrepreneurship capital is close to that of social capital (e.g. Putnam, 1993), though not identical. See Audretsch and Keilbach (2004a) for an in-depth discussion of this issue.

[4] See Wennekers and Thurik (1999) for further discussion.

1700   *D.B. Audretsch, M. Keilbach / Research Policy 37 (2008) 1697–1705*

edge that become trapped in the knowledge filter of incumbent firms and organizations and therefore generate entrepreneurial opportunities. This would imply that knowledge-spillover entrepreneurship is greater in contexts with a high level of investments creating new knowledge.

Because of the interaction and interdependence involving knowledge, entrepreneurship and economic growth, a unidirectional model would lead to biased results. Therefore, in this paper we consider simultaneously the impact of entrepreneurship capital on regional economic growth and *vice versa*. Knowledge measures will be included in all of the equations. The virtue of this approach is not only in the correction of the statistical bias. While the emergence of a statistical link between economic performance and entrepreneurial activity is of substantial interest to both scholars and policy makers alike, it considers the amount of entrepreneurial activity specific to a region as an exogenous endowment. By explicitly instrumenting entrepreneurship capital in a second equation, we are able to analyze how policy could actually influence economic performance by generating more entrepreneurial activity.

With this two-equation approach, we implicitly link two disparate literatures. On the one hand is a series of studies, dating back at least to Carlton (1983) and Bartik (1989) and more recently Reynolds et al. (1994), which have tried to identify characteristics specific to particular regions that account for variations in startup activity across geographic space. On the other hand is a literature that has examined the impact of new-firm startups on economic performance for spatial units of observation at the regional level. Most recently, this has generated a series of studies suggesting that economic growth is systematically and positively related to the degree of entrepreneurial activity across geographic space (see Acs and Storey, 2004).

3. An interdependent estimation framework

The main thrust of this paper is to suggest that not only is entrepreneurship induced by high investments in knowledge within the regional context, and that entrepreneurship promotes regional growth, but that they both influence each other. Thus, an augmented production function that includes an explicit measure of regional entrepreneurship capital is estimated. On this basis we are able to test the impact of entrepreneurship on economic growth on the one hand, and the impact of knowledge investments and growth on entrepreneurship, on the other. The first equation is a Cobb-Douglas function of the form

$$Y_i = K_i^{\alpha} L_i^{\beta} R_i^{\gamma} E_i^{\delta} \qquad (1)$$

where Y_i is economic performance of region i, measured as GDP, K_i is region i's endowment of capital, L_i is labor, R_i is region i's R&D intensity and E_i represents its endowment of entrepreneurship capital. Hence, this specifies formally that entrepreneurship capital contributes to the economic output of regions. With Eq. (1) our approach is an extension to that chosen by Mankiw et al. (1992, p. 416) who emphasize the impact of regional human capital, while we instead focus on entrepreneurship capital.

The specification of Eq. (1) assumes implicitly that entrepreneurship capital is exogenous. However, as argued above, the inverse causal relationship is also at work, i.e. entrepreneurship and regional performance are linked recursively. We therefore specify a second equation in order to take this recursive structure explicitly into account. In its general form, this equation takes the form

$$E_i = f(y_i, x_i) \qquad (2)$$

where y_i is a vector of measures of region i's economic performance and x_i is a vector of other variables influencing entrepreneurial activity in i. These variables are specified in detail in the following section. We estimate this set of equations simultaneously using three-stage least-squares regression (3SLS) to correct for the simultaneity bias (e.g. Intriligator et al., 1996).

The specification suggested here also incorporates public policy. While Eq. (1) specifies our hypothesis of a positive impact of entrepreneurship capital on economic performance, it does not give any hindsight for policy makers on what actually drives a region's endowment with this form of capital. Eq. (2) will provide at least some insights in this direction.

4. Measurement issues

4.1. Measuring the impact of entrepreneurship capital

We measure the variables used in Eq. (1) as follows. All variables are measured for the year 2000, unless stated otherwise. Output Y_i of region i is measured as Gross Value Added of the manufacturing industries corrected for purchases of goods and services, VAT and shipping costs. The stock of Physical Capital K_i used in the manufacturing sector of the region (Kreise, or German counties) has been estimated using a perpetual inventory method, which computes the stock of capital as a weighted sum of investments in the producing sector in the period 1980–2000. For a more detailed description of this procedure see, e.g. Audretsch and Keilbach (2004b). Statistics including output and investment are published every 2 years on the level of the Kreise by the Working Group of the Statistical Offices of the German Länder, under 'Volkswirtschaftliche Gesamtrechnungen der Länder'. Labor L_i is expressed as the number of employees in the manufacturing industries. These data are published by the Federal Labor Office, Nürnberg that reports the number of employees liable to social insurance on the Kreise level. R_i is the region's R&D intensity, and is measured as the number of public and private R&D employees in 1999 relative to our measure of labor for each region. These data were provided by the Stifterverband für die Deutsche Wissenschaft. This measure covers all fields or industries, i.e. it is not limited to manufacturing. Hence, we implicitly measure knowledge spillovers from R&D in the service sector to the manufacturing sector.

The variable for Entrepreneurship Capital E_i is based on a latent measure reflecting the underlying but unobservable concept of regional entrepreneurship capital—the startup of a new firm. The new-firm startup rate, defined as the number of startups in a region divided by the population, is an indicator of the underlying unobservable entrepreneur-

D.B. Audretsch, M. Keilbach / Research Policy 37 (2008) 1697–1705   1701

ship capital; *ceteris paribus*, higher startup rates would indicate a greater extent of entrepreneurship capital.

Entrepreneurship is not a homogeneous concept or activity. Some types of entrepreneurship may involve a greater extent of knowledge spillovers than other types. At least somewhat to reflect the homogeneity inherent in entrepreneurship, especially with respect to knowledge spillovers, four different measures of entrepreneurship capital are used, which presumably reflect different degrees of knowledge spillovers.

The first measure incorporates new-firm startups in *all* industries and is the broadest and most inclusive of the four measures. More than 50% of these new-firm startups are in the retail and catering sectors, i.e. shops and restaurants. The next two measures presumably reflect the greatest extent of knowledge-spillover entrepreneurship, the first being start-ups in the high-tech industries, i.e. industries with an average R&D intensity of more than 2.5%.[5] Start-ups in these industries account for 7.5% of all start-ups on average, ranging from 1.6% to 17.9% within the Kreise. A second measure of knowledge-based entrepreneurship capital is start-ups in the ICT industries. This sub-aggregate represents a mix of startups in ICT-oriented manufacturing and service industries, hence for IT manufacturing, there is an overlap between this measure and the high-tech measure. Our observation period has been very dynamic in terms of startup activities in these industries and 7.7% of all startups have been made in these industries, ranging from 1.5% to 19.0% over the regions. As a "counterfactual" we consider the aggregate of the remaining industries, which we denote 'low-tech' entrepreneurship capital: 63–95% of all start-ups are in these industries (85% on average). The 'low-tech' notion refers to the average R&D intensity of the industry and not to the actual R&D intensities of the firm; this is due to unavailability of corresponding data.

The data on startups is taken from the ZEW foundation panels that are based on data provided biannually by Creditreform, the largest German credit-rating agency. These data contain virtually all entries – hence startups – in the German Trade Register, especially for firms with large credit requirements, e.g. high-technology firms.[6] As of 2000, there were roughly 5 million entries for Germany, covering the period 1989–2000. Since the number of startups is subject to a greater level of stochastic disturbance over short time periods, it is prudent to compute the measure of entrepreneurship capital based on startup rates over a longer time period. We therefore used the number of startups from 1998 to 2000 (covering 780,000 start-ups).

Table 1 shows correlations between these measures of entrepreneurship capital as well as between these measures and population density. This table shows that both knowledge-based measures of entrepreneurship capital are strongly correlated while the correlation between these and the "low-tech" measure of entrepreneurship capital is

much weaker. On the other hand, our general measure of entrepreneurship capital and the "low-tech" measure are strongly correlated. This is due to the large proportion of startups characterized as being "low-tech". It is also noteworthy that all variables are significantly correlated with population density of regions, however the correlation of the knowledge-based measures is stronger.

4.2. Assessing the determinants of entrepreneurship capital

A priori, there are two groups of factors that shape the extent of entrepreneurship capital: (1) the generation of region-specific opportunities for entrepreneurial activity, and (2) a favorable general economic environment. Put simply, while the first set of factors increases entrepreneurial opportunities through the creation and adoption of new knowledge, the second set of factors is responsible for the creation of a fertile environment, i.e. an absence would impede the creation of new firms even if opportunities were abundant.

4.2.1. Factors creating or stimulating entrepreneurial opportunities

4.2.1.1. Economic output. Above we argued that while entrepreneurship capital can be expected to drive economic output, the inverse relationship might hold as well. Large economic output implies a large market size, hence a high intensity in economic exchange and therefore a high level of entrepreneurial opportunities. Including the regions' level of Gross Value Added of manufacturing industries, we proxy the level of these opportunities in a very general sense. With this variable, we include the dependent variable of Eq. (1) as an explanatory variable in Eq. (2).

Strong *GDP Growth* of a region implies increasing wealth, increasing market size, increasing intensity in economic exchange and consequently increasing general opportunities for new businesses. Since it measures the increase in the general economic activity, this variable again proxies general entrepreneurial opportunities. We compute this variable for each region as $g_Y = \ln(Y_{t_1} - Y_{t_0})/(t_1 - t_0)$, with $t_0 = 1992$ and $t_1 = 2000$, measuring a region's average growth rate between years 1992 and 2000. Rather than the stock measure of GDP, GDP growth is a measure of the region's past economic performance. We assume that nascent entrepreneurs derive their expectations about the future regional evolution from this past performance.

With *R&D Intensity*, we describe the region's potential for creating new knowledge. We assume that a high regional R&D activity increases regional opportunities to start up new knowledge-based businesses by the mechanisms described in Section 2. Hence, this variable is more knowledge-specific as compared to mere GDP growth in terms of opportunity creation. We expect a positive impact of this variable on a region's level of knowledge-based entrepreneurship capital.

Table 1 indicates that entrepreneurship capital is positively correlated with *Population Density*. Glaeser et al. (1992) and Ciccone and Hall (1996) argue that spatial density, hence proximity, eases local knowledge flows and

---

[5] Here, we follow the classification used in the reports to the Federal Ministry of Education and Research. See, e.g. Grupp and Legler (2000).

[6] Firms with low credit requirements, with a low number of employees or with non-limited legal forms are registered only with a time lag. These are typically retail stores or catering firms. See Harhoff and Steil (1997) for more detail on the ZEW foundation panels.

Table 1
Correlations between different measures of entrepreneurship capital and population density

	PopDens	General	High-tech	ICT
General	0.3419 (0.000)			
High-tech	0.4325 (0.000)	0.6515 (0.000)		
ICT	0.4147 (0.000)	0.6063 (0.000)	0.8411 (0.000)	
Low-tech	0.2638 (0.000)	0.9714 (0.000)	0.4667 (0.000)	0.4110 (0.000)

p-Values of a *t*-test of correlations to be stochastically different from zero in brackets.

therefore increases labor productivity. Similarly, we expect that in densely populated regions, ideas and knowledge flow faster and the provision of ancillary services and inputs is also greater; therefore entrepreneurial opportunities are generated faster and can be appropriated more easily by economic agents. Hence, entrepreneurship capital should be higher in more densely populated regions than in less densely populated regions.

4.2.2. Factors influencing the general economic situation
4.2.2.1. Unemployment rate. That unemployment is linked to entrepreneurship dates back at least to Oxenfeldt (1943), who pointed out that individuals confronted with unemployment and low prospects for wage employment turn to self-employment as a viable alternative. This was an extension of Knight's (1921)Knight (1921) view that individuals make a decision among three states—unemployment, self-employment and employment. The actual decision is shaped by the relative prices of these three activities but there was a clear prediction that entrepreneurship would be positively related to unemployment. However, as Storey (1991) documents, the empirical evidence linking unemployment to entrepreneurship is fraught with ambiguities. While some studies find that greater unemployment serves as a catalyst for startup activity (Evans and Jovanovic, 1989; Yamawaki, 1990; Evans and Leighton, 1990; Reynolds et al., 1994, 1995), still others have found that unemployment reduces the amount of entrepreneurial activity (Audretsch and Fritsch, 1994; Audretsch, 1995). We test this relationship for our data by including the regional unemployment rate in our regressions.

Florida (2002) has argued that *social diversity* in a society is a proxy for the openness of this society with respect to new ideas. Such openness is important in an environment where new ideas are transformed into business ideas and ultimately to new-firm startups. Thus, openness contributes to the entrepreneurship capital of that society by enhancing new ideas and the spillover of knowledge. We measure social diversity with an entropy index of the voting behavior on the occasion of the last parliament vote (1998). The measure takes into account all major political parties but also smaller ones. We transform the entropy index to the range [0,1] such that 0 indicates maximum and 1 indicates no variety.

4.2.2.2. Industrial diversity. In the 1990s, there was a debate on what type of spatial industry concentration served as the stronger 'engine of growth': strong concentration of industries (leading to 'Marshall–Arrow–Romer' externalities) or strong variety of industries (leading to 'Jacobs'

externalities).[7] The first hypothesis states that firms benefit from a strong concentration of industry-specific knowledge while the second states that firms benefit from the variety of knowledge coming from different industry sources. Both concepts can be important in the entrepreneurial processes described above. The empirical literature[8] did not come to a unanimous conclusion, suggesting that both effects are important, depending, e.g. on the life cycle of the industry. We test which of the two effects dominates in the creation of entrepreneurship capital by including a Herfindahl index of industrial diversity in the regressions. As our measure of social diversity, the range of this index is [0,1], where 0 indicates maximum diversity.

We also investigate whether a high tax burden reduces the propensity to start up a new business, and hence the region's entrepreneurship capital. Generally, the German tax system does not make regional distinctions with the exception of business tax, whose multiplier, and hence level, is fixed by regional authorities. With these taxes, regional authorities finance their local budget. Consequently, there are two points in relation to the regional business tax. While one side argues that a high business tax prevents firms from settling on a high tax multiplier but rather settling in other regions, the other side argues that the corresponding services attract the firms. We test these arguments by including the *regional business tax multiplier* (which is the German *Gewerbesteuerhebesatz*) in the regressions.

5. Estimation results

The top part of Table 2 shows the regression results of Eq. (1), the bottom part those of Eq. (2), both estimated simultaneously using 3SLS. The four columns represent estimates, including one out of the four measures of entrepreneurship capital, respectively.

5.1. Impact of entrepreneurship capital on regional economic performance

The regression results estimating the production function exhibit positive and significant results for the production factors. The estimates for capital and labor are in the usual range, and are close to those reported by Cobb and Douglas (1928) and numerous production function regres-

---

[7] This description is very simplified. See, e.g. the literature in the following footnote for more detailed descriptions of the underlying processes.
[8] See, e.g. Glaeser et al. (1992), Henderson et al. (1995), Henderson (1997), Ellison and Glaeser (1997).

D.B. Audretsch, M. Keilbach / Research Policy 37 (2008) 1697–1705

Table 2
Estimating entrepreneurship and economic performance

	Dependent variable: regional output			
Constant	1.5622*** (0.000)	0.3305 (0.334)	−0.5641* (0.064)	1.6545*** (0.000)
Capital	0.1031*** (0.000)	0.1301*** (0.000)	0.1300*** (0.000)	0.0859*** (0.000)
Labor	0.7945*** (0.000)	0.7379*** (0.000)	0.7449*** (0.000)	0.8276*** (0.000)
Private R&D intensity	0.0147*** (0.003)	0.0204*** (0.000)	0.0302*** (0.000)	0.0174*** (0.000)
General entrepreneurship	0.6056*** (0.000)			
High-tech entrepreneurship		0.1796*** (0.000)		
ICT entrepreneurship			0.0629** (0.041)	
Low-tech entrepreneurship				0.6346*** (0.000)
Pseudo R^2	0.927 (0.000)	0.941 (0.000)	0.940 (0.000)	0.924 (0.000)

	Dependent variable: entrepreneurship			
	General	High-tech	ICT	Low-tech
Economic output (GDP)	0.0226*** (0.006)	0.0206 (0.113)	−0.0050 (0.689)	0.0222*** (0.009)
GDP growth	0.3165*** (0.000)	0.4896*** (0.000)	0.0043 (0.974)	0.3188*** (0.000)
R&D intensity	0.8619 (0.250)	5.2191*** (0.000)	6.0824*** (0.000)	−0.0988 (0.897)
Population density	1.0366*** (0.000)	2.1215*** (0.000)	2.4347*** (0.000)	0.8595*** (0.002)
Unemployment rate	0.0015 (0.582)	−0.0445*** (0.000)	−0.0550*** (0.000)	0.0080*** (0.003)
Social diversity index	−0.0834 (0.442)	−1.1053*** (0.000)	−0.1389 (0.410)	−0.0011 (0.992)
Industry diversity index	1.0258*** (0.000)	1.1920***ᵃ (0.000)	1.4235*** (0.000)	1.0011*** (0.000)
Regional tax multiplier	−0.1136*** (0.001)	−0.0566 (0.283)	−0.0904* (0.076)	−0.1155*** (0.000)
Constant	−5.8677*** (0.000)	−7.8314*** (0.000)	−8.4191*** (0.000)	−6.1138*** (0.000)
Pseudo R^2	0.247 (0.000)	0.497 (0.000)	0.631 (0.000)	0.219 (0.000)
Number of observations	429	429	429	429

Note: p-Values in brackets.
* Statistically significant on two-tailed test at 90% level of confidence.
** Statistically significant on two-tailed test at 95% level of confidence.
*** Statistically significant on two-tailed test at 99% level of confidence.

sions that followed. The result for R&D intensity is also significant and positive throughout as was expected from the discussion above. The coefficients of entrepreneurship capital are positive and significant. This confirms our hypothesis of entrepreneurship capital creating a positive impact on regions' economic performance.

5.2. Variables influencing entrepreneurship capital

Regression results from the estimation of the four different measures of entrepreneurship capital are provided in the bottom part of Table 2. Some of the variables show a different impact on the different measures of entrepreneurship capital. It is also remarkable that the share of explained variance (expressed through the pseudo R^2) is more than twice as large for the knowledge-based measures of entrepreneurship capital. This indicates that the chosen model and the set of variables are more appropriate for knowledge-based start-up processes. Since the R^2 of the second equation expresses the fit for Eq. (1) in the second step of the regression, a higher R^2 implies that the 3SLS approach is more appropriate and the results are more reliable.[9] Let us discuss the regression results in turn.

The two GDP-based measures show a slightly different behavior. The measure of the contemporary stock of *GDP* shows a positive and significant impact on the "low-tech" measure of entrepreneurship capital (and consequently on the "general" measure) but not on the knowledge-based measures. *GDP growth* has also a positive impact on the low-

tech measure. However it has an even stronger impact on our high-tech oriented measure of entrepreneurship capital. Our results indicate that an increase of GDP growth by one percentage point will increase the regions start-up rate by roughly 50%. On the other hand, neither the stock measure of GDP nor GDP growth have an impact on the regions' ICT startups. We assume that this is due to the fact that ICT startups were especially strong in the late 1990s and probably decoupled from macroeconomic trends.

The impact of our more specific measure of economic opportunity, *R&D intensity*, is positive and significant for the knowledge-based measures of entrepreneurship capital while it is insignificant for the others. Hence R&D creates localized generally available knowledge and thus opportunities for knowledge-based entrepreneurship. We see this as evidence for our arguments given in Section 1.

Entrepreneurial activity is stronger in regions with high *population density*. Apparently, the propensity to start up a new firm is larger in cities and surrounding areas. This effect is roughly twice as large for the knowledge-based measures of entrepreneurship capital. Along with the arguments given above, we take this as evidence that spatial proximity increases the dissemination of publicly available knowledge and thus increases the opportunities for entrepreneurship.

Let us now turn to the class of variables that are responsible for the creation of entrepreneurial opportunities. An interesting effect occurs when considering the effect of the local *unemployment rate*. As for the general measure of entrepreneurship, we do not observe a significant impact of unemployment rate, its impact being significantly negative for the subset of knowledge-based

---

[9] See the discussion in Intriligator et al. (1996), Section 10.5.

measures and significantly positive for the subset expressing low-tech entrepreneurship capital. Hence regions with high unemployment generate a larger number of low-tech startups but a smaller number of knowledge-based startups. We conclude from this finding that the relationship between unemployment and entrepreneurship has actually two faces: start-ups in the 'low-tech' industries have been generated out of unemployment. Apparently this has been chosen as a strategy for self-employment from a state of unemployment. High-tech start-ups, however, do not follow this strategy. Rather, the high level of employee qualifications that is necessary to start up a firm in a high-tech industry does not match the knowledge structure of regions with high unemployment. Rather, high regional unemployment reflects a lack of opportunities for knowledge-based start-ups. Therefore a policy measure that aims to encourage knowledge-based start-ups out of unemployment is probably doomed to fail.

Considering the two diversity measures, *social diversity* does not seem to play a general impact on the regions' entrepreneurship capital. It is insignificant for all but high-tech entrepreneurship capital. For that case, increasing social diversity has s positive and significant impact. We take this as confirmation of the arguments of Florida (2002), i.e. a high level of social tolerance is positively correlated with the acceptance of new ideas and thus increases a region's entrepreneurship capital. The positive and significant sign of *industry diversity* implies that strong industry concentration has a positive impact on the region's propensity to start up new businesses. Hence we find external effects of the Marshall–Arrow–Romer type as having a positive impact on the regions' entrepreneurship capital.

The regression results for the *regional tax multiplier* show a strongly significant negative impact on the startup intensity (the regional entrepreneurship capital) for our measure of low-tech entrepreneurship capital as well as for the general measure. ICT start-up activities are less though still negatively affected, while high-tech start-up activities are insensitive with respect to this tax burden. Obviously, the decision to start-up or where to locate a high-tech firm is not influenced by the regional tax burden. It is rather influenced by other factors (such as the regional R&D intensity discussed above). If these factors are present, an entrepreneur will accept a higher tax burden. ICT start-ups exhibit a more intermediate behavior, which is discussed below.

5.3. Overall findings

Overall, a rather heterogeneous picture emerges for the different types of entrepreneurship. 'Low-tech entrepreneurship', covering 85% of all entrepreneurial activity, is promoted in regions with a strong economic performance. It is strongly positively correlated with the regional unemployment rate. On the other hand, this type of entrepreneurial activity is weaker in regions with a high business tax multiplier and with high industry diversity. Still it has a positive impact on regional economic output.

'High-tech entrepreneurship' exhibits a different behavior. While it is positively correlated with GDP growth, it is also strongly positively correlated with R&D intensity and stronger in regions with a large social diversity, hence with a higher acceptance of newness. On the other hand, this type of entrepreneurship is negatively correlated with regional unemployment; it is uncorrelated with the regional tax multiplier.

Just as for high-tech entrepreneurship, ICT-oriented entrepreneurship is positively correlated with the regional R&D intensity, hence we conclude that a strong regional R&D intensity has a positive impact on knowledge-based entrepreneurship but no impact on other types of entrepreneurship. Just as for high-tech entrepreneurship, ICT entrepreneurship is also negatively related to a high level of regional unemployment. Unlike high-tech entrepreneurship, however, ICT start-up activity is not influenced by regional economic performance (at least for the observation period which saw a technology-driven startup boom in the ICT industries). As for the other types of entrepreneurial activity, ICT is stronger in an environment with homogeneous industries, however, it is unrelated to social diversity. Finally, unlike for high-tech, ICT entrepreneurship is sensitive to the regional level of tax rate (though less so than low-tech entrepreneurship).

6. Summary and conclusions

Investments in knowledge have not proven to be the panacea for stagnant growth and rising unemployment as had seemingly been implied by endogenous growth theory. Rather, as first the Swedish Paradox and subsequently the European Paradox underscored, knowledge may be necessary but not sufficient to ensure competitiveness and growth. This paper has explained why investments in knowledge almost inevitably have an imbalanced impact on individuals, firms and regions. The knowledge filter impedes the spillover of knowledge for commercialization. Such knowledge left uncommercialized by incumbent firms generates opportunities for entrepreneurship. Those regions endowed with entrepreneurship capital are able to actualize those opportunities, resulting in higher levels of economic growth.

Based on a data set consisting of 440 German counties (Kreise) we are able to provide empirical evidence suggesting that entrepreneurship capital exerts a significant and strongly positive impact on regional economic growth. In addition, the empirical evidence suggests that high investments in knowledge have a positive impact on knowledge-based entrepreneurship.

Thus, the creation of new technological opportunities through R&D increases economic performance directly but also indirectly through inducing knowledge-spillover entrepreneurship. This is consistent with our argument that entrepreneurship serves as a conduit transforming knowledge that otherwise might have remained uncommercialized into new products. We conclude from these findings that entrepreneurship plays an important role in the knowledge-spillover process.

The policy implications from this paper suggest that to generate competitiveness and growth investments in knowledge may not suffice. Such knowledge investments may not automatically spill over into commercialization. Rather, an important function for public policy is to facilitate the spillover and commercialization of knowledge by encouraging entrepreneurship.

Acknowledgements

Financial support from the European Commission (FP6) Project: KEINS—Knowledge-Based Entrepreneurship: Innovation, Networks and Systems, Contract no. CT2-CT-2004-506022 is gratefully acknowledged. We are grateful to two anonymous referees for helpful comments.

References

Acs, Z., Audretsch, D., Braunerhjelm, P., Carlsson, B., 2004. The missing link: the knowledge filter, entrepreneurship and endogenous growth. Working Paper. Centre for Economic Policy Research, London.

Acs, Z., Storey, D., 2004. Introduction: entrepreneurship and economic development. Regional Studies 38, 871–877.

Agrawal, R., Echambadi, R., April, F., Sarkar, M., 2004. Knowledge transfer through inheritance: spin-out generation, development and performance. Academy of Management Journal 47, 501–522.

Arrow, K.J., 1962a. The economic implications of learning by doing. Review of Economic Studies 29, 155–173.

Arrow, K.J., 1962b. Economic welfare and the allocation of resources for invention. In: Nelson, R.R. (Ed.), The Rate and Direction of Inventive Activity. Princeton University Press, Princeton, NJ.

Audretsch, D.B., 1995. Innovation and Industry Evolution. MIT Press, Cambridge, MA.

Audretsch, D.B., 2007. The Entrepreneurial Society. Oxford University Press, New York.

Audretsch, D.B., Fritsch, M., 1994. The geography of firm births in Germany. Regional Studies 28, 359–365.

Audretsch, D.B., Keilbach, M., 2004a. Does entrepreneurship capital matter? Entrepreneurship Theory and Practice 28, 419–429.

Audretsch, D.B., Keilbach, M., 2004b. Entrepreneurship capital and economic performance. Regional Studies 38, 949–959.

Audretsch, D.B., Keilbach, M., Lehmann, E., 2006. Entrepreneurship and Economic Growth. Oxford University Press, New York.

Bartik, T., 1989. Small business start-ups in the United States: estimates of the effects of characteristics of states. Southern Economic Journal 55, 1004–1018.

Baumol, W.J., 2002a. Entrepreneurship, innovation and growth: the David–Goliath symbiosis. Journal of Entrepreneurial Finance and Business Ventures 7 (2), 1–10.

Baumol, W.J., 2002b. The Free Market Innovation Machine: Analyzing the Growth Miracle of Capitalism. Princeton University Press, Princeton, NJ.

Burton, M.D., Sorensen, J., Beckman, C., 2002. Coming from good stock: career histories and new venture formation. Research in the Sociology of Organizations 19, 229–262.

Carlton, D., 1983. The location and employment choices of new firms: an econometric model with discrete and continuous endogenous variables. Review of Economics and Statistics 65, 440–449.

Chatterji, A.K., 2005. Spawned with a silver spoon? Entrepreneurial performance and innovation in the medical device industry. Working Paper. Duke University.

Ciccone, A., Hall, R., 1996. Productivity and the density of economic activity. American Economic Review 86, 54–70.

Cobb, C.W., Douglas, P.H., 1928. A theory of production. American Economic Review 18 (Suppl.), 139–165.

Cohen, W., Levinthal, D., 1990. Absorptive capacity: a new perspective on learning and innovation. Administrative Science Quarterly 35, 128–152.

Ellison, G., Glaeser, E., 1997. Geographic concentration in the US manufacturing industries: a dartboard approach. Journal of Political Economy 105, 889–927.

Evans, D., Jovanovic, B., 1989. Estimates of a model of entrepreneurial choice under liquidity constraints. Journal of Political Economy 97 (2), 657–674.

Evans, D., Leighton, L., 1990. Small business formation by unemployed and employed workers. Small Business Economics 2, 313–330.

Feldman, M.P., Audretsch, D.B., 1996. R&D spillovers and the geography of innovation and production. American Economic Review 86 (3), 630–640.

Florida, R., 2002. The Rise of the Creative Class. Basic Books, New York.

Gartner, W.B., Carter, N.M., 2003. Entrepreneurial behavior and firm organizing processes. In: Acs, Z.J., Audretsch, D.B. (Eds.), Handbook of Entrepreneurship Research, vol. 1. Kluwer Academic Publishers, Dordrecht, pp. 195–222.

Geroski, P.A., 1989. Entry, innovation, and productivity growth. Review of Economics and Statistics 71 (4), 572–578.

Glaeser, E., Kallal, H., Scheinkmann, J., Shleifer, A., 1992. Growth in cities. Journal of Political Economy 100, 1126–1152.

Grupp, H., Legler, H., 2000. Hochtechnologie 2000, Neudefinition der Hochtechnologie für die Berichterstattung zur technologischen Leistungsfähigkeit Deutschlands. Gutachten für das BMBF, Karlsruhe and Hannover.

Harhoff, D., Steil, F., 1997. Die ZEW-Gründungspanels: Konzeptionelle Überlegungen und Analyse potential. Unternehmensgründungen—Empirische Analysen für die alten und neuen Bundesländer. Nomos, Baden-Baden.

Henderson, V., 1997. Externalities and industrial development. Journal of Urban Economics 42, 449–470.

Henderson, V., Kuncoro, A., Turner, M., 1995. Industrial development in cities. Journal of Political Economy 103 (5), 1067–1090.

Intriligator, M., Bodkin, R., Hsiao, C., 1996. Econometric Models, Techniques and Applications, second ed. Prentice Hall, Upper Saddle River.

Jacobs, J., 1979. The Economy of Cities. Vintage Books, New York.

Klepper, S., 2001. Employee start-ups in high-tech industries. Industrial and Corporate Change 10, 639–674.

Klepper, S., 2006. Spinouts. Unpublished manuscript.

Knight, F.H., 1921. Risk Uncertainty and Profit. Houghton Mifflin, Boston and New York.

Lucas, R.E., 1988. On the mechanics of economic development. Journal of Monetary Economics 22, 3–42.

Mankiw, G., Romer, D., Weil, D., 1992. A contribution to the empirics of economics and growth. Quarterly Journal of Economics 107, 407–437.

Marshall, A., 1920. Principles of Economics, eighth ed. Macmillan, London (Reprint 1994).

Oxenfeldt, A.R., 1943. New firms and free enterprise: pre-war and post-war aspects. Working Paper. American Council of Public Affairs, Washington DC.

Putnam, R.D., 1993. Making Democracy Work: Civic Traditions in Modern Italy. Princeton University Press, Princeton, NJ.

Reynolds, P., Miller, B., Maki, R., 1995. Explaining regional variation in business births and deaths: US 1976–1988. Small Business Economics 7, 389–407.

Reynolds, P., Storey, D., Westhead, P., 1994. Cross-national comparisons of the variation in new firm formation rate. Regional Studies 28, 443–456.

Roberts, M., Tybout, J., 1996. Industrial Evolution in Developing Countries: Micro Patterns of Turnover, Productivity, and Market Structure. Oxford University Press for World Bank, New York.

Romer, D., 1996. Advanced Macroeconomics. McGraw-Hill, Columbus.

Romer, P.M., 1986. Increasing returns and long-run growth. Journal of Political Economy 94 (5), 1002–1037.

Romer, P.M., 1990. Endogenous technical change. Journal of Political Economy 98, S71–S102.

Saxenian, A., 1994. Regional Advantage. Harvard University Press, Cambridge, MA.

Shane, S., Stuart, T., 2002. Organizational endowments and the performance of university startups. Management Science 48 (1), 154–170.

Storey, D.J., 1991. The birth of new firms—does unemployment matter? A review of evidence. Small Business Economics 3, 167–178.

Wennekers, S., Thurik, R., 1999. Linking entrepreneurship and economic growth. Small Business Economics 13 (1), 27–55.

Yamawaki, H., 1990. The effects of business conditions on net entry: evidence from Japan. In: Entry and Market Contestability: An International Comparison, Basil Blackwell, Oxford.

[11]

Small Bus Econ (2009) 32:15–30
DOI 10.1007/s11187-008-9157-3

The knowledge spillover theory of entrepreneurship

**Zoltan J. Acs · Pontus Braunerhjelm ·
David B. Audretsch · Bo Carlsson**

Accepted: 5 November 2008 / Published online: 13 December 2008
© The Author(s) 2008. This article is published with open access at Springerlink.com

Abstract Contemporary theories of entrepreneurship generally focus on the recognition of opportunities
and the decision to exploit them. Although the
entrepreneurship literature treats opportunities as
exogenous, the prevailing theory of economic growth
suggests they are endogenous. This paper advances the
microeconomic foundations of endogenous growth
theory by developing a knowledge spillover theory of
entrepreneurship. Knowledge created endogenously
results in knowledge spillovers, which allow entrepreneurs to identify and exploit opportunities.

Keywords Opportunity · Knowledge ·
Entrepreneurship · Endogenous growth · Start-ups ·
New product innovation

JEL Classifications J24 · L26 · M13 · O3

Any course of action must expose the chooser to
numberless different sequels, rival hypotheses,
some desired and some counter-desired…The
entrepreneur is a maker of history, but his guide
in making it is his judgment of possibilities and
not a calculation of certainties.

G.L.S. Shackle (1982, vii)

Z. J. Acs (✉)
School of Public Policy, George Mason University,
Fairfax, VA, USA
e-mail: zacs@gmu.edu

P. Braunerhjelm
Department of Transport and Economics, The Royal
Institute of Technology, Stockholm, Sweden
e-mail: pontusb@infra.kts.se

D. B. Audretsch
School of Environmental and Public Affairs, Indiana
University, Bloomington, IL, USA
e-mail: daudrets@indiana.edu

B. Carlsson
Weatherhead School of Management, Department of
Economics, Case Western Reserve University, Cleveland,
OH, USA
e-mail: Bo.Carlsson@case.edu

1 Introduction

Where do entrepreneurial opportunities come from?
Endogenous growth models suggest R&D activities
are "purposeful investment in new knowledge"
undertaken by profit-maximizing firms, where knowledge is an input in the process of generating
endogenous growth (Romer 1990; Segerstrom et al.
1990; Aghion and Howitt 1992).[1] The set of technological opportunity is endogenously created by

---

[1] Griliches (1979) formalized the knowledge production
function. In this model, firms are also exogenous and pursue
new economic knowledge as an input into future innovative
activity.

investments in new knowledge. Technological change is central in explaining economic growth: The rate of per capita GDP growth equals the rate of technological change on the steady state growth path. This explanation assumes that efficiency of knowledge production is enhanced by the historically developed stock of scientific-technological knowledge.[2]

In addition to facilitating technological change, knowledge also generates opportunities for third-party firms (Jaffe et al. 1993; Thompson and Fox-Kean 2005), which are often entrepreneurial start-ups (Shane 2001). This occurs through intra-temporal knowledge spillovers. Therefore, entrepreneurial activity involves both arbitrage of opportunities (Kirzner 1973) and exploitation of new opportunities created, but not appropriated by incumbent firms (Schumpeter 1934).

Endogenous growth models are based on strong assumptions for the technical ease and analysis. However, these advantages impose drawbacks of deviations from real-world behavior.

The endogenous growth framework offers no insight into what role, if any, entrepreneurial activity plays in the intra-temporal spillover of tacit knowledge. While the new growth theory enhances our understanding of the growth process, the essence of the Schumpeterian (1934) entrepreneur is missed. As a result, endogenous growth models fail to incorporate a crucial element in the process of economic growth: Transmission of knowledge spillovers through entrepreneurship (Audretsch 1995). This implies that knowledge by itself is only a necessary condition for the exercise of successful enterprise in a growth model. An interesting approach recently focuses on the allocation of societal resources spent on R&D and entrepreneurship. Michelacci (2003) concludes that low rates of return to R&D may be due to lack of entrepreneurial skills. Hence, the ability to transform new knowledge into economic opportunities involves a set of skills, aptitudes, insights and circumstances that is neither uniformly nor widely distributed in the population.

This paper develops a knowledge spillover theory of entrepreneurship to improve the microeconomic foundations of endogenous growth models, in which the creation of knowledge expands technological opportunity. The theory shifts the unit of analysis from exogenously assumed firms to individual agents with new knowledge endowments. Agents with new economic knowledge endogenously pursue the exploitation of such knowledge, implying that the existing stock of knowledge yields spillovers. This further suggests a strong relationship between such knowledge spillovers and entrepreneurial activity. The theory provides an explanation for the role of the individual and the firm in an economy. According to Romer (1996, 204), such an approach "...removes the dead end in neoclassical theory and links microeconomic observations on routines, machine designs, and the like with macroeconomic discussions of technology."

The model is one where new product innovations can come both from either incumbent firms or start-ups (Acs and Audretsch 1988).[3] We can think of incumbent firms as reliant on incremental innovation from the *flow* of knowledge, such as product improvements. Start-ups with access to entrepreneurial talent and intra-temporal spillovers from the *stock* of knowledge are more likely to engage in radical innovation leading to new industries or replacing existing products.[4] According to Baumol (2004, 9): "...the revolutionary breakthroughs continue to come predominantly from small entrepreneurial enterprises, with large industry providing streams of incremental improvements that also add up to major contributions." Entry by start-ups has played a major role in radical innovations, such as software, semiconductors, biotechnology (Zucker et al. 1998) and the information and communications technologies (Jorgenson 2001). Start-ups are especially important at early stages of the life cycle, when technology is still fluid. Therefore, this paper makes the strong assumption that radical innovation comes from new firm start-ups.

---

[2] This is not a fixed stock of knowledge. For example, change introduced by an entrepreneur can make part of the existing stock of knowledge obsolete.

[3] Acs and Audretsch (1988) find that, *ceteris paribus*, the greater extent to which an industry comprises large firms, the greater will be innovative activity, but increased innovative activity will tend to come from small firms rather than large firms.

[4] A large amount of literature exists that shows how entrepreneurial start-ups use networks to access the stock of knowledge.

The main predictions of the model are:

1. An increase in the stock of knowledge has a positive effect on the level of entrepreneurship.
2. The more efficiently incumbents exploit knowledge flows, the smaller the effect of new knowledge on entrepreneurship.
3. Entrepreneurial activities decrease under greater regulation, administrative burden and market intervention by government.

Thus, entrepreneurship contributes to economic growth by acting as a conduit[5] through which knowledge created by incumbent firms spills over to agents who endogenously create new firms. Opportunities are created when incumbent firms invest in, but do not commercialize, new knowledge. In this theory, entrepreneurship is a response to these opportunities. We suggest that, *ceteris paribus*, entrepreneurial activity will be greater where investments in new knowledge are relatively high, since start-ups will exploit spillovers from the source of knowledge production (the incumbents). In an environment with relatively low investments in new knowledge, there will be fewer entrepreneurial opportunities based on potential spillovers.

Our theoretical model explains entrepreneurship as a function of the following factors: knowledge stock, R&D exploitation by incumbents and barriers to entrepreneurship. It considers factors such as risk aversion, legal restrictions, bureaucratic constraints, labor market rigidities, taxes, lack of social acceptance, etc. This explains why economic agents might decide against starting up, even when in possession of knowledge that promises potential profit opportunity. In addition, culture, traditions and institutions are more difficult factors to identify than strictly economic factors, but they also play an important role in entrepreneurship. To capture such country-specific differences, we estimate a reduced form equation with a fixed-effect panel-regression technique.

The paper is organized as follows. The next section examines knowledge spillovers as a source of entrepreneurial opportunity in the endogenous growth framework. We present a formal model in Sect. 2. We test and discuss results in Sects. 3 and 4, using data for the period 1981–2002 for 19 OECD countries. Our

results show that entrepreneurial activity is strongly influenced by knowledge created but not exploited by incumbent firms. We conclude in the final section.

2 Knowledge spillovers as source of entrepreneurial opportunity

In order to enable more realistic applicability, the theory relaxes two central assumptions of the endogenous growth model. The first is that all knowledge is economic knowledge. Arrow (1962) emphasized knowledge as inherently different from traditional factors of production, resulting in a gap between new knowledge (K) and what he termed economic knowledge (K^c).[6] The second assumption is the assumed spillover of knowledge. In endogenous growth models, the existence of the factor of knowledge is equated with *inter-temporal spillover*, which yields endogenous growth. In our model we assume *intra-temporal knowledge spillovers* from incumbent organizations to start-ups. Moreover, *institutions* impose a gap between knowledge and economic knowledge ($0 < K^c/K < 1$), yielding a lower volume of intra-temporal knowledge spillovers (Acs et al. 2004).

Romer (1990) separates economically useful scientific-technological knowledge into two parts: The total set of knowledge consists of non-rival, partially excludable knowledge elements, and the rival, excludable elements of knowledge. Codified knowledge published in books, scientific papers or patent documentations belongs to the first set. This can be only partially excludable: The right of applying a technology for production of a particular good is guaranteed by patenting, but the same technology can be used in other applications as others learn from the patent documentation. Rival, excludable knowledge elements comprise personalized (tacit) knowledge of

---

[5] It is not, of course, the sole conduit.

[6] New knowledge leads to opportunities that can be exploited commercially. However, harnessing new ideas for economic growth requires converting new knowledge (K) into "economic knowledge" that holds commercial opportunity. For example, only about half of the invention disclosures in US universities lead to patent applications. Of these applications, about half result in patents issued, of which only 1/3 are actually licensed. Between 10–20% of licenses actually yield significant income (Carlsson and Fridh 2002, 231). In other words, only 1 or 2% of the inventions are successful in reaching the market and yielding income.

individuals and groups, including experiences and insights of researchers and business people. This does not go far enough. In the model proposed by Romer (1990), the movement of knowledge from firms producing it to other firms is exogenous. That model explains the effect of knowledge spillovers on technological change without elaborating *why* or *how* these spillovers occur.[7]

Why should entrepreneurship play an important role in the intra-temporal spillover of knowledge? New knowledge is characterized by greater uncertainty and asymmetry than other economic goods. Therefore, both the mean expected value of any new idea and its *variance* will differ across economic agents. If an incumbent firm decides the expected economic value of a new idea is not sufficiently high to warrant its development and commercialization, other economic agents may (or may not) assign a higher expected value to the idea. These agents can operate within or outside of the incumbent firm. This divergence in expected valuation can lead to market entry by economic agents to appropriate new knowledge. The knowledge that induces the decision to start new firms is generated by investments made by an incumbent firm. Thus, the start-up serves as the mechanism through which knowledge spills over from sources that produced it (such as a university or research laboratory in an incumbent firm) to a new organizational form where it is actually commercialized.

One way to reconcile the difference in the role of opportunities in models of entrepreneurship and endogenous growth models is the unit of analysis. Most models of entrepreneurship focus on the individual as the decision-making unit of analysis, whereas the literature on endogenous growth focuses on the firm as the decision-making unit of analysis. In such theories, the firm is exogenous, but its role in generating technological change is endogenous. Therefore, our theory focuses not on exogenously assumed firms, but rather, on the individual agent

endowed with new economic knowledge. With this new focus, the issue of appropriability remains, but the central question is: How can economic agents with a given endowment of new knowledge best appropriate its returns (Audretsch 1995)?

In the knowledge spillover theory of entrepreneurship, the knowledge production function is reversed. The agent decides to start a firm based on expected net return from a new product. Accordingly, the inventor would expect compensation for the future value of the potential innovation. In both cases, the employee in the incumbent firm will weigh the alternative of starting a new firm. If expected return from commercialization is sufficiently different for the inventor and for the incumbent decision-maker, and if the cost of starting a new firm is sufficiently low, the employee may choose to leave the incumbent firm to start a new firm. These start-ups typically do not have direct access to a large R&D laboratory. Rather, they rely on knowledge and experience gained in R&D laboratories of previous employers, i.e., the incumbents.

This type of labor mobility is likely to be an important source of intra-temporal knowledge spillovers (Pakes and Nitzan 1983). Essentially, R&D capital is knowledge that can earn a monopoly rent, and this potential rent motivates investment in R&D. To a large extent, R&D capital is embodied in R&D employees (L_R).[8]

Hellmann (2007), Lazear (2005), Hvide (2006) and Anton and Yao (1994) proposed models to examine conditions under which agents pursue entrepreneurial activity by starting rival enterprises. Most of this literature addressed incentives where potential externalities could be internalized (Moen 2005), while some have examined circumstances under which employees take advantage of intellectual human capital (L_E) through start-ups (Bhide

---

[7] Knowledge spillovers operate more strongly in some parts of the economy than in others. Particular characteristics tend to be associated with locations with high density of opportunities, such as those hosting high-tech industries. Most innovations occur in high-technology opportunity industries and not low-technology opportunity industries (Scherer 1965). The extent to which the results of innovation can be appropriated by incumbent firms also varies among industries.

[8] Such *intellectual human capital* is human capital that is neither publicly available nor perfectly protected. This distinguishes it from *ordinary human capital* that is widely diffused knowledge and can be acquired at a cost and earns a normal rate of return (Zucker et al. 1998). This distinction between intellectual human capital and ordinary human capital is almost identical to the distinction between rival and non-rival knowledge found in Romer (1990) where rival, excludable knowledge elements are primarily the personalized (tacit) knowledge of individual agents. We assume that the firm owns the intellectual property that results in a start-up.

1994). If an innovation makes the incumbent firm a true monopolist, it will not be profitable for the agent to pursue a start-up, since the sum of rents in a duopolistic market will be less than monopoly rent. This paper does not model the incentive structure under which individual agents become mobile. Instead, it focuses on institutions that prevent the creation of a monopoly in the first place.

3 Theoretical framework

To model entry, we partly draw on previous contributions in the endogenous growth literature. In particular, those models introduce a mechanism that fosters innovative entry through investments in R&D. We will retain that channel of entry, but also demonstrate how knowledge investment by incumbents can spur entry by entrepreneurs that do not engage in R&D themselves. Since our emphasis is on entry and not growth per se, our aim is not to derive a full-fledged growth model, but rather to focus on the mechanism for entry.[9]

Consider an economy with demand, supply and a financial market.[10] There are two types of firms: Incumbents undertaking R&D to *improve existing products* and start-ups exploiting knowledge spillovers and the existing stock of knowledge to *innovate new products*. Firms that develop an improved or new variety demanded by consumers are rewarded by temporary monopoly profits until new products out compete old ones.

3.1 Demand side

Starting with the demand side, consumers maximize standard linear intertemporal utility,

$$U = \int_0^\infty e^{-\rho t} \ln[h(x)] \mathrm{d}t, \qquad (1)$$

where $\rho t > 0$ equals consumer rate of time preference (discount rate) and h is the sub-utility function.

---

[9] See Braunerhjelm et al. (2006) for a growth model.

[10] For details, see Intriligator (1971), Aghion and Howitt (1992) and Dinopoulos (1996).

Assume that different varieties of the x-goods are perfect substitutes and that v^I refers to the most recent innovated product or variety, with improved quality or novel features. If $vp_t < p_{t-1}$, then all consumers will prefer the new product,

$$h(x_o, x_1, x_2, \ldots\ldots) = \sum_{I=0}^{\infty} v^I x_I, \quad v > 1. \qquad (2)$$

The novel products/qualities demanded by consumers may range from research-intensive varieties to products characterized by combining existing knowledge. Hence, high R&D intensity by itself does not guarantee successful introduction of a new product.

3.2 Supply side

On the production side, new products/qualities can be invented either by incumbent firms investing in R&D or by entrepreneurial start-ups.[11] Successful entry means a temporary monopoly, where the price of the new product/quality equals the improved property of the product, $v = p_I$. The only factor of production is labor, which is allocated among three different activities: R&D production (L_R), self-employment through start-ups (L_E) or a residual sector employing R&D findings and producing final goods (L_F),

$$L_R + L_E + L_F = \bar{L}. \qquad (3)$$

Perfect mobility across sectors assures that wages are equalized.[12] Initial profit conditions for firms/products that successfully enter the market are

$$\pi = (p_I - 1)Y/p_I = (v - 1)Y/v \qquad (4)$$

where p_I represents the price of the new good, corresponding to the quality improvement (v), and wage is set equal to one. Total consumption expenditure is captured by **Y**, that is, demand for a new variety. In the long run, free entry implies zero profits. Hence, in the period preceding the introduction of a new product/firm, prices equal wage costs,

---

[11] The general production function is $x = AL^\gamma$, $0 < \gamma \le 1$.

[12] The final good sector is not modeled in order to enhance transparency. It can be viewed as a sector with constant returns to scale, where labor embodied with findings in the R&D sector at each given time "t" is employed (i.e., labor does not possess skills related to ongoing R&D).

which are set to one. The first-order condition implies $v = p_I \geq 1$.

The introduction of new product innovations occurs either through R&D outlays by incumbents or through start-ups where existing knowledge is combined in innovative ways. The latter does not require any investment in R&D.[13] Instead, individuals combine their given entrepreneurial ability ($\bar{e}_j$) with the overall knowledge stock (K) in an economy to discover commercial opportunities. The societal knowledge stock is a composite of previous knowledge stemming from activities by incumbents and start-ups, i.e., knowledge refers not only to scientific discoveries, but also to novel ways of production and distribution in traditional businesses, changing business models, new marketing strategies, etc. Both types of entry are assumed to occur through a Poisson process.

Hence, the first type of product improvement is related to R&D expenditures, i.e., it is a *flow* variable, taking previous scientific knowledge as the departure point. The second type of innovative new product draws instead on the overall *stock* of knowledge and applies it in a novel way. All innovation implies that some fixed costs are incurred, such as for R&D or marketing. Innovation is thus modeled consistently with real world behavior.

Starting with incumbents, the aggregate probability of a successful product improvement increases in an economy's R&D outlays, measured as R&D

employees.[14] As shown above, labor is the only input. The production technology is characterized by decreasing returns to scale ($0 < \gamma < 1$). At the firm level, each firm i's probability (μ) of successfully launching a new product increases with higher R&D investments. Thus, innovation by incumbents can be modeled as

$$\mu \sum_{i=1}^{n} (\text{R\&D})dt = \mu \left(\sum_{R=1}^{\bar{L}} l_R \right) dt \equiv (1/\sigma) L_R^{\gamma} dt \qquad (5)$$

where dt denotes an infinite increment of time and (σ)refers to an efficiency parameter that reflects how smoothly a new discovery is introduced to the market. The second type of innovative new product occurs through start-ups, where the probability of a successful start-up (η) is related to the given knowledge stock $\bar{K}$ (at each point in time) times the average entrepreneurial ability ($\hat{e}$) in the economy,

$$\eta \left(\sum_{j=1}^{\bar{L}} \bar{e}_j \right) \bar{K} dt = \eta\,(\hat{e}\bar{K})dt \equiv (1/\sigma)\bar{K}^{\gamma} dt. \qquad (6)$$

At the individual level, the probability of success depends on each individual j's given endowment of entrepreneurial talent, which is unevenly distributed across the population of $\bar{L}$ individuals in an economy (Lucas 1978).[15] Also here, decreasing returns to scale ($0 < \gamma < 1$) prevail since an increase in entrepreneurial ability will not translate into a proportional increase in start-ups.[16]

The total rate of innovative entry in an economy can be calculated by employing the additive property of Poisson distributions,

$$\kappa\, dt = \mu\, dt + \eta\, dt = (1/\sigma)(\bar{K}^{\gamma} + L_R^{\gamma})dt. \qquad (7)$$

---

[13] To some extent, this parallels the classification of horizontal and vertical innovations (Howitt 1999; Gancia and Zilibotti 2005). The former refers to new products, whereas the latter implies quality improvements in existing products. In the model specification used by Howitt (1999), an increase in R&D directed towards horizontal innovations may decrease the profit flow accruing to vertical R&D, thereby undermining incentives to undertake vertical innovations. This impairs growth. However, there are considerable differences between the models. The previous literature refers to the discussion on "scale effect" and growth, initiated by Jones (1995). Moreover, in Howitt's model, different production technologies but identical inputs (R&D staff) are assumed for the two types of innovation, whereas in the present context, identical technologies are assumed, but different factors of production are employed. Finally, the line between an improved quality of an existing variety or a new product that replaces the former product is thin and not necessary for our argument.

---

[14] The assumed Poisson entry process means that the time frequency with which entry will occur is a random variable whose distribution is exponential with parameter μ, i.e., μ is the probability per unit of time.

[15] We follow Lucas (1978), who assumes that managerial talent is distinct from labor talent. Lazear (2005) assumes that workers and managers have the same two skills in different combinations. Those with more balanced skills are more likely to become entrepreneurs. Those with varied work and educational backgrounds are much more likely to start their own businesses than those who have focused on one role at work or concentrated in one subject at school. The implications for the size distribution of firms are similar in both models.

[16] Moreover, it would not be optimal for all economic activities to be undertaken by entrepreneurs.

Hence, incumbents may now be replaced by rival firms in an R&D race or by start-ups.[17]

3.3 The financial market

To cover investment costs in R&D or other costs, such as marketing, both incumbents and Schumpeterian entrepreneurs must turn to the financial market.[18] Investors take a risk since start-ups may replace firms, or entrepreneurs may fail. Start-ups are included in investor portfolios prior to entering the market.

Assume that investors can buy shares in all firms in order to minimize risk, implying an average return of $r(t)$. Investors calculate expected returns on their investments over time in the following way. First, a firm's instantaneous profits ($\pi = (p_I - 1)(Y/p_I)$) and the discounted return (V)—or the value of the firm—are linked through the financial market. The (expected) discounted profit is simply the value of the firm at a given time, times the probability it will succeed in inventing (μ_j) or innovating (η_j) new varieties, minus incurred labor costs.

In each period of time (dt) the shareholder receives a dividend, which is related to profits, and the firm appreciates in value $\dot{V}(t)dt = (dV/dt)dt$. However, incumbents (whether R&D-based or the entrepreneurial type) run the risk of being replaced by the introduction of new qualities (κ), thereby risking a loss of $V(t)$,

$$[\pi(t)/V(t)]dt + \dot{V}(t)/V(t)[1-\kappa]dt$$
$$+ \left[(\dot{V}(t) - V(t))/V(t)\right]\kappa dt = r(t)dt \qquad (8)$$

where $(1 - \kappa)$ is the probability that the firm survives and κ represents the probability that the firm will be forced out of business. Consequently, investors will incur losses on previous investments. From Eq. 8, as dt goes to zero,

$$\dot{V}(t)/V(t) + \pi/V(t) = r(t) + \kappa, \quad \dot{V}(t) = 0 \qquad (9)$$
$$\pi/V(t) = r(t) + \kappa \equiv \tilde{r} \qquad (10)$$

i.e., the higher risks associated with an investment in incumbents (because they may become replaced and a capital loss may be incurred) require a higher return in steady state.

To close the model intertemporal consumption must match intertemporal production—i.e., entry of new goods and start-ups reliant upon access to capital. Such an exercise implies solving a dynamic consumption (growth) model subject to a budget constraint (returns on savings and wages). This will not be undertaken here since our predominant interest is entry, not growth. However, in equilibrium the standard dynamic equilibrium condition will apply, implying that the consumer rate of time-preferences (ρ) must equal the rate of return ($\tilde{r}$) of investments over time. Then capital flows to the financial market (savings that is invested in new ventures) correspond exactly to demand for new products of intertemporally utility-maximizing consumers. Note that this does not imply a continuous flow of innovation for each period of time.

Embarking from a traditional consumer utility function, where utility is increasing in new and high quality goods, it was shown how either incumbents or start-ups supply such goods. The production technology only requires labor. Incumbents will employ labor in R&D, whereas new entrepreneurs will engage in production by drawing upon the existing stock of knowledge. Both types of firms depend on capital injections to finance innovation. This is supplied by the financial market through savings by households. Since firms may be threatened by innovation, investors require a risk-adjusted rate of return to invest in either incumbents or start-ups. Equilibrium in the labor market is assured by the assumption of free mobility across sectors, while free entry in the long-run drives profits to zero.

4 Empirical analysis

According to this model, expected profits from entrepreneurship are enhanced by the magnitude of new knowledge, but constrained by the commercialization capabilities of incumbent firms.

---

[17] The same factors that are identified by the theory developed here, as influencing entrepreneurship is also likely to influence imitation in the same direction. This paper does not explore the implications of replictive entrepreneurship.

[18] To improve tractability, we do not consider self-financing as a viable possibility. This connects with Schumpeter (1911 [1934]), who was adamant that the entrepreneur is not a risk-bearer. Risk bearing is the function of the capitalist who lends his funds to the entrepreneur.

4.1 The hypotheses

Given that entrepreneurial activity exceeds zero, the following testable hypotheses are derived from our model (see Appendix A):

Hypothesis 1   An increase in the stock of knowledge is expected to positively impact the degree of entrepreneurship.

Hypothesis 2   The more efficient incumbents are at exploiting R&D, the smaller the effect of a given knowledge stock on entrepreneurship.[19]

Hypothesis 3   Entrepreneurial activities can be expected to decrease under higher regulations, administrative barriers and governmental intervention in the market.

Our model explains entrepreneurship as a function of the following factors: knowledge stock (KSTOCK), R&D exploitation by incumbents (INC) and barriers to entrepreneurship captured by σ (BARR). It considers factors such as risk aversion, legal restrictions, bureaucratic constraints, labor market rigidities, taxes, lack of social acceptance, etc. (Parker 2004). The existence of such barriers is reflected by a low value of σ. This explains why economic agents might decide against starting up, even when in possession of knowledge that promises potential profit opportunity. In addition, culture, traditions and institutions are more difficult factors to identify than strictly economic factors, but they also play an important role in entrepreneurship. To capture such country-specific differences, we estimate a reduced form equation with a fixed-effect panel regression technique,[20]

$$\text{ENT}_{j,t} = \lambda_j + \alpha \text{KSTOCK}_{j,t} + \text{BARR}'_{j,t}\beta + \text{INC}'_{j,t}\gamma \\ + \alpha_4 Z'_{j,t}\delta + \varepsilon_{j,t}$$

where j denotes country, t represents time and Z is a vector of control variables. The error term is expected to exhibit standard properties: That is, $\varepsilon_{j,t}$ is assumed to have an independent and identical distribution with a zero mean and variance σ^2 for all j and t.

4.2 The variables

The dependent variable, entrepreneurship (ENT), proxies country share of self-employed as a percentage of the labor force.[21] There are several reasons to expect the self-employment rate to decrease as economies become more developed. Blau (1987) argues this is a fundamental economic change. He shows that the time series of self-employment is correlated with a measure of the extent to which technological change has been biased towards industries in which self-employment is important. Acs et al. (1994a) document the diversity in self-employment across countries and in time-series by examining variations in self-employment rates across OECD countries. However, the convergence of several factors, notably the decline in heavy manufacturing, growth of services and possibly the bias towards technological change in the 1990s tended to stem the decline in self-employment for most OECD countries. The self-employment rate is the best available measure across-countries and over time, and it serves as an acceptable proxy for high-impact entrepreneurship.[22]

With respect to explanatory variables, our main focus is the endowment of knowledge within an economy. We first elaborate a stock measure composed of accumulated annual R&D flows, assuming an annual depreciation rate of ten percent (KSTOCK). For the time period we are investigating (1981–2002), this implies a rapid accumulation of knowledge stock in the first 10 years (up to 1991) followed by more stable development where change in the knowledge stock is determined by annual outlays on R&D. Obviously, this can insert biases into the estimations. We have therefore chosen to approximate knowledge stocks over the entire period with annual R&D flows,

---

[19] The efficiency with which incumbents exploit knowledge is, in part, related to the incentive structure and intellectual property rights of the firm (Moen 2005; Hellmann 2007; Hvide 2006).

[20] The choice of empirical model is based on an F-test to check the validity of using a fixed-effect regression technique as compared to OLS. The test clearly rejects the null hypotheses of all fixed effects jointly being zero. We also estimated the model without fixed effects, which yields unstable results. A dynamic panel estimation is also a possible approach, but is more appropriate for limited time series data with many panels. The current paper has rather long time series with few panels.

---

[21] The agricultural sector has been excluded.

[22] Start-up data are available from the World Bank, but for a different set of countries across a considerably shorter period (1997–2004). See Klapper et al. (2007) for more. The data are shown to be positively (but weakly) correlated with the self-employment data used in the current study.

which actually constitutes variation in the stock variable once the stock has been built up. Considering that the correlation between the knowledge stock variable and R&D flows was very strong, annual R&D outlays are an acceptable approximation for knowledge stocks.[23] In line with our model, we expect an increase in relative knowledge endowment to increase the profitability of entrepreneurial activity by facilitating the recognition of entrepreneurial opportunities. The knowledge variable is normalized by GDP.

The most difficult variable to model empirically is incumbent intra-temporal exploitation of knowledge. We use two variables that are important indicators of the extent to which incumbents draw upon knowledge flows. The first is the number of patents (PATENTS) in relation to population, where a higher proportion implies that incumbents use more of the existing knowledge flows (Griliches 1986).[24] The second approximation is the gap between actual and potential GDP (GAP). The argument is that full employment of the economy resources, a small percentage difference between actual and potential GDP, diminishes possibilities for start-ups through exploitation of knowledge flows. Both variables are assumed to influence entrepreneurship negatively.

We use two variables to capture the extent of barriers to entrepreneurship in an economy. First, we incorporate public expenditure in relation to GDP (GEXP) as an approximation of total tax pressure and the extent of regulatory interventions in the economy (Nicoletti et al. 2000). As an alternative, we also include tax share in GDP for both individual (TAXPERS) and corporate firms (TAXCORP). Start-ups are less likely to occur if incentive structures are distorted through high taxes (Henrekson 2005). We expect these variables to be negatively associated with entrepreneurship.[25]

In addition to the above variables, we also include a number of control variables where previous research indicates influence on entrepreneurship. Numerous studies claim urban environments are particularly conducive to entrepreneurial activities, innovation and growth because of agglomeration economies (Jacobs 1969; Krugman 1991). Information flows are denser in cities, where different competencies and financial resources are more accessible, and market proximity is obvious (Acs et al. 1994b). We therefore include a variable to capture the share of the population living in urban areas (URBAN). We expect greater urbanization to be reflected in higher entrepreneurial activities. Studies on demographic variables conclude that individuals in the age cohort 30–44 are most likely to undertake entrepreneurial activities. A large share of population in this cohort (AGE) is expected to relate positively to the share of entrepreneurs. In order to smooth out business fluctuations, we control for economic growth, defined as a 5-year moving average (GROWTH). Finally, we control for time-specific effects by implementing either period dummies, annual dummies or a time trend.[26]

All regressions are based on data for 19 OECD countries for the period 1981 to 2002. Data come predominantly from the OECD, but other sources are also used (see Appendix B).[27] Summary statistics and correlations are listed in Tables 1 and 2, respectively.

5 Regression results

Regression results estimating the entrepreneurship rate (ENT) for 1981–2002 are presented in Tables 3 and 4. These results are consistent with the predictions of our model. Entrepreneurial opportunities do not appear to be exogenous but rather systematically created by a high presence of knowledge spillovers. As the positive and statistically significant coefficients of the knowledge stock suggest, entrepreneurial activity tends to be greater where knowledge is more prevalent.

---

[23] For the full sample the correlation coefficient between knowledge stocks and R&D flows varied between 0.95 and 0.98 (5-year averages), depending on the lag-structure. There are some variations across countries. R&D data are not available prior to 1981; hence, it was not possible to construct knowledge stocks using data from the 1970s.

[24] Giuri et al. (2007) and Braunerhjelm and Svensson (2008) provide evidence that large companies hold the dominating part of patents.

[25] We could also use the World Bank cost of doing business as an alternative measure barrier to entry.

[26] For instance, Jorgenson (2001) argues that increased technological change enhanced entrepreneurial activity, particularly in the 1990s.

[27] The following countries are included: Australia, Austria, Belgium, Canada, Denmark, Finland, France, Germany, Ireland, Italy, Japan, The Netherlands, New Zealand, Norway, Portugal, Spain, Sweden, the UK and US. For some variables with missing values, we have used the closest year available.

Variable	Minimum	Mean	Maximum	SD	Observations
Table 1 Descriptive statistics					
ENT	2.83	4.90	8.41	1.37	418
KSTOCK	.28	1.77	4.63	.75	411
GEXP	30.2	47.87	72.93	8.43	412
TAXPERS	3.83	11.54	26.22	4.74	410
TAXCORP	.27	2.87	8.92	1.31	410
PATENT	$9.8\mathrm{E}^{-4}$	.28	1.38	.26	414
GAP	−10.90	−.65	6.83	2.65	418
GROWTH	−3.02	2.64	9.77	1.51	418
URBAN	43.3	74.13	97.10	11.66	418
AGE	16.87	21.88	25.60	1.72	418

Table 3 reports results where no lags are implemented on the knowledge stock variable. In the first three regressions, variables are defined as 5-year averages, while the remaining three implement annual data.[28] Different versions of the time variables are used in the estimations, albeit the results are quite robust regardless of variable specification. When data are defined as 5-year averages in the estimations, the knowledge stock is shown to be positive in all regressions and significant in two of three. With respect to the remaining variables, only demographic structure (AGE) has a consistent and significant impact on entrepreneurship. Incumbent exploitation of knowledge (PATENT and GAP) and barriers to entrepreneurship (GEXP and taxes) have the expected negative signs but are insignificant. Only personal income taxes have a weak negative and significant impact on entrepreneurship.

One reason for the relatively low explanatory value of these regressions may be the limited number of observations from using 5-year averages for the estimations. When the regressions are repeated using annual data, the significance of the knowledge stock variable is strengthened considerably. This is also the case for variables representing entrepreneurial barriers and the impact of incumbents. Note that the patent variable is significant in all regressions, suggesting that extensive knowledge exploitation by incumbents is negatively related to entrepreneurial activity. The lower the ability of incumbents to appropriate new knowledge, the more knowledge will spill over to third parties, as predicted by the theory. Hence, to the degree

that incumbent firms take advantage of opportunities, there will be less entrepreneurial activity. The GAP variable, admittedly defined at an aggregate level, fares less well. Public expenditure (GEXP), which indicates a wide set of barriers to entrepreneurship, has a negative and significant effect on entrepreneurship. As we substitute government expenditure for the two tax variables, the negative and statistically significant coefficient of the personal tax rate indicates that personal taxes are a barrier to entrepreneurship. The positive and weak significance of the corporate tax rate may actually indicate that a higher rate of corporate taxes reduces the propensity for incumbent firms to appropriate returns from opportunities. This can generate more entrepreneurial opportunities.

A lag structure ranging from 1 to 3 years is imposed on the knowledge stock variable, as shown in Table 4. One regression is shown with variables defined as 5-year averages; remaining regressions use annual data. We only present results for estimations using annual dummies.[29] In general, the estimations conform with the results in Table 3, particularly for variables related to knowledge stock, barriers to entrepreneurship and incumbents exploitation of knowledge. The patent variable always presents a negative sign (as does the GAP variable with one exception), and is significant in four of the five regressions using annual data.

Table 2 reports a relatively high correlation coefficient (.74) between the knowledge stock variable (KSTOCK) and the patent variable (PAT-ENT). A similar but weaker coefficient (.47) is

---

[28] Averages are calculated for the periods 1981–85, 1986–90, 1991–95 and 1996–2002. The average for the last period is based on 7 years.

[29] Independent of the time variable used (trend, period dummy or year dummy), the results are quite robust. Regression results using alternative time specifications are available from the authors on request.

Table 2 Correlation matrix, independent variables, 5-year averages, period dummies

	KSTOCK	KSTOCK-1	GEXP	TAX-PERS	TAX-CORP	PATENT	GAP	GROWTH	URBAN	AGE
KSTOCK	1									
KSTOCK-1	.95	1								
GEXP	.11	.02	1							
TAXPERS	.15	.02	.45	1						
TAXCORP	.09	.10	−.44	−.17	1					
PATENT	.74	.76	.35	.05	−.19	1				
GAP	−.04	−.00	−.26	.00	.20	.02	1			
GROWTH	−.20	−.22	−.46	−.16	.29	−.32	.47	1		
URBAN	.19	.24	.11	.44	−.00	.08	.02	−.18	1	
AGE	.09	.11	−.06	.14	.01	.04	−.01	−.16	.19	1

Note: Period dummies not shown. The correlation matrix for annual data is highly similar and is not shown, but of course available on request

Table 3 Regression results, country fixed-effect panels, 5-year averages and annual data

Dep. var: ENT	5-year averages, trend or period dummies			Annual data, trend or year dummies		
KSTOCK	.54**	.51*	.19	.35***	.44***	.19**
	(2.09)	(1.97)	(.67)	(4.02)	(4.93)	(1.95)
GEXP	−.03	−.03	–	−.02***	−.02***	–
	(−1.60)	(−1.58)		(−2.59)	(−3.62)	
TAXPERS	–	–	−.11*	–		−.08***
			(−1.98)			(−4.67)
TAXCORP	–	–	.04	–		.05*
			(.53)			(1.81)
PATENT	−.89	−.56	−.50	−.30*	−.74***	−.66***
	(−1.27)	(−.91)	(−.82)	(−1.68)	(−3.39)	(−3.04)
GAP	.01	−.01	.00	−.01	.01	−.01
	(.14)	(−.25)	(.01)	(−.71)	(.75)	(−.59)
GROWTH[a]	−.04	−.04	.04	.03	−.02	.06***
	(−.45)	(−.66)	(.58)	(1.54)	(.87)	(2.79)
URBAN	.07	.07	.01	.09***	.08***	.03
	(1.46)	(1.56)	(.20)	(5.21)	(4.70)	(1.49)
AGE	.21***	.23***	.22***	.23***	.21***	.19***
	(3.55)	(4.37)	(4.19)	(12.79)	(10.29)	(10.12)
TREND[b]	–	.01	.10	−.00	–	–
		(.09)	(.86)	(−.33)		
YEAR/PERIOD DUMMIES	YES	NO	NO	NO	YES	YES
CONSTANT	−3.99	−4.94	−.08	−6.69***	−6.16***	−1.19
	(−.92)	(−1.19)	(−.02)	(−4.57)	(−3.51)	(−.76)
R^2	.64	.63	.64	.60	.63	.61
F	8.04	9.88	8.64	71.87	22.13	19.15
No. of obs.	73	73	72	408	408	403

[a] Growth is defined as a 5-year moving average when annual data are implemented

[b] Linear time trend

Table 4 Regression results, country fixed-effect panels, 5-year averages (first column) and annual data, lagged knowledge stock variable

Dep. var: ENT	5-year average	Annual data				
KSTOCK-1	.85*	.23**	–	–	–	–
	(1.70)	(2.26)				
KSTOCK-2	–	–	.47***	.26**	–	–
			(4.52)	(2.38)		
KSTOCK-3	–	–	–	–	.46***	.27**
					(3.95)	(2.28)
GEXP	−.06*	–	−.03***	–	−.03***	–
	(−1.77)		(−3.44)		(−3.49)	
TAXPERS	–	−.09***	–	−.09***	–	−.09***
		(−5.10)		(−5.26)		(−5.34)
TAXCORP	–	.04	–	.02	–	.02
		(1.44)		(1.01)		(.87)
PATENT	−.26	−.59***	−.57***	−.50**	−.45*	−.40
	(−.25)	(−2.63)	(−2.32)	(−2.09)	(−1.74)	(−1.62)
GAP	−.06	−.01	.00	−.01	−.00	−.02
	(−1.56)	(−.61)	(.10)	(−.92)	(−.28)	(−1.18)
GROWTH[a]	−.05	.06***	.03	.05***	.03	.06***
	(−.60)	(2.82)	(1.07)	(3.00)	(1.07)	(2.97)
URBAN	.13**	.03*	.10***	.04**	.10***	.05***
	(2.18)	(1.80)	(5.52)	(2.20)	(5.44)	(2.48)
AGE	.23***	.21***	.22***	.21***	.21***	.21***
	(3.22)	(10.30)	(10.19)	(10.40)	(9.83)	(10.32)
TREND[b]	−.17	–	–	–	–	–
	(−1.01)					
YEAR/PERIOD DUMMIES	NO	YES	YES	YES	YES	YES
CONSTANT	7.66	−1.71	−6.47***	−2.30	−6.50***	−2.72*
	(−1.39)	(−1.07)	(−4.19)	(−1.42)	(−4.01)	(−1.66)
R^2	.60	.61	.62	.60	.60	.59
F	5.28	18.88	20.82	17.80	18.74	16.44
No. of obs.	55	385	372	367	353	349

[a] Growth is defined as a 5-year moving average when annual data are implemented

[b] Linear time trend

obtained for the variables GROWTH and GAP, i.e., the difference between potential and actual GDP. Finally, the variables GROWTH and governmental expenditure (GEXP) display a similar degree of correlation (.46). This may introduce multicollinearity into the regressions, making the estimators less efficient, albeit still unbiased. We therefore rerun the regressions where we have excluded GAP (all regressions) and control for the impact of the exclusion in the regressions of either PATENT or GEXP on the other estimates.

As shown in Tables 5 and 6, removing the patent variable from the regressions does not influence the estimates of the knowledge stock variable. However, when we omit GEXP the control variable GROWTH turns significantly positive, but the remaining variables are basically unaffected (if the growth variable is omitted, the significance of the GEXP variable is strengthened). Hence, these correlations have only a minor influence on the results.

Thus, the empirical findings that entrepreneurship tends to be systematically greater in the presence of

Table 5 Regression results, country fixed-effect panels, 5-year averages and annual data

Dep. var: ENT	5-year averages, trend			Annual data, trend		
KSTOCK	.42*	.51**	.51**	.31***	.35***	.36***
	(1.71)	(1.96)	(2.03)	(3.63)	(4.12)	(4.13)
GEXP	–	−.02	−.03	–	−.02***	−.02***
		(−1.11)	(−1.60)		(−2.62)	(−2.57)
PATENT	–	–	−.58	–	–	−.30*
			(−.96)			(−1.67)
GROWTH[a]	.03	−.01	−.05	.06***	.03	.02
	(.75)	(−.11)	(−.77)	(4.10)	(1.60)	(1.43)
URBAN	.11***	.11***	.07	.09***	.10***	.09***
	(2.54)	(2.60)	(1.56)	(5.89)	(6.09)	(5.17)
AGE	.26***	.25***	.23***	.25***	.25***	.23***
	(45.55)	(3.55)	(4.41)	(14.07)	(14.26)	(12.78)
TREND[b]	−.08	−.09	.01	−.01	−.01*	−.01
	(−.88)	(.1.05)	(.10)	(−1.42)	(−1.83)	(−.34)
CONSTANT	−9.38***	−8.74***	−4.81	−8.08***	−7.57***	−6.50
	(−2.72)	(−2.50)	(−1.18)	(−6.04)	(−5.63)	(−4.52)
R^2	.64	.65	.63	.60	.61	.60
F	17.88	15.17	11.52	117.53	100.57	182.17
No. of obs.	74	74	73	411	411	408

[a] Growth is defined as a 5-year moving average when annual data are implemented

[b] Linear time trend

Table 6 Regression results, country fixed-effect panels, annual data, lagged knowledge stock variable

Dep. var: ENT						
KSTOCK-1	.46***	.41***	–	–	–	–
	(3.87)	(4.39)				
KSTOCK-2	–	–	.39***	.45***	–	–
			(3.96)	(4.44)		
KSTOCK-3	–	–	–	–	.43***	.48***
					(3.99)	(4.32)
GEXP	–	−.02***	–	−.02***	–	−.02***
		(−2.64)		(−2.65)		(−2.63)
PATENT	–	−.22	–	−.12	–	−.02
		(−1.17)		(−.58)		(−.07)
GROWTH[a]	.06***	.02	.05***	.02	.05***	.02
	(3.88)	(1.20)	(3.73)	(1.05)	(3.57)	(.88)
URBAN	.10***	.09***	.11***	.10***	.11***	.11***
	(6.23)	(5.69)	(6.48)	(6.19)	(6.52)	(6.18)
AGE	.25***	.24***	.25***	.24***	.25***	.24***
	(13.98)	(12.91)	(13.71)	(12.91)	(13.32)	(12.67)
TREND[b]	−.01*	−.01	−.01*	−.01	−.01*	−.01*
	(−1.71)	(−.97)	(−1.86)	(−1.54)	(1.86)	(−1.86)

(continued overleaf)

Table 6 continued

Dep. var: ENT						
CONSTANT	−8.79***	−7.32***	−9.30***	−8.07***	−9.58***	−8.25***
	(−6.40)	(−5.07)	(−6–62)	(−5.58)	(−6.66)	(−5.54)
R^2	.60	.61	.60	.60	.58	.58
F	11.73	78.80	102.43	73.52	91.17	64.60
No. of obs.	392	390	373	372	354	353

[a] Growth is defined as a 5-year moving average when annual data are implemented

[b] Linear time trend

knowledge spillovers are strikingly robust. Although the significance and even sign of some control variables are more sensitive to time period and variable specification, entrepreneurial activity responds positively to economic knowledge, regardless of time and variable specification.

6 Conclusions

This paper has developed a Knowledge Spillover Theory of Entrepreneurship in which the creation of new knowledge expands the set of technological opportunity. Therefore, entrepreneurial activity does not involve simply the arbitrage of opportunities, but also the exploitation of intra-temporal knowledge spillovers not appropriated by incumbent firms. The theory focuses on individual agents with endowments of new economic knowledge as the unit of analysis in a model of economic growth, rather than exogenously assumed firms. Agents with new knowledge endogenously pursue the exploitation of knowledge. This suggests that knowledge spillovers come from the stock of knowledge, and there is a strong relationship between such spillovers and entrepreneurial activity. If incumbent firms appropriated all the rents of R&D, there would be no intra-temporal knowledge spillovers.

There are several implications of these findings for future research. First, theories of entrepreneurship need to explain where opportunities come from, how intra-temporal knowledge spillovers occur, and the dynamics of occupational choice leading to new firm formation. Prevailing theories of entrepreneurship do not address these questions. Second, the theory helps better understand the contradictions in Smith's *Wealth of Nations* between increasing returns (the pin factory) and how the market economy can harness self-interest to the common good, leading individuals to unintentional ends (the invisible hand). The real challenge in endogenous growth theory is not that the firm will under-invest in new knowledge, but how to balance increasing returns with competition. The theory provides an explanation of the role of the individual and the firm in the economy. If Romer inspired a new economics of knowledge, The Knowledge Spillover Theory of Entrepreneurship brings us a step closer to understanding the essential role of the entrepreneur in the market economy. Finally, the role of intellectual property rights protection needs to be revaluated in light of the theory. If intellectual property protection becomes too strong, and all rents accrue to the producer of knowledge, it will reduce intra-temporal knowledge spillovers, and ultimately innovation and growth (Acs and Sanders 2008).

Acknowledgements We thank discussants at the 2007 DRUID conference in Copenhagen, Sameeksha Desai, Larry Plummer, Mark Sanders, Scott Shane, Mariagrazia Squicciarini, Siri Terjesen and two anonymous referees for valuable comments. We would also like to thank Per Thulin and Benny Borgman for excellent research assistance and the Marianne and Marcus Wallenberg Foundation for generous financial support.

Appendix A

From Eqs. 5, 6 and 7, the impact of a change in the knowledge stock (K), R&D efforts by incumbents (L_R) and in the efficiency parameter (σ, $0 < \sigma < 1$), where values close to zero in the efficiency variable implies fewer obstacles in introducing new products, can be derived as

Table 7 Definition of variables and data source

Variable	Definition	Sources
ENT	Dependent variable. Non-agricultural self-employed, as percentage of total non-agricultural employment	EIM, The COMPENDIA Database
KSTOCK	Gross domestic expenditure on R&D as percentage of GDP. KSTOCK-t refers to different lag structures	OECD, Main Science and Technology Indicators
GEXP	Total government disbursements as percentage of GDP	OECD, Economic Outlook
TAXPERS	Taxes on personal income, as percentage of GDP	OECD, Revenue Statistics
TAXCORP	Taxes on corporate income, as percentage of GDP	OECD, Revenue Statistics
PATENT	Number of patents applications to the EPO by residence of the inventor (date of grant) divided by total population expressed in 10,000	OECD, Patent Database
GAP	Difference between actual annual GDP and potential GDP, divided by potential GDP	OECD, Economic Outlook
GROWTH	Average growth over 5 years. Alternatively (see notes in the regression tables), 5-year moving average of gross domestic product growth (at the price levels and PPPs of 1995)	OECD, National Accounts vol. 1, Main Aggregates; OECD, Economic Outlook for Germany
URBAN	The share of the total population living in urban areas	World Bank, World Development Indicators
AGE	Share of population between 30 and 44 years of age. Data published every 5th year. Intermediate values estimated by cubic splines	United Nations; OECD, Economic Outlook
TREND	Linear time trend	

$$\kappa_K = (1/\sigma)\gamma K^{\gamma-1} > 0,$$
$$\kappa_{KK} = (1/\sigma)(\gamma - 1)\gamma K^{\gamma-2} < 0 \quad (\gamma < 1), \quad (A.1a)$$
$$\kappa_{L_R} = (1/\sigma)\gamma L_R^{\gamma-1} > 0,$$
$$\kappa_{L_R L_R} = -(1/\sigma)(\gamma - 1)\gamma L_R^{\gamma-2} < 0 \quad (\gamma < 1) \quad (A.1b)$$
$$\kappa_{\sigma} = -[(K^{\gamma}) + (L)^{\gamma}]/\sigma^2 < 0,$$
$$\kappa_{\sigma\sigma} = 2[(K^{\gamma}) + (L)^{\gamma}]/\sigma^3 > 0, \quad (A.1c)$$

implying that the probability of entrepreneurial start-ups is increasing in the knowledge stock (weighted by average entrepreneurial ability), but at a decreasing rate (A.1a). By increasing R&D staff, incumbent firms increase the probability of launching a new quality, albeit at a decreasing rate (A.1b). Both types of innovation are positively affected by a more efficient economy, but at a decreasing rate (A.1c).

Appendix B

See Table 7.

References

Acs, Z. J., & Sanders, M. (2008). *Intellectual property rights and the knowledge spillover theory of entrepreneurship.* Working paper. Jena: Max Planck Institute of Economics.

Acs, Z. J., Audretsch, D. B., Braunerhjelm, P., & Carlsson, B. (2004). *The missing link: The knowledge filter and entrepreneurship in endogenous growth.* Discussion Paper no. 4783. London, UK: Center for Economic Policy Research.

Acs, Z. J., Audretsch, D. B., & Evans, D. S. (1994a). *The determinants of variations in self-employment rates across countries and over time.* Discussion Paper no. 871. London, UK: Centre for Economic and Policy Research.

Acs, Z. J., Audretsch, D. B., & Feldman, M. P. (1994b). R&D spillovers and recipient firm size. *The Review of Economics and Statistics, 76,* 336–340.

Acs, Z. J., & Audretsch, D. B. (1988). Innovation in large and small firms: An empirical analysis. *The American Economic Review, 78,* 678–690.

Aghion, P., & Howitt, P. (1992). A model of growth through creative destruction. *Econometrica, 60,* 323–351.

Anton, J. J., & Yao, D. A. (1994). Expropriation and inventions: Appropriable rents in the absence of property rights. *The American Economic Review, 84,* 190–209.

Arrow, K. (1962). Economic welfare and the allocation of resources for invention. In R. Nelson (Ed.), *The rate and direction of inventive activity.* NJ: Princeton University Press and NBER.

Audretsch, D. B. (1995). *Innovation and industry evolution.* Cambridge, USA: MIT Press.

Baumol, W. J. (2004). Entrepreneurial enterprises, large established firms and other components of the free-market growth machine. *Small Business Economics, 23,* 9–21.

Bhide, A. (1994). How entrepreneurs craft strategies that work. *Harvard Business Review, 72,* 150–161.

Blau, D. M. (1987). A time-series analysis of self-employment in the United States. *The Journal of Political Economy, 95,* 445–467.

Braunerhjelm, P., & Svensson, R. (2008). The inventor's role: Was Schumpeter right? *Journal of Evolutionary Economics,* forthcoming.

Carlsson, B., & Fridh, A.-C. (2002). Technology transfer in United States universities: A survey and statistical analysis. *Journal of Evolutionary Economics, 12,* 199–232.

Dinopoulos, E. (1996). Schumpeterian growth theory: An overview. In E. Helmstädter & M. Perlman (Eds.), *Behavioral norms, technological progress and economic dynamics.* Ann Arbor: The University of Michigan Press.

Gancia, G., & Zilibotti, F. (2005). Horizontal innovation in the theory of growth and development. In P. Aghion & S. Durlauf (Eds.), *Handbook of economic growth.* North Holland, Amsterdam: New York Elsevier.

Giuri, P., Mariani, M., Brusoni, S., Crespi, G., Francoz, D., Gambardella, A., et al. (2007). Inventors and invention processes in Europe: Results from the PatVal-EU survey. *Research Policy, 36,* 1107–1127.

Griliches, Z. (1979). Issues in assessing the contribution of R&D to productivity growth. *Bell Journal of Economics, 10,* 92–116.

Griliches, Z. (1986). Productivity, R&D, and basic research at the firm level in the 1970s. *The American Economic Review, 76,* 141–154.

Hébert, R. F., & Albert, N. (1982). *The entrepreneur: Mainstream views and radical critiques.* New York: Praeger.

Hellmann, T. (2007). When do employees become entrepreneurs? *Management Science, 53,* 919–933.

Henrekson, M. (2005). Entrepreneurship: A weak link in the welfare state? *Industrial and Corporate Change, 14,* 437–467.

Howitt, P. (1999). Steady endogenous growth with population and R&D inputs growing. *Journal of Political Economy, 107,* 715.

Hvide, H. K. (2006). Firm size and the quality of entrepreneurs. *Economic Journal,* in press.

Intriligator, M. D. (1971). *Mathematical optimization and economic theory.* NJ: Prentice-Hall Englewood Cliffs.

Jacobs, J. (1969). *The economy of cities.* NY, USA: Random House.

Jaffe, A. B., Trajtenberg, M., & Henderson, R. (1993). Geographic localization of knowledge spillovers as evidenced by patent citations. *Quarterly Journal of Economics, 108,* 577–598.

Jones, C. I. (1995). R&D-based models of economic growth. *Journal of Political Economy, 103,* 759–784.

Jorgenson, D. W. (2001). Information technology and the US economy. *The American Economic Review, 91,* 1–32.

Kirzner, I. M. (1973). *Entrepreneurship and competition.* Chicago: University of Chicago Press.

Klapper, L., Amit, R., Guillén, M. F., & Quesada, J. M. (2007). *Entrepreneurship and firm formation across countries. Development Research Group Working Paper.* Washington DC: World Bank.

Krugman, P. (1991). Increasing returns and economic geography. *The Journal of Political Economy, 99,* 483–499.

Lazear, E. P. (2005). Entrepreneurship. *Journal of Labor Economics, 23,* 649–680.

Lucas, R. E. J. R. (1978). On the size distribution of business firms. *The Bell Journal of Economics, 9,* 508–523.

Michelacci, C. (2003). Low returns in R&D due to the lack of entrepreneurial skills. *The Economic Journal, 113,* 207–225.

Moen, J. (2005). Is mobility of technical personnel a source of R&D spillovers? *Journal of Labor Economics, 23,* 81–114.

Nicoletti, G., Scarpetta, S., & Boylaud, O. (2000). *Summary indicators of product market regulation with an extension to employment protection legislation. Concepts and measurement of labour markets flexibility/adaptability indicators.* Paris: OECD Economics Department.

Pakes, A., & Nitzan, S. (1983). Optimum contracts for research personnel, research employment, and the establishment of "Rival" Enterprises. *Journal of Labor Economics, 1,* 345–365.

Parker, S. C. (2004). *The economics of self-employment and entrepreneurship.* New York: Cambridge University Press.

Romer, P. M. (1990). Endogenous technological change. *The Journal of Political Economy, 98,* 71–102.

Romer, P. M. (1996). Why, indeed, in America? Theory, history, and the origins of modern economic growth. *The American Economic Review, 86,* 202–206.

Scherer, F. M. (1965). Firm size, market structure, opportunity, and the output of patented inventions. *The American Economic Review, 55,* 1097–1125.

Schumpeter, J. (1911 [1934]). *The theory of economic development,* New York: Oxford University Press.

Segerstrom, P. S., Anant, T. C. A., & Dinopoulos, E. (1990). A Schumpeterian model of the product life cycle. *The American Economic Review, 80,* 1077–1091.

Shackle, G. L. S. (1982). Foreword. In R. F. Hebert & A. Link (Eds.), *The entrepreneur: Mainstream views and radical critiques.* New York: Praeger Publishers.

Shane, S. (2001). Technological opportunities and new firm creation. *Management Science, 47,* 205–220.

Thompson, P., & Fox-Kean, M. (2005). Patent citations and the geography of knowledge spillovers: A reassessment. *American Economic Review, 95,* 450–460.

von Hayek, F. A. (1937). Economics and knowledge. *Economica, 4,* 33–54.

Zucker, L. G., Darby, M. R., & Brewer, M. B. (1998). Intellectual human capital and the birth of us biotechnology enterprises. *The American Economic Review, 88,* 290–306.

[12]

J Technol Transf (2009) 34:245–254
DOI 10.1007/s10961-008-9101-3

The entrepreneurial society

David B. Audretsch

Published online: 23 December 2008

Abstract This paper explains why and how entrepreneurship has emerged as an engine of economic growth, employment creation and competitiveness in global markets. The entrepreneurial society reflects the emergence as entrepreneurship as an important source of economic growth.

Keywords Entrepreneurship · Economic growth · Growth · Innovation · Knowledge · Spillovers

JEL classification D03 · O40 · L26

1 Introduction

A generation ago, public policy looked to the great corporations as the engine of economic growth. Charlie "Engine" Wilson, then the Chairman of General Motors, admonishment, "What's good for General Motors is good for America,"[1] reflected a sense that it was the large manufacturing corporation in industries based on large-scale production with high investments in physical capital that shaped economic performance. Scholars in economics (Scherer 1970) and management (Chandler 1977 and Chandler 1990) generally backed this view up with compelling empirical evidence.

However, more recently, a very different view has emerged about the sources of economic growth and therefore the appropriate role for public policy. With the 2000 Lisbon Proclamation emanating from the European Council of Europe, Prodi (2002, p. 1),

---

[1] Quoted from Halberstam (1993, p. 118).

D. B. Audretsch (✉)
Institute for Development Strategies, School of Public and Environmental Affairs (SPEA), Indiana University, Bloomington, IN 47405, USA
e-mail: daudrets@indiana.edu

D. B. Audretsch
Max Planck Institute of Economics, Jena, Germany

President of the European Commission, committed the European Union to becoming the world's entrepreneurship leader in order to ensure prosperity and a high level of economic performance in the EU, "Our lacunae in the field of entrepreneurship needs to be taken seriously because there is mounting evidence that the key to economic growth and productivity improvements lies in the entrepreneurial capacity of an economy."

As Breshsnahan and Gambardella (2004, p. 1) observe, "Clusters of high-tech industry, such as Silicon Valley, have received a great deal of attention from scholars and in the public policy arena. National economic growth can be fueled by development of such clusters. …Innovation and entrepreneurship can be supported by a number of mechanisms operating within a cluster." Mowery (2005, p. 1) similarly observes, "During the 1990s, the era of the 'New Economy', numerous observers (including some who less than 10 years earlier had written off the U.S. economy as doomed to economic decline in the face of competition from such economic powerhouses as Japan), hailed the resurgent economy in the United States as an illustration of the power of high-technology entrepreneurship. The new firms that a decade earlier had been criticized by authorities such as the MIT Commission on Industrial Productivity (Dertouzos et al. 1989) for their failure to sustain competition against non-U.S. firms, were now seen as important sources of economic dynamism and employment growth. Indeed, the transformation in U.S. economic performance between the 1980s and 1990s is only slightly less remarkable than the failure of most experts in academia, government, and industry, to predict it."

The purpose of this paper is to explain how and why the driving force of economic growth, employment creation and global competitiveness has evolved so dramatically in the past half century. The changing role of entrepreneurship in the economy reflects three disparate views of the economy, which correspond not only to three historical periods but also three economic models. The first emphasizes the importance of physical capital and corresponds to the public policy debate framed by the Solow model. The second emphasizes the importance of knowledge and corresponds to the Romer model. The third focuses on the role of knowledge-based entrepreneurship and corresponds to a shift in the public policy debate as to how to create an entrepreneurial society.

2 The Solow economy

Something of a consensus emerged about the driving force underlying economic growth emerging from the second world war and the Great Depression before it—physical capital. Robert Solow was awarded the Nobel Prize for formalizing the neoclassical model of economic growth, where two factors of production—physical capital and labor—were econometrically linked to economic growth.[2] As Nelson (1981, p. 1032) wrote, "Since the mid-1950s, considerable research has proceeded closely guided by the neoclassical formulation. Some of this work has been theoretical. Various forms of the production function have been invented. Models have been developed which assume that technological advance must be embodied in new capital…Much of the work has been empirical and guided by the growth accounting framework implicit in the neoclassical model."

---

[2] Solow in fact pointed out that technical change was essential for economic growth. However, in the econometric specification, the impact of technical change was inferred from the unexplained residual, which "falls like manna from heaven." According to Nelson (1981, p. 1030), "Robert Solow's 1956 theoretical article was largely addressed to the pessimism about full employment growth built into the Harrod-Domar model…In that model he admitted the possibility of technological advance.".

In fact, the public policy debate to generate growth and employment reflected, if not was guided by, the framework provided by Solow and his disciples. The Solow model focused economic growth and employment policy on investments in physical capital. This certainly reflected the popular perception of physical capital as the engine for economic growth. As the historian Robert Payne reflected at the U.S. post World War II economic performance, "There never was a country more fabulous than America. She sits bestride the world like a Colossus; no other power at any time in the world's history has possessed so varied or so great an influence on other nations...Half of the wealth of thee world, more than half of the productivity, nearly two-thirds of the world machines are concentrated in American hands, the rest of the world lies in the shadow of American industry."[3]

If the Solow model provided the crucial link between physical capital and economic growth for the macroeconomic unit of analysis, a concomitant focus on how the organization and deployment or strategy involving the factor of physical capital emerged for the unit of analysis of the firm (Chandler 1977 and 1990) and industry (Scherer 1970). In fact, the entire field of industrial organization had emerged as a response to a public policy concern over large corporations possessing too much market power as to corrupt the functioning of markets and ultimately the economy. Industrial organization had its roots as a response to the so-called *Trust Problem* emerging in the mid- to late-1800s. The first stirring of industrial organization as a field came as response to the emergence of the trusts of the late 1900s and their perceived adverse impact on performance criteria such as prices and profits. Not only were their trusts attributed to demolishing family businesses, farms in the Midwest and entire communities, but the public policy debate at the time accused them of threatening the underpinnings of democracy in the United States. In arguing for the passage of the 1890 Act, Senator Sherman argued, "If we will not endure a King as a political power we should endure a King over the production, transportation, and sale of the necessaries of life. If we would not submit to an emperor we should not submit to an autocrat of trade with power to prevent competition and to fix the price of any commodity."

It became the task of the scholars toiling in the field of industrial organization to explicitly identify what exactly was gained and lost, as a result of large-scale production and a concentration of economic ownership and decision-making. During the post-war period a generation of scholar galvanized the field of industrial organization by developing a research agenda dedicated to identifying the issues involving this perceived trade-off between economic efficiency on the one hand, and political and economic decentralization on the other. Scholarship in industrial organization generated a massive literature focusing on essentially three issues:

(1) What are the gains to size and large-scale production?
(2) What are the economic welfare implications of having an oligopolistic or concentrated market structure (i.e. Is economic performance promoted or reduced in an industry with just a handful of large-scale firms?)
(3) Given the overwhelming evidence that large-scale production resulting in economic concentration is associated with increased efficiency, what are the public policy implications?

Oliver Williamson's classic 1968 article "Economies as an Antitrust Defense: The Welfare Tradeoffs," published in the *American Economic Review*, became something of a final statement demonstrating what appeared to be an inevitable trade-off between the gains in productive efficiency from increased concentration and gains in terms of

---

[3] Quoted from Halberstam (1993, p. 116).

competition, and implicitly democracy, from decentralizing policies (Williamson 1968). But it did not seem possible to have both; certainly not in Williamson's completely static model.

Thus, one of the most fundamental policy issue confronting Western Europe and North America during the post-war era was how to live with this apparent trade-off between economic concentration and productive efficiency on the one hand, and decentralization and democracy on the other. The public policy question of the day was, *How can society reap the benefits of the large corporation in an oligopolistic setting while avoiding or at least minimizing the costs imposed by a concentration of economic power?* The policy response was to constrain the freedom of firms to contract. Such policy restraints typically took the form of public ownership, regulation, and competition policy or antitrust. At the time, considerable attention was devoted to what seemed like glaring differences in policy approaches to this apparent trade-off by different countries. France and Sweden resorted to government ownership of private business. Other countries, such as the Netherlands and Germany, tended to emphasize regulation. Still other countries, such as the United States, had a greater emphasis on antitrust. In fact, most countries relied on elements of all three policy instruments. While the particular instrument may have varied across countries, they were, in fact, manifestation of a singular policy approach—how to restrict and restrain the power of the large corporation. What may have been perceived as the disparate set of policies at the time appears in retrospect to comprise a remarkable singular policy approach.

Western economists and policy-makers of the day were nearly unanimous in their acclaim for large-scale enterprises. It is no doubt an irony of history that this consensus mirrored a remarkably similar gigantism embedded in Soviet doctrine, fueled by the writing of Marx and ultimately implemented by the iron fist of Stalin. This was the era of mass production when economies of scale seemed to be the decisive factor in determining efficiency. This was the world so colorfully describe d by Galbraith (1956) in his Theory of Countervailing Power, in which big business was held in check by big labor and by big government.

With a decided focus on the role of large corporations, oligopoly, and economic concentration, the literature on industrial organization yielded a number of key insights concerning the efficiency and impact on economic performance associate with new and small firms:

(1) Small firms were generally less efficient than their larger counterparts. Studies from the United States in the 1960s and 1970 revealed that small firms produced at lower levels of efficiency.
(2) Small firms provided lower levels of employee compensation. Empirical evidence from both North America and Europe found a systematic and positive relationship between employee compensation and firm size.
(3) Small firms were only marginally involved in innovative activity. Based on R&D measures, SMEs accounted for only a small amount of innovative activity.
(4) The relative importance of small firms was declining over time in both North America and Europe.

Thus, while a heated debate emerged about which approach best promoted large-scale production while simultaneously constraining the ability of large corporations to exert market power, there was much less debate about public policy toward small businesses and entrepreneurship. The only issue was whether public policy-makers should simply allow small firms to disappear as a result of their inefficiency or intervene to preserve them on social and political grounds. Those who perceived small firms to contribute significantly to growth, employment generation, and competitiveness were few and far between.

In the post-war era, small firms and entrepreneurship were viewed as a luxury, perhaps needed by the West to ensure a decentralization of decision-making; but obtained only at a cost to efficiency. Certainly the systematic empirical evidence, gathered from both Europe and North America documented a short trend toward a decreased role of small firms during the post-war period.

Public policy toward small firms generally reflected the view of economists and other scholars that they were a drag on economic efficiency and growth, generated lower quality jobs in terms of direct and indirect compensation, and were generally on the way to becoming less important to the economy, if not threatened by long-term extinction. Some countries, such as the former Soviet Union, but also Sweden and France, adapted the policy stance of allowing small firms to gradually disappear and account for a smaller share of economic activity.

The public policy stance of the United States reflected long-term political and social valuation of small firms that seemed to reach back to the Jeffersonian traditions of the country. Thus, the public policy toward small business in the United States was oriented toward preserving what was considered to be inefficient enterprises, which, if left unprotected, might otherwise become extinct.

Even advocates of small business agreed that small firms were less efficient than big companies. These advocates were willing to sacrifice a modicum of efficiency, however, because of other contributions—moral, political, and otherwise—made by small business to society. Small business policy was thus "preservationist" in character. For example, the passage of the Robinson-Patman Act in 1936, along with its widespread enforcement in the post-war era, was widely interpreted as one effort to protect small firms, like independent retailers, that would otherwise have been too inefficient to survive in open competition with large corporations. Preservationist policies were clearly at work in the creation of the U.S. Small Business Administration. In the *Small Business Act* of July 10, 1953, Congress authorized the creation of the Small Business Administration, with an explicit mandate to "aid, counsel, assist, and protect...the interests of small business concerns."[4] *The Small Business Act* was clearly an attempt by the Congress to halt the continued disappearance of small businesses and to preserve their role in the U.S. economy.

3 The Romer economy

Globalization did not change the importance of physical capital but rather drastically altered the geography of its location. The post-war distribution of physical capital highly concentrated in the United States, as Payne observed, did not prove to be sustainable. Rather, as first Western Europe and Japan recovered, but subsequent to 1989 eastern Europe, and other parts of Asia as well, the comparative advantage of production based on physical capital shifted from the high-cost OECD countries to lower cost regions. As a result, employment in traditional manufacturing industries in the most developed countries plummeted (Audretsch 2007).

Economics had an answer. If physical capital was at the heart of the Solow economy, knowledge capital replaced it in the Romer economy. Most significantly, while it had proven feasible to locate economic activity based on physical capital at foreign locations in

---

[4] http://www.sba.gov/aboutsba/sbahistory.html

a manner that had been predicted by Vernon (1966), outsourcing and offshoring economic ideas based on ideas, and in particular tacit knowledge, was less feasible. This suggested that the comparative advantage of high cost locations was shifting away from physical capital and towards knowledge or economic activity based on new ideas that could not costlessly be copied. While the policy goals of economic growth remained relatively unchanged, the Romer model reflected the emergence of a new emphasis on a strikingly different policy mechanism, knowledge capital, involving very different policy instruments, such as investments in human capital, research and a focus on intellectual property protection (Romer 1986; Lucas 1993).

Entrepreneurship and small firms seemed at least as incompatible with the knowledge-based Romer economy as they were in the capital-based Solow economy (Solow 1956). The most prevalent theory of innovation in economics, the model of the knowledge production function, suggested that knowledge-generating inputs, such as research and development (R&D) were a prerequisite to generating innovative output. With their limited and meager investments in R&D, at least in absolute terms, new and small firms did not seem to possess sufficient knowledge capabilities to be competitive in a knowledge-based economy.

However, investments in knowledge, such as human capital, R&D and patents, as well as broader aspects such as creativity, did not prove to be an automatic panacea for stagnant economic growth and rising unemployment. In what became known first as the *Swedish Paradox*, which was later adapted as the *European Paradox*, described the disappointment of economic growth that did not seem to respond to high levels of investment in knowledge.

4 The entrepreneurial society

The resolution of the Swedish Paradox and European Paradox (Audretsch & Keilbach 2008) came from rethinking the fundamental model of innovation. in searching for the innovative advantage of different types of firms, Acs & Audretsch (1988, 1990) surprisingly found that small firms provided the engines of innovative activity, at least in certain industries. The breakdown of the model of the knowledge production function at the level of the firm raises the question, *Where do innovative firms with little or no R&D get the knowledge inputs?* This question becomes particularly relevant for small and new firms that undertake little R&D themselves, yet contribute considerable innovative activity in newly emerging industries such as biotechnology and computer software. One clue supplied by the literature on new economic geography identifying the local nature of knowledge spillovers is from other, third-party firms or research institutions, such as universities, that may be located within spatial proximity (Audretsch 1995). Economic knowledge may spill over from the firm conducting the R&D or the research laboratory of a university for access by a new and small firm.

How can new and small firms access such knowledge spillovers? And why should new and small firms have a competitive advantage accessing knowledge produce elsewhere via-a-vis their larger counterparts? That is, what are the mechanisms transmitting the spillover of the knowledge from the source producing that knowledge, such as the R&D laboratory of a large corporation, or a university, to the small firm actually engaged in commercializing that knowledge.

The discrepancy in organizational context between the organization creating opportunities and those exploiting the opportunities that seemingly contradicted the model of the firm knowledge production function was resolved by introducing the Knowledge Spillover

Theory of Entrepreneurship, "The findings challenge an assumption implicit to the knowledge production function—that firms exist exogenously and then endogenously seek out and apply knowledge inputs to generate innovative output... It is the knowledge in the possession of economic agents that is exogenous, and in an effort to appropriate the returns from that knowledge, the spillover of knowledge from its producing entity involves endogenously creating a new firm" (Audretsch 1995, pp. 179–180).

What is the source of this entrepreneurial opportunity that endogenously generated the startup of the new firms? The answer seemed to be through the spillover of knowledge that created the opportunities for the startup of a new firm, "How are these small and frequently new firms able to generate innovative output when undertaken a generally negligible amount of investment into knowledge-generating inputs, such as R&D? One answer is apparently through exploiting knowledge created by expenditures on research in universities and on R&D in large corporations" (Audretsch 1995, p.179).

The empirical evidence supporting the knowledge spillover theory of entrepreneurship was provided by analyzing variations in startup rates across various industries reflecting different underlying knowledge contexts. In particular, those industries with a greater investment in new knowledge also exhibited higher startup rates while those industries with less investment in new knowledge exhibited lower startup rates, which were interpreted as a conduit transmitting knowledge spillovers (Audretsch & Keilbach 2007).

Thus, compelling evidence was provided suggesting that entrepreneurship is an endogenous response to opportunities created but not exploited by the incumbent firms. This involved an organizational dimension involving the mechanism transmitting knowledge spillovers—the startup of new firms. Additionally, Jaffe (1989), Audretsch and Feldman (1996) and Audretsch and Stephan (1996) provided evidence concerning the spatial dimension of knowledge spillovers. In particular, their findings suggested the knowledge spillovers are geographically bounded and localized within spatial proximity to the knowledge source. None of these studies, however, identified the actual mechanisms which actually transmit the knowledge spillover; rather, the spillovers were implicitly assumed to automatically exist (or fall like Manna from heaven), but only within a geographically bounded spatial area.

The knowledge spillover theory of entrepreneurship contests the view that entrepreneurial opportunities are exogenous and only individual-specific characteristics and attributes influence the cognitive process underlying the entrepreneurial decision to start a firm. Rather, the Knowledge Spillover Theory of Entrepreneurship explicitly identifies an important source of opportunities – investments in knowledge and ideas made by firms and universities that are not completely commercialized. By linking the degree of entrepreneurial activity to the degree of knowledge investments in a specific place, systematic empirical evidence was provided suggesting that entrepreneurial opportunities are not at all exogenous, but rather endogenous to the extent of investments in new knowledge. In a comprehensive study with colleagues at the Max Planck Institute, we found that regions rich in knowledge generated a greater amount of entrepreneurial opportunities than regions with impoverished knowledge (Audretsch et al. 2006). This empirical evidence confirmed the theory suggesting that entrepreneurial opportunities are not exogenous to the context but, rather, systematically related to the knowledge context.

The Knowledge Spillover Theory of Entrepreneurship identified one such mechanism by which knowledge created with one context and purpose spills over from the organization creating it to the organization actually attempting to commercialize that knowledge. Entrepreneurship has emerged as a vital organizational form for economic growth because it provides the missing link (Acs et al. 2004) in the process of economic growth. By serving as a conduit for the spillover of knowledge, entrepreneurship is a mechanism by which investments, both private and public, generate a greater social return, in terms of economic growth and job creation.

Audretsch et al. (2006) suggest that in addition to labor, physical capital, and knowledge capital, the endowment of entrepreneurship capital also matters for generating economic growth. Entrepreneurship capital refers to the capacity for the geographically relevant special units of observation to generate the startup of new enterprises.

The concept of *social capital* (Putnam 1993; Coleman 1988) added a social component to the traditional factors shaping economic growth and prosperity. (Audretsch et al. (2006), suggest that what has been called social capital in the entrepreneurship literature may actually be a more specific sub-component, which they introduce as *entrepreneurship capital*. The entrepreneurship capital of an economy or a society refers to the institutions, culture, and historical context that is conducive to the creation of new firms. This involves a number of aspects such as social acceptance of entrepreneurial behavior but of course also individuals who are willing to deal with the risk of creating new firms and the activity of bankers and venture capital agents that are willing to share risks and benefits involved. Hence entrepreneurship capital reflects a number of different legal, institutional and social factors and forces. Taken together, these factors and forces constitute the entrepreneurship capital of an economy, which creates a capacity for entrepreneurial activity.

By including measures of entrepreneurship capital along with the traditional factors of physical capital, knowledge capital, and labor in a production function model estimating economic growth, Audretsch et al. (2006) found pervasive and compelling economic evidence suggesting that entrepreneurship capital also contributes to economic growth.

Public policy did not wait for the painstaking econometric evidence linking entrepreneurship to economic growth. The mandate for entrepreneurship policy has generally emerged from what would superficially appear to be two opposite directions. One direction emanates from the failure of the traditional policy instruments, corresponding to the Solow model, or those based on instruments promoting investment into physical capital, to adequately maintain economic growth and employment in globally linked markets. The emergence of entrepreneurship policy as a *bona fide* approach to generating economic growth and job creation has been rampant through the old rust belt of the industrial Midwest in the United States, ranging from cities such as Cleveland and Pittsburgh to states such as Wisconsin and Indiana who are pinning their economic development strategies on entrepreneurship policies.

The second push for the entrepreneurship policy mandate is from the opposite direction—the failure of the so-called new economy policy instruments, corresponding to the Romer model, or those promoting investment into knowledge capital to adequately generate economic growth and employment. Recognition of the *European Paradox*, where employment creation and economic growth remain meager, despite world-class levels of human capital and research capabilities triggered the Lisbon Proclamation stating that Europe would become the entrepreneurship leader by 2020.

Although coming from opposite directions, both have in common an unacceptable economic performance. The mandate for entrepreneurship policy is rooted in dissatisfaction—dissatisfaction with the *status quo*, and in particular, with the *status quo* economic performance.[5]

---

[5] A third direction contributing to the mandate for entrepreneurship policy may be in the context of less developed regions and developing countries. Such regions have had endowments of neither physical capital now knowledge capital but still look to entrepreneurship capital to serve as an engine of economic growth.

5 Conclusions

The entrepreneurial society refers to places where knowledge-based entrepreneurship has emerged as a driving force for economic growth, employment creation and competitiveness in global markets. As the initial capital-driven Solow model and the more recent knowledge-driven Romer model have not delivered the expected levels of economic performance by themselves, a mandate for entrepreneurship policy has emerged and begun to diffuse throughout the entire globe. Whether or not specific policy instruments will work in the particular contexts is not the point of this paper. What is striking, however, is the emergence and diffusion of an entirely new public policy approach to generate economic growth—the creation of the entrepreneurial society. It is upon this new mantel of entrepreneurial society that locations, ranging from communities to cities, states and even entire nations, hang their hopes, dreams and aspirations for prosperity and security.

References

Acs, Z. J., & Audretsch, D. B. (1988). Innovation in large and small firms: An empirical analysis. *American Economic Review, 78*(4), 678–690.
Acs, Z. J., & Audretsch, D. B. (1990). *Innovation and small firms.* Cambridge: MIT Press.
Audretsch, D. B., & Keilbach, M. (2007). The theory of knowledge spillover entrepreneurship. *Journal of Management Studies, 44*(7), 1242–1254.
Audretsch, D. B., & Keilbach, M. (2008). Resolving the knowledge paradox: Knowledge-spillover entrepreneurship and economic growth. *Research Policy, 37*(10), 1697–1705.
Audretsch, D. B. (1995). *Innovation and industry evolution.* Cambridge: MIT Press.
Audretsch, D. B. (2007). *The entrepreneurial society.* New York: Oxford University Press.
Audretsch, D. B., Keilbach, M. C., & Lehmann, E. E. (2006). *Entrepreneurship and economic growth.* New York: Oxford University Press.
Breshsnahan, T., & Gambardella, A. (2004). *Building high tech clusters: Silicon valley and beyond.* Cambridge: Cambridge University Press.
Chandler, A. (1977). *The visible hand: The managerial revolution in american business.* Cambridge: Belknap Press.
Chandler, A. (1990). *Scale and scope: The dynamics of industrial capitalism.* Cambridge: Harvard University Press.
Coleman, J. (1988). Social capital in the creation of human capital. *American Journal of Sociology, 94*, 95–121.
Dertouzos, M., Lester, R., & Solow, R. (1989). *Made in America: Regaining the productive edge.* Cambridge: MIT Press.
Galbraith, John K. (1956). *American capitalism.* Boston: Houghton Mifflin.
Halberstam, D. (1993). *The fifties.* New York: Villard Books.
Lucas, R. (1993). Making a miracle. *Econometrica, 61*, 251–272.
Mowery, D. (2005). The Bayh-Dole Act and High Technology Entrepreneurship in U.S. Universities: Chicken, Egg or Something Else? Paper presented at the Eller Centre Conference on Entrepreneurship Education and Technology Transfer, University of Arizona, 21–22 January.
Nelson, R. (1981). Research on productivity growth and differences: Dead ends and new departures. *Journal of Economic Literature, 19*, 1029–1064.
Prodi, R. (2002). For a New European Entrepreneurship, Instituto de Empressa in Madrid.
Putnam, R. (1993). *Making democracy work: Civic traditions in modern Italy.* Princeton: Princeton University Press.
Romer, P. (1986). Increasing returns and long-run growth. *Journal of Political Economy, 94*, 1002–1037.
Scherer, F. M. (1970). *Industrial market structure and economic performance.* Chicago: Rand McNally.
Solow, R. (1956). A contribution to theory of economic growth. *Quarterly Journal of Economics, 70*, 65–94.

Vernon, R. (1966). International investment and international trade in the product cycle. *Quarterly Journal of Economics, 80,* 190–207.

Williamson, O. (1968). Economies as an antitrust defense: The welfare tradeoffs. *American Economic Review, 58,* 18–36.

1042-2587
© 2009 Baylor University

Agency and Governance in Strategic Entrepreneurship

David B. Audretsch
Erik E. Lehmann
Lawrence A. Plummer

This paper aims to highlight the opportunity to contribute to our understanding of strategic entrepreneurship by exploring the construct through the lens of agency theory. In particular, we claim a fundamental link between a new venture's control of critical resources and the distribution of equity between the principal and agent. According to agency theory, assigning top executives ownership in the firm provides arrangements that are compatible with the incentives of the owners of the firm. This paper suggests that agency theory has special relevance when considered in a strategic entrepreneurship context. This is because the function of managers in entrepreneurial new ventures is fundamentally different from their counterparts in large established, incumbent corporations. While both types of managers have to provide managerial and organizational expertise, managers in entrepreneurial new ventures have an additional function that is essential to the competitive advantage and performance of the new venture—providing knowledge and human capital, which, in many cases, is intrinsically linked to the capital resources of the new venture. Our framework is tested using patent ownership as a proxy for both relationship-specific investments and indispensable human capital of the top manager of the new venture. The empirical results support the main hypotheses posited by the entrepreneurial governance model. In particular, patent ownership of the top manager significantly increases the percentage of equity held, while the number of patents held by the firm significantly decreases the percentage of ownership.

Introduction

Strategic entrepreneurship involves simultaneous opportunity-seeking (i.e., entrepreneurial) and advantage-seeking (i.e., strategic) behaviors (Ireland, Hitt, & Sirmon, 2003). As the introduction to this special issue suggests, strategic entrepreneurship includes those "organizationally consequential" innovations, "representing the means through which opportunity is capitalized upon" while "in pursuit of competitive advantage." The innovations made possible by strategic entrepreneurship are manifest in either the basis by which a firm differentiates itself competitively from its industry rivals or changes from the firm's past organizational structure and/or business model. In the case of the latter, a new firm's transition from a private to a public equity structure by means of an initial public

Please send correspondence to: David B. Audretsch, tel.: (812) 855-6766; e-mail: daudrets@indiana.edu.

offering (IPO) constitutes a setting rife with strategic entrepreneurship implications (Certo, Covin, Daily, & Dalton, 2001).[1]

Among the implications is the ownership and control of valuable resources used in pursuit of a given opportunity. As Ireland et al. (2003) contend, much of the firm's ability to seek opportunity and competitive advantage depends largely on the resources *owned or controlled by the firm* and the capacity to manage them effectively. In fact, in addition to an entrepreneurial mindset, entrepreneurial culture, and entrepreneurial leadership, "managing organizational resources provides the *foundation* for the firm's opportunity-seeking and advantage-seeking behaviors (Ireland et al., p. 967, emphasis added). We have no dispute with this perspective, and accept, as Mosakowski (2002) suggests, that a unique strength of strategic entrepreneurship is the firm's ability to develop new advantage-granting resources through an entrepreneurial process.

We are instead intrigued by the premise that a firm may need to control resources it does not own. A pivotal question that arises is how, and with what implications for strategic entrepreneurship does a firm gain control over resources owned by others? In this vein, we confine our focus to those cases in which *individuals within a new firm—the chief executive in particular—own the key resources the firm seeks to control.* This is particularly relevant for strategic entrepreneurship in which the top executive is expected to provide inputs (e.g., knowledge and human capital) critical to opportunity seeking in addition to managerial (i.e., advantage-seeking) expertise.[2] A useful framework for answering this question comes from economic theories of the firm, including property rights and agency theory (Hart, 1995; Jensen & Meckling, 1976). Here, the premise is that the firm seeks control of the assets held by the top executive by aligning her interests with those of the firm's principals.

What makes this an interesting question is that the instances where a top manager owns a key resource may exacerbate the agency problem that otherwise inhibits the firm's ability to engage effectively in strategic entrepreneurship behaviors. That is, in these cases, not only must the new venture's governance structure align managers' interests with those of shareholders, it must also establish safeguards against contractual hazards (i.e., the hold-up problem) in the controlling arrangements for resources held by the manager. In this context, the contractual arrangements over the *control* rights of such resources—i.e., the right of the owner to grant the firm the use of a resource—are the matter of concern (Hart, 1995). As a result, among the many determinants of equity ownership (Agarwal & Samwick, 1999; Bitler, Moskowitz, & Vissing-Jörgensen, 2006; Himmelberg, Hubbard, & Palia, 1999), one would expect larger equity shares for those managers owning valuable resources upon which the firm depends.

Thus, the purpose of this paper is to suggest a view of agency theory that considers the governance of entrepreneurial new ventures within a strategic entrepreneurship context. This view revolves around the entrepreneur's dual role of providing both managerial expertise, as well as knowledge inputs to knowledge-based new ventures. In particular, we surmise that in addition to aligning the top manager's (i.e., chief executive officer [CEO]'s) interests with those of the firm's principals by means of equity ownership, the *ex-post* bargaining position of the top executive owning needed knowledge inputs—

---

1. For comparable perspectives, see Beatty and Zajac (1994); Brunninge, Nordqvist, and Wiklund (2007); Uhlaner, Wright, and Huse (2007); and Zahra, Neubaum, and Naldi (2007).
2. In a large incumbent firm, many of these knowledge inputs emerge from the firm's formal opportunity-seeking activities in the form of research and development (R&D). The situation with younger, more entrepreneurial firms, which presumably have no such formal R&D, suggests that the need for controlling knowledge inputs not owned by the firm would seem particularly acute.

captured by patents in this study—leads to her holding a larger share of equity than she would otherwise. Conversely, when it is the firm that owns the knowledge inputs (i.e., the patents are held by the firm), the superior *ex-post* bargaining position of the firm's principals leads to the top executive holding a smaller share of equity than she would otherwise.

Given this, the paper flows as follows: in the next section of this paper, we explain how the door is open, as it were, for applying agency theory to advance our understanding of strategic entrepreneurship. After that, we discuss the extent to which agency theory lends itself to the question of how a firm might gain control over resources it does not own. This leads to the fourth section of this paper where we develop the two main hypotheses linking managerial equity ownership with the holding of assets or inputs needed by the firm. The fifth section details the research design and methodology of this study, and the sixth section reports the results. The final section discusses the results and offers some concluding comments.

Resource Ownership and Control in Strategic Entrepreneurship

As a conceptual framework, strategic entrepreneurship—encompassing simultaneous opportunity-seeking (i.e., entrepreneurial) and advantage-seeking (i.e., strategic) behaviors (Ireland et al., 2003)—offers a more expansive perspective on the wealth creation and maximization of firms than do the constructs of strategic management and entrepreneurship individually. As Hitt, Ireland, Camp, and Sexton (2002) suggest, firms able to identify, yet incapable of exploiting entrepreneurial opportunities, cannot realize their full wealth-creation potential. Similarly, firms with current competitive advantages—no matter how sustainable—lacking the ability to identity and pursue new opportunities expose their investors to greater risk and diminished rates of return. Thus, provocatively, the claim is that "wealth is created *only* when firms combine effective opportunity-seeking behavior (i.e., entrepreneurship) with effective advantage-seeking behavior (i.e., strategic management)" (Ireland et al., p. 966, emphasis added).

Pivotal to this view of strategic entrepreneurship is the entrepreneurial leader's ability to manage—i.e., structure, bundle, and leverage—the firm's resource portfolio. Indeed, in addition to fostering a collective entrepreneurial mindset and culture, the entrepreneurial leader's function of "managing organizational resources provides *the foundation* for the firm's opportunity-seeking and advantage-seeking behaviors" (Ireland et al., 2003, p. 967, emphasis added). Thus, contained in this conception is the premise that the behaviors that constitute strategic entrepreneurship cross at least three levels of analysis—the leadership, capabilities, and human capital of *individuals*; the operational structure, collective mindset, and culture within *firms*; and the availability of advantage-granting resources and new market opportunities from the firm's external *environment*.

With this in mind, we are particularly intrigued by two key questions to strategic entrepreneurship posed by Ireland et al. (2003, pp. 983–984): First, how do entrepreneurial leaders within firms manage resources strategically to create competitive advantage, and, second, how are the firm's resource bundles (i.e., capabilities) leveraged in the identification and exploitation of new market opportunities? However, we also recognize that much of the discussion leading to these questions hinges on the assumption that "differences in firm performance are affected by both *owned or controlled* resources as well as how *the firm* manages those resources" (Ireland et al., p. 977, emphasis added). Thus, reframing the questions above, we ask, how does the firm come to control resources *it does not own* and manage them for entrepreneurship ends (Audretsch & Lehmann, 2006)?

One issue in answering this question, as we see it, is that when viewed across multiple levels of analysis, firms *per se* neither control nor own resources in any strict meaning. Instead, it is the individual managers (i.e., *agents*) hired by the owners of the resources that comprise the firm (i.e., *the principals*) that provide the management of organizational resources. Indeed, from this perspective, the phrase "owned by the firm" can be taken to mean "owned by the principal(s)." Thus, the problems associated with the separation of ownership and control and the accompanying agency costs are very much at play in strategic entrepreneurship. Indeed, if managing or controlling resources provides the "foundation" for the firm's strategic entrepreneurship behaviors, we suggest that it is particularly important to get the governance structures "right" to mitigate the agency problem.

Despite this observation, we find little reference to the agency problem or agency theory in the current conversation of strategic entrepreneurship. An exception is given by Michael, Storey, and Thomas (2002). They argue that in a strategic entrepreneurship setting, top managers provide expertise in the form of entrepreneurial management (i.e., expertise in the identification and recognition of opportunities) *and* administrative management (i.e., expertise in the operational coordination and loss prevention of the firm's activities). It is their contention that agency costs associated with administrative management are "solved" by proper compensation incentives, such as stock option awards. Given incomplete theoretical and empirical treatment of the matter, however, it is not clear that such incentives also resolve any agency costs associated with the agent's provision of entrepreneurial management.

Our key point here is not to claim that the strategic entrepreneurship construct is somehow a house of cards, because it does not explicitly encompass or invoke agency theory as a cornerstone. Instead, in recognizing that the concept of strategic entrepreneurship already builds on an array of theoretical perspectives including, among others, the resource-based view, real options, corporate entrepreneurship, and innovation (Hitt et al., 2002), we aim only to highlight the opportunity to advance strategic entrepreneurship by exploring aspects of it through the lens of agency theory. In particular, a central focus of such work should be to explore the governance structures that enable the ownership or control of those resources needed for both advantage-seeking and opportunity-seeking behaviors. Nevertheless, even if there seems to be room for agency theory in strategic entrepreneurship, the next question is whether agency theory lends itself to such application.

Agency Theory as a Strategic Entrepreneurship Lens

Agency theory is typically applied in the context of large and diversified firms as described by Chandler (1990). As such, competitive advantage often derives in terms of scale and scope. These economies of scale and scope make the firm too large to have ownership rest only in the hands of management, so outside investors are needed to finance assets and to bear the risk associated with such large ownership stakes (Rajan & Zingales, 2000). Competitive advantages arise through large size and extensive brand image from mass advertising to pose formidable barriers to competition from new entrants. The only critical resource is to raise money from the capital market to finance size and brand image. In providing the capital, outside owners delegate the control to salaried managers, which then leads to the logical outcome of the separation of ownership and control and the potential for disinterested managers to appropriate corporate resources for their own benefit at the expense of the shareholders.

In contrast, the competitive advantage of new knowledge-based ventures is less the result of scale and scope and more from building complementarities between resources and capabilities. We follow recent research that has emphasized the importance of intangible assets and human capital in entrepreneurial new ventures as their main source of competitive advantages (Audretsch, Keilbach, & Lehmann, 2006; Rajan & Zingales, 1998, 2000, 2001a,b). In these new ventures, equity ownership may not only serve as a mechanism to ensure managerial effort or to internalize the costs of misbehavior (Jensen & Meckling, 1976), it also provides incentives for the top executive to make firm-specific investments beyond their managerial expertise. Equity ownership of the firm's assets provides parties with bargaining power in negotiations after they have made investments in their relationships with new ventures. Especially in human capital intense firms, strategic advantages stem from specializing human capital to the firm's assets. Thus, the study of governance in a strategic entrepreneurship context has to go beyond the Jensen and Meckling framework.

In its simplest form, agency theory focuses on the internal incentives between the owners of the firm's assets (principals) and the managers (agents) hired to run it. Thus, the agency problem—and the costs associated with it—lies in the misalignment between the interests of the asset owners and the hired managers. To solve the problem, the principal searches for a perfect contract to align the managers' interests to her own (see Fiegener, Brown, Dreux, & Dennis, 2000). Theoretically, the efficient way to resolve the agency problem is to optimize not just the compensation contract between principal and agent, but also optimize the agent's equity ownership. In particular, because the future value of the firm's assets is not contractible, having the agent own a portion of the firm's assets can provide incentives for maximizing the firm's performance in a way that cannot be replicated via contract. Thus, the agent's ownership of firm equity not only helps solve the incentive problem, it also influences the strategic decisions made by the agent to the benefit of the firm.

With that said, empirical findings of top manager ownership, particularly those studies grounded in agency theory, are remarkably inconsistent (Daily & Dalton, 1993; Daily, Dalton, & Rajagopalan, 2003; Dalton, Daily, Certo, & Roengpita, 2003; Himmelberg et al., 1999). This is most likely because strategic decisions are based on expected returns *in the future*. In agency theory, both the decision of which strategy to pursue and the incentive to implement this strategy derives from the prospect of being paid out of the firm's future returns. While an agent's ownership of assets suggests that both the strategic decision and her incentives are interdependent (see Gibbons, 2004, Kräkel, 2004), the uncertainty associated with these future returns—along with other factors—leads to the problem of incomplete contracts between principal and agent.

Incomplete contracts lead to an additional problem. In their seminal papers, Grossman and Hart (1986) and Hart and Moore (1990) develop a property-rights framework for examining how changes in the distribution of asset ownership affects the incentives of the individuals who work with those tangible and physical assets. They highlight the central role of nonhuman (e.g., physical) assets because these can be owned and more readily traded compared with human assets (or human capital). Brynjolfsson (1994) extended the Grossman–Hart–Moore framework by including productive knowledge and information as an intangible asset that affects agents' marginal product when they have access to it.

The main result of the Grossman–Hart–Moore framework is that the allocation of ownership rights of the nonhuman assets has an important effect on the bargaining position of the parties after they have made firm-specific investments. In the absence of comprehensive contracts, property rights over the firm's physical assets largely determine which *ex-post* bargaining position—the agent's or the principal's—will prevail. In fact, because future returns are uncertain, ownership arrangements over nonhuman assets are routinely renegotiated *ex-post* after the agent or principal has made *ex-ante* relationship-specific investments. Thus, as Mahoney (2005, pp. 135, 136) summarizes, since "a firm's nonhuman assets represent the glue that keeps the firm together," it follows that "control over economically relevant nonhuman resources leads to control over human resources."

Mahoney's (2005) summation nicely encapsulates our claim that in a strategic entrepreneurship context, agency theory has a role in explaining how a firm gains control of resources, especially those that it does not own. In particular, a resource can be controlled if the firm (or principal) owns resources or assets complementary to the given resource. Despite this point, the question remains whether such an agency perspective is valid in a strategic entrepreneurship context. Michael et al. (2002) contend that it is a valid lens for exploring questions specific to strategic entrepreneurship. In particular, it has already been applied extensively to matters pertaining to strategic management (Mahoney), and is equally applicable to questions specific to entrepreneurship, especially if one adopts a view of entrepreneurship in which the key function of the entrepreneurial process is the coordination of resources (Casson, 2003).

To accentuate this point, we offer an example of how agency theory may be applied to strategic entrepreneurship questions. In particular, we focus on the question of how a firm (i.e., owners) manages and controls resources it does not own. Thus, for the remainder of this paper, we focus our attention on the relationship between the agent's and owner's residual claims on knowledge assets (i.e., the owning of patents) and the prevailing equity ownership shares that result from *ex-post* bargaining. We assume that the number of patents owned by the top manager is a reasonable proxy for her relationship-specific investment and indispensable human capital.[3] In doing so, we assume that two assets are necessary for the production process, patents, and physical assets.

Agency, Resource Control, and Equity Ownership

Revealed in the discussion of agency theory is a natural tension in the effect of equity ownership: on the one hand, granting agents ownership of the firm's resources—and thus residual claims on future returns—aligns their interests with those of the principals and maximizes the profit incentives for both parties. On the other hand, according to the Grossman–Hart–Moore framework, granting agents ownership also implies that principals lose authority and control over their hired managers (Mahoney, 2005). Thus, while *ex-ante* (i.e., hiring) negotiations presumably result in an initial distribution of equity ownership that optimizes each party's profit incentives, repeated *ex-post* bargaining results in "adjustments" to the ownership distribution as a function of whose bargaining position prevails. In other words, in the case of the agent, she can expect to receive compensation commensurate with the performance of the firm *plus* some adjustment to her equity position reflecting the value of the assets she owns.

Does this have relevance in a strategic entrepreneurship context? According to Ireland et al. (2003), for example, newer ventures relative to established firms tend to excel at

---

3. Patents are less than ideal as measures of firm or industry-level intangible asset stocks (Cockburn & Griliches, 1988; Griliches, 1990). Patents, on the other hand, by granting an inventor monopoly rights over a given idea (itself being unique and non obvious), are a reasonable measure of the intangible assets owned by an individual. Indeed, given the assumptions of our framework, CEO-owned patents indicate her investment of codified knowledge assets specific to the new venture and—since the accompanying tacit knowledge is necessary for successful use of the codified knowledge (Mowery, Oxley, & Silverman, 1996; Patel & Pavitt, 1997)—her contribution of indispensible human capital.

Table 1

Patent Ownership, Equity Ownership, and Hold-Up

	Patents owned by the CEO	Patents owned by the firm
Equity ownership of the CEO is high	Residual control rights, with the CEO as the inventor Strategic advantage (I)	Hold-up problem through the CEO Strategic advantage (II)
Equity ownership of the CEO is low (zero)	Hold-up problem through the shareholder(s) Strategic advantage (III)	Residual control rights, with the shareholders Strategic advantage (IV)

CEO, chief executive officer.

opportunity-seeking behaviors, but tend to rely largely on the availability of resources external to the firm. As a result, the top manager of such a firm is expected to provide not only managerial expertise that emphasizes advantage-seeking behaviors, but also the capacity for acquiring external resources, including financial, human, and social capital (Ireland et al.). This is especially true for knowledge-intensive (i.e., technology-based) ventures. The problem is that the growth and performance of knowledge-based ventures depends largely on *intangible* human and nonhuman assets. As a result, because the value of intangible assets is difficult to assess, one could argue that in this particular case, the logic of agency theory breaks down.

Indeed, as Mahoney (2005) contends, absent the dependence on nonhuman assets common with more traditional manufacturing firms, such as machinery or buildings, the question is what stops workers in a knowledge-intensive firm from quitting entirely (to act as a contractor) or leaving to form their own firms? According to agency theory (Mahoney), the answer lies in the value of the firm's other nonhuman and intangible assets, such as its reputation or explicit intellectual property (i.e., patents, trademarks, or copyrights). These intangible resources are more difficult to assess, especially in terms of future expected value, and thus tend to exacerbate the problem of optimizing the agent's ownership of the firm's assets. Indeed, on its face, the premise that "control over economically relevant nonhuman resources leads to control over human resources" seems less viable in a knowledge-based venture since in these instances, the firm's intangible resources, and not its physical assets, are weaker in function as the organizational "glue" for the firm.

Thus, since it is not readily evident that an agent's share of equity is greater when she holds valuable assets the firm seeks to control, we suggest a governance framework applicable to a strategic entrepreneurship context as summarized in Table 1.[4] As Audretsch et al. (2006) show, the competitive advantage of a knowledge-based new venture is typically bestowed by the human capital and knowledge capabilities of the top executive, who may or may not be the founder. If the critical resources are the human capital of the top executive *and* her contribution of a venture-specific resource, then equity ownership giving her residual rights grants her power in any negotiations over the use of

---

4. For purposes of this study, the level of equity ownership—either high or low in Table 1—is taken as the dependent variable. As such, we assume an optimal distribution of equity based on whether the firm or the agent owns patents. We leave exploration of the performance ramifications of the CEO's equity ownership being "too high" or "too low" for future study.

the resource. Given this, if the top manager is the owner of the patents, but has no power over the use and access to this critical resource expressed by low or no equity ownership of the firm, the firm may be at a strategic disadvantage. Thus, given the need to align the agent's interests with those of the principals and her *ex-post* bargaining position, the amount of equity ownership held by the entrepreneur or top manager is greater when she also owns an intangible resource (i.e., a patent) the principals of the firm seek to control. In contrast, the equity ownership held by the agent is less when the firm owns the intangible resource (i.e., patent) given the prevailing *ex-post* bargaining position of the principals.

If this argument holds, we expect that equity ownership of the firm and the ownership of knowledge assets are strong complementarities. In particular, if the agent owns critical assets and thus has the option of acting as an independent contractor (Hart, 1995), she receives compensation based not only on the firm's performance, but also on the resource's value after production occurs. Thus, in *ex-post* bargaining, she has two sources of incentives to invest in future projects (i.e., remain with the firm) and maintain the competitive advantage of the firm. Conversely, disadvantages occur when the incentives are misaligned in the sense that she owns a critical resource—like patents or specific human capital—but has weakened bargaining power because her equity stake is too low to motivate her to invest in future projects with the firm. Thus, our model assumes there is an optimal fit between equity ownership and intangible assets that circumvents under-investment decisions (see Gibbons, 2004; Rajan & Zingales, 1998, 2000, 2001a,b). Correspondingly, we also assume that a firms' competitive advantage is determined by its equity ownership structure, given the *ex-post* bargaining position of the party's holding intangible knowledge assets.

Given this, we assume that patents are a proxy of both knowledge assets and specific human capital as critical resources held by and embodied in the top manager and/or the employees of a firm. As a result, an individual person—in our case, the agent, or the firm's shareholders—could own the patents used in the production process.[5] In the first scenario, the top manager personally owns at least one patent. If she owns no equity shares of the firm, and if her cooperation is necessary to the production process, she risks going uncompensated for work that is not specifically stipulated in an explicit contract. However, if she owns at least some of the firm's equity, she will be in a position to reap at least some of the benefits accruing from the relationship-specific investments she makes. Indeed, her *ex-post* bargaining position derives from her ability to "veto" any allocation of the residual rewards that she considers to be unfavorable by threatening to withdraw the patents from the production process. Equity ownership of the firm's assets therefore leads to *ex-post* bargaining power and thus mitigates the hold-up problem, enabling the agent's interest in maximizing the firm's competitive advantage.

Moreover, it may also be possible for her to sell her patents or allow other firms to use the patents she holds. This kind of threat is only credible if the agent has outside opportunities. One outside opportunity is the ability to raise money to invest in new production technologies. This, however, leads to the same agency problem if she needs other sources of equity financing. That is, she still needs a comprehensive contract that specifies all the relevant circumstances for these outside opportunities. If such a contract is feasible, the question arises why she needs some ownership of the physical asset to protect and ensure her relationship-specific investments. Following the Grossman–Hart–

---

5. For underinvestment and other incentive problems in firms when employees are the inventors but not the patent holders, see Harhoff and Hoisl (2004).

Moore framework, it follows that the agent should own a share of equity as a function of her owning a needed resource in the form of a patent. Thus,

Hypothesis 1: The share of equity held by the agent (i.e., the CEO) increases with the number of patents she owns.

The second case is when the firm as a legal entity owns the patents. The essential claim is that, in this instance, it is the principal's *ex-post* bargaining position that is strengthened. This premise assumes that as long as the knowledge resources in question are tied to the assets of the firm (i.e., the value of the agent's knowledge assets is determined by the extent to which they complement the firm's assets), the resources remain relatively immobile (Barney, 1986; Barney & Clark, 2007). As long as this assumption holds, if the firm owns a share of the knowledge resources employed, the principals are granted power over the use and misuse of the patents owned by the agent. In other words, the agent's ability to hold-up other shareholders by applying the patents to outside opportunities is curtailed, and her optimum equity stake in the firm is now less than it would be, all things equal (see Brynjolfsson, 1994, p. 1651). This suggests the second hypothesis,

Hypothesis 2: The share of equity held by the agent (i.e., the CEO) decreases with the number of patents owned by the firm.

Although not explicitly tested here, these hypotheses are in sharp contrast to the usual predictions of agency theory and empirical evidence on corporate governance in larger established firms (see, e.g., Himmelberg et al. [1999] or Bitler et al. [2006]). In particular, if the economic value of patents is associated with high risk, the equity ownership held by the top manager as a patent holder should *decrease* with the number of her patents. Indeed, for a risk averse top manager, it should be optimal to cash out (at IPO) and diversify her risk. This disparity between the results commonly verifying corporate governance in the agency theory and the arguments in this paper based on our framework of entrepreneurial governance suggests that the governance in a strategic entrepreneurship context may be markedly different and even contrary to what by now constitutes conventional wisdom concerning the governance of large incumbent corporations.

Research Design

We test the hypotheses regarding the link between managerial equity ownership and patents using a unique dataset consisting of all of the knowledge-based and high-technology German IPO firms that were publicly listed between 1997 and 2002. We excluded all firms located outside Germany, as well as holding companies, resulting in an underlying dataset consisting of 285 publicly listed German firms. We collected information from the IPO prospectuses and combined it with publicly available information from online data sources, including the *Deutsche Boerse AG* (http://www.deutsche-boerse.com). This database includes firms in high-technology sectors including biotechnology, medical devices, life sciences, e-commerce, and other high-technology industries. From this dataset, we excluded all the firms older than 8 years at the time of the IPO, resulting in a sample 127 "new ventures." All data are taken at the time of IPO.

For empirical purposes, we equate the top manager with the person identified in the prospectus as the CEO. The share of equity ownership as the dependent variable is measured by the percentage of firm assets owned by the CEO at the time of the IPO. While there is no minimum percentage the CEO must own following the IPO, regulations limit the maximum percentage of CEO ownership following the IPO to 75%. The truncated variable suggests our use of Tobit estimation as a complement to the ordinary least squares (OLS) estimates, as discussed below. For the key independent variables, the number of patents owned by the CEO and the number of patents owned by the firm are taken from the German patent database. The skewed distribution of these variables suggests that we also report quantile regression estimates to further validate the OLS results is also discussed below.

In addition to the patent variables, we also include several control variables. First, evidence shows that the percentage of equity shares held by a CEO is shaped both by firm size and firm age (Audretsch & Lehmann, 2005; Daily, Dalton, & Cannella, 2003; Fiegener et al., 2000; Huse, 2000). According to Agarwal and Samwick (1999), firm size is a proxy for firm risk. They found a significant negative relationship between firm size and the amount of equity held by managers. They interpret their findings as being in line with the predictions from agency theory that the amount of variable compensation as equity shares is negatively affected by firm risk. Firm size is measured by the number of employees.

Second, as with firm size, research examining the survival of new ventures has shown that firm age is a proxy for firm risk. One interpretation of the negative relationship between new venture age and the likelihood of survival is that the entrepreneur and managers of the new venture are uncertain about their capabilities, the underlying production technology, or market conditions. As the new venture matures and gains experience, the degree of entrepreneurial uncertainty increases (Audretsch et al., 2006; Jovanovic, 1982). Moreover, there is a pure evolutionary argument: the older a firm, the longer it has survived on the market and thus the lower is the associated risk (Audretsch & Lehmann, 2005). Firm age is measured in years founded prior to the IPO. We also included dummy variables to control for the year of the IPO.

Finally, in our estimates, we control for specific industry effects by including dummy variables based on recently improved *Deutsche Börse AG* classifications of the following high-technology industries: medicine technology; information and communication technology; nano-, micro-, and optical technologies; biotechnology; chemistry; software development; computer technologies; and solar energy technology. As mentioned, we include a set of dummies to control for any effects specific to the year of the IPO. Having done so, we are concerned that the IPO and industry dummies are not independent; however, there is no clear theoretical argument that an interaction of these two effects should depend on the number of patents.[6]

To ensure the robustness of our findings, we use different estimation techniques to alternatively analyze CEO-owned and firm-owned patents as determinants of equity ownership by the CEO. First, to establish our base results, we report simple OLS estimates. In particular, we estimate the following model,

$$y(\text{CEO ownership}) = f(\text{CEO patents, new venture patents, firm size,}$$

$$\text{firm age, control dummies}) + u. \tag{1}$$

Second, since the dependent variable is truncated at low and high values (minimum 0% equity ownership and a maximum at 75%), the Tobit model produces results preferable to

---

6. Given our data, we could not derive a valid chi-square test of the independence of the IPO and industry dummies. As a result, our assumption of the independence of the control dummies could not be validated empirically. We also cannot deny that some industry effects may remain, but the estimates do not show robust effects of one or more industries across all the results.

the OLS approach. Thus, let $y_i^* = \beta' x_i + u_i$, with y_i^* as the latent variable, which represents the desired or potential equity holding by the CEO. Further, x_i is a vector of exogenous variables, including the number of patents of the CEO and those of the new venture, and u_i are disturbances with $E(u_i) = 0$. The observed variable y_i is given by

$$
y_i = \begin{cases} \underline{c}_i & \text{if } y_i^* \leq \underline{c}_i \\ y_i^* & \text{if } \underline{c}_i < y_i^* < \overline{c}_i \\ \overline{c}_i & \text{if } \underline{c}_i < y_i^* \end{cases} \tag{2}
$$

where $\underline{c}_i, \overline{c}_i$ are fixed numbers representing the censoring points of equity ownership by a CEO (0 and 75%). We use the same model specification as used for the OLS estimates

Finally, a concern in estimating the above regression model is the degree to which the variables are highly skewed. As examples from the labor market literature show (Buchinsky, 1998; Koenker & Hallock, 2001), the method of quantile regression estimation is appropriate in the case of such highly skewed endogenous variables. This semiparametric technique provides a general class of models in which the conditional quantiles have a linear form. In its simplest form, the least absolute deviation estimator fits medians to a linear function of covariates. The method of quantile regression is potentially attractive for the same reason that the median or other quantiles are a better measure of location than the mean. This technique also has the useful feature of being robust against outliers while using the likelihood estimator, which are in general more efficient than the least squares estimator.[7]

Let (y_i, x_i), $i = 1, \ldots, n$, be a sample of new ventures, where x_i is a $K \times 1$ vector of regressors. Assume that $Quant_\theta(y_i, x_i)$ devotes the conditional quantile of y_i, conditional on the regressor vector x_i. The distribution of the error term $\mu_{\theta i}$ satisfies the quantile restriction $Quant_\theta(\mu_{\theta i}, x_i) = 0$. Thus, $y_i = Quant_\theta(y_i, x_i) + \mu_{\theta i}$ or $y_i = Quant_\theta(y_i, x_i) = x_i' \beta_\theta$ is estimated. We again estimate the model consistent with the OLS and Tobit specifications:

$$Quant(\text{CEO ownership}) = f(\text{CEO patents, new venture patents, firm size,}$$

$$\text{firm age, control dummies}) + u. \tag{3}$$

Results

Tables 2 and 3 report the descriptive and correlation statistics, respectively. On average, 33.6% of the asset of the firms in the sample are owned by the CEO. In half of the firms, the CEO owns more than about one quarter of the firm (25%). In these cases, it would seem the owners of the firm other than the CEO retain the capacity to block the strategic decisions of the CEO and thus hold significant power in *ex-post* bargaining position. As Table 2 also shows, on average, each CEO owns one patent. However, the number of patents is highly skewed in the dataset with a maximum of a CEO holding 49 patents. The same holds for the number of patents owned by a new venture. On average, a new ventures holds four patents, with a maximum of one firm owning 96 patents. The firms differ in their age and especially in their size as measured by the number of employees. While the median firm is about 3 years old and has about 66.5 employees, the

---

7. See Buchinsky (1998) for a survey of the method and some applications in the labor market.

Table 2

Descriptive Statistics ($N = 127$)

	Mean	SD	Min	Max	Median
CEO equity after IPO	33.68	30.20	0	75.0	25.45
Patents owned by the CEO	1.01	4.78	0	49	0
Patents owned by the firm	4.053	15.381	0	96	0
Firm age (years)	3.2	2.258	1	7	3
Firm size (no. of employees)	143.494	227.627	2	1,400	66.5

SD, standard deviation; CEO, chief executive officer; IPO, initial public offering.

Table 3

Correlation Matrix ($N = 127$)

	CEO patents	Firm patents	Firm age	Firm size
CEO equity ownership	.0352	−.1133	.1132	−.1157
Firm size	−.0135	.119	−.0653	—
Firm age	−.0062	−.0828	—	—
Firm patents	.2314	—	—	—

CEO, chief executive officer.

average age is about 3 years, and employs on average about 143 employees. The correlation matrix in Table 3 indicates little concern for multicollinearity.

The estimation results provided in Table 4 support both hypotheses 1 and 2. The first row shows the results from the OLS estimation. As the positive and statistically significant coefficient of the number of patents held by the manager suggests, the greater the number of patents held by the CEO, the greater is the share of her equity ownership. In contrast, the number of patents owned by the firm shows the statistically significant negative impact on the share of equity held by the CEO. As the positive and statistically significant coefficient of firm age suggests, the share of equity ownership by managers tends to increase as the new ventures becomes more mature. By contrast, a firm size as measured by the number of employees has no significant effect on the shares of ownership held by the CEO. This also seems to support the two hypotheses, albeit indirectly. Power from ownership results from voting power, which is expressed by the percentage of shares held by the CEO. In contrast, a risk-averse CEO may have an incentive to diversify her risk, and thus we would expect that the percentage of ownership would decrease with firm size.

The second row of Table 4 shows the results from estimating the regression model using the Tobit regression method. The results are strikingly similar to those obtained from OLS estimation. Both regression estimation methods confirm the two hypotheses that the percentage of equity held by a CEO is positively influenced by the number of

Table 4

Regression Results Estimating CEO Equity Ownership (N = 127)

	CEO patents	Firm patents	LNSize	LNAge	Industry dummies	IPO dummies	Constant	Pseudo R²
OLS	.6324 (2.61)***	-.5418 (3.3.1)***	-.3030 (.26)	2.440 (1.98)*	Insig.	1997 (+)	23.275 (2.71)**	.1413
Tobit	.9421 (1.77)*	-.676 (2.21)**	.2259 (.14)	3.007 (2.04)**	Insig.	1997 (+)	18.984 (1.46)	.0201
.2 quantile	.6273 (15.94)***	-.187 (6.81)***	-.004 (.01)	.803 (4.33)***	Technology (+), software (+)	1999 (+)	3.130 (1.71)*	.050
.3 quantile	.338 (3.02)***	-.214 (2.98)***	-.005 (.01)	1.758 (3.85)***	Insig.	1997 (+), .998 (–)	14.496 (2.43)**	.093
.4 quantile	.281 (1.61)*	-.223 (-1.19)	-.01 (.01)	3.572 (3.26)	Insig.	1998 (–)	17.735 (1.67)*	.115
.5 quantile	.501 (1.63)*	-.263 (.53)	-.435 (.14)	3.091 (1.07)	Insig.	Insig.	22.623 (.92)	.126
.6 quantile	.544 (1.71)*	-.394 (1.75)*	.619 (18)	1.587 (.49)	Insig.	Insig.	31.693 (1.15)	.103
.7 quantile	.596 (2.18)**	-.521 (2.46)**	-.337 (.16)	3.556 (1.90)*	Medtec (+)	Insig.	33.412 (2.11)**	.124
.8 quantile	.561 (1.80)*	-.484 (1.63)*	.225 (.09)	4.506 (2.05)**	Medtec (+)	Insig.	28.372 (1.66)*	.144
.9 quantile	.525 (1.53)	-.475 (-1.46)	.397 (.06)	7.169 (.90)	Insig.	Insig.	11.569 (.30)	.211

* statistically significant at the 10% level; ** statistically significant at the 5% level; *** statistically significant at the 1% level.
CEO, chief executive officer; IPO, initial public offering; OLS, ordinary least squares; Insig., insignificant; Medtec, medical technology.

patents she owns and is negatively influenced by the number of patents owned by the firm. The third and subsequent rows report the results from the quantile regressions. For all quantiles between the .2 quantile and the .8 quantile, the percentage of equity held by the CEO increases with the number of patents owned by the CEO. In contrast, the number of patents held by the firm is negative and significant in only five of the quantiles. Thus, the results continue to support the two hypotheses, but they also indicate a nonlinearity between ownership and patents.

According to our theoretical framework, granting equity ownership is a means for new ventures to gain control of key resources owned by individuals—in this case, the CEO or entrepreneur. In other words, if the intellectual property of the entrepreneur or CEO in the form of a patented invention is essential for production because of complementarities with her expertise, then she is effectively indispensable to the new venture.[8] Thus, the above empirical results may explain why an entrepreneur or CEO holding assets essential to the success of the new venture is likely to own more of the new venture relative to other shareholders. However, if it is the firm that holds the intellectual property assets, then the bargaining position of the CEO is weakened, and thus her ownership of the firm is less. Thus, the empirical results provide compelling evidence for the two hypotheses posited earlier in this paper.

Two important qualifications regarding the results presented in Table 4 must be considered. First, empirical studies—including this one—on corporate governance may suffer from reverse causality and heterogeneity (see Börsch-Supan & Köke, 2002; Himmelberg et al., 1999). The problem of reverse causality may exist to the degree that patents are influenced by CEO ownership of the physical assets. However, as Holmström (1999) shows by analyzing the costs and benefits of litigation, such reverse causality is more likely to apply to established large corporations than for small and new ventures. Second, no information was available to determine if the CEO was also the firm's founder and thus presumably a principal. Certo et al. (2001) find that investment banking firms are less likely to underprice a firm's stock if the top manager is a "professional manager" as opposed to the firm's founder. Thus, because investors may value the founder's managerial expertise less than that of a professional manager, it is possible that the founder–CEO holds a smaller equity share following the IPO on this basis. With this said, since our model emphasizes the *ex-post adjustments* to equity distributions, this issue does not inherently invalidate our results.

Discussion and Conclusion

This paper has suggested that agency theory is readily applicable to the development and improvement of strategic entrepreneurship as a theoretical construct by introducing analysis at the level of the individual within the firm. In particular, a strategic entrepreneurship perspective of agency theory is offered to explain the link between the agent's share of equity ownership and the critical knowledge assets she may own. According to our framework, the boundaries of the new venture define the allocation of residual control rights. If contracts are incomplete as is typical, then managerial equity ownership serves not just as a mechanism to render managerial incentives compatible with the owners' goals, as agency theory predicts, but more importantly, also as an instrument enabling residual control rights in ongoing negotiations between principal and agent. The ability to

---

8. Hart and Moore (1990) emphasized this.

exercise residual control rights improves the *ex-post* bargaining position of the CEO as an asset owner, thereby increasing her incentive to make investments that are specific to the new venture.

Our framework of entrepreneurial governance was tested using patent ownership as a proxy for both relationship-specific investments and indispensable human capital of the CEO. The empirical results confirm the main hypotheses posited by our model. In particular, patent ownership of the CEO significantly increases the percentage of equity held, while the number of patents held by the firm significantly decreases the percentage of ownership. As a result, the findings of this paper imply that strategic decisions involving the governance of new ventures do not mirror the conventional wisdom already established for large incumbent corporations. Rather, the decision to provide equity ownership to managers of new ventures, especially in small and high-tech new ventures, is not entirely explained by agency theory, as suggested by Bitler et al. (2006), among others. More importantly, we are able to conclude that a firm (or its shareholders) can gain control of a resource by making the owner of the resource an owner of the firm.

One implication of our arguments is that resolving the agency problem is particularly crucial in a strategic entrepreneurship setting. In particular, optimizing the governance structure through equity ownership serves not only to align the interests of principal and agent; it also serves as a mechanism for effectively managing and leveraging the firm's resources. Beyond this point, it is also seems likely that any such equity arrangements are pivotal in allowing the *collective* entrepreneurial mindset and entrepreneurial culture upon which strategic entrepreneurship is grounded (Ireland et al., 2003). How, we wonder, can a setting conducive to entrepreneurial thinking and collective action emerge if the interests of principal and agent are in conflict? In short, we suggest that resolving any misalignments in incentives and equity structures serves many (perhaps conflicting) ends, with implications beyond the management of resources alone. Indeed, it implies a two-way street in which agency theory informs strategic entrepreneurship and vice versa, given a unique context for considering matters of governance.

We readily acknowledge that there may be other theoretical explanations for our results, that our analysis warrants further exploration with alternative specifications and variables—particularly the founder status of the CEO—and that our sample frame may not constitute a valid strategic entrepreneurship context.[9] Nonetheless, we contend that these and other qualifications—which are themselves quite valid and in need of exploration—reinforce our point that applying agency theory to strategic entrepreneurship questions contributes to our understanding of the field by raising new questions and helping us understand what strategic entrepreneurship *is* or *is not*. Indeed, among the most pressing questions our study appears to highlight is how best to represent empirically not only the strategic entrepreneurship context, but also how to measure or observe at the individual level when top managers are engaged in advantage-seeking versus opportunity-seeking behaviors. Given the set up of our model, we have in effect assumed the importance of this distinction away.

In addition to such empirical matters, future research should incorporate the role of other stakeholders who own resources the firm needs to control (see Demougin & Fabel, 2006). Ownership of the firm's assets may have little value for these stakeholders, since the expectation that they provide expertise and knowledge inputs akin to the CEO may not hold. A candidate stakeholder for such analysis is the venture capitalist (VC), since, in

---

9. We gratefully acknowledge a reviewer of this manuscript for raising these issues.

addition to their provision of financial capital, VCs often also invest their specialized human capital and capabilities in the new venture. This dual role of the VC—like the dual role of the top executive of a new venture—may exacerbate the "double moral hazard" problem associated especially with new ventures (Demougin & Fabel).[10] Then, the ownership rights of both patents and the firm's assets may be part of the agency problem as well as a mechanism to mitigate it.

REFERENCES

Agarwal, R. & Samwick, A.A. (1999). Executive compensation, strategic competition, and relative performance evaluation: Theory and evidence. *Journal of Finance, 54,* 1999–2043.

Audretsch, D.B. & Lehmann, E.E. (2005). The effects of experience, ownership and knowledge on IPO survival: Empirical evidence from Germany. *Review of Accounting and Finance, 4*(4), 13–33.

Audretsch, D.B. & Lehmann, E.E. (2006). Entrepreneurial access and absorption of knowledge spillovers: Strategic board and managerial composition for competitive advantage. *Journal of Small Business Management, 44*(2), 155–166.

Audretsch, D.B., Keilbach, M., & Lehmann, E.E. (2006). *Entrepreneurship and economic growth.* New York: Oxford University Press.

Barney, J.E. (1986). Strategic factor markets: Expectations, luck and business strategy. *Management Science, 42,* 1231–1241.

Barney, J.E. & Clark, B.N. (2007). *Resource-based theory: Creating and sustaining competitive advantage.* New York: Oxford University Press.

Beatty, R. & Zajac, E. (1994). Managerial incentives, monitoring, and risk bearing: A study of executive compensation, ownership and board structure in initial public offerings. *Administrative Science Quarterly, 39,* 313–335.

Bitler, M., Moskowitz, T.J., & Vissing-Jörgensen, A. (2006). Testing agency theory with entrepreneur effort and wealth. *Journal of Finance, 60*(2), 539–576.

Börsch-Supan, A. & Köke, J. (2002). An applied econometrician's view of empirical corporate governance studies. *German Economic Review, 3,* 295–326.

Brunninge, O., Nordqvist, M., & Wiklund, J. (2007). Corporate governance and strategic change in SMEs: The effects of ownership, board composition and top management teams. *Small Business Economics, 29*(3), 295–308.

Brynjolfsson, E. (1994). Information assets, technology, and organization. *Management Science, 40,* 1645–1662.

Buchinsky, M. (1998). Recent advantages in quantile regression models. *Journal of Human Resources, 33*(1), 88–126.

Casson, M. (2003). *The entrepreneur: An economic theory.* Northampton, MA: Edward Elgar.

---

10. A VC faces moral hazard in the entrepreneur's "behaviors" that determine the return on investment. VCs, however, also contribute managerial and consulting services to the new venture. Thus, the moral hazard problem is "double-sided" in that the return on investment is affected by the behaviors of both the entrepreneur and the VC.

Certo, S., Covin, J., Daily, C., & Dalton, D. (2001). Wealth and the effects of founder management among IPO-stage ventures. *Strategic Management Journal*, 22(6/7), 641–658.

Chandler, A. (1990). *Scale and scope*. Cambridge, MA: Harvard University Press.

Cockburn, I. & Griliches, Z. (1988). Industry effects and appropriability measures in the stock market's valuation of R&D and patents. *American Economic Review*, 78, 419–423.

Daily, C.M. & Dalton, D.R. (1993). Board of directors leadership and structure: Control and performance implications. *Entrepreneurship Theory and Practice*, 17(3), 65–81.

Daily, C.M., Dalton, D.R., & Cannella, A.A. (2003). Corporate governance: Decades of dialogue and data. *Academy of Management Review*, 28(3), 371–382.

Daily, C.M., Dalton, D.R., & Rajagopalan, N. (2003). Governance through ownership: Centuries of practice, decades of research. *Academy of Management Journal*, 46(2), 151–158.

Dalton, D.R., Daily, C.M., Certo, S.T., & Roengpita, R. (2003). Meta-analysis of financial performance and equity: Fusion or confusion? *Academy of Management Journal*, 46, 13–26.

Demougin, D. & Fabel, O. (2006). The division of ownership in new ventures. *Journal of Economics and Management Strategy*, 16(1), 111–128.

Fiegener, M.K., Brown, B.M., Dreux, D.R., & Dennis W.J., Jr. (2000). CEO stakes and board composition in small private firms. *Entrepreneurship Theory and Practice*, 24(Summer), 5–24.

Gibbons, R. (2004). *Four formal(izable) theories of the firm?* Discussion paper. Cambridge, MA: MIT and NBER.

Griliches, Z. (1990). Patent statistics as economic indicators: A survey. *Journal of Economic Literature*, 28, 1661–1707.

Grossman, S. & Hart, O. (1986). The costs and benefits of ownership: A theory of vertical and lateral integration. *Journal of Political Economy*, 94, 691–719.

Harhoff, D. & Hoisl, K. (2004). *Institutionalized incentives for ingenuity—Patent value and the German employees' invention act*. Discussion paper. Munich: LMU Munich.

Hart, O. (1995). *Firms, contracts, and financial structure*. Oxford: Clarendon Press.

Hart, O. & Moore, J. (1990). Property rights and the nature of the firm. *Journal of Political Economy*, 98, 1119–1158.

Himmelberg, C.P., Hubbard, G.R., & Palia, D.N. (1999). Understanding the determinants of managerial ownership and the link between ownership and performance. *Journal of Financial Economics*, 53, 353–384.

Hitt, M., Ireland, D., Camp, M., & Sexton, D. (2002). *Strategic entrepreneurship: Ceating a new mindset*. Malden, MA: Blackwell Publishers.

Holmström, B. (1999). The firm as a subeconomy. *Journal of Law, Economics, and Organization*, 15, 74–102.

Huse, M. (2000). Boards of directors in SMEs: A review and research agenda. *Entrepreneurship and Regional Development*, 12, 271–290.

Ireland, R.D., Hitt, M.A., & Sirmon, D.G. (2003). A model of strategic entrepreneurship: The construct and its dimensions. *Journal of Management*, 29(3), 963–989.

Jensen, M.C. & Meckling, W. (1976). Theory of the firm. Managerial behavior, agency costs and ownership structures. *Journal of Financial Economics*, 3, 305–360.

Jovanovic, B. (1982). Truthful disclosure of information. *Bell Journal of Economics*, *13*(2), 36–44.

Koenker, R. & Hallock, K.F. (2001). Quantile regression. *Journal of Economic Perspectives*, *15*, 143–156.

Kräkel, M. (2004). Managerial versus entrepreneurial firms: The benefits of separating ownership and control. *Schmalenbach Business Review*, *6*, 2–19.

Mahoney, J.T. (2005). *Economic foundations of strategy*. Thousand Oaks, CA: Sage Publications.

Michael, S., Storey, D., & Thomas, H. (2002). Discovery and coordination in strategic management and entrepreneurship. In M.A. Hitt, R.D. Ireland, S.M. Camp, & D.L. Sexton (Eds.), *Strategic entrepreneurship: Creating a new mindset* (pp. 45–65). Malden, MA: Blackwell Publishers.

Mosakowski, E. (2002). Overcoming resource disadvantages in entrepreneurial firms: When less is more. In M.A. Hitt, R.D. Ireland, S.M. Camp, & D.L. Sexton (Eds.), *Strategic entrepreneurship: Creating a new mindset* (pp. 106–126). Malden, MA: Blackwell Publishers.

Mowery, D., Oxley, E., & Silverman, S. (1996). Strategic alliances and interfirm knowledge transfer. *Strategic Management Journal*, *17*, 77–91.

Patel, P. & Pavitt, K. (1997). The technological competencies of the world's largest firms: Complex and path-dependent, but not much variety. *Research Policy*, *26*, 141–156.

Rajan, R. & Zingales, L. (1998). Power in a theory of the firm. *Quarterly Journal of Economics*, *108*(2), 387–432.

Rajan, R. & Zingales, L. (2000). The governance of the new enterprise. In X. Vives (Ed.), *Corporate governance: Theoretical and empirical perspectives* (pp. 201–226). Cambridge, UK: Cambridge University Press.

Rajan, R. & Zingales, L. (2001a). The firm as a dedicated hierarchy: A theory of the origins and growths of firms. *Quarterly Journal of Economics*, *116*(4), 805–851.

Rajan, R. & Zingales, L. (2001b). The influence of the financial revolution on the nature of the firm. *American Economic Review (Papers and Proceedings)*, *91*(2), 206–211.

Uhlaner, L., Wright, M., & Huse, M. (2007). Private firms and corporate governance: An integrated economic and management perspective. *Small Business Economics*, *29*(3), 225–241.

Zahra, S.A., Neubaum, D.O., & Naldi, L. (2007). The effects of ownership and governance on SME's international knowledge-based resources. *Small Business Economics*, *29*(3), 309–327.

David B. Audretsch is the director of the Entrepreneurship, Growth and Public Policy group of the Max Planck Institute of Economics and the Ameritech Chair of Economic Development at Indiana University.

Erik E. Lehmann is a professor of organization at the University of Augsburg and a research professor in the Department of Entrepreneurship, Growth and Public Policy of the Max Planck Institute of Economics.

Lawrence A. Plummer is an Associate Professor in the Department of Management, Clemson University and a Management Research Fellow in the Department of Entrepreneurship, Growth and Public Policy of the Max Planck Institute of Economics.

An earlier version of this paper was presented at the *Conference on Strategic Entrepreneurship*, Schloß Ringberg, Germany, June 2007. We thank the participants for their helpful comments and suggestions. We also thank two anonymous referees for their comments and suggestions that helped to improve the paper. Any errors or omissions remain our responsibility.

[14]

J Manag Gov (2012) 16:369–376
DOI 10.1007/s10997-010-9155-0

Transnational social capital and scientist entrepreneurship

David Audretsch · Taylor Aldridge

Published online: 6 August 2010
© Springer Science+Business Media, LLC. 2010

Abstract This paper provides a link between social capital and the entrepreneurial activity of university scientists in the life sciences. The two main hypotheses are that social capital promotes scientist entrepreneurship and transnational social capital is conducive to scientist entrepreneurship. These hypotheses are tested using a large data base of US scientists in the life sciences. The empirical results support the two main hypotheses. Social capital in general, and transnational social capital in particular, are found to enhance scientist entrepreneurship in the life sciences.

Keywords Entrepreneurship · Life science · Social capital · University scientists

1 Introduction

Perhaps more than for any other industry, university scientists play a key role in the entrepreneurial activities of life science companies. As Orsenigo et al. (1998), Owen-Smith et al. (2002), Owen-Smith and Powell (2003), Patzelt and Brenner (2008) show, university scientists are central to the competitiveness and performance of life-science companies.

D. Audretsch
Indiana University, Bloomington, IN, USA
e-mail: daudrets@indiana.edu

D. Audretsch
King Saud University, Riyadh, Saudi Arabia

D. Audretsch
WHU-Otto Beisheim School of Management, Vallendar, Germany

T. Aldridge (✉)
Max Planck Institute of Economics, Jena, Germany
e-mail: aldridge@econ.mpg.de

A number of previous studies have examined why some scientists engage in entrepreneurial activity in the life sciences while others do not (Zucker et al. 1998). However, these studies have generally not incorporated the impact that social capital plays, which has recently been found to be a key ingredient in entrepreneurship. The purpose of this paper is to link not just social capital to scientist entrepreneurship in the life sciences, but also to identify whether the geographic dimension of that social capital, in particular transnational social capital, contributes to scientist entrepreneurship. Transnational social capital might be particularly conducive to scientist entrepreneurship in the life sciences, because it provides access to crucial resources, such as clinical testing, that may face barriers and impediments in the host country of the scientist.

The second section of this paper explains the link between scientist entrepreneurship and social capital and presents the main hypotheses posited in this paper. The third section presents the data base that is used, which consists of a large sample of life-science scientists. The fourth section of the paper presents the empirical results testing the main hypotheses linking social capital and transnational social capital to scientist entrepreneurial activity. The final section provides a summary and conclusions. In particular, the empirical results of this paper provide support for the two main hypotheses that social capital promotes scientist entrepreneurship and that transnational social capital is conducive to scientist entrepreneurship.

2 Scientist entrepreneurship & social capital

Social capital refers to meaningful interactions and linkages among individuals. Thus, in the context of scientists, social capital highlights interactions and linkages that the scientist has with others. Social capital can be contrasted with the more traditional forms of capital. Physical capital refers to the importance of machines and tools as a factor of production. Human capital refers to the accumulation of the stock of skills and knowledge required to perform labor in a manner that generates positive economic value. The concept of social capital (Putnam 1993; Coleman 1988) is a complement to human capital and physical capital in that it contributes a social component to those factors generating positive economic value. According to Putnam (2000, p. 19), "Whereas physical capital refers to physical objects and human capital refers to the properties of individuals, social capital refers to connections among individuals—social networks. By analogy with notions of physical capital and human capital—tools and training that enhance individual productivity—social capital refers to features of social organization, such as networks that facilitate coordination and cooperation for mutual benefits".

The decision for individuals to engage in entrepreneurial activity has been found in an extensive literature to be influenced by the social capital accessed by that individual. (Aldrich and Martinez 2003; Thorton and Flynne 2003). Studies have generally found that the likelihood of an individual engaging in entrepreneurial activity is greater when they have access to higher levels of social capital. Thus, in the case of scientist entrepreneurship, interactions and linkages involving scientists reflect social capital and would be expected to enhance the likelihood of a scientist engaging in entrepreneurial activity.

However, it is important to emphasize that the literature on social capital does not suggest that linkages and interactions are homogeneous. Rather, some types of social interactions with particular individuals generate richer social capital than do others, depending upon the complementarities between the individuals. Linkages between academic scientists are expected to be particularly rich in complementarities with respect to commercialization when the linkage involves a scientist employed by private industry. This is because working with a scientist employed in the commercial context of a private firm is more conducive to an orientation towards commercializable research. In addition, the information and experience with commercializing research is richer in the context of scientists working in a private firm.

The geographic aspect involving the linkage may also enhance scientist social capital. In particular, interactions involving scientists located in the Asian context may be more conducive to commercialization of research, since they have access to clinical testing and other key steps to commercialization that have been impeded in the United States due to legal restrictions. This would suggest that an important ingredient of social capital is not just the activity and commercial orientation of the social partner, but also their geographic location (Onetti et al. 2010; Onetti and Zucchella 2008). Linkages and interactions involving transnational partners, or partners located in different key countries may provide access to critical steps towards commercialization, enabling the scientists to overcome barriers and other impediments in the host country where the university scientist is located. Thus, the fundamental hypothesis of this paper is that not only does social capital promote scientist entrepreneurship, but that social capital with a commercial orientation and with a transnational linkage with an industry scientist located in a key country will also enhance scientist entrepreneurship.

3 Measurement and data

To text the main hypothesis of this paper, that transnational social capital is conducive to scientist entrepreneurship, a data set is required that provides measurement of scientist entrepreneurship along with measures of social capital, and in particular transnational social capital.

To measure the decision by scientists to engage in entrepreneurial activity a new base was analyzed. This data base identifies scientists awarded a research grant by the National Cancer Institute (NCI). Of those scientists receiving a research grant from the National Cancer Institute, the top 20%, which amounted to 1,693 scientists, were selected to constitute the high-award scientists included in the data base. These high-award scientists received more than $5,350 million in research funded by the National Cancer Institute.

The first step in forming the dependent variable involved identifying whether or not the scientist had patented, which is the operational measure for scientist entrepreneurship in this paper. The patent activity of each scientist contained in the data base was identified from the records contained in the United States Patent and Trademark Office (USPTO). The patent database spans 1975–2004 and contains over three million patents. This enabled the identification of 1,204 patents held by 398 distinct scientists between 1998 and 2004. This data base was used to create a dependent variable taking on the value of one if the scientist had patented and zero otherwise.

The main hypothesis of this variable links the social capital of the scientist, and in particular social capital involving transnational linkages, to entrepreneurial activity. To measure scientist social capital two distinct variables are used. The first measure of social capital (Copublications) reflects linkages between a university scientist and her counterparts in private industry. It is measured by the co-authorship between the university scientist and an industry scientist in the Science Citation Index using the ISI web of science citation database. If the hypothesis that social capital enhances entrepreneurial activity is verified, the coefficient of this variable would be positive.

The second measure of scientist social capital reflects the geographic dimension of the interaction, and in particular, whether it is a transnational interaction involving an industry scientist located in Asia (Industry Co-publication Asia). This variable reflects social capital and linkages between university scientists and their counterparts located in Asia. This variable is measured as co-authorship between a university and an Asian scientist in the Science Citation Index using the ISI Web of Science citation database. Using the address fields within each publication value of the ISI Web of Science citation index Industry Co-publication Asia was identified if any of the terms of China, Japan, South Korea and Taiwan were found in the ISI Web of Science address field. A binary variable was then created, taking on the value of one for all scientists with linkages in Asia and zero otherwise. A positive coefficient of this variable would support the main hypothesis of this paper that transnational social capital enhances scientist entrepreneurial activity.

In addition to the two main variables reflecting different aspects of scientist social capital, several control variables, based on findings from the extant literature, are also included in the regression. These control variables reflect the influence of scientist-specific factors, university-specific factors, and locational-specific factors, all of which have been found to influence scientist entrepreneurship or at least the entrepreneurial activity associated with universities.

There are several important characteristics specific to each scientist which are included in the regression. These are measures of scientific reputation, the age of the scientist and gender. A measure of citations divided by the number of publications is used to reflect scientific reputation. A dummy variable with the value of unity for males and otherwise zero reflects the gender of the scientist. The age of the scientist is measured in terms of years.

Different universities have different policies towards scientist entrepreneurship. The heterogeneity of university policies towards scientist entrepreneurship is reflected by two different measures reflecting the importance of the university technology transfer office. The first measure reflects the focus of the technology transfer office on patent activities, and is the mean annual number of TTO employees dedicated to licensing and patenting as a share of total employees. The

Table 1 Variable means and standard deviations for scientists with and without transnational social capital

Variable	Scientists with no Asian copublications		Scientists with Asian copublications	
	Mean	SD	Mean	SD
Copublications	.39	.49	.73	.45
TTO employees	8.53	1.14	8.93	1.16
TTO efficiency	1.20	1.51	1.28	1.63
TTO age	1981	11.31	1981	11.45
NCI grant	$3,042,304	$2,993,584	$3,382,192	$3,525,449
Gender	.75	.44	.84	.37
Public institution	.54	.50	.54	.50
NCI center	.55	.50	.57	.50
Ivy league	.12	.34	.07	.26
North east	.35	.48	.34	.48
California	.13	.34	.14	.35
Great Lakes	.13	.33	.13	.34
Previous patents	1.69	7.12	2.67	6.19

second measure reflects the age of the technology transfer office. In addition, a dummy variable taking on the value of one is included or public universities, which may consider part of their mission to be technology transfer, as well as a dummy variable taking on the value of one for universities with an NCI center, which may also promote scientist entrepreneurship are also included. A third variable reflecting university heterogeneity is a dummy variable taking on the value of one for the Ivy League universities is also included in the regression.

Scientists who have previously patented may have a higher propensity to patent again in this time period. Thus, a control dummy variable indicating whether or not the scientist had previously patented is included. Finally, a series of dummy variables are included in the regression to control for the location of the university where the scientist is employed.

The mean and standard deviation of each variable for the scientists with Asian transnational social capital is shown in Table 1. Scientists with transnational social capital clearly exhibit a higher propensity to patent. They also have a higher degree of social capital, as measured by co-publications with industry scientists. However, there does not seem to be any difference in terms of the type of university where they are employed, or in terms of geographic location.

4 Empirical results

The empirical results from estimating a probit regression for scientist entrepreneurship is provided in Table 2. As the positive and statistically significant coefficient of the variable co-publications with industry scientists indicates, those

Table 2 Probit regression results

	1	2	3
Co-publications	0.061 **(5.82)*****	0.043 **(3.45)*****	0.055 **(5.06)*****
Asia co-publications	0.269 **(3.47)*****	0.228 **(2.64)*****	0.222 **(2.78)*****
TTO employees	0.042 **(1.75)***	−0.006 (−1.00)	0.039 (−1.51)
TTO efficiency	1.006 **(3.23)*****	0.894 **(2.41)****	**0.867 (2.60)*****
TTO age	−0.015 **(3.40)*****	−0.004 (0.76)	−0.010 **(2.14)****
Scientist citations	–	0.045 (0.33)	0.022 (1.45)
NCI grant	–	0.007 (0.55)	0.004 (0.36)
Gender	–	0.245 **(2.30)****	0.397 **(3.95)*****
Public institution	–	−0.129 (1.24)	−0.175 **(1.94)***
NCI center	–	0.021 (0.24)	0.018 (0.22)
Ivy league	–	−0.082 (0.53)	0.042 (0.30)
North east	–	0.013 (0.11)	0.087 (0.79)
California	–	0.262 (1.25)	0.154 (1.31)
Great Lakes	–	0.048 (0.35)	0.064 (0.50)
Previous patents	–	0.230 **(12.14)*****	–
Constant	27.50 **(3.25)*****	6.343 (0.60)	19.142 **(1.98)****
Observations	1,431	1,431	1,431
LR chi2	**83.75*****	**341.44*****	**112.65*****
R-squared adjusted	0.05	0.22	0.07

Absolute value of z statistics in brackets

* significant at 10%; ** significant at 5%; *** significant at 1%

scientists with a greater degree of social capital exhibit a higher propensity to patent. This result is robust and does not depend upon the inclusion of control variables. This would suggest that the hypothesis that social capital is conducive to scientist entrepreneurship is supported by the empirical evidence provided by this data set.

Similarly, the positive and statistically significant coefficient of the variable measuring scientist co-publications with industry scientists located in Asia suggests that those scientists with a greater degree of Asian transnational social capital also exhibit a higher propensity to patent. This result again proves to be robust with and without the inclusion of the control variables. Thus, the empirical evidence supports the hypothesis that transnational social capital is conducive to scientist entrepreneurship.

The statistical significance of the control variables are less robust. Aspects of the university technology transfer office have an impact on scientist entrepreneurship. In particular, TTO efficiency is found to be positively related to scientist entrepreneurship, but the age of the TTO is found to be negatively related to scientist entrepreneurship. Two scientist-specific characteristics are important for scientist entrepreneurship. Males are found to have a higher propensity to engage in entrepreneurial activity. Similarly, those scientists who had previously patented are found to be more likely to engage in entrepreneurial activity.

5 Conclusions

University scientists play an important role in the entrepreneurial activity of life-science companies. They make key contributions as founders, providers of knowledge resources, and in some cases CEOs and key employees. This paper has examined the entrepreneurial behavior of university scientists in the life sciences. In particular, the findings suggest that not only is social capital important in generating scientist entrepreneurship, but in particular, a particular type of social capital, transnational social capital is conducive to scientist entrepreneurship in the life sciences.

While this paper has identified transnational social capital as having a positive impact on scientist entrepreneurship, the exact nature of the transnational relationships and linkages and exactly how they contribute to entrepreneurial activities remains beyond the scope of this paper. Future research may find it rewarding to examine in greater detail how transnational social capital is created, enhanced and ultimately used to generate entrepreneurship in the life sciences.

References

Aldrich, H. E., & Martinez, M. (2003). Entrepreneurship as social construction. In Z. J. Acs & D. B. Audretsch (Eds.), *The international handbook of entrepreneurship*. Dordrecht: Kluwer Academic Publishers.

Coleman, J. (1988). Social capital in the creation of human capital. *American Journal of Sociology, 94*, 95–121.

Onetti, A., & Zucchella, A. (2008). *Imprenditorialità, internazionalizzazione e innovazione. I business model delle imprese biotech*. Roma: Carocci.

Onetti, A., Zucchella, A., Jones, M. V., & McDougall-Covin, P. P. (2010). Internationalization, innovation and entrepreneurship: Business models for new technology-based firms. *Journal of Management and Governance.* doi:10.1007/s10997-010-9154-1.

Orsenigo, L., Pammolli, F., Riccaboni, M., Bonaccorsi, A., & Turchetti, G. (1998). The evolution of knowledge and the dynamics of an industry network. *Journal of Management and Governance, 1*(2), 147–175.

Owen-Smith, J., & Powell, W. W. (2003). The expanding role of university patenting in the life sciences: Assessing the importance of experience and connectivity. *Research Policy, 32*(9), 1695–1711.

Owen-Smith, J., Riccaboni, M., Pammolli, F., & Powell, W. W. (2002). A Comparison of US and European university-industry relations in the life sciences. *Management Science, 48*(1), 24–43.

Patzelt, H., & Brenner, T. (2008). *The handbook of bioentrepreneurship*. New York: Springer.

Putnam, R. (1993). *Making democracy work: Civic traditions in modern italy*. Princeton: Princeton University Press.

Putnam, R. (2000). *Bowling alone: The collapse and revival of American community*. New York: Simon and Schuster.

Thorton, P. H., & Flynne, K. H. (2003). Entrepreneurship, networks and geographies. In Z. J. Acs & D. B. Audretsch (Eds.), *The international handbook of entrepreneurship*. Dordrecht: Kluwer Academic Publishers.

Zucker, L. G., Darby, M. R., & Brewer, M. B. (1998). Intellectual human capital and the birth of US biotechnology. *American Economic Review, 88*, 290–306.

Author Biographies

David Audretsch is a Distinguished Professor and Ameritech Chair of Economic Development at Indiana University, where is also serves as Director of the Institute for Development Strategies. He also is an Honorary Professor of Industrial Economics and Entrepreneurship at the WHU-Otto Beisheim School of Management in Germany. In addition, he serves as a Visiting Professor at the King Saud University in Saudi Arabia. He was awarded the 2001 Global Award for Entrepreneurship Research by the Swedish Foundation for Small Business Research.

Taylor Aldridge is a Senior Research Fellow at the Max Planck Institute of Economics and Research Fellow at the Institute of Development Studies, Indiana University, Bloomington. He has recently published in journals such as Research Policy, Journal of Technology Transfer and the Annals of Regional Science. His general area of research studies firm strategy and public policy implications of innovation and entrepreneurship.

[15]

Ann Reg Sci (2010) 45:55–85
DOI 10.1007/s00168-009-0291-x

Cultural diversity and entrepreneurship: a regional analysis for Germany

**David Audretsch · Dirk Dohse ·
Annekatrin Niebuhr**

Received: 15 October 2007 / Accepted: 17 July 2008 / Published online: 13 March 2009
© The Author(s) 2009. This article is published with open access at Springerlink.com

Abstract   In this paper, we investigate the determinants of entrepreneurial activity in a cross section of German regions for the period 1998–2005. Departing from the knowledge spillover theory of entrepreneurship, the focus of our analysis is on the role of the regional environment and, in particular, knowledge and cultural diversity. Our main hypothesis is that both, knowledge and diversity, have a positive impact on new firm formation. As the determinants of regional firm birth rates might differ considerably with respect to the necessary technology and knowledge input, we consider start-ups at different technology levels. The regression results indicate that regions with a high level of knowledge provide more opportunities for entrepreneurship than other regions. Moreover, while sectoral diversity tends to dampen new firm foundation, cultural diversity has a positive impact on technology oriented start-ups. This suggests that the diversity of people is more conducive to entrepreneurship than the diversity of firms. Thus, regions characterized by a high level of knowledge and cultural diversity form an ideal breeding ground for technology oriented start-ups.

JEL Classification   M13 · O18 · R11

D. Audretsch (✉)
Max Planck Instiute of Economics, Kahlaische Strasse 10, 07745 Jena, Germany
e-mail: audretsch@econ.mpg.de

D. Dohse
Kiel Institute for the World Economy, Düsternbrooker Weg 120, 24105 Kiel, Germany
e-mail: dirk.dohse@ifw-kiel.de

A. Niebuhr
Institute for Employment Research (IAB Nord), Projensdorfer Straße 82, 24106 Kiel, Germany
e-mail: Annekatrin.Niebuhr@iab.de

1 Introduction

The start-up and running of new business is central to modern economies' dynamics and their ability to innovate and grow. It is therefore not surprising that entrepreneurs, a species long-time neglected by mainstream economics, recently seem to regain the profession's attention.[1] They are, however, no longer viewed as "lone giants" but rather as very interactive people who heavily depend on other people, resources and opportunities in their respective context.

If it is true that the spillover of new knowledge, which is arguably the most important input into the entrepreneurial process, is geographically localized (for empirical evidence see for instance Jaffe 1989; Audretsch and Feldmann 1996; Audretsch and Stephan 1996; Jaffe et al. 1993) then the regional context should be a particularly important determinant of entrepreneurship. Indeed, recent studies have shown the importance of regional factors such as agglomeration economies, regional R&D or regional income growth in explaining differences in the entry rates of firms (Rosenthal and Strange 2003; Stuart and Sorenson 2003; Lee et al. 2004). The way in which regional diversity impacts entrepreneurial opportunity, which is the core issue of this paper, is, however, rarely explored.

We analyse the regional determinants of entrepreneurship as measured in terms of firm start-ups in Germany. The purpose of the analysis is threefold:

- The main focus of the paper is on investigating the role of the regional environment and, in particular, *regional diversity* with respect to new firm foundation. Our main hypothesis is that regional diversity—by which we mean the diversity of people (i.e. *cultural diversity*) and not necessarily the diversity of firms or industries within a region—fosters the recognition, absorption and realization of entrepreneurial opportunities and should therefore have a positive impact on new firm formation.
- Secondly, we ask whether regions with high levels of *knowledge*, measured by R&D and human capital, do indeed provide more entrepreneurial opportunities than other regions, as recent theoretical papers suggest.
- And thirdly we conjecture that the factors driving firm start-ups might differ considerably with respect to the *technology* (or knowledge) input necessary to start and run a certain business. We therefore consider different kinds of start-ups (i.e. total start-ups, technology oriented start-ups, start-ups in technology oriented services and high tech start-ups) and investigate whether the factors that influence the variation in regional firm birth rates differ systematically with respect to the technology level of the start-ups.

The paper is organised as follows. Section 2 provides the theoretical background on firm formation and regional diversity and specifies the econometric model in its basic form. Section 3 contains a detailed description of the data set and a discussion of the variables used in the estimations. Section 4 presents and discusses the results of the econometric analysis. Section 5 concludes.

---

[1] See, for example, the influential contributions by Blanchflower and Oswald (1998), Lazear (2004) or Acemoglu et al. (2006).

2 Knowledge spillovers, cultural diversity, and entrepreneurship: theoretical background and econometric model

2.1 Theoretical background

Economists have long observed that entrepreneurial activity tends to vary systematically across geographic space (Carlton 1983; Storey 1991; Reynolds et al. 1994). In searching for a theoretical framework to provide a lens through which spatial variation of entrepreneurship could best be interpreted and explained, scholars have gravitated towards models highlighting the extent to which entrepreneurial opportunities prevail or are impeded within a spatial context. This has generated an exhaustive literature linking region-specific characteristics that either promote or impede entrepreneurial opportunities to various measures of regional entrepreneurship. Most notably, region-specific measures, such as growth, unemployment, population density, taxes, and industry structure have been found to influence the extent of entrepreneurial activity within a region. Steil (1999) presents a comprehensive survey of the literature before 1999. Empirical studies for Germany are provided by Audretsch and Fritsch (1994, 2002), Fritsch and Falck (2007) as well as by Rocha and Sternberg (2005).

Just recently, the *knowledge spillover theory of entrepreneurship* (Acs et al. 2004, 2005) was introduced to establish an explicit link between knowledge and entrepreneurship within the spatial context. The knowledge spillover theory of entrepreneurship posits that investments in knowledge by incumbent firms and research organizations such as universities will generate entrepreneurial opportunities because not all of the new knowledge will be pursued and commercialized by the incumbent firms. As Arrow (1962) pointed out, new knowledge is inherently uncertain and asymmetric, so that incumbent firms and other organizations are unable to recognize and act upon all of the knowledge created by their own investments. What one (knowledge) worker perceives to be a potentially valuable idea may not actually be acknowledged as being valuable by the decision-making hierarchy of the firm. The knowledge filter (Acs et al. 2004) refers to the extent that new knowledge remains uncommercialized by the organization creating that knowledge. It is these residual ideas that generate the opportunity for entrepreneurship. By pursuing ideas and knowledge created but left uncommercialized in an incumbent firm or organization, the entrepreneurial venture serves as a conduit of knowledge spillovers. In other words: knowledge spillovers are viewed as a major cause of entrepreneurship.

Recent empirical studies have found that new-firm start-ups are systematically greater in regions rich in knowledge than in regions poor in knowledge (Audretsch and Keilbach 2007; Audretsch et al. 2006).[2] These studies implicitly assume that, given a certain investment in knowledge, economic agents will automatically identify and act upon entrepreneurial opportunities. That is, the capabilities of economic agents

---

[2] Moreover, Audretsch and Dohse (2007) are able to show that being located in an agglomeration rich in knowledge resources is more conducive to firm growth than being located in a region that is less endowed with knowledge resources.

within the region to actually access and absorb the knowledge and ultimately utilize it to generate entrepreneurial activity are implicitly assumed to be invariant with respect to geographic space.

However, such an assumption violates one of the most significant insights by Jane Jacobs (1969), later echoed by Porter (1990), Glaeser et al. (1992), Feldman and Audretsch (1999), that regions with more diversity will facilitate the spillover of knowledge, which in turn should trigger more entrepreneurial activity. According to Jacobs, it is differences among people that foster looking at a given information set differently, thereby resulting in different appraisal of any new idea. After all, if all economic agents were perfectly homogeneous, a total consensus would reign with respect to any new idea, and there would be no reason to start a new firm. As Jacobs emphasized, it is differences across economic agents that lead to divergences in the valuation of new ideas, and it is these divergences in the value of ideas that trigger people to start a new venture. Diverse backgrounds and perspectives embedded in a diverse set of agents may lead one person to decide an idea is potentially valuable while others, including the decision making hierarchy of incumbent organizations, do not. The more different kinds of people evaluate any given idea, the higher will be the probability that one of these persons will arrive at the conclusion that she wants to commercially exploit it.

Thus, while knowledge may be important to generate new ideas, it is the assessment of those new ideas by diverse economic agents characterized by differences in experiences, backgrounds, and capabilities that leads to divergences in the valuation of such ideas which ultimately induce agents to resort to entrepreneurship to appropriate the value of their knowledge endowments. This suggests that for knowledge spillovers to occur, more than investments in new knowledge is required. Rather, economic agents with the capabilities to access, absorb and commercialize that knowledge through the spillover conduit of entrepreneurship are also essential for generating knowledge spillovers. Diversity will enhance such entrepreneurial activity because diverse economic agents will value new ideas differently, leading them to respond to different ideas in a different way. It is this diversity in economic agents that triggers divergences in the evaluation of new ideas that is the basis for knowledge spillover entrepreneurship. Thus, those regions with more diversity would be expected to generate more entrepreneurial activity. By contrast, less diversity, or more homogeneity, would be expected to generate less entrepreneurship. In particular, diversity with respect to backgrounds, experience and interest should generate diversity with respect to evaluations of new ideas, which, as explained above, should trigger more individuals to reach the decision to become an entrepreneur.

Glaeser et al. (1992) and Feldman and Audretsch (1999) provided compelling evidence linking diversity to regional economic growth. However, in both of these influential studies, diversity was measured in terms of economic activity within the region, which reflects firms, but not in terms of the people actually living and working in the region. This misses the essential diversity argument by Jacobs, which is first and foremost about people and not necessarily firms. Thus, a major contribution of this paper is not only to link regional entrepreneurial activity to diversity in terms of firms but also people. So, unlike earlier papers we consider the significance of different dimensions of diversity for firm foundation, namely sectoral diversity and cultural diversity.[3] *Sectoral diversity* is probably the most common concept. The indicators of sectoral diversity used in this paper are calculated with employment shares of industries documented in the appendix. More important—and from a theoretical point of view more adequate—we apply an indicator that refers directly to the diversity in terms of people. We use information on regional employment by nationality to calculate our measure of *cultural diversity* (see Sect. 3 for details). Cultural diversity is supposed to capture diversity of economic agents (with respect to their experience, background and capabilities) which is expected to facilitate exploitation of a given regional knowledge base and thus promote entrepreneurial activity.

2.2 The econometric model

In order to arrive at robust results regarding the impact of different diversity measures, the regression analysis departs from a model that includes a number of factors that have turned out to be important determinants of the regional firm birth rate in the empirical literature. These *control variables* include measures of the density of economic activities (such as population density), the disposable income in the region under consideration and in neighbouring regions (spatially lagged exogenous variable), growth of disposable income, growth of disposable income in neighbouring regions, unemployment and an indicator of the firm size structure of the region (share of small firms in total employment).

The econometric model in its basic version has the form:

$$\text{SU}_{it} = \alpha_0 + \sum_{l=1}^{L} \alpha_l \text{KNOW}_{lit} + \sum_{m=1}^{M} \beta_m \text{DIV}_{mit} + \sum_{n=1}^{N} \gamma_n \text{CONTROL}_{nit} + u_{it} \quad (1)$$

where SU_{it} is the start-up intensity (start-ups per 10.000 inhabitants) in region i and year t, DIV_{mit} is diversity measure m in region i and period t, CONTROL_{nit} is control variable n in region i and period t. Moreover, we include two knowledge variables KNOW_{lit}, the share of R&D workers in total employment, and the percentage of highly skilled employees. Spatial lags of the knowledge variables are considered as well since the spatial range of spillover effects might exceed the borders of our observational units. The error term is denoted by u_{it} and assumed to be identically and independently distributed with mean μ_u and variance σ_u^2.

---

[3] The reader might ask how sectoral and cultural diversity relate to the notions of localization economies and urbanization economies introduced by Hoover (1937). According to Hoover, localization economies are economies external to the firm and internal to a specific industry, whereas urbanization economies are external to the industry and internal to the city. Thus, a high level of sectoral concentration in a region (reflected by a low value of the sectoral diversity index) may indicate that there exist localization economies. On the other hand, there is no simple correspondence between our diversity measures and urbanization economies. Our concepts are rather specific, either relating to the sectoral distribution (=sectoral diversity) or the ethnic/cultural distribution (=cultural diversity) of a region's employees. The concept of urban diversity which underlies the notion of urbanization economies is, by contrast, much broader as it refers to diversity with respect to virtually any type of characteristic(s) within an urban or geographic unit of observation.

To check the robustness of results emerging from the pooled model given in Eq. (1), we apply additional regression models. Panel data models are used to control for unobserved time-invariant explanatory variables:

$$\text{SU}_{it} = \alpha_0 + \sum_{l=1}^{L} \alpha_l \text{KNOW}_{lit} + \sum_{m=1}^{M} \beta_m \text{DIV}_{mit} + \sum_{n=1}^{N} \gamma_n \text{CONTROL}_{nit} \quad (2)$$
$$+ \eta_i + \lambda_t + \nu_{it}$$

where η_i denotes a region-specific effect, controlling for unobservable regional characteristics that are time-invariant. λ_t captures unobservable time effects and ν_{it} is a white noise error term. We estimate fixed effects as well as random effects specifications.

Another innovation of the paper is that we consider start-ups at different technology levels as the factors driving start-ups might differ considerably with respect to technology level. The models given by Eqs. (1) and (2) are estimated for different technology levels, i.e. we consider overall start-up intensity, technology oriented start-ups, firm birth in technology oriented services and high tech start-ups as dependent variables. Simply comparing the estimates of the four models will provide first insights into variations regarding determinants of regional firm birth rates at different technology levels. This analysis is complemented by a more detailed investigation of corresponding differences. We pool the data of different firm birth rates, estimate coefficients specific to a particular technology level and perform F tests on equality of the slope estimates in order to check whether the impact of the explanatory variables differs systematically among technology levels.[4]

3 Data description

3.1 Units of observation

The cross section consists of 97 functional regions, so-called Raumordnungsregionen, which comprise several counties (NUTS 3 level) linked by intense commuting.[5] Thus, the observational units represent regional labour markets. Since this definition of regions does not account for other forms of economic activity such as consumption, we care for possible spillover effects caused, e.g. by demand linkages and other kinds of spatial interaction via spatial econometric methods, i.e. including spatial lags of explanatory variables.

---

[4] We pool the data and estimate the model without constraining the residual variances of different start-up intensities to be the same. Constraining the variances might severely affect the results of the F tests.

[5] According to a definition by the German Federal Office for Building and Regional Planning (BBR) Raumordnungsregionen are intended to be comparable regions "that reflect in acceptable approximation the spatial and functional interrelation between core cities and their hinterland" (BBR 2001: 2).

Table 1 Correlations of firm birth rates at different technology levels

	Start-Up Rates			
	Total	High tech	Technology oriented services	Not technology oriented
Total (*Su_all*)	1.00			
High tech (*Su_ht*)	0.13	1.00		
Technology oriented services (*Su_tos*)	0.66	0.42	1.00	
Not technology oriented (*Su_nto*)	0.99	0.05	0.53	1.00

Source: ZEW start-up panel, own calculations

3.2 Dependent variables

We measure regional entrepreneurship in terms of start-up intensity, i.e. start-ups per 10.000 inhabitants. As the annual variation in birth rates of innovative firms is high we follow the recommendation of the data provider (ZEW Mannheim) and use 4-year averages (1998–2001 and 2002–2005, respectively) of firm birth rates as dependent variables in the regression analyses.[6] Unlike earlier papers, we do not only consider total start ups but differentiate between firm birth rates at different technology levels. In the remainder of the paper we focus on four different groups of start-ups, namely total start-ups (*Su_all*), technology oriented start-ups (*Su_to*) which make out roughly 10% of all start-ups, and two particularly interesting and important sub-groups of technology oriented start-ups, i.e. start-ups in technology oriented services (*Su_tos*) and the small but classy group of high tech start-ups (*Su_ht*).[7] A detailed description of the data set and the classification of start-ups according to their technology level can be found in the documentation by Metzger and Heger (2005).[8]

As the majority of start-ups are not technology oriented, the firm birth rate of low tech businesses (*Su_nto*) is highly correlated with the measure for overall firm foundation (*Su_all*) which can be seen from Table 1. We therefore refrain from considering *Su_nto* as a category of its own in the empirical part of the paper.

Moreover, the spatial pattern of firm birth rates at different technological levels is subject to a considerable variation, as indicated by the correlation coefficients in Table 1. The correlation between total firm birth and start-ups in technology oriented services (*Su_tos*) amounts to 0.66, whereas the coefficient between the overall rate

---

[6] It should be noted that the information on start-ups only relates to headquarters and that new subsidiaries are not contained in the ZEW-data.

[7] As Armington and Acs (2002, 34) observe, while "… much of the literature on new firm formation in the 1980s was motivated by high levels of unemployment in traditional industrial regions, much of the focus on new firm start-ups today is motivated by high technology start-ups that are thought to be driving the new economy."

[8] It should be noted that according to ZEW the start-up rates for some regions tend to be upward biased due to regional differences in the data survey mode. We therefore exclude the corresponding observations (Hamburg, period 1998–2001; Oberfranken, Westpfalz and Rheinpfalz, period 2002–2005 and Braunschweig, both periods) from the database.

of firm foundation and high tech start ups (*Su_ht*) is merely 0.13. There are also pronounced disparities within the class of technology oriented start-ups as shown by the
modest correlation among new high tech firms and technology oriented services (0.42).
This suggests that firm birth of different technological categories might be driven by
different factors.

The substantial spatial variation of firm birth rates at different technological levels
is also illustrated in Figs. 1 and 2. While regions with a total start-up intensity (*Su_all*)
in the upper tail of the distribution can be found in the northern and eastern parts of
the country as well as in the south and the west, we observe a striking concentration
of regions with particularly high start-up intensities in technology oriented industries
(*Su_to*) in the southern parts of the country, i.e. in the states Bavaria, Baden-Württemberg and (the south of) Hesse.

Figures 3 and 4 in appendix show that the spatial distribution of start-ups in technology oriented services (*Su_tos*) is quite similar to the spatial distribution of technology
oriented start-ups in general while the high tech start-up-rate (*Su_ht*) appears to be
particularly high in the outmost south-west (Baden-Württemberg).

3.3 Explanatory variables

In order to arrive at robust results regarding the impact of different diversity measures the regression analysis departs from a model that includes a number of factors
that have turned out to be important determinants of the regional firm birth rate.
We deal with potential endogeneity of some influential factors by using predeter-
mined explanatory variables. Thus, as regards the average firm birth rate 1998–2001
(2002–2005) the explanatory variables refer to 1997 (2001)—unless stated otherwise.
Several explanatory variables used in the regression model are based on employment
data provided by the German Federal Employment Agency. The employment statistic covers all employment subject to social security contributions.[9] The information
refers to workplace location. We use employment data differentiated by nationality,
educational level, industry and firm size to generate several diversity measures and
control variables that enter into the regression model.

As mentioned before there is a rich and growing literature on regional variation in
new firm formation. The first larger wave of papers published in the early 1990s found
significant regional variation in firm start-ups, and the explanatory variables that were
usually found to be most important were various measures of unemployment, population density, industrial structure, taxes and regional (income) dynamics. These more
traditional variables are considered as control variables in our econometric analysis
and they are described in Sect. 3.3.1 in more detail.[10]

Recent theoretical developments such as the rise of the endogenous growth theory,
the new economic geography and—most recently—the knowledge spillover theory

---

[9] Hence, civil servants and self-employed are not recorded in the employment statistic.

[10] We do not consider taxes because business tax rates in Germany are either set at the federal level (corporate income tax) or at the level of municipalities, and there are no data available that aggregate taxes levied
at the level of municipalities to the level of counties or planning regions.

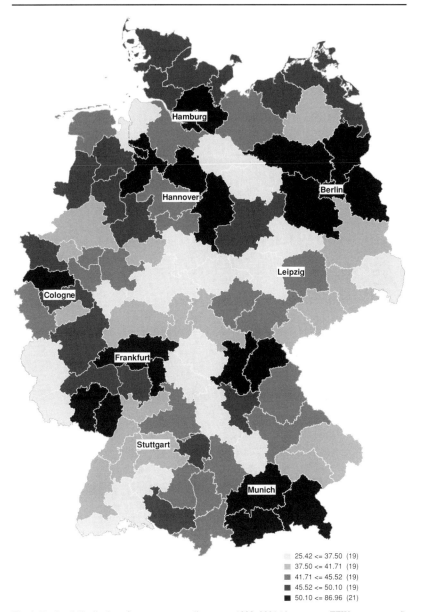

Fig. 1 Regional distribution of start-up rates—all start-ups 1998–2001 (data source: ZEW start-up panel)

of entrepreneurship led to a shift in the research focus to knowledge variables such as R&D and human capital. These knowledge variables form the second group of explanatory variables in our empirical analysis, and they are described in Sect. 3.3.2.

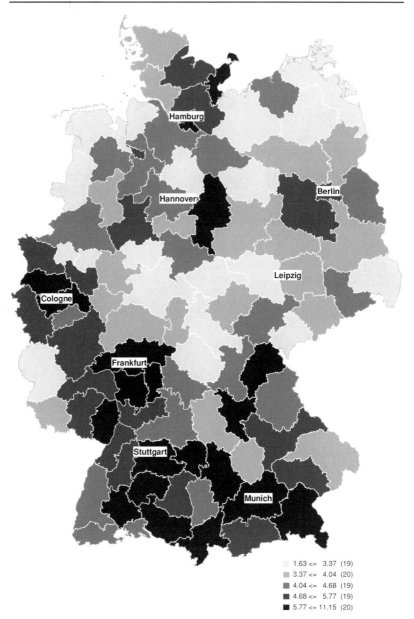

1.63 <=   3.37 (19)
3.37 <=   4.04 (20)
4.04 <=   4.68 (19)
4.68 <=   5.77 (19)
5.77 <= 11.15 (20)

Fig. 2 Regional distribution of start-up rates—technology oriented start-ups 1998–2001 (data source: ZEW start-up panel)

Finally, as argued in Sect. 2, the spillover of new knowledge and the realization of entrepreneurial opportunities depends for various reasons on the composition of the regional population. Our central hypothesis is that the higher the ethnic (and thus cultural) diversity of the economic agents living and working in a region the higher is the chance that entrepreneurial opportunities are recognized and put into practice. Regional diversity measures are discussed in more detail in Sect. 3.3.3.

3.3.1 Control variables

As a first control variable we consider the regional unemployment rate, i.e. the number of unemployed as a percentage of the regional labor force (UR). Conflicting hypotheses are discussed in the entrepreneurship literature regarding the impact of unemployment. Some authors argue that in case of high unemployment the propensity of people to start their own business might increase because of lacking alternative job opportunities. Based on this argument, one might expect that regions characterized by high unemployment rates realize high rates of new firm foundation. However, high unemployment can also indicate economic decline and low consumer demand. In this case a high rate of unemployment is likely to exert a dampening effect on entrepreneurship. The empirical evidence concerning the impact of unemployment on start-ups is rather contradictory and unclear. While Wagner and Sternberg (2004) find that being unemployed increases the propensity to start one's own firm, other studies find no significant or even a significantly negative impact of the unemployment rate (Reynolds et al. 1994; Sutaria and Hicks 2004).

The density of economic activity in a region is typically found to have a positive impact on start-ups (Reynolds et al. 1994; Armington and Acs 2002; Fritsch and Falck 2007). The density measure PD (population density) used in the context of this paper is defined as inhabitants per square kilometer in the German planning regions. In contrast to the knowledge variables discussed in Sect. 3.3.2 the variable PD is included in order to capture the impact of agglomeration economies not directly related to knowledge.

The share of employment in small businesses has been found to be an important start-up determinant in previous studies (Reynolds et al. 1994; Armington and Acs 2002; Sorensen and Audia 2000). A high percentage of small enterprises is generally held to be positive as it may be viewed as a proxy for the entrepreneurial climate and/or entrepreneurial tradition of the region (reflecting the start-up activity of previous periods). A slightly different argument is that working in a small firm fosters the emergence of an entrepreneurial attitude, because smaller businesses have a less extensive internal division of labor such that employees are more likely to get access to knowledge and attain capabilities necessary to run a firm (Beesley and Hamilton 1984; Sorensen and Audia 2000; Fritsch and Falck 2007).[11] We capture impacts of

---

[11] Fritsch and Falck (2007) offer another interesting interpretation of this phenomenon. They argue that the employment share of small firms may be viewed as a proxy for an industry's minimum efficient business size. "The smaller an industry's minimum efficient business size, the fewer the resources that are needed to enter the market successfully, which makes it more likely that new businesses will emerge in that industry" (Fritsch and Falck 2007: 159).

the firm size structure by a variable *SE*, measuring the share of small firms (less than 20 employees) in total employment.

To capture effects linked to the size of the local market and the dynamics of the economic development of the region we include the disposable income of the regions (*INC*) and the growth rate of disposable income (*INC_G*). Information on regional disposable income is available from the national accounts. Spillover effects resulting from a market size that does not correspond with our functional regions is taken into account by spatial lags of explanatory variables. The regression model is extended by spatial lags of disposable income (*W_INC*) and of the growth of disposable income (*W_INC_G*). Therefore, we investigate whether purchasing power in neighbouring regions has a significant impact on the firm birth rate.

Modelling spillover effects requires some information on the structure of spatial interaction summarized by a spatial weight matrix. We apply two alternative specifications of weight matrices. The first specification involves a binary matrix such that the weights $w_{ij} = 1$ if the regions i and j share a border and $w_{ij} = 0$ otherwise. Secondly, a weighting scheme based on distance between regions' capitals is considered. We fix a cut-off point of 100 km, i.e. $w_{ij} = 0$ if the distance between i and j exceeds this threshold. The weights within the maximum range are calculated as the inverse of distance. All weight matrices are row standardized.

3.3.2 Knowledge variables

Creation, diffusion and application of new knowledge are viewed as key drivers of growth in modern economic theories, and knowledge is also a key factor in explaining entrepreneurship. The knowledge spillover theory of entrepreneurship claims that entrepreneurial opportunities emerge as an external effect of R&D activities pursued by incumbent firms. These R&D activities create knowledge spillovers which can be exploited by would-be-entrepreneurs. To capture the impact of R&D and the spillovers it creates we include the share of R&D workers in total employment (*RD*) as a central explanatory variable in our model.[12]

Moreover, there is rich empirical evidence of a positive relationship between educational attainment and the propensity to start a business (see for instance Bates 1990). We therefore consider the share of highly qualified employees[13] in total employment (*HQ*) as a second knowledge variable in our regressions. To allow for knowledge spillovers that exceed the borders of our functional regions we also consider spatial lags of the knowledge variables (*W_RD* and *W_HQ*). Again, a binary spatial weight matrix and a distance based weighting scheme are applied alternatively.

It should be emphasized that these explanatory variables do not directly measure knowledge spillovers but, rather, investments in new knowledge. The extent to which

---

[12] R&D employment is defined on the basis of occupations. We consider engineers, chemists, physicists, mathematicians, technicians, other specialised technical staff and natural scientists as R&D employees.

[13] Regionally disaggregated data on highly qualified employees are available from the German Federal Office for Building and Regional Planning (BBR). Highly qualified employees are—according to the definition used by the BBR—employees who hold a university degree, a degree by a technical college (Fachhochschule) or who have graduated from a higher vocational school (Höhere Fachschule).

such knowledge spills over is reflected by the impact of these knowledge variables on the dependent variable, new firm start-ups.

3.3.3 Diversity measures

In most empirical studies regional diversity is measured in terms of sectoral diversity.[14] However, as argued in Sect. 2, for knowledge spillovers to occur and entrepreneurial opportunities to be perceived and put into practice what really matters is the diversity of people rather than the diversity of aggregates such as firms or sectors. For it is the diversity at the level of individuals (i.e. the level of potential entrepreneurs) that increases a region's absorptive capacity for new ideas and facilitates the matching of entrepreneurial opportunities and people able to perceive and realize them. To test this hypothesis we use measures of sectoral diversity (which is still the dominating concept in the literature) alongside with measures of cultural diversity which we argue is the more important concept with respect to the absorption of knowledge spillovers and the exploitation of uncommercialized ideas.

Cultural diversity

Cultural diversity is sometimes measured by the so-called index of fractionalization[15] which is identical with the inverse Herfindahl index of ethnic concentration. It may be written as:

$$\text{FRACT}_i = 1 - \sum_{m=1}^{M_i} s_{im}^2, \tag{3}$$

where s_{im} is region i's population (or labour force) share belonging to nationality m and M_i is the number of different nationalities actually present in region i.

This simple index has, however, a very unpleasant characteristic. As the Herfindahl index weights the highest share (in our case the share of Germans in the regional labour force) disproportionately high, the index is largely determined by the share of the dominant population group, i.e. the natives. This means that in the present case the unweighted Herfindahl measure in essence only reflects the share of Germans (foreigners, respectively) and does not account for the distribution of different nationalities within the foreign population.

A more adequate way of measuring cultural diversity is therefore the use of an entropy index.[16] The simplest and most popular member of the family of entropy indices is the Theil index. For a given region i the Theil index of cultural diversity is defined as the summation of the products of the shares and log shares of each ethnic group in the region's total labor force, i.e.:

---

[14] The most prominent studies in this context are Glaeser et al. (1992) and Feldman and Audretsch (1999).

[15] The index may be interpreted as the probability that two randomly selected individuals in a community belong to the same group (Ottaviano and Peri 2006).

[16] See Shorrocks (1980) and Cowell (2005) for a general discussion and Aiginger and Davis (2004) or Brülhart and Träger (2005) for economic applications of entropy measures.

$$\text{DIV}\_C_i = - \sum_{m=1}^{M_i} s_{im} \cdot \ln(s_{im}) \qquad (4)$$

Note that, if the region has equal sized shares of all population groups ($s_{im} = 1/M_i$) then the entropy index reaches its maximum value $\ln(M_i)$ which is, of course, rising with M_i, the number of different nationalities that are actually present in the region.[17] If the region is completely specialized (in the sense that the labour force consists of just one ethnic group) the index takes the value $\ln(1) = 0$. More generally, the index increases the more evenly a region's population is spread over the M ethnic groups. This implies that the marginal contribution of an additional individual to regional cultural diversity is—ceteris paribus—the higher the smaller the ethnic group to which that individual belongs. An increase in the share of foreign workers—which is equivalent to a decrease of the share of Germans, who are the largest group in all regions—will thus lead to an increase of the index. In a nutshell, the Theil index is an adequate measure of cultural diversity as it reflects the share *and* the variety[18] of the foreign population in the region considered.[19]

An alternative way to overcome the conceptual problems of the simple inverse Herfindahl index in measuring cultural diversity is to drop s_{i1}, the share of domestic workers, in the inverse Herfindahl index—which could then be seen as a real diversity measure of the region's foreign labour force—and to multiply this with the share of foreign workers fw_i:

$$\text{DIV}\_C_i = fw_i \cdot \left(1 - \sum_{m=2}^{M_i} s_{im}^2 \right) \qquad (5)$$

This weighted and modified Herfindahl index given in Eq. (5) is another acceptable measure of cultural diversity, although it is less elegant and comfortable than the Theil index. In our econometric analysis we use the Theil index as default and the modified Herfindahl as alternative in order to check the robustness of our results.

Sectoral diversity

In measuring sectoral diversity the unadapted (inverse) Herfindahl index is less problematic than in measuring cultural diversity because the structure of the data is quite different.[20] Therefore, it does not matter too much if we use the unadapted Herfindahl

---

[17] Note that a total of $M = 213$ nationalities are considered in our analysis (with $M_i \le M, i = 1, \ldots, 97$). Thus, the maximum value of cultural diversity that could theoretically be reached is $\ln(213) = 5,36$.

[18] Note that both elements are important: A high share of foreigners in itself does not necessarily imply a high cultural diversity if all foreigners belong to the same ethnic (and thus cultural) group. Accordingly, a high diversity of ethnic groups in a region is not sufficient for a high level of cultural diversity if the overall share of foreigners in the region is small.

[19] "Variety"—as we understand it—has two dimensions: the "richness" of the foreign labor force (i.e. the number of different nationalities actually present in the region) and the distribution of these different nationalities within the foreign labor force. The Theil index accounts for both.

[20] There is no single sector that dominates the industrial structure of all regions and thus the value of the Herfindahl index.

or the Theil index to measure sectoral diversity. In accordance with the analysis of cultural diversity we will use the Theil index as default and the inverse Herfindahl as control (robustness check) in the econometric part of the paper. The employment shares of 28 industries listed in the appendix were used to calculate the indicators of sectoral diversity.

4 Empirical analysis

4.1 Results of the basic model

4.1.1 Knowledge variables

The results of the basic model as reflected in Eq. (1) are given in Table 2. As can be seen from Table 2, the share of R&D employees (variable *RD*) has a significantly positive impact on new firm formation, regardless of the technological level of the start-ups. This is in line with our theoretical expectations that R&D activities generate entrepreneurial opportunities, as not all of the new knowledge created by R&D can be recognized and commercialised by those (incumbents) who finance the R&D. Our findings correspond with evidence provided by Audretsch and Keilbach (2007) as well as Audretsch et al. (2006), indicating that the number of start-ups tends to increase with the regional stock of knowledge. Moreover, one may argue that R&D employees dispose of a very specific human capital such that people belonging to this group have a particularly high propensity to found new enterprises. Human capital, reflected by *HQ*, the share of highly qualified employees, has a statistically significant positive impact on technology oriented start-up activities in general as well as on start-ups in technology oriented services.[21,22]

The impact of knowledge resources in neighbouring regions is, however, in most cases rather weak.[23] The estimates suggest that human capital in neighbouring regions (*W_HQ*) has a weakly significant positive impact on entrepreneurial activity in technology oriented services and no significant impact in all other cases. The weighted share of R&D employees in neighbouring regions (*W_RD*) has a significantly negative impact on total start-ups but no significant effect on technology oriented start-ups. A possible explanation for the negative sign of *W_RD* is that regions with a high level of

---

[21] Although the correlation between RD (R&D employees) and HQ (employees with higher levels of educational attainment) is rather modest (see Table 8 in the appendix) one cannot exclude with certainty that multicollinearity affects the regression results. To check the robustness of our findings with respect to possible multicollinearity we dropped the HQ variable (and, of course, also the spatial lag of HQ) and re-estimated the model in its 12 different versions (four different kinds of start-ups times three different specifications, i.e. pooled OLS, fixed effects and random effects). The omission of HQ and W_HQ resulted in a lower R^2 and changed some parameter values. The impact of the key diversity and knowledge variables is, however, by and large unchanged by the omission of HQ. We therefore conclude that multicollinearity is negligible as regards our main findings.

[22] The results of these robustness checks are available from the authors upon request.

[23] This may be due to the fact that our sample regions are rather large such that most knowledge spillovers are intraregional rather than interregional.

Table 2 OLS regression results—pooled model

	Start-up rates			
	Total	Technology oriented	Technology oriented services	High tech
R&D employment (RD)	109.37* (66.10)	30.17** (11.82)	19.26*** (7.36)	1.86*** (0.71)
Highly qualified employees (HQ)	45.99 (35.44)	15.18** (6.24)	9.15** (3.88)	−0.49 (0.44)
Spatial lag R&D employment (W_RD)	−273.27*** (89.72)	−16.13 (16.81)	−11.86 (9.93)	0.16 (1.05)
Spatial lag highly qualified employees (W_HQ)	84.01 (52.20)	12.75 (7.60)	8.68* (4.58)	1.16 (0.74)
Cultural diversity (DIV_C)	5.77 (9.67)	6.77*** (1.75)	3.62*** (1.04)	0.42*** (0.12)
Sectoral diversity (DIV_S)	−15.27** (6.39)	−1.92* (0.97)	−1.11* (0.58)	0.06 (0.12)
Unemployment rate (UR)	−68.32*** (20.33)	−13.03*** (2.65)	−7.27*** (1.63)	7.67E-02 (0.26)
Population density (PD)	4.99E-03*** (1.84E-03)	3.53E-04 (3.03E-04)	2.24E-04 (1.61E-04)	1.20E-05 (1.43E-05)
Share of small firms (SE)	73.32*** (17.82)	9.07*** (2.75)	5.63*** (1.68)	0.15 (0.20)
Disposable income (INC)	1.43E-07 (8.72E-08)	9.46E-09 (1.48E-08)	3.71E-09 (8.37E-09)	−1.83E-09 (1.11E-09)
Spatial lag disposable income (W_INC)	−1.23E-07 (1.08E-07)	−6.66E08*** (1.87E-08)	−3.64E-08*** (1.10E-08)	−6.11E-09*** (1.28E-09)
Growth disposable income (INC_G)	78.19 (72.46)	4.08 (11.88)	2.92 (6.36)	−1.27E-02 (0.80)
Spatial lag growth disposable income (W_INC_G)	−283.06*** (79.96)	−57.58*** (10.81)	−35.72*** (6.59)	−3.23*** (1.08)
Constant	76.30*** (21.27)	6.61** (3.29)	3.72* (1.95)	−0.13 (0.40)
	$R^2 = 0.39$	$R^2 = 0.69$	$R^2 = 0.64$	$R^2 = 0.31$
	$R^2_{\text{adj.}} = 0.35$	$R^2_{\text{adj.}} = 0.67$	$R^2_{\text{adj.}} = 0.62$	$R^2_{\text{adj.}} = 0.26$
	$F[13, 174] = 8.63$	$F[13, 174] = 29.75$	$F[13, 174] = 24.04$	$F[13, 174] = 6.09$

Observations marked by upward biased start-up rates are excluded. Standard errors in parentheses are heteroscedasticity consistent
*** Significant at the 0.01 level; ** significant at the 0.05 level; * significant at the 0.10 level

R&D attract potential entrepreneurs from neighbouring regions, thereby dampening entrepreneurial activity in the home region.

Regional diversity

Of particular interest with respect to the objective of this paper is the impact of regional diversity on entrepreneurial activity. As can be seen from Table 2, the empirical results for sectoral diversity (*DIV_S*) are somewhat ambiguous. Sectoral diversity tends to exert a negative effect on new firm formation which is significant in the model for total start-ups and weakly significant in the case of technology oriented start-ups in general and technology oriented services, but has no statistically significant impact on high-technology start-ups. This suggests that—at least for start-ups that do not fall into the high tech category—the regional concentration of industries and the localization economies associated herewith appear to be more important than economies resulting from the co-location of a wide variety of industries. This is in line with evidence provided by Capello (2002) who investigates the role of urbanization and localization economies with respect to entrepreneurship. According to her results, it is in particular localization economies that matter for firm productivity.

However, as argued above, the essential diversity argument by Jane Jacobs is first and foremost about people and not about firms or sectors, such that *cultural* diversity—and not sectoral diversity—is the pivotal variable when it comes to perceive and realize entrepreneurial opportunities. Cultural diversity (*DIV_C*) has a positive sign in all models and is highly significant in the case of technology oriented start-ups in general, technology oriented services and high tech start-ups.[24] This suggests that the diversity of people is indeed more conducive to entrepreneurship than the diversity of firms and that it matters in particular for technology (and thus knowledge) intensive start-ups.[25] We may thus conclude that regions characterized by a high level of R&D and a high degree of cultural diversity form an ideal breeding ground for technology oriented start-ups.

Control variables

As concerns the control variables, the unemployment rate (UR) has a significantly negative impact on all kind of entrepreneurial activities, except for the high tech case. This corresponds with the findings in Sutaria and Hicks (2004). The dampening effect of high unemployment on regional start-up activities might be explained by the fact that more prosperous regions marked by a favourable labour market situation offer better conditions for start-ups than problem regions. Especially in East Germany the dampening impact of high unemployment might considerably reduce start-up

---

[24] In the case of total start-ups *DIV_C* is positive but not significant at the 10% level.

[25] The results displayed in Table 2 are obtained with diversity measures that are based on the Theil index. However, the identified impact of cultural diversity is rather robust with respect to measurement. We get a positive and significant effect of cultural diversity on firm birth rates for an appropriately modified Herfindahl index as well. The results for sectoral diversity are also robust to measurement. See Sect. 4.2.2 for details.

intensity. However, the regression results also suggest that entrepreneurial activity in East German regions is not generally lower than in the western part of the country. A dummy variable for East German regions is not significant in all regression models.[26]

Another important factor is the firm size structure of the region (variable *SE*). In line with previous evidence as, e.g. in Armington and Acs (2002), a high percentage of small enterprises (less than 20 employees) in a region appears to be conducive to start-up activity, except for the case of high tech start-ups. This is not surprising since a high percentage of small enterprises may be seen as a proxy for the entrepreneurial climate and/or entrepreneurial tradition of the region, reflecting the start up activity of previous periods.[27] The population density (PD) variable has a positive sign for all kinds of start-ups we investigated—which is in line with earlier investigations—but is statistically significant only for total start ups.

The region's disposable income (*INC*) and the growth rate of disposable income have in most models a positive sign but they are not significant at the 10% level. By contrast, the weighted disposable income of neighbouring regions (*W_INC*) and it's growth rate (*W_INC_G*) have a clearly negative and mostly significant impact on start-ups. A possible explanation is that regions with a high disposable income might attract entrepreneurs from neighbouring areas, thus reducing the firm birth rate there. Potential founders might prefer to start their business in neighbouring regions if these locations offer a large market, as measured by purchasing power, or a particularly dynamic economy, as measured by the growth rate of disposable income in neighbouring regions.[28]

It is noteworthy that the impact of different determinants on firm birth rates appears to differ considerably with respect to the technology level of the start-ups. These differences across start-ups on various technology levels will be analysed more systematically in Sect. 4.3.

4.2 Robustness checks

4.2.1 Panel estimates

To check the robustness of the pooled regression results discussed so far we include the estimation of panel data models with fixed effects and random effects, i.e. we control for unobserved time-invariant explanatory variables (see Eq. (2) in Sect. 2). Table 3 reports estimates for the fixed effects model, and Table 4 summarizes the estimates for the random effects specification, together with the results of the Hausman tests comparing the fixed effects and the random effects models. The panel models we estimated are consistent with the pooled OLS model, (in other words, they contain all control

---

[26] Additional regression results are available upon request.

[27] We have no direct measure for the average firm age in a region, but there is, of course, a correlation between firm age and firm size, such that a high percentage of small firms also points to a high percentage of young firms.

[28] It should be noted that the correlation between most explanatory variables is relatively low, such that multicollinearity issues should not cause major problems in the regressions (see Table 8 in the appendix).

Table 3 Results of fixed effects model

	Start-up rates			
	Total	Technology oriented	Technology oriented services	High tech
R&D employment (RD)	98.37*** (35.96)	43.23*** (8.28)	27.01*** (4.84)	3.07*** (0.75)
Highly qualified employees (HQ)	4.02 (21.60)	2.36 (4.37)	1.38 (2.73)	−1.53** (0.50)
Spatial lag R&D employment (W_RD)	−113.71* (66.98)	−8.33 (15.13)	−5.66 (8.47)	−0.43 (1.14)
Spatial lag highly qualified employees (W_HQ)	134.03** (53.07)	−6.68 (8.46)	−1.54 (4.62)	−0.53 (0.98)
Cultural diversity (DIV_C)	23.00** (10.23)	7.82*** (1.59)	4.00*** (0.90)	0.52*** (0.18)
Sectoral diversity (DIV_S)	−13.48* (7.85)	−1.64 (1.32)	−0.70 (0.72)	−0.34** (0.14)
	$R^2 = 0.80$	$R^2 = 0.89$	$R^2 = 0.88$	$R^2 = 0.67$
	$R^2_{adj.} = 0.54$	$R^2_{adj.} = 0.73$	$R^2_{adj.} = 0.71$	$R^2_{adj.} = 0.25$
	$F[107, 80] = 3.05$	$F[107, 80] = 5.88$	$F[107, 80] = 5.41$	$F[107, 80] = 1.58$

Observations marked by upward biased start-up rates are excluded. All models also include time fixed effects. Standard errors in parentheses are heteroscedasticity consistent
*** Significant at the 0.01 level; ** significant at the 0.05 level; * significant at the 0.10 level

variables displayed in Table 2). However, for facility of inspection we only report the results for the most important variables, i.e. the knowledge variables and the diversity measures in Tables 3 and 4.[29] The Hausman test statistics in Table 4 show that in the cases of technology oriented start-ups in general and of technology oriented services the fixed effects specification is the adequate specification, whereas for total start-ups and high tech start-ups the random effects model is preferred.

Comparing Table 3 (results of fixed effects estimation) with Table 2 (pooled OLS) reveals some differences. In the fixed effects specification, HQ is no longer significant in the models for Su_to and Su_tos and becomes (negatively) significant in the case of Su_ht. Moreover, we arrive at a significant positive effect of W_HQ on total start-ups. Thus, once unobserved heterogeneity is taken into account, we detect a favourable effect of human capital in neighbouring regions on entrepreneurial activity. However, the results for the R&D variable and the spatially lagged R&D variable do by and large resemble those of the pooled OLS model. Most important, with respect to regional diversity the results appear to be quite robust: Again, sectoral diversity tends to exert a negative impact on new firm foundation, whereas cultural diversity has a positive impact. Interestingly, in the fixed effects specification cultural diversity is not only

---

[29] The complete tables including the results for the control variables are available from the authors upon request.

Table 4　GLS regression results—random effects model

	Start-up rates			
	Total	Technology oriented	Technology oriented services	High tech
R&D employment (RD)	121.40** (60.35)	32.71*** (9.69)	21.17*** (5.82)	2.28*** (0.67)
Highly qualified employees (HQ)	36.59 (34.51)	13.43** (5.51)	7.59** (3.32)	−0.77** (0.39)
Spatial lag R&D employment (W_RD)	−236.53** (93.73)	−14.09 (14.98)	−10.05 (9.03)	3.53E-03 (1.05)
Spatial lag highly qualified employees (W_HQ)	84.74 (55.51)	10.78 (8.80)	7.28 (5.33)	0.85 (0.64)
Cultural diversity (DIV_C)	5.03 (9.38)	6.93*** (1.48)	3.74*** (0.90)	0.45*** (0.11)
Sectoral diversity (DIV_S)	−15.13** (7.61)	−1.67 (1.19)	−0.90 (0.73)	−0.05 (−0.09)
Hausman test[a]	18.34 (0.15)	27.29 (0.01)	27.68 (0.01)	8.28 (0.83)

Regions marked by upward biased start-up rates are excluded. All models also include time fixed effects
*** Significant at the 0.01 level; ** significant at the 0.05 level, * significant at the 0.10 level
[a] Test statistic and probability value in parentheses

significant in the three classes of technology oriented start-ups but also in the model for total start-ups.

Comparison of the OLS estimates of the pooled model (Table 2) and the results of the random effects specification (Table 4) confirms that most findings are robust. We detect almost no changes of sign and only a few changes of significance levels. As in the case of the fixed effects specification, especially the evidence regarding the R&D variables and cultural diversity is highly robust. The corresponding coefficients of the random effects model do very much resemble the estimates of the pooled OLS regression model.

Taken together, our main results are fairly robust with respect to different model specifications. Most important, the prominent role of the R&D variable and cultural diversity is underscored by the panel estimates.

4.2.2 Alternative diversity measures

As a further robustness check we have replaced our original, Theil index-based diversity measures by the alternative, Herfindahl index-based measures discussed in Sect. 3.3.3. Again, the presentation of results in Table 5 focuses on the knowledge and diversity variables.[30] As can be seen from Table 5 (in comparison with Table 2) the alternative diversity measures only lead to marginal changes regarding the influence of knowledge variables and regional diversity on entrepreneurial

---

[30] The complete tables including the results for the control variables are available from the authors upon request.

Table 5 OLS regression results—pooled model with alternative diversity measures

	Start-up rates			
	Total	Technology oriented	Technology oriented services	High tech
R&D employment (RD)	108.13* (64.83)	34.39*** (12.15)	21.37*** (7.54)	2.73*** (0.75)
Highly qualified employees (HQ)	47.26 (36.68)	13.20** (6.40)	8.13** (4.00)	−0.40 (0.44)
Spatial lag R&D employment (W_RD)	−277.87*** (86.26)	−6.48 (15.04)	−6.81 (8.98)	2.38** (1.07)
Spatial lag highly qualified employees (W_HQ)	86.07 (53.11)	10.99 (7.42)	7.87* (4.51)	0.34 (0.71)
Cultural diversity alternative measure	72.38 (96.83)	57.48*** (15.81)	31.09*** (9.66)	0.86** (1.08)
Sectoral diversity alternative measure	−128.52** (60.87)	−13.94 (9.65)	−8.84 (5.53)	−0.18 (1.27)
	$R^2 = 0.39$	$R^2 = 0.68$	$R^2 = 0.64$	$R^2 = 0.27$
	$R^2_{adj.} = 0.35$	$R^2_{adj.} = 0.66$	$R^2_{adj.} = 0.61$	$R^2_{adj.} = 0.22$
	$F[13, 174] = 8.62$	$F[13, 174] = 28.48$	$F[13, 174] = 23.34$	$F[13, 174] = 4.94$

Observations marked by upward biased start-up rates are excluded. Standard errors in parentheses are heteroscedasticity consistent
*** Significant at the 0.01 level; ** significant at the 0.05 level; * significant at the 0.10 level

activity.[31] As concerns the impact of the diversity measures, the coefficients do, of course, deviate from those in Table 2, as the Herfindahl index-based measures have a range from 0 to 1 that differs from the range of the Theil index based-measures, varying from 0 to $\ln(M)$.[32] The important thing is, however, that cultural diversity still has a positive effect on start-ups while sectoral diversity still tends to exert a negative impact.

While the significance of cultural diversity is virtually unchanged when using the alternative measure, sectoral diversity is only significant in the case of total start-ups.[33] Again, these findings emphasize the importance of distinguishing between different types of diversity. Cultural diversity is found to have a positive impact on entrepreneurship, whereas the impact of sectoral diversity on entrepreneurship tends to be ambiguous or negative.

---

[31] We observe only minor changes of significance levels. Worth mentioning is only the significant impact of neighbouring regions' R&D (W_RD) in the case of high tech start-ups (which was not significant before).

[32] Remember that M is the number of nationalities in the index of cultural diversity and the number of sectors in the index of sectoral diversity.

[33] In contrast, sectoral diversity also exerted a weakly significant impact on technology oriented start-ups and technology oriented services in the original model.

Table 6 OLS regression results—alternative spatial weights matrix

	Start-up rates			
	Total	Technology oriented	Technology oriented services	High tech
R&D employment (RD)	111.18* (62.98)	29.68** (11.56)	19.36*** (7.17)	1.69** (0.72)
Highly qualified employees (HQ)	50.56 (36.19)	16.86*** (6.22)	10.30*** (3.87)	−0.45 (0.42)
Spatial lag R&D employment (W_RD) (distance weights)	−118.21 (94.90)	−5.86 (15.49)	−7.99 (9.66)	−0.75 (1.31)
Spatial lag highly qualified employees (W_HQ) (distance weights)	89.24 (78.97)	12.65 (11.84)	7.51 (7.32)	2.11* (1.25)
Cultural diversity (DIV_C)	4.88 (8.03)	6.07*** (1.35)	3.21*** (0.82)	0.46*** (0.12)
Sectoral diversity (DIV_S)	−19.60*** (6.66)	−2.17** (0.94)	−1.20** (0.57)	5.77E-02 (0.12)
	$R^2 = 0.37$	$R^2 = 0.69$	$R^2 = 0.64$	$R^2 = 0.32$
	$R^2_{adj.} = 0.32$	$R^2_{adj.} = 0.67$	$R^2_{adj.} = 0.61$	$R^2_{adj.} = 0.27$
	$F[13, 174] = 7.80$	$F[13, 174] = 29.51$	$F[13, 174] = 23.62$	$F[13, 174] = 6.23$

Observations marked by upward biased start-up rates are excluded. Standard errors in parentheses are heteroscedasticity consistent
*** Significant at the 0.01 level; ** significant at the 0.05 level; * significant at the 0.10 level

4.2.3 Alternative spatial weights matrices

Working with alternative spatial weights matrices (a distance-based weighting scheme instead of the standard binary matrix) has little effect on the impact of the diversity and intra-regional knowledge variables as can be seen by a comparison of Table 6 and Table 2. The influence of knowledge in neighbouring regions remains weak although there are some minor changes: R&D in neighbouring regions has no longer a significant impact on total start-ups, whereas a high percentage of highly qualified workers in neighbouring regions has a weakly significant (positive) impact on high tech start-ups. These are, however, only marginal changes that leave our main findings unaffected.

To sum up, our main results concerning the impact of cultural diversity and knowledge on start-ups at different technology levels appear to be rather robust with respect to alternative specifications regarding diversity measures or spatial weighting matrices.

4.3 Tests of parameter stability across different technology levels

A comparison of the different models summarized in the columns of Table 2 reveals that there are significant differences with respect to the factors that turn out to be

Table 7 *F* test on equality of slope estimates

	Reference			
	Start-up rate			
	Not technology oriented firms			Technology oriented services
	Technology oriented	Technology oriented services	High tech	High tech
R&D employment (RD)	0.23	0.45	0.94	7.97***
Highly qualified employees (HQ)	0.69	1.04	1.75	8.01***
Spatial lag R&D employment (W_RD)	1.22	1.43	1.82	2.02
Spatial lag highly qualified employees (W_HQ)	7.11***	7.51***	8.36***	1.70
Cultural diversity (DIV_C)	0.76	0.26	0.02	12.6***
Sectoral diversity (DIV_S)	2.70	3.15*	3.83*	2.69
Unemployment rate (UR)	4.27**	5.63**	7.58***	12.3***
Population density (PD)	10.7***	11.6***	12.9***	2.58
Share of small firms (SE)	10.8***	12.4***	15.0***	9.78***
Disposable income (INC)	3.12*	3.44*	3.76*	0.49
Spatial lag disposable income (W_INC)	0.01	0.03	0.22	7.99***
Growth disposable income (INC_G)	1.33	1.41	1.54	0.24
Spatial lag growth disposable income (W_INC_G)	4.23**	5.52**	7.67***	15.2***
All coefficients	5.93***	6.23***	7.31***	21.5***

The *F* statistics given in the table have an asymptotic distribution with (1,348) degrees of freedom for the tests of individual coefficients and (13,348) degrees of freedom for the test of the entire model. Observations marked by upward biased start-up rates are excluded

*** Significant at the 0.01 level; ** significant at the 0.05 level; * significant at the 0.10 level

important determinants of entrepreneurial activity at different levels of technology. This is confirmed by the results of *F* tests for parameter stability across different technology levels (see Table 7). In the columns 2 to 4, the coefficient estimates for start-ups that are not technology oriented are confronted with the results for different technology oriented categories. Significant test statistics indicate that the impact of various influential factors differs between start-ups depending on the technology level.

Distinct differences in the size of effects are detected for a number of control variables, but not for our knowledge indicators—apart from the spatial lag of highly qualified employees. With respect to the diversity measures, there is some indication for significant differences between high tech start-ups and low tech firm foundation. However, this evidence is restricted to sectoral diversity.

The findings in column 5 suggest that there are also differences among technology oriented start-ups. If we compare the impact of the explanatory variables on technology oriented services and high tech start ups, significant differences arise for some control variables, the knowledge indicators as well as for cultural diversity.

Taken together, these findings clearly suggest that it is important to differentiate between technology levels when the regional determinants of start-up rates are analysed.

5 Conclusions and outlook

In this paper we have combined the knowledge spillover theory of entrepreneurship with the diversity argument from urban economics. Our empirical analysis has shown that the determinants of new firm formation differ significantly with respect to the technology level and that it is therefore necessary to distinguish start-ups at different technological levels. We find evidence for the hypothesis that regions with a high level of R&D and human capital provide more opportunities for entrepreneurship than other regions, whereas the impact of knowledge variables in neighbouring regions appears to be ambiguous.

Regional diversity has a crucial impact on entrepreneurship. However, the relationship between diversity and entrepreneurship depends crucially upon the exact type of diversity considered. While most previous papers have considered regional diversity to be a homogeneous concept, an important contribution of this paper is to distinguish between different types of diversity. In particular, measures of both cultural and sectoral diversity are included in the analysis. The results provide compelling evidence that, in fact, the impact of diversity on entrepreneurship is highly sensitive to the type of diversity measured. While sectoral diversity tends to exert a negative effect on new firm foundation, cultural diversity has a positive and highly significant impact on technology oriented start-ups in general, technology oriented services and high tech start-ups. This suggests that the diversity of people is indeed more conducive to entrepreneurship than the diversity of firms and that regions characterized by a high level of R&D and a high degree of cultural diversity form an ideal breeding ground for technology oriented start-ups.

The research presented in this paper may be viewed as a modest first step towards a more comprehensive research program. The issue of cultural diversity and entrepreneurship is of high political relevance in modern societies and deserves more attention. Future research should aim at broadening the evidence on this issue by investigating the relationship for other countries. Cross-country studies might also allow to analyse whether there are systematic differences regarding the impact of cultural diversity between classic immigration countries, such as the US and Canada, and highly developed countries characterised by a much shorter migration tradition (e.g. Italy, Spain).

Moreover, a more detailed differentiation of foreigners could provide insights into the significance of specific nationalities, professions and ethnic groups in fostering the start-up of new businesses at the regional level.

Acknowledgments We would like to thank participants of the international workshop on "Agglomeration and Growth in Knowledge-based Societies" at the Kiel Institute for helpful comments on an earlier version. We are particularly grateful to Rui Baptista, Eckhardt Bode and two anonymous referees for valuable comments and suggestions.

Appendix

Industry classification

The indicator for sectoral diversity is based on employment data by region and industry. The following classification is applied:

1. Agriculture, hunting and forestry
2. Energy
3. Mining
4. Chemical industry
5. Rubber and plastic products
6. Non-metallic mineral mining
7. Glass and ceramics
8. Basic metals and fabricated metal products
9. Machinery
10. Transport equipment
11. Electrical and optical equipment
12. Manufacturing n.e.c.
13. Wood and wood products
14. Pulp, paper and paper products, publishing and printing
15. Leather and textiles
16. Food, beverages and tobacco
17. Construction
18. Wholesale and retail trade
19. Transport and communication
20. Financial intermediation
21. Hotels and restaurants
22. Health and social work
23. Business services
24. Education
25. Leisure-related services
26. Household-related services
27. Social services
28. Public sector

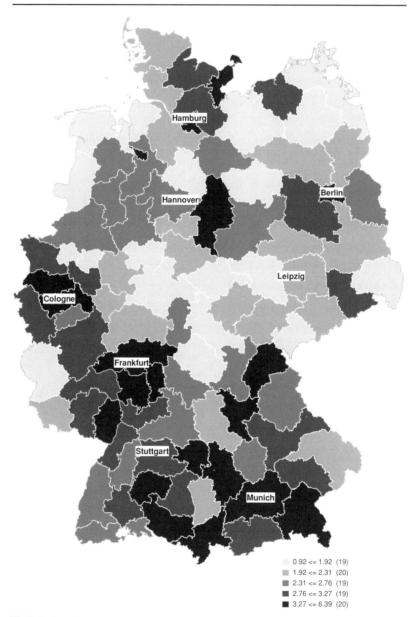

Fig. 3 Regional distribution of start-up rates—technology oriented services 1998–2001 (data source: ZEW start-up panel)

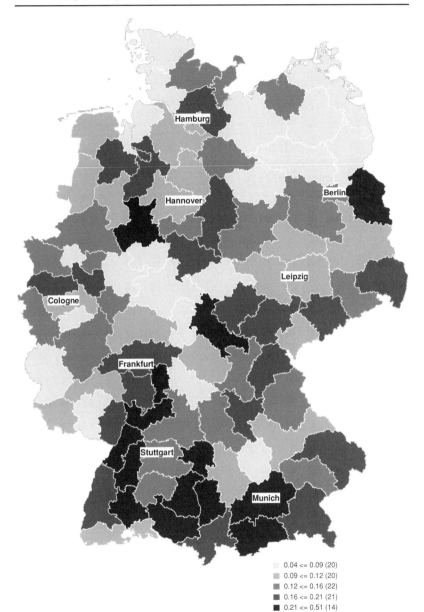

Fig. 4 Regional distribution of start-up rates—high-tech firms 1998–2001 (data source: ZEW start-up panel)

Table 8 Correlation analysis—explanatory variables

	1	2	3	4	5	6	7	8	9	10	11	12	13
1 R&D employment (RD)	1.00												
2 Highly qualified employees (HQ)	0.43	1.00											
3 Spatial lag R&D employment (W_RD)	0.43	-0.08	1.00										
4 Spatial lag highly qualified employees (W_HQ)	-0.11	0.44	0.11	1.00									
5 Cultural diversity (DIV_C)	0.06	0.71	-0.35	0.67	1.00								
6 Sectoral diversity (DIV_S)	-0.33	0.02	-0.07	0.42	0.20	1.00							
7 Unemployment rate (UR)	0.38	-0.37	0.50	-0.56	-0.70	-0.41	1.00						
8 Population density (PD)	0.35	0.33	-0.06	-0.02	0.29	-0.25	0.06	1.00					
9 Share of small firms (SE)	-0.42	-0.71	0.12	-0.20	-0.45	0.10	0.13	-0.49	1.00				
10 Disposable income (INC)	0.47	0.56	-0.08	0.19	0.58	-0.13	-0.17	0.63	-0.57	1.00			
11 Spatial lag disposable income (W_INC)	-0.09	0.28	0.14	0.57	0.39	0.25	-0.36	0.10	-0.18	0.24	1.00		
12 Growth disposable income (INC_G)	0.10	-0.00	0.05	0.14	0.09	-0.08	-0.26	-0.27	0.07	-0.08	0.15	1.00	
13 Spatial lag growth disposable income (W_INC_G)	-0.08	0.17	-0.12	0.23	0.35	0.11	-0.50	0.13	-0.08	0.15	0.01	0.18	1.00

Results refer to diversity measures based on the Theil index and spatial lags of explanatory variables calculated with a binary weights matrix. The modified Herfindahl measure and the spatial lags with the distance-based weighting scheme largely resemble the results in this Table

Table 9 Descriptive statistics

	Mean	SD	Minimum	Maximum	Data source
Start-up rates: Total (*Su_all*)	45.0	10.1	25.4	104.9	1
Not technology oriented (*Su_nto*)	40.1	8.97	23.6	89.2	1
Technology oriented (*Su_to*)	4.84	1.86	1.63	15.7	1
Technology oriented services (*Su_tos*)	2.81	1.04	0.92	8.81	1
High tech (*Su_ht*)	0.19	0.09	0.03	0.58	1
R&D employment (RD)	0.06	0.02	0.03	0.11	3
Highly qualified employees (HQ)	0.07	0.03	0.03	0.16	2
Spatial lag R&D employment (*W_RD*)	0.06	0.01	0.05	0.09	3
Spatial lag highly qualified employees (*W_HQ*)	0.07	0.02	0.04	0.12	2
Cultural diversity (*DIV_C*)	0.21	0.13	0.02	0.57	3
Sectoral diversity (*DIV_S*)	2.86	0.08	2.65	3.00	3
Unemployment rate (UR)	0.11	0.05	0.04	0.23	2
Population density (PD)	328.2	489.0	51.2	3867.5	2
Share of small firms (SE)	0.30	0.04	0.20	0.42	3
Disposable income (INC)	13,627,863	10,914,335	2,959,175	57,580,486	4
Spatial lag disposable income (*W_INC*)	14,204,702	5,671,739	4,402,156	32,526,385	4
Growth disposable income (*INC_G*)	0.10	0.01	−0.01	0.06	4
Spatial lag growth disposable income (*W_INC_G*)	−0.08	0.01	−0.01	0.04	4

Results refer to diversity measures based on the Theil index and spatial lags of explanatory variables calculated with a binary weights matrix

Data sources: (1) ZEW start-up panel (http://www.zew.de/en/forschung/datenbanken.php3), (2) INKAR data base of the Federal Office for Building and Regional Planning, (3) Employment statistic of the Federal Employment Agency, (4) National accounts of the Federal Statistical Office

References

Acemoglu D, Aghion P, Zilibotti F (2006) Distance to frontier, selection and economic growth. J Eur Econ Assoc 4(1):37–74. doi:10.1162/jeea.2006.4.1.37

Acs Z, Audretsch D, Braunerhjelm P, Carlsson B (2004) The missing link: the knowledge filter and endogenous growth, Discussion paper. Center for Business and Policy Studies, Stockholm

Acs Z, Audretsch D, Braunerhjelm P, Carlsson B (2005) The knowledge spillover theory of entrepreneurship. CEPR Discussion Paper 5326, London

Aiginger K, Davis S (2004) Industrial specialisation and geographic concentration: two sides of the same coin? Not for the European Union. J Appl Econ 8(2):231–248

Armington C, Acs ZJ (2002) The determinants of regional variation in new firm formation. Reg Stud 36(1):33–45. doi:10.1080/00343400120099843

Arrow K (1962) Economic welfare and the allocation of resources for invention. In: The rate and direction of inventive activity. Princeton University Press, Princeton, pp 609–626

Audretsch DB, Dohse D (2007) Location: a neglected determinant of firm growth. Rev World Econ 143(1):79–107. doi:10.1007/s10290-007-0099-7

Audretsch DB, Feldmann M (1996) R&D spillovers and the geography of innovation and production. Am Econ Rev 86:630–640

Audretsch DB, Fritsch M (1994) The geography of firm births in Germany. Reg Stud 28:359–365. doi:10.1080/00343409412331348326

Audretsch DB, Fritsch M (2002) Growth regimes over time and space. Reg Stud 36:113–124. doi:10.1080/00343400220121909

Audretsch DB, Keilbach M (2007) The theory of knowledge spillover entrepreneurship. J Manage Stud 44(7):1242–1254. doi:10.1111/j.1467-6486.2007.00722.x

Audretsch DB, Keilbach M, Lehmann E (2006) Entrepreneurship and economic growth. Oxford University Press, New York

Audretsch DB, Stephan P (1996) Company-scientist locational links: the case of biotechnology. Am Econ Rev 86:641–652

Bates T (1990) Entrepreneur human capital inputs and small business longevity. Rev Econ Stat 72:551–559. doi:10.2307/2109594

Beesley ME, Hamilton RT (1984) Small firms' seedbed role and the concept of turbulence. J Ind Econ 33:217–231. doi:10.2307/2098510

Blanchflower D, Oswald A (1998) What makes an entrepreneur? J Labor Econ 16(1):26–60. doi:10.1086/209881

Brülhart M, Träger R (2005) An account of geographic concentration patterns in Europe. Reg Sci Urban Econ 35:597–624. doi:10.1016/j.regsciurbeco.2004.09.002

BBR (Bundesamt für Bauwesen und Raumordnung) (2001) Aktuelle Daten zur Entwicklung der Städte, Kreise und Gemeinden. Berichte. Band 8: Bonn

Capello R (2002) Entrepreneurship and spatial externalities: theory and measurement. Ann Reg Sci 36:387–402. doi:10.1007/s001680200106

Carlton D (1983) The location and employment choices of new firms: an econometric model with discrete and continuous endogenous variables. Rev Econ Stat 54:440–449. doi:10.2307/1924189

Cowell F (2005) Theil inequality indices and decomposition. ECINEQ Working Paper 2005-1, London

Feldman M, Audretsch D (1999) Innovations in cities: science-based diversity, specialization and localized monopoly. Eur Econ Rev 43:409–429. doi:10.1016/S0014-2921(98)00047-6

Fritsch M, Falck O (2007) New business formation by industry over space and time: a multidimensional analysis. Reg Stud 41(2):157–172. doi:10.1080/00343400600928301

Glaeser E, Kallal H, Scheinkman J, Shleifer A (1992) Growth in cities. J Polit Econ 100:1126–1152. doi:10.1086/261856

Hoover E (1937) Location theory and the shoe and leather industries. Harvard University Press, Cambridge

Jacobs J (1969) The economy of cities. Vintage Books, New York

Jaffe A (1989) The real effects of academic research. Am Econ Rev 79:957–970

Jaffe A, Trajtenberg M, Henderson R (1993) Geographic localization of knowledge spillovers as evidenced by patent citations. Q J Econ 63:577–598

Lazear E (2004) Balanced skills and entrepreneurship. Am Econ Rev 94(2):208–211. doi:10.1257/0002828041301425

Lee SY, Florida R, Acs Z (2004) Creativity and entrepreneurship: a regional analysis of new firm formation. Reg Stud 38(8):879–891. doi:10.1080/0034340042000280910

Metzger G, Heger D (2005), Die Bereitstellung von Standardauswertungen zum Gründungsgeschehen in Deutschland und Österreich für externe Datennutzer, Version 2005-02, Zentrum für Europäische Wirtschaftsforschung (ZEW), Mannheim

Ottaviano G, Peri G (2006) The economic value of cultural diversity: evidence from US cities. J Econ Geogr 6:9–44. doi:10.1093/jeg/lbi002

Porter M (1990) The comparative advantage of nations. Free Press, New York

Reynolds P, Storey D, Westhead P (1994) Regional variations in new firm formation—-special issue. Reg Stud 28:343–456. doi:10.1080/00343409412331348306

Rocha H, Sternberg R (2005) Entrepreneurship: the role of clusters. theoretical perspectives and empirical evidence for Germany. Small Bus Econ 24:267–292. doi:10.1007/s11187-005-1993-9

Rosenthal S, Strange W (2003) Geography, industrial organizations and agglomeration. Rev Econ Stat 85(2):377–393. doi:10.1162/003465303765299882

Shorrocks A (1980) The class of additively decomposable inequality measures. Econometrica 48(3):613–625. doi:10.2307/1913126

Sorensen O, Audia PG (2000) The social structure of entrepreneurial activity; geographic concentration of footwear production in the United States 1940–1989. Am J Sociol 106:224–262. doi:10.1086/303116

Steil F (1999) Determinanten regionaler Unterschiede in der Gründungsdynamik. Baden-Baden: Nomos

Stuart T, Sorenson O (2003) The geography of opportunity: spatial heterogeneity in founding rates and the performance of biotechnology firms. Res Policy 32:229–253. doi:10.1016/S0048-7333(02)00098-7

Storey D (1991) The birth of new firms—docs unemployment matter? A review of the evidence. Small Bus Econ 3:167–178. doi:10.1007/BF00400022

Sutaria V, Hicks D (2004) New firm formation: dynamics and determinants. Ann Reg Sci 38:241–262. doi:10.1007/s00168-004-0194-9

Wagner J, Sternberg R (2004) Start-up activities, individual characteristics, and the regional milieu: lessons for entrepreneurship support policies from German micro data. Ann Reg Sci 38:219–240. doi:10.1007/s00168-004-0193-x

[16]

Small Bus Econ (2010) 34:105–125
DOI 10.1007/s11187-009-9235-1

The missing link: knowledge diffusion and entrepreneurship in endogenous growth

Pontus Braunerhjelm · Zoltan J. Acs ·
David B. Audretsch · Bo Carlsson

Accepted: 10 September 2009 / Published online: 30 October 2009
© The Author(s) 2009. This article is published with open access at Springerlink.com

Abstract The intellectual breakthrough contributed by the new growth theory was the recognition that investments in knowledge and human capital endogenously generate economic growth through the spillover of knowledge. However, endogenous growth theory does not explain how or why spillovers occur. This paper presents a model that shows how growth depends on knowledge accumulation and its diffusion through both incumbents and entrepreneurial activities. We claim that entrepreneurs are one missing link in converting knowledge into economically relevant knowledge. Implementing different regression techniques for the Organisation for Economic Co-operation and Development (OECD) countries during 1981 to 2002 provides surprisingly robust evidence that primarily entrepreneurs contributed to growth and that the importance of entrepreneurs increased in the 1990s. A Granger test confirms that causality goes in the direction from entrepreneurs to growth. The results indicate that policies facilitating entrepreneurship are an important tool to enhance knowledge diffusion and promote economic growth.

Keywords Endogenous growth · Knowledge · Innovation and entrepreneurship

JEL Classifications O10 · L10 · L26

P. Braunerhjelm (✉)
Department of Transport and Economics, Royal Institute of Technology, 100 44 Stockholm, Sweden
e-mail: pontusb@infra.kth.se

Z. J. Acs
George Mason University, 4400 University Drive, MSN 3C6, Fairfax, VA 22030, USA
e-mail: zacs@gmu.edu

D. B. Audretsch
Indiana University Bloomington, 1315 E. 10th Street, SPEA Suite 201, Bloomington, IN 47405, USA
e-mail: daudrets@indiana.edu

B. Carlsson
Case Western Reserve University, Peter B. Lewis Building, Cleveland, OH 44106-7235, USA
e-mail: Bo.Carlsson@case.edu

1 Introduction

Endogenous growth theory has provided two fundamental contributions that constitute intellectual breakthroughs. The first is that the formation of knowledge and human capital takes place as a response to market opportunities. The second is that investment in knowledge is likely to be associated with large and persistent spillovers to other agents in the economy. However, empirical evidence supporting the hypotheses derived from these models is ambiguous at best.[1]

---

[1] See Jones (1995a, b), Young (1998), and Greenwood and Jovanovic (1998). Jones proposed a semi-endogenous growth model in which it becomes more difficult over time to discover new products. Educational variables have been more successful

Fig. 1 Expenditures on R&D and economic growth in 29 OECD countries 1981–2000. *Source*: OECD, Statistical Compendium on CD, 2002:2

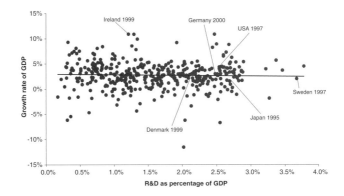

The simple correlation between research and development (R&D) expenditure and gross domestic product (GDP) growth reveals no systematic relationship (Fig. 1).[2] Thus, the model seems to offer no explanation as to why countries with large R&D stocks grew slowly (such as Sweden in the 1980s and Japan in the 1990s), while other countries less endowed with knowledge—such as Ireland and Denmark—experienced persistent and high growth rates. We believe that the ambiguous empirical support for endogenous growth models is associated with far too mechanistic a view on the spillover of knowledge (Acs et al. 2009, Carlsson et al. 2009).

We go back to Arrow's (1962) recognition that knowledge is not the same thing as economically relevant knowledge. The endogenous growth proponents (Romer 1986, 1990, Lucas 1988, Rebelo 1991, and others) picked up the thread suggested in the earlier literature.[3] Their aim was to introduce spillovers explicitly into models of growth. Aggregate knowledge capital was defined as a composite of R&D and human capital, not embodied in processes or products. Accumulation of capitalized knowledge assets was shown to lead to increased growth in a

general equilibrium setting. This result could be traced to the assumptions of nonexcludability and nonrivalry attached to knowledge, implying that marginal productivity of knowledge capital does not need to diminish as it becomes available to more users.

Still, the first wave of endogenous growth models paid little attention to how spillovers actually took place and treated the process as exogenous. Their emphasis was on the influence of knowledge spillovers on growth without specifying *how* knowledge spills over.[4] However, as pointed out by Schumpeter (1947), "the inventor produces ideas, the entrepreneur 'gets things done' … an idea or scientific principle is not, by itself, of any importance for economic practice." Indeed, the Schumpeterian entrepreneur, by and large, remains absent in those models. We intend to highlight how the introduction of the "pure" Schumpeterian entrepreneur influences knowledge spillover and how knowledge thereby can be more or less smoothly turned into business activity.

Footnote 1 continued

in explaining growth (Barro and Sala-i-Martin 2004). See Dinopoulos and Thompson (1998) and Aghion and Howitt (1998b) for a discussion of empirical problems.

[2] In Fig. 1, changing or removing the time lag does not materially change the results.

[3] A version of a R&D-driven growth model was first presented by Shell (1967).

---

[4] This was to some extent remedied in the second generation of endogenous growth models (Segerstrom et al. 1990, Segerstrom 1991, Aghion and Howitt 1992, 1998a, b, 2005, Cheng and Dinopoulos 1992, Segerstrom 1998, Aghion and Griffith 2005). These neo-Schumpeterian models design entry as an R&D race where a fraction of R&D is turned into commercially successful innovations. While this implies a step forward, the essence of the Schumpeterian entrepreneur is missed. The innovation process stretches far beyond R&D races that predominantly involve large incumbents and concern quality improvements of existing goods. An alternative mechanism was presented by Schmitz (1989), where imitative behavior of entrepreneurs fostered growth.

The purpose of this paper is to explain how knowledge is converted into economic knowledge and how economic knowledge influences growth. First, in contrast to previous endogenous growth models, we explicitly introduce a transmission mechanism—entrepreneurship—that influences the rate at which the stock of knowledge is converted into economically useful firm-specific knowledge. Thus, whether regions or countries experience higher growth depends just as much on the distribution between entrepreneurial activities and R&D in the economy as on how much resources are spent on knowledge creation. Second, we implement different regression techniques over different periods to assess the impact of entrepreneurs and researchers on growth. Third, we claim that this implies a new policy approach that reduces the obstacles to entrepreneurship to enhance commercialization of knowledge.

The paper is organized as follows. The next section discusses exogenous knowledge diffusion in endogenous growth models, and provides a suggestion as regards the missing link in the knowledge spillover process. Section 3 presents models for how the individual decision to become an entrepreneur is linked to the risk–reward possibilities that potential entrepreneurs encounter, while Sect. 4 provides a link between microbehavior, entrepreneurship, and growth. In Sect. 5 we provide empirical support for the contribution of entrepreneurship to economic growth. The following Sect. 6 discusses the implications of growth policy. The final section provides a summary and conclusions.

2 The missing link in the endogenous growth models

In the endogenous growth models the opportunity to exploit knowledge spillovers accruing from aggregate knowledge investment is not adequately explained. In essence, these models assume that knowledge (normally defined as codified R&D) is automatically transformed into commercial activities, or what Arrow (1962) classifies as economic knowledge.

New knowledge indisputably leads to opportunities that can be exploited commercially. Economic growth, however, requires that new knowledge be converted into economic knowledge that constitutes a commercial opportunity, a considerably more unpredictable and complex process. For example, only about half of the invention disclosures in US universities result in patent applications; half of the applications result in patents; only one-third of patents are licensed, and only 10–20% of licenses yield significant income (Carlsson and Fridh 2002). In other words, only 1% or 2% of inventions are successful in reaching the market and yielding income.

Hence, opportunities rarely present themselves in neat packages; rather they have to be discovered and applied commercially. Notably such discoveries are made in all types of economic activities, not only in R&D-intensive activities, even though knowledge is used—or combined—in new ways. Precisely for this reason, the nexus of opportunity and enterprising individuals is crucial in order to understand economic growth (Shane and Eckhardt 2003). This implies that knowledge by itself is only a necessary condition for the exercise of successful enterprise in a growth model. The ability to transform new knowledge into economic opportunities involves a set of skills, aptitudes, insights, and circumstances that is neither uniformly nor widely distributed in the population.[5]

In particular, the uncertainty, asymmetries, and high transaction costs inherent to knowledge generate a divergence in the assessment and evaluation of the expected value of new ideas (Arrow 1962). This divergence in the valuation of knowledge across economic agents and within the decision-making process of incumbent firms can induce agents to start new firms as a mechanism to appropriate the (expected) value of their knowledge. This would suggest that entrepreneurship facilitates the spillover of knowledge in the form of starting a new firm.

That entrepreneurship may constitute a missing link in contemporary growth models corroborates with recent empirical studies that have found an empirical regularity in the form of a positive relationship between various measures of entrepreneurial activity, most typically start-up rates, and indicators

---

[5] An interesting approach presented by Michelacci (2003) focuses on the matching mechanism between inventors (doing R&D) and entrepreneurs who commercialize such inventions. Michelacci stresses the importance of having access to both R&D and entrepreneurial skills.

Fig. 2 Entrepreneurship
and employment growth

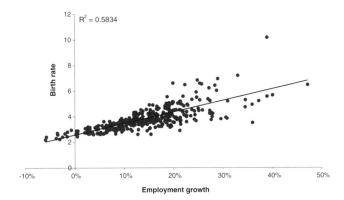

Fig. 3 High growth firms
and employment growth

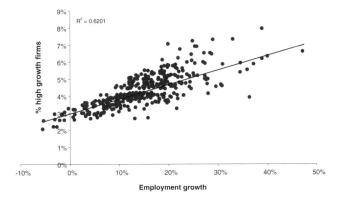

of economic growth (Figs. 2, 3).[6] Other measures are small and medium-sized enterprises (SMEs), self-employment, and business ownership rates in relation to total population or labor force. For instance, Thurik (1999) provides empirical evidence from a 1984–1994 cross-sectional study of 23 OECD countries. He shows that increased entrepreneurship, as measured by business ownership rates, is associated with higher rates of employment growth at the country level. In another study for the OECD, Audretsch and Thurik (2002) undertake two separate empirical analyses to identify the impact of changes of entrepreneurship on growth.[7]

There are undoubtedly many mechanisms that impede the commercialization of knowledge. By serving as a conduit for the spillover of knowledge that might not otherwise be commercialized, entrepreneurship is *one* conceivable mechanism that links knowledge to commercialization and economic growth.

---

[6] See, for instance, Callejon and Segarra (1999), Audretsch and Fritsch (2002), Acs and Armington (2004), Audretsch and Keilbach (2004), Braunerhjelm and Borgman (2004), and Beck et al. (2005). The Global Entrepreneurship Monitoring (GEM) report has found a similar correlation at the country level (Reynolds et al. 2003).

[7] See Braunerhjelm (2008) for a recent survey on the entrepreneurship-growth literature.

3 Incumbents, entrepreneurs, and knowledge

3.1 Basic assumptions

In order to model the role of the entrepreneur in the endogenous growth process, the mechanisms that impede knowledge exploitation contribution, and the choice of economic agents to become entrepreneurs or remain employees, we impose the following assumptions:

1. A given set of individuals $\bar{L}$ can either be employed in the goods producing sector (L_F), the knowledge (invention) producing sector (L_R) or in the entrepreneurial (innovation) sector (L_E).
2. Entrepreneurial ability is distributed unevenly (and exogenously) across individuals. They deploy their endowments of entrepreneurial capabilities to evaluate the knowledge accessible to them in reaching a decision on how best to appropriate the returns from that knowledge, i.e., they make profit-maximizing intertemporal choices of whether to remain employees or become entrepreneurs (see the following section).
3. Efficiency (σ) in transforming knowledge into economic knowledge is impacted by a nation's or region's policy, institutions, and path dependence, which influences technology transfer mechanisms.
4. There are two channels to develop and transform knowledge (A) into economically useful knowledge. The first involves incumbent firms and the second involves the entrepreneurial start-up of new (Schumpeterian) firms.
5. Incumbent firms develop and transform available knowledge into economically useful knowledge by employing researchers (L_R), which results in new inventions and new varieties of products (x_i). How smoothly incumbents develop and transform knowledge into goods and services (commercialization) is determined by the efficiency variable σ_R,

$$0 \prec \sigma_R \prec 1.$$

The closer σ_R is to zero, the less efficient the exploitation of knowledge.
6. A start-up (innovation) represents any kind of new combination of existing or new knowledge, where individuals (L_E) draw on their (given) entrepreneurial ability ($\bar{e}_i$) and the aggregate stock of knowledge (A) to develop new products.[8] Also, entrepreneurial activities are governed by how efficiently knowledge is exploited and transformed into goods,

$$0 \prec \sigma_E \prec 1.$$

Entrepreneurs do not engage in research but develop new products and new business models (organizing production).
7. The production activities of incumbents and entrepreneurs imply that the societal stock of nonrivalrous and partly nonexcludable knowledge increases.

These assumptions imply that two conditions are decisive for an increasing stock of knowledge to materialize higher economic growth. First, knowledge has to be transformed into economically useful knowledge, and, second, an economy must be endowed with factors of production that can select, evaluate, and transform knowledge into commercial use. If these conditions are not fulfilled, an increase in the knowledge stock may have little impact on growth. Moreover, economies endowed with small knowledge stocks may experience higher growth than regions more abundantly endowed with knowledge due to a higher efficiency in converting knowledge into products.

3.2 The entrepreneurial choice

Consider an economy endowed with a population of L individuals that live for two periods. In the first period incumbents employ all individuals, but between periods they make intertemporal choices as regards remaining an employee or becoming an entrepreneur.

Individuals at the higher end of the distribution of entrepreneurial ability identify more opportunities to exploit commercially as compared with individuals with lower ability. By combining given entrepreneurial capacity ($\bar{e}$) with the aggregate knowledge stock (A) in an economy operating at an efficiency level (σ_E), a certain number of the population (L_E) will identify profitable opportunities in running their own firms and become entrepreneurs (e_i). Thus, at a given point in time,

---

[8] Schumpeter (1911).

Expected utility

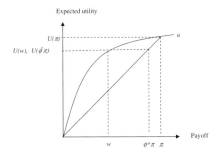

Fig. 4 Expected utility of becoming an entrepreneur

$$e_i = f(\bar{e}_i, A, \sigma_E), \quad \sum_{i=1}^{L} e_i \equiv L_E, \tag{1}$$

where aggregate entrepreneurial ability in an economy is increasing in e, A, and σ_E.

The intertemporal choice between becoming an entrepreneur or remaining an employee depends on the expected payoff accruing to the respective alternatives. Suppose that individuals' preferences are characterized by von Neumann–Morgenstern utility functions allowing a strictly increasing utility representation of the expected utility form. Moreover, assume that individuals are strictly risk-averse and that $u(0) = 0$. The decision regarding whether to become an entrepreneur or not is illustrated in Fig. 4.[9]

The individual who chooses to remain an employee will receive a wage (w) with certainty, yielding utility

$$U^{\text{Worker}} = u(w) = u^w(x), \tag{2}$$

which we will refer to as the individual's expected utility from remaining an employee, allowing

consumption of x goods. If, on the other hand, the individual chooses to become an entrepreneur, expected utility is dependent on the probability of success ($\varphi \in [0, 1]$) and the expected pay-off (π),

$$U^{\text{Entrepreneur}} = \varphi u(\pi) = \varphi u^\pi(x). \tag{3}$$

To engage in entrepreneurial activities the individual's expected net payoff from entrepreneurial activities (φu^π) must be larger than the expected net payoff from remaining an employee (u^w). As shown in Fig. 4, if $\pi \geq w$, then there exists a probability $\varphi*$ such that the choice of being an entrepreneur is optimal for the individual for all $\varphi > \varphi*$. Assume that there exist a $\pi > w$ and a $\varphi > \varphi*$ for a subset of individuals (since $\bar{e}$ is assumed to be unequally distributed). Then a share of the population will shift from employees to entrepreneurs, thereby using knowledge to commercialize new products, which simultaneously also result in new knowledge.[10]

At the aggregate level, entrepreneurial activity in the economy (L_E) depends on entrepreneurial ability and factors influencing the filter (σ_E). A policy that increases the probability of success (φ)—given π— e.g., reducing the regulatory burden or making knowledge more accessible, increases the expected utility from becoming an entrepreneur. This can be illustrated as a move along the straight line in Fig. 4 toward the "northeast" corner.

The share of entrepreneurs can also increase due to a policy that increases the expected payoff (π) for an entrepreneur (e.g., through lowered taxes). In the figure, this implies a shift downwards of the straight line and the intersection with the u-curve would take place further to the "east" in Fig. 4. Thus, even though the probability of success is held constant, the expected utility of becoming an entrepreneur may increase through other measures.

4 A simple endogenous growth model with entrepreneurship

In Sect. 3 we modeled individuals' intertemporal occupational choice, i.e., providing the analysis with a solid microeconomic base. Linking individual behavior to the macrolevel, and to illustrate the role

---

[9] The concave curve in Fig. 2—the Bernoulli utility function— is associated with certain outcomes and the straight line—the von Neumann–Morgenstern utility function—with uncertain outcomes. The certain utility of π is $u^\pi(x)$ and the certain utility of a zero payoff is $u(0) = 0$. If, as is the case for the entrepreneur, the outcomes are uncertain and can only be described in probability terms, we have to look at the von Neumann–Morgenstern utility function. This utility function gives the expected utility of becoming an entrepreneur as the linear weighted average of the certain outcomes (wage earner), where the weights are the probabilities of the respective outcomes. The expected utility of the choice to become an entrepreneur is therefore $\varphi u^\pi(x) + (1 - \varphi)u(0) = \varphi u^\pi(x)$.

[10] Compare Murphy et al. (1991).

of entrepreneurs in growth, we suggest a modification of the Romer (1990) model to incorporate "pure" Schumpeterian entrepreneurs (Schumpeter 1911).[11] Hence, there are now two methods of developing new products: research laboratories in incumbent firms (inventions) and entrepreneurs (innovations). Just as in Romer's original work we think of these products as either new types of physical capital, blueprints or "business models" that are being rented or sold to final goods producers, thus making production of final goods more effective. As, e.g., Grossman and Helpman (1991) have shown, the new varieties of capital goods can just as well be thought of as new varieties of consumer goods entering consumers' utility function directly. The different varieties appear on markets characterized by monopolistic competition, meaning that they never become obsolete and earn an infinite stream of profits.

4.1 Linking entrepreneurs to knowledge exploitation

Before the role of entrepreneurs in knowledge exploitation and growth is considered, we first briefly recapitulate the production function for researchers working in incumbent firms. Research departments within incumbent firms employ labor (L_R) as the only production factor, and research activities are influenced by the available stock of knowledge (A) and an efficiency parameter (σ_R) related to research activities.[12] The latter is a composite of a multitude of different factors. Thus, in its simplest form, the production function for research activities can be written

$$Z_R(L_R) = \sigma_R L_R A, \qquad (4)$$

where research production is positively influenced by a larger knowledge stock and higher efficiency.

Table 1 Notation and definitions of variables in the theoretical model

Variable notation	Definition
Y	Final good
x_j	Capital good j
A	Aggregate knowledge stock
K	Capital stock
L	Total population, assumed constant
L_Y	Number of people in final good production
L_E	Number of entrepreneurs
L_R	Number of researchers
$\bar{e}_i$	Given entrepreneurial ability of individual i
e_i	Probability that individual i becomes an entrepreneur
σ	Efficiency level of economy
Z	Production function, new technology
$\dot{A}$	Change in aggregate stock of knowledge
$\dot{K}$	Change in capital stock
κ	Units of capital goods to produce one unit of capital
ρ	Subjective discount rate
θ	Inverse of intertemporal elasticity of substitution

In order to include the Schumpeterian entrepreneur, we first assume that entrepreneurial ability is embodied in labor, but in contrast to raw labor, it is distributed unevenly across the population. Thus, entrepreneurial activities are assumed to be characterized by decreasing returns to scale ($\gamma < 1$). The production function for entrepreneurial activities takes the following form:

$$Z_E(L_E) = \sigma_E L_E^{\gamma} A, \ \gamma < 1. \qquad (5)$$

Hence, similar to R&D workers, the representative entrepreneur takes advantage of existing knowledge. On the other hand, the production technology differs (decreasing returns to scale), and they do not engage in research. Rather, they combine their entrepreneurial ability with the existing stock of knowledge to introduce new products and business models.[13] The different varieties of capital goods (x_i) produced by

---

[11] The model involves a large number of variables. To simplify for the reader, these variables are—in addition to being explained in the text—listed and defined in Table 1.

[12] Following Romer we ignore the distinction between new knowledge created in incumbent firms and that created in academic institutions. For simplicity we assume constant returns to scale in knowledge production by incumbents. Choosing decreasing returns to scale—which is more likely—would not qualitatively affect the results but yields expressions that are less transparent and harder to interpret.

[13] Starbucks (USA) and Ikea (Sweden) would be two examples of entrepreneurial start-ups that exploit the current knowledge stock with regard to logistics, distribution, and organization of the production in an innovative way, while the products have no R&D content.

entrepreneurs and researchers are employed in the final goods (Y) sector together with labor,

$$Y = (L - L_E - L_R)^\alpha \int_0^A x(i)^{1-\alpha} di, \tag{6}$$

where α ($0 < \alpha < 1$) represents the scale parameter. Given that the demand for all varieties in equilibrium is symmetric, i.e., $x_i = \bar{x}$ for all $i \le A$, we rewrite Eq. 6 as

$$Y = (L - L_E - L_R)^\alpha A \bar{x}^{(1-\alpha)}. \tag{7}$$

Assume that capital goods (K) are produced with the same technology as final goods and that it takes κ units of capital goods to produce one unit of capital (Chiang 1992). Then it can be shown that

$$K = \kappa A \bar{x}, \tag{8}$$

and substituting Eq. 8 into Eq. 7 gives

$$Y = (L - L_R - L_E)^\alpha A^\alpha K^{1-\alpha} \kappa^{\alpha-1}. \tag{9}$$

Thus, the economy employs three factors of production, i.e., raw labor (producing finals), together with researchers and entrepreneurs that produces varieties of capital goods. Labor market equilibrium is attained when employment in R&D, entrepreneurship, and final production equals total supply:

$$L = L_F + L_E + L_R. \tag{10}$$

4.2 Knowledge production in an economy

As a side-effect of their efforts, researchers and entrepreneurs produce new knowledge that will be publicly available for use in future capital good development, positively influencing coming generations of research and entrepreneurial activities. Equation 11 describes the production of new knowledge, i.e., the evolution of the stock of knowledge, in relation to the amount of labor channeled into R&D (L_R) and entrepreneurial activity (L_E).

$$\dot{A} = Z_R(L_R) + Z_E(L_E). \tag{11}$$

Substituting from Eqs. 4 and 5 yields

$$\dot{A}/A = \sigma_R L_R + \sigma_E L_E^\gamma, \tag{12}$$

where, again, σ:s represents the knowledge efficiency in invention activities (R&D) and innovation

(entrepreneurship), whereas A is the stock of available knowledge at a given point in time. The rate of technological progress is thus an increasing function in R&D, entrepreneurship, and the efficiency of these two activities.

4.3 Endogenous growth with knowledge-exploiting entrepreneurs

Assuming that demand is governed by consumer preferences characterized by constant intertemporal elasticity of substitution ($1/\theta$), the maximization problem can be expressed in following way:

$$\max_{C, L_E, L_R} \int_0^\infty \frac{C^{1-\theta}}{1-\theta} e^{-\rho t} dt \tag{13}$$

subject to the laws of motion for knowledge and capital

$$\dot{A} = \sigma_R L_R A + \sigma_E L_E^\gamma A, \tag{14a}$$

$$\dot{K} = Y - C = (L - L_E - L_R)^\alpha A^\alpha K^{1-\alpha} \kappa^{\alpha-1} - C. \tag{14b}$$

The current value Hamiltonian for the representative consumer is then

$$H_C = \frac{C^{1-\theta}}{1-\theta} + \lambda_A (\sigma_R L_R A + \sigma_E L_E^\gamma A) + \lambda_K \left(\kappa^{\alpha-1} A^\alpha K^{1-\alpha} (L - L_R - L_E) - C \right). \tag{15}$$

The first-order conditions for a maximum, letting $\Delta \equiv (L - L_E - L_R)^\alpha A^\alpha K^{1-\alpha} \kappa^{\alpha-1}$, are as follows:

$$\frac{\partial H_C}{\partial C} = C^{-\theta} - \lambda_K = 0,$$

$$\lambda_K = C^{-\theta} \rightarrow \frac{\dot{\lambda}_K}{\lambda_K} = -\theta \frac{\dot{C}}{C}, \tag{16}$$

$$\frac{\partial H_C}{\partial L_E} = \lambda_A \gamma \sigma_E L_E^{\gamma-1} A - \lambda_K \alpha (L - L_E - L_R)^{-1} \Delta = 0, \tag{17}$$

$$\frac{\partial H_C}{\partial L_R} = \lambda_A \sigma_R A - \lambda_K \alpha (L - L_E - L_R)^{-1} \Delta = 0. \tag{18}$$

Combining Eqs. 17 and 18 gives

$$L_E = \left(\frac{\sigma_R}{\gamma \sigma_E} \right)^{\frac{1}{\gamma-1}}. \tag{19}$$

Thus, on a balanced growth path, where both R&D and entrepreneurship are profitable, the amount of resources engaged in entrepreneurial activities is independent of consumer preferences (ρ). As γ is less than 1, entry into entrepreneurship is increasing in σ_E and decreasing in σ_R.

Maximization of Eq. 15 also gives the equations of motion for the shadow prices of capital (K) and knowledge (A) as

$$\frac{\partial H_C}{\partial A} = \lambda_A(\sigma_R L_R + \sigma_E L_E^\gamma) + \lambda_K \alpha A^{-1}\Delta = \rho\lambda_A - \dot{\lambda}_A,$$

$$\frac{\dot{\lambda}_K}{\lambda_K} = \rho - (1-\alpha)K^{-1}\Delta, \tag{20}$$

$$\frac{\partial H_C}{\partial K} = \lambda_K(1-\alpha)K^{-1}\Delta = \rho\lambda_K - \dot{\lambda}_K,$$

$$\frac{\dot{\lambda}_A}{\lambda_A} = \rho + \sigma_R L_E - \sigma_R L - \sigma_E L_E^\gamma, \tag{21}$$

$$\frac{\partial H_C}{\partial \lambda_A} = \dot{A}, \tag{22}$$

$$\frac{\partial H_C}{\partial \lambda_K} = \dot{K}. \tag{23}$$

A balanced growth path, i.e., where $\frac{\dot{Y}}{Y} = \frac{\dot{C}}{C} = \frac{\dot{K}}{K} = \frac{\dot{A}}{A}$, requires that $\frac{\dot{\lambda}_K}{\lambda_K} = \frac{\dot{\lambda}_A}{\lambda_A}$. From (16) and the law of motion for knowledge (14a),

$$\frac{\dot{\lambda}_K}{\lambda_K} = -\theta\frac{\dot{C}}{C} = -\theta\frac{\dot{A}}{A} = -\theta(\sigma_R L_R + \sigma_E L_E^\gamma). \tag{24}$$

Equating Eqs. 20 and 21, using Eq. 24, yields the following expression:

$$-\theta(\sigma_R L_R + \sigma_E L_E^\gamma) = \rho + \sigma_R L_E - \sigma_R L - \sigma_E L_E^\gamma. \tag{25}$$

Solving for employment in the research sector gives

$$L_R = \frac{1}{\theta\sigma_R}(\sigma_R(L - L_E) + (1-\theta)\sigma_E L_E^\gamma - \rho). \tag{26}$$

Inserting the expressions for equilibrium employment in the entrepreneurial (19) and research sectors (26) into the law of motion for knowledge, the steady-state growth rate (g) can be derived as

$$g = \frac{\dot{A}}{A} = \sigma_R L_R + \sigma_E L_E^\gamma,$$

$$g = \sigma_R\left(\frac{1}{\theta\sigma_R}(\sigma_R(L - L_E) + (1-\theta)\sigma_E L_E^\gamma - \rho)\right) + \sigma_E L_E^\gamma,$$

$$g = \sigma_R\left(\frac{1}{\theta\sigma_R}\left(\sigma_R\left(L - \left(\frac{\sigma_R}{\gamma\sigma_E}\right)^{1/(\gamma-1)}\right)\right.\right.$$

$$\left.\left. + (1-\theta)\sigma_E\left(\frac{\sigma_R}{\gamma\sigma_E}\right)^{\gamma/(\gamma-1)} - \rho\right)\right) + \sigma_E\left(\frac{\sigma_R}{\gamma\sigma_E}\right)^{\gamma/(\gamma-1)},$$

$$g = \frac{1}{\theta}\left(\sigma_R L - \rho + (1-\gamma)\gamma^{\gamma/(1-\gamma)}\left(\frac{\sigma_E}{\sigma_R^\gamma}\right)^{1/(1-\gamma)}\right). \tag{27}$$

Note that some entrepreneurial activity (Eq. 19) will always be profitable, i.e., $L_E > 0$, as long as the stock of knowledge exceeds zero ($A > 0$), which does not, however, always apply to R&D activities (Eq. 26).[14] The model shares a number of characteristics with previous models, e.g., growth is decreasing in the discount factor (ρ) and increasing in a larger labor force.

Apart from these properties, the specification of the model implies that the impact on growth of the distribution of labor between R&D and entrepreneurial activities can be derived. Similarly, the optimal distribution of labor between final goods production and knowledge production (R&D and entrepreneurs) can also be inferred from the model. The following propositions follow from the model:

Proposition 1 *Given that an economy has an optimal distribution of workers between the final goods sector and the knowledge producing sectors (R&D and entrepreneurs), optimal steady-state growth implies that a marginal redistribution between entrepreneurship and R&D workers has no effect on growth (assuming that the efficiency parameters is constant and that the knowledge stock exceeds zero).*

---

[14] This depends in a nontrivial way on a range of parameters. The degree of entrepreneurial activity is, for instance, decreasing in the productivity of R&D as long as R&D is profitable. Thus, R&D and entrepreneurship are to some extent substitutes. If R&D is not sufficiently profitable, then we cannot combine Eqs. 16, 17, 20, and 21 to derive the reduced-form growth. The resulting expression provides little insight and is not shown here.

Proof In steady state $\frac{\dot{A}}{A} = \frac{\dot{K}}{K} \Rightarrow \frac{\dot{Y}}{Y} = \frac{\dot{A}}{A}$, i.e., an optimal distribution of labor between final goods and knowledge production implies that a marginal increase in either sector is exactly counterbalanced by a decrease in the other sector. This is, however, not equivalent to an optimal distribution of labor in the knowledge producing sector (L_A) between R&D workers and entrepreneurs, $L_A = L - L_F = L_R + L_E$. Using this relationship and Eqs. 27 and 10, growth can be rewritten as $g = \frac{\dot{A}}{A} = \sigma_R(L_A - L_E) + \sigma_E L_E^\gamma$. Differentiating with respect to L_E yields $\frac{\partial g}{\partial l_*} = -\sigma_R + \gamma \sigma_E L_E^{\gamma-1} = 0$, which is equivalent to Eq. 19, $L_E^* = \left(\frac{\sigma_R}{\gamma \sigma_E}\right)^{1/(\gamma-1)}$, where L_E^* represents an optimal allocation between R&D workers and entrepreneurs. Consequently, $\frac{\partial g}{\partial L_E} > 0 \Rightarrow L_E < \left(\frac{\sigma_R}{\gamma \sigma_E}\right)^{1/(\gamma-1)} = L_E^*$, i.e., social optimum is not attained. Given that there is an optimal allocation of labor between the final goods sector and the knowledge sector ($dL_A = 0$), there is also a direct mapping to R&D workers ($dL_R = -dL_E$); too few entrepreneurs is mirrored by too many R&D workers.

A second, and rather obvious, implication of the model concerns the efficiency of an economy in accumulating and exploiting knowledge, which should influence the rate of growth. Moreover, if the efficiency in converting knowledge to commercial use is influenced asymmetrically over time due to events that are exogenous to firms (national and international institutional change), there may be time-inconsistent effects of R&D and entrepreneurship on growth over time.

Proposition 2 *Growth is increasing in higher efficiency of research (σ_R) and of entrepreneurship (σ_E).*

Proof First, differentiating the growth Eq. 27 with respect to the efficiency parameter of research,

$$\frac{dg}{d\sigma_R} = \frac{1}{\theta}\left[L - \left(\frac{\sigma_R}{\gamma \sigma_E}\right)^{-\frac{1}{\gamma-1}}\right] = \frac{1}{\theta}[L - L_E],$$

which is unambiguously nonnegative.

Second, differentiating the growth Eq. 27 with respect to the efficiency parameter of entrepreneurial activities,

$$\frac{dg}{d\sigma_E} = \frac{1}{\theta}\left[\left(\frac{\sigma_R}{\gamma \sigma_E}\right)^{\frac{\gamma}{\gamma-1}}\right] = \frac{1}{\theta}[L_E^\gamma],$$

which is unambiguously nonnegative.

From these two propositions the following testable hypotheses emerge: If countries have attained an optimal growth path there will be no growth effect of a (i) marginal redistribution of labor *between sectors* (the final goods sectors and the knowledge producing sectors), (ii) marginal redistribution of labor *within* the knowledge producing sectors (R&D and entrepreneurial activities), (iii) marginal redistribution of knowledge workers *between time periods*, while growth should be positively influenced by (iv) altering variables that influence how efficiently an economy works.

5 Empirical analysis

5.1 Variables

The dependent variable is defined as the annual difference in log real GDP growth (expressed in 1995 prices) for 17 OECD countries over the period 1981–2002. The main explanatory variables of interest and relevance to the model derived in the previous section include measures of R&D activities and entrepreneurship. These variables are defined as either the number of (full-time equivalent) scientists and entrepreneurs in the respective country, which most closely corresponds to the model, or normalized by population.[15]

Measuring entrepreneurship (ENT) is at least as challenging and elusive as measuring knowledge. While start-up rates are perhaps the ideal measure capturing entrepreneurship, no such comparable measure exists across the sample of countries chosen for the current analysis. When such measures do exist, they normally comprise a limited subset of countries and tend to be measured in significantly differently ways, rendering their application in cross-country comparisons and regressions inappropriate and misleading. Instead, the same measure as

---

[15] As an alternative we have also used only R&D undertaken in the business sector in the estimations which, however, only had a marginal impact on the results. The reason is of course that the business sector accounts for the overwhelming part of R&D in most countries.

Evans and Jovanovic (1989), Evans and Leighton (1989), and Blanchflower and Oswald (1998) is used: the nonagricultural self-employed. Self-employment is a proxy reflecting underlying entrepreneurial activity and has the advantage of being available for a cross-country time-series context. Obviously there are differences across countries, but we argue that our chosen econometric method to a large extent controls for these differences provided that they are consistent over time. The number of self-employed is used to represent L_E in the model introduced in the previous section.

The degree of trade union activity will be used as a measure of how efficiently an economy work (the $\sigma : s$ used in the model). The prevalence of trade unions (TUD), measured as the share of employment in the labor force belonging to a trade union, is expected to be negatively related to growth since trade unions may pose institutional rigidities and poorly functioning labor markets. Thereby optimal allocation of labor between different occupations may be distorted. In addition, labor market rigidities have been shown to correlate strongly with other market regulations that impede productivity and the functioning of an economy (Nicoletti et al. 1999).

Barro and Sala-i-Martin (2004) include a number of variables controlling for other influences. We follow their approach by including variables reflecting the human capital endowment of an economy (average years of schooling), its openness (imports and exports in relation to GDP), the degree of urbanization (population living in urban areas), and other factors of production (capital–labor ratio). All control variables are expected to exert a positive impact on growth. In addition dummies are used to control for time-specific effects, either annual or defined as periods. Definitions of the variables, and their sources, are shown in Table 2.

5.2 Econometric specification

Data has been pooled over countries and years for the period 1981–2002. In the regressions generalized least-squares (GLS) techniques, taking into account "within" and "between" effects simultaneously as we control for heteroskedastic panels and panel autoregressive (AR) error structures, will be implemented together with ordinary least squares

(OLS).[16] The regressions will use both 5-year averages of the data and annual observations.

The following growth (g) equation will be estimated:

$$g_{jt} = \beta_0 + \beta_1 ENT_{j,t} + \beta_2 R\&D_{j,t} + \beta_4 TUD_{j,t} + \delta' Z_{j,t} + \varepsilon_{j,t}, \tag{28}$$

where j refers to country and t to the time period. The error term either has a common AR1 structure where the error terms for the different panels follow a common process $\varepsilon_{j,t} = \rho \varepsilon_{j,t-1} + \mu_{j,t}$, ($\mu_{j,t}$ is white noise) or a panel-specific AR1 structure which allows for the correlation coefficient to differ between panels, $\varepsilon_{j,t} = \rho_j \varepsilon_{j,t-1} + \mu_{j,t}$. Besides the key variables, defined as the numbers of entrepreneurs (ENT), the numbers of researchers (R&D), and the efficiency variables (TUD), a set of control variables is contained in the vector Z.

The regression analysis will implement both levels of data—which closely corresponds to the theoretical model—and estimations where the data are normalized by country size for the variables of principal interest in the analysis, i.e., entrepreneurs and researchers. The bivariate correlations when the variables are expressed in levels are sufficiently low as not to suggest any problems with multicollinearity. We will also control for different lag structures on the ENT and R&D variables. The population variable will be implemented in all estimations to control for country size.

5.3 Regression results

We start by presenting the results when the variables are defined as 5-year averages. The first run of regressions is presented in Table 3 where only the level of entrepreneurs and researchers, together with population and period dummies, are used. The entrepreneurship coefficient turns out to be positive

---

[16] An autoregressive (AR) structure implies that the error term is serially correlated, such that the current error term is partly a function of previous error terms. Autoregressive structures are likely to occur in growth estimations. An AR1 process implies that the current error term depends on just one lagged error term. The panel-specific autoregressive structure is considered to be most adequate for regressions using annual-level data, while the common AR1 structure is preferred for the 5-year average estimations due to fewer degrees of freedom. As will be shown in the next section, the results are quite similar irrespective of the assumption of the autoregressive error structures.

Table 2 Notation and definition of variables in the empirical model

Growth	Difference in log real GDP, 1995 year's prices and in purchasing power parity (PPP)	OECD, Statistical Compendium on CD, 2004-2002
Entrepreneurs (ENT)	Total nonagriculture self-employed	EIM, The COMPENDIA database.
Researchers (R&D)	Total number of researchers, full-time equivalent	OECD, Statistical Compendium on CD, 2004-2
Trade union density (TUD)	Share of labor force that is unionized	Visser (2006), Schnabel and Wagner (2003), OECD Labour Market Statistics
Capital stock per worker (CAPW)	Business capital stock divided by employment valued at 1995 price level and in PPP	OECD, Statistical Compendium on CD, 2004-2
Openness (OPEN)	The sum of exports and imports of goods and services measured as a share of gross domestic product	OECD, Statistical Compendium on CD, 2004-2
Urban population (URBAN)	The share of total population living in areas defined as urban in each country	OECD, Statistical Compendium on CD, 2004-2
Average years of schooling (TYR)	Average years of schooling among population aged 25 years and above	Barro and Lee (2000), International Data on Educational Attainment. Updates and Implications, CID Working Paper No. 42
Population (POP)	Total population	OECD, Statistical Compendium on CD, 2004-2

Table 3 General least-squares regressions with heteroskedastic panels and panel-specific and common AR1 structures, and OLS regressions

	GLS, common AR1		GLS, panel-specific AR1		OLS	
	Level	Share	Level	Share	Level	Share
Self-employed,	1.10***	1.10***	1.15***	1.15***	1.21**	1.20**
1,000	(3.88)	(3.88)	(6.85)	(6.87)	(2.12)	(2.11)
Researchers,	0.18	0.18	−0.14	−0.02	0.12	0.13
1,000	(0.88)	(0.88)	(−0.11)	(−0.12)	(0.45)	(0.44)
Population	−1.40***	−0.12*	−1.31***	−0.17***	−1.15**	−0.23*
	(−3.65)	(−1.63)	(−5.95)	(−3.81)	(−2.06)	(−1.89)
Time dummy,	1.11***	1.11***	1.27***	1.27***	1.12***	1.13***
Period 2	(7.77)	(7.77)	(18.76)	(19.01)	(2.87)	(2.87)
Time dummy,	−0.49***	−0.49***	−0.22**	−0.23**	−0.34	−0.34
Period 3	(−3.20)	(−3.20)	(−2.25)	(−2.28)	(−0.82)	(−0.81)
Time dummy,	0.48***	0.48***	−0.72***	0.72***	0.63	0.63
Period 4	(2.88)	(2.87)	(−0.03)	(5.03)	(1.40)	(1.41)
Constant	7.80***	1.99*	7.20***	1.95***	8.97**	2.84**
	(3.85)	(1.89)	(5.62)	(2.88)	(2.48)	(2.03)
Wald	181***	181***	1329***	1432***	–	–
F	–	–	–	–	4.12	4.11
Adj.R^2	–	–	–	–	0.20	0.20
No. of obs.	74	74	74	74	74	74

Note: Standard errors are in parentheses; ***, **, and * indicate significance at the 1%, 5%, and 10% level, respectively. All variables expressed in logarithms

Regressions based on the following 17 OECD countries: Australia, Austria, Belgium, Canada, Denmark, Finland, France, Germany, Ireland, Italy, Japan, The Netherlands, Norway, Spain, Sweden, UK, and USA

Levels and shares of entrepreneurs and researchers, 5-year averages (1981–1985, 1986–1990, 1991–1995, 1996–2002), 17 OECD countries. Dependent variable: difference in log real GDP, 1995 year's prices, multiplied by 100

and strongly statistically significant, irrespective of econometric specification, albeit somewhat lower when OLS estimation techniques are used, suggesting that there is a positive relationship between economic growth and the degree of entrepreneurial activity. Due to the limited degrees of freedom, the estimations implementing a common autoregressive structure can be expected to yield the most robust results.

Turning to the variable capturing researchers, a conspicuous result is that in no case does this variable reach significance.

In Table 4 the full model is tested with all the control variables included. Similar results appear, where it is shown that entrepreneurial activities exert a strongly significant and positive impact on growth, while no such effect could be found for researchers.

Table 4 General least-squares regressions with heteroskedastic panels and panel-specific and common AR1 structures, and OLS regressions

	Specific AR, 5-year average		Common AR, 5-year average		OLS	
	Level	Share	Level	Share	Level	Share
Self-employed, 1,000	1.35***	1.36***	1.23***	1.23***	1.51**	1.51**
	(5.15)	(5.17)	(2.90)	(2.89)	(2.59)	(2.59)
Researchers, 1,000	−0.34	−0.34	0.26	0.26	0.24	0.24
	(−1.31)	(−1.31)	(0.65)	(0.65)	(0.48)	(0.47)
Trade union density, %	−0.09	−0.09	−0.20	−0.20	−0.31	−0.31
	(−0.49)	(−0.49)	(−0.82)	(−0.82)	(−0.78)	(−0.78)
Population	−0.95**	0.06	−1.47**	0.02	−1.80*	−0.04
	(−2.13)	(0.45)	(−2.03)	(0.12)	(−1.90)	(−0.19)
Capital stock per worker, 1,000 USD	−0.85*	−0.85*	−1.41**	−1.42**	−1.51**	−1.51**
	(−1.93)	(−1.92)	(−2.35)	(−2.35)	(−2.23)	(−2.23)
Openness, %	0.42	0.42	0.73*	0.73*	1.10**	1.11**
	(1.27)	(1.29)	(1.71)	(1.71)	(2.53)	(2.53)
Average years of schooling	1.25**	1.26**	0.60	0.59	0.51	0.51
	(2.37)	(2.40)	(0.64)	(0.63)	(0.43)	(0.43)
Urban population, %	−1.81***	−1.83***	−1.48*	−1.48*	−3.46***	−3.46***
	(−3.41)	(−3.44)	(−1.66)	(−1.65)	(−3.53)	(−3.53)
Time dummy, Period 2	1.27***	1.27***	1.09***	1.09***	0.89**	0.89**
	(9.97)	(9.93)	(4.71)	(4.71)	(2.30)	(2.30)
Time dummy, Period 3	−0.04	−0.04	−0.33	−0.33	−0.40	−0.40
	(−0.18)	(−0.20)	(−1.02)	(−1.02)	(−0.85)	(−0.85)
Time dummy, Period 4	0.84***	0.84***	0.50	0.47	0.40	0.38
	(2.71)	(2.69)	(1.05)	(1.05)	(0.61)	(0.61)
Constant	10.95**	6.28**	16.33**	9.49**	26.01***	17.95***
	(2.41)	(1.87)	(2.43)	(1.97)	(3.34)	(3.05)
Wald	1357***	1359***	99***	99***	–	–
F	–	–	–	–	4.44	4.43
Adj. R^2	–	–	–	–	0.35	0.35
No. of obs.	70	70	70	70	70	70

Note: Standard errors are in parentheses; ***, **, and * indicate significance at the 1%, 5%, and 10% level, respectively. All variables expressed in logarithms

Regressions based on the following 17 OECD countries: Australia, Austria, Belgium, Canada, Denmark, Finland, France, Germany, Ireland, Italy, Japan, The Netherlands, Norway, Spain, Sweden, UK, and USA

Levels and shares of entrepreneurs and researchers, 5-year averages (1981–1985, 1986–1990, 1991–1995, 1996–2002), 17 OECD countries. Dependent variable: difference in log real GDP, 1995 year's prices, multiplied by 100

Table 5 General least-squares regressions with heteroskedastic panels and panel-specific and common AR1 structures, and OLS regressions

	GLS, common AR1		GLS, panel-specific AR1		OLS	
	Levels	Shares	Levels	Shares	Levels	Shares
Self-employed,	0.69	0.70	1.29***	1.29***	1.45***	1.44***
1,000	(1.31)	(1.31)	(3.16)	(3.16)	(3.67)	(3.67)
Researchers,	0.28	0.28	0.22	0.22	0.15	0.16
1,000	(1.10)	(1.10)	(0.74)	(0.74)	(0.71)	(0.71)
Population	−1.09	−0.11	−1.51	−0.01	−1.90***	−0.30***
	(−1.53)	(−0.92)	(−2.80)	(−0.03)	(−3.68)	(−3.64)
Annual dummies	Yes	Yes	Yes	Yes	Yes	Yes
Constant	5.62*	1.11	6.08**	−0.87	9.52***	2.16**
	(1.68)	(0.94)	(2.17)	(−0.67)	(3.79)	(2.13)
Wald	242***	242***	292***	293***	–	–
F	–	–	–	–	6.82	6.82
Adj. R^2	–	–	–	–	0.27	0.27
No. of obs.	371	371	371	371	371	371

Note: Standard errors are in parentheses; ***, **, and * indicate significance at the 1%, 5%, and 10% level, respectively. All variables expressed in logarithms

Regressions based on the following 17 OECD countries: Australia, Austria, Belgium, Canada, Denmark, Finland, France, Germany, Ireland, Italy, Japan, The Netherlands, Norway, Spain, Sweden, UK, and USA

Levels and shares of entrepreneurs and researchers, annual data (1981–2002), 17 OECD countries. Dependent variable: difference in log real GDP, 1995 year's prices, multiplied by 100

As regards the efficiency variable captured by trade union density, it attains a negative value but remains insignificant in all estimations. Thus, the econometric results presented in Tables 3 and 4 involving the main variables of the analysis (entrepreneurs, researchers, and the efficiency variable) seem to exhibit a satisfactorily level of robustness irrespective of the definitions of variables (levels or shares) or the econometric specification implemented. The Wald statistics are also satisfactorily high. The results for the control variables fluctuate somewhat and the results are not always as expected.

We then rerun the regressions for annual data but retain the remaining specifications. The results are presented in Tables 5 and 6. The results are almost identical for our core variables (entrepreneurship, researchers, and efficiency), while the significance of some of the control variables is affected. Considering the increased degrees of freedom, the estimations implementing specific autoregressive structure should be the focus. The entrepreneurial variable is shown to display a strong impact on growth, while researchers fail to attain significance. Again the definition of variables (levels or shares) does not influence the

results, and the choice of econometric method only marginally changes the results between the different regressions.

The period dummies implemented in Tables 3 and 4 suggest that there are reasons to suspect a structural break in the data over time. It may be that the sources of growth shifted from accumulation of knowledge towards exploiting the stock of knowledge, rendering the role of conduits facilitating the spillover of the knowledge, such as entrepreneurship, more important in the latter period. Thus, in Table 7 results are presented, estimating the model where data has been distributed on two decades: the 1980s (1981–1993) and the 1990s (1994–2002).[17] The results reveal some interesting dynamics between the two periods. First, entrepreneurial activities seem to have become increasingly important in the 1990s, while researchers continue to have negligible impact on growth. In addition, the efficiency variable is shown to be

---

[17] The time periods are chosen such that they start and end in roughly the same sequence in the business cycle.

Table 6 General least-squares regressions with heteroskedastic panels and panel-specific and common AR1 structures, and OLS regressions

	Specific AR		Common AR		OLS	
	Level	Share	Level	Share	Level	Share
Self-employed,	1.24***	1.24***	1.16**	1.16**	1.72***	1.73***
1,000	(2.65)	(2.65)	(2.02)	(2.02)	(4.28)	(4.28)
Researchers,	0.25	0.25	0.24	0.25	0.41	0.40
1,000	(0.55)	(0.55)	(0.58)	(0.58)	(1.16)	(1.15)
Trade union density, %	−0.26	−0.26	−0.18	−0.18	−0.40	−0.40
	(−0.84)	(−0.84)	(−0.59)	(−0.59)	(−1.44)	(−1.44)
Population	−1.48*	0.10	−1.42*	−0.02	−2.23***	−0.09
	(−1.77)	(0.54)	(−1.61)	(−0.05)	(−3.45)	(−0.56)
Capital stock per worker,	−1.60**	−1.60**	−2.06***	−2.06***	−1.65***	−1.65***
1,000 USD	(−2.48)	(−2.48)	(−3.29)	(−3.29)	(−3.60)	(−3.61)
Openness, %	0.93**	0.94**	1.01**	1.01**	1.31***	1.31***
	(2.13)	(2.13)	(2.28)	(2.28)	(4.28)	(4.28)
Average years of schooling	0.77	0.77	0.04	0.04	0.39	0.39
	(0.75)	(0.75)	(0.03)	(0.04)	(0.45)	(0.45)
Urban population, %	−1.95*	−1.95*	−2.08	−2.08**	−3.73***	−3.73***
	(−1.91)	(−1.91)	(−2.28)**	(−2.28)	(−5.48)	(−5.48)
Annual dummies	Yes	Yes	Yes	Yes	Yes	Yes
Constant	17.00**	10.10*	20.36***	13.87***	28.69***	18.86***
	(2.23)	(1.88)	(2.86)	(2.66)	(5.36)	(4.66)
Wald	310***	310***	292***	291***	–	–
F-test	–	–	–	–	8.65	8.65
Adj. R^2	–	–	–	–	0.38	0.38
No. of obs.	371	371	371	371	371	371

Note: Standard errors are in parentheses; ***, **, and * indicate significance at the 1%, 5%, and 10% level, respectively. All variables expressed in logarithms

Regressions based on the following 17 OECD countries: Australia, Austria, Belgium, Canada, Denmark, Finland, France, Germany, Ireland, Italy, Japan, The Netherlands, Norway, Spain, Sweden, UK, and USA

Levels and shares of entrepreneurs and researchers, annual data (1981–2002), 17 OECD countries. Dependent variable: difference in log real GDP, 1995 year's prices, multiplied by 100

statistically significantly negative in the 1990s, but not so in the 1980s. In addition, even though research fails to impact growth, education becomes strongly significant in the 1990s. The results suggest a change in the sources that promotes growth between the two decades, where entrepreneurship, trade union density (efficiency proxy), and education have become more important. That is likely to reflect the structural changes that most OECD countries have undergone in the 1990s, characterized by globalization and increased competition.

To conclude, the empirical analysis basically rejects the hypotheses presented in Sect. 3: In particular, there seems to have been a suboptimal distribution of labor between sectors and within the knowledge producing sector. According to the regression results, more labor should have been shifted towards entrepreneurial activities. Similarly, low efficiency seems to have hampered growth in the latter part of the time period we are considering, and entrepreneurial activities are indicated to exert a stronger impact on growth over time. The results indicate a wedge between private and social welfare optimization. These results also imply that a different set of policy instruments should be used in order to attain sustainable higher growth rates.

Table 7 General least-squares regressions with heteroskedastic panels, panel-specific and common AR1 structures, and OLS regressions

	Specific AR		Common AR		OLS	
	1981–1993	1994–2002	1981–1993	1994–2002	1981–1993	1994–2002
Self-employed, 1,000	1.09*	1.66***	1.27*	1.81***	1.03*	2.16***
	(1.73)	(2.89)	(1.70)	(2.77)	(1.79)	(3.97)
Researchers, 1,000	0.06	−0.85	−0.10	−71	0.01	−1.03
	(0.11)	(−1.50)	(−0.16)	(−0.99)	(0.01)	(−1.48)
Trade union density, %	−0.25	−1.05**	−0.29	−0.86**	−0.25	−1.12***
	(−0.58)	(−2.30)	(−0.79)	(−2.10)	(−0.65)	(−2.78)
Population	−1.08	1.55*	−0.99	−1.92*	−0.90	−2.08*
	(−1.02)	(−1.81)	(−0.91)	(−1.76)	(−1.03)	(−2.01)
Capital stock per worker, 1,000 USD	−1.71**	0.44	−2.02**	−0.18	−1.64***	0.08
	(−1.98)	(0.46)	(−2.37)	(−0.21)	(−2.58)	(0.11)
Openness, %	0.72	0.57	0.88	−0.04	0.75*	1.03**
	(1.30)	(1.22)	(1.49)	(−0.08)	(1.70)	(2.27)
Average years of schooling	0.79	6.89***	1.04	4.28**	0.37	5.66***
	(0.68)	(3.07)	(0.75)	(2.07)	(0.37)	(3.02)
Urban population, %	−2.70***	−3.25***	−2.30**	−1.38	−2.74***	−4.64***
	(−2.45)	(−3.11)	(−2.11)	(−1.18)	(−2.93)	(−5.17)
Annual dummies	Yes	Yes	Yes	Yes	Yes	Yes
Constant	19.06**	9.12	16.24*	13.14	18.80***	19.24**
	(2.07)	(1.05)	(1.80)	(1.30)	(2.61)	(2.19)
Wald	159***	203***	173***	154***	–	–
F-test	–	–	–	–	6.31	10.96
Adj.R^2	–	–	–	–	0.33	0.52
No. of obs.	221	150	221	150	221	150

Note: Standard errors are in parentheses; ***, **, and * indicate significance at the 1%, 5%, and 10% level, respectively. All variables expressed in logarithms

Regressions based on the following 17 OECD countries: Australia, Austria, Belgium, Canada, Denmark, Finland, France, Germany, Ireland, Italy, Japan, The Netherlands, Norway, Spain, Sweden, UK, and USA

Levels of entrepreneurs and researchers, annual data, distributed on two time periods (1981–1993 and 1994–2002), 17 OECD countries. Dependent variable: difference in log real GDP, 1995 year's prices, multiplied by 100

5.4 Testing for robustness

In order to check the robustness of the results and how causality runs between growth and entrepreneurship, some additional results will be presented. First, a Granger causality test is presented in the appendix, showing that causality runs predominantly from entrepreneurial activities to growth and not the other way around.

We have also implemented different lag structures on the variables (from 1 to 4 years) on our key variables entrepreneurship and researchers to control for growth effects appearing in subsequent periods.

Table 8 reports some of the findings when the variables are lagged 1 and 4 years, respectively.[18] The results for the remaining variables are quite stable and not shown in the table. Similarly, the results change only marginally if we define the variables in terms of shares, or if we split the data set between the 1980s and the 1990s. As shown in Table 8, the entrepreneurial variable attains significance in all but one regression, while the number of

---

[18] Regression results for other lag structures are very similar to those in Table 8 and are available on request.

Table 8 Regression results. General least-squares regressions with heteroskedastic panels and panel-specific AR1 structures, and OLS

Regression	Variable	SpecificAR1	OLS
1	Self-employed lagged 1 period	0.93**	1.51***
		(1.98)	(3.70)
	Researchers	0.20	0.36
		(0.43)	(1.02)
2	Self-employed	0.98*	1.57***
		(1.93)	(3.78)
	Researchers lagged 1 period	0.23	0.29
		(0.46)	(0.78)
3	Self-employed lagged 1 period	0.60	1.35***
		(1.17)	(3.22)
	Researchers lagged 1 period	0.16	0.24
		(0.33)	(0.64)
4	Self-employed lagged 4 periods	1.11**	1.37***
		(2.27)	(3.27)
	Researchers	0.23	0.30
		(0.51)	(0.84)
5	Self-employed	1.13*	1.49***
		(1.95)	(3.38)
	Researchers lagged 4 periods	−0.70	−0.23
		(−1.24)	(−0.56)
6	Self−employed lagged 4 periods	1.30**	1.33***
		(2.15)	(2.97)
	Researchers lagged 4 periods	−0.79	−0.39
		(−1.44)	(−0.94)

Note: Standard errors are in parentheses; ***, **, and * indicate significance at the 1%, 5%, and 10% level, respectively. All variables expressed in logarithms. In addition to self-employed and researchers, the regressions contain the following variables: population, trade union density, capital stock per worker, openness, average years of schooling, and urban population

Regressions based on the following 17 OECD countries: Australia, Austria, Belgium, Canada, Denmark, Finland, France, Germany, Ireland, Italy, Japan, The Netherlands, Norway, Spain, Sweden, UK, and USA

Annual data, different lag structure of self-employed and researchers, levels; 17 OECD countries. Dependent variable: difference in log real GDP, 1995 year's prices, multiplied by 100

researchers remains insignificant in all estimations. The results support our previous findings.

Finally we have checked for different kinds of spurious correlations between the independent variables. Again, the results remain stable as we run the regressions excluding some of the variables. One obvious candidate is the education variable, which could be linked to both the variable capturing researchers but also to the urbanization variable. The results when we exclude the education variable are presented in Table 9. The remaining variables are barely affected; particularly, the research variable remains insignificant while the entrepreneurial variable continuous to display a positive and statistically significant impact on growth. These results are independent with respect to the definition of the variables or the specification of the autoregressive structure. Hence, we conclude that the regression results are robust.

6 Policy implications

A significant and compelling contribution of the endogenous growth theory was to refocus the policy

Table 9 General least-squares regressions with heteroskedastic panels, excluding the education variable

	Specific AR, annual data		Common AR, 5-year average	
	Level	Share	Level	Share
Self-employed, 1,000	1.18**	1.18**	1.21***	1.20***
	(2.53)	(2.53)	(2.82)	(2.82)
Researchers, 1,000	0.43	0.43	0.41	0.41
	(1.20)	(1.19)	(1.28)	(1.28)
Population	−1.61**	0.002	−1.61**	0.006
	(−2.00)	(0.01)	(−2.35)	(0.004)
Trade union density, %	−0.23	−0.23	−0.18	−0.18
	(−0.75)	(−0.74)	(−0.75)	(−0.75)
Capital stock per worker, 1,000 USD	−1.79***	−1.79***	−1.59***	−1.59***
	(−2.97)	(−2.97)	(−2.89)	(−2.89)
Openness, %	0.94**	0.94**	0.77*	0.77*
	(2.14)	(2.14)	(1.80)	(1.79)
Average years of schooling	–	–	–	–
Urban population, %	−1.77*	−1.77*	−1.41	−1.41
	(−1.78)	(−1.78)	(−1.58)	(−1.58)
Time dummy, period 2	–	–	1.10***	1.10***
			(4.78)	(4.78)
Time dummy, period 3	–	–	−0.29	−0.29
			(−0.91)	(−0.91)
Time dummy, period 4	–	–	0.52	0.52
			(1.18)	(1.18)
Annual dummies	Yes	Yes	–	–
Constant	19.58***	12.16***	18.85***	11.42***
	(2.93)	(2.58)	(3.46)	(2.99)
Wald	308***	308***	100***	100***
No. of obs.	371	371	70	70

Note: Standard errors are in parentheses; ***, **, and * indicate significance at the 1%, 5%, and 10% level, respectively. All variables expressed in logarithms

Regressions based on the following 17 OECD countries: Australia, Austria, Belgium, Canada, Denmark, Finland, France, Germany, Ireland, Italy, Japan, The Netherlands, Norway, Spain, Sweden, UK, and USA

Annual data (1981–2002) and 5-year averages (1981–1985, 1986–1990, 1991–1995, 1996–2002), 17 OECD countries. Dependent variable: difference in log real GDP, 1995 year's prices, multiplied by 100

debate away from the emphasis on enhancing capital and labor with a new priority on knowledge and human capital—in particular through a combination of taxes and subsidies. As Lucas (1993) concluded, "The main engine of growth is the accumulation of human capital—of knowledge—and the main source of differences in living standards among nations is differences in human capital. Physical capital accumulation plays an essential but decidedly subsidiary role."

Lucas also elaborates on specific policy instruments designed to enhance investments in human capital and knowledge. Thus, the policy debate on how to generate growth revolves around the efficacy of a combination of taxes and subsidies in order to promote education, public and private investments in research and development, training programs, and apprentice systems.

By contrast, the extension of the endogenous growth model suggested in this paper implies the central, although not exclusive, role played by a very different set of policy instruments. This policy focus is on instruments that will influence the "entrepreneurial choice" as discussed in Sect. 3, thereby converting knowledge into economic knowledge. Such institutional changes are targeted to enhance the commercialization of knowledge.[19]

The point emphasized in this paper is that entrepreneurship policies are important instruments in the arsenal of policies to promote growth. As this paper suggests, while generating knowledge and human capital may be a necessary condition for economic growth, it is not sufficient. Rather, a supplementary set of policies focusing on enhancing the conduits of knowledge spillovers also plays a central role in promoting economic growth.

7 Conclusion

A careful examination of the basic structure of the knowledge-based endogenous growth theory reveals that the model is limited by the assumption that knowledge not only spills over but also that it is automatically transformed from knowledge to economic knowledge. Such an assumption violates the basic premise of Arrow's (1962) insights into the economics of knowledge. These misspecifications may account for the somewhat ambiguous empirical results the model has generated in explaining growth differences across countries.

Recent literature on entrepreneurship suggests that it may serve as a conduit for the spillover of new knowledge. Thus, entrepreneurship is one mechanism that may augment the effect of knowledge investments. This is certainly consistent with the recent wave of statistical regularities that provide compelling, systematic empirical evidence linking measures of entrepreneurship to economic growth. Implementing different regression techniques we find surprisingly robust support for entrepreneurship being one important source of growth, while no such relationship could be established for researchers. In addition, it was also shown how R&D seems to have been overemphasized in the 1990s as compared with entrepreneurial activities, while a somewhat different picture emerged for the 1980s.

We have suggested a modification of the endogenous growth model that we believe will narrow the

gap between the model and real-world behavior. The role that entrepreneurship plays in increasing the arrival intensity of innovations, thereby generating economic growth, implies a whole new policy approach. Hence, even though the major part of entrepreneurs do not engage in R&D activities, they contribute to growth by exploiting knowledge in a way that resembles Schumpeter's approach.

In this paper we have made a first preliminary attempt to separate the contribution to growth that emanates from entrepreneurial spillovers relative to the commercialization by incumbent firms. Future research needs to identify more rigorously the different contributions to growth by entrepreneurial and incumbent firms.

Acknowledgements We would like to thank seminar participants at seminars in Amsterdam, Athens, Helsinki, Bologna, Milan, and Sophia Antipolis (Schumpeter conference 2006) for helpful comments. The paper has particularly benefited from comments by Paul Segerstrom and Henrik Braconier. We also like to thank Benny Borgman and Per Thulin, for excellent assistance. Finally, generous financial support by the Marianne and Marcus Wallenberg Foundation is gratefully acknowledged.

Appendix

Testing causality between self-employed and growth for the specification using annual data, GLS, heteroskedastic panels, and panel-specific AR1.

Test: LSELF Granger-causes DLGDPN

Step 1. Determine the relevant lag structure for DLGDPN by regressing

$$\text{DLGDPN}_t = \tilde{\beta}_0 + \sum_{i=1}^{9} \tilde{\beta}_i \text{DLGDPN}_{t-i} + \text{TDUM}'\tilde{\gamma}.$$

$$(1)$$

After looking at the significance levels for the estimated coefficients of the lagged variables, the four-lag structure was considered the relevant for the test.

---

[19]   Storey (2003) provides a set of examples.

P. Braunerhjelm et al.

Step 2. Searching for causality by regressing

$$DLGDPN_t = \beta_0 + \sum_{i=1}^{4} \beta_i DLGDPN_{t-i}$$
$$+ \sum_{j=1}^{9} \alpha_j LSELF_{t-j} + TDUM'\gamma +$$
$$+ \delta_0 LRSE + \delta_1 LPOP_t + \delta_2 LTUD_t$$
$$+ \delta_3 LCAPW_t + \delta_4 LOPEN_t + \delta_5 LTYR_t$$
$$+ \delta_6 LURBAN_t, \quad (2)$$

and testing for the joint significance of the α_js. The null hypothesis is that LSELF does not Granger-cause DLGDPN. We reject the null for high values of the test statistic, i.e., for low significance levels. Table 10 shows the significance levels for different values of j.

Hence, we conclude that the causality goes from self-employed (LSELF) to GDP (DLGDPN).

Test: DLGDPN Granger-causes LSELF

Step 1. Determine the relevant lag structure for LSELF by regressing

$$LSELF_t = \tilde{\beta}_0 + \sum_{i=1}^{9} \tilde{\beta}_i LSELF_{t-i} + TDUM'\tilde{\gamma}. \quad (3)$$

After looking at the significance levels for the estimated coefficients of the lagged variables, the eight-lag structure was considered the relevant for the test.

Step 2. Searching for causality by regressing

Table 10 Significance levels for different values of j

j	Significance level	Decision
1	0.0337	Reject
2	0.0687	Reject
3	0.0413	Reject
4	0.0232	Reject
5	0.0156	Reject
6	0.0078	Reject
7	0.0927	Reject
8	0.1376	Do not reject
9	0.0422	Reject

Table 11 Significance levels for different values of j

j	Significance level	Decision
1	0.6272	Do not reject
2	0.9213	Do not reject
3	0.8809	Do not reject
4	0.9564	Do not reject
5	0.9684	Do not reject
6	0.9515	Do not reject
7	0.8816	Do not reject
8	0.7044	Do not reject
9	0.4582	Do not reject

$$LSELF_t = \beta_0 + \sum_{i=1}^{8} \beta_i LSELF_{t-i} + \sum_{j=1}^{9} \alpha_j DLGDPN_{t-j}$$
$$+ TDUM'\gamma + + \delta_0 LRSE + \delta_1 LPOP_t$$
$$+ \delta_2 LTUD_t + \delta_3 LCAPW_t + \delta_4 LOPEN_t$$
$$+ \delta_5 LTYR_t + \delta_6 LURBAN_t, \quad (4)$$

and testing for the joint significance of the α_js. The null hypothesis is that DLGDPN does not Granger-cause LSELF. We reject the null for high values of the test statistic, i.e., for low significance levels. Table 11 shows the significance levels for different values of j.

Hence, we conclude that the causality does not go from GDP (DLGDPN) to self-employed (LSELF).

References

Acs, Z. J., & Armington, C. (2004). Employment growth and entrepreneurial activity in cities. *Regional Studies, 38*, 911–927.

Acs, Z. J., Braunerhjelm, P., Audretsch, D., & Carlsson, B. (2009). The knowledge spillover theory of entrepreneurship. *Small Business Economics, 32*(1), 15–30.

Aghion, P., & Griffith, R. (2005). *Competition and growth: Reconciling theory and evidence*. Cambridge, MA: MIT Press.

Aghion, P., & Howitt, P. (1992). A model of growth through creative destruction. *Econometrica, 60*, 323–351.

Aghion, P., & Howitt, P. (1998a) Appropriate growth policy: A unifying framework. In *mimeo*. Boston: Harvard University.

Aghion, P., & Howitt, P. (1998b). *Endogenous growth theory*. Cambridge, MA: MIT Press.

Aghion, P., & Howitt, P. (2005). Growth with quality-improving innovations: An integrated framework. In P.

Aghion & S. Durlauf (Eds.), *Handbook of economic growth*. North-Holland/Elsevier: Amsterdam.

Arrow, K. (1962). The economic implication of learning by doing. *Review of Economics and Statistics, 80*, 155–173.

Audretsch, D., & Thurik, R. (2002). Linking Entrepreneurship to Growth. OECD STI Working Paper, 2081/2.

Audretsch, D., & Fritsch, M. (2002). Growth regimes over time and space. *Regional Studies, 36*, 113–124.

Audretsch, D., & Keilbach, M. (2004). Entrepreneurship capital: Determinants and impact, papers on entrepreneurship, growth and public policy 2004-37. Max Planck Institute of Economics, Entrepreneurship, Growth and Public Policy Group.

Barro, R., & Lee, J-W. (2000). International data on educational attainment. Updates and Implications, CID Working paper No. 42.

Barro, R. J., & Sala-i-Martin, X. (2004). *Economic growth* (2nd ed.). New York: McGraw Hill.

Beck, T., Demirguc-Kunt, A., & och Levine, R. (2005). SMEs, growth and poverty: Cross country evidence. In *mimeo*.

Blanchflower, D. G., & Oswald, A. (1998). What makes an entrepreneur? *Journal of Labor Economics, 16*, 26–60.

Braunerhjelm, P. (2008). Entrepreneurship, knowledge and growth. *Foundations and Trends in Entrepreneurship, 4*, 451–533.

Braunerhjelm, P., & Borgman, B. (2004). Geographical concentration, entrepreneurship, regional growth. Evidence from regional data in Sweden 1975–1999. *Regional Studies, 38*, 929–947.

Callejon, M., & Segarra, A. (1999). Business dynamics and efficiency in industries and regions: The case of Spain. *Small Business Economics, 13*(4), 253–271.

Carlsson, B., Acs, Z. J., Audretsch, D., & Braunerhjelm, P. (2009). Knowledge creation, eentrepreneurship, and economic growth: A historical review. *Industrial and Corporate Change* (in press).

Carlsson, B., & Fridh, A.-C. (2002). Technology transfer in United States universities: A survey and statistical analysis. *Journal of Evolutionary Economics, 12*(1–2), 199–232.

Cheng, L., & Dinopoulos, E. (1992). Schumpeterian growth and international business cycles. *American Economic Review, 82*, 409–414.

Chiang, A. (1992). *Elements of dynamic optimization*. New York: McGraw-Hill.

Dinopoulos, E., & Thompson, P. (1998). Schumpeterian growth without scale effects. *Journal of Economic Growth, 3*, 315–335.

Evans, D., & Jovanovic, B. (1989). An estimated model of entrepreneurial choice under liquidity constraints. *Journal of Political Economy, 97*, 808–827.

Evans, D., & Leighton, L. (1989). Some empirical aspects of entrepreneurship. *American Economic Review, 79*, 519–535.

Greenwood, J., & Jovanovic, B. (1998). Accounting for growth. NBER WP No. 6647.

Grossman, G., & Helpman, E. (1991). *Innovation and growth in the global economy*. Cambridge, MA: MIT Press.

Jones, C. I. (1995a). R&D-based models of economic growth. *Journal of Political Economy, 103*, 759–784.

Jones, C. I. (1995b). Time series test of endogenous growth models. *Quarterly Journal of Economics, 110*, 495–525.

Lucas, R. (1988). On the mechanics of economic development. *Journal of Monetary Economics, 22*, 3–39.

Lucas, R. (1993). Making a miracle. *Econometrica, 61*, 251–272.

Michelacci, C. (2003). Low returns in R&D due to the lack of entrepreneurial skills. *The Economic Journal, 113*(January), 207–225.

Murphy, K., Schleifer, A., & Vishny, R. (1991). Thee allocation of talent: The implications for growth. *Quarterly Journal of Economics, 56*, 503–530.

Nicoletti, G., Scarpetta, S., & Boylaud, O. (1999). Summary indicators of product market regulation and with an extension to employment protection legislation. Economic Department, WP No. 226, OECD, Paris.

Rebelo, S. (1991). Long-run policy analysis and long-run growth. *Journal of Political Economy, 99*, 500–521.

Reynolds, P., Bygrave, W. D., Autio, E., Cox, L. W., & Hay, M. I. (2003). *Global entrepreneurship monitoring*. London Business School.

Romer, P. (1986). Increasing returns and economic growth. *American Economic Review, 94*, 1002–1037.

Romer, P. (1990). Endogenous technical change. *Journal of Political Economy, 98*, 71–102.

Schmitz, J. (1989). Imitation, entrepreneurship, and long-run growth. *Journal of Political Economy, 97*, 721–739.

Schnabel & Wagner (2003). Determinants of trade union membership in West Germany: Evidence from micro data 1980–2000. *Socio-Economic Review, 3*, 1–24.

Schumpeter, J. (1911). *Theorie der Wirtschaftlichen Entwicklung*. [The theory of economic development] (English Trans.). Cambridge, MA: Harvard University Press (1934).

Schumpeter, J. (1947). The creative response in economic history. *Journal of Economic History, 7*, 149–159.

Segerstrom, P. (1991). Innovation, imitation and economic growth. *Journal of Political Economy, 99*, 190–207.

Segerstrom, P. (1998). Endogenous growth without scale effects. *American Economic Review, 88*(5), 1290–1310.

Segerstrom, P., Anant, T. C., & Dinopoulos, E. (1990). A Schumpeterian model of the product life cycle. *American Economic Review, 80*, 1077–1091.

Shane, S., & Eckhardt, J. (2003). The individual-opportunity nexus. In Z. J. Acs & D. Audretsch (Eds.), *Handbook of entrepreneurship research* (pp. 161–194). Kluwer: Boston.

Shell, K. (1967). Inventive activity, industrial organization, and economic activity. In J. Mirrlees & N. Stern (Eds.), *Models of economic growth*. London: MacMillan.

Storey, D. (2003). Entrepreneurship, small and medium sized enterprises and public policies. In Z. J. Acs & D. Audretsch (Eds.), *Handbook of entrepreneurship research* (pp. 473–514). Kluwer: Boston.

Thurik, R. (1999). Entrepreneurship, industrial transformation and growth. In G. D. Libecap (Ed.), *The sources of entrepreneurial activity* (pp. 29–65). Stamford, CT: JAI Press.

Visser, J. (2006). Union membership statistics in 24 countries. *Monthly Labour Review, 129*, 38–49.

Young, A. (1998). Growth without scale effects. *Journal of Political Economy, 106*, 41–63.

[17]

Research Policy 39 (2010) 583–588

Research Policy

Does policy influence the commercialization route? Evidence from National Institutes of Health funded scientists

Taylor Aldridge [a,b], David B. Audretsch [a,b,c,*]

[a] Max Planck Institute of Economics, Germany
[b] Indiana University, USA
[c] King Saud University, Riyadh, Saudi Arabia

ARTICLE INFO

Article history:
Received 1 March 2008
Received in revised form 1 December 2009
Accepted 2 February 2010
Available online 26 March 2010

Keywords:
Entrepreneurship
Bayh-Dole
University
Commercialization
Scientists

ABSTRACT

The purpose of this paper is to provide an empirical test of the commercialization route chosen by university scientists funded by the National Cancer Institute (NCI) at the NIH and how their chosen commercialization path is influenced by whether or not the university technology transfer office is involved. In particular, the paper identifies two routes for scientific commercialization. Scientists who select the TTO route by commercializing their research through assigning all patents to their university TTO account for 70% of NCI patenting scientists. Scientists who choose the backdoor route to commercialize their research, in that they do not assign patents to their university TTO, comprise 30% of patenting NCI scientists. The findings show a clear link between the commercialization mode and the commercialization route. Scientists choosing the backdoor route for commercialization, by not assigning patents to their university to commercialize research, tend to rely on the commercialization mode of starting a new firm. By contrast, scientists who select the TTO route by assigning their patents to the university tend to rely on the commercialization mode of licensing.

1. Introduction

Link and Link (2009, p. 23), define the government acting as entrepreneur as "the provision of technology infrastructure when its involvement is both innovative and characterized by entrepreneurial risk (i.e., uncertainty)." In particular, what Link and Link (2009, p. 25) term as the government "in a Schumpeterian manner as entrepreneur" is defined as the provision of technology infrastructure, which "leverages the ability of firms and other actors in a national innovation system to participate efficiently in the innovation process and thereby to contribute to technology-based economic growth."

One important aspect of such technology infrastructure in the United States involves both the passage of the Bayh-Dole Act and its application. Not only has passage of the Bayh-Dole Act provided the requisite infrastructure enabling entrepreneurial activity to emerge out of universities, but it also has enabled "other actors", and in particular university scientists, to participate in the innovation process, when they previously might have been excluded.

Passage of the Bayh-Dole Act in 1980 was a direct response to the U.S. international competitiveness crisis of the 1970s. The Bayh-Dole Act shifted the rights for the intellectual property cre-

ated through federally funded research from the government to the university. As Senator Birch Bayh pointed out, "A wealth of scientific talent at American colleges and universities — talent responsible for the development of numerous innovative scientific breakthroughs each year — is going to waste as a result of bureaucratic red tape and illogical government regulations... What sense does it make to spend billions of dollars each year on government-supported research and then prevent new developments from benefiting the American people because of dumb bureaucratic red tape?"[1]

Passage of the Bayh-Dole Act paved the way for the widespread diffusion of the university technology transfer office (TTO), which has served as a mechanism or instrument with a mandate to facilitate the commercialization of university scientific research and to harness the ensuing revenue streams for the university. In fact, examples of the TTO existed prior to 1980, but some three decades subsequent to the Act's passage, virtually every major U.S. university now has a TTO. The main mission of the TTO is to collect the intellectual property disclosed by scientists to the university and to encourage commercialization where deemed feasible and appropriate.

---

* Corresponding author at: Max Planck Institute of Economics, Germany.
E-mail address: daudrets@indiana.edu (D.B. Audretsch).

0048-7333/$ – see front matter © 2010 Elsevier B.V. All rights reserved.
doi:10.1016/j.respol.2010.02.005

[1] Statement by Birch Bayh, 13 April 1980, on the approval of S. 414 (Bayh-Dole) by the U.S. Senate on a 91–4 vote, cited from AUTM (2004, p. 16), and introductory statement of Birch Bayh, 13 September 1978, cited from the Association of University Technology Managers Report (AUTM) (2004, p. 5).

584   *T. Aldridge, D.B. Audretsch / Research Policy 39 (2010) 583–588*

The Association of University Technology Managers (AUTM) collects and reports a number of measures reflecting the intellectual property and commercialization by its member universities. A voluminous and growing body of research has emerged documenting the impact of TTOs on the commercialization of university research. Most of these studies focus on various measures of output associated with university TTOs (Shane, 2001; Siegel and Phan, 2005; Mowery et al., 2004.) By most accounts, the impact of the TTO on facilitating the commercialization of university science research was so impressive that by the turn of the century, the Bayh-Dole Act was being celebrated as an unequivocal success: "Possibly the most inspired piece of legislation to be enacted in America over the past half-century was the Bayh-Dole Act of 1980." Together with amendments in 1984 and augmentation in 1986, this unlocked all the inventions and discoveries that had been made in laboratories through the United States with the help of taxpayers' money. More than anything, this single policy measure helped to reverse America's precipitous slide into industrial irrelevance. Before Bayh-Dole, the fruits of research supported by government agencies had gone strictly to the federal government. Nobody could exploit such research without tedious negotiations with a federal agency concerned. Worse, companies found it nearly impossible to acquire exclusive rights to a government owned patent. And without that, few firms were willing to invest millions more of their own money to turn a basic research idea into a marketable product."[2]

In an even more euphoric assessment of the Bayh-Dole Act, The Economist (2002) gushed that "The Bayh-Dole Act turned out to be the Viagra for campus innovation. Universities that would previously have let their intellectual property lie fallow began filing for – and getting patents at unprecedented rates. Coupled with other legal, economic and political developments that also spurred patenting and licensing, the results seems nothing less than a major boom to national economic growth."[3]

Despite the generally giddy assessments of Bayh-Dole, Mowery (2005, pp. 40–41) has cautioned for a more balanced perspective: "Although it seems clear that the criticism of high-technology startups that was widespread during the period of pessimism over U.S. competitiveness was overstated, the recent focus on patenting and licensing as the essential ingredient in university–industry collaboration and knowledge transfer may be no less exaggerated. The emphasis on the Bayh-Dole Act as a catalyst to these interactions also seems somewhat misplaced."

However, there are compelling reasons to suspect that not all of the intellectual property created through the university is commercialized through the TTO (Thursby and Thursby, 2005). In particular, a university's TTO may be overwhelmed with intellectual property disclosures, forcing it to select and focus on only a subset of the most promising projects. Shane (2004, p. 4) suggests that by resorting to what he refers to as the *backdoor*, scientist commercialization does not always proceed through the implicit front door of the TTO: "Sometimes patents, copyrights and other legal mechanisms are used to protect the intellectual property that leads to spin-offs, while at other times the intellectual property that leads to a spin-off company formation takes the form of know how or trade secrets. Moreover, sometimes entrepreneurs create university spin-offs by licensing university inventions, while at other times the spin-offs are created without the intellectual property being formally licensed from the institution in which it was created. These distinctions are important for a number of reasons. In particular, it is harder for researchers to measure the formation of spin-off companies created to exploit intellectual property

that is not protected by legal mechanisms or that has not been disclosed by inventors to university administrators. As a result, this book may well underestimate the spin-off activity that occurs to exploit inventions that are neither patented nor protected by copyrights. This book also underestimates the spin-off activity that occurs "through the backdoor" – that is, companies founded to exploit technologies that investors fail to disclose to university administrators."

There remains little empirical evidence supporting Shane's admonition that relying upon the data collected by the TTOs and aggregated by AUTM will obscure the extent to which scientists resort to backdoor commercialization. Field studies by Link et al. (2003, 2007) and research from a survey (Thursby and Thursby, 2002), along with two university case studies (Bercovitz and Feldman, 2006), clearly highlight the vigorous propensity of some scientists to resort to the informal and backdoor activities rather than the front door of the TTO for commercializing their research. The purpose of this paper is to identify the extent to which policy has biased the commercialization path by university scientists by resorting to the backdoor rather than using the front door of the TTO. Instead of relying on the measurement of scientist commercialization reported by the TTOs, this paper instead develops alternative measures based on the commercialization activities reported by scientists. We do this by developing a new database measuring the propensity of scientists funded by grants from the National Cancer Institute (NCI) to commercialize their research. We then subject this new university scientist-based data set to empirical scrutiny to ascertain the extent to which university scientists resort to the backdoor for commercialization, as well as to identify which factors shaping a scientist's choice of commercializing either through the TTO, or alternatively, through the backdoor.

2. Paths and modes of scientist of commercialization

Advent of the TTO has clearly facilitated the commercialization of university scientists' research. For example, the President of the Association of American Universities observed that "Before Bayh-Dole, the federal government had accumulated 30,000 patents, of which only 5% had been licensed and even fewer had found their way into commercial products". Today under Bayh-Dole more than 200 universities are engaged in technology transfer, adding more than $21 billion each year to the economy.[4] Similarly, the Commission of the U.S. Patent and Trademark Office reports that "In the 1970s, the government discovered that inventions that resulted from public funding were not reaching the marketplace because no one could make the additional investment to turn basic research into marketable products. That finding resulted in the Bayh-Dole Act, passed in 1980. It enabled universities, small companies, and nonprofit organizations to commercialize the results of federally funded research. The results of Bayh-Dole have been significant. Before 1981, fewer than 250 patents were issued to universities each year. A decade later universities were averaging approximately 1000 patents a year."[5]

Given the pervasiveness of the TTOs, why would some scientists resort to the backdoor for commercialization, while their colleagues remain within the confines of the TTO when commercializing their research? The likelihood of a scientist commercializing through the backdoor may be influenced by characteristics of the TTO, the university, the region, the scientist, and the technological nature of the invention itself.

---

[2] "Innovation's Golden Goose," *The Economist*, 12 December 2002.
[3] Cited in Mowery (2005, p. 64).
[4] Cited in Mowery (2005, p. 65).
[5] Cited in Mowery (2005, p. 65).

T. Aldridge, D.B. Audretsch / Research Policy 39 (2010) 583–588   585

As Cohen et al. (2002) point out, university TTOs are anything but homogeneous. Not every university TTO is equally equipped to absorb and assess the voluminous mountain of intellectual property disclosures. It is one thing to record and track faculty disclosures of intellectual property; it is quite another thing to assess and act on the disclosed potential innovations.

Degroof and Roberts (2004) show how policies facilitating commercialization clearly vary across universities. Di Gregorio and Shane (2003) use AUTUM data and find that the propensity for university scientists to commercialize depends upon the ability of the scientist to take equity in a spin-off rather than simply accept royalties from licensing. Markman et al. (2004a) confirm this result and attribute it to higher opportunity costs involved when the scientist is interested in starting a new firm.

Lockett et al. (2004a,b) link the resources and capabilities of TTOs in the United Kingdom to commercialization. They find a positive relationship between the resources of a TTO and the propensity for faculty to commercialize. They also find that commercialization is promoted in universities where the faculty member receives a favorable royalty distribution.

Markman et al. (2004b) find a positive relationship between the TTO compensation structure and the propensity for faculty to commercialize their research. They also show how the speed of commercialization varies significantly across TTOs.

Plan and Siegel (2006) summarize from their sweeping review of university TTO's, that there is considerable variance in management, strategies, and resources across university TTOs. Ceteris paribus, a scientist might be more likely to resort to the backdoor for commercialization if she is at a university with a less efficient TTO, or one endowed with fewer resources.

Another reason for resorting to the backdoor may have to do with the magnitude and potential value of the invention. Particularly if the TTO is inefficient and slow, the opportunity cost of commercialization through the front door may drastically reduce the value of the invention (Markman et al., 2004b). This might suggest that the best ideas and intellectual property may tend to be commercialized through the backdoor, whereas the opportunity cost of more mundane inventions is more modest with a lower opportunity cost of commercialization through the TTO.

Another factor that may influence the path of commercialization through either the front door of the TTO, or alternatively, through the backdoor, may be characteristics specific to the university where the scientist is employed. For example, Bercovitz and Feldman (2006) compare the propensity for scientists to disclose intellectual property between two top research universities and find significant differences. In particular, they conclude that it is the difference between the universities themselves that influence the disclosure behavior of scientists. Different universities apparently have different disclosure cultures. Bercovitz and Feldman (2006) show for a study based on the commercialization activities of scientists at the two universities, the likelihood of a scientist engaging in commercialization activity, which is measured as disclosing an invention, is shaped by the commercialization behavior of the doctoral supervisor in the institution where the scientist was trained, as well as the commercialization behavior and attitudes exhibited by the chair and peers in the relevant department. Similarly, based on a study of 778 faculty members from 40 universities, Louis et al. (1989) find that it is the local norms of behavior and attitudes towards commercialization that shape the likelihood of an individual university scientist to engage in commercialization activity, in their case by starting a new firm. Franklin et al. (2001, 2003) also find evidence that policies specific to a university can systematically impact commercialization activity.

There may also be systematic differences between public and private universities. Contributing to state economic development, growth, employment creation and technology transfer is often an explicit mandate at publicly funded state universities. This is rarely the case at private universities. Thus, public universities may be more sensitive to controlling, monitoring and capturing the flow of intellectual property going from university scientists to commercialization.

The region in which the university is located and the scientist is employed may also shape the propensity for a scientist to resort to the backdoor rather than the front door of the TTO when commercializing her research. In documenting the existence of regional clusters and systems of innovation, Saxenian (1994) suggests that norms and entrepreneurial culture can be regionally based. She highlights an example where even the language and vocabulary used can be particular to a region: ". . . a distinct language has evolved in the region and certain technical terms used by semiconductor production engineers in Silicon Valley would not even be understood by their counterparts in Boston's Route 128" (Saxenian, 1990, pp. 97–98). It may be that some regions have more of a culture of conforming to the TTO, where in other regional cultures, adhering to the TTO is less of a cultural norm.

The decision to commercialize through or around the TTO may also be influenced by characteristics specific to the scientist. Scientists with more experience may have less of a need for help in commercializing through the TTO. Similarly, scientists with a particularly formidable scholarly reputation may be able to more easily attract and procure external support, thus reducing their dependence upon the university in facilitating commercialization.

Inventions emanating from university research are not homogeneous. As Harhoff et al. (1999) show, the distribution of the value of innovations is highly skewed, with only exceptional innovations emerging as highly valuable. As Thursby and Thursby (2004) suggest, scientists would gain more by resorting to the backdoor for commercializing the most valuable innovations.

Finally, intellectual property protection may also influence the propensity for a scientist to commercialize through the backdoor rather than with the technology transfer office. Scientists licensing their intellectual property may have a greater propensity for using the commercialization route of the front door offered by the TTO than their colleagues commercializing by starting a new business. This is because the TTO's themselves have a greater focus, orientation on and mandate for licensing activities than startup activities. The data base reports only around 400 startups AUTM emanating from and recorded by the university TTOs. While no one knows the exact figure for the actual aggregate amount of university entrepreneurship, the TTOs records only the tip of the iceberg of startups emanating from universities. This would seemingly indicate that the decision to license intellectual property may influence whether it is commercialized through the front door of the TTO or the backdoor.

3. Measurement issues

The database used to analyze the determinants of the scientist commercialization route consists of scientists awarded a research grant by the National Cancer Institute (NCI) between 1998 and 2002. The largest one-fifth of the NCI Grant awardees, which consists of 1693 scientists, were selected to form the database used in this study. These top funded scientists received awards totalling $5,350,977,742 of funding between 1998 and 2002.

586   *T. Aldridge, D.B. Audretsch / Research Policy 39 (2010) 583–588*

Table 1
Means and standard deviations.

Variable	Observations	Mean	Standard deviation	Minimum	Maximum
Backdoor	135	.2	.40	0	1
Patent forward cites	135	1.56	6.1	0	615
License	135	.51	.50	0	1
Average cite per publication	135	2.30	1.90	1.6	130.65
Full time TTO employees	134	9.13	11.77	0	42.73
Public institution	135	.49	.50	0	1
Ivy league	135	.13	.34	0	1
Age	122	56.81	8.35	41	95
Male	135	.88	.32	0	1
New England	135	.12	.33	0	1
California	135	.16	.37	0	1
Texas	135	.10	.31	0	1
New York	135	.07	.26	0	1
Great Lakes	135	.08	.28	0	1

The dependent variable characterizes whether a scientist has commercialized her intellectual property entirely through the front door of the TTO, or resorted to the commercialization route of the backdoor. The first step in forming the dependent variable involved identifying whether or not the scientist had patented. The patent activity of NCI award scientists was identified by obtaining patent data from the United States Patent and Trademark Office (USPTO). The patent database spans 1975–2004 and contains over three million patents.[6] This enabled the identification of 1204 patents held by 398 distinct scientists between 1998 and 2004.

The dependent variable was created as a binary variable taking on the value of 0 for scientists who assigned all of their patents to their university TTO office, which reflects the TTO route to commercialization. By contrast, if the scientist failed to assign all of her patents to the university, the binary variable is assigned the value of 1, which reflects the backdoor route to commercialization. The U.S. Patent Trademark Office defines a patent assignee as "The assignee, when the patent is assigned to him or her, becomes the owner of the patent and has the same rights that the original patentee had. The statute [of law] also provides for the assignment of a part interest, that is, a half interest, a fourth interest, etc., in a patent."[7]

Of the 392 patenting scientists, 71.20% selected the TTO commercialization route, in that they assigned all of their patents to the university. However, 29.80% of the patenting scientists resorted to the backdoor for at least one of their patents.

---

[6] To match the patent records with the 1692 NCI recipient scientists, Structured Query Language (SQL) and Python programming languages were written to extract and manipulate data. A match between the patentee and NCI scientist databases was considered to be positive if all four of the following necessary conditions were met:

A positive match was made with the first, middle, and last name. If, for example, the scientist did not have a middle name listed on either the NCI award database or the patent database, but did have a positive first and last name, this first condition was considered to be fulfilled. The second criterion involved matching the relevant time periods between the two databases. Observations from both databases were matched over the time period 1998–2004, which corresponds to the initial year in which observations were available from the NCI database (1998–2002) and the final year in which patents were recorded in the patent database (1975–2004). Because applications of patents may take anywhere from 3 months to 2 years to be issued, the 2003 and 2004 USPTO patent records were included in our query. Issued patents from 1998 to 2004 by NCI scientists fulfilled the second criterion. The third criterion was based on location. If the patentee resided within an approximate radius of 60 miles from the geographic location of the university, the third condition was fulfilled. The fourth criterion was based on USPTO patent classification. Using the USPTO patent classification code, all patents were separated into respective coding groups. Patents which did not fall under the traditional categories of biotechnology were identified. All non-biotech patents were evaluated and patents such as "Bread Alfalfa Enhancer" were rejected as an NCI scientist patent.

[7] http://www.uspto.gov/web/offices/pac/doc/general.

To examine the impact of the importance of a potential innovation on the commercialization path, we rely on a method developed by Jaffee and Trajtenberg to reflect the relative importance of patents. This involves measuring this importance of a scientists potential innovation as the number of patents issued from 1998 to 2004 times the number of citations that scientist's patents were listed on other subsequent patents. According to Harhoff et al. (1999), a higher value of future patent citations should indicate more important potential innovations. By contrast, a lower value of future patent citations should indicate less important potential innovations. Thus, a positive coefficient on the forward patent citations would suggest that scientists with higher value potential innovations tend to commercialize through the backdoor.

To examine the impact of licensing on the propensity for a scientist to commercialize through the backdoor, a dummy variable was created taking on the value of 1 if she licensed her intellectual property and 0 otherwise. A positive coefficient would be consistent with the hypothesis that scientists who license their intellectual property have a lower propensity to commercialize through the backdoor.

To control for scientist-specific characteristics, we include measures of scientist output and impact, age and gender. The output and impact of each scientist were measured as the number of citations divided by the number of publications. Gender is represented by creating a dummy variable taking on the value of 1 for males and 0 for females. Age is measured in terms of years. To control for at least some aspect of the heterogeneity across offices of technology transfer, a measure of the mean annual number of TTO employees dedicated to licensing and patenting as a share of total employees is included. Presumably a greater dedication to licensing and patenting would increase the likelihood that a scientist commercializes her intellectual property through the technology transfer office rather than resorting to the backdoor commercialization path. To control for at least some aspects of the heterogeneity across universities, a dummy variable taking on the value of 1 for public universities and a dummy variable taking on the value of 1 for the Ivy League universities are included. Finally, the locational context in which the university and scientist operate is reflected by a series of regional dummy variables.

The mean values of each variable along with the associated standard deviation is provided in Table 1.

The correlation between each pair of variables is shown in Table 2.

4. Empirical results

The results from estimating a probit regression with the dependent variable as a binary variable reflecting whether the scientist

T. Aldridge, D.B. Audretsch / Research Policy 39 (2010) 583–588   587

Table 2
Correlation table.

	Backdoor	Patent forward cites	License	Average cite per publication	Full time TTO employees	Public institution	Ivy league	Age	Male
Backdoor	1								
Patent forward cites	0.2287	1							
License	−0.1202	0.1747	1						
Average cite per publication	−0.1637	0.0378	−0.0078	1					
Full time TTO employees	−0.1252	−0.0217	−0.0294	0.0738	1				
Public institution	0.0206	−0.0754	−0.0052	−0.2491	0.2685	1			
Ivy league	0.1567	−0.0498	0.0414	0.0282	−0.1175	−0.3879	1		
Age	0.0039	0.0912	0.1074	−0.1443	0.0156	0.1593	−0.0527	1	
Male	0.0503	0.0456	−0.0767	−0.0077	−0.0280	−0.0150	0.0719	0.0411	1
New England	−0.0503	−0.0719	0.1803	0.2178	−0.0568	−0.2436	0.2999	−0.0130	0.0501
California	−0.1732	−0.0376	−0.0561	0.0658	0.7707	0.1282	−0.1853	−0.0402	0.0293
Texas	0.0951	0.0255	−0.1062	0.0192	−0.0935	0.1479	−0.1403	−0.0369	0.0421
New York	0.1749	−0.0260	0.0736	−0.0038	−0.0785	−0.2089	0.3386	0.0777	−0.1929
Great Lakes	0.0765	0.2365	0.0378	−0.0962	−0.1274	−0.1077	−0.1214	0.2162	0.0147

	Public institution	Ivy league	Age	Male	New England	California	Texas	New York	Great Lakes
Public institution	1								
Ivy league	−0.3879	1							
Age	0.1593	−0.0527	1						
Male	−0.0150	0.0719	0.0411	1					
New England	−0.2436	0.2999	−0.0130	0.0501	1				
California	0.1282	−0.1853	−0.0402	0.0293	−0.1658	1			
Texas	0.1479	−0.1403	−0.0369	0.0421	−0.1255	−0.1590	1		
New York	−0.2089	0.3386	0.0777	−0.1929	−0.1025	−0.1299	−0.0983	1	
Great Lakes	−0.1077	−0.1214	0.2162	0.0147	−0.1086	−0.1375	−0.1041	−0.0851	1

commercialized through the backdoor or through the technology transfer office are shown in Table 3. The first and third columns include the regional dummy variables, while in the second and forth columns they are omitted.

As the positive and statistically significant coefficient of forward patent citations suggests, scientists with more important intellectual property are more likely to commercialize through the backdoor. Thus, there is at least some evidence suggesting that the commercialization path is not neutral with respect to the significance of the potential innovation. Rather, those innovations with

a potentially greater value are less likely to be commercialized through the technology transfer office.

By contrast, the negative and statistically significant coefficient on licenses indicates that if the scientist licenses her intellectual property she is more likely to commercialize through the technology transfer office and less likely to resort to the backdoor path for commercialization. This also suggests that those scientists not licensing their intellectual property have a greater propensity to resort to the backdoor path of commercialization.

Table 3
Probit estimations for scientist backdoor commercialization.

	(1)	(2)	(3)	(4)
Patent forward cites	1.21	1.18	1.01	9.97
	[2.55]**	[2.62]***	[2.29]**	[2.35]**
License	−7.14	−6.87	−5.54	−5.48
	[2.11]**	[2.14]**	[1.87]*	[1.91]*
Average cite per publication	−2.93	−2.97	−2.50	−2.55
	[2.01]**	[2.08]**	[1.87]*	[1.97]**
Full time TTO employees	−3.45	−2.22	−4.35	−2.33
	[0.10]	[1.40]	[0.13]	[1.56]
Public institution	4.79	4.06	5.57	5.12
	[1.27]	[1.15]	[1.62]	[1.58]
Ivy league	7.30	1.03	8.58	9.54
	[1.42]	[2.31]**	[1.77]*	[2.27]**
Age	−1.50	−7.51		
	[0.73]	[0.39]		
Male	2.74	1.11		
	[0.52]	[0.22]		
Constant	3.81	8.18	−6.84	−4.82
	[0.03]	[0.01]	[1.60]	[1.28]
Observations	121	121ujh	134	134
LR χ^2	24.55	23.50	28.35	22.94
R-squared adjusted	0.23	0.19	0.20	0.17
Observations	121	121	134	134

Absolute value of z statistics in brackets.
Regional variables included in probits' 1 and 3: New England, California, Texas, New York, and the Great Lakes.
* Significant at 10%.
** Significant at 5%.
*** Significant at 1%.

T. Aldridge, D.B. Audretsch / Research Policy 39 (2010) 583–588

Of the three measures reflecting scientist-specific characteristics, only the measure of scientist output and impact can be considered to be statistically significant. Apparently age and gender have no statistically significant relationship to the propensity of the scientist to commercialize through the backdoor. There is at least some evidence that the particular type of university may influence the commercialization path of the scientist. Scientists at Ivy League universities appear to be less likely to commercialize their intellectual property through the technology transfer office. However, whether the university is public or private does not seem to influence how the scientist commercializes her intellectual property. Similarly, the measure reflecting the priority of the technology transfer office to licensing and patents has no statistically significant impact on the commercialization mode.

5. Conclusions

A key role for the government as entrepreneur in the U.S. emerged with the passage of the 1980 Bayh-Dole Act, which shifted the intellectual property rights of government-sponsored research to the universities. However, with the subsequent emergence and diffusion of the university technology transfer office, there are reasons to suspect that an impact of this policy has been for universities to try to appropriate the economic value of government-funded research, which in turn, may skew the path of commercialization selected by scientists, away from licensing patents through the technology transfer office and towards starting a new firm, which circumvents the technology transfer office, or relies on what has been termed as "the backdoor" route for commercialization.

The purpose of this paper was to provide an empirical test of the commercialization path chosen by university scientists funded by the National Cancer Institute (NCI) at the National Institutes of Health (NIH), and how their chosen commercialization path is influenced by whether or not the university technology transfer office is involved. In particular, the paper identifies two routes for scientist commercialization. Scientists who select the technology transfer office route by commercializing their research through assigning all patents to their university technology transfer office account for 70% of NCI patenting scientists. Scientists who instead choose the backdoor route to commercialize their research, in that they do not assign patents to their university technology transfer office, comprise the remaining 30% of patenting NCI scientists. The findings show a clear link between the commercialization mode and the commercialization route. Scientists choosing the backdoor route for commercialization, by not assigning patents to their university to commercialize research, tend to rely on the commercialization mode of starting a new firm. By contrast, scientists who select the TTO route by assigning their patents to the university tend to rely on the commercialization mode of licensing.

Thus, an important finding of this paper is that, in fact, not all of the commercialization undertaken by university scientists goes through the office of technology. In particular, intellectual property that is licensed and lower in potential value tends to be commercialized through the office of technology transfer. By contrast, intellectual property that is not licensed and has a greater potential value tends to be commercialized without resorting to the office of technology transfer, or by using what has been euphemistically referred to as the backdoor. Such intellectual property has a greater propensity to be commercialized through the form of a new firm startup rather than via licensing the technology to an existing firm.

One of the striking observations from the data identifying the commercialization activities of universities as recorded by the offices of technology transfer and collected by AUTM, is the strong bias towards licensing patents and the relatively low number of new firms founded. However, the results of this study suggest that

this important government policy, in fact, does play a key role in generating entrepreneurial activity. Only by examining what the scientists actually do in terms of commercialization activity and not relying solely on what is reported by the offices of the technology transfer can the entrepreneurial role of government policy be uncovered.

Acknowledgements

We gratefully acknowledge the comments and suggestions from Albert Link and from three anonymous referees.

References

Association of University Technology Managers (AUTM), 2004. Recollections: celebrating the history of AUTUM and the legacy of Bayh-Dole.
Bercovitz, J., Feldman, M., 2006. Entrepreneurial universities and technology transfer: a conceptual framework for understanding knowledge-based economic development. Journal of Technology Transfer 31, 175–188.
Cohen, W., Nelson, R., Walsh, J., 2002. Links and impacts: the influence of public research on industrial R&D. Management Science 48 (1), 1–23.
Degroof, J., Roberts, E., 2004. Spinning-off new ventures from academic institutions in areas with weak entrepreneurial infrastructure: insights on the impact of spin-off policies on the growth-orientation of ventures. Journal of Technology Transfer 29, 327–352.
Di Gregorio, D., Shane, S., 2003. Why do some universities generate more start-ups than others? Research Policy 32 (2), 209–227.
Franklin, S., Lockett, A., Wright, M., 2001. Academic and surrogate entrepreneurs and university spin-out companies. Journal of Technology Transfer 26 (1–2), 127–141.
Franklin, S., Lockett, A., Wright, M., 2003. Technology transfer and universities' spin-out strategies. Small Business Economics 20 (2), 185–201.
Harhoff, D., Narin, F., Scherer, F., Vopel, K., 1999. Citation frequency and the value of patented inventions. Review of Economics and Statistics 81 (3), 511–515.
Link, A.N., Link, J.R., 2009. Government as Entrepreneur. Oxford University Press, New York.
Link, A.N., Siegel, D., Bozeman, B., 2007. An empirical analysis of the propensity of academics to engage in informal university technology transfer. Industrial and Corporate Change 16 (4), 641–655.
Link, A.N., Siegel, D., Waldman, D., 2003. Assessing the impact of organizational practices on the productivity of university technology transfer offices: an exploratory study. Research Policy 32 (1), 27–48.
Lockett, A., Vohora, A., Wright, M., 2004a. Critical junctures in the development of university high-tech spin-out companies. Research Policy 33 (1), 47–175.
Lockett, A., Vohora, A., Wright, M., 2004b. The formation of high-tech university spinouts through joint ventures. Journal of Technology Transfer 29 (3–4), 287–310.
Louis, K., Blumental, D., Gluck, M.E., Soto, M.A., 1989. Entrepreneurs in academe: an exploration of behaviours among life scientists. Administrative Science Quarterly 34, 110–131.
Markman, G., Phan, P., Balin, D., Giannodis, P., 2004a. Entrepreneurship from the ivory tower: do incentive systems matter? Journal of Technology Transfer 29, 353–364.
Markman, G., Phan, P., Balkin, D., Giannodis, P., 2004b. Innovation speed: transferring university technology to market. In: Paper presented at the technology transfer society meetings, Albany, N.Y., September 300.
Mowery, D., Nelson, R., Sampat, B., Ziedonis, A., 2004. Ivory Tower and Industrial Innovation: University–Industry Technology Transfer Before and After the Bayh-Dole Act. Stanford University Press, Stanford, CA.
Mowery, D., 2005. The Bayh-Dole Act and High-technology Entrepreneurship in US Universities: Chicken, Egg, or Something Else? Colloquium on Entrepreneurship Education and Technology Transfer. University of Arizona (21–22 January).
Plan, P., Siegel, D., 2006. The effectiveness of university technology transfer. Foundations and Trends in Entrepreneurship 2 (2), 77–144.
Saxenian, A., 1990. Regional networks and the resurgence of Silicon Valley. California Management Review Fall, 39–112.
Saxenian, A., 1994. Regional Advantage: Culture and Competition in Silicon Valley and Route 128. Harvard University Press, Cambridge, MA.
Siegel, D., Phan, P., 2005. Analyzing the effectiveness of university technology transfer: implications for entrepreneurship education. Advances in the Study of Entrepreneurship, Innovation, and Economic Growth 16, 1–38.
Shane, S., 2001. Technological opportunities and new firm creation. Management Science 47 (2), 205–220.
Shane, S., 2004. Academic Entrepreneurship: University Spinoffs and Wealth Creation. Edward Elgar, Cheltenham.
Thursby, J., Thursby, M., 2002. Who is selling the ivory tower? Sources of growth in university licensing. Management Science 48, 90–104.
Thursby, J., Thursby, M., 2004. Are faculty critical? Their role in university licensing. Contemporary Economic Policy 22 (2), 162–178.
Thursby, J., Thursby, M., 2005. Gender patterns of research and licensing activity of sciences and engineering faculty. Journal of Technology Transfer 30 (4), 343–353.

[18]

Journal of Economic Behavior & Organization 76 (2010) 82–89

Journal of Economic Behavior & Organization

Risk attitudes, wealth and sources of entrepreneurial start-up capital

Julie Ann Elston [a,*], David B. Audretsch [b]

[a] *Oregon State University, 228 Cascades Hall, 2600 NW College Way, Bend, OR 97701-5998, USA*
[b] *Indiana University, King Saud University and WHU-Otto Beisheim School of Management, SPEA Suite 201, Indiana University, 1315 East 10th Street, Bloomington, IN 47405-1701, USA*

ARTICLE INFO

Article history:
Received 21 August 2009
Received in revised form 20 January 2010
Accepted 18 February 2010
Available online 1 July 2010

JEL classification:
C93
G
L
L26

Keywords:
Risk
Wealth
Financing
Entrepreneurs
Experimental data

ABSTRACT

This paper empirically examines the role of risk attitudes and wealth on financing choices for successful US entrepreneurs. Our approach uses both survey data and data from economics based field experiments, which enables us control for the risk attitudes of entrepreneurs. Empirical findings suggest that lower levels of wealth increase the probability of using a Small Business Innovation Research (SBIR) grant, but lower levels of wealth also reduce the probability of using loan financing. In addition results show that higher levels of risk aversion, but not wealth, increase the probability of financing firm start-ups with earnings from a second job. Overall, findings suggest that both wealth and risk attitudes may play an important role in the financing choice of entrepreneurs.

© 2010 Elsevier B.V. All rights reserved.

1. Introduction to risk and financing

Parker (2005) concludes that we know relatively little about the economics underlying the use of alternative forms of start-up capital and their potential to help the entrepreneur by-pass credit rationing. This study directly addresses this issue by empirically examining the role of risk and wealth on the entrepreneur's choice of start-up capital for US entrepreneurs. Experimental methods are useful in this case because they can be designed to capture incentive compatible decision making and elicit risk attitudes of real entrepreneurs, no small feat since few empirical studies on entrepreneurship actually use data from entrepreneurs (Schade, 2005).[1]

Examining the role of risk attitudes is important, because conventional wisdom has long asserted that entrepreneurs are more likely to be risk takers, although there is limited empirical evidence to support this notion.[2] This study is related to a burgeoning literature on the impact of risk on the probability of becoming an entrepreneur, but this study extends our understanding in another direction, that of the role of risk attitudes on the entrepreneurs' choice of financing.[3] Generally speaking it is advantageous to empirically examine the validity of common beliefs whenever possible. One such common

---

* Corresponding author. Tel.: +1 541 322 3165; fax: +1 541 322 3139.
  E-mail address: julie.elston@osucascades.edu (J.A. Elston).
  [1] His survey article notes that only 2 out of 14 empirical studies use actual entrepreneurs as subjects.
  [2] For example, Elston et al. (2005) find that entrepreneurs are not-risk lovers, just slightly more risk averse than non-entrepreneurs on average. Palich and Bagby (1995) and Keh et al. (2002) find little or no impact of risk on entrepreneurial decision making.
  [3] Studies which examine the role of risk attitudes on entry include: Cramer et al. (2002), Caliendo et al. (2009), Elston and Audretsch (2010), and others.

0167-2681/$ – see front matter © 2010 Elsevier B.V. All rights reserved.
doi:10.1016/j.jebo.2010.02.014

J.A. Elston, D.B. Audretsch / Journal of Economic Behavior & Organization 76 (2010) 82–89   83

belief, as summed up by de Meza and Southey (1996) in arguing about why entrepreneurs have poor access to capital, is that entrepreneurs engage in the maximum use of self-financing as a self-selected group of risk-lovers. On closer examination, however, there is actually little empirical evidence on the degree of self-financing of entrepreneurs and contradictory empirical evidence that entrepreneurs are generally risk-lovers.

Risk attitudes of entrepreneurs have potentially important implications for financing behavior for several reasons. In a related literature, Parker (2005, p. 10) identifies three highly influential theoretical models to explain why liquidity constraints become more severe as firm size decreases. These models suggest that the riskiness of borrowers or their risk loving natures, and the asymmetries of information between small young firms and creditors, are all sources of agency problems which lead to credit rationing or liquidity constraints for smaller firms. Additionally, the link between sources of funding and liquidity constraints can be easily traced in the case that debt is used, as empirically debt is both a source of funding as well as evidence itself of liquidity constraints. Berger and Udell (2003) find that small firms in the US use about 50% debt financing – the same as large firms, and that even pre-IPO firms average about 33% debt. If debt is an important form of financing for entrepreneurs, any differences between borrower and lender perceptions of risk will also lead to inefficient credit markets.[4] If lenders are unable to identify the quality or risk associated with particular borrowers, Jaffe and Russell (1976) show that credit rationing will occur.[5] In addition, de Meza and Southey (1996) propose a model which predicts that risk averse entrepreneurs will be driven out of the market because the lenders cannot differentiate between riskiness of entrepreneurs, and have to therefore charge a higher average amount for financing. These theoretical studies suggest the need to control for various sources of risk when identifying the extent of liquidity constraints for small firms.[6] This study will address this issue in part by controlling for individual risk attitudes when empirically examining the financing behavior of entrepreneurs.

More generally, liquidity constraints can occur if there is a lack of capital, collateral or access to capital markets. The issue of collateral may be particularly binding in the case of the high-technology entrepreneur whose firm's assets are predominantly intangible ideas, copyrights, licenses or patents and thus not conducive to collateral based lending. Since our data has information on loans and assets, the question of credit rationing relating to collateral based lending can be directly examined.

In the empirical literature, the role of wealth (or more specifically interpreting its sign or direction) on the firm's decisions is unclear, except to say that wealth generally appears to be statistically significant. In their survey of the literature on the role of wealth on entry, Georgellis et al. (2005) find the impact of wealth on entry to be negative in 7 studies, and positive in 11 studies – including Evans and Jovanovic (1989). Others, including Kan and Tsai (2006) and Elston and Audretsch (2010), find that wealth has a positive impact on entry even when controlling for risk attitudes. This study includes a measure of wealth to test for its importance as a measure of liquidity constraints in motivating the firm's financing choice and as a measure of the importance of collateral for loan based financing.

Understanding the economics behind firm financing choices is important in order to understand how liquidity constraints can be lessened for small high growth firms. A number of public policy efforts have in fact been undertaken, such as the SBIR, to reduce liquidity constraints for nascent firms and entrepreneurs, and empirical evidence has been mounting suggesting that the SBIR does, in fact, facilitate the start-up and performance of firms.[7] The question we would like to answer is: how does risk and wealth impact the firm's choice of the financing, including the SBIR and other sources of financing?

The purpose of this paper is to extend our knowledge of how successful entrepreneurs choose alternative financing sources, controlling not only for standard demographic characteristics of the entrepreneur (such as age, gender, race, and education) but additionally key variables which are purported to impact their financing decisions such as risk and wealth.[8] The data base and methodology are introduced in the second section of this paper, which involves field based experiments complemented with survey data. These data are then analyzed in the third section to identify the impact of characteristics of the entrepreneur, including risk attitudes and wealth, on alternative sources of financing. In the fourth section a summary and conclusion are provided. In particular, findings suggest that higher levels of risk aversion lead to an increase in the probability of using earnings from a second job to fund firm start-up. Results also suggest that higher levels of wealth have a positive impact on the probability of obtaining loan financing, but lower levels of wealth actually increase the probability of using a SBIR grant – indicating that SBIR grants may alleviate to some degree firm liquidity constraints.

2. The data

The data for this study come from field based experiments complemented with survey data, both of which were collected in 2004 at two US entrepreneurship related conferences.[9] Experimental tasks yielded data on risk attitudes of individuals, among other variables, and survey questions provided general information on subject and firm characteristics. These

---

[4] In addition, according to Sarasvathy et al. (1998) the perception of risk also varies between entrepreneurs and lenders, which is not addressed in this study.

[5] This phenomenon is analogous to the lemons argument advanced by Akerlof (1970): the existence of asymmetric information prevents the suppliers of capital from engaging in price discrimination between riskier and less risky borrowers.

[6] Also see Stiglitz and Weiss (1981).

[7] Lerner (1999), Link and Scott (2010), Elston and Audretsch (2010).

[8] By "successful entrepreneurs" we mean that these entrepreneurs currently have an active firm.

[9] Details experiments and can be found in Elston et al. (2005).

Table 1
Descriptive statistics. Variable means by risk attitude.

	Entrepreneur risk groups				All entrepreneurs	
	Highly risk averse		Low risk averse		Mean	Std. dev.
	Mean	Std. dev.	Mean	Std. dev.		
Variable						
Age	45.46	10.7	43.11	12.8	44.17	11.1
Female	0.388	0.49	0.302	0.46	0.339	0.54
Race	0.889	0.32	0.704	0.46	0.788	0.41
HigherEd	0.472	0.51	0.511	0.51	0.487	0.51
Risk	0.582	0.25	−0.156	0.22	0.228	0.44
Firm revenue	3365	11912	944	2115	2030	8159
Wealth	1482	4699	1808	5321	1661	5018
n	36		44		80	

combined data enable us to investigate the financing decisions controlling for several potentially importance factors such as risk attitude, which could not have been elicited using survey methods alone.[10]

The data include 80 entrepreneurs, whose status was based on responses to various survey questions regarding the individual's employment status and entrepreneurial firm characteristics. Since survey questions were based on actual or historical behavior, the information received should minimize the type of bias that can be introduced by eliciting hypothetical responses with survey questions.[11]

The measure of risk aversion was derived from experiments which employed expected utility theory and multiple price lists to elicit risk preferences based on early studies by Holt and Laury (2002).[12] In brief, we apply a constant relative risk aversion characterization of utility, employing an interval regression model. Here the dependent variable in the interval regression model was the CRRA interval that subjects implicitly choose when they switch from lottery A to lottery B in a 10 decision lottery matrix. For each row of the lottery matrix, which is listed in Table A.1 of Appendix A, one can calculate the implied bounds on the CRRA coefficient, and thus a measure of risk aversion can be calculated for each subject in the study. The CRRA utility of each lottery prize y is defined as: $U(y) = (y^{1-r})/(1-r)$ where r is the CRRA coefficient implicitly defined when the subject switches from option A, the "safe" lottery to option B, the "risky" lottery. Risk intervals are listed in Table A.2 of Appendix A, in this context, $r=0$ denotes risk neutral behavior, $r>0$ denotes risk averse behavior, and $r<0$ denotes a risk-lover.

Table 1 provides descriptive statistics for the 80 entrepreneurs in the study, with a strong representation of high-technology entrepreneurs, with nearly half of individuals describing their entrepreneurial business as software, computers, technology or engineering.[13] Because of this strong representation of high-technology entrepreneurs, who work in sectors not conducive to collateral based lending, we hypothesize that both bankers and the capital markets will have a disproportional amount of market asymmetry regarding information on credit worthiness. In this case we would expect to see differences in the role that assets play as collateral for classes of entrepreneurs with differing risk attitudes. To explore the role of risk on the financing decision, we employ risk measures as both a control variable in regressions, as well as a sorting variable for estimates divided into high and low risk groups. In Table 1 the variable means between the data groups sorted by risk attitude are somewhat similar, except of course for risk attitude, and wealth. *Highly risk averse* entrepreneurs ($r>0.23$) are defined as those with elicited risk aversion measures above the median r for our data; and the *low risk averse* group is defined as entrepreneurs ($r<0.23$), or those with elicited risk aversion measures below the median r.

Early empirical studies on entrepreneurial behavior including Evans and Leighton (1989a,b, 1990) link individual characteristics such as education level and age to the entry decision. More recently, Douglas and Shepherd (2002) find empirical validation that both risk attitude and wealth are important in explaining the entry decision. This study also controls for these effects in order to get a clear picture of the importance of risk on the entrepreneur's financing decision. Control variables for our model therefore include, age, gender, race, education, in addition to wealth and risk attitude. *Age* is age of the subject in years and *Race* is set to 1 if the subject is non-Caucasian; and 0 otherwise. The *Female* variable is set to 1 if the subject is female; and 0 otherwise. *HigherEd* is defined as 1 if the subject had a graduate or professional terminal degree; and 0 otherwise – with our highly educated sample, this coding effectively

---

[10] We believe the field approach is also preferable to the common practice of using student subjects because it allows us to better capture the decision making process of our specific subject of choice, the high-technology entrepreneur. On the other hand, we also acknowledge the potential limitations of this approach in that results may not be easily generalizable to other types of entrepreneurs. We also acknowledge that a larger sample of high technology entrepreneurs would improve the reliability of estimates.

[11] However, self-reported data can be subject to other types of errors.

[12] The average measure of entrepreneurial risk in the data was $r=0.25$, corresponding to "slightly risk averse".

[13] Half of the entrepreneurs were from relatively low technology intensive sectors, such as business, legal, marketing, and healthcare sectors.

J.A. Elston, D.B. Audretsch / Journal of Economic Behavior & Organization 76 (2010) 82–89   85

divided the data roughly in half. *Risk*, is the interval mean for our elicited measure of the individual's degree of risk aversion. *Wealth* is a measure of the individual's estimated total assets used as a proxy for the individual's wealth. This variable can also be interpreted per Evans and Jovanovic (1989) as a measure of the liquidity constraints of the firm in the financing context, indicating the presence of liquidity constraints. The dependent variable source of financing is set to 1 if the entrepreneur reported that the specific funding source (SBIR grants, loans, inheritance, gifts, credit cards, earnings from a second job, or other) was the primary funding source used to start their firm; and 0 otherwise.

Our data also contain information from subjects on the primary sources of funding used to start-up their entrepreneurial firm, which include inheritance (3%), gifts (1%), credit cards (13%), earnings from a second job (58%), SBIR grants (9%), loans from a bank or individual (21%) and other sources (possibly lottery or gambling income).[14]

This information is coded into variables as follows. *Inherit* is set to 1 if the individual reported either gifts or inheritance as a primary source of start-up capital; and 0 otherwise. *CreditCards* is set to 1 if the individual reported credit cards as a primary source; and 0 otherwise. *Secondjob* is set to 1 if the individual reported earnings from a second or salaried job as a primary source; and 0 otherwise. *SBIR* is set to 1 if the individual reported that an SBIR grant was a primary source of start-up financing, or if they had previously received an SBIR grant; and 0 otherwise. We note that the data includes documentation that entrepreneurs have applied for (34%) and received (20%) SBIR grants with some frequency. *Loans* is set to 1 if the individual reported loans by a bank or individual were used as a primary source; and 0 otherwise. *Other* is set to 1 if the individual reported funds from other sources; and 0 otherwise.

Since the goal of this study is to examine the potential importance of risk on financing choice, we have created subsets of the data to examine the importance of these factors. *Highly risk averse* or those with elicited risk aversion measures above the median *r* for our data have a group has a mean *r* = 0.58, which denotes "risk averse" per the intervals listed in Table A.2. The *low risk averse* group or those with elicited risk aversion measures below the median *r*, have a group mean *r* = −0.156, which corresponds to the cusp between interval end points "risk neutral" and "risk loving", but closer to the later, so this group is hereafter referred to as "risk loving".

3. The model

The empirical model can be defined as:

$$\text{Source\_of\_Funds}_j = \beta_0 + \beta 1 \text{Demographics}_j + \beta 2 \text{Wealth}_j + \beta 3 \text{Risk}_j + \varepsilon_j \qquad (1)$$

where Source_of_Funds_j is the probability of using a particular source of financing for individual j, Demographics_j is a matrix of demographic variables to control for individual effects of age, gender, race, and education (to control unobservable entrepreneurial talent) of the subject j. Wealth_j is measured by the assets of the firm. Risk_j is the elicited measure of the individual j's attitude towards risk taking under the assumption of constant relative risk aversion.[15] Logistic regressions were estimated on all entrepreneurs and subsets of the data sorted by high and low risk aversion groups in order to determine how risk and wealth impact the source of financing chosen by the entrepreneur.[16] This dependent variable was based on the subjects response to the survey questions: how did you primarily finance your firm's start-up?[17]

4. Empirical results

Estimates of our model for SBIR grants and earnings from a second job are reported in Table 2. Regression 1 shows that lower levels of wealth have a weak but positive impact the probability of using an SBIR grant to start a firm. We interpret this as evidence liquidity constraints exist in the Evans and Jovanovic (1989) sense and that the SBIR grants appear to mitigate, at least to some degree, the liquidity constraints of the entrepreneurial firm. To improve the robustness of results, we estimate Eq. (1) both with and without demographic control variables, finding that the demographic information greatly improves the statistical significance of the fit of the data to the model.[18] Further, in regression 2, the negative sign and significance of the *female* coefficient indicates that being female may have a negative impact on the probability of either applying for or

---

[14] Note numbers do not always add to 100% because entrepreneurs were allowed to indicate more than one source of financing.

[15] Since the experiment elicited individual CRRA intervals rather than use ones predicted by statistical models, the CRRA measures are not subject to sampling error in this context.

[16] Data was coded and regressions estimated with binary rather than multinomial logistical methods because most subjects indicated only one particular source as their *primary source of start-up capital* leaving all other categories at zero. Further, funding categories of *Inheritance* and *Gifts* had a total of only 3 affirmative subject responses, and could not be used in estimates. The primary difference between binary and multinomial logistic models is the number of groups defined in the dependent variable, with a multinomial model becoming unstable with the presence of empty categories.

[17] The primary difference between binary and multinomial logistic models is the number of groups defined in the dependent variable. Data was coded and estimated with binary rather than multinomial logistical methods because the model becomes unstable with empty cells.

[18] Unreported estimates indicate that controlling for the entrepreneur's industry has no statistically significant impact on results. Estimates were also robust to re-groupings of data into high and low risk averse groups using alternative criteria, such as changing the switching point of *r* for including the observation in the high and low risk group.

86   *J.A. Elston, D.B. Audretsch / Journal of Economic Behavior & Organization 76 (2010) 82–89*

Table 2
Logit estimations of primary source of financing used to start entrepreneurial firm.

	1		2		3	
	SBIR		SBIR		Second job	
Parameter	Estimate	Std. error	Estimate	Std. error	Estimate	Std. error
Intercept	−2.521[**]	1.08	1.506	2.05	−1.055	1.81
Age			−0.043	0.04	0.048[***]	0.02
Race			1.859	1.39	−1.122	0.75
Female			−2.451[***]	1.23	−0.565	0.61
HigherEd			0.027	0.75	0.344	0.56
Risk	0.712	0.75	0.938	0.92	1.241[**]	0.68
Wealth	−0.198	0.23	−0.335[*]	0.26	0.073	0.18
Wealth^2	0.231[****]	0.01	0.032[**]	0.02	−0.015[*]	−0.01
Likelihood (pr.)	9.11 (0.03)		19.14 (0.00)		11.84 (0.10)	
Wald	7.04 (0.05)		11.08 (0.10)		9.63 (0.23)	

Variable definitions: The dependent variables are the primary sources of financing used for start-up, a binary variable that takes on a value of 1 if the entrepreneur used that source, and 0 otherwise. *Age* is the age of the subject in years. *Race* is coded as 0 for white and 1 for non-white. *Female* is 0 for male and 1 for female. *HigherEd* is 0 for bachelors or lower and 1 for graduate or professional degrees. *Risk* is the elicited measure of constant relative risk aversion of the subject. *Wealth* is the log of assets of the entrepreneurial firm, and *Wealth^2* is the square of this term. All other variables are defined in Section 2 of the paper.

[*] Statistical significance at the 20% levels.
[**] Statistical significance at the 10% levels.
[***] Statistical significance at the 5% levels.
[****] Statistical significance at the 1% levels.

Table 3
Logit estimations of probability of financing start-up with loans by risk attitude.

	Both		Highly risk averse		Low risk averse	
Parameter	Estimate	Std. error	Estimate	Std. error	Estimate	Std. error
Intercept	−2.385[*]	1.81	−42.68	73.0	−0.941	1.85
Age	−0.011	0.03	−0.007	0.05	−0.027	0.04
Race	0.365	0.92	10.51	23.1	−0.227	0.97
Female	−0.215	0.72	−1.015	1.13	0.903	0.94
HigherEd	−0.381	0.67	−0.879	1.00	0.153	1.00
Risk	0.864	0.77				
Wealth	0.021	0.25	4.989[**]	2.83	−0.3312	0.30
Wealth^2	0.007	0.01	−0.185[**]	0.11	0.027[*]	0.02
Likelihood (prob.)	5.62 (0.59)		13.76 (0.03)		5.21 (0.51)	
Wald	4.66 (0.70)		4.07 (0.67)		4.38 (0.62)	

Variable definitions: The dependent variable is a binary variable indicating use of loan financing as a primary source for firm start-up, which takes a value of 1 if the subject started a firm primarily with loan financing and 0 otherwise. *Age* is the age of the subject in years. *Race* is coded as 0 for white and 1 for non-white. *Female* is 0 for male and 1 for female. *HigherEd* is 0 for bachelors or lower and 1 for graduate or professional degrees. *Risk* is the elicited measure of constant relative risk aversion of the entrepreneur. *Wealth* is the log of assets of the entrepreneurial firm, and *Wealth^2* is the square of this term. Highly risk averse are those entrepreneurs with risk levels above the median $r > 0.23$ and low risk averse are those entrepreneurs with risk aversion levels below the median $r < 0.23$ for the data – with means of −0.156 indicating risk loving attitudes. All other variables are defined in Section 2 of the paper.

[*] Statistical significance at the 20% levels.
[**] Statistical significance at the 10% levels.

receiving an SBIR grant, in either case providing a fruitful direction for future research on the gender distribution of these grants.[19]

Regression 3 tests for the importance of risk and wealth on the probability of using earnings from a second job (or salaried job) to finance entrepreneurial entry. In this regression both older entrepreneurs and entrepreneurs with higher levels of risk aversion increase the probability of choosing earnings from a second job as a primary source for start-up funding. Given both the size and statistical significance of the risk coefficient, it is interesting to consider that it is not primarily a lack of wealth but risk aversion that drives taking on a second job to finance firm start-up.

In Table 3 we see that estimates on loans are not statistically significant unless we subset the data by risk attitudes. The fact that wealth is statistically significant in increasing the probability of using a loan to start the firm for highly

---

[19] One would need to compare application and acceptance rates by gender, controlling for all other variables of interest in the grant awarding process.

J.A. Elston, D.B. Audretsch / Journal of Economic Behavior & Organization 76 (2010) 82–89   87

risk averse entrepreneurs indicates that collateral has an important role to play for entrepreneurial financing. We argue that it may in fact serve to counter to some degree, the asymmetries of information associated with these technology intensive firms.[20] These results also indicate that entrepreneurs with higher risk aversion are more likely to be liquidity constrained and to use wealth to obtain loans than those with lower risk aversion – so low that they actually are risk loving. This is interesting because it suggests that lenders may be aware of the higher risk aversion attitudes of these entrepreneurs, and deduce that riskier projects are being presented to them for loan financing, thus resulting in higher collateral requirements (in the form of wealth or assets). These findings are inconsistent with de Meza and Southey (1996) suggestion that highly risk averse entrepreneurs will be driven out of the market because lender's cannot differentiate between risk attitudes and therefore charge a higher amount for financing. In this case, successful highly risk averse entrepreneurs are in the market, they are simply more liquidity constrained than the risk-lovers, and there is differentiation by risk attitude in the importance of wealth on the probability of using loans.[21] Further, these empirical results do not generally support the proposition that the banks' inability to identify entrepreneurial quality leading to excessive bank lending (de Meza and Webb, 1999), our data show that these successful entrepreneurs use other sources, such as earnings from a second job more often than loans, as well as SBIR grants.Unreported estimates indicate an absence of statistical significant for models explaining use of inheritance, gifts, and credit cards, for financing start-ups. There are at least two reasons why these findings do not appear to be significant. First, there was simply not enough observations to run statistical models for inheritance and gifts, and two, the process for determining the funding choice of credit cards for example, was apparently more complex than our data (variables) allowed us to explore. Overall, these results suggest a significant degree of heterogeneity in risk attitudes and financing behavior among entrepreneurs in our study.

5. Conclusions

While the extant literature has generally considered the impact of liquidity constraints on entry, this study seeks to clarify how particular sources of entry are chosen by entrepreneurs based on their levels of inherent levels of wealth and risk attitudes.

Based on data collected from field based experiments complemented with survey data, the empirical evidence provided in this paper suggests that, in fact, both wealth and risk attitude matter, but in different ways depending on the source of funding sought by the entrepreneur. In particular, we find that lower levels of wealth drive the entrepreneur choice for SBIR funding, suggestive that the SBIR grants are in fact a means of alleviating the liquidity constraints of low wealth entrepreneurs.

Conversely, for those financing with earnings from a second job (salaried), it is not wealth but risk aversion that causes individuals to seek this source of financing, which underscores the importance of risk attitudes in the financing choice of the nascent entrepreneur. It is interesting to note that 58% of the firms in the study used earnings from a second job as the primary source of funds for start-up capital – the most common funding source, in contrast to findings for the UK, which found that the most common external funding source (73%) was bank loans (de Meza and Southey, 1996). This finding is interesting because there appears to be little or no discussion in the literature about what role, if any, earnings from a second job may play in UK firm start-ups. More generally, this suggests that country specific institutional differences may also impact funding choices. In other words, capital and labor market differences between the US and UK may also have a role to play in explaining the respective financing choices of nascent entrepreneurs in these countries.

Empirical results also suggest that wealth has a positive impact on the probability of using loan financing to start a firm, confirming that collateral based lending may also be an issue for smaller firms seeking to alleviate liquidity constraints. Further, since this is only the case for the risk averse entrepreneurs in the study, this finding is consistent with the interpretation that creditors may in fact be able to ascertain the entrepreneur's risk attitude, and therefore request higher collateral to fund their firms or projects.

Overall, these findings, suggest that it is important to control for both risk and wealth in explaining the choice of financing for nascent entrepreneurs, and that liquidity constraints are only a partial explanation of financing choices.

Appendix A.

Tables A.1 and A.2.

---

[20] An anonymous referee has suggested that there may be some degree of reverse causality, that increases in loans may also increase wealth. However, any causality in this sense would be indirect, as wealth is measured by value of total assets, and loans is operationalized as a dummy variable, taking on a value of 1 if they were used as a primary source of funding to start the firm.

[21] Hillier (1998) qualifies the de Meza and Southey (1996) proposition to suggest that entrepreneurs may not be credit rationed if they are only optimistic about the probability of success of their firm, rather than holding biased perceptions about estimated firm payoffs. This study does not attempt to control for degree of optimism.

88   *J.A. Elston, D.B. Audretsch / Journal of Economic Behavior & Organization 76 (2010) 82–89*

Table A.1
Random lottery pairs.

ID: X......

Decision	Option A	Option B	Your choice (circle A or B)	
1	$20.00 if throw of die is 1 $16.00 if throw of die is 2–10	$38.50 if throw of die is 1 $1.00 if throw of die is 2–10	A	B
2	$20.00 if throw of die is 1–2 $16.00 if throw of die is 3–10	$38.50 if throw of die is 1–2 $1.00 if throw of die is 3–10	A	B
3	$20.00 if throw of die is 1–3 $16.00 if throw of die is 4–10	$38.50 if throw of die is 1–3 $1.00 if throw of die is 4–10	A	B
4	$20.00 if throw of die is 1–4 $16.00 if throw of die is 5–10	$38.50 if throw of die is 1–4 $1.00 if throw of die is 5–10	A	B
5	$20.00 if throw of die is 1–5 $16.00 if throw of die is 6–10	$38.50 if throw of die is 1–5 $1.00 if throw of die is 6–10	A	B
6	$20.00 if throw of die is 1–6 $16.00 if throw of die is 7–10	$38.50 if throw of die is 1–6 $1.00 if throw of die is 7–10	A	B
7	$20.00 if throw of die is 1–7 $16.00 if throw of die is 8–10	$38.50 if throw of die is 1–7 $1.00 if throw of die is 8–10	A	B
8	$20.00 if throw of die is 1–8 $16.00 if throw of die is 9–10	$38.50 if throw of die is 1–8 $1.00 if throw of die is 9–10	A	B
9	$20.00 if throw of die is 1–9 $16.00 if throw of die is 10	$38.50 if throw of die is 1–9 $1.00 if throw of die is 10	A	B
10	$20.00 if throw of die is 1–10	$38.50 if throw of die is 10	A	B

Decision row chosen by first throw of the die: ......
Throw of the die to determine payment: ......
Earnings: ......

Table A.2
Risk aversion classifications based on lottery choices.

Number of safe choices	Range of relative risk aversion for $U(x) = x^{1-r}/(1-r)$	Risk preference classification
0–1	$r < -0.95$	Highly risk loving
2	$-0.95 < r < -0.49$	Very risk loving
3	$-0.49 < r < -0.15$	Risk loving
4	$-0.15 < r < 0.15$	Risk Neutral
5	$0.15 < r < 0.41$	Slightly risk averse
6	$0.41 < r < 0.68$	Risk averse
7	$0.68 < r < 0.97$	Very risk averse
8	$0.97 < r < 1.37$	Highly risk averse
9–10	$1.37 < r$	Stay in bed

Source: Risk aversion and incentive effects, p. 10 of Holt and Laury (2002).
where r is implicitly defined when switching between 'safe' lottery A and 'riskier' B.

References

Akerlof, G., 1970. The market for lemons: quality uncertainty and the market mechanisms. Quarterly Journal of Economics 84, 488–500.
Berger, A.N., Udell, G.F., 2003. Small business and debt finance. In: Acs, Z., Audretsch, D. (Eds.), Handbook of Entrepreneurship Research. Springer, New York, pp. 299–330.
Caliendo, M., Fossen, F., Kritikos, A., 2009. Risk attitudes of nascent entrepreneurs: new evidence from an experimentally-validated survey. Small Business Economics 32, 153–167.
Cramer, J., Hartog, J., Jonker, N., Van Praag, C., 2002. Low risk aversion encourages the choice for entrepreneurship: an empirical test of a truism. Journal of Economic Behavior and Organization 48, 29–36.
de Meza, D., Southey, C., 1996. The borrower's curse: optimism, finance and entrepreneurship. The Economic Journal 106, 365–386.
de Meza, D., Webb, D.C., 1999. Wealth, enterprise and credit policy. The Economic Journal 109, 153–163.
Douglas, E., Shepherd, D., 2002. Self-employment as a career choice: attitudes, entrepreneurial intentions, and utility maximization. Entrepreneurship Theory and Practice 26, 81–90.
Elston, J.A., Audretsch, D.B., 2010. Financing the entrepreneurial decision: an empirical approach using experimental data on risk attitudes. Forthcoming in Small Business Economics.
Elston, J.A., Harrison, G.W., Rutström, E.E., 2005. Characterizing the entrepreneur using field experiments. Discussion paper, Department of Economics, College of Business Administration, University of Central Florida, http://cebr.dk/upload/harrison.pdf.
Evans, D.S., Leighton, L.S., 1989a. Some empirical aspects of entrepreneurship. American Economic Review 79, 519–535.
Evans, D.S., Leighton, L.S., 1989b. The determinants of changes in U.S. self-employment. Small Business Economics 1, 11–120.
Evans, D.S., Leighton, L.S., 1990. Small business formation by unemployed and employed workers. Small Business Economics 2, 319–330.
Evans, D.S., Jovanovic, B., 1989. An estimated model of entrepreneurial choice under liquidity constraints. Journal of Political Economy 97, 808–827.
Georgellis, Y., Sessions, J., Tsitsianis, N., 2005. Windfalls, wealth, and the transition to self-employment. Small Business Economics 25, 407–428.
Hillier, B., 1998. The borrower's curse: comment. The Economic Journal 108, 1772–1774.
Holt, C.A., Laury, S., 2002. Risk aversion and incentive effects. Andrew Young School of Policy Studies Research Paper Series No. 06-12. Available at SSRN: http://ssrn.com/abstract=893797.
Jaffe, D.M., Russell, T., 1976. Imperfect information, uncertainty and credit rationing. Quarterly Journal of Economics 90, 651–666.
Keh, H.T., Foo, M.D., Lim, B.C., 2002. Opportunity evaluation under risky conditions: the cognitive processes of entrepreneurs. Entrepreneurship Theory and Practice 27, 125–148.
Kan, K.K., Tsai, W.D., 2006. entrepreneurship and risk aversion. Small Business Economics 26, 465–474.

J.A. Elston, D.B. Audretsch / Journal of Economic Behavior & Organization 76 (2010) 82–89   89

Lerner, J., 1999. The government as venture capitalist: the long-run effects of the SBIR program. Journal of Business 72, 285–318.
Link, A., Scott, J., 2010. The government as entrepreneur: evaluating the commercialization success of SBIR projects. Research Policy 39, 589–601.
Palich, L.E., Bagby, D.R., 1995. Using cognitive theory to explain entrepreneurial risk-taking: challenging conventional wisdom. Journal of Business Venturing 10, 425–438.
Parker, S., 2005. The economics of entrepreneurship: what we know and what we don't. Discussion Papers on Entrepreneurship, Growth, and Public Policy #1805, The Max Planck Institute for Research into Economic Systems.
Sarasvathy, S.D., Simon, H.A., Lave, L.B., 1998. Perceiving and managing business risks: differences between entrepreneurs and bankers. Journal of Economic Behavior and Organization 33, 207–226.
Schade, C., 2005. Dynamics, experimental economics, and entrepreneurship. Journal of Technology Transfer 30, 409–431.
Stiglitz, J, Weiss, A., 1981. Credit rationing in markets with imperfect information. American Economic Review 71, 393–410.

Small Bus Econ (2011) 36:209–222
DOI 10.1007/s11187-009-9210-x

Financing the entrepreneurial decision: an empirical approach using experimental data on risk attitudes

Julie A. Elston · David B. Audretsch

Accepted: 11 May 2009 / Published online: 5 June 2009
© Springer Science+Business Media, LLC. 2009

Abstract This paper empirically examines the role of personal capital in the entry decision for US high-technology entrepreneurs. Our innovative approach utilizes both survey data and data from economics-based field experiments, which enables us to elicit and control for the risk attitudes of individual entrepreneurs in the study. Empirical findings suggest that (1) Small Business Innovation Research (SBIR) grants, (2) credit cards, and (3) earnings from a salaried job are among the most important sources of funds for entrepreneurs in their decision to start up a firm. Our findings support Evans and Jovanovic (Journal of Political Economy 97(4):808–827, 1989) in that wealth appears to have a positive impact on the probability of starting up a firm, even when controlling for risk attitudes; however, risk attitudes do not appear to have a strong role to play in the entry decision overall. Policy implications suggest that firm start-ups are dependent on access to capital in both initial and early stages of development, and that government funding, including SBIR grants, is an important source of capital for potential and nascent high-technology entrepreneurs.

Keywords Entry · Experimental data · High-technology entrepreneurs · Liquidity constraints · Personal capital · Risk attitudes · SBIR

JEL Classifications C93 · G32 · L26 · M13

We still know relatively little about the economics behind the use of alternative forms of start-up finance, including family lending, mutual guarantee schemes, and credit card finance. It is possible that these can be useful alternative sources of funds that can help entrepreneurs bypass credit rationing, but presently we do not know the precise extent to which this is the case. (Parker 2005)

1 Financing the entrepreneurial decision: an overview of the literature

In their interviews of randomly selected individuals, Blanchflower and Oswald (1998) found that many of those who were not self-employed, claimed that the primary reason they were not was a shortage of capital. It is clear that even if an individual correctly perceives an entrepreneurial opportunity, he may still be constrained from undertaking the opportunity if there is a lack of capital, collateral, or access to capital markets. The issue of collateral is particularly

J. A. Elston (✉)
Oregon State University, Corvallis, OR, USA
e-mail: julie.elston@osucascades.edu

D. B. Audretsch
Indiana University, Bloomington, IN, USA

binding in the case of high-technology entrepreneurs whose firm assets are predominantly intangible ideas, copyrights, licenses, or patents and thus not conducive to collateral-based lending. Further, because of the relatively complicated nature of many new technologies and innovations, both bankers and the capital markets will have more than the usual asymmetrical informational problems in assessing the risk of firm projects. As Hart and Moore (1994) put it, the threat of default is high for the investors as they cannot prevent entrepreneurs from withdrawing their human capital from a funded project. This is suggestive that access to capital is an important factor to consider in studying the entry decision.

Regarding the role of risk attitudes, conventional wisdom suggests that while entrepreneurs are more likely to be risk takers, there is actually very limited empirical evidence to suggest that risk attitudes impact the entrepreneurial decision. Palich and Bagby (1995) and Keh et al. (2002) both find little or no impact of an individual's risk taking propensity on entrepreneurial decisions. With regard to this study, we argue that risk attitudes may impact not only the individual's entry decision directly, but also indirectly, as access to external sources of funds (different from stock wealth effects) may increase the individual's willingness or ability to start a firm.[1] This suggests the need to control for risk attitudes of entrepreneurs when evaluating the importance of capital constraints on entry.

To date, few of the empirical studies have controlled for risk attitudes when attempting to measure the impact of liquidity constraints on the entry decision, an important issue that is addressed in the design of this study.[2] Further, it is it not well understood to what extent personal finances explain the individual's decision to start a firm.

According to Parker (2005, p. 10), there are three highly influential theoretical models to explain why liquidity constraints become more severe as firm size decreases,[3] which are outlined in Stiglitz and Weiss

(1981), de Meza and Webb (1987) and Evans and Jovanovic (1989). Stiglitz and Weiss (1981) argue that the riskiness of borrowers lead suppliers of capital to limit the quantity of loans; therefore, we can conclude that the inherent risk of entrepreneurial firms or the risk-loving attitudes of those that would pursue them (De Meza and Webb 1987) would lead to credit rationing alone. Another explanation stems from the fact that the amount of information about a firm is generally not neutral with respect to firm size. As Petersen and Rajan (1992, p. 3) observe, "Small and young firms are most likely to face this kind of credit rationing, which is based on asymmetrical information problems."

The role of wealth and the access to capital on the individual's decision to start a firm is unclear in the literature. In their survey article, Georgellis et al. (2005) provide a summary of study results regarding the impact of wealth (mostly inheritance) on the transition to self-employment in the US and UK. This survey finds mixed results with empirical evidence on the impact of inheritance on self-employment negative in 7 of the studies and positive in the other 11 studies. In their own research using data from the *British Household Panel Survey*, they conclude that inheritance raises the probability of transit to self employment, but also reduces the probability of firm survival, providing ample evidence of the presence of significant capital constraints for small entrepreneurs in the UK.

Evans and Jovanovic (1989) provide an approach that uses data from the *National Longitudinal Survey of Young Men* (*NLS*) to examine the role of wealth in the form of assets, wages, and earnings. They find that wealth increases the probability of becoming an entrepreneur, concluding that "...capital is essential for starting a business, and that liquidity constraints tend to exclude those with insufficient funds." Cressy (2000) later argues that as wealth increases, risk

---

[1] By direct effects, we mean that risk-averse individuals may be less likely to leave salaried employment to start their own firm (Parker 2004).

[2] Kan and Tsai (2006) control for risk attitude in their study on the importance of wealth.

[3] Stiglitz and Weiss (1981) argue that as the rate of interest rises, so does the riskiness of borrowers, leading suppliers of

Footnote 3 continued
capital to limit the quantity of loans they make. Most potential lenders have little information on the managerial capabilities or investment opportunities of such firms and are unlikely to be able to screen out poor credit risks or to have control over a borrower's investments. Also if lenders are unable to identify the quality or risk associated with particular borrowers, Jaffe and Russell (1976) show that credit rationing will occur.

aversion decreases, which increases the probability that an individual will become an entrepreneur. He further suggests EJ's results may be biased by the omission of a measure of risk aversion in their model. Kan and Tsai (2006) test this claim using data from the *Panel Study of Income Dynamics* and find that wealth has a positive impact on start-ups even when they control for risk attitudes.

A key contribution of this study is to extend this model to include the impact of other potentially important measures of personal financing on the entry decision, such as personal loans, credit cards, Small Business Innovation Research (SBIR) grants, inheritance, gifts, and earnings from a second job—while controlling for risk attitudes of the individuals. The application of experimental economics methods to elicit risk attitudes of subjects in the field (rather than relying on exclusively self reported data from surveys as most previous studies as have done) is an important contribution for several reasons. First, experimental tasks provide salient rewards to subjects to insure proper measurement of the individuals risk preferences—a crucial component in the study of the entrepreneurial decision.[4] Second, while complementary to previous studies, this particular approach attempts to improve on the inherent limitations on previous studies, which resort to generalizations about high-technology entrepreneurs from data collected either from (1) sampling the general population, (2) entrepreneurs in general, for example pooling data on both restaurateurs and high technology innovators, or (3) relying on campus laboratory experiments conducted on student test subjects.[5]

In short, while the entrepreneurship literature has made great strides in trying to identify the role that personal characteristics play in the entrepreneurial decision, few studies have examined the extent to which other forms of personal financing (besides inheritance or lottery wins) impact this decision controlling for risk attitudes on the part of the

entrepreneur. The development of our model is outlined in the next section.

2 Modeling entrepreneurial choice

To date, the economic growth and entrepreneurship literatures are replete with studies that model this decision as one of income or entrepreneurial choice, focusing on various personal characteristics. Parker (2004) provides a comprehensive survey of theories, empirical models, and recent studies on this topic. Some of the early studies include that of Evans and Leighton (1989a, b, 1990), which links personal characteristics, such as education or experience (which proxy for the ability or skill of the entrepreneur), age, and employment status of almost 4,000 white males to the decision to start a firm in the US. Other studies, such as those of Bates (1990) and Blanchflower and Meyer (1994), emphasize human capital in the entrepreneurial choice. An important insight by Douglas and Shepherd (2002) was that the intention to become an entrepreneur is stronger for individuals with more positive risk attitudes, suggesting that empirical models of entry should control for risk attitudes.[6] Therefore, we start with a benchmark model of the entrepreneurial decision controlling for age, race, gender, education, wealth, and risk preferences.[7] We can then explicitly evaluate the impact of individual risk attitudes on the decision to start a firm, reasoning that decreases in risk aversion should increase the probability of an individual starting a firm. The corresponding refutable hypothesis is:

---

[4] Salient rewards refer to an experimental design where the payoffs increase with performance in order to induce subject behavior consistent real world competitive environments. Although for smaller payouts as in this study, this appears to be less of an issue (Holt and Laury 2002).

[5] Use of experimental data by design does involve using not a random sample of the general population.

---

[6] Their study uses survey data from 300 Australian students to measure risk preferences from responses to questions regarding hypothetical preferences for salary (low risk) versus performance-based bonuses (high risk).

[7] If wealthier individuals have an easier time starting a firm then a positive relationship between wealth and the probability of starting a firm is evidence in itself that there are liquidity constraints (Evans and Jovanovic 1989, p. 819). In the absence of data on individual wealth before starting the firm, we use assets of the nascent firm as a proxy to measure and control for wealth effects—per Evans and Jovanovic (1989). This measure is consistent with the fact that there is often little distinction between personal wealth and the assets of the young entrepreneurial firm. In fact, from a lender's perspective, the corporate veil is indeed thin for new firms, with owner's personal assets often being used as collateral for firm loans.

Hypothesis 1   *Decreases in risk aversion lead to an increased probability that an individual will start a firm.*

$$Entry_j = \beta_0 + \beta 1 Demo_j + \beta 2 Ability_j + \beta 3 Wealth_j + \beta 4 CRRA_j + \varepsilon_j$$

$$(1)$$

This basic model (1) is then modified to include liquidity measures/sources of funds available to the potential entrepreneur,[8] demographic control variables, measures of individual ability, and additionally the potential impact of different sources of personal liquidity and government funding. These liquidity sources include inheritance, gifts, credit cards, earnings from a second job, SBIR grants, and private loans, allowing us to formally we test the following hypothesis regarding the potential impact of personal capital on the entry decision for the high-technology entrepreneur.

Hypothesis 2   *Having received at least one SBIR increases the probability of starting a firm.*

Hypothesis 3   *Funds from use of Credit Cards increase the probability of starting a firm.*

Hypothesis 4   *Having a salaried or second job increases the probability of starting a firm.*

Hypothesis 5   *Having received an inheritance or gift increases the probability of starting a firm.*

Hypotheses 2–5 articulate the impact of these various measures of personal capital or liquidity on the decision to start a firm. It is important to note that SBIR grants can be applied for before or after starting a firm, and by full-time, part-time, and/or salaried non-entrepreneurs alike. Some use the award as an impetus to start a firm, while others like university faculty, for example, may apply without the intention of leaving salaried employment. In larger organizations, often times salaried research staff are applicants for SBIR grants on behalf of the firm.[9]

---

[8] While the interdisciplinary literature on entrepreneurship refers to the process of starting a firm as: firm start-up, entry, the entrepreneurial decision, the entry decision, self-employment, etc., we will hereinafter use the term *entry* to denote this process.

[9] From discussions with entrepreneurs, we found that for accounting and tax reasons, some entrepreneurs chose to take

The modified model builds on previous studies by extending the standard specification to include new sources of initial start-up capital in a measure for firm liquidity constraints *LC*1, and a measure of the individual's risk preferences *CRRA*[10]: Thus, our modified entry model can be specified:

$$Entry_j = \beta_0 + \beta 1 Demo_j + \beta 2 Ability_j + \beta 3 Wealth_j + \beta 4 CRRA_j + \beta 5 LC1_j + \varepsilon$$

$$(2)$$

where *Entry$_j$* is the probability of starting an entrepreneurial firm for individual *j*; *Demo* is a matrix of demographic variables to control for individual effects of age, gender, and race characteristics of the subject. The level of education of person j is used as a proxy for entrepreneurial talent or *Ability$_j$*. *CRRA$_j$* is a measure of the individual's attitude towards risk taking under the assumption of constant relative risk aversion.[11] *Wealth* is measured by the log of total assets—an indicator of the importance of initial wealth of the potential entrepreneur—log transformed to control for variance in the data. We assert that since these entrepreneurial firms are young, their assets are a good proxy for the wealth of the entrepreneurs, who in these cases are the owners of the firm.[12] Estimates show that the assets of the entrepreneurial firm were far more statistically significant than household income as an indicator of the probability of starting a firm. *LC*1$_j$ is a matrix of variables that measure the individual's access to capital, which includes: inheritance, gifts, credit

---

Footnote 9 continued

their compensation in the form of a salary. In examining the data, there were two cases in which salaried part-time entrepreneurs received SBIR grants and five cases where full-time entrepreneurs were recipients.

[10] See Elston et al. (2005) for details on the series of experimental tasks that generated this data.

[11] In fact we elicit individual CRRA intervals rather than use ones predicted by statistical models, so the CRRA measures are not subject to sampling error in this context.

[12] Empirical studies use different measures to proxy for the importance of wealth. For example, Evans and Jovanovic (1989) use assets, wages, and earnings as proxies for individual wealth. Kan and Tsai (2006) use personal assets, and Georgellis et al. (2005) rely on the reported inheritance of individuals.

cards, earnings from another job, SBIR grants, and private loans. Since these sources are highly correlated within and across firm life stages and among each other, we test the respective hypothesis with separate regressions to avoid introducing multi-collinearity into our estimates.[13] The one exception is the liquidity measure credit cards, which is not correlated with wealth, so we include regression results for credit cards both with and without wealth or *Log(Assets)* in Table 3.

We also asked subjects if they had either (1) ever experienced a capital shortage with their firm or (2) were currently experiencing a shortage of capital, in order to evaluate the impact of various sources of capital on the early developmental stage of the firm. In particular we wanted to evaluate the firm's use of internal (cash flow from operations) versus external funds (credit cards, private loans, government grants, and loans, equity). We formalize this test of the importance of cash flow in reducing current capital shortages of the firm as:

Hypothesis 6 *Private sources of capital reduce the probability of current firm shortages of capital.*

Hypothesis 6 tests the significance of various sources of financing in reducing the firm's *current* shortage of capital, which speak to the importance of access to capital for reducing the firm liquidity constraints associated with the early growth stage of firm development. Our capital shortage equation is specified:

$$CapShortage_j = \beta_0 + \beta1Demo_j + \beta2Ability_j \\ + \beta3CRRA_j + \beta4Wealth_j + \beta5LC2_j \\ + e_j$$
(3)

Our models specified in Eqs. 1–3 will then be estimated in order to provide empirical evidence to support or refute the importance of each of these hypotheses regarding the importance of various sources of personal financing sources for the entrepreneur. Because the sources of funding available to the entrepreneur vary over time, our measures $LC1_j$ and $LC2_j$ do as well. This reflects that fact that later

stage (relatively older) firms have access to different sources, such as equity capital and cash flow from operations.

3 Data

3.1 Field data, survey data and variable definitions

3.1.1 Field data

The field experiments were conducted in April and November 2004 at two of the bi-annual SBIR national conferences. Our field data were collected from a booth set up in the exhibitor's area of the conferences. The subjects, who later would choose to participate in a series of paid experimental tasks, were first asked to complete a survey of firm and individual characteristics.

An important contribution of our approach is the ability to both measure and control for individual risk attitudes of subjects by compiling data through a series of field experiments, detailed in Elston et al. (2005). From this study, we combine the experimental data on individual risk attitudes with the survey data to analyze the entry decision controlling for risk attitudes and liquidity. We recognize this is not a sample of the general population; that was not our intention. It does allow us to test and control for the importance of risk attitudes on the decision to start a firm for high-technology entrepreneurs, which is not possible with survey data alone. This field approach is also preferable to the common practice of using students to proxy for the decision making of real life entrepreneurs because it allows us to capture more precisely the decision-making process of the high-technology entrepreneur.

3.1.2 Sample selection

It is important to note that when we study a specific field population of interest—high technology entrepreneurs in this case—this in itself does not constitute selection bias. Selection bias is a statistical sampling problem for which it is not sufficient to establish that there has been selection. Rather, one must establish

---

[13] Since our experiments were one shot, we do not have the option of lagging variables over time to control for the potential endogeneity of independent variables.

that the quantity of interest (access to capital) is systematically different in the sample (high technology entrepreneurs attending the conferences) than in the entire population of interest—all high technology entrepreneurs—in order to establish that selection bias has taken place. We argue that in the worst case, having previously received an SBIR award, it is actually *less likely* that one would attend another SBIR conference (which provides seminars on how to get an award), so that any empirical results indicating significance of the SBIR award would tend to be underestimated in our empirical results.

3.1.3 Survey data

In addition to the field experiments we also collected survey data from a total of 182 individuals. Responses to the questionnaires allowed us to stratify the sample into Entrepreneurs (E) and Non-Entrepreneurs (NE).[14] We classify 44% of these as entrepreneurs since they reported self-employment status and income. Thus, we have information on a total of 80 Es and 92 NEs. In each case we required that individuals provide information on the nature of their entrepreneurial firm before we classified them as an entrepreneur, while NE includes potential entrepreneurs. All subsequent analyses in this study use either data collected on entrepreneurs only (both part-time and full-time) or the whole sample, which includes non-entrepreneurs.[15]

3.1.4 Measuring risk aversion

Our measure of risk aversion is derived from experiments that employ expected utility theory and multiple price lists to elicit risk preferences of subjects.[16] In brief, we apply a constant relative risk aversion

characterization of utility, employing an interval regression model. The dependent variable in the interval regression model is the CRRA interval that subjects implicitly choose when they switch from lottery A to lottery B in a ten-decision lottery matrix. For each row of the lottery matrix, one can calculate the implied bounds on the CRRA coefficient, and thus a measure of risk aversion can be calculated for each subject in the study. The CRRA utility of each lottery prize y is defined as: $U(y) = (y^{1-r})/(1-r)$ where r is the CRRA coefficient.[17] In this context, $r = 0$ denotes risk neutral behavior, $r > 0$ denotes risk averse behavior, and $r < 0$ denotes a risk lover. We found that most of the subjects were risk averse with a mean $r = 0.25$ and that the E group was less risk averse on average than the NE group. The entrepreneurs in the study average 44 years of age, are 34% female, and 49% have completed at least some higher education. We also found that they were more likely to be Asian (13 vs. 5%) and had a higher income (48 vs. 42%) than the NEs.

Our entrepreneurship data are representative of US high-technology entrepreneurs rather than entrepreneurs in general, with the number of individuals describing their primary self-employment business as engineering or business technology related (47), software or information technology (22), medical or university (9), and other (2). In contrast, the non-entrepreneurs reported employment in mostly other sectors of the economy including: engineering or business technology (12), software or information technology (2), medical or university (5), goverment (16), and other (64)—which included food, textiles, and retail.

3.1.5 Descriptive statistics

Responses to questions on sources of funding are summarized in Appendix A, with key variables presented in Graphs 1 and 2. Graph 1 suggests that most entrepreneurs, 84%, reported having experienced a shortage of capital at some time, with another 48% reporting that they are currently experiencing liquidity constraints, which underscores the potential

---

[14] In a related study on part-time entrepreneurs, Levesque and Schade (2005) examine how entrepreneurs divide time between working a wage job and working in their newly formed firm.

[15] Entrepreneurs who also held salaried positions outside of their entrepreneurial firm are still classified as entrepreneurs as opposed to salaried non-entrepreneurs; in estimations we found that if we pool the two types of entrepreneurs, the data simply exhibit a wider variance in risk attitudes.

[16] For details, see Elston et al. (2005).

[17] Note when $r = 1$, $U(y) = \ln(y)$.

importance of including these factors in studying entrepreneurial decision making.

GRAPH 1

Have you ever experienced a shortage of capital?

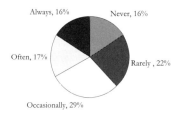

GRAPH 2

How did you primarily finance your firm's start-up?

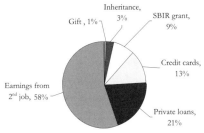

Source: All charts are based on own calculations

Focusing on the start-up phase of the entrepreneurial firm, Graph 2 shows that inheritance (3%) and gifts (1%) are not as frequent as some studies have found to be the case in the UK (Blanchflower and Oswald 1998). Our interpretation is that perhaps inheritance is less common in the US, or at least does not drive entrepreneurship in the high-technology arena. We speculate that since these entrepreneurs report working predominantly in the high-technology sector, perhaps other factors, such as education and skills, may be more important than inheritance in determining the decision to start a firm. Supporting this conclusion is the fact that earnings from another job (58%) are a common way that these entrepreneurs secure funding to start up

their firm.[18] Private loans from individuals and banks are also an important source of funds, as are, to a lesser degree, credit cards. When asked how they finance the firm currently, 74% responded cash flow from operations, which is consistent with the well-known financing hierarchy structure of most firms—that is, most firms prefer to use less expensive internal funds over more costly external capital. Of course, these findings are only suggestive, and we need to control for other factors in a regression context to determine their degree of importance.

Government loans and grants appear to have an important role in both the start-up and early growth phases of these firms. When asked how the firm is funded today, 56% reported that government support was important versus 20% for equity capital—a somewhat surprising result given the size and liquidity of US equity markets, although again these are relatively young firms. A relatively large number of these entrepreneurs have applied for, 34%, and received, 20%, government support in the form of SBIR grants, which speaks positively about both the public awareness and potential importance of this small business program for funding firm start-ups. This finding is consistent with national data analyzed by Branscomb and Auerswald (2002), who estimate that the federal government provides 20–25% of all funds for early stage technology development in the US.

While this data speaks to the potential importance of these sources of funding, the statistical significance of these sources on the entry decision are calculated by estimating our Probit equation controlling for risk attitudes and demographic factors.

3.1.6 Variable definitions

In Table 1 we list the key variable definitions with descriptive statistics. Explanatory variables are grouped into general variables of interest, those relating to sources of financing used specifically in the start-up phase of the firm, and finally sources of financing that are currently used to grow the entrepreneurial firm. Since the last two groups refer to

---

[18] One can speculate that since secondary jobs are generally less common in Europe that this may negatively impact the ability of Europeans entrepreneurs to finance new firms.

Table 1 Key variable descriptions

Variable	Variable description	Mean	SD
General			
Entry	1 If the subject started a firm and 0 otherwise	0.44	0.50
Age	Age of subject in years	42.87	12.52
Race	1 if non-Caucasian and 0 otherwise	1.64	1.70
Female	1 if gender is female and 0 otherwise	0.36	0.50
HigherEd	1 if terminal degree is graduate or professional; and 0 for a bachelors degree or less. The median education level is bachelors	5.37	0.90
CRRA	Measure of the individual's degree of risk aversion	0.25	0.43
Log(Assets)	Log of the assets of the entrepreneurial firm	4.26	8.86
Lassets2	Square of the log of assets of the entrepreneurial firm		
CapShortage	1 if currently experiencing a shortage of capital; 0 otherwise	0.91	0.85
SBIR-rec	1 if received an SBIR grant; 0 if not	1.08	0.95
Inc	Estimated annual household income from 10 categories: (1) $25K or under, (2) $25–$45K, (3) $45–$65K, (4) $65–$85K, (5) $85–$100K, etc.... (10) over $200K	4.98	2.23
LC1 variables: primary sources of start-up capital as % total			
Inherit	Inheritance reported as a primary source	2.01	14.09
Gift	Gifts were reported as a primary source	0.33	4.07
CCards	Credit cards were reported as a primary source	3.69	14.81
2nd Job	Earnings from a second job were reported as a primary source	21.93	39.86
SBIR	SBIR grant reported as a primary source	3.53	17.17
Private	Loans from an individual or bank reported as a primary source	11.01	29.64
Other	Other sources (possibly lottery or gambling income) reported as a primary source	22.57	40.69
LC2 variables: current source of firm funding as % of total capital			
Gov't	Includes all government loans or grants including SBIR	11.27	28.21
Private	Loans from bank or private persons reported as a current source	5.78	16.72
CCards	Credit cards reported as a current source	1.81	6.19
2nd Job	Earnings from a second job reported as a current source	12.88	30.12
CF	Cash flow from operations reported as a current source	28.54	39.77
Equity	Equity capital reported as a current source	6.29	18.29
Other	Other sources (possibly as lottery or gambling income) reported as a current source	7.16	22.85

financing at different stages of firm development, they allow us to distinguish the importance of different sources of capital on firm start-up and subsequent firm development and growth stages.

4 Empirical results

Table 2 lists Probit estimates for entry by subject demographic, risk attitude, and wealth—as measured by the log of total assets. Generally, the demographic variables become less important in predicting *Entry* once we control for risk attitudes and wealth, both of which are statistically significant. In column 1, the measure of risk or *CRRA* is large, negative and statistically significant, indicating that higher levels of risk aversion reduce the probability of entry or starting up a firm. This finding is important because it provides some of the first empirical evidence (which supports intuition) that individual risk attitudes—specifically risk aversion—reduces the probability that an individual will choose to start up a firm.

Table 2 Logit estimations of firm entry controlling for: demographic characteristics, risk attitude (CRRA), and wealth

Parameter	1		2		3	
	Estimate	t-stat	Estimate	t-stat	Estimate	t-stat
Intercept	−0.314	−0.23	−0.282	−0.37	−0.329	−0.50
Age	0.036	1.36	0.019	1.19	0.203	1.60
Race	1.017	1.42	−0.538	−1.18	−0.679	−1.61
Female	−0.819	−1.30	−0.234	−0.67	−0.206	−0.65
HigherEd	−0.503	−0.83	−0.409	−1.21	−0.303	−0.95
CRRA	−1.452**	−1.97	−0.158	−0.41		
Log(Assets)	0.551***	5.89				
Lassets2	−0.034***	−4.29				
Likelihood (p)	104.71 (0.0001)		3.99 (0.5511)		5.05 (0.2864)	
Wald (p)	46.90 (0.0001)		3.86 (0.5590)		4.88 (0.2997)	

Estimations on potential and nascent entrepreneurs. Dependent variable is *Entry*, which takes on a value of 1 if subject started up a firm and 0 otherwise. *Age* is the age of the subject in years. *Race* is coded as 0 for white and 1 for non-white. *Female* is 0 for male and 1 for female. *HigherEd* is 0 for bachelors or lower and 1 for graduate or professional degrees. *CRRA* is the elicited measure of constant relative risk aversion of the subject. *Log(Assets)* is the log of assets of the entrepreneurial firm that measures individual wealth, and *Lassets2* is the square of this term. (*), (**), and (***) denote statistical significance at the 10, 5, and 1% levels, respectively

It is interesting to note that the smaller and almost significant effects of race and gender found in the reduced model data both disappear when we add measures of risk attitudes and wealth, which suggests it may be important to control for these demographic characteristics, even if they are not of great import in predicting entry itself.[19] Overall, our evidence is also consistent with findings of Kan and Tsai (2006), which find that risk aversion has a negative impact on the entry decision even when we control for wealth, which supports Hypothesis 1—*Decreases in individual risk aversion lead to an increased probability that an individual would start a firm.*

Since the correlation matrix of key variables listed in Appendix B indicates that assets and liquidity sources were highly positively correlated, as we might expect, we entered these sources of financing separately in our model as reflected in Table 3. The only exception was credit cards, which were not correlated with wealth; thus, Table 3 has models that

test for the importance of *CCards* both with and without wealth effects in the model. In Table 3 estimates, *SBIR-rec* is both economically and statistically an important indicator of entry, supporting Hypothesis 2—*Having received at least one SBIR grant increases the probability of starting a firm.* This finding is consistent with national data on SBIR recipients, which indicates that almost 40% of individuals who received an SBIR award stated they would either (1) definitely not or (2) probably not or (3) might not have undertaken their research project in the absence of the SBIR award.[20] The statistical significance of the SBIR on entry is not due to the fact that the data were gathered at a SBIR conference; in fact, only seven individuals in our entry sample had actually received an SBIR award in the past, much fewer than those who received other types of funding from other sources, such as credit cards, loans, and earnings from a second job, which were statistically less significant.

Estimates indicate that *CCards* and earnings from a *2nd Job* were small but significant sources of capital for firm start-ups, thus providing support for Hypothesis 3—*Funds from Credit Cards increase the*

---

[19] An alternative interpretation is that while neither Race nor Age are statistically significant, they are *almost significant* in the model without control variables, which may indicate that the age of the entrepreneur has a potentially positive impact and being non-Caucasian has a potentially negative impact on the probability of starting a firm.

[20] Wessner (2002).

Table 3 Logit estimations of firm entry controlling for: demographic characteristics, risk attitude (CRRA), and personal sources of liquidity

Parameter	1		2		3		4		5	
	SBIR-rec		2nd Job		Inherit		CCards		CCards	
	Estimate	t-stat	Estimate	t-stat	Estimate	t-stat	Estimate	t-stat	Estimate	t-stat
Intercept	−2.984	−2.82	−1.726	−1.72	−1.72	−2.83	−2.598	−2.44	−3.156	−2.46
Age	0.023	1.08	0.026	1.23	0.027	1.19	0.008	0.37	0.037	1.52
Race	0.699	1.23	0.482	0.80	0.979	1.66	0.071	0.12	−0.624	−0.90
Female	−0.211	−0.43	−0.351	−0.73	−0.128	−0.26	−0.724	−1.43	0.022	0.04
HigherEd	−0.335	−0.69	−0.695	−1.48	−0.386	−0.81	−0.099	−0.20	0.022	0.04
CRRA	−0.740	−1.32	−0.172	−0.33	−0.204	−0.38	−0.817	−1.45	−0.634	−1.03
SBIR-rec	2.106***	6.80								
2nd Job			0.046***	3.73						
Inheritance					0.021	1.63				
Credit-Cards							0.039*	1.70	0.038*	1.75
Log(Assets)									0.889***	5.18
LAssets2									−0.044***	−3.92
Likelihood (p)	86.96 (0.0001)		55.07 (0.0001)		21.37 (0.0010)		86.56 (0.0001)		100.06 (0.0001)	
Wald	46.21 (0.0001)		21.66 (0.0029)		18.24 (0.0057)		48.18 (0.0001)		53.84 (0.0001)	

Estimations on potential and nascent entrepreneurs. Variable definitions: the dependent variable is *Entry*, a binary variable that takes on a value of 1 if the subject started a firm and 0 otherwise. *Age* is the age of the subject in years. *Race* is coded as 0 for white and 1 for non-white. *Female* is 0 for male and 1 for female. *HigherEd* is 0 for bachelors or lower and 1 for graduate or professional degrees. *CRRA* is the elicited measure of constant relative risk aversion of the subject. *Log(Assets)* is the log of assets of the entrepreneurial firm that measures individual wealth, and *LAssets2* is the square of this term. Using LC1 data on primary sources of capital used to start firm: *SBIR-rec* is a binary variable that takes a value of 1 if the firm had received an SBIR grant and 0 otherwise. *Credit-Cards* takes on a value of 1 if the subject indicated that credit cards were a primary source of start-up capital for the firm and 0 otherwise. *2nd Job* refers to earnings from another job that was identified as an important source for start-up capital for entrepreneurs. *Inheritance* takes on a value of 1 if the subject indicated that inheritance or gift was a primary source of start-up capital for the firm and 0 otherwise. All other variables (demographic) are defined in Sect. 3 of the paper. (*), (**), and (***) denote statistical significance at the 10, 5, and 1% levels, respectively

probability of starting a firm, and since the finding on the significance of *CCards* is present whether we control for wealth effects or not, see regressions 4a and 4b; so this is a particularly robust result. Earnings from a second job are also positive and statistically significant, providing evidence to support Hypothesis 4—*Having a Second Job increases the probability of starting a firm*. Results indicate that neither inheritance nor gifts were statistically significant in predicting entrepreneurial entry for high-technology entrepreneurs; thus, we find no support for Hypothesis 5—*Having received an Inheritance or Gift increases the probability of starting a firm.*[21] In

non-reported results, neither loans nor other sources of capital were statistically significant in predicting entry.

Table 4 contains Probit estimates testing whether various sources of funding (LC2: government loans, private loans, credit cards, earnings from a 2nd job, equity, cash flow from operations, and having received an SBIR grant) reduce the probability of current capital shortages for entrepreneurs. Regressions were run only on data from entrepreneurs. In regression 1 estimates are reported from a backward stepwise regression with the inclusion criteria set at 10% with all possible financing sources in the model (but controlling for all demographic variables). We note that *SBIR* grants or *SBIR-rec* is statistically significant and negative in both regressions, indicating that receiving an SBIR reduces the likelihood of

---

[21] The data on gifts and inheritance were pooled into one variable because there were too few observations on gifts.

Table 4 Logit estimations on *Is your firm currently experiencing a capital shortage?*

Parameter	1		2	
	Estimate	*t*-stat	Estimate	*t*-stat
Intercept	0.619	0.55	1.978	2.13
CRRA	−0.178	0.29		
Age	−0.018	0.65		
Race	0.295	0.41		
Female	0.203	0.35		
HigherEd	0.822	1.48		
SBIR-rec	−0.019*	1.67	−0.039*	1.77
Cash flow			−0.024*	1.69
Likelihood (p)	6.93 (0.4364)		6.37 (0.0413)	
Wald (p)	5.95 (0.5454)		4.59 (0.1004)	

Model estimated on Entrepreneurs only. Variable definitions: the dependent variable *Shortnow* is a binary variable that takes on a value of 1 if the entrepreneur responded that s/he has a current shortage of capital and 0 otherwise. *Age* is the age of the subject in years. *Race* is coded as 0 for white and 1 for non-white. *Female* is 0 for male and 1 for female. *HigherEd* is 0 for bachelors or lower terminal degrees and 1 for graduate or professional degrees. *CRRA* is the elicited measure of constant relative risk aversion of the subject using LC2 on current sources of funding for firm. *SBIR-rec* is a binary variable that takes on a value of 1 if the entrepreneur received an SBIR grant and 0 otherwise. *Cash flow* is cash flow from firm operations. Regression 1 estimates the model controlling only for demographic effects and risk attitude, while regression 2 includes only those variables statistically significant at the 10% level or higher. (*), (**), and (***) denote statistical significance at the 10, 5, and 1% levels, respectively

experiencing a shortage of capital. No other sources of funding were found to be significant in the model at the 10% level in reducing the current capital shortage. In the second model, we did not control for any demographic variables in the model. Results in regression 2 of Table 4 reveal that *Cash flow* from operations and *SBIR-rec* are both statistically significant at the 10% level. Therefore, we find weak support for Hypothesis 6—*Private sources of capital, that is specifically cash flow from operations and having received an SBIR grant, reduce the probability of current firm shortages of capital.*

5 Conclusions

This study provides insight into the entry decision of high-technology entrepreneurs in the US, which have

been an economically important source of innovation and growth in the US during the last 2 decades.

We find that capital constraints are problematic for high-technology entrepreneurs, negatively impacting the probability of firm start-up. While empirical results are consistent with previous studies on the importance of wealth in the entry decision, we find that the additional measures of personal liquidity are also significant in predicting entry. Specifically SBIR grants are found to be an important source of funds for improving the probability of entry for high-technology entrepreneurs, dominating all other sources of personal capital in the study. From an industrial policy perspective, this suggests that the SBIR program may be money well spent in terms of policy goals to increase the probability of new high-technology start-ups.

Once the firm is established and growing, SBIR grants dominate as an important source of funds for reducing the probability of a capital shortage—a finding that is robust to model specification. In context, our findings suggest that when the firm has more alternative sources of funds, including cash from operations, loans, and equity, it prefers to use cash flow from operations and SBIR rather than other sources of external funds. This is broadly consistent with the well-established preferences of firms for use of internal over external funds. It is important to note that this finding does not support the notion of "SBIR mills"—firms who subsist predominantly from SBIR grants rather than from firm income derived from successfully developing and commercializing new technologies.

Contrary to findings of previous studies, including Blanchflower and Meyer (1994), our results provide evidence that gifts and inheritance are not important indicators of entry—at least for our sample of US high-technology entrepreneurs. Our interpretation of this finding is that our data, unlike the large national survey panels, represent more accurately one type of entrepreneur—the high-technology entrepreneur—whose path to entry is less likely to be predicted by chance gifts or inheritance, but more likely by deterministic factors, such as education and skill-based sources of financing, like grant writing—e.g., SBIR grants.

We also found little evidence that risk attitudes were important in predicting entry; risk attitudes were only significant when wealth was included but access to capital was excluded from the entry model. This suggests that risk attitudes may not be as important in the entry decision as many have thought, indicative that the distribution of risk attitudes may be similar between entrepreneur and non-entrepreneur groups. This is consistent with earlier findings from Elston et al. (2005), which found that these same entrepreneurs were not risk loving; rather, they appeared to be only somewhat less risk averse than their non-entrepreneurial peers. These findings are also consistent with those of Palich and Bagby (1995) and Keh et al. (2002), which found little difference in risk propensity measures between entrepreneurs and non-entrepreneurs.

One caveat of our study is that results may or may not be easy to generalize to all entrepreneurs; the trade-off is that it does provide a better understanding of the importance of financing sources on the entry decision of US *high-technology entrepreneurs*—an economically and strategically important group about which we understand too little.

These findings suggest a number of directions for future research. Our study on the importance of sources of financing is neither exhaustive nor complete; many other sources may be important, in particular for the growth stage of the firm—including angel or venture capital financing. Future studies may also be warranted to better examine the impact of the broad spectrum of governmental support in funding the firm. The Small Business Administration, for example, has a number of programs in addition to the SBIR that support firm start-up and development, including the Small Business Technology Transfer (STTR) program, a variety of loan programs, surety bond guarantees, as well as various training programs to support small business development.

In addition, it is interesting to note our study's finding on the importance of a second salaried job on the individual's decision to start a firm. This model is less common in Europe and other places, and suggests that from a policy perspective it may be interesting to consider how impediments to holding a secondary job inhibit entry and innovation of small firms in Europe.

Acknowledgements We are grateful to Maria Minniti and Christian Schade for discussions on the material contained in this study. Elston thanks the Ewing Marion Kauffman Foundation for research support under grant no. 20070378.

Appendix A

See Table 5.

Table 5 Summary of responses to key questions on the importance of personal capital sources for the entry decision

Have you ever experienced a shortage of capital in running your firm?	
Never	16%
Rarely	22%
Occasionally	29%
Often	17%
Always	16%
	100%
Do you have a shortage of capital now?	
Yes	48%
No	52%
Gift	1%
Inheritance	3%
SBIR grant	9%
Credit cards	13%
Private loans	21%
Earnings from second job	58%
Have you ever received an SBIR grant?	
Yes	34%
No	66%
How do you finance your firm now as a %?	
Credit cards	31%
Private loans	29%
Equity capital	20%
Other	33%
Government	56%
Earnings from second job	29%
Cash from operations	74%

Percentages taken from responses from 80 entrepreneurs who participated in the experiments and survey. Government includes grants or loans. Private loans include those from individuals and banks

Appendix B

See Table 6.

Table 6 Correlation matrix

Correlation matrix of key variables

	Entre	CRRA	CapShort	Funding source for start-up phase only (LC1)						SBIR-rec	Funding source for current operations (LC2)						Assets
				Inherit	Gift	CCards	2nd Job	SBIR	Private		Gov't	Private	CCards	2nd Job	CF	Equity	
Entre	1																
CRRA	−0.05	1															
CapShort	0.63***	0.09	1														
Inherit	0.06	0.04	0.17**	1													
Gift	0.08	0.06	0.01	−0.01	1												
CCards	0.22***	−0.08	0.09	−0.03	.	1											
2nd Job	0.48***	0.03	0.38***	−0.07	0.06	−0.01	1										
SBIR	0.212**	−0.06	0.19*	−0.02	−0.01	−0.04	−0.08	1									
Private	0.22***	0.07	0.27***	−0.04	−0.03	0.01	−0.14**	−0.05	1								
SBIR-rec	0.68***	0.09	0.85***	0.13**	0.07	0.18*	0.45***	0.04	0.23***	1							
Govt	0.11	0.1	0.23***	−0.05	−0.03	−0.03	−0.16*	0.35***	0.05	0.20***	1						
Private	0.27***	−0.14**	0.16**	−0.04	−0.02	0.11	0.05	−0.06	0.48***	0.24***	0.04	1					
CCards	0.23***	0.01	0.13	−0.03	−0.02	0.49***	0.06	−0.01	0.19*	0.23***	−0.01	0.16*	1				
2nd Job	0.34***	−0.05	0.24***	−0.01	0.26***	0.04	0.53***	0.07	−0.08	0.34***	−0.12	−0.02	−0.02	1			
CF	0.48***	0.12	0.56***	0.18*	−0.05	0.19*	0.32***	−0.09	0.18	0.49***	−0.17*	−0.08	0.10	−0.15*	1		
Equity	0.17**	0.03	0.20***	−0.04	−0.02	−0.04	0.04	0.16*	0.1	0.23***	0.06	0.03	0.00	−0.02	−0.02	1	
Assets	0.65***	−0.01	0.67***	0.16**	−0.07	0.12	0.26***	0.15	0.35***	0.67***	0.28***	0.33***	0.16**	0.11	0.46***	0.27***	1

(*), (**), and (***) denote statistical significance at the 10, 5, and 1% levels, respectively

References

Bates, T. (1990). Entrepreneur human capital inputs and small business longevity. *The Review of Economics and Statistics, 72*(4), 551–559.

Blanchflower, D. G., & Meyer, B. (1994). A longitudinal analysis of young entrepreneurs in Australia and the United States. *Small Business Economics, 6*(1), 1–20.

Blanchflower, D. G., & Oswald, A. G. (1998). What makes an entrepreneur? *Journal of Labor Economics, 16,* 26–60.

Branscomb, L. M., & Auerswald, P. A. (2002). *Between invention and innovation: An analysis of funding for early-stage technology development.* NIST GCR 02-841 (p. 23). Gaithersburg, MD: NIST.

Cressy, R. (2000). Credit rationing or entrepreneurial aversion? An alternative explanation for the Evans and Jovanovic finding. *Economic Letters, 66,* 235–240.

de Meza, D., & Webb, D. C. (1987). Too much investment: A problem of asymmetric information. *Quarterly Journal of Economics, 102,* 281–292.

Douglas, E., & Shepherd, D. (2002). Self-employment as a career choice: Attitudes, entrepreneurial intentions, and utility maximization. *Entrepreneurship Theory and Practice, 26,* 81–90.

Elston, J. A., Harrison, G., & Rutström, E. E. (2005). *Characterizing the entrepreneur using field experiments.* Discussion paper, Department of Economics, College of Business Administration, University of Central Florida. http://cebr.dk/upload/harrison.pdf.

Evans, D. S., & Jovanovic, B. (1989). An estimated model of entrepreneurial choice under liquidity constraints. *Journal of Political Economy, 97*(4), 808–827.

Evans, D. S., & Leighton, L. S. (1989a). Some empirical aspects of entrepreneurship. *American Economic Review, 79*(3), 519–535.

Evans, D. S., & Leighton, L. S. (1989b). The determinants of changes in U.S. self-employment. *Small Business Economics, 1*(2), 11–120.

Evans, D. S., & Leighton, L. S. (1990). Small business formation by unemployed and employed workers. *Small Business Economics, 2*(4), 319–330.

Georgellis, Y., Sessions, J., & Tsitsianis, N. (2005). Windfalls, wealth, and the transition to self-employment. *Small Business Economics, 25,* 407–428.

Hart, O., & Moore, J. (1994). A theory of debt based on the inalienability of human capital. *The Quarterly Journal of Economics, 109*(4), 841–879.

Holt, C. A., & Laury, S. K. (2002). Risk aversion and incentive effects. *The American Economic Review, 92,* 1644–1655.

Jaffe, D. M., & Russell, T. (1976). Imperfect information, uncertainty and credit rationing. *Quarterly Journal of Economics, 90,* 651–666.

Kan, K. K., & Tsai, W. (2006). Entrepreneurship and risk aversion. *Small Business Economics, 26,* 465–474.

Keh, H. T., Foo, M. D., & Lim, B. C. (2002). Opportunity evaluation under risky conditions: The cognitive processes of entrepreneurs. *Entrepreneurship Theory and Practice, 27*(2), 125–148.

Levesque, M., & Schade, C. (2005). Intuitive optimizing: Experimental findings on time allocation decisions with newly formed ventures. *Journal of Business Venturing, 20,* 313–342.

Palich, L. E., & Bagby, D. R. (1995). Using cognitive theory to explain entrepreneurial risk-taking: Challenging conventional wisdom. *Journal of Business Venturing, 10,* 425–438.

Parker, S. (2004). *The economics of self-employment and entrepreneurship.* Cambridge: Cambridge University Press.

Parker, S. (2005). *The economics of entrepreneurship: What we know and what we don't.* Discussion papers on entrepreneurship, growth, and public policy #1805. The Max Planck Institute for Research into Economic Systems.

Petersen, M. A., & Rajan, R. G. (1992). *The benefits of firm-creditor relationships: Evidence from small business data.* University of Chicago working paper #362.

Stiglitz, J., & Weiss, A. (1981). Credit rationing in markets with imperfect information. *American Economic Review, 71,* 393–410.

Wessner, C. (Ed.). (2002). *The small business innovation research program: Challenges and opportunities.* Washington, D.C.: National Academy Press.

[20]

Research Policy 40 (2011) 1058–1067

Research Policy

The Bayh-Dole Act and scientist entrepreneurship

T. Taylor Aldridge [a,b,*], David Audretsch [a,b]

[a] Indiana University, King-Saud University, Riyadh, Saudi Arabia
[b] WHU Otto Beisheim School of Management, Vallendar, Germany

ARTICLE INFO

Article history:
Received 30 July 2010
Received in revised form 31 January 2011
Accepted 28 April 2011

JEL classification:
M13
O38

Keywords:
Bayh-Dole Act
Entrepreneurship

ABSTRACT

Much of the literature examining the impact of the Bayh-Dole Act has been based on the impact on patenting and licensing activities emanating from offices of technology transfer. Studies based on data generated by offices of technology transfer, suggest a paucity of entrepreneurial activity from university scientists in the form on new startups. There are, however, compelling reasons to suspect that the TTO generated data may not measure all, or even most of scientist entrepreneurship. Rather than relying on measures of scientist entrepreneurship reported by the TTO and compiled by AUTM, this study instead develops alternative measures based on the commercialization activities reported by scientists. In particular, the purpose of this paper is to provide a measure of scientist entrepreneurship and identify which factors are conducive to scientist entrepreneurship and which factors inhibit scientist entrepreneurship. This enables us to compare how scientist entrepreneurship differs from that which has been established in the literature for the more general population. We do this by developing a new database measuring the propensity of scientists funded by grants from the National Cancer Institute (NCI) to commercialize their research as well as the mode of commercialization. We then subject this new university scientist-based data set to empirical scrutiny to ascertain which factors influence both the propensity for scientists to become an entrepreneur. The results suggest that scientist entrepreneurship may be considerably more robust than has generally been indicated in studies based on TTO data.

© 2011 Elsevier B.V. All rights reserved.

1. Introduction

The enormous investment in physical plant and equipment propelled the United States to unprecedented post World War II prosperity. In the new era of globalization, both scholars and policy makers have been looking towards the country's unrivaled investment in research and knowledge to generate economic growth, employment and competitiveness in internationally linked markets for continued prosperity. However, it has been long recognized that investment in scientific knowledge and research alone will not automatically generate growth and prosperity. Rather, these new knowledge investments must penetrate what has been termed "*the knowledge filter*" in order to contribute to innovation, competitiveness and ultimately economic growth (Acs et al., 2010). In fact, the knowledge filter impeding the commercialization of investments in research and knowledge can be formidable. As Senator Birch Bayh warned, "A wealth of scientific talent at American colleges and universities – talent responsible for the development of numerous innovative scientific breakthroughs each year – is going to

waste as a result of bureaucratic red tape and illogical government regulations, ..."[1] It is the knowledge filter that stands between investment in research on the one hand, and its commercialization through innovation, leading ultimately to economic growth, on the other.

Seen through the eyes of Senator Bayh, the magnitude of the knowledge filter is daunting, "What sense does it make to spend billions of dollars each year on government-supported research and then prevent new developments from benefiting the American people because of dumb bureaucratic red tape?"[2]

In an effort to penetrate such a formidable knowledge filter, Congress enacted the Bayh-Dole Act in 1980 to spur the transfer of technology from university research to commercialization.[3] The goal of the Bayh-Dole Act was to facilitate the commercialization of university science (Kenney and Patton, 2009; Link et al., 2005, 2007). Assessments about the impact of the Bayh-Dole Act on penetrating the knowledge filter and facilitating the commercialization

---

* Corresponding author at: Indiana University, King-Saud University, Riyadh, Saudi Arabia.
E-mail address: aldridge@econ.mpg.de (T.T. Aldridge).

0048-7333/$ – see front matter © 2011 Elsevier B.V. All rights reserved.
doi:10.1016/j.respol.2011.04.006

---

[1] Introductory statement of Birch Bayh, September 13, 1978, cited from the Association of University Technology Managers Report (AUTM) (2004, p. 5).
[2] Statement by Birch Bayh, April 13, 1980, on the approval of S. 414 (Bayh-Dole) by the U.S. Senate on a 91-4 vote, cited from AUTM (2004, p. 16).
[3] Public Law 98–620

T.T. Aldridge, D. Audretsch / Research Policy 40 (2011) 1058–1067   1059

of university research have bordered on the euphoric,[4] "Possibly the most inspired piece of legislation to be enacted in America over the past half-century was the Bayh-Dole Act of 1980. Together with amendments in 1984 and augmentation in 1986, this unlocked all the inventions and discoveries that had been made in laboratories through the United States with the help of taxpayers' money. More than anything, this single policy measure helped to reverse America's precipitous slide into industrial irrelevance. Before Bayh-Dole, the fruits of research supported by government agencies had gone strictly to the federal government. Nobody could exploit such research without tedious negotiations with a federal agency concerned. Worse, companies found it nearly impossible to acquire exclusive rights to a government owned patent. And without that, few firms were willing to invest millions more of their own money to turn a basic research idea into a marketable product."[5]

An even more enthusiastic assessment suggested that, "The Bayh-Dole Act turned out to be the Viagra for campus innovation. Universities that would previously have let their intellectual property lie fallow began filing for – and getting patents at unprecedented rates. Coupled with other legal, economic and political developments that also spurred patenting and licensing, the results seems nothing less than a major boom to national economic growth."[6]

The mechanism or instrument attributed to facilitating the commercialization of university scientist research has been the university technology transfer office (TTO). While the TTO was not an invention of the Bayh-Dole Act, its prevalence exploded following passage of the Act in 1980. Not only does the TTO typically engage in painstaking collection of the intellectual property disclosed by scientists to the university but also the extent of commercialization emanating from the TTO. The Association of University Technology Managers (AUTM) collects and reports a number of measures reflecting the intellectual property and commercialization of its member universities. A voluminous and growing body of research has emerged documenting the impact of TTOs on the commercialization of university research (Lockett et al., 2003, 2005; O'Shea and Rory, 2008; Phan et al., 2005; Siegel et al., 2007). Most of these studies focus on various measures associated with university TTOs (Mustar et al., 2006; Mosey and Wright, 2007; Shane 2004; Powers and McDougall, 2005; Phan and Siegel, 2006; Di Gregorio and Shane, 2003; Mowery et al., 2004) By most accounts, the impact on facilitating the commercialization of university science research has been impressive.

However, in terms of scientist entrepreneurship, measured by new ventures started by university scientists, the data reported by university TTOs and collected by AUTM suggests a paucity of commercialization spilling over from universities. In the first years of this century, which also pre-dated the financial and economic crises, the number of startups emanating from U.S. universities reported by AUTM averaged 426 per year from 1998 to 2004. Given the magnitude of research budgets and investments in knowledge at American universities, an estimated total between 1998 and 2004 funded by the United States government granting agencies, this measure of university startups is both startling and disappointing.

Similarly, O'Shea et al. (2008) report that, for all its research prowess and headlines as an engine of the Route 128 high tech entrepreneurial cluster around Boston (Saxenien, 1994), the technology transfer office at MIT registered only 29 startups emanating from the university in 2001. Its counterpart, which is generally considered to have fuelled the Silicon Valley high-tech cluster (Saxenien, 1994), Stanford University, registered just six startups. Based on the TTO data measuring scientist entrepreneurship at universities compiled by AUTM, the Bayh-Dole does not seem to have had much of an impact on the economy.

However, there are compelling reasons to suspect that measuring and analyzing the commercialization of university research by relying solely upon data collected by the TTOs may lead to a systematic underestimation of commercialization and innovation emanating from university research. The mandate of the TTO is not to measure and document all of the intellectual property created by university research along with the subsequent commercialization. Rather, what is measured and documented are the intellectual property and commercialization activities with which the TTO is involved. This involvement is typically a subset of the broader and more pervasive intellectual property being generated by university research and its commercialization which may or may not involve the TTO office (Thursby and Thursby, 2005; Mosey and Wright, 2007). For example, in his exhaustive study on academic spinoffs, Shane (2004, p. 4) warns, "Sometimes patents, copyrights and other legal mechanisms are used to protect the intellectual property that leads to spinoffs, while at other times the intellectual property that leads to a spinoff company formation takes the form of know how or trade secrets. Moreover, sometimes entrepreneurs create university spinoffs by licensing university inventions, while at other times the spinoffs are created without the intellectual property being formally licensed from the institution in which it was created. These distinctions are important for two reasons. First it is harder for researchers to measure the formation of spinoff companies created to exploit intellectual property that is not protected by legal mechanisms or that has not been disclosed by inventors to university administrators. As a result, this book likely underestimates the spin-off activity that occurs to exploit inventions that are neither patented nor protected by copyrights. This book also underestimates the spin-off activity that occurs "through the back door", that is companies founded to exploit technologies that investors fail to disclose to university administrators."

There is little empirical evidence supporting Shane's (2004) admonition that relying solely upon the data registered with and collected by the TTO will result in a systematic underestimation of commercialization and ownership of university research (Thursby et al., 2009; Aldridge and Audretsch, 2010). Such an underestimation of commercialization of university research may lead to an underestimation of the impact that spillovers accruing from investment in university research have on innovation and ultimately economic growth.

If the spillover of knowledge generated by university research is viewed as essential for economic growth, employment creation, and international competitiveness in global markets, the systematic underreporting of university spillovers resulting from the commercialization of scientist research concomitantly may lead to severe policy distortions. Thus, rather than relying on measures of scientist entrepreneurship reported by the TTO and compiled by AUTM, this study instead develops alternative measures based on the commercialization activities reported by scientists. Some of this intellectual property is co-owned by the university; some is completely owned by the scientist In particular, the purpose of this paper is to provide a measure of scientist commercialization of university research and identify which factors are conducive to scientist entrepreneurship and which factors inhibit scientist entrepreneurship. We do this by developing a new database mea-

---

[4] Mowery (2005, p. 40–41) argues that such a positive assessment of the impact on Bayh-Dole is exaggerated, "Although it seems clear that the criticism of high-technology startups that was widespread during the period of pessimism over U.S. competitiveness was overstated, the recent focus on patenting and licensing as the essential ingredient in university–industry collaboration and knowledge transfer may be no less exaggerated. The emphasis on the Bayh-Dole Act as a catalyst for these interactions also seems somewhat misplaced."
[5] "Innovation's Golden Goose," *The Economist*, 12 December, 2002.
[6] Cited in Mowery (2005, p. 64).

1060   *T.T. Aldridge, D. Audretsch / Research Policy 40 (2011) 1058–1067*

suring the propensity of scientists funded by grants from the National Cancer Institute (NCI) to commercialize their research as well as the mode of commercialization. We then subject this new university scientist-based data set to empirical scrutiny to ascertain which factors influence the propensity for scientists to become an entrepreneur. This enables a comparison of the factors conducive to scientist entrepreneurship to what has already been solidly established in the literature for the more general population. We should emphasize that in this paper we are considering a specific context for scientist entrepreneurship – the creation of a new firm. While this fits within the broader definition of scientist entrepreneurship stated in the introductory paper for this special issue, it should be recognized that we are only focusing on this sole aspect and measure of scientist entrepreneurship.

Section 2 of the paper develops the main hypotheses about why some university scientists engage in entrepreneurship while others abstain from entrepreneurial activities, and why the entrepreneurial behavior of scientists may either emulate or not emulate the entrepreneurial behavior that has been identified in the literature for the more general population, enabling us to posit seven main hypotheses about what influences scientist entrepreneurship. In Section 3 the data base for university scientists funded by the National Cancer Institute of the National Institutes of Health (NIH) is explained. The main hypotheses for scientist entrepreneurship are tested in Section 4 and the results are presented. The findings are discussed and highlighted in Section 5. Finally, a summary and conclusions are presented in Section 6. In particular, by asking scientists what they do rather than the university technology transfer offices, this paper finds that the Bayh-Dole Act has resulted in a strikingly robust and vigorous amount of scientific entrepreneurship. We find that one-quarter of patenting scientists have commercialized their research by starting a firm. In addition, the results suggest that in some aspects scientist entrepreneurship emulates what the literature has found to exist for the broader population. However, in other aspects, scientist entrepreneurship diverges from what the literature has established for the more general population.

2. The scientist entrepreneurial decision

A compelling literature has been developed, both theoretically, as well as being substantiated with robust empirical evidence, explaining why some people choose to become an entrepreneur, in the form of starting a new firm, while others do not (Parker, 2010). However, a review of Parker's comprehensive and exhaustive review of the literature reveals that virtually none of these studies focused on the decision by university scientists to become an entrepreneur. What is known about entrepreneurial scientist startups originating from universities has normally been inferred from data where the unit of analysis was the university.

Thus, the starting point for analyzing the decision by a scientist to become an entrepreneur is the extensive literature on the entrepreneurial choice for the context of a broad population. To this we will add specific considerations for the scientist context. Five types of factors have been found to shape the individual decision to become an entrepreneur – characteristics specific to the individual, human capital, social capital, the institutional context, and access to financial capital.

2.1. Individual characteristics

A vast and extensive literature has accumulated linking the characteristics of individuals to the propensity to become an entrepreneur (McClelland, 1961; Roberts, 1991; Brandstetter, 1997; Gartner, 1990). While McClelland (1961) undertook pioneer-

ing work, Zhao and Seibert (2006) summarize a more focused series of studies on personality characteristics conducive to becoming an entrepreneur. For example, Reynolds et al. (2004) use the PSID to identify the key role that personality characteristics play in becoming an entrepreneur.

A particular focus for framing the decision to become an entrepreneur has been on entrepreneurial intentions (Wright et al., 2006; Ajzen, 1991; Gaglio and Katz, 2001) However, none of these studies is concerned with the particular type of individuals which are the focus in this present studies – university scientists. Thus, it is not clear whether the consistent findings concerning entrepreneurship and entrepreneurial intentions for the more general population also hold for scientists. In fact, there are reasons to suspect that the main influences underlying entrepreneurial intentions may differ for scientists when compared to the more general population. For example, studies by Levin and Stephan (1991) and Stephan and Levin (1992), posited and found empirical evidence supporting a life cycle model of scientist commercialization, which suggested that, in particular, that age may have a different impact on the propensity for a scientist to engage in entrepreneurial behavior than for the overall population. While the preponderance of studies based on the overall population tend to find that age is negatively related to the likelihood of an individual becoming an entrepreneur, Levin and Stephan (1991) and Stephan and Levin (1992) found that age is positively related to scientist entrepreneurship. Their empirical results were consistent with their life-cycle framework, which predicted that in the early stages of their career, scientists are the most productive and have the greatest incentives to invest in creating knowledge which is public in nature, in an effort to enhance their scientific reputation. As they mature and have achieved prominence, they then have an incentive to invest in knowledge which is private and can be commercialized, so that they are more likely to become entrepreneurs as they mature rather than when they are starting out in their careers.

The scientist life cycle prediction is consistent with the focus of Wright et al. (2006), Shapero and Sokol (1982) and Ajzen (1991) on entrepreneurial intentions. Such entrepreneurial intentions and the propensity to be sensitive to entrepreneurial opportunities may increase as a scientist evolves over her life cycle. Based on the life-cycle framework of Levin and Stephan (1991) and Stephan and Levin (1992) we postulate

Hypothesis 1. Age is positively related to the propensity for scientists to become an entrepreneur.

2.2. Gender

An important individual specific characteristic that has consistently been found to influence the decision to become an entrepreneur is gender (Minniti and Nardone, 2007). Studies have consistently found that females have a lower propensity to become entrepreneurs (Allen et al., 2007). For example, in 2003, the U.S. self employment rate of females was about 55% as high as the male self-employment rate; and 6.8% of women in the labor force were self-employed, compared with 12.4% of men. Similarly, according to Allen et al. (2007), the results from the Global Entrepreneurship Monitor (GEM) identify 10.73% prevalence rate of entrepreneurial activity by U.S. females, measured in terms of owning a business, as compared to 18.45% by U.S. males.

There is also at least some evidence that female scientists and engineers have a lower propensity to engage in commercialization activities, such as entrepreneurship. Elston and Audretsch (2010, 2011) find that gender is the most significant determinant of using an Small Business Innovation Research (SBIR) grant to start a firm, and that, female applicants were far less likely than males to report SBIR grants as their primary source of start-up capital. The nega-

T.T. Aldridge, D. Audretsch / Research Policy 40 (2011) 1058–1067   1061

tive effect of being female on probability of receiving SBIR funding was robust and persistent even after controlling for age, race, education, and wealth. Similarly, Link and Scott (2009) find that only 17.5% of the SBIR firms in their sample from the NIH SBIR program were owned by females, with the remaining 82.5% owned by males. Thus, the evidence suggests not only is there low participation of females in the SBIR program, but it is significantly lower than the prevalent rates for U.S. female entrepreneurs. This suggests

Hypothesis 2.   Female scientists will have a lower likelihood of being entrepreneurs.

2.3. Human capital

A large literature has emerged examining the link between human capital and entrepreneurship (Bates, 1995; Evans and Leighton, 1989; Gimeno et al., 1997; Davidsson and Benson, 2003). Higher levels of human capital facilitate the ability of individuals to recognize entrepreneurial opportunities as well as to act on them through entrepreneurial action. Studies have typically found a positive relationship between human capital and entrepreneurship. The human capital of the individual, typically measured in terms of years of education, has been found to have a positive impact on the decision to become an entrepreneur.

There is no reason to suspect that the relationship between human capital and scientist entrepreneurial behavior differs from that of the more general population, which would suggest a positive relationship. However, an important caveat is that scientists represent a highly truncated part of the overall distribution of human capital. All scientists exhibit very high levels of human capital. Still, with this caveat in mind, we propose

Hypothesis 3.   The propensity for a scientist to become an entrepreneur is positively related to human capital.

2.4. Social capital

Social capital refers to meaningful interactions and linkages the scientist has with others. While *physical capital* refers to the importance of machines and tools as a factor of production (Solow, 1956), the endogenous growth theory (Romer, 1986, 1990; Lucas, 1988) puts the emphasis on the process of knowledge accumulation, and hence the creation of *knowledge capital*. The concept of *social capital* (Putnam, 1993; Coleman, 1988) can be considered a further extension because it adds a social component to those factors shaping economic growth and prosperity. According to Putnam (2000, p.19), "Whereas physical capital refers to physical objects and human capital refers to the properties of individuals, social capital refers to connections among individuals – social networks. By analogy with notions of physical capital and human capital – tools and training that enhance individual productivity – social capital refers to features of social organization, such as networks that facilitate coordination and cooperation for mutual benefits."

Similarly, social capital is considered by Coleman (1988) to be "a variety of entities with two elements in common: they all consist of some aspect of social structure, and they facilitate certain actions of actors, . . ., within the structure." A large and robust literature has emerged attempting to link social capital to entrepreneurship (Mosey and Wright, 2007; Aldrich and Martinez, 2010; Shane and Stuart, 2002; Davidsson and Benson, 2003). According to this literature, entrepreneurial activity should be enhanced where investments in social capital are greater. Interactions and linkages, such as working together with industry, are posited as conduits not just for knowledge spillovers but also for the demonstration effect providing a flow of information across scientists about how scien-

Table 1
Technology transfer office mission statements.

Primary objectives of the UTTO	Percentage of times appeared in mission statement (%)
Licensing for royalties	78.72
IP protection/management	75.18
Facilitate disclosure process	71.63
Sponsored research and assisting inventors	56.74
Public good (disseminate information/technology)	54.61
Industry relationships	42.55
Economic development (region, state)	26.95
Entrepreneurship and new venture creation	20.57
N = 128 TTOs	

Source: Markman et al. (2005).

tific research can be commercialized (Thursby and Thursby, 2002). This leads us to

Hypothesis 4.   Social capital is positively related to the propensity for a scientist to become an entrepreneur.

2.5. Institutional influences

In addition to individual specific characteristics, the entrepreneurship literature has identified the institutional context within which the decision to become an entrepreneur is made. Henrekson and Stenkula (2010) and Karlsson and Karlsson (2002) suggest that certain institutional features are more conducive to individuals recognizing and acting on entrepreneurial opportunities, while other institutions are actually impediments to entrepreneurship. There are additional considerations that are special or unique to the scientist context. One of these is the role played by the technology transfer office (Mustar et al., 2006; Chapple et al., 2005). Studies provide evidence that offices of technology transfer are not homogeneous across universities and are likely to impact scientific entrepreneurship in different ways. In particular, some offices of technology transfer simply are larger, and have great resources, both human and financial, at their disposal (Mowery, 2005). Presumably, better endowed offices of technology transfer can offer scientists greater assistance in commercialization activities.

A second dimension of the offices of technology transfer is that some may put a higher priority on licensing of intellectual property rather than on facilitating scientist startups. For example, as shown in Table 1, Markman et al. (2005) illustrate how the mission statements of 128 university TTOs prioritize licensing intellectual property over scientist startups. Similarly, O'Shea et al. (2005), and Lockett et al. (2005) show that characteristics of the TTO influence the propensity for scientists to become an entrepreneur.

This leads us to posit two hypotheses concerning the institutional context in which the scientist is working

Hypothesis 5.   Scientist entrepreneurship is positively related to the resources available to the technology transfer office.

Hypothesis 6.   Scientist entrepreneurship is negatively related to the extent to which the TTO devotes resources to licensing.

2.6. Financial resources

Having access to financial resources to facilitate starting a new firm is one of the biggest issues confronting nascent entrepreneurs. As Kerr and Nanda (2009, p. 1) point out, "Financing constraints are one of the biggest concerns impacting potential entrepreneurs around the world." Similarly, Gompers and Lerner (2010) emphasize that such financing constraints may be even more severe for scientists, where the ideas generating entrepreneurial ventures are highly uncertain, asymmetric and characterized by high costs of transaction. This suggests

Hypothesis 7. Access to additional financial resources is positively related to scientist entrepreneurship.

In addition, Roberts and Malone (1996) and Breznitz et al. (2008) emphasize that the external environment external may also influence the propensity for scientists to start a new firm. While this paper will not posit any explicit hypotheses linking the external environment to scientist entrepreneurship, we explain in Section 3 that several control variables are included to at least control for several external influences.

3. Measurement

While AUTM collects and makes available data identifying TTO sponsored and approved scientist startups, the data are aggregated at the level of the university TTO. In fact, no large-scale, systematic data base measuring scientist entrepreneurship for the disaggregated level of the individual scientist exists.

Thus, in order to analyze scientist entrepreneurship at the level of the individual scientist, rather than at the level of the aggregated university TTO, we had to create a unique and new data base. The starting point for creating a data base measuring the entrepreneurial activity, in terms of scientist startups, was to identify those scientists awarded a research grant by the National Cancer Institute between 1998 and 2002. Of those research grant awards, the largest 20%, which corresponded to 1693 scientist awardees, were taken to form the database used in this study. The National Cancer Institute (NCI) awarded a total of $5,350,977,742 to the 1693 highest funded quintile of United States-based scientists from 1998 to 2002.

The second step in creating the scientist entrepreneurship data base was to identify which of the scientists receiving funding to support basic research from The National Cancer Institute subsequently received patent protection for an invention. This suggested a sub-set of scientists receiving support for basic research that had potential commercialization applications. NCI award scientists being granted a patent was identified by obtaining patent data from the United States Patent and Trademark Office (USPTO).

To match the patent records with the 1692 NCI recipient scientists, Structured Query Language (SQL) and Python programming languages were written to extract and manipulate data. A match between the patent and NCI databases was considered to be positive if all four of the following necessary conditions were met:

The first necessary condition was that a positive match was made with the first, middle, and last name. If, for example, the scientist did not have a middle name listed on either the NCI award database or the patent database, but did have a positive first and last name, this first condition was considered to be fulfilled.

The second criterion involved matching the relevant time periods between the two databases. Observations from both databases were matched over the time period 1998–2004, which corresponds to the initial year in which observations were available from the NCI database (1998–2002) and the final year in which patents were recorded in the patent database (1975–2004). Because applications of patents may take anywhere from 3 months to 2 years to be issued, the 2003 and 2004 USPTO patent records were included in our query. Issued patents from 1998 to 2004 by NCI scientists fulfilled the second criterion.

The third criterion was based on location. If the patentee resided within an approximate radius of 60 miles from the geographic location of the university, the third condition was fulfilled. The fourth criterion was based on USPTO patent classification. Using the USPTO patent classification code, all patents were separated into respective coding groups. Patents which did not fall under

the traditional categories of biotechnology were identified. All non biotech patents were evaluated and patents such as "Bread Alfalfa Enhancer" were rejected as an NCI scientist. Based on these four match criteria, a subset of 398 distinctly issued patentees were identified between 1998 and 2004 with a total of 1204 patents.

While the patent records identify which of the NCI Award scientists have been awarded a patent to protect the intellectual property representing an invention, they provide no indication whether or not the scientist has started a business. To identify whether a scientist had started a firm, we implemented a survey of the NCI scientists with a patent. The survey instrument was designed with two main criteria. The first was to maximize information without overly burdening the nation's top medical scientists. Reducing the time and input burden imposed on the scientist was considered to have a favorable impact on the response rate. The second was to maximize information revealing the creation of intellectual property and its subsequent commercialization through licensing and entrepreneurial activity, while at the same time respecting the need for scientist confidentiality and not confronting the scientist with information requests that might compromise such confidentiality.

Based on these two criteria, an interview instrument was designed probing four subgroups of issues: licensing, entrepreneurship, social capital and the role of the TTO. The question in the licensing section asked if the scientist has licensed their intellectual property. The question contained in the entrepreneurship section identified whether the scientist started a new firm. The questions concerning social capital asked the scientist if she sat on any industry science advisory boards (SAB) or board of directors, the extent to which the NCI grant award facilitated commercialization, along with other sources of major funding received from a governmental agency. The questions concerning the influence of the TTO asked whether the university's TTO "directly helped you to commercialize your research between 1998 and 2004".

The 398 patenting scientists were "Googled" to obtain their e-mail and telephone information. The records could, generally, be found by typing their full name, university and the word "oncology". The ensuing patentee e-mail accounts and telephone numbers were then collected and registered in the scientist database. Of those 398 scientists identified in the database, 146 responded. Six respondents indicated that they had not patented the ascribed patents, therefore reducing the number of patentees to 392. The number of respondent, therefore, reflects a response rate of 36%. Of these respondents, one in four reported that they had, in fact, started a firm. This is a strikingly high degree of entrepreneurial activity exhibited by these high profile scientists, and certainly reflects a much more robust and extensive degree of entrepreneurship than has been indicated by the TTO data collected by AUTM.

Section 2 identified from the literature five different types of factors shaping the decision by a scientist to become an entrepreneur – personal characteristics, human capital, social capital, financial resources, and TTO characteristics. These factors are empirically operationalized through the following measures:

3.1. Personal characteristics

Two measures reflecting the personal characteristics of scientists are included. The first is the age of the scientist, measured in terms of years, which was obtained from the scientist survey. Hypothesis 1, which is based on the life-cycle framework for scientists posited by Levin and Stephan (1991) and Stephan and Levin (1992), suggests that age will be positively related to scientist entrepreneurship.

The second measure is gender. This is a dummy variable assigned the value of one for males (1310) of the overall 1693 included in the NCI database. The gender of each scientist was obtained by "Googling" their names, i.e. pictures. The estimated

T.T. Aldridge, D. Audretsch / Research Policy 40 (2011) 1058–1067

coefficient will reflect whether the gender of the scientist influences the propensity to commercialize research. Hypothesis 2 suggests a positive relationship between gender and scientist entrepreneurship.

3.2. Scientist human capital

A unique computer program was used to measure scientist citations over the period 1998–2004, using the "Expanded Science Citation Index." Higher levels of human capital were inferred by a greater citation count divided by the number of publications. This measure has been used elsewhere to reflect the human capital of scientists. As Hypothesis 3 suggests, a positive relationship is expected to emerge between scientist human capital and the propensity of a scientist to start a new firm.

3.3. Social capital

Two different measures were used to reflect the extent of a scientist's social capital in the context of linkages with private industry. Such linkages are hypothesized to be conducive to generating both entrepreneurial opportunities and the access to expertise and experience in commercializing those opportunities through entrepreneurship. The first measure a binary variable taking on the value of one if the scientist has been a member of a scientific advisory board or the board of directors of a firm. A positive coefficient would indicate that social capital, as reflected by board membership, is conducive to the commercialization of university research. The second measure is *industry co-publications*, which reflects social capital and linkages between university scientists and their counterparts in industry and is measured as co-authorship between a university scientist and an industry scientist in the Science Citation Index using the Institute for Scientist Information (ISI) Web of Science citation database. The total count of papers co-authored with an industry scientist between the years of 1998 and 2004 was estimated using several search queries on the ISI database. Using the address fields within each publication value in the ISI database, co-publications were identified as a private sector address if the terms *Co., Co. Ltd., Inc.,* or *LLC*, were found. Also, in order to not misidentify the University of Colorado as a company, for example, the query forced the previously mentioned search terms to be standalone words, and not part of larger words. Hypothesis 4 suggests that the coefficient is expected to be positive, which would reflect that university–industry scientist interactions are conducive to scientist entrepreneurship.

3.4. Characteristics of the technology transfer office

Hypotheses 5 and 6 involve the relationship between the technology transfer office and scientist entrepreneurship. Two dimensions of the technology transfer office at the university are included. The first is *TTO employees*, which measures the mean number of employee. The measure is taken from the AUTM data base. A positive relationship would suggest that a greater commitment of TTO employee resources yields a higher propensity for scientists to become an entrepreneur. The second measure is *TTO licensing*, which is obtained by dividing the number of employees dedicated to licensing technology by the number of administrative employees. This variable reflects the commitment of the TTO to licensing relative to other TTO functions. This measure is derived from the AUTM data base. A positive relationship would suggest that allocating a greater share of TTO employees to licensing would increase scientist entrepreneurship.

3.5. Financial resources

There are two measures reflecting financial resources available to the scientist. The first is NCI grant, which is the mean total NCI awarded to the scientist between 1998 and 2002. The award amount was obtained from the original NCI award excel sheet. If external funding of scientific research is conducive to scientific entrepreneurship, a positive coefficient of the NCI grant would be expected. The second measure reflects the extent to which the NCI grant helped the scientist commercialize by obtaining patent protection of her invention. This measure was obtained from the survey of scientists. A positive coefficient would be consistent with Hypothesis 7, which suggests a positive relationship between additional financial resources and scientist entrepreneurship.

3.6. Control variables

Several other measures were included to control for the external context in which the scientist was working. The first is *NCI center,* which is a binary variable taking on the value of one if the scientist is employed at one of the 39 nationally recognized cancer centers, and zero otherwise. A comprehensive cancer integrates research activities across the three major areas of laboratory, clinical and population-based research. The comprehensive cancer centers generally have the mission to support research infrastructure, but some centers also provide clinical care and service, reflecting the priority that community outreach and dissemination play at the centers. A positive coefficient would reflect that being located at a comprehensive cancer center facilitates scientist entrepreneurship. The second measure is *Ivy league*, which is a binary variable taking on the value of one for all scientists employed at Brown University, Cornell University, Columbia University, Dartmouth College, Harvard University, Princeton University, the University of Pennsylvania and Yale University. The third variable is *public universities*, which is a binary variable taking on the value of one for scientists employed at public universities and zero otherwise. Because they are at least partially financed by the public, state universities tend to have a stronger mandate for outreach and commercialization of research. This may suggest a positive coefficient.

The final control variable includes a dummy variable taking on the value of one if the patent was licensed. This may preclude entrepreneurial activity by the scientist, at least in the form of a start up, so that a negative relationship would be expected.

The independent variables are summarized and described in Table 2. The mean and standard deviation of each variable is given in Table 3. The means and standard deviations are provided for three different samples – the top grant recipients from the National Cancer Institute, those top funded scientists with a patent, and those who were interviewed. There are some differences across these groups. For example, the number of citations per scientist is considerably greater for those scientists with a patent, than those who did not patent their intellectual property. The patenting scientists have a greater propensity of being male and of co-authoring an article with a scientist from industry.

The correlation coefficients for the variables are listed in Table 4. These variables do not exhibit high levels of correlation. The highest correlation coefficient is 0.292, between the scientist working at a public institution and the TTO commitment to licensing. Most of the correlation coefficients are below 0.20.

4. Model and results

The purpose of the analysis is to identify factors which are conducive to scientist entrepreneurship and those which impede it. The dependent variable, which was obtained from the interviews,

Table 2
Description of independent variables.

Independent variables	Description
Board	Binary variable, for scientists indicating that they sat on either a board of directors or science advisory board, board = 1
Industry co-publications	The number of publications an NCI scientist shared with a private industry scientist
NCI helpful	Binary variable, for scientists indicating that the NCI grant was helpful for patenting, NCI helpful = 1
Scientist age	The age of the scientist
Male	Binary variable, where a male = 1
NCI grant	Total amount of funding received by the scientist
NCI center	Binary variable, for a scientist whose institution is recognized by NCI as a comprehensive center for cancer research, NCI center = 1
Public institution	Binary variable, for a scientist whose institution is a public institution, public institution = 1
Ivy league	Binary variable, for a scientist whose institution is an Ivy league university, Ivy league = 1
Average citation per publication	Aggregate number of ISI citations divided by the number of ISI publication a scientist received from 1998 to 2004
TTO employees	The mean annual number of TTO employees dedicated to licensing and patenting
TTO licensing commitment	The number of TTO employees dedicated to licensing and patenting divided by administrative employees
Scientist patent licensed	Binary variable, for scientists indicating that the at least one of their patents were licensed, scientist patent licensed = 1

Table 3
Means and standard deviations.

Variable	NCI scientist N = 1693	Patent scientist N = 392	Interviewed scientist N = 140
Patent (%)	23.35 (0.42)	100.00	100.00
Startup (%)	–	–	25.71 (0.44)
Industry co-publications	1.83 (3.57)	3.01 (4.89)	2.56 (3.73)
Board (%)	–	–	58.00 (0.50)
TTO employees	8.66 (11.44)	9.14 (11.6)	8.95 (11.65)
TTO licensing commitment	1.68 (2.29)	1.31 (1.45)	1.22 (1.24)
NCI grant (Dollars)	3,161,943 (3,196,918)	3,484,128 (3,795,993)	3,053,465 (2,674,288)
Gender (%)	77.87 (0.42)	87.85 (0.33)	88.57 (0.32)
NCI helpful (%)	–	–	45.04 (0.50)
Scientist age	–	–	56.76 (8.40)
Scientist citations	1316.44 (2472.29)	1741.19 (2441.07)	1500.34 (1603.49)
NCI center (%)	55.86 (0.50)	56.50 (0.50)	50.70 (0.50)
Public institution (%)	53.91 (0.50)	48.10 (0.50)	49.29 (0.50)
Ivy league (%)	10.24 (0.30)	12.15 (0.33)	15.00 (0.36)

takes on a value of one if the scientist started a firm and zero if she did not. Because of the binary nature of the dependent variable, a probit regression model is appropriate.

The results from the probit estimation are provided in Table 5. The results suggest considerable support for Hypothesis 4. Both measures of social capital, the scientist serving on a scientific advisory board, and co-authoring a publication with a scientist employed in private industry are positively related to the likelihood of that scientist starting a new firm. These results for the entrepreneurial behavior of scientists are certainly consistent with those found for the more general population by Davidsson and Benson (2003), among others, and suggest that the entrepreneurial behavior of top university scientists emulates the entrepreneurial behavior of the general behavior, at least in terms of the important role played by social capital.

The positive and statistically significant coefficient of NCI helpful is consistent with Hypothesis 7. The financial resources provided

Table 4
Correlation coefficients of variables.

	Startup	Industry Co-pubs	Board	TTO employees	TTO Commit	NCI grant	NCI helpful
Startup	1						
Industry Co-pubs	0.166	1					
Board	0.346	0.031	1				
TTO employee	−0.015	0.143	0.091	1			
TTO commit	0.006	0.126	0.089	0.983	1		
NCI grant	−0.053	0.073	0.12	0.15	0.134	1	
NCI helpful	0.277	−0.01	0.213	0.205	0.2	0.106	1
Scientist age	−0.137	−0.166	−0.066	−0.038	−0.041	0.041	0.004
Gender	0.157	−0.017	0.315	−0.015	−0.007	−0.058	0.086
Avg citation per Pub	−0.066	0.066	0.104	0.07	0.078	0.193	0.09
NCI center	−0.057	0.237	−0.093	0.232	0.268	−0.089	0.079
Public institution	−0.075	−0.067	−0.031	0.278	0.292	0.073	0.132
Ivy league	−0.007	0.048	−0.1	−0.152	−0.138	0.015	0.122

	Scientist age	Gender	Average Citation per Pub	NCI center	Public institution	Ivy league
Scientist age	1					
Gender	0.056	1				
Average citation per pub	−0.103	0.053	1			
NCI center	−0.099	−0.145	0.022	1		
Public institution	0.259	0.181	−0.193	−0.108	1	
Ivy league	−0.214	−0.007	0.127	0.175	−0.376	1

T.T. Aldridge, D. Audretsch / Research Policy 40 (2011) 1058–1067   1065

Table 5
Probit regression results estimating scientist commercialization – startups.

Independent variables	1	2	3	4
Board	**1.277**···	**1.502**···	**1.525**···	**1.488**···
	[3.747]	[4.456]	[4.517]	[4.628]
Industry co-publications	6.425·	**8.687**··	**9.083**··	**9.404**··
	[3.401]	[3.997]	[4.094]	[4.229]
NCI helpful	**8.284**···	**9.148**··	**9.277**··	**8.965**··
	[3.212]	[3.682]	[3.704]	[3.787]
Scientist age		−2.102	−2.190	−2.123
		[2.487]	[2.496]	[2.499]
Male		5.649	5.718	5.997
		[1.006]	[1.008]	[1.018]
NCI grant		−8.558	−8.601	−8.289
		[9.982]	[1.004]	[9.929]
NCI center		−2.277	−2.013	−1.875
		[3.966]	[3.886]	[3.909]
Public institution		−2.652	−2.675	−2.963
		[3.995]	[3.998]	[4.008]
Ivy league		−6.405	−6.739	−7.586
		[8.085]	[8.131]	[8.396]
Average citation per publication		−1.197	−1.168	−1.160
		[1.011]	[1.012]	[1.013]
TTO employees		−4.721		
		[9.528]		
TTO licensing employees			−1.286	−1.389
			[1.705]	[1.748]
Scientist patent licensed			1.580	−1.076
				[4.046]
Constant	**−2.247**···	−9.534	−9.366	−1.076
	[4.519]	[1.715]	[1.720]	[1.768]
Observations	91	82	82	82
chi²	27.66	33.43	33.77	33.93

Standard errors in brackets. *Note:* all units have been multiplied by 10,000. The bold values mean that the coefficient is statistically significant for a two-tailed test at the 95 percent level of confidence.
· $p < 0.1$.
·· $p < 0.05$.
··· $p < 0.01$.

by the NCI grant are conducive to scientist entrepreneurship. Those scientists who suggested that the grant from the National Cancer Institute facilitated patenting their intellectual property exhibited a higher propensity to start a new firm. This would suggest that the NCI is enhancing scientist entrepreneurship. These findings are consistent with the findings for the more general population that a lack of access to financial resources tends to constrain entrepreneurial activity (Kerr and Nanda, 2009).

The empirical results are not consistent with Hypotheses 1 and 2. In contrast to the consistent findings in the literature for entrepreneurship for the general population (Reynolds et al., 2004), in the case of university scientists, age and gender have no impact on the propensity for the scientist to become an entrepreneur. While both gender and age are consistently found to influence the decision to become an entrepreneur for the population at large (Reynolds et al., 2004), these are not found to have any statistically significance impact for the scientists included in this study.

Similarly, there is no statistical evidence supporting Hypothesis 3. Human capital apparently has no statistically significant impact on the propensity for scientists to start a new firm. This is a contrast to the findings for the more general population (Davidsson and Benson, 2003; Bates, 1995). One interpretation of this disparity may be that this sample consists of scientists with exceptionally high levels of human capital. Variations in human capital for these scientists apparently have no additional impact on the decision

to become an entrepreneur. By contrast, studies focusing on the broader population include observations with a much greater variance in levels of human capital, as well as a much lower mean level of human capital, so that human capital has consistently been found to influence entrepreneurial activity.

The main hypotheses focusing on the impact of the institutional context on scientist entrepreneurship, Hypotheses 5 and 6, are not supported by the empirical evidence. Neither the resources of the technology transfer office, as measured by number of full-time employees, nor the share of TTO employees dedicated to licensing and patenting has a statistically significant on the likelihood of a scientist starting a new firm.

None of the control variables have any statistically significant impact on the likelihood of a scientist starting a new firm.

5. Discussion

The empirical results presented in Section 4 from analyzing why some scientists become entrepreneurs, while other colleagues do not, point to the importance of relationships and linkages forged through social capital, and in particular, to other scientists working in industry, as well as experiences gained by serving on a company scientific advisory board. The measures of social capital are found to be the most important influences in the decision of a scientist to become an entrepreneur. Those scientists with higher levels of social capital, in that they are members of a scientific advisory board of a company, or they have co-authored articles with scientists working for a company, exhibit a systematically higher propensity to become an entrepreneur.

Some of the more traditional explanations of entrepreneurship, and in particular, personal characteristics such as gender and age, but also human capital do not seem to play an important role.

Thus, in some aspects, scientist entrepreneurship appears to emulate the entrepreneurial behavior exhibited by the more general population. In particular, the validation of Hypotheses 4 and 7, highlighting the key roles that social capital and access to financial resources play in facilitating entrepreneurship, are also consistent with the empirical results found for the general population (Davidsson and Benson, 2003; Aldrich and Martinez, 2010; Kerr and Nanda, 2009; Gompers and Lerner, 2010). However, in other important aspects, and in particular age, gender and human capital, scientist entrepreneurship diverges from the results found for the more general population (Minniti and Nardone, 2007; Davidsson and Benson, 2003; Bates, 1995). While Blanchflower and Oswald (1998), pose the question, "What makes an entrepreneur?" the answer does not seem to be exactly identical for scientist entrepreneurship.

6. Conclusions

A number of indications suggest that the Bayh-Dole has not had much of an impact on generating entrepreneurial activity by scientists in the form of starting a new firm. Based on the respected and often cited data collected by the technology transfer offices at universities, and assembled by AUTM in a systematic and comprehensive manner, it would appear that even the most entrepreneurial universities generate only a handful of startups by scientists each year.

However, in this study, by asking scientists rather than the technology transfer offices of universities what entrepreneurial activities they actually engage in, a very different picture emerges. In fact, based on a data base of high profile scientists receiving large-scale funding from the National Cancer Institute, we find that university scientist entrepreneurship is robust and dynamic. The empirical results from this study suggest that around one in four scientists has engaged in entrepreneurial activity in the form of starting a new firm.

In addition, while most of the previous literature on scientist has been restricted to focusing on characteristics of the technology transfer offices and universities, due to the nature of the data being aggregated to the level of the university, in this study we are able to analyze the decision of a scientist to engage in entrepreneurial activity at the level of the individual scientist. The empirical results suggest that the decision to become an entrepreneur does not exactly mirror what has been found in the extensive literature for studies analyzing the broader population. Neither personal characteristics nor human capital seem to play an important role in the decision of a scientist to become an entrepreneur, as they do for the broader population. Rather, it is the levels of social capital, as measured by linkages to private industry that increase the propensity of a scientist to become an entrepreneur.

An important qualification of the findings from this paper is that they are based on a special sample of highly successful top scientists in a narrow scientific field. Whether they hold across broader groups of scientists and for other scientific fields is an important issue that needs to be addressed in future research. There is no a priori reason to expect the results from this exceptionally high performing group of scientists in a very narrow, specific scientific field to hold across other scientific fields. Subsequent research needs to identify both the prevalence and determinants of scientific entrepreneurship across a broad spectrum of scientific fields. In addition, future research could make a valuable contribution by analyzing the post-startup performance of scientist startups. For example, do the growth and survival of new firms started by university scientists emulate the growth and survival patterns that have been well documented in the literature for firms more generally? It would also be desirable to expand the analysis to include a third typology of university startups, such as those new companies founded by surrogate academic entrepreneurs, based on university owned technologies without the involvement of the inventor of the technology (Clarysse et al., 2005; Franklin et al., 2001). Thus, while the findings of this study would indicate that scientist entrepreneurship is robust and prevalent in the Bayh-Dole era, and is certainly more prevalent than previous studies have suggested, there are important research opportunities to understand how and why scientist entrepreneurship differs from entrepreneurship for the more general population.

Acknowledgements

We thank Don Siegel, Mike Wright, participants of the Conference on "30 Years after Bayh-Dole: Reassessing Academic Research," held on October 29 at the National Academy of Sciences, Washington, DC, and an anonymous referee for their valuable comments. Any errors or omissions are our responsibility.

References

Acs, Z., Audretsch, D.B., Braunerhjelm, P., Carlsson, B., 2010. The missing link: the knowledge filter and entrepreneurship in endogenous growth. Small Business Economic 34 (2), 105–125.
Ajzen, I., 1991. The theory of planned behavior. Organizational Behavior and Human Decision Processes 50, 179–211.
Aldrich, H., Martinez, M., 2010. Entrepreneurship as social construction. In: Acs, Z.J., Audretsch, D.B. (Eds.), Handbook of Entrepreneurship. Springer, New York.
Aldridge, T.T., Audretsch, D., 2010. Does policy influence the commercialization route? Evidence from National Institutes of Health funded scientists. Research Policy 39 (5), 583–588.
Allen, I.E., Langowitz, N., Minitti, M., 2007. 2006 Report on Women and Entrepreneurship. Global Entrepreneurship Monitor.
Association of University Technology Managers, 2004. Recollections: Celebrating the History of AUTUM and the Legacy of Bayh-Dole.
Bates, T., 1995. Self-employment entry across industry groups. Journal of Business Venturing 10, 143–156.
Blanchflower, D., Oswald, A.J., 1998. What makes an entrepreneur? Journal of Labor Economics 16 (1), 26–60.
Brandstetter, H., 1997. Becoming an entrepreneur – a question of personality structure? Journal of Economic Psychology 18, 157–177.
Breznitz, S.M., O'Shea, R.P., Allen, T.J., 2008. University commercialization strategies in the development of regional bioclusters. Journal of Product Innovation Management 25, 129–142.
Chapple, W., Lockett, A., Siegel, D., Wright, M., 2005. Assessing the relative efficiency effects of UK University Technology Transfer offices: a comparison of parametric and non-parametric approaches. Research Policy 34 (3), 369–384.
Clarysse, B., Wright, M., Lockett, A., Van de Velde, A., Vohora, A., 2005. Spinning out new ventures: a typology of incubation strategies from European research institutions. Journal of Business Venturing 20 (2), 183–216.
Coleman, J., 1988. Social capital in the creation of human capital. American Journal of Sociology Supplement 94, 95–120.
Davidsson, P., Benson, H., 2003. The role of social and human capital among nascent entrepreneurs. Journal of Business Venturing 18 (3), 301–331.
Di Gregorio, D., Shane, S., 2003. Why some universities generate more TLO start-ups than others? Research Policy 32 (2), 209–227.
Elston, J., Audretsch, D.B., 2010. Risk attitudes, wealth and sources of entrepreneurial start-up capital. Journal of Economic Behavior and Organization 76 (1), 82–89.
Elston, J., Audretsch, D.B., 2011. Financing the entrepreneurial decision: an empirical approach using experimental data on risk attitudes. Small Business Economics 36 (2), 209–222.
Evans, D., Leighton, L., 1989. Some empirical aspects of entrepreneurship. American Economic Review 79, 519–535.
Franklin, S., Wright, M., Lockett, A., 2001. Academic and surrogate entrepreneurs and university spin-out companies. Journal of Technology Transfer 26 (1–2), 127–141.
Gaglio, C.M., Katz, J.A., 2001. The psychological basis of opportunity identification: entrepreneurial alertness. Small Business Economics 16 (2), 95–111.
Gartner, W., 1990. What are we talking about when we talk about entrepreneurship? Journal of Business Venturing 5 (1), 15–28.
Gimeno, J., Folta, T.B., Cooper, A.C., Woo, C.Y., 1997. Survival of the fittest? Entrepreneurial human capital and the persistence of underperforming firms. Administrative Science Quarterly 42, 750–783.

Gompers, P., Lerner, J., 2010. Equity financing. In: Acs, Z.J., Audretsch, D.B. (Eds.), Handbook of Entrepreneurship Research. Springer Publishers, New York, pp. 183–216.

Henrekson, M., Stenkula, M., 2010. Entrepreneurship and public policy. In: Acs, Z.J., Audretsch, D.B. (Eds.), Handbook of Entrepreneurship Research. Springer, New York.

Karlsson, C., Karlsson, M., 2002. Economic policy, institutions and entrepreneurship. Small Business Economics 19 (2), 163–171.

Kerr, W., Nanda, R., 2009. Financing constraints and entrepreneurship. National Bureau of Economic Research Working Paper no. 15498.

Kenney, M., Patton, D., 2009. Reconsidering the Bayh-Dole Act and the current university invention ownership model. Research Policy 38 (9), 1407–1422.

Levin, S.G., Stephan, P.E., 1991. Research productivity over the life cycle; evidence for academic scientists. American Economic Review 81 (4), 114–132.

Link, A., Scott, J.T., 2009. Private investor participation and commercialization rates for government-sponsored research and development: would a prediction market improve the performance of the SBIR programme? Economica 76 (302), 264–281.

Link, A., Siegel, D., Bozeman, B., 2007. An empirical analysis of the propensity of academics to engage in informal university technology transfer. Industrial and Corporate Change 16 (4), 641–655.

Link, A., Siegel, N., Donald, S., 2005. University-based technology initiatives: quantitative and qualitative evidence. Research Policy 34 (3), 253–257.

Lockett, A., Wright, M., Franklin, S., 2003. Technology transfer and universities' spin-out strategies. Small Business Economics 20 (2), 185–201.

Lockett, D.S., Wright, M., Ensley, M., 2005. The creation of spin-off firms at public research institutions: managerial and policy implications. Research Policy 34 (7), 981–993.

Lucas, R., 1988. On the mechanics of economic development. Journal of Monetary Economics 22, 3–39.

Markman, G., Phan, P., Balkin, D., Gianiodis, P., 2005. Entrepreneurship and university-based technology transfer. Journal of Business Venturing 20 (2), 241–263.

McClelland, D., 1961. The Achieving Society. Van Nostrand, Princeton.

Minniti, M., Nardone, C., 2007. Being in someone else's shoes: the role of gender in nascent entrepreneurship. Small Business Economics 28 (2–3), 223–238.

Mosey, S., Wright, M., 2007. From human capital to social capital: a longitudinal study of technology based academic entrepreneurs. Entrepreneurship Theory and Practice (31), 909–935.

Mowery, D.C., 2005. The Bayh-Dole Act and high-technology entrepreneurship in U.S. universities: chicken, egg, or something else? In: Gary, L. (Ed.), University Entrepreneurship and Technology Transfers. Elsevier, Amsterdam, pp. 38–68.

Mowery, D., Nelson, R., Sampat, B., Ziedonis, A., 2004. Ivory Tower and Industrial Innovation: University-Industry Technology Transfer before and after the Bayh-Dole Act. Stanford University Press, Stanford, CA.

Mustar, P., Reanault, M., Columbo, M., Piva, E., Fontes, M., Lockett, A., Wright, M., Clarysse, B., Moray, N., 2006. Conceptualizing the heterogeneity of research-based spin-offs: a multi-dimensional taxonomy. Research Policy 35 (2), 289–308.

O'Shea, R., Allen, T., Chevalier, A., Roche, F., 2005. Entrepreneurial orientation, technology transfer and spinoff performance of U. S. universities. Research Policy 34 (7), 994–1009.

O'Shea, R.P., Chugh, H., Allen, T.J., 2008. Determinants and consequences of university spinoff activity: a conceptual framework. Journal of Technology Transfer 33, 653–666.

O'Shea, R., 2008. University commercialization strategies in the development of regional bioclusters. Journal of Product Innovation Management 25 (2), 129–142.

Parker, S., 2010. The economics of entrepreneurship. Cambridge University Press, New York.

Phan, P., Siegel, D.S., 2006. The effectiveness of university technology transfer: lessons learned, managerial and policy implications, and the road forward. Foundations and Trends in Entrepreneurship 2 (2), 77–144.

Phan, P., Siegel, D., Wright, M., 2005. Science parks and incubators: observations, synthesis and future research. Journal of Business Venturing 20 (2), 165–182.

Powers, J.B., McDougall, P., 2005. University start-up formation and technology licensing with firms that go public: a resource-based view of academic entrepreneurship. Journal of Business Venturing 20 (3), 291–311.

Putnam, R., 2000. Bowling Alone: The Collapse and Revival of American Community. Simon and Schuster, New York.

Putnam, R., 1993. Making Democracy Work. Civic Traditions in Modern Italy. Princeton University Press, Princeton, NJ.

Reynolds, P., Carter, N., Gartner, W., Greene, P., 2004. The prevalence of nascent entrepreneurs in the United States: evidence from the panel study of entrepreneurial dynamics. Small Business Economics 23, 263–284.

Roberts, E., Malone, R., 1996. Policies and structures for spinning off new companies from research and development organizations. R&D Management 26 (1), 17–48.

Roberts, E., 1991. Entrepreneurs in High-Technology: Lessons from MIT and Beyond. Oxford University Press, Oxford.

Romer, P., 1986. Increasing returns and long-run growth. Journal of Political Economy 94 (5), 1002–1037.

Saxenien, A., 1994. Regional Advantage. Harvard University Press, Cambridge, MA.

Shane, S., 2004. Academic Entrepreneurship: University Spinoffs and Wealth Creation. Cheltenham, Edward Elgar.

Shane, S., Stuart, T., 2002. Organizational endowments and the performance of university start-ups. Management Science 48 (1), 154–171.

Shapero, A., Sokol, L., 1982. The social dimensions of entrepreneurship. In: Kent, C.A., Sexton, D.L., Sexton, D.L., Vesper, K.H. (Eds.), Encyclopedia of Entrepreneurship. Prentice-Hall, Englewood Cliffs, NJ, pp. 72–88.

Siegel, D.S., Veugelers, R., Wright, M., 2007. Technology transfer offices and commercialization of university intellectual property: performance and policy implications. Oxford Review of Economic Policy 23 (4), 640–660.

Solow, R., 1956. A contribution to the theory of economic growth. Quarterly Journal of Economics 70, 65–94.

Stephan, P., Levin, S., 1992. Striking the Mother Lode in Science: the Importance of Age, Place, and Time. Oxford University Press, New York (1992).

Thursby, J., Thursby, M., 2005. Gender patterns of research and licensing activity of sciences and engineering faculty. Journal of Technology Transfer 30 (4), 343–353.

Thursby, J., Fuller, A., Thursby, M., 2009. US faculty patenting: inside and outside the university. Research Policy 38 (1), 14–25.

Thursby, J., Thursby, M., 2002. Who is selling the ivory tower? Sources of growth in university licensing. Management Science 48, 90–104.

Wright, M., Westhead, P., Ucbasaran, D., 2006. Habitual Entrepreneurship. Edward Elgarm, Aldershot.

Zhao, H., Seibert, S., 2006. The big five personality dimensions and entrepreneurial status: a meta-analytic review. Journal of Applied Psychology 91 (2), 259–271.

[21]

Research Policy 41 (2012) 1407–1421

Research Policy

Financial signaling by innovative nascent ventures: The relevance of patents and prototypes

David B. Audretsch[a], Werner Bönte[b,*], Prashanth Mahagaonkar[c, 1]

[a] Institute for Development Strategies, Indiana University, 1315 E. 10th Avenue, SPEA Suite 201, Bloomington, IN 47405, United States
[b] Schumpeter School of Business and Economics, Jackstädt Center for Research on Entrepreneurship and Innovation, University of Wuppertal, Room M.12-27, Gauss Str. 20, 42119 Wuppertal, Germany
[c] Schumpeter School of Business and Economics, University of Wuppertal, Room M.12-30, Gauss Str. 20, 42119 Wuppertal, Germany

ARTICLE INFO

Article history:
Received 1 October 2010
Received in revised form 27 January 2012
Accepted 14 February 2012
Available online 28 March 2012

Keywords:
Innovation
Entrepreneurship
Finance
Information asymmetries

ABSTRACT

External finance is a central issue for innovative nascent ventures. In this study, we argue that innovative nascent ventures may use patents to signal appropriability and prototypes to signal feasibility to potential investors. Using new data on 906 nascent ventures, we find that nascent ventures with patents or patent applications as well as prototyped innovations are more likely to obtain equity finance. However, nascent ventures that can solely signal appropriability by patenting are not more likely to obtain equity finance. This result may indicate that venture capitalists and business angels assign higher value to the appropriability signal when coupled with feasibility and vice versa.

© 2012 Elsevier B.V. All rights reserved.

1. Introduction

Innovative new ventures fail if they cannot attract resources needed to commercialize new ideas and inventions. Obtaining external resources is a central issue for nascent new ventures since they rarely have sufficient internal resources to finance startup activities. One important problem are information asymmetries between innovative nascent ventures and external financiers. Although the U.S. venture capital industry has grown dramatically since the 1980s, information asymmetries may still inhibit the commercialization of innovative ideas. In fact as Hsu (2004, p. 1805) mentions, "particularly for entrepreneurs without an established reputation, convincing external resource providers such as venture capitalists (VCs) to provide financial capital may be challenging".

Information asymmetries are likely to be a severe problem, especially for innovative new ventures in the *earliest stage* of the startup process. Innovative nascent ventures developing their business concepts and operating businesses that do not yet generate revenues tend to possess assets that are knowledge-based and intangible. Consequently, the quality and value of the new venture cannot be directly observed. Such knowledge based resources sometimes might take the form of patent rights, which provides

the business a strategic advantage. As expected, patents are also advantageous to gain financial resources too.

The relevance of patents for access to external financial resources is analyzed by Engel and Keilbach (2007). Using a dataset consisting of young German firms, they find that those firms with a higher number of patent applications (size corrected) have a higher probability of obtaining venture capital. This result is in line with the findings reported by Hellman and Puri (2000). Their results suggest that innovators are more likely to obtain venture capital financing than are imitators. Moreover, the results presented by Hsu and Ziedonis (2008) suggest a significant effect of patents on investor estimates of start-up firm value especially in earlier financing rounds. Haeussler et al. (2009) investigate how patent applications and grants improve the ability of capital seeking biotechnology companies in Germany and Britain to attract venture capital financing. Their results suggest that biotechnology companies obtain equity finance earlier if they filed applications for patents whereas ultimate grant decisions do not have an additional effect on the financing decision of venture capitalists.

As signaling is one way to reduce information asymmetries (Spence, 1973), there are reasons to expect that patents act as signals to investors. Patents are means to protect property rights and, consequently, innovative entrepreneurs may use them to signal to potential investors their ability to appropriate the returns of their innovations (*appropriability*). However, Gompers and Lerner (2001, p. 35) warn that "Although more tangible than an idea, patents and trademarks themselves are not enough to enable a company

* Corresponding author. Tel.: +49 202 439 2446; fax: +49 202 439 3852.
 E-mail address: boente@wiwi.uni-wuppertal.de (W. Bönte).
[1] Tel.: +49 202 439 2476; fax: +49 202 439 3852.

1408   *D.B. Audretsch et al. / Research Policy 41 (2012) 1407–1421*

to obtain financing from most lenders. A soft asset such as patent may have value only when it is combined with other assets, such as the entrepreneur's knowledge of a particular process or technology that the patent involves". In order to cope with the problem of asymmetric information and to obtain external finance, innovative entrepreneurs may therefore use other or additional signals. Patents as appropriability signals might be valued higher when coupled with signals of feasibility.

Our line of argument is that the development of a prototype may serve as such a signal to potential investors. Innovative nascent ventures may use prototypes to signal the actual *feasibility* of the proposed project and this signal may allow potential investors to improve their assessment of the commercial potential of the new venture. Prototypes may be the crucial link that actually provides additional value to patents as signals and thus making financing easier. Yet, the role of prototypes is largely neglected by empirical studies that deal with the importance of patenting in attracting investment from venture capitalists. Hence, the relevance of patents might be overrated if the positive effect of patents is to some extent resulting from the (unobserved) existence of prototypes. We contribute to the existing literature by investigating the relevance of patents and prototypes for the external finance of innovative new ventures. In particular, we argue that venture capitalists tend to assign higher value to the signal of patents if innovative nascent entrepreneurs also signal feasibility by developing a prototype and vice versa. Consequently, it can be argued that the value of sending both signals is higher than the value of the sum of separate signals. Hence, we investigate empirically whether new ventures owning a patent or filing an application for a patent is essential to the business are more likely to obtain equity finance if in addition a prototype has been developed.

Additionally, we contribute to the literature by focusing on innovative *nascent* ventures. In contrast, previous studies are restricted to analysis of *existing* firms that survived the start-up phase. Yet, it may be that financing constraints have the greatest impact on deterring potential entrepreneurs from even starting a new firm. Cassar (2004, p. 279) states that for analyses of the financing of business start-ups "the ideal sample would consist of entrepreneurs in the process of starting a venture and tracking these entrepreneurs through the initial stages of business formation". In this article we therefore shift the lens away from established, incumbent firms, to nascent ventures (entrepreneurs). We use a new dataset to address the point emphasized by Cassar (2004).

We use data obtained from a web-based survey of visitors of a web site that provides information for entrepreneurs who are seeking external finance. In our empirical analysis we focus on nascent entrepreneurs who are in the *process* of starting a new venture and who were asked to provide information about the characteristics of their *innovative nascent ventures*. Our Innovative Nascent Entrepreneurs Database (INED) allows us to identify nascent ventures with patents or patent applications, prototypes and provides information on external sources of finance. While it is likely that our data are not representative, our database has some important advantages. In contrast to existing empirical studies, we are able to eliminate the problem of *survivorship bias* because we analyze ventures at birth. Moreover, we are able to distinguish between nascent ventures that are in the planning stage and those in the very early start-up stage. Furthermore, nationally representative samples tend to be dominated by non-innovative nascent ventures whereas a large fraction of nascent ventures in our sample are ventures with patents or patents applications.

Our empirical results suggest that innovative nascent ventures possessing patents as well as prototypes have a higher probability of obtaining equity finance from business angels and venture capitalists. However, we find that the signal matters to investors only if the nascent ventures are in the early stage of the startup

rather than the planning stage. This may indicate that nascent entrepreneurs may have to use their own resources in the *planning stage* in order to file patents and to develop prototypes and those nascent entrepreneurs who successfully signaled appropriability and feasibility may have a higher probability of attracting investment from business angels and venture capitalists in the *early start-up stage*. Bank finance, however, does not seem to value any of the signals and is based only on collateral.

In the following section we discuss the issue of financial constraints for innovative firms, followed by a detailed discussion of appropriability and feasibility issues and their relation to financing constraints. Section 3 introduces the data used and provides some descriptive statistics; Section 4 presents empirical results and a final discussion section concludes the study.

2. Literature and hypotheses development

2.1. Financial constraints of innovative nascent entrepreneurs

The emerging literature on markets for technology analyzes the implications of the presence of markets for technology for firms' corporate strategies and the factors limiting the development of markets for technology (Arora and Gambardella, 2010). One important insight of this literature is that the possibility of selling and buying technologies enlarges the firms' strategy space (Arora et al., 2001). Firms do not necessarily have to commercialize their innovations themselves but may choose to sell their technology, e.g. they can license it to other firms. Hence, in the presence of markets for technology innovative nascent entrepreneurs have to make a fundamental decision between two business models: first, they may decide in favor of a focused business model where they appropriate the returns on their innovative efforts by selling technology. Biotech start-ups, for instance, may focus on research and sell their technology to large pharmaceutical firms. Second, innovative nascent entrepreneurs may decide in favor of in-house exploitation and commercialize their innovations by developing the technology in-house and by investing in complementary assets in order to manufacture goods. Of course, it is also possible that a venture combines both strategies and exploits important technologies in-house, while licensing 'non-core' technologies (Arora et al., 2001, p. 430).

The profitability of both business models and, thus, the expected future value of innovative nascent ventures is determined by the tradeoff between the costs associated with the more integrated approach and the potentially lower rents from licensing (Arora et al., 2001). This tradeoff depends, for instance, on appropriability conditions. As pointed out by Teece (1986), innovative firms should acquire complementary assets if they are not able to appropriate rents from innovation through licensing because technology cannot be effectively protected by intellectual property rights. Arora and Gambardella (2010) state that uncertainty about property rights, about the value of the technology, and about the transaction process hinder the development of a market for technology. Moreover, *asymmetric* uncertainty and opportunistic behavior may lead to an increase in transactions costs and reduce the efficiency of markets for technology. Hence, one might expect that many nascent entrepreneurs acquire complementary assets to exploit their innovation. Arora et al. (2001, p. 439), however, conclude that "to the extent that the entrepreneurial start-up may not be very efficient at building those assets in-house, in-house exploitation is probably a much riskier and possibly less efficient strategy."

Innovative nascent ventures usually rely on external finance, irrespective of whether entrepreneurs decide in favor of a focused business model or in favor of in-house application. The tremendous growth of the U.S. venture capital industry since the 1980s

D.B. Audretsch et al. / Research Policy 41 (2012) 1407–1421   1409

has helped many innovative start-ups attract external financing through the equity market and this may have reduced the cost of technology development as well as the cost of acquiring complementary assets (Arora et al., 2001, p. 439). Nevertheless, innovative nascent ventures tend to be financially constrained for several reasons. Information asymmetries, uncertainty, and the potential nonexclusive nature of investments in intangible assets make it especially difficult for potential investors to evaluate the expected future value of innovative nascent ventures (Audretsch and Weigand, 2005).

Asymmetric information between nascent entrepreneurs and potential investors is major problem. Nascent entrepreneurs have better information about the returns occurring from their investment in intangible assets than do potential investors. Hence, adverse selection and moral hazard problems may hinder firms to obtain external finance or external finance may be very costly (Carpenter and Petersen, 2002). It is likely that information asymmetries are a more severe problem for innovative nascent ventures that do not have any established track record than for already existing firms.

Uncertainty about the commercial value of technologies may negatively affect the development of markets for technology and consequently the expected future profits of innovative nascent ventures (Arora and Gambardella, 2010). It can make, for instance, a focused business model less attractive. Moreover, potential investors may start their engagement in a very early stage of the start-up when the results of the innovative efforts are not clear. As Arrow (1962) points out, uncertainty characterizes the relationship between innovative efforts, or inputs into the innovation process, and their resulting outcomes (technology). Thus, "the challenge to decision making is ignorance, the fact that nobody really knows anything" (O'Sullivan, 2006, p. 257), or at least, anything for sure. If potential investors are subject to bounded rationality (Simon, 1961), the degree of uncertainty inherent in the innovative process renders their decisions to be based on subjective judgments that may or may not coincide with the assessment of the nascent entrepreneur. This implies that innovative activity may be burdened with difficulties in obtaining finance, even at the prevailing market interest rates. While this problem exists for all firms *per se*, one can argue that in the case of nascent entrepreneurs, potential investors are especially cautious and many times will abstain from investing in the seed stage itself. Hence, nascent entrepreneurs, due to inexperience, may not qualify for finance through the subjective judgments/heuristics commonly used by investors.

Furthermore, knowledge exhibits, at least partly, characteristics and properties of a public good, i.e. it is non-excludable and non-rival in use (Arrow, 1962). Thus, in order to fully appropriate investments in innovative activity, the associated intellectual property must be protected through protection mechanisms such as patents, copyrights or secrecy. If knowledge spills over to other firms, the benefits accruing from innovation cannot be fully appropriated by the innovating firm. Hence, the expected future value of an innovative nascent venture tends to be determined by the venture's ability to protect its technology effectively.

While problems with innovation are universal, it can be expected that these are more severe for innovative *nascent* ventures than for already *existing* ventures. Nascent entrepreneurs face financing constraints at least as great, but presumably even greater, than existing ventures do, even if the latter are new ventures.

2.2. How can nascent entrepreneurs overcome financial constraints?

The decision of venture capitalists and business angels to invest in innovative nascent ventures may be influenced by various signals. Hence, innovative nascent entrepreneurs soliciting for equity finance may have a higher probability of being financed by venture capitalists or business angels if they are able to send appropriate signals. For instance, the decision of venture capitalists may be influenced by the characteristics of entrepreneurs, such as educational background or successful start-up founding experience, which may signal entrepreneurial quality (Hsu, 2007).

In this paper, we focus on two signals, namely patents and prototypes, which may help nascent entrepreneurs to attract external finance through the equity market. Nascent entrepreneurs have to assure potential investors of the future value of their innovative nascent venture. In the following we argue that innovative nascent ventures filing applications for patents and developing prototypes are signaling their ability to appropriate the returns of their innovations (*appropriability*) and the actual *feasibility* of the proposed project. Appropriability and feasibility tend to be correlated with the future value of innovative nascent ventures. Hence, these signals are valuable for potential investors since they reduce the uncertainty about property rights, the uncertainty about the value of the technology, and information asymmetries (Spence, 1973).

Although the literature on markets for technology may suggest that better appropriability tends to increase the profit of the focused business model (e.g. licensing) more than the profit of in-house application, it can be expected that better appropriability leads to an increase in the expected profits for both business models since imitation of technology is more difficult. One might therefore argue that if appropriability of innovation can be ensured, it may help innovative nascent ventures to attract external finance.

Let us consider the problem of knowledge as a public good. The markets for knowledge create opportunities for increasing investment in innovation. From the policy perspective, the intellectual property system is encouraged mainly to ensure the appropriability of innovation and induce increases in investment further. Intellectual property (I.P.) rights are the result of government intervention through which appropriability can be ensured from research and development and further investments can be encouraged (in the line of thought followed by Arrow, 1962, Nelson, 1959, and Levin et al., 1987). Most of the nascent entrepreneurs self-finance innovative activities and try to deploy protection mechanisms which, *per se*, ensure appropriability. The question remains as to whether appropriability mechanisms, such as patents, can serve as a reliable signal to external investors to obtain more investment.

Can patents serve as signals? From a legal perspective, they do. Long (2002) shows that patents serve as a signal and patentees use patents for acquiring future benefits rather than only excluding others from accessing their intellectual property. The several reasons why patents can be used as signals are summarized by Long (2002). Patents are primarily information transfer mechanisms (Horstmann et al., 1985). In this manner they convey information about both the invention and the firm. In general, market actors believe patents are correlated with various desirable firm attributes.

Anton and Yao (2004) suggest that whether an innovation becomes patented depends on the amount of the information to be disclosed to the intellectual property markets leading to 'little patents and big secrets'. In this manner appropriability (through I.P.) signals potential investors to anticipate the true value of an innovation. The entrepreneurs know this value and if a innovation, when patented, is considered to be valuable in terms of importance, radicalness and scope of the patent (Shane, 2001).

While we address the problem of public good, patents seem to somehow be utilized as a channel through which the information asymmetry problem can also be addressed. The signal through patent acts in the mode of *information* and *characteristic* about the technology employed by the innovative nascent venture. Development of an invention from an idea and a concept to a patent indicates that the firm has prospective competent characteristics

1410   *D.B. Audretsch et al. / Research Policy 41 (2012) 1407–1421*

required in the market. The benefit to the investor when the firm fails to commercialize successfully generally includes rights and conditions, which may sometimes also share royalties accruing from the patent along with other intellectual property monetary benefits. In this way investments in start-ups by entrepreneurs holding I.P. and, in particular, patents may be considered partly secured, provided contracts are properly drawn.

Increasingly patent protection is the main factor for VCs in making the decision of whether or not to invest (Hayes, 1999). As in the job market models, potential candidates observe the characteristic (degrees) potential employers value and try to obtain them beforehand to signal their productivity. Nascent entrepreneurs could also be considered to be attracted to patenting in order to signal commercial value of their innovations (Hall and Ziedonis, 2001). On the other hand, patents or patent applications are used by venture capitalists as evidence for the quality of the management of the company, that it is at a certain stage in development, and that the company has "defined and carved out a market niche" (Lemley, 2001, p. 1505). To further lend support to the value of patenting towards financing, Helmers and Rogers (2011) studies a panel of UK startups between 2001 and 2005 and finds that startups with patents show a higher asset growth compared to the startups without patents; this asset growth, in turn, indicates the lucrativeness of investing in startups with patents.

Another extension is provided by Haeussler et al. (2009). Based on a sample of German and British biotechnology companies Haeussler et al. (2009) find that as start-ups file patent applications, the hazard of obtaining venture capital financing increases. They argue that venture capitalists not only consider patent grants but also patent applications as useful signals because patent applications contain technical information that allows potential investors to assess strengths and weaknesses of the invention. Hence, patent and patent applications provide information about appropriability conditions as well as characteristics of the technology employed and therefore reduce asymmetric information, information costs for potential investors, and investor's uncertainty about property rights. With respect to the effectiveness of patents in terms of markets for technology approach Harhoff (2011, p. 60) states that patents play a role in safeguarding the asset-values, decrease the transaction costs, facilitate licensing trade, and function as important signals to investors. Thus, we propose our first hypothesis as follows:

Hypothesis 1.   Innovative nascent ventures that own a patent or have applied for a patent that is essential for the business are more likely to obtain equity finance.

However, while patents and patent applications may reduce uncertainty about the property rights and characteristics of the technology employed, there may be still uncertainty about the *feasibility* and, therefore, the economic value of the project. Signaling feasibility may not only be important for innovative nascent ventures, which develop a technology and invest in downstream assets to commercialize their innovation, but may also be relevant for nascent ventures that are technology specialists selling or licensing the technology. However, at least for nascent ventures aiming to commercialize the innovation themselves, the expected future profits tend to be higher if the nascent venture is able to demonstrate feasibility.

One indicator of feasibility is the development of a prototype. What is ability in the eyes of an investor? For instance, we can think of manufacturing ability, ability to ensure a sound pricing and costing strategy. This would mean a big step ahead of the business plan. Every principal seeks to find such agents that would signal future plans and profitability as accurately as possible. Even though advanced planning techniques exist to provide accurate numeric forecasts, the ability of a prototype to signal success or

failure of the start-up is even higher. Mitigating information asymmetries and the quality of a signal remains a crucial step in reducing financing constraints. A strong signal that can substantially reduce information asymmetry is the development of a prototype.

Prototyping is a crucial step in the commercialization process. In some cases prototyping makes patenting easier, and in some cases it serves as a crucial link to the patent and final realization of the finished marketable product.[2] When an agent possesses a prototype, she can clearly determine the processes required for large-scale production, the resources needed and the best suppliers can be charted out. Hence production plans can be strengthened. Once the production plans are clearly defined, the costs and the pricing strategy can be accurately approximated by the agent. Business plan projections become much accurate, and therefore having a prototype serves as a signal to decrease information asymmetry and, at the same time, it also reduces the uncertainty inherent in the project.

An interesting experiment at the Cranfield Institute of Technology (Hilal and Soltan, 1992) finds the following advantages with the prototyping approach as compared to the non-prototyping (structured development approach).

1. The prototyping approach was found to be more robust to sudden and major changes (such as absence of an expert due to illness).
2. It provides a 'superior environment for knowledge elicitation, where a domain expert is available, through the mechanism of allowing the expert to criticize working models of the final system'.
3. Prototyping approach allows for greater flexibility in project planning.
4. 'Testing' can be done throughout the project while in the non-prototyping approach it is left until the very end.

In a study of 46 venture capitalists and 90 deals, Tyebjee and Bruno (1984) report that almost 23 percent of financing had been received by start-ups with a fully developed prototype. Feasibility via prototyping can also signal higher ability and therefore a higher likelihood of obtaining external funding, mainly from investors who want to be part of the start-up process and be involved at every stage. This tends to be most relevant in the case of nascent entrepreneurs confronting the most severe credit rationing, as well as information asymmetry problems. Hence, we expect that innovative nascent ventures, which have developed a prototype, can signal feasibility to potential investors, which increases the likelihood of external finance.

Hypothesis 2.   Nascent ventures with prototyped innovations are more likely to obtain equity finance.

Our previous discussion suggests that patent applications and patent grants may signal "appropriability", while the development of a prototype may signal "feasibility". So far, we have not discussed a potential relationship between the signals. One could argue that, from the point of view of a potential investor, receiving both of these signals separately may not be different than receiving both signals together. We argue, however, that there may be a complementarity between both signals so that the value of one signal increases in the presence of the other signal. A nascent entrepreneur who can signal both appropriability and feasibility

---

[2] As Libik (1969) observes, a typical product-development process in a firm involves selection of feasible projects from basic research that is then further developed (applied research phase) and, if a project is successful, then a production prototype is built.

D.B. Audretsch et al. / Research Policy 41 (2012) 1407–1421   1411

may therefore have an advantage in terms of obtaining external finance.

Prototyping, for instance, may also increase the scope and scale of appropriability by enabling the agent to benefit from subsequent intellectual property rights, such as design rights (on the prototype and production designs), copyrights and trademarks, etc. If, however, a nascent venture holds just a prototype but not a patent, it offers yet another risk that licensing costs for any technology that is planned to be used might be fatal to the venture. Moreover, as mentioned earlier, the markets for technology approach stresses not just the role of appropriability but also on the role of how the technology needs to be embodied into a product. A strategy that includes appropriating rents from technology both by licensing or patenting and by embodying into a product might be viewed by potential investors as a safer strategy to ensure profitability. Moreover, potential investors may be subject to bounded rationality and may therefore use simple rules for their investment decisions, e.g. they invest in the presence of patents and prototypes.

To sum up, especially innovative nascent ventures signaling appropriability as well as feasibility by filing applications for patents and by developing prototypes may reduce the problems of information asymmetry, uncertainty and public good nature of knowledge. Therefore, the expected benefit from investing in an innovative nascent venture having prototypes tends to be high for investors, thus increasing the probability of the agent to obtain external finance.

Hypothesis 3. Nascent ventures with patents or patent applications as well as prototyped innovations are more likely to obtain equity finance.

In the empirical analysis we not only concentrate on VCs (which are well versed in receiving signals) but also business angels and show that signals work with them as well, in that VCs and business angels are different from bankers with respect to financing criteria (Mason and Stark, 2004). As Mason and Stark put it, in contrast to VCs, business angels are supposed to have prior industry experience themselves in order to assess the market risks correctly. Hence, prototypes and patents can be assessed by business angels with knowledge of the industry and can decide upon the financing of the idea. Moreover, business angels and VCs are also particular about market characteristics that might affect the innovation. Hence, one can expect that feasibility of an innovation is also better assessed by business angels and VCs.

Although we framed our hypotheses in a very general way, it is highly likely that the relevance and the effects of patents and prototypes depend on the field of technology. The results of empirical studies show, for instance, that the effectiveness of patents as a mechanism for the protection of innovations varies considerably across industries (Cohen et al., 2000). Moreover, it is likely that a prototyping strategy is not feasible in all industries and that the costs of prototyping may differ across sectors and industries. In our empirical analysis we therefore control for sector-specific fixed effects and conduct robustness checks where we exclude sectors that tend to be less qualified for exploring the effects of patent and prototypes.

To empirically test our hypotheses, we use a new dataset of nascent ventures (entrepreneurs), which is explained in the following section.

3. Data and methodology

3.1. Building the Innovative Nascent Entrepreneurs Database (INED)

To test our hypotheses, the types of data sets providing information about the financial structure of (new) firms that have been

used in previous studies are of little use. In contrast to existing studies, we focus on nascent ventures rather than established firms, however young they may be. Thus, a very different type of dataset providing information on innovative activities and financial prospects of nascent ventures is required to test the hypotheses posited in the previous section.

Finding a dataset possessing information both on nascent ventures' innovation activity and their finance is difficult. For this article a new data set is developed and applied, which is based on a survey of 4122 entrepreneurs (including individuals who are considering launching a new business), investors and others. The data set was created for the Ewing Marion Kauffman Foundation by the Center for Innovative Entrepreneurship (CIE) in May–June, 2005 and consists of a web-based survey of potential entrepreneurs. CIE surveyed visitors of the web site http://www.vfinance.com, which is a location for entrepreneurs seeking finance and interested in finding the names of potential angel investors or venture capital firms. CIE implemented the survey using two methods. This first was to send each web site visitor an email inviting them to participate in the survey. The second method involved soliciting a random sample of web site visitors to participate in the survey. An important qualification of this data base involves selection bias. The data base consists solely of individuals sufficiently interested in obtaining finance that they visited the web site. Thus, individuals not interested in obtaining finance for a new venture are not included in the data base. However, it is important to emphasize that the two major hypotheses do not imply starting with a sample of individuals representative of the overall working population and then identifying which ones constitute nascent entrepreneurs. Rather, in this study the starting point should consist of individuals who are already nascent entrepreneurs. Thus, the appropriate data base should exclude those not considering launching a new venture and include only those individuals who can be reasonably classified as being a nascent entrepreneur. Thus, while the well-known PSED (Panel Study of Entrepreneurial Dynamics), for instance, was initiated to provide representative data on important features of the entrepreneurial or start-up process (Reynolds et al., 2004), it is more appropriate for testing hypotheses distinguishing between nascent and non-nascent entrepreneurs. While the sampling mechanism used in PSED is appropriate to generate a sample that is nationally representative with respect to population characteristics, like age or education, it might not be ideal for analyzing innovative nascent entrepreneurs' sources of external finance, where a data base consisting solely of innovative nascent entrepreneurs is more appropriate.

As pointed out by Davidsson (2006, p. 55), the downside of the 'representative' sample provided by the PSED "is that the sample will be very heterogeneous and dominated by imitative, low-potential ventures". In order to get sufficient numbers of high-tech firms, Davidsson suggests to make use of other sampling mechanisms than probability sampling. In this respect, the data base used in this article based on the CIE survey is a valuable source of information about innovative nascent entrepreneurs, who are, by definition, *seeking finance*. Moreover, the share of innovative entrepreneurs included in this database is strikingly high.

3.2. Variable definitions

While the PSED data base consists of a sample presumably reflecting characteristics of the overall population, we created the Innovative Nascent Entrepreneurs Database (INED) from the CIE survey to consist solely of nascent entrepreneurs. However, in creating the INED, a similar criteria were used that a respondent had to meet in order to be considered as a nascent entrepreneur. In particular, for an individual to be classified as a nascent entrepreneur in the PSED, each record had to meet three criteria: (1) "now trying

1412   *D.B. Audretsch et al. / Research Policy 41 (2012) 1407–1421*

to start a new business", (2) "currently active in a startup effort" and "anticipates part or full ownership of the new business", and (3) "has NOT yet attained positive monthly cash flow that covered expenses and the owner–manager salaries for more than three months" (Reynolds et al., 2004, p. 268).

For the INED, an individual was similarly classified as being a nascent entrepreneur if the three following analogous conditions were met:

- The individual is seeking capital to start a new business,
- The individual intends to be owner or part owner of the business, and
- The business has not generated revenues in 2004 and 2005.

Respondents claiming zero percent ownership or having positive revenues in 2004–2005 were not classified as being nascent entrepreneurs. The questions included in the survey are presented in Appendix A. The sample can be distinguished as consisting of two major groups, or sub-samples: the group of individuals engaged in the planning stage for starting a new firm and the group of individuals actually engaged in the launch of a new venture. We identified entrepreneurs in the planning stage and entrepreneurs in the start-up stage by using interviewees' answers to the following question: "Which of these best describes you?" An individual was classified as a planning stage nascent entrepreneur, or belonging to the former group, if she declares that she is "planning to start a new business". By contrast, a respondent was classified as being in the early start-up stage if she declares: "I currently own and operate a business."

In order to ensure the integrity and consistency of the data we applied additional stringent criteria for classifying nascent entrepreneurs as either planning stage or incipient start-ups. First, we used the question "where is your business in the start-up process?" Entrepreneurs are not considered for the empirical analysis if they report that they are planning to start a business and at the same time declare that their start-up is in operation or product/service is already launched. Likewise entrepreneurs are not considered if they report that they own and operate a business and at the same time state that they are still developing a concept. Second, entrepreneurs reporting that they started their business before 2005 and/or that the number of employees, not counting the owners, exceeds one were excluded from the first group (planning stage nascent entrepreneurs). Similarly, those respondents reporting that they started their business before 2003 and/or that the number of employees exceeds ten were excluded from the second group (incipient start-ups).

3.2.1. External source of finance

The data set contains information about the sources of business financing. Entrepreneurs reported whether they used the following external financing sources to establish their business: (1) bank loans to the business, (2) home equity loan in an owner's name, (3) other bank loans in an owner's name, (4) venture funds in exchange for stock/ownership in company and (5) individual investors or companies in exchange for stock/ownership in company. While the first three sources are indicators of debt, the last two sources represent indicators of equity. The consistency of the responses was checked and verified. First, those records where respondents reported equity finance and 100 percent ownership were excluded from the sample. Second, those records where a respondent reported owning zero percent of the business and at the same time reported having equity as a source of business financing were also excluded from the sample.

3.2.2. Patents and prototype

In the survey entrepreneurs were asked the following question, "Does your business own or have you applied for a patent that is

Table 1
Sectoral distribution of nascent entrepreneurs.

Sectors	Planning stage Percent	Early start-up stage Percent
Accommodation & Food Services	8.02	0.84
Arts, Entertainment & Recreation	13.68	12.11
Broadcasting & Telecommunications	3.77	3.34
Construction	2.36	1.25
Educational Services	4.01	2.3
Finance, Insurance & Real Estate	6.13	6.89
Health Care & Social Assistance	4.72	7.31
Manufacturing	6.84	9.39
Professional, Business, Scientific & Technical Services	9.20	11.9
Publishing, Software & Information Services	6.37	11.48
Retail & Wholesale	14.86	8.98
Transportation & Warehousing	0.94	1.46
Other services	8.25	9.39
Other	10.85	13.36
Total	100.00	100.00

Total sample: 906 observations; planning stage: 426 observations; early start-up stage: 480 observations.

essential to the business?". This question was used to compute the dummy variable 'patents' which takes the value one if the answer is YES and zero otherwise. Respondents where also asked "Where is your business in the start-up process?" This question was used to compute the dummy variable 'prototype' which takes the value one if the answer is 'prototype developed' and zero otherwise.

3.2.3. Business relevant information

The data set contains additional information about the entrepreneur and the proposed startup. In particular, records indicate whether a business plan was written, whether the business has international links, whether the respondent is a serial entrepreneur, whether the business was started by a single person or a team of people and whether the respondent owns a house that can be used as collateral (see Appendix A for the questions asked).

3.3. Descriptive statistics

Table 1 displays the sectoral distribution of nascent entrepreneurs in our sample. Neither in the planning stage nor in the early start-up stage is our sample restricted to specific sectors; rather is comprises of entrepreneurial activities across multiple sectors.

Table 2 reports for each sector the fraction of nascent entrepreneurs who report that they own or are applying for a patent, who report that they have developed a prototype, and who report that they have done both. As can be seen from the table, there is a considerable variation between sectors. In some sectors the fraction of nascent ventures with patents and/or prototypes is low or even zero while the fraction is quite high in other sectors (e.g. manufacturing). However, one should interpret the data with some caution because our dataset is not representative at the sectoral level due to the low number of observations. Therefore, data do not allow us to draw definite conclusions on the relevance of patents and prototype in specific sectors.

The means and standard deviations of all variables are reported in Table 3. As can be seen from the table, 12 percent of the nascent entrepreneurs in the planning stage use debt as an external source of finance. By contrast, 19 percent of nascent incipient entrepreneurs in the very early stage of the venture rely on debt. With respect to equity finance, the difference between both the planning and incipient entrepreneurs is even larger. While only 6 percent of nascent entrepreneurs in the planning stage have equity

D.B. Audretsch et al. / Research Policy 41 (2012) 1407–1421   1413

Table 2
Sectoral distribution of patents and prototypes.

Sectors	Patents Percent	Prototype Percent	Patents & prototype Percent
Accommodation & Food Services	5.26	0.00	0.00
Arts, Entertainment & Recreation	20.69	15.52	10.34
Broadcasting & Telecommunications	31.25	15.62	6.25
Construction	6.25	0.00	0.00
Educational Services	0.00	3.57	0.00
Finance, Insurance & Real Estate	8.47	6.78	3.39
Health Care & Social Assistance	32.73	21.82	12.73
Manufacturing	52.70	31.08	18.92
Professional, Business, Scientific & Technical Services	32.29	19.79	12.50
Publishing, Software & Information Services	28.05	31.71	17.07
Retail & Wholesale	14.15	14.15	10.38
Transportation & Warehousing	9.09	9.09	0.00
Other services	17.50	8.75	6.25
Other	34.55	20.91	13.64

Total sample: 906 observations.

finance, more than 20 percent of the nascent entrepreneurs in the early start-stage have equity finance. These differences are statistically significant at the 1 percent level. Nascent entrepreneurs in the planning stage choose either debt (25 percent) or equity (50 percent), whereas only one entrepreneur of this group relies on both, debt and equity. In the early start-up stage 19 percent entrepreneurs rely on both sources of external finance while 73 percent choose only equity and 79 percent choose only debt.

The fraction of innovative nascent entrepreneurs, which includes those with a patent application or ownership of a business related patent, increases from 15.5 percent in the planning stage to more than 20 percent in the early start-up stage. An even stronger increase can be observed for the fraction of entrepreneurs who report to have developed prototypes. It is 6.1 percent in the planning stage and 25.2 percent in the early start-up stage. In the group of entrepreneurs in the planning stage, 66 applied for a patent or own one and 32 percent of these have also developed a prototype. In the early start-up stage, 155 new ventures have patents or have applied for patents, and 47 percent of these innovative start-ups have also developed a prototype. Although we do not know whether the patents are related to the prototype, it is likely

Table 3
Descriptive statistics.

Variable	Planning stage		Early start-up stage		Z-test
	Mean	Std. Dev.	Mean	Std. Dev.	
Debt	0.120	0.325	0.192	0.394	3.0[*]
Equity	0.061	0.240	0.204	0.404	6.3[*]
Patents	0.155	0.362	0.323	0.468	5.9[*]
Concept in development	0.296	0.457	N.A.	N.A.	N.A.
Concept developed	0.636	0.482	0.304	0.461	−10.0[*]
Prototype developed	0.068	0.252	0.260	0.439	7.7[*]
Start-up operation	N.A.	N.A.	0.390	0.488	N.A.
Product/service	N.A.	N.A.	0.046	0.209	N.A.
Business plan	0.601	0.490	0.835	0.371	7.9[*]
Serial entrepreneur	0.467	0.500	0.600	0.490	4.0[*]
International links	0.110	0.314	0.215	0.411	4.2[*]
Team	0.340	0.474	0.479	0.500	4.2[*]
House	0.587	0.493	0.625	0.485	1.2

All variables are dummy variables that take on the values one or zero. N.A. means not applicable.

[*] Z-test for the equality between two proportions: significant at the 1 percent level.

Table 4
Descriptive statistics: patents and sources of finance.

	No external	Debt	Equity	Both	Total
Planning stage					
No patents	299	40	20	1	360
	(85.4)	(80.0)	(80.0)	(100.0)	(84.5)
Patents	51	10	5	0	66
	(14.6)	(20.0)	(20.0)	(0.0)	(15.5)
	350	50	25	1	426
	(100)	(100)	(100)	(100)	(100)
Early start-up stage					
No patents	229	49	34	13	325
	(74.1)	(67.1)	(43.0)	(68.4)	(67.7)
Patents	80	24	45	6	155
	(25.9)	(32.3)	(56.7)	(31.6)	(32.3)
	309	73	79	19	480
	(100)	(100)	(100)	(100)	(100)

Percentage in parentheses.

that at least some of the nascent entrepreneurs try to protect their business relevant innovation (prototype) through patents.

As seen in Table 3, 63 percent of the nascent entrepreneurs in the planning stage have developed a concept while 30 percent of them are still in the process of developing a concept. As can be expected, the fraction of nascent entrepreneurs that have developed only a concept is significantly smaller for the group of nascent entrepreneurs in an early start-up stage. Most of them report 'start-up operation' but only 4.6 percent have already launched a product or services. However, this is not surprising since these are start-ups that have not yet generated revenue.

There are also significant differences between both groups with respect to the fraction of those entrepreneurs who have written a business plan, who have established links with international partners and who have previously started a business. In the group of incipient nascent entrepreneurs, these fractions are larger. Moreover, there are more serial entrepreneurs in this group and more team start-ups. The large fraction of teams (50 percent) is consistent with the prevalence of teams reported by the PSED.

Table 4 reports the number and share of nascent entrepreneurs who have chosen debt and/or equity finance for sub-samples of innovative (with a patent) and non-innovative (without a patent) nascent entrepreneurs. In the planning stage the fraction of innovative nascent entrepreneurs without external finance (14.6 percent) corresponds with their fraction in the total sample (15.5 percent). With respect to debt and equity they are slightly over-represented in this stage. In the incipient stage, however, they are underrepresented in the category 'no external finance' and they are over-represented with respect to equity finance. This points to a remarkable change in the capital structure between these early stages of the new venture.

One obvious explanation for the significant differences between nascent entrepreneurs in the planning stage and their counterparts in the incipient stage of launching a new venture is that at least some of the start-up characteristics may reflect the probability of making a transition from the a nascent entrepreneur in the planning stage to a nascent entrepreneur in the early start-up stage. Consequently, the fraction of start-ups with these characteristics would be higher in later stages of the start-up. Parker and Belghitar (2006) investigate the decision of nascent entrepreneurs to quit, to remain a nascent entrepreneur or to start a new firm. They find, for instance, that preparing business plans and having experience in business ownership do not influence the decision by nascent entrepreneurs, whereas team ventures are less likely to make the transition form planning stage to launching the new venture. Another interpretation is that many nascent entrepreneurs may begin to write business plans, intensify their innovation efforts

1414   *D.B. Audretsch et al. / Research Policy 41 (2012) 1407–1421*

or try to establish links to international partners once they make the decision to launch a new venture.

In summary, the descriptive statistics suggest that the decomposition of the sample into two groups is reasonable since both groups differ with respect to relevant business characteristics. In the econometric analysis we, therefore, investigate each group separately in order to test how innovative activity influences the capital structure of nascent entrepreneurs. Moreover, correlation coefficients that are reported in Tables 5 and 6 suggest that multicollinearity between explanatory variables is not a severe problem.

4. Empirical results

4.1. Do patents and prototypes affect external financing?

In this section we present estimates of marginal effects which are obtained from separate estimations of the multinomial logit model (MNL) for nascent entrepreneurs in the planning stage and nascent entrepreneurs in the early start-up stage. We did not differentiate between nascent entrepreneurs who rely only on equity finance and those who rely on both, equity and debt. Instead, we estimated the MNL model with the three categories 'no external finance', 'debt finance' and 'both sources of external finance'. For the group of entrepreneurs in the planning stage this distinction would be unsuitable since only one entrepreneur has both, debt and equity. For the other group, a Wald test of whether the two categories 'only equity finance' and 'both sources of finance' can be combined suggests that this is the case. Further Wald tests reject the null hypothesis that these categories can be further collapsed indicating that significant differences between the determinants of external sources of finance exist.

The *marginal effects* of the explanatory variables on the probabilities of each category are reported for the group of nascent entrepreneurs in the planning stage and for the group of nascent entrepreneurs in an early start-up stage in Table 7.[3] As seen from this table, having a patent or a prototype does not affect the probability of obtaining external finance if nascent entrepreneurs are in the planning stage. The estimated marginal effect of the dummy variable prototype on the probability of having no external finance is negative and the marginal effect of this variable on the probability of having both, debt and equity finance is positive. However, the estimates of these marginal effects are statistically insignificant. The estimated marginal effects of the dummy variable patents are also statistically insignificant.

Other variables do influence the probability of being externally financed. Nascent entrepreneurs in the planning stage who have a business plan, who have started a business before and who (or whose family members) own a house have a lower probability of having no external sources of finance. The probability of having debt finance is positively affected by the existence of a business plan and by house ownership. Obviously, the existence of collateral is very relevant for bank loans as was found by Ueda (2004). This can be seen as a timing problem that the entrepreneurs may first approach the bank and then, if they fail, they prefer equity. In this case it can be argued that banks do not recognize patents and prototypes as signals. But as Ueda (2004) shows, it is the entrepreneurs with low collateral that approach venture capitalists. Therefore it can be self-selection on the part of the entrepreneur that she chooses to approach the VC/business angel first. In this case we can conclude that the entrepreneur directly approaches the VC/BA

because she realizes that VC/BA might be the right signal receivers, and thus avoids banks altogether. Also, a business plan and a developed concept have a positive impact on obtaining equity. Moreover, being a team start-up reduces the probability of debt finance whereas it is positive for equity.

The results are strikingly different for the early start-up stage. Here, the probability of having no external sources of finance decreases if a start-up owns a patent or has applied for patent, has developed a prototype, has launched products/services or has established international links. Again, serial entrepreneurs and team start-ups have a higher probability of choosing external finance. The probability of debt finance is higher if a start-up has launched product/services and as in the planning stage team start-ups have a lower probability of debt finance and existence of collateral increases this probability. The probability of equity finance is higher for nascent entrepreneurs that have developed a prototype and that have contracted with companies or individuals outside the United States for goods or services. As in the planning stage, team start-ups and start-ups with a business plan are more likely to choose equity. The estimated marginal effect of the variable prototype is of the same order of magnitude as for entrepreneurs in the planning stage but now this effect is statistically significant at the one percent level.

Note that estimated marginal effects imply that nascent entrepreneurs with prototypes have a remarkably higher probability of having equity finance. Since the variable prototype is a dummy variable, the estimated marginal effect means that a nascent entrepreneur with a prototype has 15.3 percent higher probability of being financed by business angels or venture capitalists than other nascent entrepreneurs. In contrast, having a patent does not affect the probability of having equity finance.

The statistically insignificant effect of patents for equity finance might be explained by the fact that many start-ups with a prototype also report that they have applied for a patent or own a patent. Therefore, we performed additional estimations that take this into account by differentiating between start-ups that report only a patent, start-ups that have a prototype but no patent and start-ups that have both.

The estimation results are reported in Table 8. For the group of entrepreneurs in the planning stage the estimation results are hardly affected. For the group of entrepreneurs in an early start-up stage, however, the results now show that especially start-ups that report both, patents and prototypes, have a higher probability of being externally financed and in particular the probability of equity finance is positively affected. However, the results also show that start-ups with a prototype but no patent have a higher probability of equity finance while this is not the case for start-ups with patents but no prototype. The magnitude of the estimated marginal effects is remarkable. It implies that a nascent entrepreneur who possesses a prototype and a patent has a 26.5 percent higher probability of being financed by business angels or venture capitalists than are nascent entrepreneurs without patents and prototypes. The marginal effects of the dummy variables "only prototype" and "only patents" are positive but statistically insignificant.

4.2. Robustness checks

In order to check the robustness of our estimation results we performed additional regressions. First, we excluded sectors which might be less qualified for exploring the effects of patents and prototypes. Since previous results suggest that patents and prototypes are relevant for equity finance but not bank loans, we focus on the probability of being financed by venture capitalists and/or business angels. Marginal effects based on the results of probit model estimations are reported in Table 9. Column (1) reports the result for the total sample and it therefore simply reproduces the

---

[3] Since they are more straightforward to interpret, we report the marginal effects of explanatory variables on the probability of each category instead of reporting the estimated coefficients of the MNL model which reflect the marginal effect of a change in the respective variable on the *log-odds ratios* of the categories.

D.B. Audretsch et al. / Research Policy 41 (2012) 1407–1421

Table 5
Correlation matrix of explanatory variables (planning stage).

	(1)	(2)	(3)	(4)	(5)	(6)	(7)	(8)
(1) Patents	1							
(2) Prototype developed	0.43*	1						
(3) Concept developed	−0.12	−0.36	1					
(4) Business plan	0.09	0.03	0.27*	1				
(5) Serial entrepreneur	0.01	0.08	−0.05	0.03	1			
(6) International links	0.08	−0.07	0.0184	0.01	0.15*	1		
(7) Team	0.03	0.04	0.12*	0.18*	0.0926	0.11*	1	
(8) House	0.00	−0.06	0.03	−0.01	0.10*	0.01	−0.00	1

* Significant at the 5 percent level.

Table 6
Correlation matrix of explanatory variables (early start-up stage).

	(1)	(2)	(3)	(4)	(5)	(6)	(7)	(8)	(9)
(1) Patents	1								
(2) Prototype developed	0.33*	1							
(3) Start-up operation	−0.21*	−0.47*	1						
(4) Product/service	0.02	−0.13*	−0.17*	1					
(5) Business plan	0.14*	0.03	−0.03	−0.09*	1				
(6) Serial entrepreneur	0.09	0.10*	−0.10*	−0.07	0.07	1			
(7) International links	0.17*	0.16*	−0.06	−0.07	0.05	0.14*	1		
(8) Team	0.17*	0.02	−0.03	−0.01	0.11*	0.18*	0.20*	1	
(9) House	−0.01	0.06	−0.03	−0.04	0.01	0.11*	0.07	0.12*	1

* Significant at the 5 percent level.

results based on multinomial logit estimations reported in column ('Both') in Table 8. As can be expected, the results are very similar. Descriptive statistics presented in Table 2 show that in four sectors the number of nascent ventures having patents and prototypes at the same time is zero. Hence, these sectors may be less qualified for analyzing the effects of patents and prototypes. We therefore excluded these sectors from the analysis and the results of this

estimation are reported in column (2). The results are hardly affected by the exclusion of these sectors. Columns (3) and (4) report the results of regressions where we excluded further sectors for which patents and prototypes might be less relevant. In summary, the results indicate that innovative nascent ventures with patents and prototypes are more likely to be financed by venture capitalists and/or business angels.

Table 7
Determinants of nascent entrepreneurs' external sources of finance.

Variable	Planning stage			Early start-up stage		
	No	Debt	Both	No	Debt	Both
Patents	−0.0144	0.0196	−0.00521	−0.122**	0.0600	0.0617
	(0.0486)	(0.0463)	(0.0162)	(0.0530)	(0.0435)	(0.0392)
Prototype devel.	−0.146	−0.0210	0.167	−0.118*	−0.0355	0.153***
	(0.139)	(0.0462)	(0.142)	(0.0660)	(0.0433)	(0.0588)
Concept devel.	0.0222	−0.0545	0.0323*	N.A.	N.A.	N.A.
	(0.0372)	(0.0335)	(0.0174)			
Start-up oper.	N.A.	N.A.	N.A.	−0.0573	0.0431	0.0142
				(0.0548)	(0.0423)	(0.0425)
Product/service	N.A.	N.A.	N.A.	−0.188	0.218*	−0.0294
				(0.125)	(0.123)	(0.0763)
Business plan	−0.0890***	0.0531**	0.0359**	−0.0124	−0.0591	0.0715*
	(0.0295)	(0.0260)	(0.0159)	(0.0588)	(0.0501)	(0.0372)
Serial entrep.	−0.0434	0.0263	0.0172	−0.0921**	0.0659**	0.0261
	(0.0299)	(0.0271)	(0.0144)	(0.0442)	(0.0335)	(0.0343)
Internat. links	−0.0707	0.0291	0.0416	−0.117**	0.0113	0.106**
	(0.0560)	(0.0477)	(0.0336)	(0.0583)	(0.0435)	(0.0469)
Team	0.0266	−0.0601**	0.0335*	−0.132***	−0.0602*	0.192***
	(0.0314)	(0.0255)	(0.0188)	(0.0465)	(0.0338)	(0.0373)
House	−0.0922***	0.109***	−0.0166	−0.125***	0.113***	0.0120
	(0.0302)	(0.0273)	(0.0137)	(0.0429)	(0.0320)	(0.0335)
Sector effects	Yes	Yes	Yes	Yes	Yes	Yes
χ^2-Statistic	60.48			109.9		
Pseudo R^2	0.122			0.128		
Actual Frequ.	350	50	26	309	73	98
Pred. Frequ.	373	39	14	343	69	68

This table shows the marginal effects which are calculated at sample means using the results of multinomial logit estimations based on a sample of 426 nascent entrepreneurs in the planning stage and on a sample of 480 nascent entrepreneurs in the early startup stage. The estimates reflect the marginal effects of a change of the respective dummy variables from 0 to 1. The standard errors are reported in parentheses. Ten sector dummies are included to control of sector-specific fixed effects.

* Significant at the 10 percent level.
** Significant at the 5 percent level.
*** Significant at the 1 percent level.

1416   *D.B. Audretsch et al. / Research Policy 41 (2012) 1407–1421*

Table 8
Determinants of nascent entrepreneurs' external sources of finance.

Variable	Planning stage			Early start-up stage		
	No	Debt	Both	No	Debt	Both
Patents/protot.	−0.152	−0.0103	0.162	−0.284***	0.0190	0.265***
	(0.139)	(0.0527)	(0.141)	(0.0832)	(0.0598)	(0.0852)
Only prototype	−0.128	0.00465	0.123	−0.0810	−0.0620	0.143
	(0.179)	(0.0984)	(0.168)	(0.0901)	(0.0481)	(0.0871)
Only patents	−0.0159	0.0257	−0.00985	−0.0890	0.0397	0.0493
	(0.0543)	(0.0520)	(0.0169)	(0.0674)	(0.0532)	(0.0532)
Concept devel.	0.0222	−0.0545	0.0322*	N.A.	N.A.	N.A.
	(0.0372)	(0.0334)	(0.0174)			
Start-up oper.	N.A.	N.A.	N.A.	−0.0557	0.0419	0.0138
				(0.0547)	(0.0423)	(0.0426)
Product/service	N.A.	N.A.	N.A.	−0.192	0.219*	−0.0270
				(0.126)	(0.124)	(0.0777)
Business plan	−0.0883***	0.0529**	0.0354**	−0.0157	−0.0570	0.0727*
	(0.0295)	(0.0260)	(0.0159)	(0.0587)	(0.0499)	(0.0372)
Serial entrep.	−0.0423	0.0257	0.0166	−0.0930**	0.0654*	0.0276
	(0.0299)	(0.0271)	(0.0144)	(0.0444)	(0.0335)	(0.0345)
Internat. links	−0.0716	0.0292	0.0423	−0.117**	0.0109	0.106**
	(0.0561)	(0.0476)	(0.0339)	(0.0584)	(0.0435)	(0.0470)
Team	0.0261	−0.0603**	0.0343*	−0.133***	−0.0591*	0.192***
	(0.0315)	(0.0255)	(0.0191)	(0.0465)	(0.0338)	(0.0373)
House	−0.0932***	0.110***	−0.0164	−0.129***	0.115***	0.0137
	(0.0303)	(0.0274)	(0.0136)	(0.0431)	(0.0321)	(0.0336)
Sector effects	Yes	Yes	Yes	Yes	Yes	Yes
χ^2-Statistic	73.5			142.2		
Pseudo R^2	0.148			0.166		
Actual Frequ.	350	50	26	309	73	98
Pred. Frequ.	377	37	12	343	69	68

This table shows the marginal effects which are calculated at sample means using the results of multinomial logit estimations based on a sample of 426 nascent entrepreneurs in the planning stage and on a sample of 480 nascent entrepreneurs in the early startup stage. In this specification we test the effect of possessing both a patent and a prototype on financing. We also identify the effect of having only one of either patent or prototype. As can be observed, the effect of having only prototypes and having both is quite large on external financing. The estimates reflect the marginal effects of a change of the respective dummy variables from 0 to 1. The standard errors are reported in parentheses. Ten sector dummies are included to control of sector-specific fixed effects.
* Significant at the 10 percent level.
** Significant at the 5 percent level.
*** Significant at the 1 percent level.

So far, we used equity as a dependent variable. Hence, the previous results are based on the implicit assumption that the probability of being financed by a venture capitalist is affected by the same factors as the probability of being financed by a business angel. However, there might be differences in the decision making between venture capitalists and business angels. Again, Table 10 reports the results for the total sample. Column (1) reports the estimation results where the dependent takes the value 1 if the nascent venture is financed by equity and zero otherwise, similarly Column (2) reports estimations results where the dependent variable takes the value 1 if the nascent entrepreneur is financed by a venture capitalist and Column (3), reports on estimation results where the dependent variable takes the value 1 if the nascent venture is financed by a business angel. Again, the results are very similar. The estimated marginal effect of patents plus prototype is higher than the marginal effect of patents alone. We tested for differences between the marginal effects and the tests show that the differences are also statistically significant.

A problem of our approach might be the potentially endogenous dummy variables, prototype and patents. One might consider the dependent binary variable 'equity' as simultaneously determined with the dichotomous regressors 'patents' and 'prototype'. Reverse causality might be a problem because better-funded nascent entrepreneurs, for instance, may have more resources to devote to filing patents and developing prototypes. Moreover, venture capitalists may encourage funded nascent entrepreneurs to file patents. If this would be the case, our estimates of the marginal effects of patents and prototypes would especially be upward biased because of endogenous dummy variables.

One argument against the potential endogeneity is the statistically insignificant effect of patents and prototypes in the planning stage. Our data show that in the *planning stage* only 14.3 percent of nascent entrepreneurs with patents and prototypes are financed by venture capitalists or business angels while in the *early start-up stage* 42.3 percent of nascent entrepreneurs with patents and prototypes are financed by venture capitalist and business angels. This may suggest that nascent entrepreneurs may have to use their own resources in the planning stage in order to file patents and to develop prototypes. In the early start-up stage, however, business angels and venture capitalists may begin to support those nascent entrepreneurs who successfully signaled appropriability and feasibility.

Although these results are suggestive, they do not represent a formal test of exogeneity. Monfardini and Radice (2008) propose a test of exogeneity of a dichotomous regressor that is based on the estimation of a recursive bi-variate probit model. In our case this model consists of a reduced form equation for the potentially endogenous dummy variable 'patents' ('prototype' or 'prototype & prototype') and a structural form equation for equity. This enables a test whether the correlation between the residuals of these equations is zero which is the null hypothesis (exogeneity).

To ensure that the other variables are exogenous, we include only the variable 'team', which is very likely to be exogenous, and the sector dummies in our model. One might suspect that the variables 'business plan' and 'international links', which have a significant effect on the probability of having equity finance, are also endogenous. A venture capitalist may force, for instance, nascent entrepreneurs to write a business plan or to have international links. Although we think that this is not very likely, we

Table 9
Probability of equity finance for different sectors - results of probit estimation.

	(1)	(2)	(3)	(4)
Patents/protot.	0.271***	0.258***	0.217***	0.229**
	(0.0788)	(0.0791)	(0.0801)	(0.120)
Only prototype	0.153*	0.0927	0.0119	0.124
	(0.0847)	(0.0790)	(0.0735)	(0.132)
Only patents	0.0550	0.0416	0.0315	0.0822
	(0.0541)	(0.0536)	(0.0582)	(0.0927)
Start-up operat.	0.0186	0.0226	−0.000527	0.0333
	(0.0426)	(0.0453)	(0.0507)	(0.0867)
Product/service	−0.0325	−0.0357	−0.0756	−0.0858
	(0.0698)	(0.0722)	(0.0684)	(0.107)
Business plan	0.0774**	0.0959***	0.1000**	0.103
	(0.0364)	(0.0368)	(0.0422)	(0.0757)
Serial entrep.	0.0277	0.0226	0.0321	0.00692
	(0.0356)	(0.0378)	(0.0429)	(0.0691)
International links	0.111**	0.112**	0.0952*	0.117
	(0.0488)	(0.0510)	(0.0554)	(0.0802)
Team	0.199***	0.217***	0.194***	0.273***
	(0.0364)	(0.0378)	(0.0434)	(0.0682)
House	0.0145	0.0196	0.00808	−0.0846
	(0.0343)	(0.0358)	(0.0415)	(0.0749)
Sector effects	Yes	Yes	Yes	Yes
Wald test	$\chi^2(20)$	$\chi^2(19)$	$\chi^2(16)$	$\chi^2(13)$
	111.26	106.91	80.13	52.21
Pseudo R^2	0.2335	0.2368	0.2142	0.2178
Observations	480	452	358	193

Probit estimation was used since the dependent variable in each specification is a binary variable. The dependent variable takes on the value one if a nascent venture is financed by venture capitalists or business angels and is zero otherwise. The first column reports the marginal effects of explanatory variables on the probability obtaining equity for the total sample. In Column 2 four sectors are excluded: Accommodation & Food Services, Educational Services, Construction, and Transportation & Warehousing. In Column 3 three further sectors are excluded: Finance, Insurance & Real Estate, Broadcasting & Telecommunications, and Other Services. In Column 4 we further exclude Arts, Entertainment & Recreation, Retail & Warhousing, and Other. Robust standard errors are reported in parentheses. Sector dummies are included to control of sector-specific fixed effects.

  * Significant at the 10 percent level.
  ** Significant at the 5 percent level.
  *** Significant at the 1 percent level.

Table 10
Probability of being financed by business angels and venture capitalists – results of probit estimation.

Variable	(1) Equity	(2) Venture capital	(3) Business angel
Patents/protot.	0.271***	0.166**	0.228***
	(0.0788)	(0.0662)	(0.0768)
Only prototype	0.153*	0.126*	0.129
	(0.0847)	(0.0713)	(0.0805)
Only patents	0.0550	0.0135	0.0441
	(0.0541)	(0.0198)	(0.0514)
Start-up operat.	0.0186	0.0248	0.0357
	(0.0426)	(0.0222)	(0.0409)
Product/service	−0.0325	0.110	−0.0557
	(0.0698)	(0.0913)	(0.0580)
Business plan	0.0774**	0.0145	0.0573
	(0.0364)	(0.0150)	(0.0352)
International links	0.111**	0.0123	0.101**
	(0.0488)	(0.0171)	(0.0467)
Serial entrep.	0.0277	0.00941	0.0455
	(0.0356)	(0.0134)	(0.0329)
Team	0.199***	0.0598***	0.154***
	(0.0364)	(0.0196)	(0.0345)
House	0.0145	0.0124	−0.00179
	(0.0343)	(0.0131)	(0.0327)
Sector effects	Yes	Yes	Yes
Wald test	$\chi^2(20)$	$\chi^2(19)$	$\chi^2(20)$
	111.26	48.02	90.33
Pseudo R^2	0.2335	0.2042	0.2070

This table concentrates specifically on the private equity market made up of venture capitalists and business angels. The first column reports the marginal effects of explanatory variables on the probability obtaining equity. The results are based on the sample of 480 nascent entrepreneurs in the early startup stage. Column 2 presents the marginal effects on obtaining only venture capital and Column 3 deals with only business angel financing. Probit estimation was used since the dependent variable in each specification is a binary variable. Robust standard errors are reported in parentheses. Ten sector dummies are included to control of sector-specific fixed effects.

  * Significant at the 10 percent level.
  ** Significant at the 5 percent level.
  *** Significant at the 1 percent level.

conservatively exclude these variables from the subsequent analysis. In principle, formal identification of the recursive bi-variate model does not require additional exogenous regressors (instruments) if there is sufficient variation in the data (Wilde, 2000). However, Monfardini and Radice (2008) show that instruments are important because they preserve the validity of the LR testing approach in the presence of misspecification.

Therefore, we make use of two additional instrumental variables that do not have a direct influence on the probability of obtaining equity finance but do affect the probability of having patents and/or prototypes. In the survey respondents were asked the following question: "*How important were these factors to you in the decision to start your business?*" Among others, two possible answers were "*Be innovative and in the forefront of technology*" and "*Develop an idea for a product*". Respondents were asked to assess the importance of the factors on a four point Likert scale. We used these scores to compute two dummy variables. The dummy variable 'innovative' takes the value one if respondents assess being innovative as important or very important and zero otherwise. The dummy variable 'idea' takes the value one if respondents assess development of product ideas as important or very important and zero otherwise.

As one might expect, most nascent entrepreneurs say that their start-up is very innovative and that ideas for products are important in starting a new business. However, 25.1 percent of the entrepreneurs in the planning stage and 16.3 percent of the entrepreneurs in the early start-up stage report that their business is not very innovative. Moreover, 20.3 percent of the entrepreneurs in the planning stage and 16.1 percent of the entrepreneurs in the

early start-up stage say that the development of a business idea is not that important. The pairwise correlations between the dummy variables 'innovative' and 'idea' and the 'patent' and 'prototype' variables are positive and statistically significant. The correlations between the instrumental variables and the 'equity' variable are much lower and in the case of the 'idea' variable the correlation is statistically insignificant.

Therefore, these two dummy variables are included as regressors in the reduced form equations for the dummy variables 'patents', 'prototype', and 'patents & prototype'. Estimation results are reported in Table 11. Columns (1a), (2a), and (3a) report the results of three different estimations where the dependent variable is 'equity' and the potentially endogenous variable is 'patents', 'prototype' or 'patents & prototype'. As can be seen from the table, the estimated coefficients of these variables are positive and statistically significant which suggests the nascent entrepreneurs with patents and prototypes are more likely to be financed by venture capitalists and business angels.[4] Columns (1b), (2b), and (3b) report the results for the reduced form equations for the potentially endogenous dummy variables. The estimated coefficients of the dummy variables 'innovative' and 'idea' are positive and statistically significant, which suggests that the instrumental variables are

---

  [4] Note that the estimated coefficients reflect the influence of the explanatory variables on the log-odds ratios and are therefore not directly comparable with the marginal effects reported in the other tables.

1418   D.B. Audretsch et al. / Research Policy 41 (2012) 1407–1421

Table 11
Results of recursive bivariate probit.

	(1a) Equity	(1b) Patents	(2a) Equity	(2b) Prototype	(3a) Equity	(3b) Prototype & Patents
Patents	1.167*** (0.42)					
Prototype			1.179** (0.52)			
Prototype & Patents					1.338** (0.58)	
Team	0.752*** (0.19)	0.452*** (0.13)	0.949*** (0.17)	0.0579 (0.14)	0.888*** (0.17)	0.269* (0.16)
Innovative		0.749*** (0.23)		0.707*** (0.26)		1.355*** (0.46)
Idea		0.839*** (0.24)		1.142*** (0.32)		1.072** (0.42)
Sector effects	Yes	Yes	Yes	Yes	Yes	Yes
Likelihood-ratio test of $\rho = 0$	$\chi^2(1)$ 2.05697		$\chi^2(1)$ 0.779692		$\chi^2(1)$ 0.788504	

In this table we address the issue of the possibility of endogeneity in the model. This we do by estimating a recursive simultaneous bi-variate probit where we endogenize patents, prototypes and both in three specifications respectively. The endogenous(binary) variable in each specification is regressed on the presence of a team and on indicators reflecting whether the entrepreneur thinks that being innovative and developing ideas for new products is important for the business. The estimations are based on a sample of 465 nascent entrepreneurs in the early start-up stage. The results suggest that, after accounting for endogeneity, the results of our model still hold true. Estimated coefficients are reported which are based on a bi-variate probit model estimation. Robust standard errors are reported in parentheses. Ten sector dummies are included to control for sector-specific fixed effects.

* Significant at the 10 percent level.
** Significant at the 5 percent level.
*** Significant at the 1 percent level.

strongly correlated with the endogenous variables.[5] Moreover, the results of the corresponding LR-tests suggest that the null hypothesis of exogeneity of these dummy variables cannot be rejected at conventional significance levels. Although not reported here, we also included our instrumental variables in both equations of the bi-variate probit model and also estimated the multinomial logit model presented in Table 8 with the two instrumental variables. However, the estimated effects of the instrumental variables are statistically insignificant, which suggests that the instruments are only correlated with equity finance through their effects on patents and prototypes. Taken together, the results of the robustness checks confirm the previous estimation results.

5. Discussion

In this article we argue that innovative nascent ventures filing applications and developing prototypes may use patents and prototypes as signals to potential investors. While patents may signal the ability of nascent ventures to protect their proprietary innovation (*appropriability*), innovative nascent ventures may use prototypes to signal the actual *feasibility* of the proposed project.

We developed three hypotheses on the relationship between patents and prototypes with an innovative nascent venture's probability of obtaining equity finance. Our first hypothesis was that patents as such have a positive effect on the likelihood of obtaining equity finance, which puts forward our appropriability argument. Next we build upon the argument by proposing that for nascent ventures, which are essentially high risk investment targets, information problems make it further difficult to obtain equity and further signals are needed that show the feasibility of the proposed project. Hence our second hypothesis was that if a nascent venture develops a prototype, it will increase the possibility of obtaining equity. Innovative nascent ventures signaling

appropriability as well as feasibility by filing applications for patents and by developing prototypes may reduce the problems of information asymmetry, uncertainty and public good nature of knowledge. A nascent venture with both patents and prototypes sends a much stronger signal than a venture that has just one of the two, in essence signaling both appropriability and feasibility. Consequently, venture capitalists and business angels may value the appropriability signal more if innovative nascent entrepreneurs also signal feasibility and vice versa. Hence, we proposed our third hypothesis that nascent ventures with patents or patent applications as well as prototyped innovations are more likely to obtain equity finance.

The results of our empirical analysis, which is based on a new database of nascent ventures, suggest that innovative nascent ventures with patents *and* prototypes are indeed more likely to obtain equity finance. This confirms our third hypothesis that having both patents and prototypes increases the likelihood of obtaining equity. It seems that patents *per se* do not have a positive influence on the probability of obtaining equity finance. Hence, our first hypothesis stating a positive relationship between patents and equity finance is only partly confirmed. A significant effect only emerges if patents are combined with the development of a prototype. One explanation for this result is that the development of a prototype reduces information asymmetries and resolves the problem of uncertainty associated with the *outcome* of innovation efforts. While prototypes may signal less risk, patents may signal that the nascent entrepreneur is well positioned to appropriate the returns from her investment in intangible assets. Hence, the expected value of an innovative new venture possessing patents and prototype may be more predictable than the value of other innovative new ventures.

The timing of patenting and involvement of investors is an issue. Are start-ups innovative before they are financed by external investors or do external investors make new ventures more innovative? The results of an empirical study by Hellman and Puri (2000), which is based on cross-section data on 149 Silicon Valley firms in the computer, telecommunication, medical and semiconductor industries, suggest that new ventures following an innovator strategy have a higher probability of obtaining venture funding than firms following an imitator strategy. Hellman and Puri (2000) use

---

[5] We also performed OLS estimations and F-tests. The null hypothesis that the estimated coefficients of the dummy variables 'innovative' and 'idea' are jointly insignificant can be rejected. For the 'patents', 'prototype', and 'patents & prototype' equation the respective F-test is: $F(2,451)$ 13.33***; 12.7***; 8.65***.

D.B. Audretsch et al. / Research Policy 41 (2012) 1407–1421   1419

information *ex ante* to identify the different foundation strategies. Their results also suggest that innovators have a significantly higher number of patents than do imitators, which indicates that the *ex ante* intent is relevant (Hellman and Puri, 2000). Using a sample of young German firms, Engel and Keilbach (2007) find that start-ups that possess patents before the foundation date are more likely to obtain venture finance. This indicates that many start-ups have patents before the involvement of the venture capitalist.

Our results are consistent with these findings. While in the *planning stage* the probability of being financed by venture capitalists and business angels is not higher for nascent entrepreneurs with patents and prototypes, we find that in the *early start-up stage* nascent entrepreneurs with patents and prototypes are more likely to attract investments from venture capitalists and business angels. This may suggest that investors react to signals from nascent entrepreneurs who have at least passed through the planning stage. This would also imply that the stress on prototyping/patenting begins right in the planning stage in order to obtain financing in the start-up stage. Hence, in the planning stage nascent entrepreneurs may have to invest their own money or have to borrow money from their family or friends in order to file patents and to develop prototypes. In the early start-up stage, however, business angels and venture capitalists may begin to support those nascent entrepreneurs who successfully signaled appropriability and feasibility.

An exclusive survey targeting early stage start-ups, which was conducted in 2008 on why entrepreneurs patent, lends further support to our results. Sichelman and Graham (2011) conducted the "2008 Berkeley Plant Survey" to which about 1000 early stage start-ups across different industries responded out of a total sample of 13,500 companies. The companies were specifically asked for their reasons to patent and among others the top reason to patent was to 'avoid others copying their idea', closely followed by the reason that patents 'improve chances of securing investment'. This result was consistent across industries with biotech and medical companies placing the importance for securing investment higher than software companies. Thus, our arguments and empirical results are supported even in elicited importance factors of patenting by entrepreneurs themselves.

Our results may also contribute to the literature dealing with the relationship between patents and market value (Hall et al., 2005; Kortum and Lerner, 2000). Prior research faced the difficulty of disentangling the value of the intellectual property right *per se* from the underlying technology the patent reflects. Patents may be positively correlated with the value of a start-up because they are a measure of the start-up's innovativeness, or because they enable the start-up to exclude competitors from a market. Our results suggest that the positive relationship between patents and equity finance is partly explained by the existence of a workable prototype. Since prototypes to some extent control for the 'underlying technology', patents are closer to being a measure of the value of intellectual property.

5.1. Limitations and future work

Our result should be taken *cum grano salis*, since they may not be generalizable to all industries and sectors. While in some industries patents are an effective mechanism to protect proprietary innovations, they are less effective in other industries (Cohen et al., 2000). Likewise, a prototyping strategy may not be feasible for all innovations or the costs of prototyping may vary remarkably across sectors and industries. Although, we tried to deal with this problem by including sector controls in our empirical analysis and by conducting regressions based on sub-samples of sectors, there is still a need for further research. An obvious next step for future research

are empirical analyses that focus on certain industries or fields of technology.

The limitations as well as opportunities for future research can be observed in many aspects of this article. First, we did not track individual nascent entrepreneurs over the start-up process, so that the empirical evidence is based on cross-sections of nascent entrepreneurs in the planning-stage versus those in the early start-up stage. Availability of the data on timing of patenting/prototyping as well as obtaining finance remains a challenge. Hence, it would be preferable to use a panel structure that identifies the exact timing.

Second, our data are obtained from a web-based survey of visitors of a web site that provides information for entrepreneurs who are seeking external finance and who are interested in finding the names of potential angel investors or venture capital firms. Hence, selection might be a problem and data might not be representative. For instance, only internet users and entrepreneurs seeking external finance are surveyed. However, for our study this sampling method and the selection resulting from it tend to be advantageous, since it can be expected that innovative nascent entrepreneurs are familiar with the internet and since we are especially interested in nascent ventures seeking external finance. Moreover, the large fraction of innovative entrepreneurs reporting that they own patents or that they have applied for a patent that is essential to the business may provide at least a *post hoc* justification for this sampling method. In contrast, nationally representative samples tend to be dominated by non-innovative nascent ventures.

Third, a major drawback of our data is the measurement of patents and prototypes. We cannot distinguish between nascent ventures owning a patent and ventures having applied for a patent. Moreover, surveyed entrepreneurs only report whether they developed a prototype but there is no further information about the maturity of the prototype. Although it can be argued that filing an application for a patent is already a signal to potential investors, future research should distinguish between patent application and ownership and should use more detailed information about prototypes.

Fourth, more information is needed on other innovation efforts of innovative nascent ventures, such as R&D activities, collaborations with other firms or the role of public science institutions, as well as licensing activities. With respect to the financial sources it would be ideal to have explicit elicitation of entrepreneurs' preferences, which may suggest a future research possibility.

5.2. Policy implications

The results of our study have implications for policy programs that support innovation and start-up activity. In terms of encouraging start-up entrepreneurs, it would be worthwhile to also assess the feasibility of proposed projects. Given that markets for technology as well as financing options expand (such as bootstrapping), policies on innovation financing should also concentrate on removing barriers to innovative nascent entrepreneurs. It is also important for business plan workshops and coaches to cite the importance of creating prototypes to prospective entrepreneurs. Prototype development, depending on the industry, should be put forward as an essential step required to gain finance from VCs and business angels. On the other hand, our study indicates that patents and prototypes do not work in case of debt financing. As Harhoff (2011) argues, patents have a potential to be used as collateral for banks. In such case, policymakers should be concerned with how to secure debt which is backed by patents as a collateral. Until now, there are no visible cases of patents being used as collateral. If this is made possible, then external financing might be easier for innovative nascent ventures, with prototypes proving to be a mechanism to signal feasibility to banks. However, we think that unless a proper

1420   *D.B. Audretsch et al. / Research Policy 41 (2012) 1407–1421*

legal structure is made around patents, banks will still maintain the conservative attitude towards innovative nascent ventures.

5.3. Conclusion

Prior research on the relationship between innovation and finance focused primarily on existing firms that survived the start-up phase. Moreover, empirical research analyzing knowledge based start-ups highlights the importance of patents for external finance. The results of our empirical analysis suggest that especially innovative nascent ventures with patents and prototyped innovations are more likely to obtain equity finance. Hence, our results caution against ignoring the relevance of prototyped innovations.

Appendix A. Questions used from the CIE questionnaire

Defining and identifying nascent entrepreneurs

- Which category best describes you? (Answers: Entrepreneur seeking capital to start a new business, Entrepreneur seeking capital for an operating business; Entrepreneur interested in business planning services or seminars; Visitor searching for general information about raising capital; Investor interested in investment opportunities; vFinance Investments Client; vFinance Employee or Associate)
- Are you actively involved in running this business? (Answer: YES/NO)
- What percent of this business do you own? (Answers: 0, 1–25, 26–50, 51–75, 76–99, 100)
- Did your business generate revenue in the first quarter of 2005 (January 2005 through March 2005)? (Answer: YES/NO)
- 2004 revenue. In U.S. dollars? (Answers: Over 10 million, 5 million to 10 million, 1 million to 5 million, 500,000 to 999,999, 250,000 to 499,999, 150,000 to 249,999, 100,000 to 149,999, 75,000 to 99,999, 50,000 to 74,999, 25,000 to 49,999, 1 to 24,999, No revenue in 2004)

Distinguishing between planning stage and early start-up stage

- Which of these best describes you? (Answers: I currently own and operate a business; I am planning to start a new business; I am interested in private investments in businesses; None of the above)

External sources of finance

- What sources of business financing have you already used to establish this business? (Answers: bank loans to the business, home equity loan in an owner's name, other bank loans in an owner's name, venture funds in exchange for stock/ownership in company, individual investors or companies in exchange for stock/ownership in company)

Business characteristics

- Where is your business in the start-up process? (Answers: concept in development, concept developed, prototype developed, start-up operation or product/service launched)
- Does your business own or have you applied for a patent that is essential to the business? (Answer: YES/NO)
- Has your business contracted with any companies or individuals outside the United States for goods or services? (Answer: YES/NO)
- Do you have a written business plan for your business? (Answer: YES/NO)

- Have you started another business before this business? (Answer: YES/NO)
- Do you or anyone in your household own your residence? (Answer: YES/NO)
- Which of the following best describes how your business was started? (Answers: A new business created by a single person; A new business created by a team of people; A business inherited from someone else; Purchase of an existing business; Purchase of a franchise)

Decision to start the business

How important were these factors to you in the decisions to start your business? (Answers: very unimportant, unimportant, important and very important)

- Be innovative and in the forefront of technology.
- Develop an idea for a product.

References

Anton, J.J., Yao, D.A., 2004. Little patents and big secrets: managing intellectual property. RAND Journal of Economics 35 (1), 1–22.
Arora, A., Fosfuri, A., Gambardella, A., 2001. Markets for technology and their implications for corporate strategy. Industrial and Corporate Change 10 (2), 419–451.
Arora, A., Gambardella, A., 2010. Ideas for rent: an overview of markets for technology. Industrial and Corporate Change 19 (3), 775–803.
Arrow, K.J., 1962. Economic welfare and the allocation of resources for invention. In: Nelson, R.R. (Ed.), The Rate and Direction of Inventive Activity. Princeton University Press.
Audretsch, D.B., Weigand, J., 2005. Do knowledge conditions make a difference?: Investment, finance and ownership in German industries. Research Policy 34 (5), 595–613.
Carpenter, R.E., Petersen, B.C., 2002. Capital market imperfections, high-tech investment, and new equity financing. Economic Journal 112 (477), F54–F72.
Cassar, G., 2004. The financing of business start-ups. Journal of Business Venturing 19, 261–283.
Cohen, W.M., Nelson, R.R., Walsh, J.P., 2000. Protecting their Intellectual Assets: Appropriability Conditions and Why U.S. Manufacturing Firms Patent (or not). NBER Working Paper Series, 7552.
Davidsson, P., 2006. Nascent entrepreneurship: empirical studies and developments. Foundations and Trends in Entrepreneurship 2 (1), 1–76.
Engel, D., Keilbach, M., 2007. Firm-level implications of early stage venture capital investment: an empirical investigation. Journal of Empirical Finance 14, 150–167.
Gompers, P., Lerner, J., 2001. The Money of Invention: How Venture Capital Creates New Wealth. Harvard Business School Press, Boston, MA.
Haeussler, C., Harhoff, D., Mueller, E., 2009. To Be Financed or Not? – The Role of Patents for Venture Capital Financing. CEPR Discussion Papers, 7115.
Hall, B.H., Jaffe, A., Trajtenberg, M., 2005. Market value and patent citations. Rand Journal of Economics 36, 16–38.
Hall, B.H., Ziedonis, R.M.H., 2001. The patent paradox revisited: determinants of patenting in the US semiconductor industry, 1980–94. The RAND Journal of Economics 32 (1), 101–128.
Harhoff, D., 2011. The role of patents and licenses in securing external finance for innovation. In: Audretsch, D., Falck, O., Heblich, S., Lederer, A. (Eds.), Handbook of Research on Innovation and Entrepreneurship. Edward Elgar Publishing, Cheltenham, pp. 55–73.
Hayes, L.D., 1999. What the general practitioner should know about patenting business methods. The Computer Lawyer 16 (9), 3–18.
Hellman, T., Puri, M., 2000. The interaction between product market and financing strategy: the role of venture capital. Review of Financial Studies 13, 959–984.
Helmers, C., Rogers, M., 2011. Does patenting help high-tech start-ups? Research Policy 40 (7), 1016–1027.
Hilal, D.K., Soltan, H., 1992. To prototype or not to prototype? That is the question. Software Engineering Journal 7 (6), 388–392.
Horstmann, I., MacDonald, G.M., Slivinski, A., 1985. Patents as information transfer mechanisms: to patent or (maybe) not to patent. Journal of Political Economy 93 (5), 837–858.
Hsu, D., 2004. What do entrepreneurs pay for venture capital affiliation? Journal of Finance 59 (4), 1805–1844.
Hsu, D., 2007. Experienced entrepreneurial founders, organizational capital, and venture capital funding. Research Policy 36, 722–741.
Hsu, D., Ziedonis, R.H., 2008. Patents as Quality Signals for Entrepreneurial Ventures. Academy of Management Best Paper Proceedings.
Kortum, S., Lerner, J., 2000. Assessing the contribution of venture capital to innovation. Rand Journal of Economics 31, 674–692.
Lemley, A.M., 2001. Rational ignorance at the patent office. Northwestern University Law Review 95 (4), 1495–1532.

D.B. Audretsch et al. / Research Policy 41 (2012) 1407–1421   1421

Levin, R.C., Klevorick, A.K., Nelson, R.R., Winter, S.G., 1987. Appropriating the returns from industrial research and development. Brookings Papers on Economic Activity (3), 783–831.

Libik, G., 1969. The economic assessment of research and development. Management Science 16, 33–66.

Long, C., 2002. Patent signals. The University of Chicago Law Review 69 (2), 625–679.

Mason, C., Stark, M., 2004. What do investors look for in a business plan? A comparison of the investment criteria of bankers, venture capitalists and business angels. International Small Business Journal 22, 227–248.

Monfardini, C., Radice, R., 2008. Testing exogeneity in the bivariate probit model: a Monte Carlo study. Oxford Bulletin of Economics and Statistics 70, 271–282.

Nelson, R.R., 1959. The simple economics of basic scientific research. The Journal of Political Economy 67 (3), 297–306.

O'Sullivan, M., 2006. Finance and innovation. In: Fagerber, J., Mowery, D., Nelson, R. (Eds.), The Oxford Handbook of Innovation. Oxford University Press, Oxford, pp. 240–265.

Parker, S.C., Belghitar, Y., 2006. What happens to nascent entrepreneurs? An econometric analysis of the PSED. Small Business Economics 27 (1), 81–101.

Reynolds, P.D., Carter, N.M., Gartner, W.B., Greene, P.G., 2004. The prevalence of nascent entrepreneurs in the United States: evidence from the panel study of entrepreneurial dynamics. Small Business Economics 23 (4), 263–284.

Shane, S., 2001. Technological opportunities and new firm creation. Management Science 47, 205–220.

Sichelman, M.T., Graham, J.S., 2011. Why do entrepreneurs patent? In: Litan, R.E. (Ed.), Handbook on Law, Innovation and Growth. Edward Elgar Publishing, Cheltenham, pp. 212–243.

Simon, H., 1961. Administrative Behavior, 2nd ed. Macmillan, New York.

Spence, A.M., 1973. Job market signaling. The Quarterly Journal of Economics 87 (3), 355–374.

Teece, D.J., 1986. Profiting from technological innovation: implications for integration, collaboration, licensing and public policy. Research Policy 15 (6), 285–305.

Tyebjee, T.T., Bruno, A.V., 1984. A model of venture capitalist investment activity. Management Science 30, 1051–1066.

Ueda, M., 2004. Banks versus venture capital: project evaluation, screening, and expropriation. The Journal of Finance 59, 601–621.

Wilde, J., 2000. Identification of multiple equation probit models with endogenous dummy regressors. Economics Letters 69, 309–312.

.